T0315020

MAKING MONEY IN THE EARLY MIDDLE AGES

Making Money in the Early Middle Ages

Rory Naismith

PRINCETON UNIVERSITY PRESS

PRINCETON & OXFORD

Published by Princeton University Press
41 William Street, Princeton, New Jersey 08540
99 Banbury Road, Oxford OX2 6JX

press.princeton.edu

All Rights Reserved
ISBN: 978-0-691-17740-3
ISBN (e-book): 978-0-691-24933-9

British Library Cataloging-in-Publication Data is available

Editorial: Ben Tate and Josh Drake
Production Editorial: Jenny Wolkowicki
Jacket design: Haley Chung
Production: Danielle Amatucci
Publicity: William Pagdatoon and Charlotte Coyne
Copyeditor: Anita O'Brien

Jacket credit: Courtesy of the American Numismatic Society

This book has been composed in Miller

Printed on acid-free paper. ∞

Printed in the United States of America

10 9 8 7 6 5 4 3 2 1

For Brittany and Yseult

Now this doubloon was of purest, virgin gold, raked somewhere out of the heart of gorgeous hills, whence, east and west, over golden sands, the headwaters of many a Pactolus flows. And though now nailed amidst all the rustiness of iron bolts and the verdigris of copper spikes, yet, untouchable and immaculate to any foulness, it still preserved its Quito glow. Nor, though placed amongst a ruthless crew and every hour passed by ruthless hands, and through the livelong nights shrouded with thick darkness which might cover any pilfering approach, nevertheless every sunrise found the doubloon where the sunset left it last. For it was set apart and sanctified to one awe-striking end; and however wanton in their sailor ways, one and all, the mariners revered it as the white whale's talisman. Sometimes they talked it over in the weary watch by night, wondering whose it was to be at last, and whether he would ever live to spend it.

—HERMAN MELVILLE, *MOBY-DICK; OR, THE WHALE* (1851)

CONTENTS

Figures

Note: Figures are not reproduced exactly to scale, but images of coins are set to give an approximate indication of relative size, with the real diameter given in the caption.

Maps

All maps are drawn by the author.

Table

PREFACE AND ACKNOWLEDGEMENTS

THE GENESIS OF THIS BOOK goes back to half-formed ideas that grew out of my doctoral studies in the 2000s. Why *did* people make and use coins at all in the early Middle Ages, if cash was so scarce that they were used to getting by without? These preliminary thoughts took more defined form during subsequent years, not least during many fruitful talks with Mark Blackburn as the two of us would walk home from the Fitzwilliam Museum. I owe much to the sheer good fortune that we both happened to live on the north side of Cambridge and so usually found ourselves heading in the same general direction. But Mark's impact went much deeper than that. I remain extremely grateful for the opportunity to benefit from his insight and teaching, as well as his warmth and support, before his untimely death in 2011.

In a more direct sense, the beginning of this book came from the readers' reviews on a paper I submitted to *Past and Present* in 2012. One of the comments was that "there is enough in here for a book—I hope he writes it later." I never found out who this anonymous reader was, though I remain grateful to them, for their point hit home: indeed there was enough for a book on why coins were made and used. This was a question that I had found most numismatic literature did not address, while the assessments offered in works of economic and social history rarely went into any depth or commanded much confidence. For these reasons, I started to accumulate notes and ideas building toward the present book.

The actual writing took somewhat longer than originally planned but has benefited from extended gestation in a series of stimulating intellectual homes. Initial planning took place while I was a research fellow at Cambridge, funded by Clare College (2009–12), the Leverhulme Trust (2012–14), and finally the Mellon Foundation (2014–15), and affiliated with Clare College, the Department of Anglo-Saxon, Norse and Celtic (ASNC), the Faculty of History, and the Fitzwilliam Museum. From 2015 I was based in the Department of History at King's College London, and it was during four happy years there that I began to work on the book in earnest. A major stimulus to do so came when I was fortunate enough to receive, in January 2019, a Leadership Fellowship from the Arts and Humanities Research Council (AHRC), for a project originally entitled "Foundations of Gold and Silver" (Grant Ref. AH/S005498/1). This book

[xvii]

was due to be the major outcome of the grant, which funded a year of relief from teaching and administrative responsibilities, plus another six months on half time.

In the event, while that year proved invaluable, it did not pan out in quite the way I anticipated, for two reasons. The first was that, in spring 2019, I accepted an offer of a new post in Cambridge, returning to the Department of ASNC as a Lecturer in the history of England before the Norman Conquest, and soon after as a Fellow of Corpus Christi College. The AHRC kindly agreed that I could defer the beginning of my research leave, and with it the substance of work on this book, to the academic year 2020–21, so that I could complete the first year of the new job in-post. The second reason was one that nobody could have foreseen at that point: the onset of the Covid-19 pandemic in 2020. It quickly became apparent in spring of that year just how horrific and disruptive the virus would be. Normal academic life, and normal life of almost every kind, ground to a halt. Plans to travel in order to consult libraries and museum collections in other countries had to be jettisoned, though thanks to notes made beforehand, and the support of librarians in Cambridge and elsewhere, I was able to keep up momentum. The bulk of the work on this book was therefore completed during a bizarre and unexpected time of lockdown.

These circumstances mean that the normal rounds of thanks expressed at the beginning of books carry added weight. I have benefited from an extraordinary amount of kindness, patience, and professionalism. I owe a very large debt of gratitude to the AHRC for choosing to fund the fellowship that made this book possible. I am grateful to colleagues in Cambridge and London for discussions, advice, and general camaraderie, some of it under very trying circumstances. My agent, Lisa Adams, has been a strong supporter of this project from my first plans to write it up as a book, and she helped mould it into a viable proposal for Princeton University Press. I owe thanks to Ben Tate for his friendly and understanding help from the editorial side at Princeton, and also to Jenny Wolkowicki, Dimitri Karetnikov, Susan Clark, Anita O'Brien, and Virginia Ling for an efficient and friendly production process.

There are also many friends and colleagues who have helped in a range of ways: discussing various points in person, by e-mail or (as became all too familiar at the height of the pandemic) by video call; giving feedback on drafts or related papers; and kindly sharing their own work. I am grateful to all. These include Martin Allen, Anders Andrén, Florent Audy, Paul Beliën, John Blair, Roger Bland, Lorenzo Bondioli, Simon Coupland, Oliver Creighton, Damián Fernández, Svante Fischer, Richard von Glahn, Caroline Goodson,

Toby Green, Svein Gullbekk, Ben Guy, Guy Halsall, Sophie Hemmings, Liesbeth van Houts, Peter Ilisch, Jane Kershaw, Andrew Kurt, Ivar Leimus, Chris Loveluck, Nick Mayhew, Matt McHaffie, Fraser McNair, Jens-Christian Moesgaard, Sam Moorhead, Cécile Morrisson, James Norrie, Peter Olive, Wybrand Op den Velde, Rob Portass, Stuart Pracy, Alice Rio, Levi Roach, Alessia Rovelli, Andrea Saccocci, Alexandra Sapoznik, Guillaume Sarah, Elina Screen, Alan Stahl, Naomi Standen, Alice Taylor, Paolo Tedesco, Frans Theuws, Lucia Travaini, Mariele Valci, Charles West, Gareth Williams, and Ian Wood.

The strange world in which this book was written forced all of us into small bubbles formed around home and family. Completing this project required especially close support from loved ones, as work and home life collapsed into each other and many external sources of help were closed off. And while the reasons for this were frightening, and the practicalities at times challenging, in the final analysis it has, I believe, made for a more considered and humane work. Two years in the close and constant company of my wife Brittany and daughter Yseult has been both a pleasure and an endless source of inspiration and stimulation. This book is dedicated to them.

NOTE ON VALUES

EXPRESSIONS OF VALUE in this book often follow the system known from predecimal British currency (i.e., 12 pennies or denarii to a shilling or solidus, and 20 shillings or solidi to the pound). In such cases, the traditional abbreviations for value are used: d for penny/denarius, s for shilling/solidus, and £ for pound. Expressions of weight are given in grams and kilograms when translated into modern equivalents; expressions of weight from ancient and medieval sources in pounds (librae or similar) are given in the traditional abbreviation lb(s), with the important caveat that the exact weight of the pound would vary between regions and periods.

CHAPTER ONE

Introduction

AS EUROPE DESCENDED into war in 1940, wondrous things began to emerge from beneath St. Peter's Basilica in the Vatican. The decision to lower the floor of the crypt to make room for Pope Pius XI's (1857–1939) sarcophagus uncovered a network of Roman tombs. One of these—a relatively humble one—supposedly belonged to St. Peter, and its location had dictated the unusual placement of the fourth-century basilica above it, on a hillside in the midst of a still-active cemetery. That tomb lay directly beneath the altar, several metres below the current floor level of St. Peter's, and as they dug down toward it the excavators of the 1940s came across nearly two thousand coins. The largest concentration of them lay in the "Niche of the Palliums": a recess immediately above the tomb of Peter. In the Middle Ages the niche was accessible from above, being where the clergy lowered down special strips of fabric, the *pallia* (a sign of papal favour given primarily to archbishops), so that they could touch the tomb of Peter and become contact relics. Evidently the niche was also where visiting pilgrims would throw offerings.

The coins from the Niche of the Palliums and other parts of the St. Peter's excavations offer a cross-section of monetary history. They run in date from the Roman period to the sixteenth century. The early and late parts of this spread are well represented, but after the fifth century the quantity of coins drops off sharply. Only a tiny number of coins minted in the sixth to ninth centuries appeared: about fifteen in total, or less than 1 per cent of the overall assemblage. That figure gradually picked up in the tenth and especially the eleventh centuries and ballooned thereafter. There is no question that St. Peter's remained accessible and frequented throughout the early Middle Ages. The coin finds from its innermost recesses constitute so many tiny acts of devotion, each a small spark of material piety that was once dropped away into the darkness. Visitors from across Europe chose to toss in coins from their distant homelands, making for an especially diverse assemblage. At the same time, these finds are also a rare barometer of coin-use over the *longue durée*. They point toward an important conclusion. The scarcity of early medieval coins below St. Peter's does not reflect any retreat in the veneration of St. Peter. Rather, there simply were not as many coins around to be deposited by visitors.[1] This book is about why, even when there were so few coins around, people still made them and used them to give to St. Peter, to pay rents, or to spend at markets.

The Dark Age of Currency?

Not only were early medieval coins in short supply, but they typically consisted of gold and silver pieces of relatively high value. It was not possible to go out and buy one loaf of bread, one pint of beer, or one egg on the basis of the currency available between about the sixth and eleventh centuries in western Europe. In this respect the early Middle Ages compare poorly with the periods that sandwich it. Both the Roman and later medieval currency systems were much larger in scale and also catered to the needs of diverse groups and needs. In the Roman world, that had meant a wide range of coin denominations in copper alloy, silver, and gold. Different segments of this system fared better than others as direct Roman rule faltered in western Europe. Gold was, in some areas, hardly affected at all. The Roman gold solidus, and especially its fraction the tremissis, maintained a dominant position for centuries after the empire itself was gone. The keenest loss, from the point of view of most of the population, would have been the vast base-metal coinage, which was used for small transactions. There was not really anything to fill that gap aside from reuse of old Roman coins. Early medieval currency thus represented what had been the upper tier of Roman currency. Even the silver denarius or penny, which gradually supplanted the tremissis from the seventh century onward, may have been less valuable than its gold predecessor, but was still a coin of significant worth: Charlemagne in the 790s laid down that one of the silver denarii his currency generally consisted of should buy no less than 12 two-pound loaves of wheat bread,[2] while a gold piece of the same weight would have got no fewer than 144 loaves.[3]

---

1. Serafini 1951; Toynbee and Ward-Perkins 1956; Kirschbaum 1959.
2. Council of Frankfurt c. 4 (Boretius 1883, 74).
3. See Lyon 1969, 214–16, for gold:silver ratios.

It should be stressed that this was very much a western European set of problems. Lower-value coinage could be found in the Byzantine and Muslim worlds (though not always in profusion), including southern Italy and, at least into the eighth century, other Byzantine enclaves further north. This was an age that glittered with gold and silver, all the more so for their isolation in an oppressive gloom that has tended to produce a negative outlook on early medieval coinage, at least as something that actually mediated exchange and stored value for most of the populace. The focus has fallen on what could *not* be done, and on the poor showing of early medieval coins relative to other periods or categories of material evidence. There are far more Roman coins, or far more pot sherds. For many observers, the retreat of the currency exemplifies the collapse of economic sophistication, even of "civilisation," as Bryan Ward-Perkins put it with reference to Britain in the bleak aftermath of Roman rule.[4] Henri Pirenne in the 1930s viewed the unimpressive Carolingian monetary regime as a signal of the emaciation of Mediterranean commerce and the involution of economic structures.[5] More recently, Chris Wickham's magisterial survey of early medieval economic and social structures left coinage out almost completely,[6] and Jim Bolton set up the tenth- and eleventh-century coinage of England as a foil for the larger currency of subsequent times.[7]

One of the most influential attempts to explain what role coins actually did play under these circumstances came from Philip Grierson, who argued that post-Roman gold tremisses and Carolingian denarii hardly circulated at all.[8] Nobody knew the numismatic material better than Grierson, and his work on coinage as an expression of power and an artefact of government neatly sidestepped its small quantity and supposedly negligible economic importance. Instead, the archaeological record as it stood in the 1970s and before led him to build a case for restricted, socially driven use. Coin finds at that stage were few and dominated by hoards and graves. It seemed only logical to picture these coins as the stuff of gift-giving and other socially embedded payments like fines, not buying and selling.[9] The purse of Merovingian gold pieces included in the Sutton Hoo ship-burial became, for Grierson, a fee for the spectral crew of the ship, and

4. Ward-Perkins 2005, esp. 110–13. See also Fleming 2021, 6; Gerrard 2013, 80–81.
5. Pirenne 1939, esp. 242–47.
6. Wickham 2005, 702 n. 16 (though cf. Wickham 2011, 229).
7. Bolton 2012.
8. Grierson 1959a; 1965, 534–36.
9. Grierson 1959a.

the Crondall hoard of the same period a wergild payment in waiting.[10] Grierson set himself against prevailing wisdom on the subject, which tied coins to mercantile commerce,[11] and turned for inspiration to Marcel Mauss's seminal work on gift-giving.[12] Law codes and narrative texts that mentioned coins seemed to fit that model too, focusing on use in ritual settings such as the settlement of fines.

The Dark Age of Money?

Grierson's openness to social scientific approaches helped him to avoid a cardinal sin of numismatically inclined scholars: that of taking coinage as a measure of the penetration of money in society or of monetisation as a conceptual phenomenon. It was emphatically not either of those things. Even in the early Middle Ages, people thought extensively in terms of money. They measured the value of land, livestock, market goods, and even human life, honour, and spiritual devotions in pounds, solidi, and denarii or other units predicated on weights of precious metal. In an important sense, this always was a highly monetised world. And with so few coins around, most "monetary" exchanges or obligations inevitably involved no coin at all: credit and commodities fulfilled that role, the latter sometimes so frequently or conveniently that they took on a role as a kind of money themselves. A weight of precious metal in the head did not necessarily translate to the corresponding sum of coins in the hand, even though superficially coins might seem to fit comfortably into the prevailing systems of account. Indeed, the exact relationship of coins to units of account is often difficult to grasp.[13]

Marc Bloch once described medieval coinage as "something like a seismograph which does not only signal earthquakes, but sometimes causes them."[14] Given the limitations outlined earlier, the sensitivity of coinage as an economic seismograph needs serious scrutiny. This is not just a numbers game. A situation can be imagined in which there might be a relatively complex, dynamic exchange economy with few or no coins, such as the Viking-Age Baltic (though in effect silver bullion fulfilled many of the roles of coinage elsewhere, with less formal regulation). Conversely,

10. Grierson 1961; 1970.
11. E.g., Pirenne 1925, 116, 244.
12. Mauss 1990 (originally published in French in 1925).
13. These points will be discussed in more detail in chapter 5.
14. "Quelque chose comme un sismographe qui, non content de signaler les tremblements de terre, parfois les provoquerait." Bloch 1933, 1.

a surge in the production of coin is not necessarily symptomatic of an economy in good health, as in the Roman Empire of the third century, or mid-sixteenth-century England. All depends on context: on weighing up the nature of individual coinages and the societies in which they circulated. A safe starting premise, however, is that early medieval coins factored into a small to very small slice of economic activity. The question is who and what fed into that slice. As has been seen, Grierson believed that the limited practicality of early medieval coinage translated to narrow functionality. But this particular conclusion must now be left behind, in favour of one that takes account of significantly more layers of society and exchange. More recent assessments of coin use have turned away from Grierson and rehabilitated the more upbeat interpretation by Alfons Dopsch from the early part of the twentieth century.[15] Dopsch situated his contribution as a late entry in the venerable debate on when a primitive, nonmonetary "natural economy" had given way to a "money economy" and landed firmly on the side of there being a money economy in the early Middle Ages, grounded in a dynamic rural economic landscape.[16] He argued that coined money remained a pillar of post-Roman civilisation, even if in diminished quantity, with extensive evidence for its presence in circulation and thought; an approach that has also been juxtaposed with Pirenne's emphasis on long-distance trade and its contraction after the seventh century.[17]

One reason Dopsch's conclusions about coinage have taken on a new sheen is the significant and unexpected growth of the underlying material record.[18] Far more coins have come to light since the popularization of metal detectors in the 1970s, and some modern European countries (most notably England/Wales and the Netherlands) have created databases to log their finds and put them at the disposal of scholars. The results are revelatory: now it can be seen that early medieval coins did circulate in appreciable numbers. Pennies and even gold coins turn up far and wide, including in rural areas with no known claim to political or economic significance. This cannot be squared with a vision of currency as mostly the domain of elite gift-giving and a few intrepid long-distance traders.

15. E.g., McCormick 2001, 2–6; Coupland 2014c, 259.

16. Bloch 1967, 230–43 (originally published in French in 1939); Dopsch 1937, 358–83 (the longer version in the original German edition is Dopsch 1923–1924, 2:477–538). Others had reached similar conclusions in looking at specific areas: Giuseppe Salvioli (1901) had done so for Italy two decades earlier.

17. E.g. Morrison 1963, 404–7. For the "Pirenne thesis," see chapter 2.

18. The historiography of this period is elegantly surveyed in McCormick 2001, 1–18. See also Naismith 2012b, 252–59.

Of course, those same detectors cannot be tuned to find only early medieval items, and for every one early medieval coin that comes to light, there will (at least in England and Wales) be fifty or more Roman ones, and fifteen or so later medieval ones.[19] In relative terms the early Middle Ages are still very coin-poor, yet that poverty seems less absolute than once appeared to be the case.

We are still dealing with a knot of contradictions, albeit slightly different ones. Early medieval coins were used for many things by lots of people, albeit not often. A basic tool of day-to-day life became a rare commodity, access to which was contested and tenuous, expressing gulfs in status and social connections. It might be argued that money was always thus, and contemporary experience has led researchers to emphasise its status as a kind of social relation.[20] What is needed is a recalibration of expectations regarding when, why, and on whose terms coins were used. From this point of view, coined money can be argued to gain in significance when it lacks in quantity. Choosing to use coins was a calculated decision that said something about the nature of an exchange. Choice is an important concept here. Georg Simmel, in his still electrifying *Philosophy of Money*, stressed that freedom stemmed from using money. Instead of a peasant cultivator having to produce whatever commodity their landlord demanded, paying in money meant they could produce whatever they wanted, or at least whatever they could sell.[21] One difficulty here is that choice assumes a ready flow of money, which created a large-scale form of equity and consensus structured around the handling and flow of money in the early medieval situation, but that equity and consensus existed only fleetingly, at the point of transaction. Before and after that moment, a constrained money supply offered vast scope for articulating inequality.[22] Coined money's notionally universal status worked against it, turning access into advantage. One party might have been able to demand a better price; for the other, using money may not have been a choice at all. Gender, age, status, location, and all sorts of other variables affected access to and use of money. Even if coin was free and fluid, the decision to use it, and often the decision about when and how much to hand over, was

19. These ratios derive from the totals recorded on the Portable Antiquities Scheme (PAS) for England and Wales, as of 8 August 2021: 282,141 Roman coins, 5,051 early medieval coins, and 76,517 later medieval ones (here meaning 1066–1509).

20. Ingham 1999; Graeber 2011.

21. Simmel 2004, 285–91 (originally published in German in 1900).

22. For an argument on the fundamental link between hierarchy and money (or, rather, debt) see Bell and Henry 2001; Henry 2004.

frequently not. What, exactly, might early medieval people have sought to say by using coins in this climate?

The Meanings of Money

The back and forth of money is so familiar that it is easy to think it has always and everywhere been the same. Certainly the concept is widespread, having developed independently in many cultures,[23] and there is a long tradition of seeing the impact of money as universal, at least in the case of general-purpose money that could be used in all settings (in contrast to "special-purpose" moneys of more restricted function).[24] All-embracing applicability—fungibility, as economists sometimes call it—is both the greatest strength and the greatest danger of money according to this line of reasoning. The theory is that, having the capacity to drip down into all contexts like a sociological acid, money will eat away at distinctions between them. Fear of money's potential to subvert, distort, and corrode the basic fabric of human society is of very long standing. Ecclesiastical satirists of the eleventh century fastened on it,[25] and Shakespeare put a biting speech on the transgressive power of money into the mouth of Timon of Athens around 1606: "Thus much of [gold] will make black white, foul fair, wrong right, base noble, old young, coward valiant . . . this yellow slave will knit and break religions, bless the accursed, make the hoar leprosy adored, place thieves and give them title, knee and approbation with senators on the bench."[26] Two centuries later, Karl Marx used this passage to exemplify his thinking on money as a force for change, and similar lines were followed by foundational figures in the sociology of money, including Max Weber as well as Mauss and Simmel.[27] General-purpose money stood out as a defining feature of modern society, its incitement to calculative abstraction at once both liberating and dehumanizing. Jacques Le Goff has more recently followed this logic backward, arguing that European society prior to about 1800 was distinguished by a more bounded form of monetary thought, shaped by moralizing and religious strictures on the proper and improper uses of money.[28]

23. Grierson 1977; Ingham 2000.

24. As defined classically in Polanyi 1957 and Bohannan 1959, though cf. important critique in Akin and Robbins 1999, 8–10.

25. Murray 1978, 76–77.

26. *Timon of Athens*, 4.3.30–34, 38–42.

27. Marx 1964, 165–69 (with Paolucci 1977); Simmel 1977/2004; Weber 1968, 75–85, 100–109, 166–93 (with Lallemant 2019); Mauss 1990, esp. 71–83.

28. Le Goff 2004; 2012. See also Howell 2010, esp. 261–302.

Le Goff implicitly hits on a deep problem in the macrohistory of money. If general-purpose money has a predictable, inevitable set of effects, why are they not visible in earlier times, when money had a similarly wide range of uses? One way of addressing this quandary has been to push back the history of "modern" money. Some medievalists have staked claims to the origin of monetary modernity or protocapitalism as early as the central Middle Ages.[29] This reclaims a part of the medieval period for "proper" economic history but at the same time leaves what came before as historical static, a sorry shuffle to set before the march of progress. That approach is rejected here. Early medieval money and coin are interesting in themselves, for their dogged continuity, and also for what that continuity implies. People continued to find needs and uses for currency, even in the restricted form of the era. And the degree of restriction varied considerably. In England, Francia, and Frisia between about 660 and 850, and a larger area from the late tenth century onward, coin was relatively common. Coined money can be read as a transregional phenomenon that spanned seas and continents, but also, and arguably more important, as a function of local hierarchies and economic infrastructures: part of what John Haldon has described as the core skeleton that underlies the soft tissue of society.[30] For this reason, coinage is in some ways a good seismograph for other developments within a society, in that even modest growth in use tends to accompany higher degrees of social and economic elaboration—with the important caveat that for this period coinage needs (as will be seen) to be read as a reflection primarily of the economic dominance of elites over other groups in society.

Was this a "money economy"? In its way, certainly. As Michael Postan noted already in the 1940s, historians tend to approach the emergence of a "money economy" as a deus ex machina that swoops in at a point that suits their own needs and invented criteria.[31] One way to break from that cycle is to recognise that different forms of money economy have prevailed over time, to be considered on their own merits rather than measured against an imaginary *real* money economy. A flexible approach of this kind was implicit in Weber's thinking on money as a technology of power that could be used in varied ways to achieve control (*Verfügungsgewalt*), meaning that it was experienced in different ways by various social groups and also enmeshed with other kinds of power and dominance.[32]

29. Postan 1973, 28–40; Little 1978; Mell 2017–18.
30. Haldon 2015, 219.
31. Postan 1944, 123, 124.
32. Weber 1968, 179.

That said, another strategy has been to query whether modern money really is all it has been claimed to be. The classic studies mentioned earlier were rooted in the aggressive industrial capitalism of nineteenth- and early twentieth-century Europe. But even in one of the crucibles of modern capitalism, the United States at the turn of the twentieth century, money did not always have the anticipated effects: Viviana Zelizer has shown that dollars and dimes were not all treated equally by urban wage labourers and their families. Money did not dissolve these households, the personhood of those who lived in them, or the boundaries between the different kinds of exchange they engaged in.[33] The concept of money as corrosive and dangerous grew up in a very specific cultural and intellectual ecosystem: one of rapid, disturbing social and economic change, on the one hand, and of growing concern with abstraction and the breakdown of barriers between humans and things, on the other. The latter has been argued to have its own distinct intellectual pedigree, linked to aspects of Protestant intellectual tradition.[34] In other words, a distinct kind of money economy (itself with variable real-life effects) and a specific way of looking at it have been taken as universal, when in fact they were highly particular.

Underlying the approaches to money outlined here is the effect money has on society. But economic processes need not be approached just as detached, impersonal forces: they are the product of, as well as an influence on, currents in thought and society.[35] It is therefore just as important to examine what societies do to money.[36] Views on the effects of general-purpose money have moved on from what Zelizer calls the "hostile worlds" scheme, meaning one that sets a supposedly inviolate traditional sphere against a threatening modern and monetary one.[37] Those who have tried to put their finger on broader patterns in the impact of money have shifted to how it factored into long- or short-term "transactional orders," or "modalities of exchange" like sharing between family groups, deferred gift-giving, or market trading.[38] This is effectively a death blow to the idea that money—even general-purpose money—has a single social outcome. Many Pacific Island societies have embraced general-purpose money enthusiastically and integrated it into traditional forms of exchange; the

---

33. Zelizer 1994. See also Parry and Bloch 1989, 4–7.
34. Keane 2007, 270–84; 2008, 37–38.
35. Haldon 2015, 220–36.
36. Maurer 2006.
37. For this term see Zelizer 2005.
38. Parry and Bloch 1989, 23–30; Akin and Robbins 1999, 14–16.

potential for destabilization is there but is not activated by money in and of itself, instead depending on a range of political and economic factors.[39] Most recently, the focus has pivoted to how materiality and social networks continuously reinvent money's significance in different situations. In modern Vietnam, dollars and local money play complementary roles that are embedded in display and family dynamics.[40] Digital money in modern Africa has a material form in the technology needed to access it, and a human dimension in that it creates much-desired institutional and financial identity.[41] Embedded local developments carry as much interest as abstracted universals. The message is that what people do to money matters as much as what money does to people.

Two of the most stimulating recent assessments of money as a wider phenomenon exemplify this principle and combine the sweep of the big picture with the finesse of finely detailed examples. Tellingly, both acknowledge the painful awareness of money's fragility and artificiality brought on by the financial crash of 2008. David Graeber has examined money as one example of the coercive machinery erected to enforce obligation or debt, from ancient Mesopotamia to the twenty-first century. From this perspective, coins represent a material form of credit relations in morally, socially meaningful packaging.[42] Christine Desan has looked at a deep and well-evidenced case study, England from the seventh century onward, in which money emerged as a tool for mediating between institutions and the population. Like Graeber, Desan saw its underlying basis as a promise to repay debts, especially those owed to or from the state.[43] The latter's role quietly transformed at the end of the seventeenth century: money became something that the government issued without charge in order to stimulate and reward profit-oriented commerce, in effect making money fuel for capital and the market rather than a responsibility of public power created in return for a fee. These two works each take a functional approach to money, viewing it not just as an abstraction, but as something dynamic and open to modification. Graeber and Desan recognise that money was not monolithic, and that it gains in interest when the multiplicity of its effects is recognised, as a proxy for how groups and individuals mediated material value.

39. Akin and Robbins 1999, 20–25, and other papers in the same volume.
40. Truitt 2013.
41. Maurer 2015.
42. Graeber 2011.
43. Desan 2014.

Situating Early Medieval Money

There is perhaps a risk here of money as a historical phenomenon becoming submerged in a roiling froth of incommensurable special cases. It is therefore important to stress what made the early medieval example (or examples) distinct. Some of its qualities align closely with the anthropological interpretations previously outlined. Wealth given to the Christian Church for furtherance of its mission or charitable activities underwent something very like a leap from short- to long-term transactional orders, for example: money disposed of in this way metamorphosed from transient earthly dross to eternal treasure in heaven, as eloquently explored by Peter Brown.[44] There was a remarkable degree of openness about the use of early medieval money. It is extremely difficult to identify sectors of thought and society that were hived off from monetary valuation or settlement in coin. Money could be used for more or less everything, so long as its context was made clear. Where there was anxiety, it was not about the use of money as such, but about whether its proper role as pious gift (or whatever) was correctly signposted. The performative aspect of using money, and by extension its materiality, therefore carried considerable weight.

Concern with presentation rather than the basic presence of money perhaps relates to one of the main differences between early medieval money and the examples anthropologists have concentrated on. Most of the latter relate to the introduction of modern, Western general-purpose money into traditional societies that already have well-established exchange mechanisms. The interest is in the impact of a new element. There was, in contrast, nothing new about money in early medieval Europe. It had been a fact of life from Britain to North Africa since the early Roman imperial period or before. That in itself might have been one reason for the ubiquity of money as a unit of account that related to coins and *could*, but need not always, be represented by them: there was less prospect of money overwhelming ideas of propriety. What it offered was a kind of contained, instrumentalised transactional approach.

All this still leaves the question of why coins were made and used at all, especially if it was perfectly possible to get by without them. What did having some coins, but usually not many of them, actually achieve? Part of an answer lies in their connotations. Coins could be given to anyone for anything, backed up by trust that the next person would accept

44. Brown 2012; 2013; 2015.

them at the same value. That was a serious principle in the early Middle Ages, and not one that could be taken for granted: rulers from the sixth century onward enacted legislation mandating that people had to accept good coins or, more revealingly, not refuse them, on pain of heavy punishment.[45] By extension, coins thus reflect acceptance of the authority behind them, emblematized by the more or less carefully engraved name, image, or symbol of the ruler.[46] This is true of state-sponsored moneys across history, and in modern times currency forms part of a multifaceted state-building project: people see, hear, and touch many other manifestations of central authority.[47] This was not the case in the early Middle Ages. Manifestations of state authority were far fewer, and their impact slighter, the further one moved in social terms from the centre. For the typical early medieval peasant, coins would not have been just a minor prop in a complex edifice constituting royal and central power: they were one of the few visible, direct ways in which that infrastructure impinged regularly on people's lives. To deal in coins, then, was to deal with others as common members of the same ideological project—to enter into what Jonas of Orléans in the 820s called the "willing compact of seller and buyer" (*pactio vendentis et ementis grata*).[48] Coined money reified the means of exchange and cast the participants into a scheme of values closely and clearly dependent on authority, power, and social relations: they needed to be able to believe that the next person to whom they offered the coins would accept them at the same value. Coins created a sense of transactionality, that one thing had been given for another in a discrete and concrete act of exchange. In a sense this is "hostile worlds" turned on its head: instead of the detached nature of coin consuming everything it touched, people involved in diverse kinds of exchanges and power dynamics instrumentalized the finite, transactional quality of money, using it to frame different ways in which value changed hands. Use of coined money hence had a demonstrative, public quality to it. It was a way of defining and encapsulating value that could be taken up in any kind of exchange. In the immediate context of a transfer of goods or services, coined money might be seen as introducing a degree of fairness and transparency, even though on a larger level it was anything but.[49]

45. See chapter 4.

46. An idea developed by Georg Friedrich Knapp (1924).

47. Hart 1986. Helleiner 2003 develops this idea in relation to the crystallization of nineteenth-century nation-states.

48. See chapter 4.

49. Feller 2017b, esp. 78–80. This duality is elegantly brought out in Kuchenbuch 2019, esp. 64–65, 69.

The embedded transactionality of early medieval money tempered Simmel's famous idea of it bringing freedom and equality. It was there: an English monk of the early eleventh century saw the attraction of silver coins being that "one who has coins or silver can get everything he wants."[50] Paying rent in coin meant peasant tenants had a degree of autonomy in what to cultivate and an inducement to deal in coin on their own account. But in a situation where money reflected larger power structures, it served and benefited whoever loomed large in them. In the early Middle Ages, that meant landholding elites first and foremost. There was little or no bureaucracy separate from them. Government generally remained local, vested in dominant groups, with larger-scale governance being a matter of negotiation between locally powerful elites and the ruler's immediate entourage.[51] The scale of elite wealth and power varied and included an important indirect element as patrons and powerbrokers for others, but the role of elites as both the major holders of local resources and the primary agents of the state had important consequences in relation to exchange systems, and especially coined money.[52]

Cui bono is the essential question. Early medieval western European coinage did not work according to the same logic as that of the Roman Empire, or for that matter its eastern (Byzantine) successor or the Muslim world. There, the manufacture and distribution of coin remained within a more detached, bureaucratic framework. Access to fresh coin depended on direct involvement with the machinery of the state. Like other mechanisms once associated with more centralized government, the impetus behind the manufacture and initial distribution of coinage in the post-Roman West gradually came to depend on locally vested power structures. Elites and their needs therefore played a critical role in minting, either on their own account or as the arm's-length agents of the state. This is not quite the same thing as private minting, though in practice it could come close.[53] In effect, elites were in a position both to set and to play by their own rules when it came to the use of coined money.[54]

One distinction that helps clarify the consequences of this dynamic is between primary and secondary uses of coin. Primary refers to the demands that precipitated minting, and the uses to which those new coins

---

50. "Qui denarios uel argentum habet, omnia quę sibi placent, ualet adipiscere." Ælfric Bata, *Colloquia* 24, ed. and trans. Gwara and Porter 1997, 134–35.

51. Innes 2000, looking at the Carolingian example.

52. A cogent and lucid study of elites and commercial exchange is Wickham 2021.

53. Pace Hendy 1988.

54. Cf. Hudson 2020, who explores this point with reference to debt relations.

were first put. Secondary refers to everything that happened subsequently. It is of course not always possible to distinguish the two in practice. But there was a real difference between them. Most uses of coin did not require freshly minted tremisses or denarii. When kings or others were in a position to dictate terms (such as fines or tributes paid directly to them, or money for the maintenance of armies), they might demand fresh coin of a specific type. But broadly speaking, access to fresh coin was an exclusive privilege, restricted to—or at least channelled through—elites. In contrast, those who depended on the coins in circulation often faced an uphill struggle in getting what they wanted or needed. Most references to nonelite engagement with coin certainly or probably reflect secondary usage (e.g., obtaining necessary coins from market trading). But not even all members of the elite had ready access to coin: loans in cash generally took place within the elite and suggest deep imbalances in the distribution of cash even at that level.

Coined money in early medieval Europe was not just a neutral, fungible means of exchange. It carried a large social premium, and at any one time most coins in circulation were probably concentrated in very few hands, meaning that secondary users of coin had a small slice of an already small pie available to them.

Investigating Early Medieval Money

The final parts of this introduction address some of the essential preliminaries to what is to come. The chronological starting point is the later Roman Empire, and subsequently the collapse of central Roman rule, along with Roman ways of making and distributing coined money. Both of these changes were drawn out and affected various regions at different times, mostly within the fifth century, though Italy and North Africa arguably remained within a Mediterranean Roman sphere for rather longer. At its other end, the close of this study comes roughly around 1100. Demographic and urban growth reached new heights in the twelfth century, especially its second half, at about which time the supply of coined money also started to expand radically, partly on the back of major new silver mines being tapped in central Europe. These are interlocking developments and, as with their precursors in the eleventh century, are best explained as an ensemble.[55] But together they represent the beginning of a quantum leap in terms of access to coin. This is an important story, though it is one that is

55. Spufford 1988, 109–31; Wickham 2016, 121–40; 2017.

best told separately. The point here is to concentrate on the more qualified role of money in the earlier Middle Ages, and to show that it was in many ways less different than might initially be thought.

Three pivotal shifts can be isolated in this period, though they did not start or finish everywhere at the same time. The first was the end of Roman monetary organization, which tended to follow the end of central Roman rule, albeit not always immediately. This entailed the effective cessation of new base-metal coinage and the dominance of gold, which survived in relatively rude health as the workhorse of regional fiscal systems. It also attenuated and eventually broke the fiscal axis that supported a large proportion of Roman minting. The second sea-change was the move from gold to silver as the principal component of the currency. This began on the shores of the English Channel in the later seventh century and spread soon after into Francia and the rest of England. Here, the advent of the penny meant a boom in the minting and use of coin. The new denomination took considerably longer to take hold in Italy (toward 800), where the penny had less effect on use and production, while—with the exception of Catalonia—it did not take hold in Christian Iberia at all until the eleventh century. From a fairly early stage silver pennies or denarii became identified more explicitly with the expression of royal authority: coins frequently carried the name and title of the current ruler, which had not been so common in the immediately post-Roman centuries when the visual point of reference was still the imperial coinage itself. This role as a metallic mouthpiece for rulers stimulated, and developed alongside, important changes in the manufacture of coinage, as elites took on new roles in the minting system—more or less directly in the Frankish world, and probably indirectly in England. The third main shift leads on from the second and took place in the later tenth and eleventh centuries. It consisted of a widespread and noticeable upturn in the use of coin, visible from Rome to England in both finds and written references to the use of coin.[56] This has in the past been seen as essentially a reaction to new supply, specifically the opening of new silver mines in Germany. Fresh supplies of bullion were indeed important, yet the sources they came from were generally already known and just exploited on a larger scale; they point, therefore, to an intensification of demand. Strengthening local appetite for coin, encroaching into areas of economic action where it had before been a smaller element, was a leitmotif of this era. A change on such a large scale cannot and should not

---

56. Coins also started to be used on a larger scale in northern Europe too, in Ireland and Scandinavia for example, though this development stems from a different background. See chapter 9.

be pigeonholed in a monocausal niche. There were different regional conditions in play. But a common and important element was more aggressive elite intervention in the human landscape. Even regions that had, in terms of money and exchange, previously marched to the beat of their own drum were touched by this last upsurge: the Scandinavian kingdoms, together with several kingdoms in central and northwest Europe. Most had in earlier times known imitative coins, or silver bullion as a means of exchange; what changed was a reorientation of means of exchange into the purview of ruling elites and their allies.

To be clear, this is primarily a book on Western Europe, with selective extensions to the north and into the Mediterranean. There are several reasons for this focus. Especially as Roman ways of making and handling money receded, there were important points of contact between England, the Frankish lands, and central and northern Italy. Similar sources occur in these regions and show comparable developments, which extended by the eleventh century into what Chris Wickham has called "outer Europe,"[57] meaning Ireland, Scandinavia, and parts of central and eastern Europe (chapter 9). These areas are not all the same by any stretch of the imagination, but they are different in ways that can be used to make meaningful observations.

There is still value and interest in focusing on this part of Europe. Yet it is increasingly apparent that this is not the only direction from which the subject might be approached.[58] Western Europe was also just one corner—and generally a poor corner—of a large, loose, and long-standing sphere of cultural and economic contacts; one that embraced Central and Eastern Europe along with the whole Mediterranean, modern Iraq, Iran, Central Asia, and parts of Africa, as well as Central and Eastern Europe. This was only a unity in the broad sense that its segments sometimes impinged on one another in relation to bullion and coin, either directly or indirectly. At times that effect could be large and impressive, as with the vast haul of Islamic silver dirhams that flowed some 5,000 km from the Caliphate to the Baltic (chapters 2 and 5). Another tack is to acknowledge that there were important similarities in how various monetary economies worked, meaning that comparisons between (say) the Geniza merchants' handling of coin as part of their international trading network might trigger helpful insights into the circulation of coin in contemporary Northern

---

57. Wickham 2009a, 472. Cf. Robert Bartlett's "outer zone" or "fringe zone" (1993, 199, 247).

58. Global medieval history has grown rapidly to become a substantial field: a major series of studies is Holmes and Standen 2018; a good recent review is Ertl and Oschema 2022.

Europe, at least if one allows for a significant difference in scale (chapter 2). Indeed, taste for precious-metal coin was one of the few things that united most parts of this vast zone (though the viking world was a case apart in this respect).[59] Gold or silver in the form of coin, or destined to play a monetary role, therefore offers a good lens through which to examine these "global" dimensions of the early Middle Ages, and to follow the cultural effects that often went with economic contacts. There are limits to this. Trade between far-flung regions within this vast Eurasian sphere was often tenuous, and some of the most important developments in this period came about precisely because those links broke down. Trade could also be "business only," with negligible cultural impact from the region that supplied coins or bullion. Everything unfolded on a case-by-case basis and changed easily. Finally, all this is to home in on things or people that actually moved. It is possible to go even further by setting societies side by side that are similar in certain regards, and perhaps contemporary, but different enough to cast what is special about each into relief, as is done with Tang and Northern Song China in chapter 5. This exercise tells us something about the hierarchy of forms of money, and about state and private involvement with coin, but without any realistic prospect of the two areas having directly affected each other. China at this time had a much larger and more centralized monetary system overall than anywhere in western Eurasia.

Sources and Approaches

It is proper to come back down to earth by turning to the major categories of evidence that will be called on to pursue these developments within western Europe. Actual coins, and finds of coins, play a major part. Often, they are the only evidence available, and even when other materials survive, coins carry special value as a real part of the circulating medium. Coins must, however, be interpreted with care. There might be uncertainty on dating and attribution. Bigger problems are likely to arise in interpreting finds of coins. Various categories of find—hoards, and individual coins or clusters from amateur finds or archaeological excavations—reveal very different things. The main challenge is that present-day countries all have their own legal procedures for handling finds of coins. Some (e.g., England and Wales, or the Netherlands) are relatively relaxed and actively

---

59. This volume generally uses lowercase viking (rather than Viking) to emphasise that this was more of an activity or occupation than an essentialised identity or ethnicity.

encourage responsible amateurs with metal detectors to go forth and hunt for ancient artefacts; others (such as France, Ireland, Italy, and some German *Länder* and Swiss cantons) are much more protective, meaning that there is little or no legitimate metal detector use outside archaeological contexts. This is not the place to discuss the merits of the various systems, but it is appropriate to note that these highly divergent modern legal practices seriously impede comparisons between regions of Europe. To set England alongside Italy, for example, is simply not comparing like with like: England now has thousands of new coin finds logged on public databases each year by detector users, while Italy may well have at least as many coins to be found, but the only ones known to scholarship are a tiny number that occur in controlled archaeological excavations, and chance finds that are declared to the authorities. Disparity is not the only problem. Far from everything that is found gets recorded, even in regions with databases, and illegal detecting is a problem everywhere.[60] Biases relating to limits of modern access also skew the sample: towns, heritage sites, military land, and national parks are off-limits, and coin finds in England tend to occur with surprising frequency in the vicinity of A-roads heading out of London, suggesting that the stomping grounds of detectorists play a significant part in shaping the apparent profile of circulation.[61] The large samples recorded in England, Wales, and the Netherlands, despite their difficulties, remain the best indications of early medieval coin circulation as a general phenomenon and will be referred to many times in the course of this book.

Written references to minting, money, and coin will play an even larger part, for people are the focus here, not the coins as such. The volume and distribution of relevant texts depend on a whole other set of variables, tied up with processes relating to the production and preservation of written material. In this period only a small minority of the populace could read, and even fewer had the training and resources to write (a quite distinct skill from reading), the latter largely being members of the clergy. In some

60. There is little one can do except note the few cases of the finders and purveyors of illegal hoards being successfully prosecuted. From England alone in the period 2016–20, two such finds (from undisclosed locations in west Norfolk and Herefordshire) resulted in very public sentences for the offenders involved: "Police Officer Jailed for Gold Coins Sale Faces Longer Term," *BBC*, 15 September 2017, https://www.bbc.co.uk/news/uk-england-norfolk-41283961; and Rebecca Mead, "The Curse of the Buried Treasure," *New Yorker*, 9 November 2020, https://www.newyorker.com/magazine/2020/11/16/the-curse-of-the-buried-treasure. But many others are known only from rumour and from suspicious clusters of coins appearing on the market.

61. Richards, Naylor, and Holas-Clark 2009.

parts of early medieval Europe, laypeople would have used documentary materials (and even books) quite regularly. But because church archives were the only ones that survived the Middle Ages, these are the institutions about which most is known, and the perspective of monks and priests bulks large in knowledge of the period. One upshot of this is that many written accounts of coinage have a moral, religious slant to them. They deal in lessons: what should be, and what should not be, rather than what is. Their value is not diminished by this, but they do need to be read with care as a source for the social realities of the early Middle Ages.

This book is divided into two parts. Part 1, consisting of chapters 2, 3, 4, and 5, looks at larger structural issues. These four chapters address, respectively, mining and sources of bullion, the making of coin, the use of coin and money beyond coin (i.e., commodities and bullion, as well as moneys of account). Part 2 is chronological in structure. Chapter 6 sets out the late Roman background. Chapter 7 then considers the gold-dominated post-Roman centuries, down to the seventh century. Chapter 8 looks at the first appearance and rise of the silver penny, in the era of the later Merovingians and Carolingians. Finally, chapter 9 turns to the tenth and eleventh centuries, considering in turn the institutional and organizational developments of coin production in the period, and changes in coin.

PART I

CHAPTER TWO

Bullion, Mining, and Minting

ONE OF THE MOST REMARKABLE objects uncovered at the Viking-Age trading site of Kaupang in Norway was an unprepossessing-looking lump of silver. This coagulated mass is a snapshot of what has long been inferred from other kinds of evidence but was never expected to emerge among surviving finds: a batch of silver from a crucible, lost halfway through being melted, with its varied contents still visible. These include several cut-up fragments of coins (Arabic dirhams), but also pieces of ingot and hacksilver (figure 2.1).[1] Diverse kinds of silver object, brought from far and near, were being blended together for a new use.

The mix of material in the Kaupang crucible melt hints at the complex material reality that lies behind the gold and silver of early medieval coined money. Supply of bullion was a matter of sporadic pulses punctuated with spells of dearth or drips of miscellaneous character. Yet for obvious reasons this intermittent flow mattered considerably. Being made of gold or silver, early medieval coins depended on availability of the necessary metal.[2] Without bullion, there could be no coinage, and currencies eked out in the absence of new metal tended to wither swiftly.[3] The potential sources are easily outlined. Freshly extracted and refined ore was one possibility. Others included metal recycled from other coins, or from other objects.[4] The possibility of melting down diverse gold and silver items to turn them into coin is by no means unlikely. Book covers, jewellery, rings,

---

1. Blackburn 2007, 32–34.

2. A sweeping and ambitious survey of this topic is Blanchard 2001–05, vol. 1. Mining also features prominently in Spufford 1988.

3. Matzke 2011a, 271. For the example of clipped siliquae in post-Roman Britain, see Patterson 1972; Guest 2005; Naismith 2017b, 31–34.

4. Naismith 2017b, 16–17.

FIGURE 2.1. Crucible melt excavated at Kaupang, including several fragmentary dirhams. Museum of Cultural History, University of Oslo, Norway. Photo by Eirik Irgens Johnsen.

and other church adornments fabricated from gold or silver always had a semimonetary character. Æthelwold, bishop of Winchester (d. 984), had church plate "broken in pieces and turned into money" to feed the poor during a famine,[5] while the *Liber pontificalis* from Rome rarely dwells on much about offerings to or from the papacy, or on the details of how and why they were given, but it does minutely record the weight of gold and silver objects.[6] All were in their way still money, and potential coins in waiting.

The interplay of coin and bullion in actual transactions will be revisited in chapter 5; the point of the present chapter is to examine the most basic premise of early medieval minting—where the precious metal used in mints came from. Mines will be addressed first, with reference to methodology, known examples in western Europe, and their operation in relation to networks of power and authority. Thereafter the focus shifts to the general dynamic behind movements of bullion: why it went where it did, and at what pace. The principal modes of circulation are then examined with reference to three brief case-studies, namely, the Viking-Age circulation of dirhams, gold in the Mediterranean from the fifth to the seventh centuries, and gold and silver in the tenth- and eleventh-century Mediterranean trading networks of the Cairo Geniza. What emerges brings

5. "Minutatim confringi et in pecunias redigi." Wulfstan of Wincester, *Vita sancti Æthelwoldi* c. 29 (ed. and trans. Lapidge and Winterbottom 1991, 44–47).
6. Delogu 1988.

us back to the Kaupang crucible melt. Early medieval sources of bullion were numerous and flexible but also unpredictable and easily fell short or dried up, meaning that it was commonplace to cast around and use metal of several different origins and forms. People played the hand they were dealt, whether that meant a glut of dirhams or a meagre handful of miscellaneous fragments.

Tracing the Origins of Gold and Silver

It is fitting to begin where the metals themselves began: mines and also, in the case of gold, alluvial deposits (i.e., metal mixed with waterborne sediments, which could be removed by panning). Early medieval mining has left a mixed footprint, and generally a light one. Some sources are well known from a range of archaeological, scientific, and historical sources; others, only from one of those three. An added complication is that modern scholars can only work backward from what survives into modern times and need to allow for the possibility that some deposits were mined away to nothing in earlier times: they are simply gone, and all one can do is speculate about their nature and quantity.[7]

Fortunately, coins and other metallic objects do survive, and their constituent parts sometimes betray a clue to the origin of the metal when subjected to various forms of scientific analysis. These techniques remain problematic with regard to gold but can work very well for silver. Medieval silver typically derived from galena, a naturally occurring form of lead sulphide.[8] It follows that lead mines could also represent silver mines. Massive amounts of effort and material resources went into the extraction of silver from galena, the minimal viable amount for refining being around 0.1–0.5 per cent silver relative to lead.[9] Silver refined from galena generally kept a residue of lead, which modern scholars can extract and analyse.[10] The balance of different isotopic variants of lead—that is, with different numbers of neutrons in the nucleus of each atom—can distinguish between sources of silver, if they have clearly separate and well-known

7. Merkel 2020, 42–43.

8. Silver did also occur in other forms, including "dry" silver that needed no further refinement; silver of this kind (as well as galena) was used for minting in eighth- and ninth-century Muslim lands: Merkel 2021.

9. For the varied richness of medieval silver ores, see Merkel 2020.

10. Metcalf and Northover (1986, 36) note that "silver" should really be assessed as the sum of silver plus key trace elements that were not easily removed (gold, lead, copper, and tin).

isotopic signatures.[11] The process poses more challenges if the isotopic signature corresponds to a large area, or to one with highly varied isotopic evidence.[12] Another, complementary approach is to examine the quantities of other trace elements besides silver and lead,[13] while a more oblique signal of the impact of mining comes from trace evidence for pollution, such as minute deposits of lead recently extracted from layers of glacial ice in the Colle Gnifetti in northern Italy. The latter point to a significant uptick in lead (and plausibly also silver) extraction in the mid-seventh century.[14] Finally, it is possible to apply both direct and circumstantial historical references to mines, and the evidence of excavations of mining sites and settlements. Yet because productive mines would continue to be worked, ultimately to oblivion, archaeologically identifiable remains frequently represent smaller, more temporary operations.[15]

Local sources of gold remain difficult to pin down, but over a dozen areas of Europe (map 2.1) can be identified where silver was definitely or probably extracted between about 500 and 1100.[16] At least five of these (southern Spain, the Colline Metalliferi, the Harz mountains, Mont Lozère, and Wiesloch) had been exploited to some degree in antiquity,[17] and only a couple—southern Spain and Melle—are known to have been active on a really large scale (at least for silver) between about 600 and 900. The southern Spanish mines fed the large silver currency of al-Andalus, specimens of which have been found in southern France, though at this stage isotopic evidence does not point to these being a large contribution to the local currency.[18] Melle is now recognised as the first great new mining operation of medieval Europe. At its height, between the mid-seventh century and the early tenth, it has been argued to have produced an average of about fifteen tons of silver per year.[19] Melle contracted in

11. A mix of distinct sources will produce a balance of their isotopic signatures: Merkel 2016, 68–69.

12. Loveluck et al. 2018, 2020.

13. Sarah 2008, 1:19–174; Merkel 2016, esp. 19–34.

14. Loveluck et al. 2018.

15. As, for example, at Mont Lozère: Baron et al. 2006.

16. This figure represents a minimum: there were surely other sources that have not been pinned down. Carolingian denarii from Toulouse, for example, indicate one or two more sources of silver besides Melle further north in Aquitaine: Geneviève and Sarah 2018, 189–91.

17. Bartels and Klappauf 2012, 121–22.

18. For Spanish dirhams in southern Gaul, see Parvérie 2007; 2010; 2012; 2014.

19. Téreygeol 2018; for the impact of Melle on Alpine glaciers as a gauge for its impact over time, see Loveluck et al. 2018. Some other assessments, however, argue for a much smaller output, including Bettenay 2022.

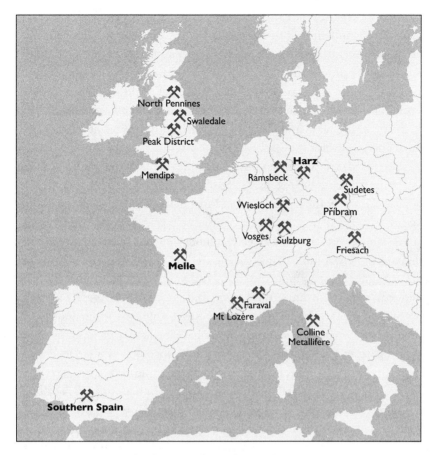

MAP 2.1. Known or probable areas of significant silver extraction in western and central Europe c. 500–1100. The most important sources have bold labels.

output and importance over the tenth century, while the Harz went from strength to strength; so much so that it is often thought the mines of the Harz only started to be worked in the tenth century, when Widukind of Corvey, Thietmar of Merseburg, and others record the discovery of new seams of silver, although other minerals (and to a small extent silver) had been exploited there in earlier times.[20] Other areas where production of silver took off at sites previously active for other minerals, include

20. Thietmar of Merseburg, *Chronicon* 2.13 (Holtzmann 1935, 52–53; trans. Warner 2001, 101); Widukind of Corvey, *Res gestae Saxonicae* 3.63 (Lohmann and Hirsch 1935, 138; trans. Bachrach and Bachrach 2014, 138). On the identification of Thietmar's mines, see Ehlers 1997, 47. Early mining activity in the Harz can be traced back to the seventh century, though at first more focused on copper: see Segers-Glocke and Witthöft 2000; Roseneck 2001; Brachmann 1992; Straßburger 2013, 16–17; Bartels and Klappauf 2012, 122,129.

the Colline Metalliferi, Faravel, Mont Lozère, and Wiesloch.[21] It was also in the tenth and eleventh centuries that silver mining probably began at other locations such as Ramsbeck and Sulzburg in Germany, the Vosges in France, and Příbram and Sudetes in Czechia.[22] Several locations in western and central Britain have now produced archaeological evidence for lead exploitation in the ninth to eleventh centuries, though it remains difficult to estimate the scale and duration of these efforts, or whether they produced much silver.[23]

This rundown of mining in western Europe tells only half the story, however. It misses the extensive use of gold and silver from sources elsewhere, especially the Byzantine and Muslim worlds. But it also skirts the larger question of whether mines stimulated minting or minting stimulated mining. Was the stock of coined money pushed more by supply or by demand? Peter Spufford's magisterial study of medieval monetary history argued generally for supply: newly opened mines seemed to stimulate new and expanded minting in the central and later Middle Ages.[24] A different sort of relationship is suggested by the chronology of the major mining enterprises of earlier times. These had frequently been known long before production surged. Melle had been tapped on a limited level since the fifth century,[25] but it expanded rapidly from the mid-seventh century. Something similar probably took place in the Harz mountains: although the region more widely had been a source of lead, silver, copper, and other minerals for centuries, production stepped up from about 700, with a noticeable expansion and intensification in the later tenth and eleventh centuries. At Wiesloch, the spread-out networks that had been used for the washing and refining of lead and silver ore in the ninth century, which involved carting it to locations several miles away, gave way in the mid-tenth to a more concentrated and active operation.[26] These step-changes coincide with periods of growth in the coined currency. Melle scaled up at the time when silver started to be added to the Frankish and English

21. Straßburger 2013; Bartels and Klappauf 2012, 126–27, 136–38; Bianchi 2018; Py 2009; Py et al. 2014.

22. Straßburger 2006; 2013, 18–28; Bartels and Klappauf 2012, 144–46; Cabała et al. 2019, 2; Fluck 1993.

23. Bayley 2018; McFarlane, Lundberg, and Neff 2014. Some Northumbrian lead was being used at Kaupang in Norway: Skre 2011b, 428; Pedersen 2016a, 158, 194–95; 2016b, 156–59. For more discussion of lead and silver mining in early medieval Northumbria, see Maddicott 2000, 29, 31–32; Booth 2000, 84–87; Metcalf 1993–1994, 3:639.

24. Spufford 1988, 74–75. Cf. Matzke 2011a, 271.

25. Téreygeol 2007, 125.

26. Bartels and Klappauf 2012, 122, 126, 128, 136–38.

gold coinage in significant quantity, soon to be replaced by an entirely silver currency, and the widespread amplification in mining activity of the Harz Mountains later in the tenth and eleventh centuries sits alongside contemporary growth in the monetary economy. Once these mines had got going, the relationship with minting shifted more to supply, but in the world of limited scale and on-off supply of bullion that characterised the early Middle Ages, demand probably stimulated initial increase in supply. That in turn suggests conscious agency behind the increase of silver exploitation.

Bullion, Profits, and Power

Several constituencies were responsible for the extraction of metal from the ground and its processing into usable form. Somewhat fewer were in a position to benefit substantially therefrom, or to exert serious change over the process, and the argument made here is that elite and/or state interests typically kicked in with the growth of mining operations.

The actual work, of course, was carried out by miners. Many would be low-skilled, often active only on a seasonal basis, but some highly skilled individuals were also needed. Those more specialised miners may already have had a degree of freedom of movement: miners are thought to have gravitated to the Harz from Francia (possibly from Melle itself) in the tenth century, if only on late and thin evidence. In principle mining communities could undertake the whole operation on their own, without intervention from outside. In the Harz, seventh- and eighth-century smelting sites for lead and silver are isolated and not marked by anomalies in vegetation or soil suggestive of larger activity, so they are thought to represent refining under the auspices of individual families or small communities, outside the orbit of major settlements or power structures.[27]

But miners faced significant structural obstacles. Some related to the seigneurial dimensions of mining. Whoever held the relevant land by default had an interest, and early medieval kings and emperors sometimes followed Roman tradition in asserting regalian rights over mineral deposits.[28] A royal diploma of 1028 granted the bishop of Basel "certain veins and excavations of silver" (*quasdam venas et fossiones argenti*) in the Breisgau; from these, the bishop received "whatever pertains from

27. Bartels and Klappauf 2012, 127–28, 134–35.
28. Hirt 2010, 107–356; Jones 1964, 435–36, 838–39; Täckholm 1937, 97–115. In the Harz, the king himself was the major landowner: Bartels and Klappauf 2012, 176–79.

[the mines] to our [i.e., royal] jurisdiction" (*quicquid inde nostrum ius attingit*).[29] Presumably that meant a cut of profits from selling silver and/or of the silver itself. How large this share was is not specified. In the Roman period, the state share could be as high as half of all produce (and a demand that the rest be sold to the state at fixed prices), while some thirteenth-century and later owners of the land on which mines sat demanded a tenth.[30] The income taken by the abbey of Lorsch from Wiesloch later in the eleventh century amounted to two or three marks of silver a year, or about 0.2 per cent of production estimated from archaeological finds.[31] Similarly, the eight thousand pounds of lead from Melle allocated by the king to Saint-Denis every two years (according to the ninth-century *Gesta Dagoberti*) would represent at most 1.3 per cent of annual output, and probably a lot less.[32]

The relatively small perquisites that came from mining represent a balancing act: lords needed to attract labour by keeping the demanding process of mining profitable. Even the most exacting seigneurial regime still probably allowed the bulk of silver to be distributed and sold through the initiative of miners. Crucially, though, lords were in a position to profit in other ways. The expectation was that normally the whole process of cleaning and smelting metal would take place on the same landholder's property: at Mont-Lozère in southern France, this was probably why the miners did *not* use the ore deposits in closest proximity to the smelting sites.[33] Smelting could have been where a small share of produce was taken, or else an occasion for another fee to use the lord's facilities. Redistribution of bullion offered a further opportunity for income. There were tolls to be levied on wagons and boats. If metal was taken to a market, as it very probably was, the lord might stipulate that it be taken in the first instance to one under his control, where there would be a toll:

29. MGH DD CII 133. For discussion, see Zotz 1993, 195–96; Bartels and Klappauf 2012, 165–66.

30. Ørsted 2000, 74–75; Spufford 1988, 123.

31. Bartels and Klappauf 2012, 166. For the Lorsch income, see Glöckner 1929–36, 1:413 (no. 139).

32. *Gesta Dagoberti* c. 40 (Krusch 1888, 419). This figure is calculated from data given in Téreygeol 2018. Annual output of silver is estimated, for the period between 650 and 900, at between 13.8 and 16.9 tons of silver, with silver occurring at from one to five parts per thousand of lead. It is assumed that the *Gesta Dagoberti* used either a Roman pound of 322.9 grams (Duncan-Jones 2012) or a larger Carolingian pound of 489.6 grams. For background to this complicated text, see Prelog 1989; Hageneier 2004, 241–45; Goethe 2016, 16–58.

33. Baron et al. 2006, 250–51.

potentially every ninth or tenth coin spent there.[34] It is not possible to put a precise figure on how much silver might have ended up in the hands of elites with interests in and around a mining area, but it was a lot more than the dues owed directly from mining and needs to be seen in terms of what would now be called vertical integration: every stage in the lifespan of the metal involved a cost.

The other main hurdle impeding large-scale mining was logistical. Mining itself needed extensive support, and the processing of extracted ore even more so, especially if it was galena with a low yield of silver. Wood would be needed to reinforce mine shafts and feed furnaces, watercourses were needed for washing the ore, and buildings were needed for storage. Distribution compounded those needs: men, horses, and carts were required to move the ore and metal from place to place.[35] A significant increase in mining activity therefore had to be met with exponential intensification in the resources devoted to systems of support. Theoretically miners and merchants could provide the necessary investment themselves: that was sometimes the case in central and western Europe later in the Middle Ages,[36] and in the early medieval Islamic world, where Ibn Ḥawqal (d. after 978) quotes a sum of 300,000 dirhams raised by miners for a new mine shaft at Panjhīr.[37] In practice, responsibility for growth in early medieval European mining probably came from above and took the form of centralisation and specialisation. At Melle, the scale and close concentration of all the necessary activities indicates a strong hand at work: probably that of the king (and, later, the count).[38] The *Gesta Dagoberti's* account of Melle lead suggests a system of distributing the king's share of metal to royal estates, which could have been handled using portage (corvée) services similar to those that can be detected for salt in the abbey of Prüm's polyptych.[39] At Melle itself, a rich cluster of funerary epitaphs perhaps reflects some of the figures who oversaw mining and associated processes and profited from them.[40] Wiesloch's formerly dispersed setup, with mining, washing, smelting, and other activities distributed several

34. Endemann 1964, 56–57

35. Bartels and Klappauf 2012, 144–48.

36. Hielscher and Husted 2020; Bartels and Klappauf 2012, 181–87, 217–30.

37. Ed. and trans. Kramers and Wiet 1964, 2:448–49; Cowell and Lowick 1988, 65–66. See also Morony 2019, 212–13.

38. Bourgeois 2014; Bourgeois and Téreygeol 2005; La Coste-Messelières 1950; 1957–58.

39. Polyptych of Prüm, c. 41 (Schwab 1983, 197–98). Cf. Kuchenbuch 1978, 293–97; Thome 1972.

40. Bourgeois 2014, esp. 16; Treffort and Uberti 2010, 203.

miles apart, gave way in the mid-tenth century to a much more focused arrangement, at the heart of which was a set of large new facilities and a colossal dump of slag eventually totalling over 220,000 tons.[41] At Düna (Niedersachsen), on the western edge of the Harz, a similar process can also be seen in action. Three individual farmsteads that had each been engaged in smelting iron and nonferrous metals were replaced, after being destroyed in the course of the tenth century, by a stone building that became a new focus of settlement. Smelting and other metalworking activities were concentrated in a single area beside a stream, and ironworking was abandoned in favour of copper, lead, and silver. There was further elaboration of the central stone building in the eleventh and twelfth centuries, leading to the addition of fortifications and a palisade, as well as a kitchen.[42] Several sites in the Colline Metalliferi show a similar pattern. These rolling hills, full of diverse mineral resources, contained mining settlements that started out as clusters of huts near seams of ore in the eighth and ninth centuries but gave way in the decades around 900 to more overt focuses of seigneurial power (what Giovanna Bianchi calls "off the scale" [*fuori scala*] sites).[43] Interestingly, one well-studied site of this kind, Cugnano, probably did not actually see large-scale refinement, for pieces of slag metal are few. That could be an indication that these new lordly encroachments were based on collecting and moving the ore from surrounding sites, most likely by selling it to smelters or other buyers.[44] The Colline Metalliferi had a high concentration of public land, so the king and local agents working on his behalf are the most likely agents behind the stronger interest in mining and metalworking that these changes imply.[45] Some of these sites could have been granted, temporarily or permanently, to other members of the elite, whose initiative became more visible in the eleventh and especially twelfth centuries.[46]

The unknown quantity in all this is what happened next: how silver made its way from mines and refinement centres to mints or other destinations. Most would probably have been sold through channels shaped by the local seigneurial and economic conditions. Silver destined for long-distance distribution perhaps remained in ingot form. Otherwise,

41. Bartels and Klappauf 2012, 136.

42. Klappauf, Linke, and Both 2004.

43. Bianchi 2020.

44. Bianchi 2018, 400; Francovich and Wickham 1994, 19–20.

45. Bianchi 2020.

46. Bianchi 2018; Bianchi and Collavini 2018; Bianchi and Rovelli 2018. The model was first postulated, in a study focused on the twelfth and thirteenth centuries, by Francovich and Wickham 1994, esp. 22–26.

minting—at Melle, or one of the several mint-towns in the vicinity of the Harz—lent added trustworthiness to the metal, for a further fee. Jewish responsa of the early eleventh century show that there was indeed a well-developed market in Germany that capitalised on the fees of exchanging bullion into different kinds of coin.[47]

CIRCULATION OF BULLION: DYNAMICS

In a sense it is misleading to treat movement of bullion as separate from mining. All metals used in early medieval coinage ultimately came from mines, and most of them not by very many or very long removes.[48] The percolation of metal from mines to mints probably followed one of two broad patterns, here termed "fast" and "slow." A fast scenario would run thus: Silver has been mined from the Panjhir in the Samanid emirate. After refinement, it is rapidly struck into dirham form, probably with export in mind, at the nearby mint-city of Balkh.[49] With many others, the new coin would be taken north and west, out of the emirate, on a route similar to that documented by Ahmad ibn Fadlan (d. c. 960) as part of an embassy undertaken in the early 920s. Ibn Fadlan's journey took him to the great city of the Volga Bulgars, situated on the bend in the Volga near modern Kazan. There the dirhams would change hands, probably in return for slaves and other commodities brought from the North by people ibn Fadlan called the Rus.[50] It would then travel north again, in the hands of those Rus visitors, to enter circulation in the Baltic.

Fast circulation of bullion involved treating the metal as a commodity in itself, with well-developed routes taking it, via relatively few exchanges, from the point of production to a particular destination, after which it might be reminted or (in the case of the dirhams) circulate in its original state. The slow scenario worked through multiple smaller steps and only sporadic treatment as commodity rather than coin (which was not always a clear distinction). Silver mined from the mines in the Harz mountains in the later tenth century might be used as an illustration. The metal— heavy and bulky in its unrefined state—would be refined and minted in

47. Eidelberg 1955, no. 29; trans. and comment in Toch 2008, 185; see also Toch 2012, 212–14.

48. The one exception is gold that had been panned. This was probably not a major source in the early Middle Ages, although a charter from Passau—a forgery in the name of Arnulf (887–899) (MGH DD Arn 163) but created during the tenth century—notes that the city's goldsmiths had the right to pan in nearby rivers.

49. Kovalev 2011, 7–9.

50. For ibn Fadlan's celebrated account of the Rus, see Lunde and Stone 2012, 45–55.

fairly close proximity to the mines, if still far enough to require an elaborate system of portage, at Gittelde or one of the mint-places responsible for the "Otto-Adelheid Pfennige."[51] But instead of being minted with the intention of rapid and long-distance redistribution, these coins (or at least some of them) might have started by entering more local use. They could have first been minted under the auspices of an ecclesiastical institution or secular aristocrat, and thereafter spent on consumables, luxury goods, or wages for labour; the key point is that they would enter into circulation in the same way as other coins. And, just like other coins, they would have been spent and circulated multiple times. By incremental steps those coins would have moved outward, their general trajectory being guided by the distribution of major holders of wealth and of centres of circulation such as markets: in the case of coins from the Harz, they might have gravitated west toward the major cities of the Rhineland, or south to Bavaria and the Alps. They could have been reminted multiple times even just within Germany and certainly would have been if they penetrated into Italy or were taken to England. The supposition is that people would come to a mint-place with external gold or silver and trade it for acceptable coin.[52] That process could have been in the hands of moneyers who doubled as exchangers, while others may have been set up like Strasbourg in the early twelfth century, with a set of money changers distinct from the moneyers,[53] or like in the Muslim Mediterranean where powerful officials called *murid* managed the purchase of bullion for the mint.[54] The custom was effectively for the mint or moneyer to buy the bullion offered to them, in return for so many coins. These would not necessarily have been the same exact batch of gold or silver as the patron had handed over: mixing metal from different sources would have been normal and made little difference to either party as long as what each got in return was of the correct quality and value.[55] In any case, mints and moneyers would often have kept a float of ready-made coin to handle this eventuality. Mints were therefore a literal melting pot of metal.

These two models represent opposite extremes. In practice, it is likely that coins and bullion circulated on both fast and slow circuits, the two

51. Hatz et al. 1991.

52. See chapter 3.

53. Naismith 2016c, esp. 58. This is perhaps implied for Langres and Soissons in the ninth century, where *moneta* and *trapezeta* were specified separately: Bautier 1967, no. 13; Odilo, *Translatio S. Sebastiani*, c. 43 (Holder-Egger 1887b, 388);

54. Goitein 1967–93, 1:267.

55. Cf. practice in later medieval Venice, where all gold and silver was refined into ingots before minting: Stahl 2000, 321–39.

being interdependent. A German merchant specialising in trade with England might (for example) have gathered as much coin as he could from Harz miners, or from locally circulating specie in Cologne or Tiel, perhaps even favouring issues he knew to be of good silver, before taking them to England. Meanwhile, dirhams would often have entered something more akin to slow circulation after reaching the Baltic. All this is of course informed speculation, starting from the fact that gold and silver must have come from one or more points of origin to its last point of minting and thence its point of deposition. What lies between these steps is the question. Metallurgical evidence indicates that it was not necessarily a simple and straightforward process. Gold and silver were liable to be changed to some degree every time they were melted and reworked, mixed to some extent with metal from other sources. Bullion several removes from its source stands only a limited chance of reflecting its dominant original trace elements or lead isotope values. It is perfectly possible that once our imaginary merchant from Cologne arrived in Canterbury or London and presented his coins for reminting, the moneyer mixed them in molten form with silver from other sources—perhaps brought by a merchant from further south in the Rhineland with coins mostly made from Wiesloch silver, some Samanid dirhams from a recent visitor to Scandinavia, or for that matter an English thegn from just a few miles away with coins of previous local issues made from all these different sources, recycled many times over. And just to add further complexity, the moneyer or his employees might have used locally sourced lead, copper alloy, or other minerals in the course of refining and manufacturing. These could be brought over long distances, too: a charter refers to transportation of lead from Derbyshire to Kent, and archaeological evidence suggests lead from northern England was taken to Norway.[56] Michael Matzke has stressed the importance of such regional traditions of alloying and refining in the creation of distinct metallurgical profiles of metal.[57] If silver from one or more outside sources was melted and then brought to a standard fineness by the addition of local supplies of lead or other metals (with their own trace elements), the ensuing coins will end up resembling the local profile, or a blend of that and their original source. This might explain why the trace elements of late Anglo-Saxon pennies do not map exactly onto Harz or Rhenish silver or any other single known source,[58] even though it is very

56. S 1624 (Brooks and Kelly 2013, no. 66); Skre 2011b, 428.
57. Matzke 2018, 165–67.
58. Merkel 2016, 108–10.

likely that English bullion by at least the end of the tenth century came mostly from German sources.

Most bullion that went into coins probably came together in something like the way imagined here. Complexity, that is to say, was the norm. Coinages made wholly or predominantly from a single and readily identifiable source of primary (that is, mined) gold or silver are the exception.

IMPORTS OF BULLION: THREE CASE STUDIES

Bullion never moved itself; nor was it moved without reason. These reasons and the people behind them will be addressed in this section, with reference to three case studies. Two (dirhams moving to the Northern Lands in the Viking Age, and gold in the fourth- to seventh-century Mediterranean) primarily address fast circuits known largely from actual coins. The third calls on the better-attested movements of coin in and around Fatimid Egypt, which shows just how messy and interwoven fast and slow circuits could be.

Imports of Muslim silver dirhams into the Baltic and eastern Europe travelled some 2,000 miles down the winding rivers and through the open grasslands (map 2.2) of Russia and Ukraine.[59] This influx began shortly before the year 800 and can be followed in close detail because so many of the coins carry both a mint name and an exact date. They came from across the Muslim world, from North Africa to Baghdad and Iran.[60] As the ninth century went by they arrived in larger and larger numbers, with a significant contraction after about 850, probably stemming from disruption to the transit routes rather than an actual drop-off in minting.[61] A new and even larger phase of importation began at the end of the ninth century, which looked further east, to the massively productive mints operated by the Samanid emirs of what is now Afghanistan and Pakistan; these in turn were fed by silver mines in the Tien Shan mountains (running from the western border of modern China into Central Asia).[62] Samanid dirhams continued to move north in vast quantities until the middle of the tenth century. As in the ninth century, they did not stop coming because of any

59. See chapter 5.

60. Several potential silver sources existed in the Muslim world at this time, with distinct metallurgical characteristics: Sarah 2008, 1:429–41; Ilisch et al. 2003. A distinctive feature of Muslim silver extraction is that it did not rely exclusively on low-yield lead-silver ores, as elsewhere; native silver and high-yield ores were also available: Merkel 2021. An older survey relying mostly on literary sources is Lombard 1974, 151–250.

61. Kilger 2008a, 228–35; Noonan 1985, 42–48.

62. Merkel 2016, 52–54; Cowell and Lowick 1988; Kovalev 2003.

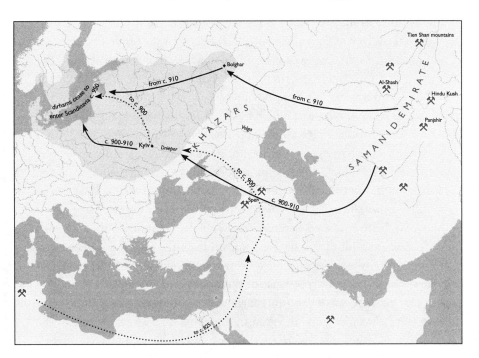

MAP 2.2. Main routes of dirhams from the Muslim world, with possible Islamic silver mines (based on Lombard 1974, 151–250); the shaded area represents the territory in which dirham hoards are concentrated.

shock or shortfall at the point of production; rather, there was some sort of break that cut off the coins from reaching the Baltic, while they continued to arrive in eastern Europe in bulk down to the 980s and 990s.[63] It was at around this time, in the later decades of the tenth century, that western (German and English) silver started to circulate in the Baltic on a larger scale, in some sense picking up where the dirhams had left off.

Hoards are the main evidence for this traffic and survive in vast numbers, containing hundreds of thousands of coins overall.[64] These stand in for a great many more dirhams that were brought but met a different fate. The hoards suggest that coins could have reached northern Europe relatively fast, moving in the wake of long-distance networks focused on specialised, valuable commodities. Their subsequent treatment reflects how various regions and communities interfaced with those networks.[65]

63. Noonan 2000–2001. Kovalev 2011, 12–19, argues that state-building activities by the Rus in the mid-tenth century were to blame.

64. For overviews see Kovalev 2007; Kilger 2008a; Jankowiak 2020.

65. Jankowiak 2019, esp. 28.

In the ninth century, dirhams tended to be hoarded soon after arrival, with a limited degree of fragmentation; in the tenth, they tended to circulate for longer before being deposited, often in a very fragmented state.[66] The impact of the dirhams goes beyond surviving coins: arm rings and many other metal objects of Scandinavian and Baltic origin can be shown to be made from melted-down dirhams.[67] Dirhams had more mixed influence in areas outside the Baltic and Eastern Europe, where they circulated on a smaller scale and as part of a more diverse landscape of silver and coin. In Britain and Ireland, eastern silver circulated alongside, and mixed with, western European silver (often from Melle, at least in the ninth century).[68] In the mid-tenth century the Spanish traveller Ibrāhīm ibn Ya'qūb encountered Samanid dirhams from Samarkand being used at Mainz: no finds of this date are known from the region around Mainz, though, so these coins may have been a small element of the local currency, remarked on only because of their unexpected presence.[69]

The dirham imports of northern and eastern Europe in the Viking Age can be set alongside the gold that arrived in western Europe in the fifth to seventh centuries. Here, the problem is the opposite: the source was probably somewhat closer, in the eastern Mediterranean, but is significantly more difficult to pin down. The stream from the east was probably never completely reliable and may have contended with a parallel tendency for gold to drain out of the west toward the east in payment for lucrative luxury imports.[70] Shortages of gold occurred sporadically from as early as the decades around 500. In Ostrogothic Italy, Theoderic (493–526) at one point sent a royal agent to break into ancient tombs in search of gold and silver coin, and Athalaric (526–34) encouraged gold mining on a royal estate in Bruttium (though not with any known success).[71] The situation went from bad to worse around the middle of the seventh century when finds of Byzantine gold in the West dried up,[72] and Frankish and English gold coins underwent rapid debasement. Gold in the West was hence liable to be recycled, perhaps many times: this context of a shrinking, increasingly heterogenous supply could lie behind

---

66. Blackburn 2007, 34–47; Rispling 2007.

67. Merkel 2019; Hårdh 1976, 110–27; Kershaw et al. 2021. See also chapter 5.

68. Kruse 1992. Research in progress by Jane Kershaw and Stephen Merkel points more strongly to a mixed picture, especially in the context of viking silver.

69. Jacob 1927, 31.

70. McCormick 2001, 84–85.

71. Cassiodorus, *Variae* 4.34 and 9.3 (Mommsen 1894, 129, 269–70; trans. Bjornlie 2019, 188, 358–60).

72. Lafaurie and Morrisson 1987; Morrisson 2014.

the miracle of St, Eligius (d. 660) being able to make two gold thrones out of the raw material meant for one, in a saint's life written before 684.[73] Fineness was no longer so critical in assessing the worth of coins: debased solidi might be mounted in fittings of finer gold than the actual coin.[74]

Seeing this sequence of developments, Henri Pirenne latched the decline and end of gold coinage in Gaul to the disruption to Mediterranean trade caused by the Muslim conquests.[75] Even after nearly a century, versions of his argument are still being debated, for Pirenne was the first to identify a rupture that went much deeper than coin.[76] Although the "Pirenne thesis" is often still used as shorthand for studies of this break, the emphasis has long since shifted away from Muslim military expansion to a general weakening of economic structures in the seventh century that affected both the North and the Byzantine world. But these internal developments also had direct and damaging consequences for the long-distance flows that brought gold from east to west. East-west trade had been in gradual decline for a long time before the seventh century, even if it never ended altogether,[77] and needs to be seen alongside gifts and subsidies that came as part of the eastern empire's chequebook diplomacy, like the 50,000 solidi paid by Emperor Maurice (582–602) to the Merovingian Frankish King Childebert II (575–96) in the 580s.[78] Indeed, there was legislation in force in the East Roman (Byzantine) Empire that forbade the private export of gold;[79] this may not have blocked trade in gold completely, but it is an impediment to explanations of bullion flow that rely too heavily on high-level commerce. The break may also have been a facet of fiscal reorientation around the time of Constans II (641–668). The East Roman Empire under his rule was still accessible, and still in touch, but had bigger problems on its eastern and southern frontiers that

73. Audoin, *Vita Eligii* 1.5 (Krusch 1902, 672–73).

74. Codine-Trécourt 2014, 36–38.

75. Pirenne 1939, 173, 243–47. Responses to the Pirenne thesis are legion: for a selection, see Effros 2017; Delogu 1998; Hodges 1989, 6–28; Lyon 1974, 441–56.

76. For western Europe, the classic analysis is Hodges 1989, 29–46. For Byzantium, an important general study is Haldon 1997, esp. 41–124; 2016, esp. 26–78. See also the relevant sections of Wickham 2005, 693–824.

77. McCormick 2001, 783–84.

78. Gregory of Tours, *Historiae* 4.42 (Krusch and Levison 1951, 314; trans. Thorpe 1974, 375); Paul the Deacon, *Historia Langobardorum* 3.17 (Bethmann and Waitz 1878, 101; trans. Foulke 1907, 117–18). For discussion, see Fischer 2019.

79. *Codex Justinianus* 4.63.2 (Blume and Frier 2016, 2:1055). Reiterated in the *Book of the Eparch* 2.4 and 2.6 (Koder 1991, 86–87). Cf. Laiou 2004.

had slashed the empire's income and output of gold coins and forced what remained to be spent more on internal, military needs.[80]

Of course, to attribute western gold coinage and its decline to ebbing imports from the East is just passing the buck. Where Byzantium got its gold is just as debatable. A new source came online in the fourth to seventh centuries, when solidi were minted on a vast scale.[81] Where this was located is unclear: historically known sources lay in Ethiopia and Nubia to the empire's south, Armenia and the Caucasus to the east, and the Arabian Peninsula to the southeast; it is also possible that West Africa emerged as a source for gold as early as the sixth century.[82] Access to all these routes grew more difficult over time. Sassanian Persia contested Roman-Byzantine influence in Armenia and neighbouring regions, most successfully in the fifth and sixth centuries, while the expansion of Islamic rule wrested Egypt and North Africa from Roman control in the 640s and 680s/690s, respectively, and also disrupted the routes and states that facilitated the flow of Arabian and Armenian gold into the empire. Restriction of access to these sources of bullion by the mid-seventh century was an important factor in the contraction of Byzantine gold coinage.[83] More emphasis fell on the recycling of gold in subsequent times, supplemented by confiscations, tributes from neighbours at certain times and smaller commercially driven inflows of coin and bullion from elsewhere.[84] Internal sources of fresh gold were scarce. The one gold mine that has been identified archaeologically in the East Roman-Byzantine Empire, at Bir Umm Fawakhir in eastern Egypt, demonstrates the determination of the state to stretch its available sources of gold as far as possible.[85] The difficulty of extracting gold from the "granite-hard" seams of quartz at this inhospitable and remote location must have been daunting and led the excavators of the site to posit that only a large and well-organised regime—presumably the imperial authorities—that was truly desperate for gold would have devoted the manpower and resources needed for the relatively slim pickings available.[86] Importantly, the restricted scale of its

80. Esders 2013, esp. 220–38; Hendy 2002.

81. Morrisson et al. 1985, 92–95.

82. Lombard 1974, 9–73. For the sub-Saharan connection, see Phillipson 2017.

83. Shahîd 1995–2010, 2.2, 47–57; Shaddel 2021.

84. Haldon 1997, 176; Hendy 1985, 284–303; and Banaji 1996.

85. Meyer et al. 2000 and 2003; Meyer 2011. For the early Islamic reopening of a Pharaonic and Hellenistic gold mine at Samut, again in eastern Egypt, see Marchand et al. 2019. For the bleak state of late-antique gold extraction more widely, see Edmondson 1989; Gianichedda 2008.

86. Meyer 1997, esp. 15–16.

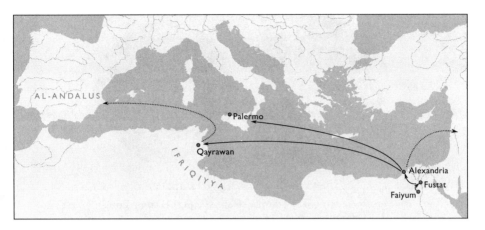

MAP 2.3. Major routes for trade in the late tenth and eleventh centuries, including in gold and silver, used by merchants known from the Cairo Geniza.

output as well as lack of evidence for its trace element signature in coins or other objects mean that Bir Umm Fawakhir cannot have been a major overall contributor of gold to the empire's stocks.[87]

Byzantium's loss in terms of gold was the caliphate's gain, and before long it would capitalise on a strong start by developing existing gold and silver mining operations and opening new ones, in Spain, North Africa, the Arabian Peninsula, Iran, and Central Asia. This metallic richness fed into the caliphate's enormous circulating currency, though the flow was not constant or even between regions; also, with the important exception of the Central Asian mines, there is still considerable work to be done on tracing what gold and silver went where, both within and beyond the Muslim world.[88]

The impact of both silver dirhams in the North and gold in the Mediterranean has to be extrapolated largely from coins and coin finds. Who moved the coins, how, and why, are largely a matter of inference. That is why the last case study presented here is important for comparative purposes. The activities of Jewish merchants in Fatimid Egypt (969–1171) are recorded in magnificent, richly anecdotal detail from thousands of letters and other records that were deposited in a Geniza (or documentary elephant's graveyard) in the Ben Ezra Synagogue of Fusṭāṭ (Old Cairo).[89]

---

87. Borek 2012, 63–64.

88. Lombard 1974, 151–250; Heck 1999; Morony 2019. Jane Kershaw and Stephen Merkel are carrying out important new work on silver sources in the Muslim world.

89. Goitein 1967–93, 1:1–28; Goldberg 2012, 5–29; Rustow 2020, 29.

FIGURE 2.2. Silver dirham of al-ʿAzīz, Fatimid caliph (975–96), minted in Damascus in AH 385/AD 995–96 (diameter 22 mm). Ashmolean Museum, Oxford.

The Ben Ezra collection is especially rich in material from the later tenth to thirteenth centuries, including a large amount of correspondence between merchants whose business flowed mainly between Egypt, Tunisia (Ifrīqiya), and Sicily (map 2.3). Gold and silver featured prominently in their trade. There were large—sometimes very large—transfers of precious metal treated as a good for trade in much the same way as flax or pepper. Merchants engaged in this business paid close attention to the exchange rates being offered for gold and silver, and to the quality and weight of specific types of coin. One Egyptian around 1050 wrote back home from Syria to ask about the price in Egypt of a batch of silver dirhams minted in Damascus under al-ʿAzīz (975–96)[90] (figure 2.2). Another merchant from Alexandria near the end of the eleventh century wrote to a correspondent in an unnamed western location about a group of silver ingots weighing 2,900 dirhams in total. With these the correspondent was asked to buy "dinars, Murabitis, Aghmatis or quarters, but not one shred of textiles."[91] It is worth emphasising that the silver circulating in Fatimid Egypt is thought to have come overwhelmingly from outside, including from the western Mediterranean, where this correspondent now was, but after various political reverses in Ifrīqiya that limited access to bullion it was apparently now viable to take Egyptian silver back to the West.[92] Also, the Egyptian merchant was interested in acquiring specific, highly desirable currencies. Playing exchange rates and obtaining versatile coins were

90. Goitein 1967–93, 1:233 (citing Cambridge, University Library, Or 1080 J, 42v).

91. Goitein 1967–93, 1:236 (citing Cambridge, University Library, Taylor-Schechter Collection, 20.121).

92. Goitein 1967–93, 1:235.

recurrent features of the Geniza bullion market, where gold and silver pieces of various kinds were bought and sold frequently.

Like most of the business recorded in the Geniza, bullion trade operated on a diversified, opportunistic basis. Merchants dealt in a wide range of commodities: the house of Ibn 'Awqal in the early eleventh century handled no fewer than eighty-three different goods flowing in and out of just one port.[93] Gold and silver fitted in with whatever range of goods a merchant took on a trip and did not always command special status. Their flexibility is demonstrated by another letter, from a merchant of Ifrīqiya temporarily working at the great Egyptian flax centre of Būṣīr, who gave instructions to a colleague in Alexandria on what to do with the proceeds of a sale. Evidently he wrote before the transaction was completed, for the letter runs through thirteen eventualities based on what form the proceeds would take. The first of these was cash, which would be deposited with a named merchant in Cairo to be held for the writer. But there follow a dozen other possibilities: wax, lead, vegetable oil, cloth, dark-blue wrappings, hides, two kinds each of shoes and silk, olive oil and wood.[94]

Bullion, then, was an important commodity in the world of the Geniza, yet also part of a bigger tapestry woven from individuals and the trust between them. Purses of gold and silver representing the proceeds of sales or settlement of debts criss-crossed the Mediterranean (and Egypt) in the hands of many merchants. At any one time, a merchant might have in his possession a number of such purses, most of them the property of trusted colleagues, the expectation being that they would be used for profitable trade or returned as and when the opportunity presented itself. That process could take time yet was watched carefully. One merchant berated another about a specific purse that had gone astray: "I have already asked you several times to clarify for me the matter of the Gabesians' money, namely the 100 dinars which they had sent with Abū Zikrī Judah and which should have reached you several years ago. There has been a good deal of correspondence and controversy since that time, and we do not know what became of it."[95] Another letter (from the 1050s) illustrates a relatively local interaction between a merchant in Old Cairo, 'Ayyāsh ibn Ṣadaqa, and Nahray ibn Nissīm, who was at Būṣīr in the agriculturally rich Fayyūm region of Egypt some 85 km away to buy flax. Flax dominates Ayyash's missive, but among other subjects he

93. Stillman 1973, 29.

94. Goitein 1967–93, 1:153 (citing Cambridge, University Library, Taylor-Schechter Collection, 8 J 22).

95. Stillman 1970, 243 (translating Antonin 904).

also brings up what Nahray should do with three purses of money: one belonging to him, one to his master Abu al-Faraj, and a third to 'Ayyāsh's uncle. Later he discusses another merchant, Qāsim, who was in 'Ayyāsh's eyes something of a liability, not to be counted on to make the best deal with the hundred dinars entrusted to him. 'Ayyāsh advised changing them for silver dirhams and recommended his preferred money changer in Cairo.[96]

The conditions reflected in the Geniza letters are in many respects unique to Egypt and its neighbours. The Fatimid Caliphate had a dynamic monetary economy with a large gold element.[97] Even the peasantry was accustomed (at least in the rich flax-producing areas) to handling gold. One peasant farmer (*muzari'*), Jirja ibn Bifam, is known in rich detail thanks to an archive of thirty-nine documents he buried in a pot beneath a house near the monastery of Naqlun. These texts show how Jirja disposed of dozens of gold dinars to purchase lands, at a time when one dinar was a substantial sum, enough to purchase 125–143 kg of wheat.[98] Men of such stature could afford to be picky on the quality of dinars they would accept.[99] This reflects the relative abundance of cash rather than a position of strength for the peasants, as the coin-driven fiscal system of Egypt forced peasants to sell their crop in advance at a knockdown rate in order to get the gold and silver needed to pay their taxes; in practice, those taxes would often be paid directly by the merchants who acted as middlemen between peasants and the state.[100] This system fostered close interaction between farmers and local flax traders, or even important merchants from the cities, and despite its flaws still presents a striking contrast to western Europe in both structural and material terms.[101] This was a highly commercialised society, with widespread use of cash. It also had an elaborate fiscal machinery that relied on and cooperated with commerce and was supported by highly bureaucratised mechanisms of local revenue collection.[102] That said, there are important points of comparison with western Europe. Shortfalls and imbalances in distribution of money were still commonplace. One merchant in the early eleventh century paid the large sum of five hundred dinars in tax for a group of flax farmers,

96. Goldberg 2012, 56–61 (translating TS 13 J 13.11v).

97. Heidemann 2010, 661–63; 2015, 47–52; Kool et al. 2011, 35–37.

98. Eds and trans. Gaubert and Mouton 2014, 37–161, with Wickham 2019, 79–80.

99. Udovitch 1999, esp. 273–78; Smith 2015a, 19–22. For the buying power of gold, see Ashtor 1977, 99–101.

100. Bondioli 2021, 105–58, 199–211.

101. Wickham 2021, 22; Udovitch 1999; Goldberg 2012, 99–106.

102. Rustow 2020, 355–61.

in return for which he was paid directly in flax;[103] and a mosque in the 1020s was at risk of dissolving because its (urban) tenants had fallen into arrears and the mosque's staff could not be paid.[104] The patterns of circulation visible from the Geniza invite comparison with the patchier evidence from Europe, where it is surmised that there was a similar mix of a few large-scale movers of bullion and a mass of smaller, often slower and incidental movements of coin. Something of this sort can possibly be detected in the Viking-Age Baltic, where Søren Sindbæk has shown that the circulation of goods revolved around major hubs that had the widest variety of goods on offer, with capillary routes and subsidiary centres extending out from them: these suggest networks that revolved around links between nodal points in long-distance trade like Egypt, Ifrīqiya, and Sicily in slightly later times.[105]

There is a temptation in looking at movement of bullion to imagine that there was a "real" stratum of circulation, commercial in character, and driven by fast circuits of commoditised gold and silver that were fed by something lucrative at the opposite end—possibly slaves from the Baltic for dirhams, or English wool for German silver, or Egyptian flax for Ifriqīyyan gold and silver.[106] Conversely, seigneurial renders and slow circulation via the tortuous back-and-forth of local exchange stand as somehow separate. Yet the Egyptian case shows things were not so simple. Small-scale exchanges could gradually build up to a large flow, even if they took longer and were less direct, and fast circuits did not operate in isolation from other goods. Movement of bullion was, in an important sense, the sum of circulation of coin, and of the people who carried it, and needs to be understood as one part in a mechanism that combined and interlinked long-distance with local interaction.

Conclusion

This chapter is of necessity speculative. While it is *sometimes* possible to identify where the metal in a particular coin ultimately came from, the historical processes that led to its extraction and movement are much more difficult to grasp, along with the question of who drove each leg of the journey. Some possibilities have been identified here, guided by what

103. Bondioli 2021, 138–41.
104. Rustow 2010.
105. Sindbæk 2007a, 128–29; 2007b; 2009, esp. 75–76.
106. Wyatt 2020; Howard-Johnston 2020; Jankowiak 2020; Sawyer 2013, 65–69, 104–5.

is known of Roman, Muslim, and later medieval mining. Certainly there would not have been a single model, even in the straitened circumstances of early medieval western Europe. A great deal remains to be found out about mining and processes of refining and distributing bullion; all one can be confident of is that these activities were, by the standards of the day, substantial operations that dealt with a high-value good. They were therefore shaped by elite demand and resources in many respects, yet still involved many others too, as gold and silver shifted in its primary role from raw commodity to worked good to means of exchange.

CHAPTER THREE

Why Make Money?

PETER DAMIAN (1007–72) had a talent for painting arresting rhetorical pictures of the filth that soiled humanity. As a leading member of the ecclesiastical movement in Rome that would later be known as the "Gregorian" or "reform" party, he and his allies set their crosshairs on shortcomings in the church: the institution that was supposed to set and exemplify moral standards. Money and its abuse featured prominently in Peter's invective, not least when castigating the sin of simony, or commerce in ecclesiastical office and services. This was one of the vices that Peter singled out in a withering report of a visit he had made in 1059 to the church of Milan. "In this way, alas, Simon Magus converted the holy church of St Ambrose into his perverted workshop. This moneyer and money changer of wickedness was equipped with bellows, hammers and anvil, and manufactured nothing other than universal peril for the souls of all men."[1]

To get and deal in coin was one thing, but actually to make coin was quite another. Minting, supposedly turning the cathedral itself into a workshop full of the sounds, smells, and detritus that accompanied hard labour, encapsulated the sordid state of Milan. It sent a powerful message: to traffic in salvation was to put corrupt money into circulation, with the simoniac priests and their ministrations being the coin. This was not the only occasion Peter Damian called on monetary

---

1. "Hoc itaque modo Symon Magus, heu prodolor, hanc sanctam Ambrosianam aecclesiam perversitatis suae velut officinam fecerat. Follem, malleos et incudem trapezita ac monetarius iniquitatis habebat, nichilque aliud nisi animarum omnium commune periculum fabricabat." Peter Damian, *Epistolae* 65 (Reindel 1983–93, 2:240–41; adapted translation from Blum and Resnick 1989–2005, 3:33–34).

metaphors in his writing,[2] and in later times something like what he described would actually be put into effect: in Italy in the thirteenth and fourteenth centuries the cathedrals, city walls, and harbours of vanquished foes would sometimes be turned temporarily into mints by the victors.[3] Making coin in the most cherished places of one's enemy was a way of symbolically claiming them; a practice that relied on the associations that charged minting with identity and tied it to worldly, sullying labour.

How coins actually came into being and entered circulation is a basic question—so basic it is easily taken for granted. Peter Damian expected his audience (in this instance his educated clerical associates in Rome) to be familiar enough with the processes involved that it would work as an explanatory device. It meant hammers and stamps or dies to impress designs onto pieces of metal: precisely the tools that were shown on coins of Louis the Pious from Melle, the implication being that this was a place defined by the extraction and minting (figure 3.1) of silver.[4] Yet despite these rhetorical and visual deployments of minting, and despite clear evidence for the physical trappings of mints in terms of metalworking tools, it is surprisingly difficult to determine why early medieval coins were actually made. For the most part, coins simply appear on the scene, already as part of the circulating medium, with no indication of how and where they were first obtained. Why did people actually mint coins rather than obtain them from the existing pool of circulating currency? How much of the population interacted directly with mints and moneyers? What forces dictated the size of their output? Questions like these are easily asked but rarely answered, and they form the major theme of this chapter. It is not giving anything away to acknowledge that the reasons for making any individual coin remain a mystery. What this chapter will do is review the possibilities and how they may have evolved over time.

The first sections will address basic preliminaries: the physical making of the currency and scale of production, which was most likely small, driven by sporadic production that was tied closely to specific needs or demands. These points lead to a sketch of the underlying structures of

2. Dinkova-Bruun 2015, 83–84; Naismith 2015, 25–26; Naismith 2020a, 201–2.

3. Grierson 1979.

4. See Grierson and Blackburn 1986, 213, and n. 758; and now Coupland 2018c. Minting implements were probably also shown on a Merovingian tremissis (Lafaurie 1964).

FIGURE 3.1. Silver obol of Louis the Pious, minted at Melle 814–c. 816 (diameter 15 mm). Classical Numismatic Group, LLC.

early medieval minting, before turning to selected major needs or demands that might have prompted minting: fiscal requirements; reminting of foreign coin; *renovatio monetae*; and a raft of private demands, including commercial need.

How to Make Coined Money

Early medieval coins were effectively pieces of metal manufactured to be of acceptable alloy, weight, and size. They would then be struck using a pair of stamps, known as dies. This final step is what leaves the imprint and therefore makes a blank disc into a coin, but most of the effort and technical expertise went into the preliminary steps. In practical terms, minting was essentially a subset of metalworking: a fact that is easily forgotten if coins are treated only as manifestations of jurisdiction and power. Several kinds of equipment and support were needed to undertake the physical processes involved. Most obviously, that included the requisite metal, plus any other minerals needed to produce the desired alloy, along with weights and scales for verifying weight. A good furnace was essential, along with fuel to keep it burning. Crucibles and metalworking tools were also indispensable. Dies had to be made from iron and steel. The tally goes on.

It is worth stressing that these tools and roles may not all have been the work of one person, or solely of dedicated moneyers. The latter may well have been goldsmiths or some other kind of metalworker first, and a moneyer only when needed.[5] A large background network of metalworking expertise and support should be assumed, at least for minting operations of any significance.[6] This is one reason why mobile minting facilities of the kind set up in Italian cathedrals were small, tokenistic operations, or why the products of minute "mints" were few and poorly made: they simply lacked the support to be sustainable. In the case of larger, better recorded minting establishments in the ancient world and the later Middle Ages,

5. For selected examples, see Heinzelmann 2013, 257–63 (St. Eligius); and Nightingale 1982, esp. 40, 47 (Deorman and his family in eleventh-century London).

6. For an overview from a numismatic perspective, see Grierson 1975, 94–123.

there might be top-down, state-driven mechanisms that marshalled most or all of the resources needed to keep churning out coins on a large scale, though even major mints depended on a sometimes precarious supply of bullion that could wax and wane precipitously.[7] Also like other kinds of metalworking, coin production can be thought of in terms of *chaînes opératoires*, as the product of complex, interwoven networks of cooperation, supply, and demand that sustained economic processes but were not necessarily driven by an overarching commercial logic, or by a single kind of patronage. Archaeologists working on Viking-Age Scandinavia,[8] and even more so on prehistoric societies, are alive to the human complexities of metal production and distribution: their work emphasises the complex organisation of metalworking and affiliated crafts, and the ritual and social interests that stimulated them, including long-distance contacts and elaborate social structures.[9]

How Large Was the Early Medieval Currency?

Scale is always important, but it is critical with regard to the coinage. All minting operations produce coins; scale is what separates an industrial-level operation, keyed into elaborate systems of supply and distribution to feed demand, from Michael Dolley's memorable description of the eleventh-century Manx "mint": "two men and a boy," who would knock out a few coins of distinctly ropy quality as the need arose.[10] While their products might look much alike, the mechanisms behind them were entirely different.

The actual number of coins made is one way into this question. On the face of it, written references to movable wealth, and large finds of gold and silver treasure, suggest considerable quantities; certainly far more than the surviving body of coins. One land transaction in Lombard Italy involved the handover of over 11,500 freshly minted tremisses: more than 12 kg of metal, though by this stage the coins were only about 50 per cent or less fine, so roughly 6 kg of gold.[11] The will of the English King Eadred (946–55) asked that two thousand mancuses of gold (by weight) be minted into mancuses (coins).[12] In the abstract, this is a kingly amount of gold: about

7. See, for example, Stahl 2000, 245–406 (on Venice); Allen 2012a, 73–133 (on later medieval English mints); Howgego 1995, 26–30 (on major ancient mints).

8. Pedersen 2017; Croix, Neiß, and Sindbæk 2019. See also Ashby and Sindbæk 2020.

9. Kuijpers 2012; Stöllner 2012; O'Brien 2015, 245–302; Fontanals et al. 2019.

10. Dolley 1976, 83. See also Naismith 2019b, esp. 415.

11. See also chapter 9.

12. S 1515 (Miller 2001, no. 17).

8.5 kg, only slightly more than the almost 2,700 gold dinars and fractional dinars (weighing some 7.5 kg) lost in a shipwreck in Caesarea harbour around 1035,[13] or more than twice as much as was found in the Staffordshire hoard (just under 4 kg).[14] It is also likely that Eadred and others like him could dispose of far larger quantities of silver. The vast Cuerdale hoard may have contained as much as 42.6 kg in silver (only about a quarter of which was made up of coins);[15] even bigger was the pair of contemporary hoards buried beneath a ninth-century building at Spillings, Gotland, totalling some 67 kg of silver in the form of dirhams and silver objects in whole and cut form.[16] And there are accounts—the veracity of which is undeterminable—of even larger caches of precious metal.[17] When Charlemagne's armies claimed the Avars's royal treasure in the 790s, it allegedly took fifteen wagons to bring all the spoils back to Aachen.[18]

How many assemblages like these actually went into moneyers' melting pots is less clear. Traditionally, the decisive evidence for the scale of minting has been solidly numismatic, coming from analysis of how many dies are represented among the surviving corpus of coins of a given type.[19] It may or may not be straightforward to arrive at this number. Coins can be difficult to track down, or very similar in appearance, and those in poor condition might be too damaged to be usable. In any case, the theory is that once the numbers of coins and of dies represented among them are established, these figures provide the basis for an estimate of the number of dies originally used. The principle, drastically simplified, is that if the ratio of dies to coins is very high, then many dies were used, and if the ratio is very low, then few were used. Various statistical models have been developed to translate numismatic data into estimated numbers of dies. These offer different levels of reliability and precision. The more subtle techniques have the benefit of offering a range of likely answers rather than just a single number, and also a measure of how confident one can be in those numbers.[20] All are solidly based in mathematical and numismatic rigour, with some obvious caveats. Coinages dominated by a few large hoards that contain samples fresh from the mint might massively overrepresent one or two sets of dies, skewing any estimate based on them. Meanwhile, a corpus

13. Kool, Baidoun, and Sharvit 2018.
14. Fern 2019, 30.
15. Graham-Campbell 2011b, 34–35.
16. Pettersson 2009. See also chapter 5.
17. Hardt 2004.
18. *Historia regum/York Annals* s.a. 795 (Arnold 1882–85, 2:57). Cf. Hardt 2018.
19. Grierson 1975, 155–57.
20. Esty 2006; 2011.

dominated by modern collections chosen to be as diverse as possible might give a misleading impression of heterogeneity. But on the whole the equations themselves are reliable.

One steps onto much thinner ice in attempting to extrapolate from surviving numbers of coins and dies, or projected numbers of dies, back to the original output of coins. Early medieval coinage was in fact an early battleground on the merits of this sort of analysis, as Michael Metcalf and Philip Grierson spent the 1960s exchanging increasingly pointed barbs over how many pennies were minted under Offa of Mercia (757–96).[21] The primary point of contention lay in how to translate estimates of the number of dies into an estimate of how many coins were actually made. Metcalf worked on the basis that dies would normally have been used to capacity and so multiplied the projected number of dies by the average number of coins that dies produced at the first time when detailed data on output becomes available, in the thirteenth and fourteenth centuries, by which time obverse dies generally made between twenty thousand and sixty thousand coins, reverse dies between ten thousand and twenty-five thouand.[22] Grierson contended that "the factor which determines how many times a die will be used is not how many coins it can strike—this is only a limiting factor—but how many coins people want."[23] He has not been alone in doubting the reliability of calculations of mint output by back-projecting data from the later Middle Ages.[24]

Grierson tended to take a very negative view of early medieval monetisation, but on this point his observations carry weight.[25] Minting depended on demand. It simply is not possible to know how many coins were made in the early Middle Ages, and the production tolerance of dies is unlikely to have been the main restriction. Availability of bullion and demand were crucial (and closely intertwined). Numismatic data needs to be read with caution, and with several possible intepretations in mind. At the lower end of the spectrum are coinages that, from circumstantial evidence, one would not expect to have been vast, yet where almost every coin comes from a different set of dies. A good example is the set of western imitations of Abbasid gold dinars, produced at the end of the eighth century (after

21. Metcalf 1963a; 1963b; 1964; 1965; Grierson 1963a, 1963b; 1967; etc.

22. Allen 2004, 48–49; 2007, 199. The difference reflects which die occupied the upper position, taking the more direct impact of each hammer blow. The die that would be considered the obverse on typological grounds did not always occupy the obverse position during production.

23. Grierson 1963b, 223.

24. Buttrey 1994.

25. See chapter 7.

AH 157/AD 773–74, the date most of them carry). It is highly unlikely that the numerous dies represented among them reflect large-scale production: much more probably, new dies were produced frequently to strike individual consignments of gold into hundreds or (at most) thousands of coins at a time, along the lines of King Eadred's bequest of two thousand gold pieces.[26] In this instance, an appearance of vastness could plausibly be quite the opposite. At the other extreme, demand could rise to sufficient levels for dies to be used to capacity: one thinks of large mint-places like ninth-century Dorestad or eleventh-century London. Very large holdings of silver undoubtedly existed, which would have needed more than one die to mint. If a viking leader had decided to liquidate the Cuerdale hoard or the Spillings hoards, for example, they would have produced about thirty thousand and forty-five thousand coins, respectively, probably needing several sets of dies. And even if there were not many "high rollers" coming in with gold or silver in such huge quantity, some mint organisations may have had a steady enough stream of smaller customers that they were using dies near to capacity. But it should be stressed that this is unlikely to have been the norm, and as in the later Middle Ages, recoinages may have been the only times that major mints regularly used dies to capacity, and the only times some smaller mint-places operated at all.[27] There must have been many moneyers and mint-places that never came close to using up their dies. Grierson's point is simple but powerful, its heat often lost in the harsh light of his feud with Metcalf. It bears repeating: coin production was driven by need rather than maximum capacity, and only occasionally did the former rise to match the latter.

Why Were Early Medieval Coins Made?

What, then, were the needs that drove minting? A great many situations can be identified in which coin might be used, but it is deceptively difficult to identify ones that called specifically for the making of fresh coins. Three principal forces were at work: minting *by* larger state structures; minting *for* the state; and minting for more dispersed, effectively private needs. These also relate to the location and organisation of minting, and their characteristics can be summarised as follows:

1. A state expenditure model, in which the primary motor for production is the expenditure of the state on military and

26. Pace Ilisch 2004, 104. See also MacKay and Naismith 2022.
27. Grierson 1963a, 114.

bureaucratic pay, tributes or subsidies, and the direct needs of the ruler and their circle of dependants. Typically, this model involved a degree of centralisation at relatively large and stable mint-places, as far as the fiscal system permitted, with allowance for short-lived mints to help with particular military campaigns or governmental projects. The Roman Empire, its successor in Byzantium, and the Muslim caliphates all generally worked along these lines; not coincidentally, all three also had well-developed fiscal systems that often (though not always) exploited a high degree of coin use and commercialisation.[28]

2. A state demand model, in which state needs were still the largest factor governing production of coined money, and the bulk of production was still seen as the prerogative of a larger, perhaps still centralised power, but with an important change: demand for taxes (and potentially other dues) now guided production, not state expenditure. The burden and responsibility of producing new coins hence shifted to individuals or groups who dealt with the state. This tended to suit the more dispersed state structures of early medieval western Europe and sometimes resulted in much more atomised systems of production, as seen in Merovingian Gaul and Visigothic Spain.[29] At many such mint-places, the makers of coin would no longer have been full-time professionals, instead being drawn from among artisans and officials with appropriate skills as and when those abilities were needed—though larger mint-places in this model could still accommodate more regular and dedicated minting.

3. A local demand model, which often evolves out of a state demand model. Again, production is more dispersed, vested in individuals, groups, or institutions with local power, who will in some cases also be agents of a larger state apparatus. But in this model, a wider range of private needs replaces the demands of a larger state system as the driving force, collapsing primary and secondary uses. Most coins would, at least initially, stay within the area instead of being conveyed to a dominant supralocal authority. The move from state demand to local demand might be gradual, perhaps even with periods when state pressures resumed, but the tendency was toward minting as a response to the economic, administrative,

28. For this cycle in relation to a later case-study, see Haldon 1993, 233–37.
29. See chapter 7.

and social requirements of local patrons—above all elites with more resources, who will in many cases also be in de facto control of minting. In Francia, for example, it is likely that a state demand model led to the establishment of the mint-moneyer coinage of the late sixth century, but that this gave rise to, and was eventually supplanted by, a local demand model.

In general terms, most regions of western Europe started out on a state expenditure model (at least if they lay within the Roman Empire) and eventually worked along the lines of a local demand model. Individual strands of this story will be addressed elsewhere. Individual mint-places or regions could also vary. There was no single or natural progression, and some regions might leap straight into the second or third model without any prior history of the first (as with England in the seventh century). Nevertheless, common factors affecting development in this direction can be pinpointed. A major one is social. Development toward state demand and local demand led to dispersal of minting and its passage into the hands (directly or indirectly) of locally powerful figures, which meant that access to fresh coinage became tied to the interests of these groups. Minting came to depend on wealth, patronage, and being embedded in the right networks. This is not to say that fresh coins were inaccessible outside the elite; just that others had to play by their rules and piggyback on systems set up primarily to benefit elites.

FISCAL MINTING

The association of minting with state power, however loosely, means that historically payments to and from the state have been seen as a major motivation for making coin. Indeed, the late Roman monetary system, together with its institutional successors in Byzantium and the Muslim world, maintained a firewall between mints and potential customers or taxpayers.[30] Military spending on salaried armies being the biggest single expense, army pay is typically seen as the dominant factor behind classical and Byzantine minting.[31] The model as summarised by Leslie Brubaker and John Haldon is state > bureaucracy/army > producers, and back to the

30. Hendy 1988, 29: "Late Roman and early Byzantine coinage was primarily a fiscal instrument." See also Hendy 1985, 371–439; Brubaker and Haldon 2011, 464–88; Heidemann 2010, 656–57.

31. Howgego 1990, 7–9; Duncan-Jones 1994, esp. 67–94; von Reden 2010, 19, 54, 138.

state, with the market as a catalysing element.[32] When one element of the cycle was removed, the whole system seized up. That was what happened when, in the sixth century, a short-sighted prefect abolished the postal service (*cursus publicus*) in inland Anatolia: landowners who had once handed over their crops as a tax payment, which the *cursus* had then carried off to where they were needed, now had to pay in gold but had no one to sell their produce to, so they found themselves ruined.[33] Here the pressure came from misguided economising, at least as it was portrayed by John Lydus and Procopius, but money and tax were also a tempting form of extortion if pushed to extreme levels. Ibn Hazm (d. 1064) lambasted the robber-barons of eleventh-century al-Andalus for their multilayered monetary oppression. Miners extracted gold and silver, lost some of it to the state, and then used what remained to buy goods from peasants. But the peasants then lost their coins to tax collectors, through whom the coins passed to soldiers who inflicted violence on the populace but also spent their money—which began the process all over again: hence ibn Hazm's vivid characterisation of coins as "wheels that turn in the fires of hell."[34]

Michael Hendy saw the collapse of this wall between minting and populace as a symptom of the general erosion of government institutions in the West and, as he summed it up, a move from public to private motivations for minting.[35] But what remains murky is when and how new coins actually entered into the mix in a fiscally driven monetary system. One recent proposition has been that in Byzantium during the seventh to ninth centuries annual donatives known as *rhogai* and other forms of largesse from the imperial government were the primary context for making and distributing new coin—and that the demand and scope for new coins was driven by symbolic and political factors.[36] Something similar took place in the entourage of the caliph and his chief minister in Fatimid Egypt.[37] In other words, payments as part of state income and expenditure had special dimensions to them that made minting into a performance of authority, even where it was not strictly necessary. The act of distribution could itself call for fresh, homogenous coins.

32. Brubaker and Haldon 2011, 484; Haldon 2009, 220, 225–29.

33. John Lydus, *De magistratibus* 3.61 (Wuensch 1903, 151–52); Procopius, *Historia arcana* 30.5–7, 11 (Haury 1905–13, 3:181–83). Hendy 1985, 295; Belke 1998, 271–22.

34. See chapter 4.

35. Hendy 1988, esp. 29–32.

36. Jarrett 2017, 527.

37. Sanders 1994, 84–85.

It is thought that fiscal minting continued to play a dominant role in Byzantium and the Muslim world throughout the early Middle Ages and beyond; in parts of western Europe, it may also have been important down to about 700 but grew attenuated over time. By the time of the First Crusade, westerners saw the "public" model as just another piece of Greek chicanery: Albert of Aachen marvelled at how the money given to crusaders by Alexius I (1081–1118) at Constantinople quickly found its way back into the emperor's hands, meaning that "the royal treasury was perpetually overflowing with money and could not be emptied by the presentation of gifts."[38] Again, the difficulty comes in identifying cases where new coin specifically was required. Exceptional payments such as viking tributes may have led people to turn to moneyers for fresh coins.[39] Current coin, often meaning new minting, may have been mandated for other, more routine demands in a similar way. There were fines and fees paid to the king and his agents, as well as money raised to pay for military supplies or as commutation for not serving.[40] Even though there was no salaried army to dominate state spending and minting, an important if variable collection of smaller, broadly state-related payments can often still be identified, from Roman successor states to the Carolingian Empire, larger French counties of the tenth century, and late Anglo-Saxon England. These could have sustained elements of state income-driven minting, but it is less clear whether such demands needed fresh coin or (if they did) whether they constituted the dominant strand of demand.

IMPERMEABLE BORDERS

When the Frankish abbot Lupus of Ferrières (d. c. 862) planned a visit to Rome at some uncertain point in the mid-ninth century, he was startled to find out from other travellers that "the silver money of Italy ... will from now on be the only one in use."[41] He asked his correspondent (an unnamed ecclesiastic in Italy) to have a supply of local coin ready for him when he arrived, perhaps so he could avoid delay, or indeed avoid the costs of going through a more formal exchange system. In principle, this could

---

38. "Regis erarium assidua pecunia habundans, nulla datione uacari potest." Albert of Aachen, *Historia Ierosolimitana* 2.16 (ed. and trans. Edgington 2007, 86–87).

39. E.g., Coupland 1999, 72–73. A possible case is discussed in Moesgaard 2014.

40. For the latter in the Carolingian Empire and later Anglo-Saxon England, see Coupland 2004, esp. 54–56; Abels 1988, 132–45.

41. "Italicae monetae argento, quod solum usui futurum," Lupus of Ferrières, *Letter* 75 (Levillain 1927–35, 2:18).

have been another situation that required people to avail themselves of local mints, to obtain any coins they wished to spend.

The monetary barrier Lupus feared was apparently of recent creation and may in fact have been a misunderstood reference to the distinct local coinage of Rome.[42] A unified coinage, acceptable everywhere from Catalonia to Saxony and from Tuscany to Brittany, was one of the casualties of the civil war that wracked the Carolingian Empire in the 840s. This was not the first barrier to coin circulation erected in early medieval Europe. Already in the time of Sigismund, king of the Burgundians (516–24), a law in the additions to the *Lex Burgundionum* stipulated that all gold solidi were acceptable, save for four groups, one of which was the coins of the Visigoths, "which have been debased since the time of King Alaric [II]" (484–507).[43] From the later sixth century, it is apparent from coin finds that both the Visigothic kingdom and the Merovingian kingdom established a more or less effective block on coins from outside territories, in contrast to the relatively relaxed circulation of gold coin in the fifth and earlier sixth centuries.[44] Justinian had previously upheld open circulation in the *Pragmatica sanctio* for Italy in 554, in which he forbade merchants and money changers from selling coins of the current emperor to his taxpaying subjects at a marked-up rate, the inference being that some believed only coins of Justinian were acceptable in settling debts to the state. In contrast, Justinian asserted that any solidus bearing the image of a Roman emperor was acceptable.[45] Yet even here the law specified only coins of Roman emperors. In principle this excluded Persian coins or those from western Europe that did not adhere to the norms of Roman currency. Many more such barriers are suggested by the disappearance of coins of other jurisdictions from finds, perhaps combining the establishment of a block on external coin with an initial recoinage: in Northumbria from the time of Eadberht (737–58), the extended Mercian kingdom from later in Offa's reign (757–96), and Norway from the time of Harald Sigurdsson (1046–66).[46] The mechanisms needed to uphold rejection of foreign coin are silently assumed. Charlemagne's 794 decree that "the new denarii should circulate in every place and every city as well as in every market,

42. Coupland 2001, 178.

43. "Qui a tempore Alarici regis adaerati sunt." *Constitutiones extravagantes* 21.7 (de Salis 1892, 120–21).

44. Carlà 2010, 62–87; Arslan 1998.

45. *Pragmatica sanctio* c. 20 (Krueger et al. 1877–95, 3:801–2).

46. Naismith 2012a, 304–6; Naismith 2012b, 203–9; Skaare 1976, 70–71; Gullbekk 2009, 29–31.

and be accepted by all" implicitly excluded foreign coins as well as old Frankish ones.[47]

It is worth considering what currency control measures meant in real terms. Someone at some stage must have been checking the coins that were in use, to weed out any foreign specimens. Theoretically everyone everywhere might have been on the lookout for coins that were not acceptable. The Old English version of the *Legend of the Seven Sleepers of Ephesus* (an eleventh-century adaptation of a late-antique Latin text) brings to life the hostility and nosiness that accompanied an accusation of using bad money: tradesmen who found one of the sleepers trying to pass off coins more than a century old raised the hue and cry and passed the offending coins round one another to examine them in detail.[48] They then took the matter up with the town-reeve and the bishop, who also examined the coins.[49] The setting—a marketplace in a city—is also appropriate. What Charlemagne and his agents sought to police was the exchange of coin; they did not stop people from carrying purses of foreign currency with them, as long as they did not try to pass them off as local.

This is important in considering what people did with foreign coin and where. How regularly did large quantities of it pass through mints? What about those who moved from areas preferring gold to silver, or base to fine metal? Movement of coin between zones of restricted monetary circulation weighed heavily on those who undertook long-distance travel involving goods and/or money, meaning above all merchants.[50] They risked a significant loss through one or two processes of reminting.[51] If possible, then, it may have been more attractive for a merchant to travel with commodities for sale and use the proceeds on the spot to acquire more commodities that could be passed on for a profit at home. Dealing in large amounts of coined money would have been a short-term function of trading in particular markets: merchants might receive coins in return for commodities they had sold and spend them in short order on other goods to take home, meaning that often they brought only small amounts of cash, if any, on either leg of the journey with them.[52] This

---

47. "In omni loco, in omni civitate et omni empturio similiter vadant isti novi denarii et accipiantur ab omnibus." Council of Frankfurt, c. 5 (Boretius 1883, 74).

48. Whitelock 1961; Cubitt 2009, 1022–28.

49. *Old English Legend of the Seven Sleepers of Ephesus* § 82 and 96 (ed. and trans. Kramer, Magennis, and Norris 2020, 630–31, 636–39).

50. With the important caveat that pilgrims, diplomats, and other travellers could also indulge in side ventures of a mercantile nature: McCormick 2001, 275, 621, 640, 677–80.

51. A point Dolley and Metcalf 1961, 154, note in relation to Anglo-Saxon coinage.

52. Kershaw 2017, esp. 185–87.

was the practice of Ælfric of Eynsham's (d. c. 1010) idealised merchant, who declared, "I embark on a ship with my wares, and I sail overseas, then sell my goods and buy precious things that are not known in this land."[53] For large amounts of precious metal (as coin or otherwise) to be moved, there had to be some sort of special attraction in the form of a good rate of exchange offered by the local money changers or mints, or a currency of sufficient repute to offset the costs of travel and exchange. In other words, it had to be thought of as a commodity in itself.

Reminting of foreign coin can sometimes slip into the role of a deus ex machina: an explanation for why gold and silver occurred anywhere without a significant local source of metal. And it clearly could be important. From the point of view of rulers and minting authorities, reminting could be a source of metals in short supply. Production of Byzantine *miliaresia* of the eighth century depended heavily on imported dirhams.[54] And despite the drawbacks, people clearly did take tranches of coin between different monetary spheres, as occasionally seen in out-of-place hoards, such as a find of Norman denarii deposited in Southampton around 1030.[55] When purchase rolls from the main English mints were produced in the thirteenth century, the principal source of bullion outside times of recoinage was from merchants (mostly foreign) bringing in quantities of coin to change.[56] The major role of mint-places on the borders of the Carolingian Empire, such as Dorestad and Venice, suggests they depended on incoming silver.[57] But the main point to be stressed here is that reminting of foreign coin did not just happen as a matter of course, at least on a significant scale. It depended on a conjunction of strict legal enforcement with the commodified handling of gold and silver. Both these conditions depended on important background developments. There needed to be a relatively assertive administrative infrastructure. There also needed to be a particular configuration of supply and demand to produce large-scale transfers of gold and silver (which could go back and forth between different regions numerous times). Prices had to be worthwhile and predictable for those who moved bullion. Regular, routinised long-distance trade of this kind was rare and fragile in the early Middle Ages. It represents a middle stratum, with more localised trade in basic raw materials and

53. "Ego ascendo nauem cum mercibus meis, et nauigo ultra marinas partes, et uendo meas res et emo res pretiosas, quae in hac terra non nascuntur." Garmonsway 1978, 33.

54. Gordus and Metcalf 1970–72.

55. *Checklist* 213.

56. Cassidy 2011; 2013.

57. Coupland 2022.

foodstuffs below, and luxury goods above: the former moved a lot but over short distances; the latter, over long distances but in small volume.[58] Gold and silver in small quantities fell into the last of these three categories, but when large amounts changed hands, bullion had the potential to shift, functionally, into a middle category of bulk goods that travelled over long distances and achieved wider penetration in society.

RENOVATIO MONETAE

Although it is deeply entrenched in the literature, the term *renovatio monetae* was never actually used in the early Middle Ages: it has been imported from usage of the twelfth and thirteenth centuries.[59] The core principle is that, as well as requiring their subjects to eschew coins of foreign authorities, rulers from time to time demanded that they switch to a new kind of domestic coinage. The motives behind reminting should be addressed first, for these shaped the overall approach taken by different states. Recoinage was emphatically not always just a profit-making scheme. Few of the well-recorded early medieval recoinages resembled those of the later Middle Ages or after that generated a handsome profit for the ruler by sharply debasing the coinage.[60] Recoinage was instead associated with the prevention of forgery, and rhetoric of morality and purity. The expectation when Charles the Bald commanded a recoinage at an assembly at Pîtres in 864 was that everyone involved in producing the coinage, from the king downward, would share in the same ideological concept of Carolingian government. Reform of the currency was an act of Christian good governance, and a poor coinage was implicitly situated alongside other wrongs of the age that Charles now sought to put right.[61] The edict of Pîtres thus also addressed military service and organisation, the protection of royal agents, and the payment of royal income. England's ruling circle in the decades around 1000 was even more charged with Christian anxiety. As Archbishop Wulfstan (d. 1023) put it, "improvement of the coinage" (*feos bot*) stood next to the avoidance of adultery and murder in securing England's collective spiritual well-being.[62]

---

58. Wickham 2005, 696–700; 2008, esp. 23–25.

59. Svensson 2013. However, a similar verbal form was used in GDB (179r) in the 1080s and at Verdun in 1099 (Jesse 1924, no. 57).

60. Sussman 1992; 1993; Munro 2012. A possible example is the new coinage of Harald Harðráði (1046–66) in Norway: see Skaare 1976, 65–110.

61. Nelson 1992, 207–9.

62. References collected in Keynes and Naismith 2011, 198.

Coinage was especially responsive to moralising discourse because it combined a unique range of attributes. It carried the name of the king and was made under the supervision of figures answerable to him. At the same time, most people in the kingdom would probably handle coins at some point, so it was the closest thing early medieval rulers had to mass-market penetration, its purity and quality charged with symbolic meaning. Moreover, exchanging coin invoked relations of trust, not least in the coin itself, which was manufactured from a material that could easily be adulterated without any outward sign. Damage to the reputation of a coinage, and hence to the good name of its master, was not taken lightly: in the eleventh century the abbot of Corbie forbade adulterating his coinage below 80 per cent pure lest "by this expansion the coinage might be brought into disrepute."[63] The nexus between coined money and moral integrity tapped into a long-standing Christian tradition of monetary metaphors, going back to the New Testament and the "sayings" (*agrapha*) ascribed to Christ, one of which encouraged the good Christian examining their soul to be like a shrewd money changer scrutinising a coin for defects.[64] That image of examining a coin took on a life of its own in subsequent centuries. It also gave rise to a scaled-up feedback loop in the eyes of rulers of a particularly pious, self-reflective bent: if one defective coin reflected a tainted soul, a whole currency of defective coins reflected a godless society. High standards of coinage were therefore a way to assert collective moral well-being.

Recoinages undertaken on this basis tended to come at times of anxiety, introspection, or general reassertion of moral and social standards at the top of the political establishment. That was certainly the case for most Carolingian recoinages. Charlemagne's in 793 took place in the midst of a famine, as part of a broader shake-up of weights and measures, and also between two serious revolts.[65] The second reform in the reign of Louis the Pious (822/23), which came relatively hot on the heels of a previous one (818), took place at a time of deep concern with office and its proper fulfilment in a godly empire.[66] In England, the long string of frequent coin reforms that took place between the late tenth and mid-twelfth centuries began late in the reign of Edgar (959–75), but real responsibility for turning a one-off into a routine lies with his son Æthelred II (978–1016).

63. "Ea pluralitate moneta vilisceret." Bompaire et al. 1998, 314.

64. Naismith 2020a, 199–203; Vos 1997; Dinkova-Bruun 2015; Ohly 1999, 17–32; Weinrich 1958.

65. Verhulst 1965; Ganshof 1946; Garipzanov 2016.

66. Coupland 1990; de Jong 2009, 112–47.

Æthelred's own new coinages should be seen in a highly moralised light, as part of the king's wider efforts to enlist divine support through collective and personal action.[67] The most arresting example is the remarkable *Agnus Dei* coinage of 1009, which temporarily replaced the usual iconography with the Lamb of God and the Holy Dove (see figure 9.11).[68] This was an extreme case, but the other recoinages under Æthelred can also be explained in similar terms. New coinages instituted after Æthelred's death did seemingly become more routine, and potentially more financially motivated, but only on the basis of a long-standing practice undertaken for other reasons.[69]

If there were diverse motives for decreeing a recoinage, there were just as many ways of implementing one. The touchstone example is Charles the Bald's recoinage instituted at the assembly of Pîtres in summer 864 (figure 3.2). Elements of the exercise were not so dissimilar from the replacement of a certain kind of coin or note in modern times, such as allowing a grace period (in this case of about five months) during which both old and new coins were acceptable. Anyone trying to use old money for buying and selling after that time would have it confiscated, and there were also penalties for anyone who rejected the new coins.[70] Charles's demands depended heavily on the moneyers, who were clearly expected not only to make the new coinage but to exchange it as well. Frustratingly, the text does not elaborate on how this would actually be done, but each moneyer was promised a starting float of five pounds of silver, to be supplied by the king, presumably so that they could have a stock of coin on hand to make immediate exchanges, rather than force customers to wait while individual batches of coin were reminted.[71]

If recoinages worked on these terms, there is no doubt that they would have been a powerful factor in bringing new coins into being.[72] But the question is whether in practice recoinages worked as Charles envisaged on the banks of the Seine in 864. One side of the problem is that virtually all written information about early medieval recoinages comes from a solidly top-down point of view. Laws and capitularies reflect the concerns of rulers first, manufacturers second, and users of coin a distant third. The

67. Naismith 2016a; Roach 2016. See also chapter 9.
68. See chapter 9.
69. Naismith 2016a, 133.
70. Suchodolski 1983; Coupland 2017.
71. Edict of Pîtres (no. 260), c. 8–15 (Boretius and Krause 1897, 313–16).
72. For the reform of 864 and its impact on the coinage, see Metcalf 1990; Grierson 1990.

FIGURE 3.2. Silver denarius of Charles the Bald, minted at Liège, after the edict of Pîtres in 864 (diameter 19 mm). Classical Numismatic Group, LLC.

edict of Pîtres is not addressed to the moneyers, let alone to coin users, but to counts and their agents, who were expected to implement and enforce the decrees. A frustrating consequence of this is that hardly anything is known about how people actually obtained new coins as part of a recoinage. Theoretically there could have been long lines of customers from all walks of life turning up at mints, clutching bags of soon-to-be proscribed coins. But the distribution of moneyers and mint-places, which correlates poorly with likely population density, points in a different direction. It is more probable that dealing directly with mints, especially at times of recoinage, was primarily the prerogative of local elites who had greater resources and mobility.[73]

The process could have worked in this way. Charles the Bald declared a recoinage and his counts marshalled their moneyers, and their five pounds of start-up money. The count's men and peers, including the bishop and any monasteries of the region, got wind of the decision at a local assembly. These figures had first access to the new coinage, followed by those who worked directly for them, such as *villici* (bailiffs) responsible for overseeing specific properties. Both groups, but especially the latter, would have gathered coins from tenants that needed to be exchanged and handed them over in a job lot, probably profiting from the process. Other arrangements—possibly related to those used to assess and collect tribute payments—would have come into play for peasants living on land outside great estates, where aristocratic landholding was limited or fragmented. The new coins would then be distributed. England would have been similar, but with the moneyers providing a larger number of social points of

73. See also chapter 4.

contact with the world of minting, especially in the tenth and eleventh centuries.[74] This was not the only conceivable mechanism for accessing new coinage. Some individuals, such as wealthier peasants, might have been in a position to interact with moneyers on their own account, especially when dealing with the more granular infrastructure of late Anglo-Saxon England. Alternatively, those who could not or would not go directly to moneyers to obtain new coin for its own sake might simply have waited for the new issues to filter through into use on the market, though by this stage it may well have carried a significant premium over older types. The central point is that access to mints was limited, and at times of recoinage their business would have increased, though very likely while remaining concentrated in the hands of relatively few parties.

Even recoinages about which more is known, like that ensuing from the edict of Pîtres, often did not pan out like they were meant to. Ten mint-places were expected to issue coins for Charles in Aquitaine and Neustria. In the event, neither of the two in Aquitaine formed part of the scheme: Melle minted a different type, and it is not clear that Narbonne ever minted any coins at all around this time, while more than one hundred did so in Neustria (and, after a few years, parts of Lorraine).[75] The edict of Pîtres is also not representative of how other Carolingian recoinages unfolded. In contrast to Charles's five months of grace before banning old coin, Louis the Pious in the early 820s allowed a period of three years for a new coinage to circulate alongside the old and get settled in.[76] The new type he had established also marked a new departure. It did away with mint names to create a truly homogenous coinage for the whole empire, usually referred to by its reverse inscription: *Christiana Religio* (figure 3.3). But his sons walked this back after his death, and the idea was not revived.[77]

It is sometimes debatable whether we are dealing with a recoinage at all, as opposed to a change in the design of coinage that replaced older issues through gradual turnover. Even where the new coinage gained ground quickly, which suggests forced obsolescence rather than a slow trickle out of circulation, there are other models available beyond the one put forward at Pîtres. The English parallel is again instructive.[78] There are

74. See also chapter 9.

75. See chapter 8.

76. *Admonitio ad omnes regni ordines* (825), c. 20 (Boretius and Krause 1897, 306).

77. Coupland 1990, 35–45.

78. For the late Anglo-Saxon model compared with that of Dublin and other locations, see Woods 2019, 82–86.

FIGURE 3.3. Silver denarius of Louis the Pious, *Christiana religio* type, minted c. 822/23–40 (diameter 21 mm). Classical Numismatic Group, LLC.

references in legislation of the tenth and early eleventh centuries to coins and protection against forgery (including enforced changing of defective coin),[79] but this says almost nothing about how recoinages worked: the closest one gets is Domesday Book referring to points "when the money was changed" and moneyers had to obtain new dies from London.[80] Systematic recoinage is never directly referred to at all. Finds of coins suggest that each successive issue from the time of Edgar onward was dominant in circulation—which is to say, many hoards consist only or very largely of the current type—but there was also a not insignificant layer of older coins that continued to circulate.[81] That is enough to undermine the presumption that there was a total ban on the use of old coin. There must have been some sort of push factor that induced people to get new coins but did not ban older types from circulation outright. One possibility is that current coin was mandated for some but not all purposes. Which these might have been is a matter of educated guesswork; attractive possibilities include the settlement of fines, payments to soldiers, and contributions to tribute or land tax—all direct payments to agents of the king. Something similar might have applied in tenth- and eleventh-century West Francia, where numerous local coinages were made, but hoards show that there was healthy interpenetration among them.[82] And in twelfth-century England, the *Dialogus de scaccario* describes close attention being paid to the type and quality of coins rendered to the Exchequer by sheriffs.[83] Even

79. IV Æthelred c. 7.2 (Liebermann 1903–16, 1:236–37).
80. GDB 172r, 179r.
81. Naismith 2017b, 229–31.
82. See chapter 9.
83. Richard Fitzneal, *Dialogus de scaccario* (Johnson 1950, 8–12, 40–43).

if it was not required for every transaction, stipulating the use of current coin for certain purposes would have given it a strong boost in terms of use and perhaps led to old types circulating only at discounted value.[84]

Recoinages, of whatever form, would have stimulated minting operations. That much is clear. But almost everything else about them in this period is up for debate. That includes why they happened, who benefited, and how they were put into practice, especially in terms of distribution. It should also be stressed that recoinages were really quite rare if one looks across the period. Even in England, where recoinages later became so routine, they were occasional during the eighth and ninth centuries, with a long gap between about 880 and the 970s. After the time of Charles the Bald, they were unusual in the Frankish world, with the important possible exception of Normandy.[85] Elsewhere, recoinages sometimes took place relatively early in the development of a new coinage, as in Scandinavia and possibly Dublin, both of which were heavily influenced by English practice—but they were still far from common.[86] Their impact needs always to be seen in relation to the specific regime and society that instituted them.

PRIVATE DEMAND

Private demand for minting has been left until last because it is in some ways the most nebulous of the main sources of demand for minting, yet taken as a whole it is likely to have been a major force. Its underlying importance is suggested by the deep-rooted early medieval view that dealing with mints and moneyers was a matter of "buying" silver and "selling" coins. At one point in the eleventh-century poem *Unibos*, an avaricious village provost tries to convince his companions to join him in what he expects to be a miraculously profitable commercial venture; as an enticement, he cites the vast number of coins the eponymous Unibos now has and underlines the point by saying that "if the [moneyers] should know" about the easy pickings supposedly on offer, "they would never coin

---

84. Naismith 2017b, 230. Fairbairn 2013, 237–99, presents a stimulating argument, claiming that there was no systematic recoinage as such, but rather a naturally fast turnover in the currency.

85. Moesgaard 2011. Since the number of relevant hoards is limited (especially from Norman territory), it is not possible to determine whether each issue completely replaced the one before it. The Norman coinage may therefore have been closer to that of England in changing type but not necessarily forcing recoinage (indeed, as Moesgaard emphasizes, it could have been a model Edgar and Æthelred II looked to).

86. Skaare 1976, 65–110; Woods 2013, 137–50, 218–32.

silver."[87] In other words, moneyers with easy access to other kinds of silver coin would have no need to make more. The ability of moneyers to eke out bullion could seem like alchemy. Christian of Stavelot marvelled at this skill: "moneyers are accustomed to taking other people's silver and turning it into coins, and at the end of the year they return what they received and, out of their ingenuity, half again on top."[88] Doing so required diligent husbanding of precious metal supplies. Specialists existed to supplement the flow that came from regular business, such as a group of scrap metal dealers who travelled the towns of eleventh-century England, extracting minute amounts of gold and silver from metalworking detritus and selling it to moneyers and related artisans.[89] The transformation of metal in the course of minting also meant that moneyers could fence stolen or otherwise illicit bullion with ease, which was one reason—alongside the risk of adulterating coin—that they were often seen as untrustworthy.[90]

In addition to this basically commercial dynamic of minting, mints and moneyers were also seen as an important source of coins to be used for commercial purposes. The puzzle here is why someone would seek out new coins, probably at considerable expense, as opposed to acquiring existing coins on the market. Scarcity is one possibility: the lack of sufficient coin to fulfil the needs of patrons was, counterintuitively, cited as a motive in some of the first recorded Carolingian grants of minting rights, to Prüm in 861 and to Châlons-en-Champagne in 865, with mixed results (no coins at all survive from Prüm in this period, and Châlons was not especially productive).[91] Going to a moneyer could be thought of as precisely the thing to do when *without* coins. When Ælfric of Eynsham (d. c. 1010), the great English homilist and scholar, rendered into Old

87. "Si trapezetae saperent, argentum nunquam tunderent." *Unibos* v. 40 (Klein 1991, 854; trans. Ziolkowski 1999, 19).

88. "Et solent monetarii accipere argentum ab aliquibus et solent denarios firmare et post annum integrum reddere quod acceperunt et medietatem de ingenio suo super acceptum." Christian of Stavelot, *Expositio super Librum generationis*, c. 25 (Huygens 2008, 462).

89. Goscelin of Saint-Bertin, *Miracula sancti Augustini* (AASS 6 May, 402). See discussion in Tsurushima 2012, 35–38, identifying the men in question among eleventh-century moneyers.

90. For two early-eleventh-century examples, see *Miracula sanctorum Ursmari et Ermini*, chap. 22 (Holder-Egger 1888a, 834–35, referring to events in the 1040s); *PL* 132, 536B (a letter from the monks of St. Gall to abbot Burchard II [1001–22]) For discussion of the latter, see Cahn 1911, 56–57.

91. DD Kar, 3:16; Tessier et al. 1943–55, no. 277. The authenticity of the latter document has been brought into question (Bur 1991), though not the section granting minting rights, and in any case the earliest surviving copy dates from the eleventh century.

English a homily of Gregory the Great that included a discussion of the parable of the talents,[92] he came across the idea of giving coin to the money changers (*nummulariis*) as a metaphor for spreading divine knowledge, on the understanding that those money changers would turn it into appropriate coin for wider circulation.[93] Ælfric did not live in a society with dedicated money changers, and so instead of saying money should have been given to them to be exchanged, he said it ought to have been handed over "to the moneyers to be struck" (*myneterum to sleanne*).[94] The implication here is that Ælfric thought of *feoh* (money) as something other than current coin: most likely old coin or bullion, but possibly cattle, for like Latin *pecunia*, *feoh* could refer to either money or livestock.[95] Moneyers could in theory change any kind of commodity for coin, though probably at a premium, for anything other than silver would require dipping into their float of precious metal without replenishment. Agreements for cash in advance might have been framed as a loan rather than buying and selling of coin, and indeed moneyers are known to have issued loans.[96] The saintly John of Gorze (d. 974) was praised by his hagiographer precisely for *not* taking advantage of "that which minting lawfully demands" (*ipsum quod moneta iure extorquet*) when silver was loaned or exchanged at the mint in his charge.[97]

Demand for minting could also be framed as coming from commercial activity, as at Rorschach in 947, where the flow of travellers passing through en route to Italy and Rome was seen as a good reason to establish a market and mint, for the benefit (figure 3.4) of the abbey of St. Gall.[98] Again, the inference here should probably be that the travellers, the monks, and others had noticed a shortfall in local supply relative to local demand; the new coins might also have been mandated for use within the market. The same basic idea lies behind dozens of other Ottonian and Salian diplomas that grant minting privileges in conjunction with rights for a toll and a market.[99]

Supplying coins simply because they were in short supply is one side of the commercial role of mints. Another is that there were transactions

92. Matthew 25:14–30; Luke 19:11–27.

93. Gregory the Great, *Homiliae in evangelia* no. 9 (Étaix 1999, 61).

94. Ælfric of Eynsham, *In natale unius confessoris* (Godden 1979, 319).

95. Casquero 2005; DOE s.v. *feoh*.

96. López 1953, 22–23.

97. John of Saint-Arnoul, *Vita Iohannis Gorzie coenobii abbatis*, c. 88 (ed. and trans. Jacobsen 2016, 352–54).

98. DD OI 90.

99. Kluge 1991, 101–4.

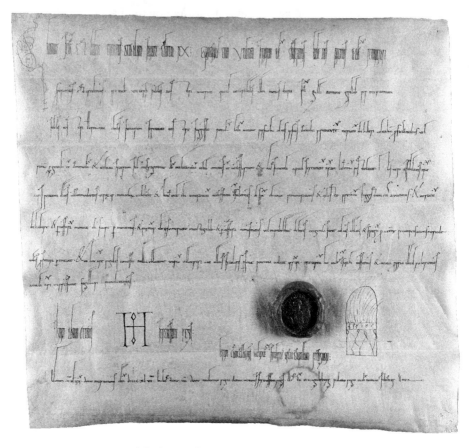

FIGURE 3.4. Original diploma of Otto I (936–73), granting the right to a market and mint at Rorschach, Switzerland, to St. Gall; issued on 12 June 947 (St. Gall, Stiftsarchiv, X2 A1; DD OI 90). It says that Gerloh, abbot of St. Gall, had suggested to Otto that "it would be appropriate, as well as necessary for the benefit (*utilitas*) of the brothers serving under his rule, to hold a market for travellers going to Italy or Rome in the place belonging to his monastery called Rorschach"; Otto therefore granted that a market and "the striking of money" (*percussuram monetae*) should be established there.

where fresh coin was thought particularly appropriate. To pay in new coin was a powerful statement: a signal of good faith or, quite simply, wealth and power. A figure or institution with resources would commission a run of fresh coins as a way of quite literally stamping their own identity onto an important purchase or gift. This could have been a driving force behind England's remarkably numerous and diverse coinages in the age of the early pennies (c. 670–750);[100] it also probably lies behind King Eadred's

100. See chapter 8.

decision to have gold bullion minted into coins before distribution to high-profile recipients, and the fact that some of the rare portrait coins of Charlemagne possibly minted in connection with the terms of his will carried the inscription EX METALLO NOVO.[101] For a time in eighth-century Italy, new coins were sometimes specified in land sales. The most impressive case comes from 759, when an abbot from Brescia bought half an estate from the bishop of Lodi, who had the intention of distributing the proceeds to the deserving poor. He could afford to be generous, for the sum in question was huge: 3,850 solidi (presumably taking the form of 11,550 tremisses), paid in new gold coins that were tested, weighed, and of appropriate colour (*auri solidos novos protestatos acoloratos pensantes*).[102] The abbot had drawn these from the treasury (*ex sacolo*) of his monastery, implying that it kept or could obtain a large stock of freshly minted gold pieces.[103] In principle the manufacture of so many tremisses could have been a major task for the moneyers of one of the north Italian mint-towns of the time, funded perhaps by the monastery's gold objects.

Commercial thinking was hardwired into the mechanics of early medieval minting, and it also clearly did have a relationship with all kinds of exchange. Yet in practical terms "private" minting would have been largely the preserve of those patrons who could present a mint or moneyer with a substantial quantity of bullion.

Conclusion

The reasons for making early medieval coins remain frustratingly elusive. That in itself is interesting, however. Whatever mechanisms did bring people to have new coins made were routine and unremarkable. One has to dig deep to find any specific references to why coins were minted. Three general points stand out. First, coins were made for many reasons. The same moneyer might move between several kinds of demand in the

101. The case of EX METALLO NOVO is not clear-cut: it could also refer to a new mine, though analysis of the alloy suggests it was made from Melle silver: Sarah 2009, 82; Coupland 2018a, 444–45.

102. Later (e.g., Olivieri 2011, 90–91, on the early twelfth century), *novus* more often referred to coins of a newly instituted issue, possibly though not necessarily freshly minted. But it is not clear that successive reigns or issues were differentiated in this way in the eighth and ninth centuries; moreover, some of the Italian documents in question were written when the current reign or issue was a decade or more old.

103. *ChLA* XXVII, no. 814. Unusually, several witnesses were specifically included to testify to the handover of this very large sum of money. For other examples, see Porro-Lambertenghi 1873, nos. 36–37 and 261; *ChLA* XXVIII, no. 845.

course of a few days or hours. Second, diversity of demand probably fed into the general lumpiness of early medieval minting. Production might have intensified temporarily when a big consignment of silver was brought by an aristocrat, when a recoinage was demanded, or when particular payments to the king or to landlords were due. Third is that it is misleading to imagine that there must be a "real" economic force somewhere just out of view. In the context of coinage, the tapestry of forces assessed here was probably it. What follows is that, relative to the overall stock of coin in circulation, the amount being minted would have been relatively small and shaped by a range of factors quite different from those that affected the bulk of the currency. Production, or primary use, was its own beast.

CHAPTER FOUR

Using Coined Money

THE MONKS OF MARMOUTIER (near Strasbourg) faced a problem in the 1060s. A local troublemaker called Thibault had brought a legal case against the monastery. This was not the first time he had locked horns with the monks, and it would not be the last. The case in question—a technicality concerning the cleric attached to a church Thibault's kinsman had sold to the abbey—was essentially a shakedown. Thibault wanted a payout. He got one, agreeing at a gathering in Vendôme to back off in return for the monastery paying him 40s and a sow to his wife Helia. So far so good: a payment was determined among the interested parties that might be seen as either compensation or a pay-off. All that remained was actually to make the handover, which was recorded in a supplementary note to the relevant charter. A monk called Joscelin did the honours, arriving at Thibault's home with the money, the pig, and the document recording the agreement. But a problem presented itself to Joscelin: a noisy and playful issue that would have been immediately apparent as he neared the house. Thibault and Helia had many children, the three youngest of whom (*infantes*, implying they were below the age of seven) had not been at the meeting in Vendôme and therefore might, in principle, grow up and rekindle the dispute. Joscelin thought fast and undertook what was essentially an extension of the agreement made by the charter. For this to stick he also needed to extend the material satisfaction that had been given to Thibault and his wife. So the three little boys, named Burcard, Aremburg, and John, stepped up and touched the document, and each received from Joscelin a single coin. The terse narrative of the charter does not elaborate on this scene or what followed it, but it is easy to picture the three little boys marvelling at their coins as they were shepherded through the motions of witnessing a charter, before turning to the more important matter of what they might spend their pocket money on.[1]

This series of exchanges exemplifies several of the main ways in which coins changed hands in the early Middle Ages. They served as a desirable way of settling obligations, with an implication of finality. Strikingly, they were used alongside a payment in kind, the wife's sow. There might be a gendered dimension here, with coin for the men and livestock for the wife, though other, less formal contexts could work very differently. Finally, there is a performative, ritual element to the use of coin. Giving a penny to each of the three little boys served little practical purpose, however pleased they might have been in the moment: it was more for the benefit of the parents and the attendant witnesses, who could testify that they had seen Thibault's sons receive payment in return for agreeing to the terms of the charter. Coined money was an effective way of signalling acts of this kind, being a tangible and immediately recognisable encapsulation of value. Just as its value and circulation depended on consensus and agreement, the act of exchanging coins demonstrated consensus and agreement more broadly. A point that emerges several times in this chapter is that transfers of coin were above all a way of reifying a transfer of wealth: handing over coin imparted a transactional quality, demonstrating implicitly that both participants recognised and accepted the value at stake, and that a line had been drawn under this particular exchange. Importantly, this aspect of using coin did not subsume other areas of social interaction; on the contrary, the transactional, finite dimensions of using coin were adopted unabashedly into all sorts of settings.

This chapter considers five major categories of coin use, and the effect coins had in each case. These do not account for absolutely every kind of use, and the division could be arranged in other ways, but the point is to emphasise how diverse and interconnected the whole picture was. The first of these is gift-giving: a context that has loomed very large historically in assessments of the period. Gifts of money did happen—often, in fact—but their dominance in terms of the overall circulating mass of coin is questionable. The second includes any handover of coin in hierarchical contexts, such as payments of rent from tenants to lords, the point being that coin, or rather acts of handing over coin, had important status connotations. Payments to the king or his representatives, and to the church, are treated separately. These too were tied up with notions of status and obligation, albeit on a more global level. The fifth main category

1. de Trémault 1893, no. 7. For context see Teunis 2006, 83–84.

considered here is commerce, buying and selling, where the presence of coin is perhaps most expected, but by no means universal or economically rational. Commercial use is treated at greater length, with consideration of the larger implications of how imbalances in use and access to coin played out for elites and others. Coinage played a role in shaping the meaning of acts of exchange, and so to control the flow of coin was to control expressions of social dominance on a much deeper level than just having money to spend on what one wanted.

Money and Gift-Giving

In November 1883 excavators were seeking to uncover the House of the Vestal Virgins in the Roman Forum. Their main interest lay in the classical remains, and to reach them they ploughed through metres and metres of accumulated later material. One of the more surprising finds they made along the way—though not quite arresting enough to halt the inexorable digging—was a vessel full of coins; at least 830 all told. It soon emerged that these coins were mostly Anglo-Saxon pennies of the early tenth century, known ever since in Anglophone scholarship as the "Forum hoard." But the most interesting part of the find was a pair of silver "hooked tags" or fasteners, with an inscription that spanned the two: + DOMNO MARINO PAPA[e],[2] "for the lord pope, Marinus" (see figure 4.1). Marinus is thought to refer to Pope Marinus II (942–46), whose tenure coincides exactly with the date of the latest coin in the hoard (a penny of Edmund, king of the English, minted at York between 944 and 946).[3]

On the basis of the hooked tags, the Forum hoard was, within days of its discovery, touted as an early example of Peter's Pence: an annual donation from England to the papacy.[4] But this practice was only becoming established in the mid-tenth century, so the Forum hoard cannot be straightforwardly identified as a cache of Peter's Pence gone astray. It may represent a transitional stage, during which specific dioceses or other groups offered money to Rome, on an occasional rather than a regular basis. This reading depends in part on the inscription of the hooked tags, which identifies the Forum hoard as an assemblage of coins intended for a donative purpose. They represent a gift, together with some highly elaborate packaging.[5]

---

2. The final e is perhaps implied by the double crossbar of the final letter a, creating a simple a-e ligature.

3. For a full catalogue of the hoard, see Naismith and Tinti 2016.

4. Naismith and Tinti 2016.

5. Naismith 2016e.

FIGURE 4.1. Hooked tags found in the Forum hoard, identifying the assemblage as a gift for Pope Marinus II (length 45 and 43 mm). Courtesy of the Italian Ministry of Culture, Museo Nazionale Romano: Medagliere and Servizio Fotografico MNR.

Traces of fabric adhered to some of the coins, from a long-decayed bag or purse. The tags themselves contain the equivalent of about five pennies each in silver and were the equivalent of an extremely opulent and highly visible gift tag. That implies an occasion for giving in which the offering was meant to be seen, even if only by an audience of one (i.e., the pope or St. Peter). Moreover, the tags are interesting for what they do *not* say: the name of the donor, which is otherwise very common on donation inscriptions in other media. To refer only to the recipient was highly unusual but might be explained if the expectation was that the donor would be there in person to make the handover. That in turn suggests a donor who was of some status and could realistically expect an audience with the pope.

There were many English visitors to Rome in the tenth century, but few would have had the resources to make an offering on the scale of the Forum hoard.[6] Fewer still would have been of sufficient standing to meet the pope in person. A plausible candidate for bringing the hoard to Rome can in fact be identified: Theodred, bishop of London (elected between 909 and 926; died between 951 and 953).[7] He was one of the more prominent bishops of the time and possessed considerable wealth, as revealed through his will.[8] Crucially, this will mentions a pair of chasubles acquired at Pavia, in the course of a visit to Italy. It is not specifically said that Theodred had been going to or coming from Rome, though that is entirely plausible, and the date for this visit is also compatible with the likely assemblage date of the Forum hoard. Finally, the most recent coins in the hoard include a particularly strong London element, not least a string of eleven pennies all made using the same pair of dies. These had probably remained together ever since production, having seen less attrition through circulation, like a tenth-century equivalent of sequential banknotes.[9]

6. Naismith and Tinti 2019, 525–26.

7. Naismith and Tinti 2016, 44; Naismith 2018b, 149–52.

8. S 1526 (Kelly 2004, 225–28).

9. For a full catalogue of the hoard, see Naismith and Tinti 2016.

Theodred thus had the means, motive, and opportunity to take the Forum hoard from England to Rome. The hoard stands as a vivid but far from unusual deployment of coin in a Christian donative context. There were some who had misgivings about the presence of money in sacred settings. The most absolute and shrill opposition grew out of concern over simony: the sin of buying and selling holy office, which was supposed to be freely given. There was a long history of condemning simony in Christian texts, but the accusation was applied very selectively before the eleventh century, when simony rocketed up to the forefront of the agenda within the circle of the "reform" papacy.[10] Payments and gifts came under scrutiny, and the presence of money was seen as a hallmark of impropriety. In rhetoric of the period, money served as a metonym for avarice and corruption. The ascetic John Gualbert (d. 1073) supposedly refused even to speak to a priest who visited him with a bag of coins,[11] and as Humbert of Silva Candida put it in one of the most strident diatribes against simony, "he who puts coinage first puts God utterly second."[12]

The simony panic generated more light than heat, however, and even then only within select clerical circles. For most users, giving coin as such was not an issue. But there was a sense that, in donative settings, not all coins were created equal. For coin to reflect a virtuous and unfeigned gift, donors had to avoid giving any coins tainted by undesirable prior uses; a contextually specific inversion of Vespasian's famous dictum that money doesn't stink.[13] A visitor to Bury St. Edmunds in the eleventh century had set aside a specific coin for donation to the saint; one that came "from his own rightful earnings" (*ex iustissimis rerum suarum*) and was readily distinguishable by him, as opposed to others that were not appropriate for donation. In this case, disaster struck: the man found the designated coin missing from his purse when he came to the altar. He retraced his steps through the town and eventually found the lost coin glinting in the dirt of the marketplace.[14] A similar point is made in the miracles of St. Bavo, from Ghent around the year 1000, in the story of a young man who sold

---

10. West 2015 suggests that opposition to simony among the papal "reform" faction arose from confrontation of northerners accustomed to simpler notions of ecclesiastical economy with the richer, more involved ecclesiastical exchange system of Italy. For more general surveys see Meier-Welcker 1952–53; Münsch 2006; McCready 2011, 66–111.

11. Andrew of Strumi, *S. Ioannis Gualberti vita*, c. 6 (*PL* 146, col. 792B–C).

12. "Immo penitus postponit sibi Deum, cui praeponit nummum." Humbert of Silva Candida, *Contra simoniacos*, 1.2 (Thaner 1891, 151).

13. Suetonius, *Vespasian* c. 23 (ed. and trans. Rolfe 1914, 302–3).

14. Herman of Laon, *Miracles of St. Edmund*, c. 44 (ed. and trans. Licence 2014, 340–41).

himself into servitude. Material poverty at a time of famine is said to have been the cause; a recurring trope, but a plausible one.[15] Being pious, the young man wished to give a penny from the proceeds of his sale to the church. But when he tried to put the coin down on the altar, his arm and hand froze and remained immobile. Shocked, he began to have doubts about what he had just done. He regained movement in his arm only when he replaced the coin with one he had acquired from his "dutiful labour" (*officioso sudamine*).[16] The story revolves around the protagonist's youth and place in the monastic *familia*: that is to say, he did not yet have a fixed position in society and was already a servant beholden to St. Bavo, so selling himself to someone else was, if not quite stealing, at least depriving the saint's church of his labour. The spiritual benefit of the sale, represented by the coin, was hence being misplaced.[17]

There is a strong performative element here, which could raise a different set of concerns about the proper place of money. All depended on showing, demonstratively, how coin was appropriate for a pious donation. This can be seen in action in a story from Einhard's narrative of the translation and miracles of Saints Marcellinus and Peter, written in the early ninth century about the arrival of a group of Roman relics in Germany. Einhard describes seeing a man named Willibert among the many pilgrims approaching the altar with an offering, but he was apparently taken aback when Willibert placed a handful of coins onto the altar. Confounded, and perhaps concerned for the reputation of his new shrine, Einhard confronted the giver of the coins and asked pointedly who he was and "what he hoped to get for himself by offering this sort of gift."[18] A subtle hint of something improper is coded in this question: when describing the mass of pious pilgrims, Einhard wrote of them each bringing a *donum* to the saints, but when challenging Willibert's offering of coins he switches to *munus*. A *donum* was an open and honourable gift, in contrast to a *munus*, which implied a more transactional exchange; in other words, a quid pro quo.[19] On those grounds Willibert was asked to account for himself, and fortunately for him he had a good story up his sleeve, about how the money he offered—no small sum of 40d—represented the proceeds of

15. Rio 2012, 672–73, notes that this is a commonplace of self-sales, even when the seller was able to negotiate a better outcome; it is therefore possible that poverty was more relative than absolute.

16. *Miracula S. Bavonis* c. 5 (O. Holder–Egger 1888b, 592).

17. Rio 2012; 2017, 42–74.

18. "Quidque sibi vellet huiusce muneris oblatio." Einhard, *Translatio et miracula SS. Marcellini et Petri*, 3.3 (Waitz 1887, 249; trans. Dutton 1998, 93).

19. Nelson 2010; Wickham 2010, 242–47.

selling his last pig, which he had pledged to the saints when desperately ill. The whole tale revolves around how this was a very proper gift after all, but its history needed to be known; Willibert did not make this sufficiently clear from the manner of his offering.

The Forum hoard exemplifies this presentational aspect of monetary giving, as a rare example of a large assemblage still visibly earmarked for donation. Among other actual finds, only coins in burials present a comparably clear identity, but it is not clear whether these should be interpreted as gifts for the deceased, symbolic gifts from the deceased, or something else entirely. More productive comparisons come from other accounts of how money was presented in special ways to signify its status as a gift. These extend beyond religious donations. Conrad II (d. 1039), on his way through Italy to be crowned emperor in Rome, took pity on one of his men who had lost a leg in fighting at Ravenna. The soon-to-be-emperor's imaginative compensation took the form of a pair of leather greaves filled with coins.[20] A bishop in seventh-century Gaul left various bequests of gold solidi in his will and asked that these be put into little bags, each marked with a small tag bearing the name of its recipient.[21] Sacks of gold pieces were also the preferred medium for giving out salaries from the emperor to palace functionaries in tenth-century Constantinople, some being so large the recipients had to stagger away awkwardly.[22] A widespread tradition involved placing coins for presentation to a superior in a bowl or cup. One tenth-century English will describes money to be given to its recipient this way, and the practice is apparently depicted in one early twelfth-century church mural (figure 4.2) from Catalonia.[23]

A necessary complement to packaging was stage management: handing over the coins in such a way that their identity as a gift was apparent. A short narrative from St. Gall describes a visiting English bishop in 929 doing just that. Koenwald, bishop of Worcester, arrived as part of a tour of German monasteries, armed with "a not insubstantial offering of silver" (*oblatione de argento non modica*) from the king for distribution on his journey. His actual giving of that silver was carefully choreographed. It took place on the anniversary of the burial of St. Gall (16 October), when he entered the monastic church put some money on the altar and gave another sum for the monks. Immediately afterward, he was inducted into

20. Wipo, *Gesta Chuonradi* c. 13 (Bresslau 1915, 35).

21. Weidemann 1986, 45–46.

22. Liudprand of Cremona, *Antapodosis* 6.10 (Chiesa 1998, 149; trans. Squatriti 2007, 200–202).

23. Naismith 2018b, 148–50.

FIGURE 4.2. Apse painting from Santa Maria, Taüll, Catalonia, Spain (c. 1123), showing an offering of silver coins in dishes. Museu Nacional d'Art de Catalunya, Barcelona; author's photograph.

the monastic community, who promised to include him and a series of other English worthies in their prayers. The donation of cash was a central element of Koenwald's welcome.[24]

What Koenwald engaged in at St. Gall was almsgiving: charitable donation to churches. Alms consisted of food and clothing as well as coined money, which would either be retained by the church for its own use or redistributed by church authorities to the poor. Disbursement of alms offered one of the few reliable outlets of charitable support in the early Middle Ages, and each church had its own established cohort of orphans and widows who would receive those alms on a regular and indefinite basis. The actual amount was relatively small, portioned out to ensure sustenance rather than to allow an escape from poverty. The point was to maximise the spiritual benefit of the donors rather than empower the recipients; the "proud pauper" (*pauper superbus*) who did not know his place as the recipient of modest worldly goods was one of the characters to be met with in the influential Hiberno-Latin tract *De duodecim abusivis saeculi*.[25] In practice, almsgiving offered a direct line from the wealthy

24. Keynes 1985, 198–99. For context, see also Georgi 1995.
25. Hellmann 1909, 49–51.

and the powerful to the poor. Offerings could range from individual coins given during church collections—some of which fell and rolled beneath the floorboards of Scandinavian and Swiss churches, to be found centuries later[26]—to very large amounts. Odilo, a monk of Soissons, boasted to a deacon in the early tenth century of how pious visitors to the shrine of St. Sebastian from all parts of Gaul, Germany, and elsewhere brought immense offerings in diverse forms: "the heap of varied kinds of silver coin exceeded 85 *modii*,"[27] and this did not include the male and female ornaments (*monilia virorum ac mulierum*) and vessels of gold and silver that amounted to another 900 lbs.[28] This was an unambiguously good thing in Odilo's eyes. But Odo of Cluny (d. 942) lamented at one point how laymen would compete with one another in the scale of their almsgiving, "since things expended profusely for foolish glory are better called consumption or extravagance than charity."[29] Big spenders sometimes even had coins specifically made for eleemosynary purposes, with inscriptions stating as much,[30] and it is entirely possible that other coins (including some of those in the Forum hoard) were produced with this purpose in mind even if it is not inscribed onto them.

Alms raise three final and important observations. The first is that coined money *could* be entirely appropriate for giving, if it was fairly won and its status as a gift made clear. These caveats imply a degree of hesitation. Yet money was at the same time a deep-rooted Christian metaphor for the soul, and the need to scrutinise and cherish inner goodness. It exemplified the capacity to turn tawdry things of the earth into heavenly

---

26. Gullbekk 2015, 232–42. These become plentiful later in the Middle Ages, though the earliest specimens date to the eleventh century.

27. "Octoginta quinque modiorum diversorum nomismatum argenti cumulus excresceret." How many actual coins this translated to is a matter of educated guesswork. If Odilo meant Roman *modii* of about 8.62 litres each (Duncan-Jones 2012), he would have been describing 732.7 litres of coins. About 1,826 modern British one-penny coins can fit into a litre; these are similar in diameter to pennies and denarii of the tenth century but somewhat thicker, so a guess based on them will be an underestimate. The amount Odilo claimed to have been deposited at Soissons would have amounted to some 1.3 million modern British pennies. This is clearly a wild exaggeration, meant to convey the idea of "a great many."

28. Odilo, *Translatio S. Sebastiani* c. 36 (Holder-Egger 1887b, 386). The text is traditionally dated c. 930 on the basis of material adjacent to it in one manuscript copy, though it is likely to be earlier, perhaps c. 900 (Lifshitz 1992, 334–37).

29. "Cum res ad inanem gloriam profuse dispensae, comestio vel effusio magis dicendae sunt quam charitas." Odo of Cluny, *Collationes* 1.41 (*PL* 133, 548B).

30. Examples are known in the name of Pippin III (Kluge 2014, Pippin no. 18—though the author notes that the coin inscription ELIMOSINA has sometimes been read as a place-name, perhaps for Angoulême) and Alfred the Great (Dolley 1954).

treasure.[31] This openness to monetary gifts might seem surprising. A gift of money, like a gift of food or drink, was not expected to last, at least as a physical object. It also offered no disguise as to the real value of a gift, if one was predisposed to look at it in this way.[32] That depended, though, on value being the main concern. Parallels from other traditions show that there might be other kinds of logic at work. In modern China, there is a very strong tradition of offering money as a gift at major life events, typically in a red envelope. Money handed over in this way is expected and socially valorised as a gift, and it carries no stigma; nor is there any particular tendency toward exact reciprocation, or one-upmanship.[33] As in early medieval Europe, contextual and presentational transformation reworked money into a gift, not the gift into money.

The second point relates to status, in that much more is known about gifts that involved members of the clergy and of the secular elite. This is not to say gifts were exclusive to these groups: *xenia* and *munuscula* consisting of small, tokenistic gifts were expected from tenants to landlords as a supplement to rents, for example,[34] and we have seen instances of poor yet pious individuals giving single coins to churches. Lower-status gifts are surely underrepresented in extant sources, and a whole spectrum of small gifts should probably be imagined, largely below the radar of surviving texts.[35] Nonetheless, the greater material resources of the elite, and the complexity of their vertical and horizontal social entanglements, probably did lead to a higher volume of gifts and a more diverse and developed engagement with them.

The third observation concerns exactly this question of scale. While there is no question that coins were extensively used for making gifts, did gift-giving account for much coin circulation as a whole? And at a larger level, were gifts ever the principal form of exchange supporting early medieval coin use? Both questions must be answered with a qualified negative. Gifts were, on the whole, driven by social concerns rather than economic ones and did not represent a secure basis for fulfilling day-to-day material needs.[36] The scale, timing, and form of gifts, along with their value, could only be roughly predicted.[37] Even among people of con-

---

31. See chapter 6.
32. Wickham 2010, 254–55.
33. Hudik and Fang 2020; Kipnis 1996.
34. Jussen 2003; Kuchenbuch 2003.
35. Wickham 2010, 243–44.
36. Wickham 2010, 259–60; Curta 2006, 673–74.
37. Though Curta 2006 explores the competitive side of gift-giving, in which giving or reciprocating with something of much greater or lower value than expected was a potential power play.

siderable means, gifts were often symbolic tokens of negligible monetary worth; gifts exchanged by the network of St. Boniface (d. 754), which linked England and Germany, included money and books, but also towels and other small items, all chosen with carefully calculated resonance in mind.[38] Coins were not quite so negligible. But whether gift-giving represented the majority of monetary circulation is doubtful, certainly in the case of the larger silver-based currencies of the seventh century and later. Such is suggested by the body of coin finds. These do not cluster at likely focuses of donative activity such as churches, or even elite settlements. Although the history of each individual coin is lost, and it is possible that they had passed in and out of use as gifts, collectively the pattern of finds points to circulation being governed by density of population and complexity of exchange.[39] That is difficult to reconcile with the idea of a "gift economy" shaping the general landscape of coin use in the early Middle Ages, and there are good reasons for consigning this term to the historical attic.

There are of course exceptions. Individual offerings consisting of coins could be large, with a considerable local impact. One will from ninth-century Canterbury provided for a thousand paupers a year to receive one penny each.[40] In some specific contexts there are also grounds for seeing gifted coins as a large and ongoing part of the monetary economy. Early medieval coinage always represented a very small part of exchange, and in general the smaller the body of coin, and the higher its value, the larger a share of its use will be accounted for by gift-giving. One place that met these conditions was Rome between the late eighth and tenth centuries, where gift-giving governed extensive flows of foreign coins into the city and generated a separate sphere of circulation. The latter existed alongside the local "money of St. Peter": the so-called *antiquiores*, penny-size silver coins issued in the names of the popes (often in conjunction with the current emperor), which were the standard currency of the city.[41] Strikingly, finds of Anglo-Saxon coins from Rome in this period are at least as numerous as those of *antiquiores*.[42] These seem to have had some sort of preferential status or else reflect a particular kind of devotional practice

38. Clay 2009.

39. See chapter 9.

40. S 1414 (Brooks and Kelly 2013, no. 64). See Naismith 2012b, 283–84.

41. Toubert 1973, 1:566; Valci 2021. The latter records a total of sixteen single finds of *antiquiores* from Rome and Lazio.

42. Naismith 2014c; Naismith and Tinti 2016, with some additional finds identified by Mariele Valci. There are at least sixteen certain or probable single finds of English coins of the appropriate period from Rome and Lazio, plus three hoards.

FIGURE 4.3. The Offa dinar, imitating an original Abbasid
dinar of AH 157 (AD 773/74) (diameter 19 mm). British
Museum, image from Sylloge of Coins of the British Isles.

by English visitors, for contemporary coins from the Carolingian Empire
are very rare finds in Rome.

Rome was a special case, distinct for its unusually well-developed
economy of devotional gifts, and for its relatively small local coinage.[43]
Gift-giving may similarly have accounted for a higher share of the circulation of gold coinage in western Europe after about 700 (i.e., after
gold had ceased to be the default denomination). High in value, low in
quantity, and dominated by the elite, these coins followed quite different
patterns from contemporary silver issues. Few barriers impeded their
circulation: Arabic dinars (or imitations of them), Byzantine solidi, and
others travelled over long distances and could be used interchangeably.
Written references to this segment of the currency are disproportion-
ately numerous, for gold coinage was the stuff of high-status exchange,
brought out to impress and make a statement. When St. Gebhard, bishop
of Constance (979–95), appeared at the site where work was about to
begin on the new abbey of Petershausen in 983, he marked the four cor-
ners of its soon-to-be-built church with a gold coin dropped into the
soil that would lie beneath its foundations.[44] Two centuries earlier, Offa
of Mercia pledged to make an offering of 365 mancuses (gold pieces)
per year to the pope. It may well have been that the famous imitative
dinar carrying Offa's name (figure 4.3) was made precisely to fulfil this

43. The best illustration of its rich donative economy is the lavish expenditure of gold
and silver on ecclesiastical ornamentation by the popes, as catalogued in the *Liber pontificalis*: Delogu 1988.

44. *Casus monasterii Petrishusensis* 1.16 (Feger 1956, 54–55; trans. Beach, Shannon,
and Sutherland 2020, 52). On this and other placed deposits in religious settings, see
Travaini 2019; 2022.

promise.[45] If so, gift-giving set the agenda for producing a certain group of coins.

Making a Statement: Money, Status, and Ritual

Stabilis—whose name is an unsubtle clue to the moral of his tale—appears as a protagonist in a miracle story told by Andrew of Fleury in the eleventh century. He was a peasant, of servile status, who lived and worked on the lands of St. Benedict at Fleury. This was not necessarily a difficult or unpleasant life relative to some others, but it did not suit the ambitions of Stabilis. He found the poverty of his condition restrictive, and so decided to pack up and relocate to a distant region on the other side of France. In Burgundy Stabilis found success. For a time, he lived the high life of a *miles*, gaining wealth, a wife of noble lineage, servants, horses, and all the accoutrements needed for hunting; in short, "he traded the ignoble office of peasant for the business of knighthood."[46] Crucially, Stabilis also stopped paying the nominal annual head-tax he owed to St. Benedict, forgetting all about his unglamorous earlier life and even about the saint himself. His happiness lasted until one day in the 960s, when a monk of Fleury who knew him happened to visit the area to look after some of the monastery's property. The monk called out Stabilis as a fugitive peasant who by birth owed tribute and service to St. Benedict. After Stabilis denied the charge, the case had to be taken to the count of Troyes, who decided that the outcome should be put into the hands of God through a trial by combat. Stabilis's idyll was beginning to collapse. His downfall was assured when a doughty local volunteered to fight on behalf of the saint. As he stepped into the ring, Stabilis felt a pang of remorse (doubtless sharpened by fear) and quietly slipped an obol (halfpenny) out of its place in the fold of his sleeve.[47] Muttering that this was the last payment he would make to Benedict, Stabilis threw it to the ground. The coin immediately grew to the size of a shield, resonating with the name of St. Benedict. Not surprisingly, this miraculous turn of events put a stop to the fight. Stabilis decided discretion was the better part of valour and agreed to return to his

45. This promise is known from a letter written to Offa's successor by Leo III (Dümmler 1895, no. 127; trans. Whitelock 1979, no. 205). For discussion, see Naismith 2012b, 113–14.

46. "Militari commercio rusticanae ignobilitatis mutat officia." Andrew of Fleury, *Miracula sancti Benedicti* 6.2 (Davril, Dufour, and Labory 2019, 348).

47. This was apparently a standard way to carry small change in the tenth and eleventh centuries: an addition to the Old English version of the *Seven Sleepers of Ephesus* notes that coins were kept in a fold of clothing (Kramer, Magennis, and Norris 2020, 630–31).

proper status as a servile tenant of the saint. The coin, meanwhile, shrank back to its normal size a few hours after the combat but was kept as a relic in the church.

It would have been fascinating to know what went through visitors' minds when confronted with this humble silver halfpenny among Fleury's relic collection.[48] But the story in itself is telling. It has been widely disscussed for its insight into attitudes toward status and knighthood,[49] less so for its relevance to coin. The two are related, however. Exchanging coined money could be a kind of ritual. It inserted an independent, externally validated token of value into human interaction: a focal point that introduced a transactional character into proceedings. Giving one or more coins signified that an exchange was legitimate, settled, and complete— very literally in tenth-century England, where the handover of the last penny in a land purchase, publicly and before witnesses, was the moment when the property became the buyer's.[50] We have already seen this with gifts as well as purchases, and performative handovers of coin called attention to any change or action that could be valued in terms of money, or even as a symbol of trust: the "willing compact of seller and buyer," as a Carolingian Church council put it in 829.[51] This went back much further. The Frankish king, Childeric (d. 481), at one point had to leave the kingdom of the Franks because of his lascivious conduct and take refuge in Thuringia. But before leaving he arranged with a trusted friend for a signal that could be sent between them. They broke a gold coin into two pieces, and when the situation had stabilised in Francia, Childeric would receive the missing part of his coin and know that it was time to make his move.[52] The only direct mention of coin in Bede's *Ecclesiastical History* is similar. Eorcengota, daughter of Eorcenberht of Kent (640–64), spent much of her life at the nunnery of Brie in France but in her old age experienced a vision that warned of her impending death. She saw a troop of men clad in white

48. There are many coin relics from later times (Travaini 2022); one of the very few others from this period is a Byzantine gold piece kept as a relic and used to perform miracles of healing by St. Wulfstan of Worcester (1062–95): William of Malmesbury, *Life of Wulfstan* 2.9 (Winterbottom and Thomson 2002, 78–81).

49. For a small selection, see Dejardin-Bazaille 2007; Barthélemy 2009, 130, 220–21; Head 1992, 230–31; Reynolds 1997, 40–41. See also the similar story of Albericus the peasant (Andrew of Fleury, *Miracula sancti Benedicti* 5.8 [Davril, Dufour, and Labory 2019, 332–36]).

50. *Libellus Æthelwoldi* 45/*Liber Eliensis* 2.34 (Blake 1962, 109; trans. Fairweather 2005, 132–33); S 1448a (Kelly 2009, no. 30[xii]).

51. Council of Paris (829), c. 52 (Werminghoff 1908, 2:645).

52. Gregory of Tours, *Historiae* 2.12 (Krusch and Levison 1951, 61–62; trans. Thorpe 1974, 128–29).

coming into the monastery. They told her they had been sent "to take back with them the golden coin that had been brought thither from Kent"—in other words, Eorcengota herself was being fetched back to heaven.[53] This was the opposite of Simmel's interpretation of money's effect: instead of affecting all it touched, the transactional quality of money was instrumentalised as a strategy for social interaction.[54]

Using coin in itself did not reflect on personal status, but its associations with the transfer of value made it an effective way of marking shifts of individual standing. Manumission by coin had a long pedigree, extending from the Merovingian era to the twelfth century in the Frankish kingdom and its successors.[55] Details varied slightly over time, but the core principle was that by knocking a coin out of a servile person's hand, they became free.[56] One eleventh-century Italian text adds the picturesque detail that the coin should then go flipping over the person's head.[57] In the earliest references to this practice, which appear in Merovingian legal texts and formularies, it was the owner of the slave who did the knocking, or rather throwing the coin at or from the manumittee, but they were expected to carry out the act before the king. In Carolingian and later occurrences, the master slips into the background, and it was now the king who would knock the coin out of the slave's hand, and the ceremony only or mostly applied to slaves of the king.

The origins of manumission by coin are shrouded in obscurity. It simply appears out of nowhere under the Merovingians. Various suggestions have been advanced for what the exchange of a coin at the point of manumission might signify. A single denarius could be a metonym for *census* that had hitherto been paid to the master, or for the price that the slave would have been worth if the manumittee had been sold.[58] But the coin was refused, so it should perhaps be seen as a kind of quittance, with the lord refusing to accept any further payment from his or her subordinate.[59] It was closer to the confirmation of an agreement. Earlier rituals of manumission include no exact precursor, but a possible precedent may be the Roman tradition of finalising a pact with the sacrifice of coin. This tradition is best known in connection with the *stips*: a coin cast into a holy

53. "Ut aureum illud nomisma, quod eo de Cantia uenerat, secum adsumerent." Bede, *Historia ecclesiastica gentis Anglorum* 3.8 (Colgrave and Mynors 1969, 238–39).

54. Algazi 2003; Bourdieu 1990 (the latter in conjunction with Silber 2009).

55. The key recent studies are Maass 2007; Kano 2013.

56. The status of the person being freed varies: Kano 213, 44–47.

57. *Liber Papiensis* c. 224 (Boretius 1868, 353).

58. Kano 2013, 51; Schmidt-Wiegand 2006, 155.

59. Winogradoff 1876, 600; Brunner 1886, 250.

place as a symbol of an agreement with the gods, sometimes inscribed to emphasise that purpose.[60] People continued to deposit *ex stipe* offerings of coin across the Roman period: some whole temples were rebuilt from the proceeds of coins left by grateful visitors. After the adoption of Christianity, people found new ways to perpetuate the custom: putting coins into the font at baptism, for example.[61] Of course, to use coins—small, handy, and relatively accessible objects—as a symbol for personal presence or participation does not necessarily have to derive from a specific prior custom. It could develop spontaneously, as it did in many times and places.[62] Another possible parallel would be the habit of making gifts of individual coins at holy places, forcing them into tombs or other secret places.[63] The assemblage of coins from beneath Old St. Peter's belongs to this category and might be set aside smaller groups of low-value coins that had been pushed into the cracks of sarcophagi of St. Ambrose and diverse others by generations of pilgrims. These were left as a token of the givers' visits from afar, in perpetual contact with the holy place: a sort of contact relic in reverse.[64]

Demonstrative handling of coin could, then, be a way of marking a shift in status. To put it in the terms of Florence Weber, money could be found in a great many "social scenes" and so helped define people's place within them.[65] It enabled the relationship between slave, master, and king to be reframed as a negotiated agreement, which fits well with the varied forms of early medieval slavery.[66] To be able to pay one's own way was another signal of autonomy and could in theory be done willingly, even enthusiastically, especially if dues were collected and/or spent publicly. Using cash in a world of scarce and high-value coins was a meaningful act, even if on a modest scale. In tenth-century England, a tract on the rights and obligations of people of various conditions on a rural estate (known as *Rectitudines singularum personarum*) states at one point that the cottager or *kotsetla*—a freeman of humble standing—should pay his "hearthpenny . . . as behoves every freeman."[67]

---

60. Desnier 1987, esp. 226–27. For broader context, Aarts 2005, esp. 22–23.
61. See chapter 6.
62. E.g., Houlbrook 2018.
63. Possibly into water at Little Carlton (Lincolnshire): Willmott et al. 2021.
64. Travaini 2004.
65. Weber 2012; Cardon 2021, 308–18.
66. Rio 2017.
67. "Heorðpænig . . . ealswa ælcan frigean men gebyreð." *Rectitudines singularum personarum* 3.4 (Liebermann 1903–16, 1:446). For discussion, see Naismith and Tinti 2019, 538–39.

Strikingly, coin also featured prominently in payments that meant the precise opposite of manumission: entry *into* servitude, or recognition of servile status. Owners of slaves did not want to be seen as getting something for nothing, not least because this might leave their status as owner in jeopardy.[68] Precisely this worry was voiced in another Marmoutier charter, in which a knight gave a miller and his family into the possession of the church. The knight was given 20s in return, not so much as a price, but "so that it not be thought that this was done for nothing."[69] Money payments, either as coin or in a commodity rated by its value in pennies (most often wax), were also a defining characteristic of a whole class of people who had undertaken autodedition, or voluntary entry into servitude to a church. That status would then be passed on to their heirs, tying them to the piece of land they brought with them. Such figures were known as *colliberti* in Carolingian and post-Carolingian western Francia, or (on a much larger scale) *censuales* or *cerocensuales* in eastern Francia.[70]

Actual coins featured prominently in the ceremony of autodedition, in which the offerand approached the altar and put coins directly onto it, sometimes coins that had been carried on their head (hence the payment being called *capitatio* or, in French, *chevage*, "head tax"),[71] which would drop down with a clink when the person bowed. This ceremony is best known from the remarkable "Book of Serfs" (*liber de servis*) preserved at the monastery of Marmoutier, a collection of deeds concerning members of the extended monastic *familia* in the eleventh century.[72] To take one example from among many, Acfred of Luzone, his wife Guitburga, and their two children gave themselves into servile status at some point between 1032 and 1064. In a formulation that recurs many times, the document of their submission states, "In order that this spontaneous offering might seem more certain and done by the individual in question, [Acfred] placed 4d upon his head in recognition of his servitude (as is customary), and thus gave himself to the perpetual service of God and St. Martin, under our then abbot Albert."[73]

---

68. Cf. Campbell 2000, 227–45.

69. "Unde ne id totum gratis fecisse videretur." de Grandmaison 1864, no. 55.

70. A crucial study of this phenomenon is now Fouracre 2021, 154–80.

71. *Capitatio* was also the term used for a standard poll tax in the Roman period, leading to the proposition that it was transmitted to members of ecclesiastical *familiae* when fiscal resources were put into the hands of the church (Esders 2010, 37–38, 65–69).

72. de Grandmaison 1864. For discussion, see Fouracre 2005; 2006; 2011.

73. "Et ut haec ejus spontanea traditio certior et ab ipso facta appareret, iiiior denarios, ut est conuetudinis, pro recognatione servi, super caput posuit, et sic se Deo sanctoque

The four pennies offered here were nominal in terms of real value, intended to equate to the value of a pound of wax that would burn on the altar in the church, and offerings to other churches were of much the same order.[74] Their payment was less about monetising the status of these ecclesiastical tenants and more about support for a key part of ecclesiastical ceremonial, and about confirming a new status quo. *Censuales* and *colliberti* were generally distinguished from *servi*; one of the Marmoutier charters concerns a man named Engelric who asserted that he was a *collibertus*, although the man who gave Engelric's father to the abbey claimed to have offered him as a *servus*, and it was this view that won out.[75] Being a *collibertus* or *censualis* meant not only low rent but also a degree of autonomy and legal protection.[76] The church took such people under its wing, and for some (such as widows) this might have been an attractive prospect, shielding them from predatory secular lords. It could also be a halfway house for individuals who had been freed by secular owners, but whose former masters wanted them to have the benefit of ongoing and hopefully benign patronage.[77] In the ninth century two women, Johanna and Otgeld, were freed on this basis by a priest named David in recognition of their years of dutiful service and passed into the protection of the church of St. Stephen at Dijon, with each paying a single penny per year in recognition of this arrangement.[78] Similar practices can be traced as far back as the eighth century, and it was a payment of this kind that aggrieved Stabilis so much in the tenth century.

But although the sums involved were small, they still mattered as a tangible token of status and symbolised much more real restrictions that came into play if that status were ever put on the line. Another large collection of autodeditions from St. Peter's in Ghent stipulated that those who entered into the monastic *familia* would have to pay a significantly higher fee if they ever wished to marry outside that *familia* (6d), and even more as a death duty (12d).[79] At Marmoutier, the payments may have been small, but they were accompanied by some extremely potent ceremonial designed to hammer home the offerands' change in

Martino perpetuo serviendum, sub domno Alberto abbata tunc nostro." de Grandmaison 1864, no. 69.

74. Fouracre 2020; 2021, 166.

75. de Grandmaison 1864, no. 101.

76. Fouracre 2021, 168–76.

77. Rio 2017, 99–101.

78. Courtois 1908, no. 6.

79. Fouracre 2021, 167.

status: specifically, a rope was worn around the neck as the head of a household giving themselves over to the abbey went through the ritual of autodedition.[80]

All of this leads to the conclusion that coin did not have any particular connotation of freedom or servitude. Sometimes it is not even certain that actual coins were paid: several of the payments by slaves, or by freedmen and women, could also be made in wax or other commodities, to the value of one penny or more.[81] But expressing such dues in coin (and often receiving them in coin) mattered, as a demonstration of change in a relationship founded to some degree on material resources. Coins were a metonym for agency, economic and otherwise, and hence provided an effective symbolic shorthand for the fulfilment of promises and pledges. This property left wide room for interpretation in ritual terms. Reading those actions, and what they reflected back onto views of coined money, is often a speculative exercise. Frustratingly, some of the most interesting cases are the least certain. There is, for example, the practice of putting coins into Carolingian and late Anglo-Saxon graves. Often found in the hand, or else near the head, chest, or hips, these are unlikely to be residual deposits of whatever the dead had about their person at the time of death—not least because the English examples occur in association with "deviant" or "execution" burials.[82] These are deliberate, conscious deposits, with a ritual, symbolic character. Unfortunately, what their inclusion conveyed is a matter of conjecture.

Giving God, King, and Lord Their Due

In May 877 the elderly Charles the Bald (843–77) agreed to pay off the last of many viking incursions into his kingdom. This was not the first time tribute had been paid to forestall pillage or combat. In 866 another army had ravaged the heartlands of Francia before the king decided to buy it off with the sum of 4,000 lbs, paid in a mix of silver and wine.[83] A sophisticated system was adopted in 866 for apportioning these tribute

80. Barthélemy 2009, 43–51.

81. E.g. Glöckner and Doll 1979, no. 191, from 806, in which five slaves given to the church are to have their own land, in return for paying 4 d in wax or other goods.

82. For Carolingian examples, see Schulze-Dörlamm 2010; Martin-Kilcher 1977; Cardon 2021, 276. For Italy, see Travaini 2004. For the late Anglo-Saxon cases, see Reynolds 2009, 116, 141, 153, 178. A coin of Æthelred II was found in the hand of a body in another execution cemetery at Andover, Hampshire: Walker, Clough, and Clutterbuck 2020, 100.

83. *Annales Bertiniani* s.a. 866 (Waitz 1883, 81; trans. Nelson 1991, 130). These two payments and their consequences are discussed in Coupland 2000, esp. 61–67.

payments. Its basis was the *mansus*, or unit of land assessed as fulfilling the needs of one family. Each of those *mansi* held under free tenure was expected to pay 6d, each held under servile tenure 3d.[84] Smaller landholdings paid 1d or 2d. Each trader owed a tenth of the value of their goods, and priests also made a payment according to the extent of their property. Free Franks owed the "army tax" (*heribannus*), though the rate at which this was paid is not clear.[85] These efforts apparently did not raise enough money, for a second top-up tribute had to be imposed, at a flat rate of 1d from every *mansus*.[86] No one could escape from this imposition. Lords were made responsible for gathering the tax paid from all the land in their territory and passing it on to the king. Charles and his men were no strangers to tribute payments by this stage, but evidently there was still room for improvement in calculating and extracting them. Strikingly, when the vikings reappeared in 877 the distribution of payment was adjusted to benefit tenants at the expense of lords. Tenants of free *mansi* were on this occasion asked to cough up only 4d (not 6d), but another 4d was also diverted from the rent that they would have paid to the landlord. Servile *mansi* paid 2d from the tenant and the lord's rent, respectively. A new tier of payment was also introduced: a full solidus (12d) from every *mansus* in the lord's demesne, which would generally have been the most productive, intensely exploited land, paying directly into the profit of the lord. Members of the clergy saw themselves as losers in this process: in their view, the aristocrats charged with defending the land had failed in their task, and yet the churches were being asked to pay a significant proportion of the resultant costs.[87] Bishops collected contributions from their priests, which varied widely from 5s to 4d, and also made unspecified offerings from church treasuries. Another difference in 877 was that a larger area was included—Burgundy as well as Francia—and a larger sum had to be attained: £5,000 rather than 4,000.[88] Apparently it was reached without difficulty.[89]

84. This referred to the conditions under which that particular piece of land was held, not the status of the tenants: unfree people could occupy free land, or vice versa. But on the whole servile land was more heavily burdened and exploited.

85. Joranson 1923, 75; Coupland 2004, 54–56.

86. Following Nelson 1991, 130 n. 7, in contrast to Grierson 1990, 63; Joranson 1923, 62–92; and Lot 1924, 76–78, who read this as describing three stages of payment: an initial one and two top-ups.

87. Coupland 2000, 71–72.

88. *Annales Bertiniani*, s.a. 877 (Waitz 1883, 135; trans. Nelson 1991, 200–201).

89. For discussion of these payments, see Coupland 1999; Nelson 1992, 213, 250–51, with Joranson 1923 and Lot 1924.

Paying one's way with the king and his agents was an important, if occasional, demand that impelled people to use coins, and that could be bolted onto rents or other hierarchical payments. Rents and religious dues would often have been annual, or at a small number of fixed points over the year, their timing dictated by agrarian rhythms when peasants are likely to have had full purses.[90] Charles the Bald at least sought to mitigate and share out the impact of his exactions, in a developing effort to make the richer elements of society (including the church) pay a larger share, and even for peasants the amounts demanded are unlikely to have been too onerous.[91] Other rulers took a less nuanced approach. One of the best expressions of the practicalities and shortcomings of monetary tax comes from al-Andalus, where Ibn Ḥazm (d. 1064) outlined the pressure and exploitation inflicted by the monetary system of the Taifa rulers. He fastened on coins as "wheels that turn in the fires of hell," burning everyone as they went, and it is worth quoting his perceptive account in full:

> The gold that stays in the hands of those who extract it is—after a portion of it is seized through violence—in effect as licit and good as a clear river, but only up to the moment when dirhams are minted and dinars are refined, since then they fall into the hands of the peasants; these buy dirhams and dinars in return for comestibles and provisions [from the miners] that they alone possess, and that can only be acquired by haggling with them. . . . The extractors of gold are forced to buy all this from the peasants who live there and work the earth. In this way, dirhams fall miserably into the hands of peasants but do not stay in their possession for long, since they must hand them over to the army, violently and unjustly, as taxes, just like the *jizya* of the Jews and Christians. This wealth, extracted from [the peasantry] against all right, becomes the property of the tyrant who rules them and is turned into fire. Afterwards, this [tyrant] presents the wealth to his followers in the army, from whom he seeks help to reinforce his own power and the smooth running of his regime, in order to be able to subdue enemies and launch invasions and raids against subjects who depart from obedience, or against those from whom he demands submission. And in this way, the heat of that fire is doubled, because the *jund* [army]

---

90. Spufford 1988, 382–83. Spufford dated the onset of this tidal cycle of money going out into the countryside and rapidly back in again through rents and taxes to the thirteenth century, though the plethora of rural finds from earlier times now suggests something similar existed in earlier times.

91. Coupland 1999, 64.

uses it to do business with traders and artisans, and it becomes scorpions, serpents and vipers in the hands of those merchants. In turn those merchants buy what they need from the peasants, and thus dinars and dirhams come to be—as you can see with your own eyes—wheels that turn in the fires of hell.[92]

Ibn Ḥazm's ruthless Taifa kings were probably pushing this cycle more aggressively than had been customary in earlier times, though the basic principle was surely far from new. The correlation between coinage, state exactions, and military activity might be a major force in the monetary economy. In al-Andalus this was especially true, and minting was a state monopoly. Western European kingdoms generally had less centralised minting and no salaried army, though costs of military supplies were important, as were tolls, fines, and (at times) tributes. Æthelred II of England (978–1016) is remembered for tribute payments that were exacted from a smaller area but dwarfed Charles's in scale: £10,000 in 991, £22,000 in 994, £24,000 in 1002, £36,000 in 1007, and £48,000 in 1012.[93] The reliability of these impositions has been questioned, but there is good reason to believe that they are of the right order of magnitude.[94] It is not known if Æthelred apportioned these tributes in the same way as Charles. The little information that does survive indicates that everyone who held land was liable, including the king and ecclesiastical institutions. They paid in a competitive, cutthroat way: essentially, responsibility fell, as in Francia, on units of land as assessed for fiscal purposes (hides, equivalent to *mansi*), and had to be paid by the holder of that property. No questions seem to have been asked about how the money was raised, and liability was probably often passed on to tenants or subtenants. But it was in landowners' interests to keep up the pressure, for if they could not raise the requisite amount but someone else was in a position to pay what was due, they could make the payment and then claim the land for their own.[95]

These exertions prompted a discourse on unjust taxation that continued for much of Æthelred's time as king.[96] Yet people still paid, and not only for the opportunity to deprive their neighbours of land. Paying toward a tax or tribute was a statement of belonging and identity. When a viking force descended on the Ostergau of Frisia in 873 and demanded

92. Barceló Perello 1997, 198. See also Moreno 2018, 414–15.

93. Figures summarised in Naismith 2017b, 254.

94. For a summary and references to the extensive literature, see Naismith 2017b, 253–58.

95. Lawson 1984, 723–24.

96. Cubitt 2020, 22–24.

tribute, the inhabitants supposedly retorted that they "were not bound to pay tribute to anyone except to King Louis [the German] and his sons": paying tax to the right ruler formed part of a display of bravado.[97] The principle of paying tribute when necessary was part and parcel of submission to higher authority, tied up with oaths of loyalty to the king, and prayers for the success of him and his armies that would have been heard in churches all over ninth-century Francia and in England under Æthelred.[98] Taxes in the late Roman Empire had similar connotations: by paying what was due according to imperial assessment fixed in local census records, subjects gained entitlement to the protection and benefits of the state. When people remonstrated with the authorities in fourth-century Egypt or in fifth-century Gaul, it was after they were pressed for more than what they had been assessed to pay. They complained using the rhetoric of injustice and oppression, and they cited the virtue that came from paying one's taxes like a responsible citizen.[99] There was a very deep sense of reciprocity at work: in presenting their case to the courts, litigants positioned themselves as dutiful taxpayers, who should be able to expect equitable treatment from the ruling powers, and protection from their armies.[100]

Tithes and other kinds of church due called on a similarly generalised kind of reciprocity, whereby the congregation was meant to support its spiritual caretakers and store up treasure for themselves in heaven.[101] Like taxes for a king or emperor, ecclesiastical renders could take several forms and were not always monetary, not least because—more so than taxes—they would often be spent fairly locally on the maintenance of the clergy, and on charitable works.[102] Also like taxes, these payments were universal: everyone in a Christian society would benefit from the ministrations of the church, to the extent that paying but not receiving a reasonable level

97. "Se non debere tributa solvere nisi Hludowico regi eiusque filiis." *Annals of Fulda* 873 (Pertz and Kurze 1891, 80; trans. Reuter 1992, 72).

98. McCormick 1984; 1990; Keynes 2007, 187–88; Roach 2016, 171, 272–73 (drawing on Lapidge 1991).

99. Clark 2017, esp. 59–68. Compare with the diatribe of Salvian, which rails against unfairly distributed taxation that let the rich off lightly but burdened the poor (*De gubernatione Dei* 4.6 [Lagarrigue 1975, 252–56]).

100. Slootjes 2004, 6.

101. Constable 1964; Wood 2006, esp. 68–71, 459–518; Eldevik 2012, 34–102. For the Carolingian world, see Patzold 2020, 241–303. For England, where tithe as such was a later development, see Tinti 2005.

102. Cf. the law-code VIII Æthelred, c. 9–13 (ed. and trans. Whitelock, Brett, and Brooke 1964–1981, 1:392–93), written in 1014, which gives separate deadlines in the liturgical calendar for tithes of livestock and crops, and for other dues, including Peter's Pence, church-scot, plough-alms, and light-dues.

of support was a distinct embarrassment. The venerable Bede noted with some consternation that, in the vast diocese of York in the early eighth century, there were many people in remote places who could not escape paying their dues to the bishop but had seen neither hide nor hair of him for years. Any bishop who took people's tribute but refused or neglected his duty to preach and minister had, in Bede's view, been overtaken by avarice.[103] But Bede's story is also telling for its implication that even "our people's villages and hamlets . . . located in out-of-the-way, hilly places and thick woodland" were paying their way with the church.[104] That is impressive testimony to the effectiveness of mechanisms for collection. Across Europe, tithes constituted a substantial and, just as important, predictable stream of income. But for that reason they were also hotly contested. Several layers of the ecclesiastical hierarchy staked a claim to tithes and related payments, from local churches to mother churches or minsters, and finally bishops. Disputes frequently arose over what share of tithes and other income should go to which church, and what cut secular patrons should be entitled to.[105] The actual amount at stake was sometimes secondary to the relationship and rights it implied. This is surely the best way to explain the extraordinary peregrinations of St. Symeon of Trier (d. 1035), a Sicilian with a gift for people and languages who wound up living at St. Catherine's monastery on Mount Sinai. His abbot sent him on a dangerous mission all the way from Egypt to Normandy to retrieve a monetary gift for the monastery that Duke Richard II (996–1026) had pledged. After suffering shipwreck on the Nile and then travelling circuitously via Antioch, Belgrade, and Rome, Symeon finally made it to Rouen—where he discovered that the old duke had died and nobody could tell him anything about the money promised to his monastery.[106]

In 857 the bishop of Piacenza reformed the paying of tithes, partly to help bring remote parts of the diocese into line, but in the process shifting the focus away from labour and service to money.[107] Tithes and related dues like these were constitutive of local and regional identities: they indicated belonging in a very tangible way. The boundaries, form, scale, and timing of church dues were all a process of negotiation, sometimes a fraught and

103. Bede, *Letter to Bishop Ecgberht*, c. 7–8 (ed. and trans. Grocock and Wood 2013, 134–39).

104. "Multae uillae ac uiluli nostrae gentis in montibus . . . inaccessis ac saltibus dumosis positi."

105. Wickham 1998, on Tuscany in the eleventh and twelfth centuries, where rights over *pievi* (baptismal churches) were an important source of income.

106. Eberwin, *Vita S. Symeonis heremitae* 2 (*AASS* Jun 1, cols. 89A–101E).

107. *ChLA²*, LXVIII, 19.

disputed one that dragged in the clergy of competing churches as well as lords and the local inhabitants themselves. Lords who supported the establishment of small, local churches probably expected to benefit from the income that church would generate. For peasants, paying to a particular church—sometimes on a supplementary, voluntary basis—helped build a local communal identity. A group of eighteen peasant households dwelling on Mount Spiola near the rural church of Varsi came together in 854 to volunteer an annual tithe to the local priest, diverting or revitalising whatever they had done with their church renders before.[108] Around Exeter in the late eleventh century, hundreds of peasants (in some cases whole settlements) formed gilds that offered small sums of money in return for voluntary association with the cathedral church, in a process that supplemented their affiliation with and obligations to other minster churches.[109] Ecclesiastical renders could even bestow a certain kind of status. Some large church estates in ninth-century Francia contained *luminarii* or *cerarii*, who owed nominal monetary rents to the landlord that were earmarked for maintenance of lights in church. Whether these payments were settled in actual coin is incidental, as indeed is the amount (which was often fixed at 4d); what mattered was what the sum was meant to do, what it meant for the status of those who paid it, and that it was denominated in money.[110]

Tithes were sometimes paid in cash, especially if their redistribution was complex and spread over long distances, though on a local level they seem more often to have been collected in kind. For large-scale state structures, gathering tax or other income in coin was generally desirable, simply for practical reasons. In-kind payments were costly and slow to relocate, and liable to spoil.[111] This was a challenge that later Roman emperors had to deal with, and it did not go away: Gregory of Tours, writing in the late sixth century, claimed it was precisely because rendering wheat and wine to the imperial warehouse was so cumbersome that Clermont's fourth-century bishop Illidius won his city the right to pay in gold.[112] Coin—and, in the late and post-Roman world, gold coin in particular—served as a

---

108. *ChLA²*, LXIX, no. 4. Cf. Bougard 2018 for this example and others in Italy, with wider discussion in Zeller et al. 2020, 95–98. This was not an uncontested process: in the same year, one individual from this community found himself in court over his refusal to transfer tithes to this church: Manaresi 1955–1960, 1, no. 59.

109. Naismith 2020b, 653–55.

110. Fouracre 2021, 113–22.

111. Treadgold 2014, with reference to the later Roman Empire.

112. Gregory of Tours, *Liber vitae patrum* 2.1 (de Nie 2015, 28–29).

metonym for tax payments.[113] That association had remarkable staying power, even when taxes as an institution were ebbing.[114] Of course, this is not to say that all tax was coin or that all coin was for tax. At Clermont, and doubtless many other places, the baseline was payment in kind, and the survival of gold currency in the early medieval west depended on its attachment to other kinds of use and demand in the ambit of the elite.[115] By the ninth and tenth centuries, when both the Roman state and gold coinage were long gone, the specific circumstances facing Charles the Bald and Æthelred II meant that precious metal again became the principal form of tax income. Both rulers were confronted with viking raiders who would, if left unchallenged, pillage and extort valuable goods from the country and either go home with them or sell them en route and take home the proceeds (as the *Anglo-Saxon Chronicle* says one viking fleet did in 1048).[116] What they desired was movable wealth, the most agreeable form of which was precious metal, rated according to their own measure.[117] It was therefore monetary income that Charles and Æthelred sought from their subjects, under extraordinary conditions.

Payments to agents of the king, or to the church in return for pastoral care, often took place alongside renders of monetary rent to landowners. Monetary rents have historically been a focal point of interest in the early medieval monetary economy. They were there at least on some scale throughout the period, from the gold and silver pieces offered by the tenants of an abbot in sixth-century Gaul,[118] to silver pennies offered by a large swathe of society in the ninth, tenth, and eleventh centuries, including the small, customary offerings given by *colliberti* and *censuales* in recognition of servitude to a church.[119] These use the same terminology as rents demanded from *servi* and tenants and can be seen as an outgrowth of the practice of recognisory payments from lands held by lease from the church (called *precaria* in Frankish tradition).[120] The clas-

113. See chapter 6.

114. For the general outline of its later development, see Wickham 1997. E.g., a tax on Tours in the sixth century could be described as an *aureus*: Gregory of Tours, *Historiae* 9.30 (Krusch and Levison 1951, 448–49; trans. Thorpe 1974, 515–17).

115. Naismith 2014a, and chapter 7.

116. *ASC* E 1048 (Irvine 2004, 78–79).

117. A phrase found both in ninth-century Francia (*Annales Bertiniani* 866 [Waitz 1883, 81; trans. Nelson 1991, 130]) and, later, in England (S 912 [Crick 2007, no. 11] and S 919 [K 689]).

118. *PL* 71:1143B–50B.

119. See chapter 9.

120. Fouracre 2021, 70–71, 90–93.

sic windows onto monetary rents are estate survey documents, above all the polyptychs from ninth-century Francia. An example, composed in the 810s, covers the property of the abbey of Wissembourg in the rich lands of the modern Franco-German border. Altenstadt, an estate very close to the monastery, consisted of at least forty-four farms that owed diverse services to the abbot. Many of these had apparently been commuted to a monetary buyout. In lieu of doing the monastery's pruning, for example, the inhabitants would pay 5d; for digging up vines, 10d; for digging them up a second time, 4d; for cutting back hay, 6d. For other labour services, "the work [was] sufficient" (*opus sufficiens*). The details of what was expected varied farm to farm: some owed substantial renders in kind of tiles, wood, or livestock, while a few paid everything through work, and a couple had idiosyncratic conditions of labour outlined in detail. Arrangements in other settlements were different again. At Klingen, some 15 km to the north, services and foodstuffs featured much more prominently than money payments, and some farms paid cloths of specified dimensions. Haßloch, still farther away (about 50 km), produced strikingly larger payments of commodities and cash and seems to have been a rich wine-growing estate; its farms had the option of producing wine (either twenty or fifteen vessels), or 30s instead, and another 40d was expected at a second point in the year.[121]

Arrangements such as these could be outlined for hundreds of other places in Francia, England, Germany, and Italy. Some will be considered in more detail in later chapters. The Wissembourg polyptych, however, effectively illustrates a common feature of relevant records: just how varied and complex the dues owed from peasant to lord could be. Taken out of context they seem labyrinthine. Individual settlements varied, and even individual tenants within those settlements owed varying amounts. For the two parties involved, however, each set of obligations in kind, service, and cash had its own background and rationale. That might be as straightforward as more land equalling a proportionately heavier obligation, and a higher rent. Inconvenience of transport for very distant lands privileged payments in cash or more portable commodities, as opposed to perishable goods or service. But it was clearly not always that simple. Landless Carolingian peasants domiciled on ecclesiastical property owed coin to the landlord, presumably gained either through wage labour,

---

121. Most accessibly available at "Carolinguian Polyptyques," University of Leicester, School of Historical Studies, https://www.le.ac.uk/hi/polyptyques/wissembourg/latin2english.html. For polyptychs in general, see Fossier 1978; Devroey 2006.

artisanal skills, or market engagement.[122] High variation in the presence
and scale of money rents suggests that these impositions might not always
have been directly proportionate to the availability of coin—though they
do presuppose that tenants had or could get cash if needed. A survey of
lands, tenants, and other dues of the bishopric of Lucca in the later ninth
century stands as an example: there is no strong geographical rationale to
the prevalence of money rents, and it was commonplace for tenants to owe
part of their obligations in cash alongside labour and commodities, indicating that access to cash was commonplace and not necessarily proportionate to cash rents (map 4.1). The lands of Prüm were similar: renders in
coin, kind, and labour did not correlate directly with the size of holdings,
and it is likely that the numerous fractional landholdings reflect a society
in which many households got by only partially on the basis of agriculture.
Members of the same family could devote their time to a mix of farming
and semispecialised other roles like mining or crafts. The result could be
that a family owing low rent, and possibly occupying a small landholding,
actually engaged in more monetary exchange than neighbours who had
greater resources yet stayed with renders in kind where they could.[123]

This assumes a significant degree of input from tenants, and it was
in the interests of landlords and tenants to reach agreements that both
sides were comfortable with. If the lord sacrificed a degree of the income
that could have been squeezed out of the peasantry, he gained ease and
efficiency in having them on side. And there were other ways to get some
of that income back: through tolls on bridges, roads, and markets, for
example.[124] But the lord's will was the most likely determining factor in
whether and how much rent was to be charged. Sometimes money rents
went up considerably between the ninth and eleventh centuries, if not
consistently.[125] How much the money element was worth relative to other
elements within a mixed rent is more difficult to determine: commodities
and services are not always quantified; when they are, price information is
vanishingly scarce; and even when a given service is commuted, the value
is inconsistent.[126] Similarly, the reason for taking a partial or completely

122. Devroey 2015, 216.
123. Devroey and Schroeder 2020, 192–97.
124. McCormick 2001, 640–47; Ganshof 1959a; 1959b; Stoclet 1999.
125. Devroey 2015, 216–17.
126. Guérard, in his edition of the polyptyque of Saint-Germain (1844, 1:134–54)
offered figures for the mutual value of cash, service, and commodities, which have often
been requoted (esp. from Spufford 1988, 47). However, Guérard's methodology for arriving
at these figures—which involved converting Carolingian coins and prices into 1840s equivalents based on a bread price index from 1789 and after—is not reliable.

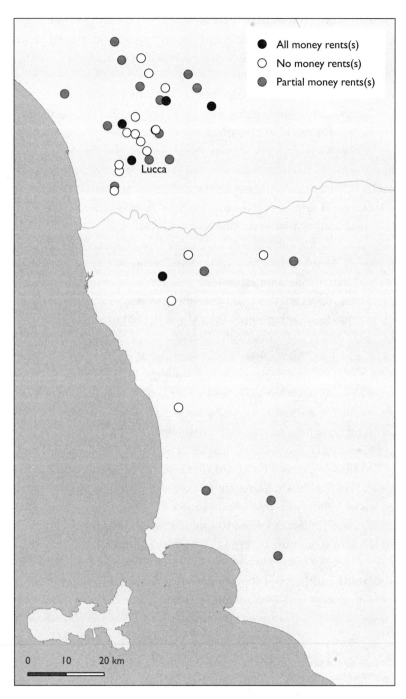

MAP 4.1. Distribution of properties owing monetary rent to the bishop of Lucca, according to a survey from the later ninth century (Castagnetti 1979, 205–24).

monetised rent is almost never expressed, and modern assessments differ. Commuting rents in kind or labour to money took away stable, predictable labour and subjected lords as well as peasants to market pressures, so cash rent can be read as "easy" rent, a sign of weakness on the lord's part, or of favour to tenants.[127] When rents were charged only in money and at a very low rate, something along these lines is likely. But they could mean something else. Cash might have been used to pay wage labour, which was more flexible than obligated service. Furthermore, the absence or retreat of money rent does not spell the absence of coin from exchange systems as a whole. In the later Middle Ages, resurgence of rent in kind has been read as a strategy for lords to obtain commodities to sell on the market and at the same time deny that opportunity to peasants.[128]

Rents, monetary and otherwise, were thus about much more than paying the rent. They represented constant and complex negotiation between lords and tenants, meaning that their character depended partly on the kind of lordship in question. Large-scale landlords such as major aristocrats or churches, perhaps operating through subtenants or local estate managers, presented a relatively distant and potentially more flexible kind of oversight,[129] whereas smaller-scale lords such as up-and-coming *milites* or (in England) thegns were more present and inclined to apply greater pressure.[130] That said, the greater resources and probably more elaborate documentation of a major landholder could also be a powerful force to bring to bear on uncooperative tenants. At Limonta near Como in northern Italy, the Milanese abbey of Sant'Ambrogio can be seen to have gradually squeezed its tenants for more cash, as well as labour services and renders in kind, over the course of the tenth century.[131] Earlier in 828 four *coloni* (peasants who were free yet tied to a particular estate) from Antoigné, which belonged to a monastery on the Loire, came to Pippin I, king of Aquitaine (817–38). They complained that the abbot and his agents had demanded more in "rent and renders" (*de censum vel de pro soluta*) than they and their fellow villagers should pay, defined with reference to what had been customary in the past. The abbot's advocate, however, had come forearmed. He produced an estate survey (*descriptio*)

127. Herlihy 1959, 61–62.

128. Wickham 2021, 27.

129. Devroey 2006, 491–99; 2019c; Feller 2007, 81–99.

130. For the English case, see Faith 1997, 153–77; Blair 2018, esp. 354–80. See also chapter 9.

131. Balzaretti 2019, 438, 443–49. There are issues with the authenticity of some of the relevant pieces of documentation, though the overall point is not in doubt.

executed in 801 and swore that nothing demanded since then had gone beyond what the peasants themselves swore to offer twenty-seven years earlier. Oaths of this kind would have been one of the key products that a polyptych or more targeted inquest elicited, even though they are rarely referred to directly.[132] In this instance the *descriptio* and oath played directly into the abbot's hands: the plaintiffs lost and superficially had no leg to stand on, but it is possible that what they really hoped for was to get back to was the status quo before the 801 survey, when impositions may have been lower.[133]

This power dynamic could work on a very granular level. A variegated seigneurial landscape as seen in Prüm's lands would actually have worked in the landlord's interest. Peasants who all shared the same status or obligation had a common cause, which they could use against their lord. But if the lord offered individualised and more desirable terms to some tenants and not others, village society could be split and turned against itself, thereby undercutting collective bargaining power. This effective but nasty tactic lay behind a legal case in northern Francia in 861, when forty-one *coloni* from Mitry brought a complaint to the king that the abbot of Saint-Denis was forcing them into "inferior service" (*inferiorem servicium*), unbefitting their free status.[134] Legal freedom was meant to bring a less onerous set of services, in part because it provided a better platform for negotiating them.[135] What "inferior service" meant at Mitry is not specified, but it probably extended to greater services and rents than the *coloni* were comfortable with. The abbot's countermove was to bring in another twenty-two men from Mitry, who swore the exact opposite to the first group: that they and their ancestors were all in fact *servi* who had always done inferior service and greater labours "by right and by law, as is manifest" (*per drictum et per legem ... sicut manifestum est*). What was really going on here is difficult to perceive. The forty-one litigants felt strongly enough to make the long journey to the king's palace at Compiègne, and several went so as far as to bring their children with them. Screaming babies and impatient toddlers were perhaps meant to evoke sympathy and speed things along (hopefully in the right direction). It is also unlikely that the plaintiffs were genuinely in the dark about their legal condition, and that they had been labouring under a misapprehension of freedom for years. What makes most sense is that the new and more onerous services

132. Naismith 2017a, 375–76.
133. Levillain 1926, no. 12.
134. Tessier 1943–55, no. 228.
135. Wickham 2003, 560–61; Rio 2017, esp. 209–11.

introduced by Saint-Denis had driven a wedge into the community, fuel-ling the debates that ensued on what level of imposition was acceptable and in turn on who was free or servile in a community that was legally free but in practice tied to their land. Acceptance of the landlord's general wishes could have been precisely how one group—those who swore in sup-port of the abbot—ended up paying lighter dues than their neighbours who put up resistance.[136]

Frustratingly, this give-and-take is usually invisible to modern observ-ers. Altering customary dues was difficult enough, but rents are seen only when written down, and once committed to parchment they could become just as tough to tear up. Some of the rents recorded in Domesday Book in 1086, which mostly focused on monetary rather than in-kind income, remained static for more than a century thereafter, even through a period of rapid inflation at the end of the twelfth century.[137] Others were changed only when a new tenant took over, after the death of his or her predeces-sor: a note added to the oldest English cartulary, written at the beginning of the eleventh century, on the amounts in cash due from certain named individuals probably refers to a new arrangement for one of the properties named earlier in the collection.[138] This stability worked in tenants' favour and left lords who depended too heavily on rent vulnerable to inflation, as the abbey of Cluny discovered in the twelfth century after monetising a high proportion of its income in the eleventh.[139] But lords had other options up their sleeves. In his *De administratione* Suger, abbot of Saint-Denis (d. 1151), lamented how his efforts to restore and improve the income of his abbey had been beset by problems. One of these arose at Guillerval, a village halfway between Paris and Orléans. Theoretically it ought to have been the pride of the abbey's patrimony, being one of its first grants from Dagobert I (629–39). But by Suger's time it was in disarray, partly subject to a feud between two lay aristocrats, and its inhabitants paid a shockingly low rent. What stands out here is that despite Suger's avowed interest in doing whatever he could to raise income, he complained that he could *not* change the rent. To compensate, he developed an area of demesne land and also enhanced some of the other customary dues owed by the tenants, such as the *champart* (*campipartis*), or tax on salt.[140]

---

136. Rio 2017, 196–97; Wickham 2003, esp. 562–63.
137. Bridbury 1992, 111–25.
138. London, British Library, Cotton Tiberius A.13, f. 109v. Printed in Ker 1948, 174.
139. Duby 1973, 61–82.
140. Suger, *De administratione* 14 (ed. and trans. Gasparri 1996, 74–76).

Money rents therefore came as part of a package and were the product of an ecosystem with many variables. Polyptychs, charters, and related texts tend to flatten this out. Rents were not just abstract numbers: when and how they were paid mattered deeply to their meaning as part of a larger social whole. Tenants of the cathedral of Rheims in the ninth century paid their main dues on St. Remi's feast day (1 October), while the day before—the mass of the vigil of St. Remi—was when the *capitalicum* of 4d needed to be paid by any servants of the saint who had relocated to another territory.[141] Theoretically, rents and services were provided in return for the privilege of using the lord's property, based on the idea that lords had always held the land.[142] These obligations sometimes retained an element of hospitality,[143] and there was a strong tradition of offering customary gifts (*xenia, eulogiae*, etc.) of eggs or small amounts of money on top of rent.[144] The lord could be thought of as providing protection and patronage in return for his income from tenants, most explicitly in the case of *milites* or thegns: the prospect of the latter being starved of land led Bede to fear for the military safety of Northumbria.[145] The reciprocal principles that underlie rents and services were of course largely fictions, "strategies for concealing strategies" in the words of Pierre Bourdieu, but they were nonetheless important and could be exploited by both sides as a posture when the need arose—or set aside if, as at Mitry, the lord was determined to make their wishes felt.

As the most visible monetary element in the seigneurial economies of early medieval Europe, rents matter deeply to historians, and they undoubtedly mattered to those who paid them too, as both a material imposition and a barometer of standing within a community. The fact that rents and services were structured around moral, social, and symbolic contours does not make them any less "real": all early medieval transfers of wealth, through coined money and otherwise, were circumscribed in this way. But a few reservations need to be made in closing. The first is specific to coin. Although coined money featured frequently in rents, there is strikingly little comment on its presence, or opposition to it. Records of disputes between peasants and lords tended to focus more on status and

---

141. Devroey 2006, 497–98.
142. Faith 2019, 37–45.
143. Faith 2019, 49–57.
144. Devroey 2006, 503.
145. Bede, *Letter to Bishop Ecgberht*, c. 11 (ed. and trans. Grocock and Wood 2013, 142–45).

services than on specifics of rent.[146] Equally, in only some cases was cash all that lords extracted. It more often features as a supplement to the other main ingredients of tenant obligations (services and payment in kind). Cash rent was, to put it bluntly, just there. That speaks to its normalisation, but explicit evidence of either tenants or lords pushing for more monetisation is limited: even when cash dues do increase, the moment and context of the change are rarely seen. Second, it is unclear how much weight should be put on surviving attestations of money rents. Carolingian polyptychs are now recognised as products of a very specific, and in many ways unrepresentative, kind of landholding based on great estates held by ecclesiastical institutions.[147] They say little or nothing about wage labour, for example, even though this certainly took place, sometimes possibly on a large scale, with payment in money being commonplace.[148] The exactions of smaller-scale secular lords, which may have been heavier, are poorly known. It is also possible that peasants themselves extracted higher rates of rent from their subtenants than lords did.[149] Broadly speaking, money rents should not be taken as the be all and end all of hierarchical monetary relations—but, if properly contextualised, they can be broadly indicative of economic complexity.

Monetary Obligations: Credit, Compensation, and Fine

CREDIT

Over the first half of the eleventh century, the abbey of Saint-Vanne in Verdun built up a relationship with a family of minor local landowners. The links in this association were expressed by agreeing, again and again, to advance money to members of the family in return for chunks of their land given as a pledge. Odo, patriarch of the family, kicked things off by giving a piece of land in return for 10s 8d. His two sons, Herbert and Hugo, continued this tradition over subsequent decades. Herbert mortgaged some or all of his ancestral property (*allodium*) for 65s and half the harvest the land produced. Later he would go a step further and actually enter the monastic community as a lay brother (*sub laico habitu*), and when he decided to go on pilgrimage to Jerusalem he made a donation out

---

146. Wickham 2003; Eggert 1975.
147. E.g., Davies 2012; Tange 2012.
148. Naismith 2017a, 360.
149. Campbell 2005.

of what he had already given as a pledge. Dealings between Herbert and the abbey seem to have been mutually beneficial, and not just on a financial level. Hugo, his brother, presents a different impression. Probably over a number of years, he obtained at least seven loans: five from the abbey and two from his brother. These amounted to a total of 35s 3d in cash, plus two horses worth 20s and 15s, respectively (the second one being obtained after the first died). Each is introduced by some statement of his need— "with necessity pressing" (*insistente necessitate*), "driven by need" (*necessitate compulsus*) or just "troubled" (*anxiatus*) or "forced" (*coactus*)—but there must be a question mark over the gravity of these needs that arose so frequently and could sometimes be satisfied only with a good horse. The document in which this long series of interactions is recorded was prompted by the last of Hugo's loans. It is not clear how many, if any, of the earlier advances were ever repaid, while the transactions that involved just the brothers must have been included as background information, perhaps related to the fact that Herbert had ended up joining the church and handing over his property for good (presumably including those lands Hugo had given as a pledge for his loans). In any case, what stands out is the thirst for money on the part of Herbert and especially Hugo, and the willingness of Saint-Vanne to feed that thirst.[150]

Getting money on credit, usually against land, was relatively common in the early Middle Ages.[151] Most recorded loans come from the tenth and especially eleventh centuries, largely because of the increasing number of archives with relevant charter material, and secondarily because of the growing scale and complexity of coin use.[152] There is no doubt, however, that loans could be obtained long before the tenth century, or that they existed in areas with few records. Many loan agreements would never have been committed to writing, or preserved in ecclesiastical archives where they stood a better chance of surviving. From England, for example, loans are known only from incidental references in other documents.[153] In Francia, the possibility of loans at village level from bailiffs (*iudices*) to

---

150. Bloch 1902, no. 44.

151. The critical general study of the practice is now Bougard 2010.

152. See chapter 9.

153. See, for example, S 1211 (Brooks and Kelly 2013, no. 124), where land given as security became the focus of a long-running dispute, which is the point of the document; S 1488 (Kelly 2000–2001, no. 133); a will that refers to loans incurred by shires remitted after death (Whitelock 1930, 163, suggests these could have been toward viking tribute payments); a redeemed mortgage, taken out under Edward and redeemed under William, is mentioned in GDB 215v; Whitelock 1930, no. 39, refers to a mortgage on Skillington, owed to Archbishop Ealdred, perhaps advanced to finance the testator's pilgrimage to Rome

peasants is mentioned as one abuse that Louis the German was implored to avoid in 858.[154] A further problem is that some cases of what looks like a sale in fact represent a mortgage, with the hope that the debtor would eventually regain the land that they "sold" to the creditor.[155] From regions where records are fuller (Italy and parts of Francia), early medieval credit revolved very largely around land. As in the case of Herbert and Hugo, the landholder would offer the creditor a piece of their property as collateral. The debtor would have a set amount of time in which to repay that loan and regain the land, or else risk losing it for good. Interest might be charged on loans and mortgages of this kind, though not always, as the proceeds of the land itself (which went to the creditor) fulfilled that role.

The elasticity of credit in relation to the supply of coin has been hotly debated for the later Middle Ages.[156] In earlier times credit seems primarily to have served as a key to unlock liquidity for those who were rich in assets but poor in cash. Those without land could access credit, but at significantly greater cost. Frankish formularies include documents by which debtors accepted interest rates of 33 per cent a year or subjected themselves to servitude for a few days a week to pay off a loan.[157] It is not clear how often loans were made on such terms. Only a few documents concerning credit relate to service or interest;[158] instead, they overwhelmingly relate to loans in return for pledges of land. This could be a result of their much higher chances of preservation, but there is also a strong likelihood that access to credit depended heavily on access to land as the most stable and reliable form of collateral.

The nexus between early medieval credit and landholding relates to how money flowed through society in two principal ways. Hugo and the abbey of St. Vanne are a case in point for the first: Why was it that a man with lots of outstanding credit could keep getting more? In modern parlance, Hugo was very heavily leveraged, with a worryingly high level of debt, and no banker in their right mind would advance him more money.

(though GDB 376v says simply that Ealdred bought the land from the same man, implying that a mortgage could be represented as a sale).

154. Council of Quierzy (858), c. 14 (Hartmann 1984, 422–23).

155. For Italy, see Bougard 1995, 328; Feller, Gramain, and Weber 2005, 90–91.

156. Bolton (2012, esp. 274–93) sees credit as more able to expand to fill shortfalls in specie, while Nightingale (2013) views credit as more dependent on the volume of available coin (with a rejoinder in Bolton 2013).

157. Formulary of Angers no. 18 and 38 (Zeumer 1886, 10, 17; trans. Rio 2008, 63–64, 79–80); Formulary of Marculf 2.25–27 (Zeumer 1886, 92–93; trans. Rio 2008, 210).

158. See, for example, a document from Nocera (Italy) in 882: Piazzi et al. 1873–2015, 1:95.

It is possible that there are mitigating circumstances not visible from the relevant texts. Hugo might have had a large patrimony of land to draw on, or been dutifully paying back his earlier loans. But there were also extra-economic factors. Lending, if one had the money, was a good way to build up clients and contacts among landowning society, and if there was a realistic possibility of Hugo defaulting on his debts, the monastery stood to gain a large amount of land. An obligated Hugo would have had a vested interest in staying on good terms with the monastery, just as his brother did, eventually joining the community. For the abbot, bankrolling men like Hugo put him at the centre of the local elite and gentry. It was about managing obligations and relations, not just about the money.

But the second major point is that these considerations were never completely divorced. Put differently, obligations and relations were also about money. Debts could be transferred, which is difficult to square with loans underpinned by affective considerations: the debt itself became a commodity and source of income that could be transferred and negotiated.[159] From the perspective of the borrower, too, loans were more about the money, in that they enabled Hugo and others like him to do things they did not have the cash for. They did not come and ask for money without a reason, even if the only explanation given relates vaguely to "need." Those needs could be very diverse, sometimes related directly to upward social mobility.[160] Horses, for which Hugo mortgaged two pieces of land, were an important trapping of elevated status. Marriage, and specifically the cost of marrying up, was another reason that churches sometimes had to advance money. Another charter of Saint-Vanne tells how a minor aristocrat or knight (*miles*) named Wido had undertaken to marry one Herberga, but the members of her *nobilissima* family expected gifts appropriate to their standing: hence he needed to borrow £12 of silver from the abbot.[161] The purpose of loans mattered, even if it is not always readily apparent, and the crucial point is that since loans were often monetary, they tended to relate to pressures that could be solved with hard cash. The purchase of valuable or bulk commodities, including those needed to uphold elevated status, is one possibility. Another would be the payment of a fine, tribute, or (as will be seen later) compensation: a widespread viking tribute might have prompted a burst of lending, and those faced with actually settling a large wergild compensation, or even a share of one, frequently would not have had the

---

159. For examples, see Bartoli Langeli 2005, no. 12; Lelong 1903, 1, no. 220.
160. Bougard and Le Jan 2010, esp. 49–51, for wealth and social mobility.
161. Bloch 1898, no. 28.

money or equivalent movable goods to do so and would therefore need to obtain the shortfall via credit.[162] Pilgrimage was another big expense that could prompt the mortgage of land, sometimes with the term being linked to the duration of the trip. Abbots and bishops seem to have been willing to offer especially generous terms for loans toward pilgrimage.[163]

For all these reasons, loans prominently feature real cash.[164] Many references to credit are quite specific that coin was meant. A record of a loan in Lucca in 813 offers one of the most detailed and explicit references to coin in the city's archives: the creditors obtained "twelve silver solidi that are of good, clean, full-weight, and spendable denarii, of the mint/money of either Pavia, Milan, or Lucca, and reckoned at twelve denarii to each solidus."[165] Repayment, in contrast, was much more variable, and its form not always specified, most likely for the same reason that the creditors needed an advance of money in the first place: they did not currently have the means to pay. Credit arrangements illustrate how uneven the early medieval distribution of cash was. Virtually everyone could encounter difficulty in raising cash, even members of the elite. While those in higher positions and with widespread landed property tended on the whole to have more money, that was not universally the case, and there are striking instances of reaching downwards to borrow. An ealdorman of Kent in the 890s borrowed £30 from a layman of unspecified status named Goda,[166] while a century later the archbishop of Canterbury promised a large estate to the bishop of Dorchester in return for £90 advanced toward a viking tribute.[167] Debt was simply a fact of life in a world where the supply of coin was chronically short and lumpy. Borrowers endured onerous rates of interest and grievous penalties for defaulting.[168] The imbalance is exacerbated by documents generally ironing out the time factor, to present the impression that large amounts of gold or silver could be secured at whim. Quite the contrary: paying in instalments, and allowing time for people to gather requisite funds,

---

162. Esders 2015, esp. 125; 2021b, 14.

163. E.g., Whitelock 1930, no. 39. See also Bull 1993, 213–15.

164. Loans in kind are known but rare outside northern Iberia, where they fit into a tradition of thinking about money as a measure of agricultural commodities rather than coin: Bougard 2010, 464–66; cf. Davies 2002; Jarrett 2014; Portass 2017, 163–66 (showing that loans could be made from monasteries to peasants).

165. "Argentum solidus duodecim, quot sunt denarii boni mundi grossi expendivilis, de moneta de Pipia et Mediolano seo Lucana duodecim denarios rationati per singulos solidos." Barsocchini 1833, no. 389 (ChLA LXXIV, no. 4).

166. S 1211 (Brooks and Kelly 2013, no. 124).

167. S 882 (Brooks and Kelly 2013, no. 134).

168. Balzaretti 2019, 487–89 (citing ChLA XXVIII, no. 859, of 796).

must have been entirely commonplace and is occasionally seen in detailed narratives concerning transactions. Bishop Æthelwold (d. 984), whose outlays in gold and silver were staggering, occasionally had to pay for lands in two or more parts.[169] Sometimes people were completely strapped for cash: at Marseille in the 1050s, a sale of land agreed at a price of 4s failed because the buyers fell short of the full amount by 3d and in the end had to pay 3s 2d in cash plus 2 solidi in kind—that is, a premium of an extra solidus on the original price.[170] Most people, including elites, in the early Middle Ages are very likely to have lurched frequently from being flush with movable wealth to relative penury. An inheritance or compensation payment could temporarily make them rich, as could diligent nurturing of seigneurial income, harvest-time sale proceeds, or sale of landed property.[171] But for those who did not wish to dissolve their links to land completely, credit provided a way to bridge the gap between monetary wealth and its lack.

All this revolves around a more substantial and formal form of credit. There could have been many others, smaller in scale or less formal, that reached much further socially. Mercantile credit to women buying luxuries or lords dealing with trusted merchants in rural settings is mentioned in eleventh-century Germany.[172] Societies that combined any degree of exchange complexity with monetary systems as limited as those of early medieval Europe probably relied heavily on credit from family, friends, and neighbours. One of the great unknown quantities of the period is how prevalent such systems may have been and how they worked in practice.

FINES AND COMPENSATION

Fines and compensation have already been mentioned as a potential reason why credit might be sought. The two overlap but present their own issues. Both fines and compensation arose from legal interactions, either from losing a case or from a negotiated settlement. Fines were payments to a higher authority that was not directly involved in a dispute, or for dereliction of that authority's commands (e.g., for disobedience, lack of military service or failure to attend a key assembly): they reflected acceptance

---

169. *Libellus Æthelwoldi* 10, 45 (ed. and trans. Kennedy and Keynes forthcoming); cf. *Liber Eliensis* 2.49a (Blake 1962, 116–17; trans. Fairweather 2005, 139–40).

170. Guérard 1857, no. 53.

171. Æthelwold must have been rich in inherited property (Yorke 1988, 68–69), and gradual sale of these assets is a plausible explanation for his deep pockets.

172. *Vita Meinwerci episcopi Patherbrunnensis*, c. 153 (Tenckhoff 1921, 81). See also Eidelberg 1955, no. 36; translated with comment in Toch 2008, 185; and Toch 2012, 206.

of a wider jurisdiction over conduct and are a barometer of royal or lordly insertion into legal processes.[173] Larger fines imposed through the machinery of royal government are the most visible, along with those that members of the elite levied against one another. In eleventh-century western France, fines for violence were commonplace, but often pardoned, and functioned as a kind of retrospective legitimisation for violent acts, with their own ceremonial.[174] Fines and compensatory payments, even if they were never coughed up, were a way to negotiate and settle disputes without resorting to violence. They could also be paid preemptively, to the kin of a vendor of land, for example, as a way of forestalling future dispute. There was a strong element of performativity in these payments, both in their recording and in their enactment, as we have seen with the three little sons of Thibault in eleventh-century France.

There was as much meaning, though probably rather fewer niceties, in the settlement of fines and compensation outside the elite. Actual collection of fines at the village level lay in the hands of various kinds of middlemen living cheek by jowl with the peasants.[175] The abuse of such fines, especially when imposed on less powerful members of society with less capacity to resist and less chance of others sticking up for them, was one aspect of the so-called evil customs (*malae consuetudines*) that loom large in French historiography for the tenth and especially eleventh centuries.[176] To frame exactions in this way was a rhetorical posture, but the demands were considerable: the abbey of Saint-Aubin in Angers around 1080 listed the abuses committed by one Raginald the treasurer against the population near its priory of Méron, mostly against peasants, who had been forced to come up with surprisingly large sums: fines included 30s for taking a measure of grain to sell at Saumur, 18s for a woman taking 12d in bread to sell across the river Thouet, and so on.[177]

Compensation, meanwhile, was a payment between parties in a dispute, to satisfy any material and symbolic loss that had occurred. The two were central elements of the legal process in most parts of early medieval Europe, lending a strongly monetary flavour to legislation of the period.[178]

173. Evolution in this direction is especially apparent in England: Lambert 2017b.

174. McHaffie forthcoming.

175. Esders 2019, 296–98, on abuses of financial privilege by this group. See also Devroey 2019c for the role of these figures.

176. Poly and Bournazel 1991, 28–34. For an alternative view see Barthélemy 2009; and West 2013, esp. chaps. 2 and 6, who argues for patchier but still sometimes aggressive lordly handling of peasants at least as far back as the Carolingian period.

177. Lelong 1903, no. 220. See further discussion in Lemesle 2008, 123–47; McHaffie 2018.

178. Oliver 2011, 26–71.

Fines or compensations of so many monetary units are ubiquitous. That said, it is far from clear that all such payments were made using actual coin, and fines and compensation could be handled differently. A short document from ninth-century Reichenau outlines the way in which four named men had each raised the sum, or at least the pledge, of £30 by calling on several guarantors (*fideiussores*), while each also owed the sum of 60s to the count. The latter payment was presumably the royal *bannus*: a fine imposed for breaking the king's peace. Notably, it was reckoned using a different and smaller unit, for which coin could have been mandatory; also, each offender was directly liable for it and did not call on the financial assistance of others.[179] The fact that the £30 payments had to be made with the help of guarantors is far from surprising. A liability of this magnitude was a serious burden, far beyond what all but the wealthiest members of society could afford on their own account. It is not stated what this sum was for, but wergild is a strong candidate: the *Pactus legis Salicae* gave a wergild of 600s (i.e., £30) for boys under twelve, child-bearing women, a pregnant woman (and the same for her foetus if male), or free men killed at home or while serving in the army.[180]

The Reichenau document illustrates one strategy for dealing with such a liability: spreading the burden among friends and family. In seventh-century England, kin were obligated to step up in this way.[181] This could be a mechanism for lasting group formation,[182] and it had the secondary effect of distributing liability for the future good behaviour of the offender: having gone round the houses to win enough financial support, it would have been much harder to do so a second time. But not everyone could count on having kin willing or wealthy enough to part with the requisite funds at relatively short notice: the laws of Alfred allowed only thirty days for friends and family to be notified and any requisite money raised.[183] Those with no recourse could find temporary sanctuary in a church. One such man, Cunzo, fled to seek sanctuary at St. Gall when he fell liable to two wergild payments at an unknown date in the ninth century. Fortunately for him, the monastic community took pity on his predicament and gave him 100s toward these costs, though he and his heirs were expected to pay them off with an annual render in kind.[184] Again, shortfalls

179. Esders 2015; see also Esders 2014.

180. *Pactus Legis Salicae* 24:1, 8–9; 41:15, 17–19, 21; 43:1, 65e:1–4 (Eckhardt 1962, 89, 92, 160–61, 229, 235; trans. Drew 1991, 86, 105–6, 124, 127).

181. Ine 74.2 (Jurasinski and Oliver 2021, 434–35).

182. Esders 2021b, 23.

183. Alfred 44.1 (Jurasinski and Oliver 2021, 342–43).

184. Clavadetscher et al. 1983–, no. 207 (between 784 and 812).

in cash were a recurrent problem for those who had to pay a big sum. Even if neither friends, family, churches, nor others could come up with the necessary funds, other options remained open. Lands could be sold, as at least one charter from ninth-century Bavaria records,[185] or, as a last ditch, the offender could enter debt servitude, though that cannot have been an appealing option if it meant subjection to a family he or she had wronged.[186] It was only sheer poverty (meaning powerlessness as well as lack of economic resources), according to Venantius Fortunatus, that prevented a poor couple in sixth-century Gaul from sticking up for their daughter when she was accused of theft, convicted, and promptly sold into servitude, presumably to cover a fine beyond the means of her family.[187]

Money carried great social weight as a measure for binding obligations. It had the potential to shift the balance of power considerably. Crucially, it was also a choice: quarrels could always be resolved through violence. Choosing not to settle was a realistic, if risky, option: the highest elites in particular might actually prefer violence to negotiated compensation, if their position was strong enough.[188] Making a dispute about money through fines and compensation was tantamount to saying that a settlement might be possible. Agreed tariffs laid out in law codes served an essential stabilising purpose; otherwise, there was a risk of spiralling costs and grave insults perpetuating conflict.[189] To offer monetary satisfaction was a material recompense as well as a measure of honour for the recipient and of the degree of goodwill the giver wanted to establish.[190] Money became a currency of status and a path to stability, with fines, settlements, and compensation payments seeming to multiply in proportion to violence and litigation, most prominently in eleventh-century France,[191] or in the vicinity of Ely in the late tenth century.[192]

---

185. Bitterauf 1905–09, no. 592a. For discussion of this and the previous example, see Esders 2015, 123–25.

186. See chapters 7 and 9; Rio 2017, 42–74.

187. Venantius Fortunatus, *Carmina* 5.14 (Leo 1881, 121).

188. Pancer 2001, 116–18; Lambert 2021. Cf. also the references to criminals with too much wealth and power to be punished according to normal channels in III As 6 and IV As 3 (Liebermann 1903–16, 1:170–71).

189. Lambert 2017b, 35–39; 2021; see also Oliver 2011. Miller 2006 explores this theme. Viviana Zelizer (1985) has discussed a similar problem in modern times: the move for compensating deceased children based on calculated loss of lifetime income to the family to a token compensation in recognition of the pricelessness of a lost child.

190. Lambert 2021, 150–57.

191. Teunis 2006.

192. Kennedy 1995; Keynes 2003, 18–30; Naismith 2016f, 29–32.

Damage to property may not have elicited quite the same depth of feeling or else might simply be better recorded. In any case, there was more willingness to bargain over land and use the possibility of either pressing, alleviating, or withdrawing compensation as a bargaining chip. Bishop Æthelwold showed strategic magnanimity of this kind at the end of protracted negotiations over land at Downham, Cambridgeshire. Their former owner, Leofsige, used various stratagems to create problems for the bishop, in the course of which other properties were temporarily wrested away and went unploughed for years. Eventually, a large assembly at London found in Æthelwold's favour and decided that Leofsige should return the lands he had seized and pay a penalty of over £100. The lands promptly came back to the bishop, but Leofsige died before he could begin settling the compensation payment, and his widow and children were left liable. Sigeflæd, as the widow was called, threw herself on the bishop's mercy. Crucially, she had the support of local society in her plea that the debt of over £100 be settled by writing off a debt of £5 the bishop owed her—a twentieth of the amount adjudicated. Æthelwold not only accepted but went one better, writing off the debt completely, repaying the £5 to Sigeflæd and even paying another £7 for the grain from her land. Magnanimity on the bishop's part helped save face for both sides, drew a line under further losses, and kept the status quo intact.[193]

Because the basis of loans and most compensation was to go beyond normal financial means, the ability to enforce and receive them—or to pay them back—was a sharp indicator of power as well as its absence. These obligations call attention in a stark way to the role of money in social interactions as a form of pressure. Hard cash was a part of this equation, with varied significance. For those seeking credit, it was usually preferable to get actual gold or silver pieces. Repayment was more negotiable, as was compensation. But most relevant transactions were regulated in abstracted monetary terms, which is the central point. When people thought about large transferrals of wealth, they typically did so using a monetary framework.

Getting Whatever You Want: Money and Commerce

The commercial dimension of coin use has deliberately been kept until last, because it is the one that carries the most baggage. There is a long tradition of interpreting finds of coins, or written references to coined

---

193. *Libellus Æthelwoldi* chap. 9–10 (ed. and trans. Kennedy and Keynes forthcoming).

money, as signals of commerce and the presence of merchants. That is undoubtedly too simplistic: it is unrealistic for gold coins of high value, while silver ones are now so plentiful that they must often have been used by a much wider range of people. But it remains true that direct buying and selling must have accounted for a significant proportion of monetary circulation, from a merchant in Gregory of Tours's *Historiae* who swindles his way from his first *trians* to a profit measured in gold pieces,[194] to the rough-and-tumble world of *Unibos* where coin, commerce, and greed all stand closely linked as destabilising factors.[195] Of all the major categories assessed here, commerce is the one where coined money features most often. Commerce played a special role as the glue that held most other kinds of use in place.[196] To raise cash for rents or tributes, peasants were expected to use markets; in turn, the sums raised by lords or kings might also be spent in market settings, albeit not necessarily immediately or in the same place. Offerings of alms from churches were also expected to be spent commercially. Even if a wide range of uses are recorded, they will generally presuppose commensurate commerce in coin, going on quietly in the background.

Early medieval commerce was deep and economically important, and moreover lent itself to the transactional, fluid qualities of coinage. But it was at the same time highly fragmented and socially embedded. This meant that it worked according to its own logic, and early medieval commerce did not operate in quite the same way as modern capitalist economies. This part of the chapter first discusses aspects of how monetised commerce worked, with particular reference to markets and prices, before turning to the social dynamics that underpinned monetary buying and selling.

MARKETS AND PRICES

Markets came in many shapes and sizes in the early Middle Ages. Dedicated, designated marketplaces did exist, and some of them were also major centres of minting and coin use, such as Dorestad, London, Marseille, and Venice. These were the poles around which regional and long-distance economic networks pivoted. They witnessed not only the exchange of goods and coins, but also the transfer of ideas and conceptual commodities.[197] Such places were the exception, however. Markets should

---

194. Gregory of Tours, *In gloria confessorum* 110 (Krusch 1869, 369–70).
195. See chapter 9.
196. Wickham 2021, esp. 23–24.
197. Sindbæk 2007a; 2007b; 2009; Loveluck 2013, 178–212, 302–60.

really be understood as a mindset: the idea of a time and place where one could buy commodities from others. Markets were not ubiquitous, or integrated, but they were nonetheless significantly more common than the thin textual record would imply. Every estate survey that stipulated rent in coin anticipated peasants engaging in market exchange to get them. That was exactly what an aggrieved ninth-century peasant named Waremund had been doing when his horse was stolen from a market held under the patronage of St. Hubert at Liège. He angrily remonstrated with the saint: "I came into your protection, so that I could get more of the things I need, and also so that I could acquire those things that I owe as an obligation to my lords [meaning the monks of St. Hubert]."[198]

Waremund's gripe encapsulates the twin roles of markets. They provided an outlet for him to sell surplus and obtain the cash that he owed to his lord. The second of these was a starkly vertical payment, though the actual market engagement is likely to have been more horizontal in character. But Waremund could piggyback on seigneurial demands by indulging in commerce for his own benefit. Both processes involved an element of choice and autonomy and had the potential to be self-stimulating: if lords and peasants needed more money, they would encourage others to sell. This cycle was known and encouraged. A diploma granting ecclesiastical immunity to the abbey of Tournus in 875 specifically exempted *servi, coloni,* or free peasants (*franci*) who belonged to the abbey or dwelt on its land from tolls in all markets regardless of whether they were "trading on the brothers' behalf, or their own."[199] The degree of flexibility depended on whether and how well participants knew each other. Familiarity brought advantages in terms of trust and reliability.[200] Cases of early medieval people attempting to take commercial advantage of one another typically emphasised a faceless setting: a town or religious site with many comings and goings, or travellers passing through rural settlements. Peasants overcharging travellers in the Carolingian Empire was so severe a problem that Emperor Carloman had to command a stop to it in 884.[201]

Lords benefited from markets in other ways too. Most important, they generally would not have lived entirely off produce in kind. Any degree

---

198. "Veni enim ad tuam tutelam, ut et meis aliquid utilitatulis adaugere, atque ea quae meis senioribus debitor sum impertiendo adquirere valerem." *Miracula sancti Hucberti,* c. 3 (*AASS* Nov I, col. 819–20). Waremund retrieved his horse the following day, when he apprehended the thief who had taken it.

199. "Sive de fratrum negotiis, sive de suis." Tessier 1943–55, no. 378.

200. See the classic example of Clifford Geertz's North African bazaar (1979).

201. Capitulary of Ver c. 13 (Boretius and Krause 1897, 375).

of dispersal in landed property brought logistical challenges in trying to maintain a steady supply of consumables. Churches were in a stronger position, and it is known that some—above all those responsible for polyptychs like Saint-Germain and Prüm—built up formidably complicated and long-distance webs of redistribution, founded on service obligations.[202] But these also relied on coordination with markets: Prüm expected some tenants to sell its produce on the market, or to bring goods to market centres for sale as part of their labour service.[203] Travel on this basis offered a golden opportunity for peasants to buy and sell on their own account too.[204] Moreover, although the segment of the rural economy the polyptychs illuminate so brightly is probably unusual for its level of elite intervention, and not necessarily a good guide to the rural economy as a whole, it is likely that the market engagement and dependence they show was matched in many areas beyond the "great estate" or *grands domaines*.

Money was a major part of the rural economy, even if as a background player that only occasionally steps into the spotlight. Importantly, rents in kind and the produce of land farmed directly for the lord's profit (*dominium* or inland) were not necessarily all meant for consumption by the recipient. A case can be made that payments in kind were destined all or in part for the market, giving lords something to sell, and on their own terms. This is a strong possibility when there was extensive monetisation in the countryside but little sign of monetised rents, as in the case of England in the late seventh and early eighth centuries.[205] It is also a plausible explanation for a switch in charters or leases back to rents in kind at a time when other sources indicate burgeoning commercialisation. That is the interpretation put on renders in kind in northern Italy in the eleventh century: lords wanted the profit of selling for themselves.[206] Sale of renders can sometimes also be inferred from their size and nature. The 26,275 eels that the abbey of Ely received from just two estates in Norfolk in the early eleventh century would have provided nearly 72 eels per day for a year, and this must have been just a fraction of the eels that Ely was receiving.[207] Preserving and storing all these eels was one option; others could be used for alms in kind; but another very

202. Devroey 2003b; Kuchenbuch 1978, 138–45.

203. Morimoto 2018, 715–18.

204. Kohl 2019, 158–59, noting that *angariae* involving travel typically came with a stipend for expenses.

205. See chapter 8.

206. Norrie 2017, 138–40.

207. Naismith 2017a, 358.

likely outlet was to sell them. In other words, Ely's plethora of eels may be an example of maximising produce in kind for marketing purposes. That, of course, leaves the question of what elites and their substantial households actually did eat. At Ely, part of the answer seems to have been buying food on the open market. The *Libellus Æthelwoldi* refers to the bishop and brothers buying grain and other produce from estates,[208] and the same collection of memoranda that lists the thousands of eels also describes purchases of grain and sheep.[209] All this is to say that elite use of markets—normally mediated through tenants and perhaps local agents of a larger landowner—went much further than pushing for monetary rent, which is only a partial guide to the intensity and extent of market dependence. Elite households bought and sold alike, with a range of partners from lower social strata including peasants, gentry, urban populations, and, in some cases, armies.[210]

Prices—the bread and butter of economic history in other periods—are difficult to follow in a meaningful way for this period because the available data is so poor. Virtually no regular price indexes can be constructed, with the important but problematic exception of prices for land. Payments for land followed several imperatives, sometimes with a commercial, assessed element, but also a large social component, meaning prices were fixed based on who sold to whom and why.[211] Care and rigour might be taken to ensure equity with the starting price. Adalhard of Corbie (d. 826), in his capacity as imperial *missus* for northern Italy, at one point had to negotiate a transfer of lands between two monasteries at Brescia and Nonantola. He brought in expert assessors (*estimatores*), who arrived at a monetary valuation for each property, taking into account its location, size, and value, this last determined with reference to productivity and current market prices for grain. The whole process presupposes a rigorously objective commercial valuation of land, and mechanisms for determining what that was.[212] But the level of scrutiny Adalhard exercised also reflects what was distinctive about land. It carried a relatively high value and had implications for status and for family and community interests.[213] That is precisely why the purchase of land was often far from open or neutral;

208. *Libellus Æthelwoldi* 11/*Liber Eliensis* 2.11 (Blake 1962, 86; trans. Fairweather 2005, 109).

209. Naismith 2017a, 354.

210. Astill 2011, 270–71.

211. Wickham 1994, 257–74; Feller and Wickham 2005.

212. Bougard 2008.

213. Selected discussions of this include Wickham 1994, 257–74; Reuter 1995, esp. 175–81; Rosenwein 1989, 47–48, 202–7.

who one sold to and why mattered deeply. A "market" price was possible, but usually as a jumping off point for further negotiations based on the relationship between buyer and seller, so that the sum actually paid bore little relation to the commercial value.[214]

Land was special, not least because so much is known about it compared to other kinds of transaction. Yet the land market may not have been completely unrepresentative in showing the negotiability of market prices, and how several kinds of market mentality fed into the formation of prices for other commodities. Odo of Cluny (d. 942) used an episode in the life of St. Gerald of Aurillac (d. c. 909) to explore proper commercial conduct for a lord. When Gerald was returning from a pilgrimage, he supposedly showed a group of Venetian merchants at Pavia some cloaks he had bought in Rome and asked them if he had "bought well" (*bene negotiatus*). They told him that he had inadvertently bought the cloaks at a very good price, much less than he would have paid in Constantinople. Gerald was aghast and insisted on giving the difference in money to some passing pilgrims so that they could convey it to the seller in Rome. For a man of Gerald's station, to pay less than he should (defined for Gerald as top-dollar price) was an insult to his sense of status and propriety.[215] This was not the only time Odo imagined Gerald turning to coin to make more equitable, socially responsible exchanges: Odo described how, when Gerald's men commandeered cherries for their lunch one day, he insisted on paying in cash the peasant who claimed them.[216] Silver was a swift, discrete alternative to violent requisition of commodities, and paying the appropriate price constituted a show of noblesse oblige.[217] But what Odo praised in Gerald suggests failings he saw around him: lords of his own day, who could afford not to haggle, may have been forcing unfavourable prices onto partners. This was one of the practices that Jonas of Orléans and other bishops condemned at the Council of Paris in 829.[218]

For basic agricultural goods, the exceptional prices of famine years, and the few examples of controlled prices that central authorities attempted to impose, are actually better known than the regular prices that were paid. Many people would have had to pay for essential food supplies rarely: this level of the early medieval economy was geared toward topping up needs

214. Naismith 2013c, 304–8; Feller, Gramain and Weber 2005, 25–49.
215. Odo, *Life of Gerald*, 1.27 (Bultot-Verleysen 2009, 172–74; trans. Sitwell 1958, 117–18).
216. Odo, *Life of Gerald*, 1.23 (Bultot-Verleysen 2009, 170–71; trans. Sitwell 1958, 115).
217. Feller 2017b.
218. See previous discussion and chapter 8.

through "interpersonal obligations and responsibilities, rather than commercial forces or state-like structures."[219] In Italy there were precious few markets before the tenth century, even in urban settings, and those that there were usually arose from elite dominance and exploitation, not bottom-up demand.[220] That situation started to change from the late tenth and especially the eleventh century,[221] but it is nonetheless apparent that, as in the later Middle Ages, markets were poorly integrated beyond a local level, meaning that prices for the same item could vary significantly between regions.[222] This was a well-known fact of life. Archbishop Jeremiah of Sens (d. 828) sent a messenger with a wagon, some money, some local goods, and a begging letter to Frothair, bishop of Toul (813–47), trying to solicit from him some salt, because storms on the coast, his usual source, had made it unaffordable locally.[223] Two centuries later, a trader came to Conques from the Auvergne and found the price of wax at the church of St. Foi so shockingly low that he decided to stock up on as many candles as he could stuff into his clothing. The saint did not take kindly to this ruse and so set one of the candles in the trader's shirt on fire.[224]

These and similar stories revolve around the mismatch of prices between regions, and the difficulty in finding reliable information. Prices came from intensely local, personal experience: people talking with friends, acquaintances, and neighbours about whether a given price was acceptable. The English monastic teacher Ælfric Bata put his finger on this in a colloquy that pictures two students discussing the price of a book one wanted to buy from the other. The initial offer was £2 of pure silver: a high price, for "if you don't want it, somebody else will: this is an expensive thing, and somebody else should buy it more dearly than you." But the buyer was not taken in by the sales talk. "Even if someone else wants to be so foolish, I don't. I want to be careful and buy your book at the right price—at the price my friends will tell me its worth. That's a fair price."[225]

219. Goodson 2021, 116.

220. Goodson 2021 116–29.

221. Goodson 2021, 136–40.

222. Unger 2007.

223. Frothair, *Epistolae*, no. 8 (Hampe 1899, 281).

224. Bernard of Angers, *Liber miraculorum sanctae Fidis* 1.24 (Robertini 1994, 125–27; trans. Sheingorn and Clark 1995, 91–92).

225. "Si tu non uis, alius aliquis uult. Kare ualet hoc, et alius aliquis debet illum emere karius quam tu . . . Et si aliquis uult esse talis ebes, ego nolo, sed cautus uolo esse, et sic tuum librum emere sicut rectum est et sicut mei amici dicent mihi quanti pretii dignus sit, sic ualet esse bene." Ælfric Bata, *Colloquia* 24 (ed. and trans. Gwara and Porter 1997, 134–37).

Eventually the two settle on twelve mancuses (i.e., 30s, or 10s less than the initial asking price). This is a case in point of what later medieval observers called the just price: not a fixed and unchanging abstract, but a price that was considered fair and acceptable to both parties, based on their knowledge and experience.[226]

Markets were transformative places, offering both danger and opportunity. Theoretically, market participants had the freedom to choose with whom to do business, as long as a mutually agreeable price could be reached, meaning that (depending on context) whom one dealt with was less important than what one bought or sold. This was precisely the kind of exchange that money catered for, and when they worked as they should markets had the potential to flatten out power differentials.[227] Market relations therefore became unstable when the preconditions of commerce were skewed: when one party could force a price or intimidate the other. But even these abuses generally necessitated close and long-term involvement with a market. Sudden incomers, even wealthy ones, brought only their enhanced buying power. In the ribald eleventh-century poem *Unibos*, the mayor, provost, and priest of the eponymous hero's fictional village journeyed to the market town where Unibos claimed to have struck a fabulous bargain. They arrived with the hides of recently slaughtered cattle, fully expecting to make out like bandits. But once in the marketplace itself, they found that their arrogance and relative wealth did not give them any particular advantage. They haggled clumsily with a cohort of shoemakers, demanding £3 and not a penny less for a hide that the shoemakers rated as worth 10d (which was close to the 8d Unibos had received earlier in the tale). Eventually a fight broke out; the aggressive, intransigent sellers were held responsible and fined. This shambles of a deal fell down because the two parties approached the exchange with completely different frames of reference in mind, exacerbated by enough of a break in geography for them to expect a world of difference: the shoemakers were even made to say "let these three, who think that the skins of oxen are the greatest of riches, tell here and now from which region they come."[228] *Unibos* is a comedic text: peasant ineptitude in complex market settings was a trope

---

226. Wood 2002, 133–44. For earlier roots, see Cahn 1969.

227. Simmel (e.g., 1977, 463/2004, 342) was interested in the possibility that money could liberate and empower the individual, including the individual peasant (or, more relevant to his own industrial world, wage labourer). For helpful discussion, see Poggi 1993.

228. "De qua sint hi prouintia, dicant tres in praesentia qui putant boum tergora diuitiarum maxima." *Unibos* vv. 48–66 (Klein 1991, 855–58; trans. Ziolkowski 1999, 19–21).

the high-status writer could play on for laughs.[229] Nonetheless, it points to the need for equity and comparable expectations in market transactions.

The debacle with the shoemakers also relies on the premise that the three village magnates might find a big gap in prices that they could take advantage of. The fluidity of market prices left the way open for imbalance and exploitation in the short term, especially in times of need when basic commodity prices would spike. In the long run, this was a period of general stability. Where prices for similar commodities can be compared over long periods, signs of inflation are inconsistent and often very low.[230] This reflects the many factors besides neutral, organic supply and demand of coin that could make prices resiliently sticky. Law and elite or political interests played an important part, as well as the fact that money meant much more than coin.[231] So too did customary and moral imperatives, like those that Odo assigned to Gerald of Aurillac. Moralising stories and (in some cases) legal protections relied on the premise that open market practices of the day exacerbated power differentials, not least through access to coin, or the abuses that arose from imposing monetary frameworks on transactions. This is an important aspect of money and markets in the early Middle Ages: they were cutthroat and unequal, but not in the same way as those of modern capitalist societies.[232] There was a powerful temptation for the powerful and rich to prey on everyone; the weak and the poor, on the weaker and poorer. Elites had the potential to dominate markets, especially smaller-scale ones, meaning that everyone had to play by their rules: their prices, their terms for transactions. Social power, in short, meant buying power, especially in a society where commerce and coin were distributed so thinly and unevenly. That inevitably meant that elites had a very different experience of coined money to peasants.

ELITES AND COINED MONEY

In 688 the newly installed Lombard king Cunincpert (688–700) was ousted from his throne by Alahis, duke of Brescia. Alahis achieved his coup with the help of two powerful brothers from his home city, Aldo and Grauso, but according to Paul the Deacon he quickly put their support in jeopardy. One day Alahis was counting his gold tremisses on a table, and

229. Kuchenbuch 2019, 57–62.

230. Farmer 1988, 716–18. But cf. Verhulst 2002, 123–25, which argues for significant inflation in the Carolingian Empire.

231. Feller 2011; 2014.

232. Le Goff 2004, 25–70; 2012, 142–50.

when he dropped one, it was picked up and handed to him by the young son of Aldo. Thinking the boy too little to understand his remarks, Alahis (whom Paul portrayed as an out-and-out villain) said that his father, Aldo, would soon hand over many such coins to him. When the clever yet unnamed boy reported these words to his father, it began the sequence of events that would lead to Alahis's undoing.[233]

Paul's story implies that elites treasured and sought stockpiles of cash. Many other texts emanating from and portraying an aristocratic milieu likewise revolve, albeit in a looser way, around glittering treasure. But if money features at all in *Beowulf*, *Waltharius*, and their ilk, it is as the stuff of gift-giving and as a spur to acts of bloody revenge.[234] The focus was more on the results of and reactions to wealth than the material itself, the emphasis falling generally on objects that were more evocative of martial and social prowess. Money is there only implicitly: the dirty laundry of early medieval aristocratic society. Once in the hands of someone like Alahis, coins would change hands infrequently, with a drip-feed of smaller parcels entering wider distribution. In the words of Ludolf Kuchenbuch, elite reserves were "functionally demonetised" (*funktional de-monetisiert*);[235] so too were any coins that were transformed into gold or silver objects, a practice most widely associated with the vikings but feasible in any system based on precious-metal currency.[236] Faint traces of big, immobile assemblages of this kind can be detected in hoards of coins that sometimes contain numerous specimens from the same dies, because those coins had stayed together from the time of production through to deposition, circulating as a group.[237] But even though few hoards are likely to reflect the main moveable wealth of the high elite, it is still clear that elites disposed of very large sums of cash. We have already met the Lombard abbot whose institution could put down over 11,500 brand new tremisses.[238]

A good sense of what elite dominance might have looked like in practice can be gained from the later Middle Ages and especially the early modern period. It is necessary here to leapfrog over the period from about

233. Paul the Deacon, *Historia Langobardorum* 5.39 (Bethmann and Waitz 1878, 202–3; trans. Foulke 1907, 242–43).

234. Naismith 2016d; MacLean 2018.

235. Kuchenbuch 2019, 64–65.

236. See chapter 5.

237. As, for example, in the Forum hoard of the 940s (Naismith and Tinti 2016, 37). For an extreme case (264 gold solidi of the 610s, all struck from the same pair of dies), see Bijovsky 2010.

238. See earlier discussion.

1200 to 1350, when there was much more money available.[239] In contrast, long-term study of prices and money supply suggests that both the eleventh century and the fifteenth to seventeenth centuries were marked by rapid circulation of coin, indicating relatively short supply and coins changing hands many times in quick succession.[240] It is very likely that early medieval society experienced something like the same radical social imbalance of monetary wealth as early modern England.[241]

An endemic problem of economies that rely heavily on precious-metal coin was a tendency to make coins that were relatively high in value, and to minimise production of lower denominations, for demand was driven primarily by wealthy interests, and the amount of time and effort needed to make low-value coins was not significantly less than for valuable ones.[242] The coins minted in the early Middle Ages therefore remained focused on gold solidi and tremisses and latterly silver pennies. This preponderance can be quantified much more strongly in the early modern period. In 1601 only 4 per cent of silver coined by the English mint was made into coins worth less than a shilling; that proportion fell to 0.5 per cent in the 1670s, and even in the Great Recoinage of 1696 the lowest denomination coined was the sixpence.[243] Aristocrats and wealthier tradesmen hoarded coin, and especially good coin, meaning that the poor had to rely on a constricted supply of low-quality coins. There were serious practical implications that arose from this, and genuine economic disadvantages. Monetary inequality also engendered a tendency to think of coin in terms of its (and its holder's) quality as well as its strict quantitative value. Probate inventories of what deceased men and women had in their possession frequently included cash, illuminating its uneven distribution: among a hundred samples from Chesterfield in the period 1520–1600, the average amount of cash held was 12s, but that was pushed up by a few wealthy households, one of which had £32, while of the forty-two poorest, only three had any money at all.[244] England's population had suffered from a top-heavy currency for a long time by this stage. There had been clamours to king and

239. Bolton 2012, 174–223; Lucassen 2018, 63–68.

240. Mayhew 2013, esp. 37.

241. Muldrew 2001, esp. 99–101, from which much of the following is drawn.

242. Sargent and Velde 2002, 4–7; Desan 2014, 108–90. The other difficulty usually identified is that low-value coins require roughly the same amount of time and effort to make as high-value ones so are less profitable for manufacturers to produce—but it is not clear that early medieval minting was always driven by the same profit-oriented logic: see chapter 3.

243. Challis 1978, 200–202; Craig 1953, 129–30, 178.

244. Bestall and Fowkes 1977, 170–71, cited in Muldrew 2001, 91.

parliament about the poor quality and supply of coin, especially of lower-value coin, since at least around 1200.[245] Access to coin was a challenge for all levels of society in the fourteenth and fifteenth centuries, since if peasant tenants could not get coin to pay, their masters among the gentry and the aristocracy would not receive.[246] Money had to go both ways sometimes.

While the general similarities are instructive, the details of elite advantage took different forms during the early Middle Ages. A great deal of diversity is apparent. In eleventh-century England, liability for geld—national-level tax or tribute—rested with lords, but since their demesne lands were exempt, what that meant in practice was that they (or, more accurately, the reeves who ran their estates) were responsible for collecting the geld within each hundred from subtenants and peasant cultivators who actually paid, and then for transporting that sum to a shire- or national-level collection point.[247] Elite impact on coin use can be inferred most clearly in regions where the "classic" *grand domaine* was frequently found, such as northern Francia in Merovingian and Carolingian times, and the larger estates of late Anglo-Saxon and Domesday England. Great estates concentrated a lot of people and resources into a sprawling unit under a single lord. Yet they were never autonomous islands of production and consumption: great estates were part of a diverse economic and tenurial ecosystem and depended on autonomous small landholders and artisans from outside the estates, as well as on markets and complex webs of redistribution.[248] More important, many regions with substantial monetisation, such as northern and central Italy or East Anglia in the eleventh century, had few or no great estates,[249] while even the most aggressive landholding regimes created opportunities for peasants to alleviate their position. Peasants stood to benefit materially from involvement with the elite: by negotiating lower rent that could be paid willingly and

---

245. Desan 2014, 105–6.

246. Mayhew 1974, 69–72; Desan 2014, 191–230.

247. Baxter 2020, 1098–1100. For demesne exemption, see Pratt 2013. Domesday Book (especially Exon Domesday) is the best source for this, though similar arrangements probably applied earlier: Herman of Laon refers to a local man from eastern Norfolk being charged with delivering a geld to Thetford in the time of King Swein (1013–14): *Miracles of St. Edmund*, c. 10 (ed. and trans. Licence 2014, 26–27).

248. Tange 2012; Schroeder 2020. For redistribution, see Devroey 1993; 2003b.

249. Wickham 1995, 523–26; Campbell 2005. Brenner 1976 made an influential argument for the importance of rural power structures in later medieval and early modern economic development. Although the details of the argument have been very extensively discussed, the basic point remains persuasive.

comfortably, or potentially by gaining access to support in developing the productivity of lands, as when Carolingian grants of *precaria* (church lands leased at preferential rates) provided for improvements undertaken by the lessee,[250] or when decidedly primitive and economically rudimentary peasant holdings in northern Italy gave way, over the tenth to twelfth centuries, to richly developed and productive lands.[251] Not all peasants went in this direction, to be sure—conniving with the elite was one way to foster inequality within peasant communities, as will be discussed later in more detail—but an appreciable number did.

Chris Wickham has recently underlined the hollowness inherent in this kind of elite dominance.[252] Elite interests had always been important, but in the early medieval West they merged with and effectively replaced state structures as the new economic tentpole.[253] The early medieval economy was hence always restricted by the small size of the elite, even if one factors in their (relatively) much greater wealth and an "extended elite" of military retinues, significant functionaries, families, and so on who were directly dependent on, or allied with, the elite.[254] Elites in a "feudal" economic system always depended on resources extracted from the land they dominated, in the form of its produce and the labour of its inhabitants, although they did not appropriate everything.[255] A large proportion of surplus remained in peasant hands, and the crucial question was what happened to it. Wickham proposes two models for this aspect of earlier medieval economic structures. One is decidedly limited and frames lords and their entourages as the main vectors of demand, with peasants themselves not generating a dense enough exchange network to drive markets on their own account. Indeed, many peasants lay completely outside a "feudal" system of this form, not substantially beholden to a lord at all, and even those whom it did touch could have consumed whatever they did not give to the lord. The other starts from the premise of much deeper aristocratic dominance. This was the "caging" of the peasantry (*encellulement*):[256] more and wider lordships brought a greater

---

250. Kasten 2006.

251. Hodges 2020, esp. 173–74.

252. Wickham 2021.

253. An argument developed by Chris Wickham in particular: 2005, 693–824; 2008, 22–24; 2009a, 222–25.

254. Wickham 2021, 37.

255. Feller 2011, 46. As in Wickham's important study (2021, 3), "feudal" is used here in the Marxist sense, denoting an economic system based on taking surplus from those who work the land—not feudal-vassalic relationships (for a summation of which, see Roach 2015).

256. Guerreau 1980, 201–10; Fossier 1989.

proportion of the peasantry into "feudal" relationships, meaning they had to hand over a larger amount of produce on an individual basis, as well as engage more with markets to obtain the wherewithal needed to settle obligations to the lord. Counterintuitively, forcing more peasants to do this, and on a larger scale, had the side effect of stimulating economic complexity and demand below the elite, in that more and more peasants could buy and sell for themselves on the back of having to do so for their lord. Even if the latter continued to provide the basic framework, peasants operated as a penumbra of considerable size.[257] "Feudal" economies in this way stimulated peasant producers not only as cogs in seigneurial mechanisms but as autonomous economic actors, and elites anticipated that those producers would be involved in commerce, as indeed would the elites themselves and their operatives.[258]

These ideal types suffer from the difficulty of obtaining a peasant's-eye view of what was going on. There are important lessons to learn from the later Middle Ages about just how extensive the overall impact of peasant labour could be, even at times when lords too were doing well. England is the best recorded example: ecclesiastical and secular aristocratic production of wool, England's main commercial export, in the early fourteenth century amounted to less than a third of the overall production, the balance coming from the aggregate of peasant output.[259] It should be stressed that this reflected a world on the other side of a series of commercial developments that had reached only an embryonic stage in the early Middle Ages.[260] There was simply a more complex and integrated economy for peasants to tap into by 1300. In the early Middle Ages, peasants at further remove from lords would often have enjoyed greater autonomy, but also a high degree of economic isolation and simplicity, like an emaciated version of Marx's French peasants who lived like separate potatoes in a sack.[261]

Wickham roughly correlates his first model with the early Middle Ages, meaning about the sixth or seventh century to the tenth, and the second with the central Middle Ages, beginning around 1000.[262] But it can be argued that both these models operated at earlier times. Patterns of coin

257. Wickham 2021, 18–20. Wickham also identifies a third layer to this process involving rural wage labour and artisanal activity.

258. Wickham 2021, 17.

259. Masschaele 1997, esp. 52–53.

260. Wickham 2021. See also chapter 10.

261. Hodges 2020, esp. 170–73, with reference to Italy. For the potatoes, see Marx 1963 [1852], 124.

262. Wickham 2021, 20. As Wickham quite rightly notes, the major elaboration of this

use suggest an oscillating, regionalised picture of exchange complexity rather than a smooth upward curve. This is not to argue that the ninth century can be put next to the thirteenth: there was a world difference. But some access to coined money, based on some degree of commerce and exchange complexity that reached across society, can clearly be seen much earlier. Currency may have been top-down in production, but it percolated outward and downward with just a relatively small bump in scale. The major *longue durée* variable was scale, which might be envisaged as the frequency within which the oscillations of complexity fluctuated.[263] The peaks of earlier waves could replicate in incipient form some of the economic characteristics associated with later times. Wickham's model of elite dominance reflects the fifth- to seventh-century prevalence of gold coin, which must have moved overwhelmingly between layers of the elite and had little part in the lives of peasant producers,[264] though even here a case can be made for a trend downward in its use over the course of the seventh century, in the Merovingian kingdom and arguably also in England.[265] The intensity of coin use is an indicator of regions that might have moved toward Wickham's model of more broadly based exchange. It is perfectly possible to have commerce without lots of coins;[266] the opposite, however, is less easy to explain, at least in the context of the medium-value silver coins that prevailed in early medieval Europe. Coins can mean many things, and always need to be set against pottery and other indexes of economic complexity, but there is a strong case to be made that commercial uses undergirded most others. Moreover, a large rural distribution of coin finds is difficult to reconcile with anything other than widespread peasant use of cash; this in turn implies at least some level of commercial engagement by a large share of the population. There were significant differences in the superstructure that operated at higher levels. England, Frisia, and possibly parts of the Merovingian kingdom in the age of the early pennies (c. 660–750) witnessed dramatic, fast, and yet short-lived expansion of coin, which suggests the impetus came from elite disbursement of silver reserves. There must have been capacity

---

layer generally belongs to a later period, though elements of it can be found occasionally in the early Middle Ages.

263. Spufford 1988, 382–85. Kuchenbuch 2019, 71–73, helpfully summarises these dynamics in Marx-style formulas, with different arrangements for the ruled and for rulers.

264. Although not based solely on coin, a model of this kind is clearly developed for the circulation of precious items in the North Sea in Nicolay 2014, 264–94.

265. See chapters 7 and 8.

266. A point emphasized in Wickham 2009a, 227.

to absorb and use these coins, but probably not to sustain monetisation on that level for long. Growth based on a broader symbiotic relationship between elites and peasant society can be argued for England, Germany, and northern Italy at various points in the tenth and eleventh centuries. Seigneurial pressures extended downward and outward to contingents who were closer to the margins of the elite, and who worked in tandem with wider and increasingly commercialised rural and urban networks.[267] These advanced as a pair, if not always a happy one, and each depended more and more on the other. Parts of west Francia had perhaps operated in this way since about the early ninth century. Other regions also merit consideration, such as Gotland and other parts of Viking-Age Scandinavia, allowing for extensive use of silver bullion in monetary contexts. It should be stressed that Gotland is not thought to have had a high degree of elite dominance. Production might still have been focused on figures of relative wealth and importance, but coin use as a whole is better seen as arising from the actions of a broader spectrum of society.

PEASANTS AND COINED MONEY

At some point in the early ninth century, a mass of poor people (*plebeia . . . multitudo*) gathered at the shrine of St. Philibert in Noirmoutier (dép. Vendée). They came for prayer but stayed for trade, at a cross set up near the monastery. One man from among this crowd decided to stop for a drink on his way home and entered a *taberna*: this rare reference to mass-market catering suggests a stable yet lowly clientele with money to spend. The customer asked for a halfpenny of wine but only had a penny to spend, so the publican agreed to give him both the wine and a halfpenny in change. In the confusion recognisable by anyone who has ever attended a crowded bar, the customer was given a full penny's worth of wine by mistake. When the customer asked for a second round using his change, the publican quite reasonably said, "You must be having a laugh, mate: what you've got there is mine, not yours, as you took away both my wine and my money."[268] When the peasant falsely swore by St. Philibert that he was telling the truth, the saint inflicted prompt and messy retribution by having him vomit all over the floor.[269]

267. Loveluck 2013, 274–327.

268. "Bene . . . tibi jocaris, amice; non enim tuum sed meum affers. Tulisti quippe meum et vinum et pretium." Ermentarius, *De translationibus et miraculis sancti Filiberti* 1.71 (Poupardin 1905, 49–50).

269. Naismith 2014e, 33–35.

Behind the façade of just deserts, this story hints at quantitative as well as qualitative dimensions of the early medieval monetary economy. To take the former first, the drinker had about him some supply of coin. Not everything had gone to the lord, or the church, or the king. The gathering at Noirmoutier represented as down-to-earth a sector of commercial coin use as there was: one that went on *between* peasants, local traders, and casual labourers, with some level of disposable income. It follows that not all peasants subscribed to the Chayanovian logic of putting in the minimal labour needed to cover subsistence and any necessary renders to lord or church.[270] Working as a group provided even more security and had the potential to make peasants into a significant economic force.[271] Surplus, of goods also used for subsistence, of supplementary cash crops, or of labour,[272] did not necessarily mean capitalism: it offered a buffer against risk, and an economic bargaining chip. Coined money was a common corollary of these approaches, providing a good way of building up savings, while the capacity to accumulate a liquid reserve was what set the managing and the prosperous apart from the struggling.[273] Even among nonelites, cash assemblages might mount up. English manumissions from the tenth to twelfth centuries include the price paid for freedom, ranging from 2s up to over £3 and clustering at about 10s, often explicitly said to have been paid in cash. Most of these payments were made by close relatives or spouses of the enslaved person, and in several cases by the slave him or herself. Enslaved people and their families were raising large amounts that probably included savings.[274] There were many ways these self-manumittors could have acquired their money.[275] Some manumission payments could have derived from loans or gifts obtained specifically for that purpose, but this is not likely to cover every case. Tenants of Prüm in the ninth century can be seen selling surplus at market, working for wages, or plying any artisanal skill they may have picked up.[276]

270. Chayanov 1966; Masschaele 1997, 33–35.

271. Schroeder 2020, esp. 76–83. Peasants were, collectively, the largest economic bloc in the English rural economy when records first emerge in the later Middle Ages: Masschaele 1997, 42–54.

272. Arnoux 2016.

273. Bowes 2021, 30–31.

274. Pracy 2020, 18–19

275. Raftis 1996 argues for subject peasants playing a collectively large role in the later medieval English countryside. The background market and demographic developments that supported this were not present to anything like the same degree in the early Middle Ages, though the general point is an important one.

276. Devroey and Schroeder 2020, 192–97.

Multiple streams of income would have been common, translating into small nest eggs of coins put by as savings. Small hoards of coins can be read in this light.[277] And if there were several members of a household capable of contributing in this way, a family that was poor in land and of low standing could still put together a tidy little sum.[278]

The real interest of the miraculous spewing of Noirmoutier is in its implications about the qualitative aspects of coin use. On the one hand, the two central characters were lowly, earthy figures. Saints' lives and other literary narratives are replete with anecdotes about poor people—peasants or *pauperi* without land or regular employment—gathering small clutches of coin. These stories play on the radically different meanings coined money held for various layers of society.[279] On a very general level, the tales were heirs to biblical parables, but their early medieval authors consistently adapted the basic principle to current circumstances; in other words, biblical miracles inclined writers to think of present conditions, often of a very down-to-earth nature.[280] Miracle tales of money frequently concern people with disabilities, advanced age, diminished status, or limited support whose capacity to work was limited and who therefore depended more on meagre and onerously obtained coins. A poor woman with a withered hand near ninth-century Paris, who had been in the habit of giving a halfpenny to the church of St. Mary every year, once decided to celebrate the arrival of Easter by giving herself a treat and so spent the halfpenny instead on some meat to eat. That night she was stricken by illness, and the hands that had betrayed her promised offering became immobile (though eventually they healed after she made good on her gift).[281] While stories like this cannot be taken as sober accounts of actual events, they do call on scenes, people, and actions familiar from the time of the writer and so are a valuable spotlight on experiences with coin.[282]

It is worth pausing to consider how audiences would imagine the poor woman getting and spending the coin that she spent or donated. For most, lords and peasants alike, economic life moved at the tempo set by agrarian

277. For the prevalence of small hoards in the Carolingian world, see Coupland 2014c, 263–64; for late Anglo-Saxon and Norman England, see Fairbairn 2019, 113–14.

278. Devroey and Schroeder 2020, 192–97.

279. Naismith 2012b, 281–82; Bruand 2002, 160–65; Nelson 1992, 24; Coupland 2014c, 257–58.

280. Heinzelmann 1981, 244–8; Rio 2021.

281. *Historia miraculorum sancti Germani*, c. 7 (*AASS* Maii 6, col. 803B).

282. This particular story is similar to the parable of the widow's mite (Mark 12:41–4; Luke 21:1–4) in very general terms, but it should be stressed that both the message and the details depart significantly from the biblical story.

production, which would have meant a cycle of peaks and troughs in access to coin throughout the year, with knock-on effects for the price of basic commodities.[283] This may not be the case here. The poor woman near Paris with the withered hand dwelt in a developed area, with access to an outlet where she could spend half a penny on meat, which probably implies retail trade—a butcher's shop, or even an eatery.[284] It was entirely characteristic for early medieval and later women to engage in small-scale retail exchange of this kind (in contrast to men, who tended to deal in bigger sums and savings).[285] That in itself implies a high level of complexity, accommodating small sums and small quantities, and therefore geared toward the needs of a relatively humble clientele.

The nature of early medieval sources generally makes it necessary to adopt a binary-seeming approach to elites and nonelites or peasants. In practice, as is clear from some areas with richer source material,[286] there were nuances within and between these categories. Nonelites dealing with other peasants or nonelites—as apparently happened at Noirmoutier— hence did not necessarily mean treating with equals in an open, harmonious, and cooperative way. Differences in status, wealth, and power within this segment of society might be small in overall terms, but still very real and significant within urban or rural communities.[287] Unfree or heavily obligated peasants, who lived on a small portion of land that belonged to someone else, might have had neighbours who would not be classed as aristocratic or elite according to contemporary legal categories, but who held a significant amount of land and did not cultivate it themselves,[288] which for modern historians would arguably push them closer to village elite status, or even into what would later be called the gentry.[289] Paul Fouracre has noted a widespread class of richer peasants distinguished by nominal rents to ecclesiastical landlords, rated in money and intended specifically for lighting.[290] At the level of the village community, such individuals

283. Spufford 1988, 382–83.

284. Canteens existed in London by the twelfth century: William FitzStephen, *Vita sancti Thomae, Cantuariensis archiepiscopi et martyris* c. 10 (Sheppard and Robertson 1875–85, 3:5–6; trans. H. E. Butler in Stenton 1934, 28).

285. Hilton 1984; Cardon 2021, 208–9, 230.

286. As developed recently in Quirós Castillo 2020b.

287. For general guidance, see Devroey 2006, 203–12, 265–316; Faith 2019, 17–45; Loyn 1991, 299–325.

288. For this definition of a peasant (though it excludes those who worked the land but with no control over their own labour: slaves), see Wickham 2005, 386.

289. For an excellent discussion of definitions of elite status, see Bougard, Bührer-Theirry, and Le Jan 2013.

290. Fouracre 2021, esp. 113–16.

would have been firmly elite. Well-off peasants or "middling" landowners renting land to poorer counterparts may well have been the primary users of waged labour, while neighbours may have competed for tenancy of a monastery or aristocrat, at a level far below what is usually visible. In such cases, the lord was presumably concerned with who would maintain the status quo and pay the rent on time.[291]

All the same, the effects of micro-inequalities are difficult to detect and pale next to dealing with wealthier elites. Notker the Stammerer (d. 912) criticised a bishop for storing up grain and opening it up for sale only at a time of famine, when he could make a vast profit.[292] Earlier in the ninth century, the proceedings of the 829 council of Paris (written up by Jonas of Orléans) gave a detailed account of the market-related abuses that rich landowners were inflicting on their poorer neighbours.[293] Counts, bishops, and others, and their men, were using a bigger set of weights and measures when buying and a smaller one when selling or lending,[294] forcing people to sell their produce (presumably to the lord and his men) at low prices and giving desperate peasants access to stores of food only if they agreed to give up their land as collateral until harvest, or else to pay the inflated famine price in harvest-time goods, which meant having to part with three or four *modii* of grain or wine for every one borrowed in advance.[295]

The council's detailed account of asymmetry in ninth-century markets offered a succinct encapsulation of how commerce should interface with seigneurial authority: "Once those things have been given to their lords that rightfully should be given, the poor should be allowed the freedom to sell to others whatever remains to them, insofar as the willing compact of seller and buyer applies, and without the interference of their lords."[296] This was

---

291. Schroeder 2020, 84–95; Devroey 2019b; 2019c, the latter emphasising higher-grade estate workers on the lands of Saint-Germain.

292. Notker, *Gesta* 1.23 (Haefele 1959, 31–32; trans. Thorpe 1969, 74).

293. For the moralizing agenda of this council and its impact on episcopal behaviour, see Patzold 2006, 341–47.

294. Local measures would be held by agents of landlords: in *Unibos*, when the eponymous hero returns to his home village, he asks a boy to fetch the *praepositus* and his *pondus* measure, to assess how much money he has found in his hoard: *Unibos* vv. 21–24 (Klein 1991, 851–52; trans. Ziolkowski 1999, 17).

295. Council of Paris (829), c. 52–53 (Werminghoff 1908, 2:645–46). The council consisted of twenty-four bishops and archbishops from Neustria, and its provisions should be read as relating to this portion of the empire; other contemporary meetings took place at Lyon, Mainz, and Toulouse, though Paris is the only one to have left a written record. For background, see de Jong 2009, 170–84.

296. "Pauperibus libertas tribuatur, ut redditis senioribus suis quae iuste reddenda sunt, reliqua, quae sibi supersunt, liceat aliis, prout pactio vendentis et ementis grata fuerit,

idealistic rhetoric: actual markets were rife with exploitation, as differences in resources, access, and influence came into play. Economic complexity (including monetisation and coin use) did enhance nonelite agency and wealth yet at the same time worked in favour of the predatory model feared at Paris in 829. This inherent contradiction lay at the heart of the early medieval economy. Large-scale landholding depended on commercial exchange, in a fundamentally symbiotic relationship that embraced slaves, tenants, and smaller landholders.[297] As we have seen, lords possessing dispersed lands, mingled with those of others, relied on cooperation with the world around them, not least through commerce. All this took full advantage of the characteristics of coinage. Prices, fair and otherwise, were reckoned and often paid in coin. Markets were a standard venue for obtaining and spending coin, and coins embody commercial links that bound town and country together. Plentiful coin finds tend to coincide with tenurial and seigneurial complexity, as in northern Francia and eastern England. It remains true that commerce was, on the whole, limited in the early Middle Ages. But so too was use of coin—and where the one developed further, the other tended to follow.

Peasants must often have found themselves in a double bind. They had to obtain coin for basic necessities, but doing so was to enter into a potentially exploitative situation, with very little defence on the side of the powerless against the powerful. It should be stressed that pressure was not necessarily constant or ubiquitous: lords and their operatives could not be everywhere at once, and tenants could grit their teeth against exactions that would ease when the lord or bailiff moved on.[298] Others might be removed enough socially or geographically not to have to engage with elites in markets or would consciously choose to restrict all forms of market engagement.[299] But another possibility for those who could not avoid entering unequal commercial transactions was to challenge the means of exchange that underpinned the theoretically universal, compulsory acceptability of coin. While this was perhaps not a strategy for dodging all unwelcome monetary transactions, it did provide a way to stall or reject an unfair price and generally make life difficult for lords and their agents. From the point of view of rulers, any kind of rejection ran the risk of undermining a basic tenet of authority and so had to be nipped in the bud.

---

absque prohibitione seniorum suorum distrahere." Council of Paris (829), c. 52 (Werminghoff 1908, 2:645).

297. Naismith 2014e, 30–37; Wickham 2021.

298. Schroeder 2020.

299. Scott 2009, 105, emphasises this as a strategy for mobile, mountain-dwelling populations of modern Southeast Asia.

In 861 Charles the Bald was faced with just such a problem when he instructed some of his *missi* to go and deal with the rejection of good coins in markets at an unspecified location.[300] They were to punish offenders in public as a warning to others. Unusually, Charles told his *missi* to show a degree of compassion in recognition of the variable quality of contemporary coin,[301] and lenience to people who had been forced into desperation by viking tribute payments; Charles even sanctioned a reduction in the usual penalty for rejecting good coin for free men and women. The *missi* were to take into account "age, condition, and sex" when deciding what kind of punishment to inflict, "because women are accustomed to haggle":[302] first offenders would be beaten with either a big stick or light rods, while second offenders would be burned in the face with the heated-up coin they had refused. The point seems to have been display and restoration of public confidence rather than causing real, lasting harm to individuals.[303] A picture emerges of lively and contentious monetary exchange, in which women played a major role in small-scale market trade,[304] and in which *Franci, coloni,* and *servi* were not content simply to accept whatever coins were being forced onto them. Questioning the status of denarii was a strategy to dodge unfavourable transactions. It is possible that the problem of coin refusal had flared up in Charles's kingdom because of the added pressure that viking tribute payments put on peasants and lords to come up with good coin, and because of the variable quality of the coinage at this point. Crucially, though, this was not empty rhetoric. People did refuse coin, and the problem was taken seriously.[305] The king's instructions and the *missi*'s actions reflect a social problem and a symbolic challenge, as well as a threat to the economic status quo.

Conclusion

In Ælfric Bata's imaginary conversation from the dawn of the eleventh century, two monks eventually strike a deal. But before agreeing on the amount to be paid, they needed to establish what means of payment would be used, and the buyer reeled off a daunting list of thirteen possible ways

300. On *missi* under Charles, see Nelson 1992, 52–54.

301. Coupland 1991.

302. "Aetatem, et infirmitatem et sexum . . . quia et feminae barcaniare solent." *Constitutio Carisiacensis de moneta* (Boretius and Krause 1887, 302).

303. McComb 2018, 176–78; Nelson 2004, 6–7.

304. E.g., Davis 2011, 4.

305. For further discussion of the refusal of good coin see Suchodolski 1983 and Coupland 2017, who interpret the phenomenon in terms of coin reforms and forgery, respectively.

of settling the transaction, ranging from gold and silver to beans, clothing, and goats. The seller chooses, however, to keep things simple: "Nothing would suit me more than for you to give me coins, for he who has coins or silver can get everything he wants."[306] Using coin offered versatility on several levels. It could measure anything and everything, equating them with a common standard of worth. At the same time, money could be used in any kind of situation where value had to be transferred. The previous two chapters have outlined some of those situations and how coin worked in them in the early Middle Ages.

Treating some of the most important and visible uses separately should in no way imply that these formed hermetically sealed spheres of exchange. One of the great virtues of coined money was its capacity to cycle through a series of users and contexts. A silver penny could theoretically start a day by being paid as rent into the purse of a lord's *praepositus*, then be given away in alms to a church, and then spent in a market on food or clothing by a needy pauper. These transactions could begin in the countryside, go into a town or market, and then out again in quick succession. Exactly this kind of interconnection was presupposed in a will from early ninth-century Canterbury, in which a wealthy priest left rich possessions to the church on condition that they fund annual distributions of alms to the poor; this was to include 26d per year for a specified number of *pauperes* so they could buy clothes, and 1d for 1,200 other *pauperes* to buy food.[307] Crossover between uses was normal, indeed expected. The balance undoubtedly varied. Details are considered elsewhere, but on the whole the smaller and higher the value of the circulating coinage, the more likely it was to be weighted toward gifts, tributes, and fines, with a smaller share changing hands commercially. Conversely, a large coinage of less prohibitive value could have facilitated a much larger commercial element of circulation, underpinning and mingling with other uses.

At the risk of stating the obvious, it is important to close by stressing that coins did not appear, or move, on their own. They reflect the actions of people, and even when those people are silent and faceless droppers of single finds or buriers of hoards, they need to be viewed as part of a social world of money that emerges from contemporary texts; a world marked by deep contradictions. Coins typified the legitimate, discrete exchange of value: in the moment, they even represented a kind of equality based

306. "Nihil est mihi karius, quam ut des mihi denarios, quoniam qui denarios uel argentum habet, omnia quæ sibi placent, ualet adipiscere." Ælfric Bata, *Colloquia* 24 (ed. and trans. Gwara and Porter 1997, 134–35).

307. S 1414 (Brooks and Kelly 2013, no. 64).

on shared ideas of worth. This was one reason why they were used in such a wide range of settings, without apparent fear of conceptual cross-contamination. Yet at the same time, access to those coins and what they could do was profoundly uneven, and the decision as to how many should be handed over—the setting of prices in a market, or deciding whether and how much rent or toll should be paid—would likewise have very often been skewed by differentials in status and clout. While use of coined money may have been widespread, it also tended to follow and exacerbate hierarchical imbalances.

CHAPTER FIVE

Money, Metal, and Commodities

FOR HUNDREDS OF YEARS, congregants arriving at the church of Forsa in Hälsingland, about 300 km north of Stockholm, would have been presented with an imposing sight: an iron ring densely carved with runes, which hung on the inner door (figure 5.1). Long thought to date from the twelfth century, it is now recognized as a rare example of a Viking-Age "oath ring" on which people would swear binding promises. This ring carries a long inscription, which opens by demanding "one ox and two *aura*" as a fine for the restoration of a *vi* or pre-Christian cult site. *Aura* here is a term more often encountered as *aurar* or *ørar* (sing. *eyrir*), a unit of weight derived from the Latin *aureus* and applied initially to gold and subsequently to silver as well.[1] Who actually took the fine and what they did with it is not clear; the penalties (which escalated for repeat offenders) are framed simply as the prerogative of "the people" (*liuðr*) in accordance with "the people's right" (*liuðritt*).[2]

The Forsa ring stems from a society in which payment with precious metal was already standard, but so too was payment in cattle. Either could also mean goods to the value of an ox or two *ørar* of silver, though that

1. Skre 2017a, 284–87; 2017b, 295; Kilger 2008b, 280–83; Engeler 1991, 128. The actual weight of this unit is more debatable: it was probably around 26 g, with a significant degree of local variation. There is a veritable forest of literature on this topic, with the most important recent contributions being Pedersen 2008, 140–48; Kilger 2008b, 280–98; Williams 2020, 31–33; Kershaw 2019c; and Horne 2022, 181–84.

2. The text and translation here follow Brink 2008, 28–29. Brink 1996 made the case for the ring being a product of the ninth century (and possibly originally mounted on the door of another nearby church at Hög). There is extensive further discussion of the ring; for a recent analysis with reference to the earlier literature, see Sundqvist 2016, 377–86.

FIGURE 5.1. The Forsa ring, with detail of inscription. Sven Rosborn, Wikipedia Commons.

is not said explicitly, and in any case the point is that in ninth-century northern Sweden a mix of bullion and agricultural commodities provided a basis for measuring value. There are no coins mentioned at all.

After considering coined money directly in previous chapters, here the focus will be on arrangements like that of the Forsa ring: bullion and commodities alongside or instead of coins. These should not, however, be seen as mutually exclusive: even societies that had well-developed coinage systems saw extensive overlap of coin, bullion, and commodity, while others had only bullion and commodities, or commodities alone. Each system had its strengths, and it is better to emphasise how the three interfaced and benefited different groups than to arrange them in a hierarchy of sophistication.

Coinage, on the one hand, reflected developed, often overbearing, control from above that tended to work in favour of states and elites; on the other hand, it was comparatively quick, straightforward, and versatile in actual use. Bullion is in some respects like a coinage system without minting, and hence with much more limited "primary" uses; instead, everyone was a secondary user, operating in a system that was socially and functionally fluid. At the same time, bullion was more cumbersome to use than coin, and many kinds of commodity even more so, since while coins and bullion could be traded with confidence over long distances, that was both less practical and less predictable with many other goods. For these reasons, direct exchange of commodities (especially agricultural products) made most sense on a local basis.

Different kinds of money and means of exchange reflected and accentuated the structural inequalities of early medieval society. The interplay between them will be assessed more generally in the first part of this chapter, after which three case studies will be presented. These are intended to explore aspects of the monetary landscape beyond coin, especially with regard to the social contexts of transacting. The first of these is northern Spain in the ninth to eleventh centuries, where coin and bullion were sparse but commodity exchange supported a vibrant peasant land market. The second is Viking-Age Scandinavia and its cultural offshoots, which constitutes the quintessential bullion economy of the early Middle Ages, with the added interest of a different social dynamic from contemporary western Europe. The third is intended as a check on the supposed hierarchical, evolutionary spin that is often put on the categories of money, bullion, and commodity money, and provides an alternative take on the nexus between state power and commercial circulation: Tang and (Northern) Song China, where there was extensive coinage but also widespread use of silver and silk as quasi-monetary commodities, all within an empire of formidable size and sophistication.

Money and Means of Exchange

In approaching the relationship between coin, bullion and commodities, it is helpful to keep a flexible definition of money. Even if it is named and denominated after so much of a given commodity—a pound or *eyrir* of silver, a cow of a particular age, or whatever—money is fundamentally a promise to pay, a unit for measuring value, leading to the pithy formulation of Alfred Mitchell Innes: "The eye has never seen, nor the hand touched a dollar. All that we can touch or see is a promise to pay or satisfy a debt due for an amount called a dollar."[3] By this token money can be anything. Crucially, though, Innes and others working in a modern

3. Innes 1914, 155. This approach has retained purchase over the years: Ingham 2004, 70, also identifies money's role as a unit of account as its most basic defining characteristic from which assignment to commodities followed.

tradition assumed that it should be *one* thing, and also that it should become *detached* from specific commodities, with the special exception (until the 1970s) of gold and silver. Neither of these assumptions applied in the early Middle Ages.[4] There were often multiple kinds of money in circulation, many of them commodities that had a use value, or a symbolic or display value, in addition to their exchange value. In some cases, these all might be subsumed into a single unit of account such as a pound or solidus of precious metal, or a *modius* of wheat (in Spain),[5] or an enslaved woman (in Ireland),[6] or cow (also in Ireland and Spain, together with Wales and other locations).[7] The assumption must be that at some stage such items were widespread and valued enough to command consensus as a unit of account, with ramifications for the significance of raiding and/or trading in these goods, and for social structures that depended on them.[8] These implications are difficult to grasp, however, because the relevant sources often appear only when these systems of account are long ossified, and no longer refer to actual cattle or slaves.[9] This is a critical preliminary: money lived in the mind, not in the hand or in the purse. It measured obligation or, as David Graeber and others have eloquently emphasized, debt: means of exchange are, in this view, essentially a mass of endlessly circulating IOUs that people accept because they believe that others will take them on the same terms.[10] Measuring value, as what Ludolf Kuchenbuch has called a "nominal denominator" (*nominaler Nenner*), was central to the concept and practice of money;[11] everything else followed from that.

One might argue that this definition is so broad as to be useless—that money that can be everything is not really anything at all.[12] But early medieval societies in fact stand as a robust and enduring example of what Koenraad Verboven called structural monetisation.[13] Monetary units were above all tools to think and calculate with. Alcuin of York (d. 804) wrote a riddle for students that involved complicated monetary calculations:

4. Skre 2011a, 69–70. See also Skre 2017b, esp. 292–94.

5. Portass 2017, 169–70. For grain used as a unit of account in Ireland, see Kelly 1997, 588–89.

6. Jarrett 2014; Kelly 1997, 591–92; Charles-Edwards 1993, 478–82.

7. Breatnach 2014; Naismith 2017b, 371.

8. Graeber 2011, 171–75, on Ireland.

9. Breatnach 2014; McCormick 2008.

10. Graeber 2011. For other work that emphasises the nature of money as a social agreement of debt, see Innes 1914; Simiand 1934; Bell and Henry 2001; Henry 2004; Parsons 2014, 5.

11. Kuchenbuch 2019, 56–57.

12. Einaudi 2006, 159.

13. Verboven 2009, 95; cf. Murray 1978, 31–32.

how an imaginary man was to go about building a house with only 25d to spend on the wages of craftsmen and their apprentices. The riddle can be solved only by breaking the denarii into smaller parts that never existed as coins, meaning that Alcuin expected his students to *think* in denarii but not always actually *use* physical ones.[14] This is of course a highly contrived problem, though it is clear that in many real situations people exercised a similar degree of latitude in their understanding of money: laws of Alfred the Great call for compensation to the tune of a third of a penny, which never existed as a coin.[15] By this definition, early medieval societies were as monetized as contemporary imaginations permitted.

A slippery issue of terminology is that money and monetary are frequently used to refer both to the use of units of account and to the means of exchange (usually coins) that were used to pay them. These must be kept distinct. Indeed, coins did not always match up exactly with corresponding units of value or weight. It is not always apparent which was meant, and to have all three correspond exactly, as they did in the Carolingian world after 793, represented a powerful regulatory measure; the creation of a *civilisation monétaire*, in the words of Jean-Pierre Devroey.[16] But coins were far from the whole story. Means of exchange (and also storage of wealth) in premodern societies, including early medieval Europe, have traditionally been grouped into coined money, bullion, and commodities. The last of these covers several distinct things. It includes direct exchange of commodities (barter: wheat for a cow), plus exchange of goods rated using a common scheme of valuation (a cow worth five pence for wheat worth five pence), and also commodity money, defined as a good that starts being used as a benchmark to measure the worth of other things (a cow worth five sheep for wheat worth five sheep); this might be considered a commodity while it retains a clear use-value (as a sheep would do) but closer to coined money when its value consists only in its scarcity and desirability, and hence its exchange-value.[17]

For a long time these three categories were conceived of as a hierarchy, on the premise that coinage is inherently more sophisticated than others. *Naturalwirtschaft* and *Geldwirtschaft*, the latter predicated on the introduction of controlled and standardized money, formed the first two stages

14. Alcuin, *Propositiones ad acuendos iuvenes* 37 (Butzer and Lohrmann 1993, 343–44; trans. Hadley and Singmaster 1992, 119). The text and its importance are highlighted in Kuchenbuch 2016, 40–45.

15. Laws of Alfred, c. 47 (ed. and trans. Jurasinski and Oliver 2021, 350–51).

16. Devroey 2015, 204.

17. Simmel 1978, esp. 79–90, 122–30; Akin and Robbins 1999, esp. 4–5.

of a tripartite evolutionary scheme in the nineteenth century, ending in credit.[18] Although the specifics of this theory are now long abandoned, there remains a tendency to think of monetary economies as a different world from those based on bullion or (especially) commodity exchange. In the 1950s Joachim Werner drew a line between a *Feinwaagenlandschaft* and a *Monetarlandschaft* (balance region and monetary region) within the Merovingian kingdom.[19] Couched in more neutral terms yet still inheriting an implied east-west, barbarian-Roman dichotomy, Werner's approach had a strong influence on subsequent work, even if, again, the model itself has largely fallen by the wayside.[20]

The rules of the game have shifted significantly since then. Coins, notes, and other manifestations of formal currency no longer enjoy a position of unquestioned supremacy. Decentralised currency and commodity money have made a resurgence in the twenty-first century, leading to productive re-evaluation of what makes particular kinds of money effective.[21] It is more rewarding now to ask how and why various kinds of money entered use, and with what effects for different groups in society.[22] The institution of a currency (coined or otherwise) was an act of control and benefited those with most control over and access to that currency, meaning elites in this period,[23] while in a society with limited stratification and economic complexity, commodity exchange—potentially without monetary standards as such—could work effectively.[24]

Coin and Bullion: Categories or Continuum?

The Roman period was marked by a disjuncture between the supposedly ordered, monetized world within the *limes* of the empire and the primitive one that lay beyond.[25] This was not strictly a barrier, for the barbarian world depended on Rome for coin and bullion: the quantity of these

18. Formulated in starkest terms by Hildebrand 1864, more subtly and with more emphasis on the distance between production and consumption in Bücher 1901, 86–89 (first published in German in 1893). Major later contributions include Dopsch 1930, and a powerful critique is Bloch 1967, 230–43. See also Postan 1973, 1.

19. Werner 1954, esp. 17–20. See also Werner 1961.

20. For difficulties with this division, see Nicolay 2014, 267–68.

21. Maurer 2015; Maurer, Nelms, and Swartz 2013; Fitzpatrick and McKeon 2020.

22. Akin and Robbins 1999, 2–10. Kershaw 2017 does this effectively for viking-settled England.

23. See chapters 3 and 4.

24. Skre 2011a, 77–80. See also Lie 1992 for broader discussion of the impact of differing levels of complexity and stratification.

25. Kemmers 2019, 59–63; Williams 2013b, 381.

that crossed the frontier was considerable, representing a mix of the spoils of military campaigns, formal tribute payments, and the pay packets of soldiers from *barbaricum* who served with the Roman army.[26] These diverse possibilities, combined with regional tastes and varied hoarding and mortuary practices, mean that there are big differences in what forms of Roman gold and silver crossed the frontier, and how they were handled once they had. Hacksilver as well as coin (see figure 5.2) passed into northern Britain, Germany, and southern Scandinavia,[27] while Scandinavia was rich in solidi during the fifth and sixth centuries that suggest a fairly direct link with Italy.[28]

On the face of it, the circulation of gold and silver in central and northern Europe seems like a wholly different world from the empire itself. And in many respects the Roman frontier was a genuine watershed. Roman authorities mandated acceptance of coin as a means of payment, while beyond the frontier gold and silver coins circulated on a less firm basis, alongside ingots, hack-metal, and ring-money.[29] Weight and fineness hence came under close scrutiny: gold coins in England, northern Germany, and the Netherlands in the sixth and seventh centuries were sometimes cut or even added to, with extra pieces of gold soldered on to bring them up in weight.[30] Acceptable coins moved within a world of gift-giving and ritual exchange; not quite, perhaps, at the top of the hierarchy of treasure, but still within an elevated context.[31] This left less of a niche for base-metal coinage, which did not circulate extensively outside the empire.[32]

It is possible to overplay the distinction between use of coin in and outside the empire. Rather, they both sat at different points along a continuum of money- and bullion-based practices. Gold pieces pierced or looped for ornamental purposes outside or on the fringe of the former empire, most plausibly within the framework of socially driven interactions, sometimes had their holes plugged and mounts removed, apparently in order to

26. Randsborg 1998 and Fischer and López Sánchez 2016 provide good surveys.

27. Painter 2013; Voß 2013; Dyhrfjeld-Johnsen 2013; Rau 2013.

28. Fagerlie 1967; Metcalf 1995; Nicolay 2014, 212–14; Fischer 2019; Fischer and Wood 2020.

29. Williams 2013a, 127–28; Nicolay 2014, 294; Marsden and Pol 2020, 400.

30. Nicolay 2014, 153, 159–60, 303–4. For English examples of Merovingian gold tremisses with extra pieces attached, see Marsden and Pol 2020, 401–2; cut tremisses include EMC 1990.1291, 2011.0059.

31. Skre 2017a, esp. 288–92; Nicolay 2014, 264–94 (though Nicolay does, on 266, allow for a degree of horizontal exchange based on quasi-commercial interaction between holders of precious metal).

32. Base-metal did circulate beyond the frontier, though on a limited basis in an exchange context: Horsnæs 2006.

FIGURE 14.2. The Traprain Law hoard: an assemblage of late Roman silverware, most of it fragmented, found in East Lothian

bring them back into circulation.[33] Within the former empire, coins were sometimes hoarded alongside gold bullion.[34] Gold and silver also changed hands on a ceremonial, gift-giving basis within the empire, and a large part of soldiers' pay was framed as a gift (*donativum*) of the emperor.[35] Coin and bullion overlapped significantly. The gold solidus and its fractions were always thought of as sanctioned pieces of bullion, quite literally worth their weight in gold. The entire late Roman gold currency was thus in a sense a bullion economy.[36] Silver plate, with individual pieces rated by weight, had become a well-established expression of elite status by the late Roman period.[37] In the western part of the empire especially, there was a custom of cutting up such objects into pieces of carefully defined weight.[38] Silver had traditionally been treated as a more valuable version of base metal, in a fluid relationship with gold. But for a time in the late fourth century this relationship became fixed, meaning that silver started to be treated more like gold (probably to help supplement supplies of gold). The result was a surge in minting of silver coins and also in treating silver objects as stores of wealth.[39]

Precious-metal coin and bullion were complementary, intertwined categories in the Roman Empire, and would continue to be so in the early Middle Ages. Handling of gold and silver by weight in exchange or savings contexts was commonplace in regions that also had gold or silver coinage. Bede described King Oswald of Northumbria (634–42) ordering a large silver plate to be cut up and distributed in small pieces to a mass of destitute petitioners who crowded outside his hall.[40] Around the year 1000 an aristocratic Englishwoman named Æthelgifu asked in her will that twenty-five mancuses of gold (c. 106 g) should be cut from her headband and shared out among five recipients.[41] The annals of Saint-Bertin tell of Emperor Lothar's (d. 855) men cutting up and sharing out one of several silver tables formerly owned by Charlemagne in 842.[42] In Rome,

33. Nicolay 2014, 266.

34. For hoards in Spain combining coins and other objects, see Pliego Vázquez 2009, 1:249–50

35. See chapter 6.

36. Carlà 2009, 131–57.

37. Baratte 2013. For close study of a major find from Britain, see Johns 2010.

38. Painter 2013, 215–17.

39. Carlà-Uhink 2020.

40. Bede, *Historia ecclesiastica gentis Anglorum* 3.6 (ed. and trans. Colgrave and Mynors 1969, 230–31).

41. S 1497 (ed. and trans. Crick 2007, no. 7).

42. *Annals of Saint-Bertin* s.a. 842 (Waitz 1883, 27; trans. Nelson 1991, 53).

the pages of the *Liber pontificalis* positively glitter with gold and silver: lavish donations of precious metal, rated by weight, are recorded for virtually every pope.[43] Hoards also display a relationship between coins and objects. About 10 per cent of English hoards deposited c. 800–1100 contain gold or silver objects in addition to coins,[44] as do a similar proportion of hoards containing Carolingian coins deposited between 751 and about 1000.[45] Typically these are whole objects of fairly modest scale: a small silver cross from the Gravesend (Kent) hoard of the 870s,[46] and a single silver earring in a mid-ninth-century hoard from Kimswerd-Pingjum in the Netherlands.[47] Some, however, are richer, and in terms of weight and value the coins are matched or surpassed by the objects, as with the Sutton (Cambridgeshire) hoard of about 1070, where around a hundred coins were found with five gold rings and a large silver brooch,[48] or the Ilanz hoard from Switzerland, which contained 138 coins along with five gold ear-pendants, two gold earrings, two fragments of gold jewellery, and two small ingots or droplets of gold.[49] Ilanz is unusual in containing broken-up fragments of objects: although written sources describe the breaking up of gold and silver items for redistributive purposes, the resultant hacksilver or hackgold was normally irregular and probably not intended to remain in that state for long. Such items were probably meant to be melted down for coin or other objects; this was precisely why several letters and miracle stories from eleventh-century Germany revolved around intercepting thieves of church ornaments before they could whisk them off to moneyers.[50] The anxiety was that, once minted, it would be impossible to track down and recover the lost gold and silver.

What one sees on the ground did not always conform to ideal types of coin, bullion, or commodity. Elements of all three could combine and recombine depending on local circumstances. Enclaves of coin-based exchange could emerge in the midst of areas that were otherwise not

43. Delogu 1988.

44. Some 21 of 178 finds listed on https://www.fitzmuseum.cam.ac.uk/dept/coins /projects/hoards/index.list.html (though this excludes a number of very recent hoards). The total also excludes those usually identified as from a viking context, which have a higher proportion with objects.

45. Coupland 2011 and 2014d (22 hoards out of 261 include gold and silver objects, excluding hoards from outside the empire or recognized as being of viking context).

46. Wilson 1964, 134–25.

47. Coupland 2011, no. 88; Haertle 1997, no. 44.

48. *Checklist* 276.

49. Sarah 2020; Geiger 1986, esp. 402–4.

50. See chapter 3.

generally inclined to accord coins any special treatment over other kinds of bullion. It was more feasible to force a movement from bullion to coin, or (theoretically) vice versa, because the requisite precious metal was already available and familiar. Yorkshire, for example, had a complex series of interlocking monetary spheres during viking rule in the late ninth and early tenth centuries. Coin minted at York is prevalent among finds within the city so could have been required for transactions there, or for payments of fines, tolls, and other sums to the king. The urban population, who had more cause to enter into frequent, small purchases, perhaps also accorded them preference. Conversely, bullion suited larger payments and perhaps was favoured among Scandinavian settlers, explaining why its circulation was stronger in rural areas of Yorkshire. Takeover of this region by the English king Æthelstan in 927 had a swift effect, indicating a concerted effort to orient the local economy toward the king's own coins. Hoards stopped containing bullion or foreign coin soon after 927, while single finds of dirhams petered out in the 930s.[51] Adjusting an economy based on the exchange of other commodities presented more of a challenge. Even Charlemagne could not will a coin-based economy into being in Saxony as part of its conquest by the Franks in the years 772–804. Silver-based units current in Francia were imposed, but capitularies for the region suggest that payments were actually settled in commodities such as cattle, grain, and honey.[52] The Saxons may now have had to think in coin, like their counterparts to the west, but there is precious little signal that they used them on any significant scale. Finds of coin or other items of precious metal in Saxony from this time are few and far between,[53] and coined money would not become widespread until the tenth century.[54]

Scandinavia and Saxony both lay beyond the Roman frontier, which laid the basis for the boundary between *Monetarlandschaft* and *Feinwaagenlandschaft* or *Gewichtsgeldwirtschaft*.[55] In some areas that boundary shifted over time or was fuzzy to begin with. Southern Britain, unusually, fell out of the Roman monetary system in the early fifth century. Initially a coin-based economy of sorts persisted, as local authorities instituted

51. Williams 2009, 81; Kershaw 2020, esp. 126–27.

52. *Capitulare Saxonicum*, c. 11 (von Schwerin 1918, 49). For discussion, see Landon 2020, 47.

53. Steuer 2003, 163–64.

54. Ehlers 2007, 141–45.

55. For the latter term, see Steuer 1984—one of the first major studies of the bullion economy as such.

large-scale clipping of the many silver coins still available in Britain.[56] But by about the middle of the fifth century this had given way to treatment of silver as bullion.[57] The western part of former Roman Britain may have subsequently moved over to commodity-based exchange; certainly Gildas, writing probably in the early sixth century, thought of coinage as an unwelcome Roman imposition.[58] Eastern Britain, meanwhile, is more equivocal. Find evidence of hack-gold and -silver of the fifth to seventh centuries remains limited,[59] while imported and (later) English-made gold coins tended not to be cut into fragments but were sometimes adjusted in weight by having extra pieces of gold attached.[60] Sets of weights and scales of the period also suggest that whole gold coins served an important role as weight units.[61] Gareth Williams's persuasive interpretation of this complicated material is that there was "a bullion economy in which tremisses/*scillingas* . . . acted as the standard measures of weight and account, as well as the most widespread medium of currency within this bullion economy";[62] in other words, a bullion economy shaped in large part around coins drawn from or based on the currency of more coin-oriented neighbouring economies, even though many of those coins were of variable metallic quality.[63]

A coin economy with elements of bullion was far from unique. In the Muslim Caliphate, gold and silver coins had always been thought of with reference to weight, although at first close control of production meant that the weight was apparently taken as read and the coins effectively circulated by tale.[64] From the mid-ninth century this was no longer the case: precious-metal coins started to deviate from their supposed standard, and so the weight of coins became a more direct concern.[65] The Geniza letters show that those who used dinars maintained a clear distinction between the number of actual coins a given purse contained and the number of dinars they weighed, with the latter always being the meaningful variable.

56. Naismith 2017b, 31–34; Abdy 2006, 84–88; Guest 2005, 110–15; King 1981.

57. Highlighted by the recent hoard from Wem, Shropshire: White 2020.

58. Gildas, *De excidio et conquestu Britanniae*, c. 7 (ed. and trans. Winterbottom 1978, 19, 91).

59. Hines 2010, 162.

60. Williams 2014b, 41–42.

61. Scull 1990, esp. 205–8.

62. Williams 2014b, 42.

63. An issue addressed in chapter 7.

64. Bessard 2020, 183–84.

65. Ilisch 1990, 122; Jankowiak 2019, 16–19. In Ilisch's sample, the earliest hoard with a small proportion of fragments was buried in or after AD 840/41.

An eleventh-century merchant wrote from Tunisia to Egypt with details of six purses of gold pieces, giving both the number and weight of dinars in each: one weighed 300 but contained 308¼, while another weighed 300 but contained 300¾. Silver dirhams were apparently always referred to by weight.[66] Because coins were now treated essentially as sanctioned pieces of bullion that needed to be weighed again and again, there was no impediment to cutting them up.[67] Dirhams in particular might be subdivided into a huge number of small fragments. Fragmentation of silver coins has been interpreted as a response to the end of low-value copper-alloy currency; that is, as an attempt to produce low-value coinage.[68] This new form of currency was in high demand: hoards containing fragments have been recorded in many parts of the Islamic world, from al-Andalus to Iraq and Oman,[69] and a Baghdadi jurist at the beginning of the twelfth century sought to ban the sale of whole dirhams for fragments or vice versa, on the grounds that it was illicit to make a profit by selling like for like, which was essentially what this practice represented.[70] Superficially the cutting up of coins resembles a bullion economy, and as in the Viking-Age North whole and fragmented coins regularly occur side by side in hoards.[71] But for several reasons Islamic fragments should be understood as an extension of a firmly coin-based system. They were probably made for local use and not exported from the Islamic world in fragmented form: the fragmentary dirhams found in eastern Europe and the Baltic were cut up after their departure.[72] And while hoards of whole and fragmentary objects together with coins do occur from the Muslim world, they are a minority: most finds with fragmentary gold or silver coins contain no bullion.[73]

Unlikely bedfellows though they may appear, southern Britain in the fifth to seventh centuries and the Muslim world from the mid-ninth both underscore the metallic, material element within a precious-metal coin economy. But where a transaction took place was not the only factor in play. Different kinds of bullion, coin, and commodity economy could coexist, as layers superimposed on top of each other. The choice of whether to use one or the other depended on who was involved, or what kind of exchange

66. Goitein 1967–93, 1:230–35, with the letter quoted on 231–32.

67. Canto and Marsal Moyano 1988, 445–48; Heidemann 2002, 365–69; Doménech Belda 2003, 130–35.

68. Heidemann 2018, 185.

69. Ilisch 1990; García Ruiz and Ruiz Quintanar 1996; Kool et al. 2011; Heidemann 2018.

70. Heidemann 2002, 367.

71. Retamero 2006, 315–16.

72. Gruszczyński 2019, 205–11; Jankowiak 2019, 19.

73. Doménech Belda 2013, 17–18, describing examples from al-Andalus.

was taking place. Often they would intertwine, particularly when making socially loaded exchanges such as gifts, dowries, land purchases, and bequests. They corresponded to different levels of trust, power, and privacy.

The Social Dynamics of Mixed Moneys

A ruler lavishing gold pieces on preferred religious institutions lay a world away from merchants, peasants, or minor landholders measuring one another up in rural and urban communities. Coin and bullion may have worked side by side for these groups on a microregional basis, as we have seen in early tenth-century Yorkshire. Each kind of money had its own logic, both having a performative element to their use yet suited to largely separate occasions and audiences.[74] Mixed hoards and assemblages point in the same direction, to an interlocking menu of money-stuffs. The pattern in Viking-Age Ireland is similar, with mixed and coin hoards clustered in the orbit of Dublin,[75] as is that of the Isle of Man in the tenth and eleventh centuries, where many routes and traditions intersected and hoards including whole objects and ingots or hacksilver as well as coins could be likened to a wallet containing coins, notes, and credit cards.[76] Furthermore, not all pieces of bullion and coins carried the same symbolic weight. Users selected their means of exchange to satisfy social and ritual as well as economic demands. Whole, uncut objects probably carried an added display element, making them suitable for the most prestigious kinds of transaction, such as gifts that signified close and important relationships. Whole objects made of precious metal had a dual identity, the two elements of which reinforced each other: their completeness, when put on display in a society accustomed to fragmentation, signified an established place in the social order; and as so much bullion, sometimes made to conform with units of weight, refined to high purity and always with the potential to be broken up for use in a multiplicity of exchanges,[77]

74. For a modern parallel, see Kuroda 2007.

75. Sheehan 1991, 44, for a map that makes the point very effectively and has been reprinted many times since.

76. Bornholdt-Collins, Fox, and Graham-Campbell 2014.

77. Hårdh 1996, esp. 137; Merkel 2016, 44–45; Sheehan 2019, 110. It should be stressed that weight-adjusted objects do not necessarily fit into a single precise metrological system; the units they follow are variable and particular to individual workshops or regions (cf. the different units identified in Graham-Campbell 2006, 76–77; Kilger 2008b, esp. 286–88; Hårdh 2008, 111–13). Fine jewellery was more often refined than plain ingots or rings: Söderberg 2011.

which signalled the power to engage in future transactions on one's own terms.[78] Bestowing a complete, worked object hence meant something special: rings or brooches may well have been made primarily with a donative purpose in mind. Exchanges involving them are likely to have taken place close, socially and often chronologically, to the point of manufacture. Conversely, whatever aura and personal associations attached to an object are less likely to have survived or mattered as they got further removed from the point of origin, especially if they were cut up. Ingots and hackmetal would have been appropriate for a range of participants, including those of more passing or distant acquaintance.

If the value-added gift of a whole and worked object reflected Marshal Sahlins's "general reciprocity" and conveyed an expectation of ongoing tangible and intangible remuneration, handling exchange with circulated bullion lay closer to his "balanced reciprocity," meaning that relations may well have started and ended in the context of a single exchange.[79] Both, however, entailed closer and more fluid interpersonal interactions than would be necessary in a coin-based economy. Coins *might* be challenged for their weight, fineness, or some other quality but normally were not, and hence a transaction could conclude very rapidly. Trust was placed in the authority behind the coin rather than the individual piece. The problem was that, at least in this period, coins were available only in a few set denominations of high value. Intermediate amounts or small sums could not be handled effectively. Bullion, in contrast, had the advantage of pecuniary versatility, in that pieces could be cut to suit any need. But it also had the distinct disadvantage of transactional inflexibility: to cut a piece of the right size involved a degree of guesswork, and most exchanges would require the metal to be weighed, and potentially tested for purity. To dispense with those checks was to introduce an element of trust, or give rein to intimidation.[80] One might skip weighing and testing with a trusted friend; equally, one would be well advised to avoid demanding that the silver given by a person in a position of power be weighed and tested.

This was the crux of a story in the Kings' Sagas about an outspoken Icelander who challenged the quality of silver in the coins given to him by King Haraldr Harðráði of Norway (1046–66). The point was that the cowed Norwegians refused to do so.[81] If testing and weighing did go

78. Akin and Robbins 1999, 28–29; cf. Graeber 1996.

79. Sahlins 1972, esp. 174–78.

80. Pace Jarman 2021, 61.

81. Finnur Jónsson 1932, 149–52; trans. Skaare 1976, 9–11. The text, preserved in the thirteenth-century manuscript Morkinskinna (Copenhagen, Royal Danish Library, GKS

ahead, they made exchanges slow and cumbersome, requiring close, pro-longed interaction.[82] Each party weighed up the other as well as their sil-ver as the process went along: transacting with bullion might therefore have had elements closer to a poker game than a cash payment. Another of the Kings' Sagas, that of Olaf Haraldsson (1015–28), describes just such a scene in the Faeroes, where—after several attempts—the king had finally managed to send a tribute-gatherer from Norway. Þrándr, a lead-ing local man, handed over a purse of silver that was poured out onto an upturned shield in the brightest-lit part of a tent at the islands' meeting place, meaning in a public setting surrounded by observers. These details were all power plays designed to show that the tax gatherer did not trust Þrándr. And indeed the king's man and his companion found Þrándr's silver (and a second purse) wanting and did not even get to the point of weighing. Þrándr almost resorted to violence after his embarrassment was ridiculed; the situation was resolved only when he paid with a third purse of silver gathered from his own tenants.[83] In other words, the silver he had got from his own men was better, while the islanders at further social remove from Þrándr tried to fob him and the king off with substandard silver (which Þrándr had evidently not checked himself). Testing silver (Who checks? Where, when?) and weighing it (Whose weights and scales are used, or whose first?) all introduced a human element; the more so in the bullion-oriented viking sphere, for (as Svein Gullbekk has observed) "issues related to quality and trust . . . were first and foremost present in societies without a stable monetary regime."[84] Archaeological finds from Kaupang suggest testing and weighing could penetrate right down into intimate domestic settings and were not confined to a spatially distinct domain.[85] In this climate, weighing and testing might represent a perfor-mative act, the equivalent, perhaps, of a handshake or signature, or less convivially of counting and checking notes to discomfit the other party.[86]

Users of coins *could* dispense with the niceties of checking and evaluat-ing means of exchange (and, by extension, the person who offered them),

1009 fol.), belongs to a later period, though the debased state of the coinage more accu-rately reflects the situation of the eleventh century than the thirteenth.

82. Munro 2012, 317–18.

83. *Óláfs saga ins helga*, c. 143 (Bjarni Aðalbjarnarson 1941–51, 2:264–65; trans. Finlay and Faulkes 2011–15, 2:177–79). For discussion, see Gullbekk 2019, esp. 167–71. Again, the conditions implied by this story better reflect the situation of the eleventh century than the thirteenth, by which point testing and weighing coins or silver was unusual.

84. Gullbekk 2019, 171.

85. Pedersen 2008, 155–66.

86. Kilger 2006, 464–65; Archibald 2011, 56. Cf. Duczko 2002.

but that is not to say they always did. The potential to refuse good coin presented a possible strategy for the disadvantaged to reclaim a small degree of agency in the marketplace, on the basis that critique of coins perhaps offered a veil for critique of the transaction.[87] Different kinds of coin, restricted to particular people or contexts, represent what Karl Polanyi defined as "special-purpose money" and had the potential to splinter a coin-based economy into distinct and unequal segments.[88] Extensive use of highly debased Northumbrian pennies alongside silver at the viking military sites of Aldwark and Torksey in the 870s, for example, is best explained either as a facet of metalworking or as engagement by the vikings with a local currency that they could use with the nearby population. The second of these is more persuasive, though it surely added an element of inequality to an already imbalanced situation. The Scandinavians in northern England had gold and silver in relative abundance and used them intensely on their campsites. They may well have demanded that tributes or other renders collected from the locals be paid in scarcer, more valuable precious metal, "according to their [i.e., the vikings'] weight," as a Frankish contemporary put it.[89] How much precious metal entered back into local use at this early date is not clear—the suspicion is rather less.[90] But if the vikings used (and possibly even manufactured) debased Northumbrian pennies to transact with locals, they were benefiting from a weaker kind of money. In economic terms the situation was, for a short while, comparable to that of early modern West Africa, with local currencies systemically disadvantaged and destabilized by those who could bring in high-value moneys from elsewhere.[91]

The emphasis so far has fallen on the interplay of various kinds of coin and bullion economies. Commodities used as money have not been as prominent. That is because it is usually impossible to identify material remains of commodity money,[92] and even in textual sources it can be difficult to differentiate goods exchanged as goods from goods that served a quasi-monetary role. Nonetheless, there is no doubt that commodity exchange—sometimes

---

87. See chapters 4 and 8.

88. Polanyi 1957, 264–66.

89. *Annals of Saint-Bertin* s.a. 877 (Waitz 1883, 81; adapted from Nelson 1991, 130).

90. Hadley and Richards 2021, 117–40, identify about thirty sites with material that also occurs at Aldwark and Torksey, though it is less clear whether these all represent places where elements of the great army passed through.

91. Green 2019, esp. 108–48, 262–95.

92. There are possible exceptions. At the end of this period and after, standardization of *vaðmál* (homespun cloth) in Iceland probably reflects a larger and more complex exchange role: Hayeur Smith 2019.

measured in metal-based units, sometimes in commodity-money, some-times not measured in monetary terms at all—was dominant in early medi-eval Europe as a whole. Even in the most highly monetized societies, with relatively copious precious-metal coins or bullion in circulation, it is likely that the large majority of exchanges still involved commodities, especially agricultural products and livestock. It is pointless to attempt to estimate proportions, but figures from the early modern and modern worlds are sobering: in France c. 1800 the money supply relative to GDP was only about 40 per cent, while in rural India in the 1960s only about 60 per cent of trans-actions involved currency.[93] That proportion would of course vacillate and be much higher in cities. As will be seen, though, economies that depended more heavily on commodity exchange were not necessarily primitive and autarchic outposts of *Naturalwirtschaft*.

Case Study 1: Northern Spain

The kingdoms of northern Iberia in the ninth century and much more so the tenth and eleventh centuries are blessed with abundant charters, which shed revealing shafts of light on the operation of local societies across the region. A substantial proportion of these charters are sales, recording the exchange of land for other movables. In the course of the tenth and eleventh centuries, these movables often started to be described with monetary terminology.[94] It has been suggested that these reflect a vibrant circulation of coins, potentially going back to the Visigothic era (in the case of charters that speak of solidi and tremisses, not minted since the early eighth century),[95] but the absence of locally made coinage until well into the eleventh century—save on a small scale in Catalonia—and the extreme scarcity of any coin at all in archaeologi-cal finds have led to a reevaluation of the documents.[96] Their monetary refer-ences are now generally recognized as calling on a system of account that had only a nodding acquaintance with actual coins; mentions of *argentei* or similar are the most likely to denote real silver (probably dirhams from al-Andalus), and context sometimes makes it very likely that actual coins or pieces of silver

93. Figures and sources quoted in Naismith 2012b, 285–86.

94. For the chronology, and the patchiness of monetary units, see Manzano Moreno and Canto García 2020, 176–77.

95. Sánchez-Albornoz 1965, 411–39.

96. Gautier-Dalché 1998; Isla Frez 1991, 2013; Davies 2002; Martin Escudero, Mín-guez, and Canto 2011. For Catalonia, see Crusafont, Balaguer, and Grierson 2012, 29–31, 70–74; Balaguer 1999, 23–39. On eleventh-century developments and coinage, see Cru-safont, Balaguer, and Grierson 2012, 209–25; and for a neat comparison with England, see Molyneaux 2015, 239–41.

are being described, as in one charter of 986 from San Millán that records a ransom payment to the Muslims of "150 solidi *argenti*."[97] Others, however, make it clear that monetary units applied to other, typically agricultural goods: a charter of 941 rated five pregnant cows and four measures of grain as being worth 7 Galician (*gallicani*) solidi.[98] Units remained founded on specific and persistent measures of value, with a significant divergence between the buying power of a solidus in Galicia and Portugal and in lands further east, which probably reflects the prevalence of a notional gold solidus in the former and a notional silver one in the latter.[99] This silver solidus, consisting of eight argentei, was not that of the Carolingian realms but instead modelled on the "dinar of dirhams" in al-Andalus, an accounting dinar that consisted of eight silver pieces.[100] Mentions of specific types indicate that actual dirhams did indeed circulate: one charter of 943 from Portugal describes a payment of forty-five *solidos kazimis*, or *qāsimi* dirhams, minted under the authority of Qāsim b. Khālid in Cordoda between 941 and 944. Dirhams from the Muslim lands of the South constituted the dominant coin in both thought and action farther north.[101]

At the same time, far from all sales refer to solidi, and not all references to solidi necessarily mean coin. In Catalonia sums in solidi were frequently qualified as being "of goods to that value" (*in rem valentem*). For transactors immersed in the rhythms of agrarian life, units like a cow or a *modius* of grain made good sense as a benchmark of value. In 961 an orchard was sold to the abbot of Villanova "for the price of an ox and a cow with her calf, rated at 24 *modii* [of grain]", plus a quantity of linen.[102] This document is one of many showing how Villanova engaged at this time in a campaign of land acquisition, buying up property from peasant proprietors.[103] There is no sign of resistance or wariness on the part of the vendors: lively *compraventa*—back-and-forth buying and selling of small patches of property—was an established part of tenth-century agrarian life, and peasants seem to have sold voluntarily without any indication of encroaching servitude.[104] Transacting in this way served multiple

97. Ubieto Arteta 1976, no. 99, cited in Davies 2002, 161.

98. Loscertales de García de Valeavellano 1976, no. 62, cited in Manzano Moreno and Canto García 2020, 177.

99. Sánchez-Albornoz 1965, 404–7; Manzano Moreno and Canto García 2020, 178–80.

100. Manzano Moreno and Canto García 2020, 178–87.

101. Manzano Moreno and Canto García 2020, 185–87. For the charter, see *PMH*, no. 51.

102. "Precio boue et uacca cum sua agnicula, preciatos in xx et iiii modios." Andrade Cernadas 1995, no. 138.

103. Portass 2017, 153–73.

104. Portass 2017, 77–84.

purposes, creating group solidarity and (if with a monastery or aristocrat) potentially a powerful friend or patron,[105] and it is in some cases questionable whether sales are really sales or rather gifts in disguise; all the same, there is no denying that northern Spain had an active peasant land market.[106] There may well have been utilitarian motives behind what commodities changed hands, based on negotiation between buyers and sellers engaged in mixed agriculture, but other forms of exchange must also have been going on, to explain what participants did with the large quantities of livestock, produce, cloth, and other items that changed hands.[107] In other words, the existence of a land market implies the existence of other kinds of complex exchange, including markets for commodities. "Here," as Wendy Davies has put it, "is an utterly rural economy, but one that does not remotely suggest self-sufficiency: it was equipped with the apparatus for ready exchange, and commercial exchange at that."[108] Coins and bullion featured in this economy only marginally; commodities were the dominant means of exchange and store of wealth.

The Spanish situation is not necessarily representative. Dependence for exchange on what could be grown and herded worked especially well in a society that consisted largely of autonomous peasant smallholders.[109] It empowered those with the capacity to produce, and while there was stratification and some who sought to set themselves above their neighbours in terms of wealth,[110] aristocrats and monasteries were not yet the dominant force in most regions—indeed, the charters occasionally allow their establishment to be followed in real time.[111] But despite the local vigour and complexity of exchange structures in northern Spain, they were relatively small in scale and self-contained. Most of the items that were transferred would have been made within the vicinity and would in turn be kept and consumed there.[112] Coins and silver differed on both these points. They often passed over long distances during the course of their

105. See, inter alia, Wickham 1994, 257–74; Reuter 1995, esp. 175–81; Rosenwein 1989, 47–48, 202–7.

106. Portass 2017, 76. Some scholars (e.g., Feller 2005; Gurevich 1985, 257–58) have queried whether land could ever really have a market value, though the location, productivity, and other qualities of land were certainly considerations (Bougard 2008).

107. Davies 2002, 171–72.

108. Davies 2002, 172.

109. Zeller et al. 2020, 194, 212–13.

110. For the example of Bagaugano and his wife Faquilona, a power couple of tenth-century Cantabria, see Portass 2017, 66–96. For archaeological dimensions of local inequality, see Quirós Castillo 2013; 2020a.

111. Portass 2017, 174–93.

112. For a model that emphasizes this point, see Lie 1992, 512–13.

FIGURE 5.3. This later (fourteenth-century) manuscript of Icelandic law includes a marginal illustration of *vaðmál* being cut to measure (Reykjavík, Stofnun Árna Magnússonar, GKS 3269 b 4to, f. 6v). Arni Magnusson Institute for Icelandic Studies.

lifespan in use, and when they did enter local circulation, it was usually through the agency of monasteries that had good connections with the Mozarab communities in al-Andalus.[113]

Exchange based largely on agrarian goods was hence highly versatile on a local basis because it suited face-to-face communities where the acceptability of grain, cattle, or other commodities rested to a significant degree on trust and familiarity between the parties involved. Mechanisms of this kind would not have been as workable on a long-distance basis, however. The goods involved were simply not distinct enough: crops and livestock would have been much the same wherever one went. It took special configurations of demand for this to be viable, as when a group of peasants in tenth-century Lorraine travelled some 200 km to exchange their produce for salt—a specialised good, whose makers may have depended more on exchange than agriculture.[114] But while agricultural produce was probably the most widespread kind of commodity exchange in peasant communities across Europe, it was not the only kind of commodity money. Indeed, since these consumables had a clear use value, it might be argued that they were not really commodity money at all, in contrast to (for example) the small squares of fabric "which had no practical use" that Ibrāhīm ibn Ya'qūb (fl. 960s) observed circulating in Bohemia in the mid-tenth century.[115] A more borderline case is that of homespun cloth (figure 5.3), the *vaðmál* of Iceland: this served a monetary role and a

113. Manzano Moreno and Canto García 2020, 185–87.
114. Adso of Montier-en-Der, *Vita sancti Mansueti*, c. 24 (Goullet 2003, 159–60).
115. Lunde and Stone 2012, 165.

secondary practical one.[116] Strikingly, both these examples were circumscribed to a particular polity or island and not of wider applicability. Anyone attempting to use these forms of commodity money elsewhere would find themselves laden simply with goods, and not particularly desirable ones in the outside world.

Case-Study 2: The Viking World

Viking-Age Scandinavia and its Baltic neighbours have produced hundreds of finds of silver objects and hackmetal (and a much smaller number of gold ones), as well as of coins that were tested or cut. Over five hundred hoards have been found on the Baltic island of Gotland alone, with more turning up every year.[117] The biggest of these are a pair of contemporaneous hoards found about three metres apart at Spillings farm in 1999 (figure 5.4). Buried sometime in or soon after 870/71 (the latest date of the coins), they together amounted to about 67 kg of silver, which is approximately the weight of a small adult human, in the form of some 14,300 dirhams (the large majority fragmented, unusually for Gotland), 600 whole objects (mostly arm-rings and bracelets), and a large quantity of hacksilver. Exceptionally, a hoard of cut and broken copper-alloy objects was also found nearby, mostly melted together to form a single mass, in total weighing about 20 kg; even more puzzlingly, these bronze items were stored in a locked box, while the silver hoards apparently had no container at all.[118] These three vast assemblages had been buried underneath the same building, which had no hearth and so has been interpreted as a warehouse or store.[119]

The Spillings hoards are a special case because of their size and copper-alloy component, but they reflect the rich tradition of using bullion in exchange and savings contexts in the viking world. These practices can be traced across a huge area, stretching from Iceland and Ireland to Russia.[120] Indeed, many of the same kinds of object can be found across that same swathe of territory: silver dirhams from the Muslim world, which were of course made as coins but were so often cut up that they were evidently thought of as pieces of bullion; certain types of silver object

---

116. Hayeur Smith 2019.

117. Gruszczyński 2019, 25.

118. Details are effectively summarised in Östergren 2011. See also Pettersson 2009.

119. Widerström 2009; Östergren 2011, 325–26.

120. Exemplary case studies of bullion and coin from specific sites include Skre 2007b; Merkel 2016; Kershaw 2017; Hårdh 1996; Sheehan 1998.

FIGURE 5.4. Part of the enormous Spillings hoard, found on Gotland in 1999 and deposited sometime soon after 870/71. W. Carter, Wikipedia Commons.

such as "Permian" rings;[121] and copper-alloy weights, in "cubo-octahedral" and "oblate spheroid" shapes, modelled on those used in Muslim lands but made at several locations in the North as well.[122] Although not all objects in viking hoards are deliberately cut or tested, these features are very common and help to define the particular character of the viking "bullion economy." Viking handling of bullion was marked by routine checking and cutting of objects, and by the continued use of checked and cut objects in an exchange context. The most extreme form of the fragmentation process was reached in tenth-century Poland with what is sometimes referred to as "liquid silver": assemblages of thousands of tiny pieces of silver, weighing as little as 0.1 gram each.[123] Broadly speaking, fragmentation seems to have become more extreme in proportion to the number of transactions an object went through, which did not always correlate with actual distance

121. Hårdh 2007; 2008, 108–13; 2016; Callmer 2015.

122. Pedersen 2008, 121; Gustin 1997; Sperber 1996; Kruse 1992, 80–81; Steuer 1987, 460, 475–77; Balog 1970.

123. Bogucki 2011; Suchodolski 1990, 317–22.

travelled.[124] This could be a drawn-out process or a rapid one: dirhams from the viking winter campsite at Torksey are heavily fragmented, which perhaps implies intense exchange in the context of (effectively) a mobile town well supplied with booty that was active for only a short time (winter 872–73, according to the *Anglo-Saxon Chronicle*).[125] The inference here is that cutting is a plausible proxy for the commercial circulation of silver, and the increasing complexity of that commerce, on the basis that while one could use many pieces of hackmetal to pay a large sum, one had to cut a large piece into many to pay small sums.[126] This must be tempered with recognition that fragmentation could serve other roles: as a form of testing, for example, perhaps with ritual connotations (which could imply *less* familiarity with and trust in silver, not more). The occasional occurrence of fragments of the same coin in one hoard points in this direction.[127]

In very general terms, use of precious metals in Scandinavia and the Baltic has been seen as moving through three stages: "display," "bullion," and "coin."[128] At first the emphasis fell on ornamentation and display, with actual exchange concentrated heavily in elite and ceremonial contexts. Transfers of objects were of whole pieces, not hackmetal, the implication being that they did not remain in this state far beyond the social circuits in which they originated. This was the context of late Roman and early Byzantine gold,[129] and also of the early period of significant silver use in the Viking Age, when it took the form of whole silver rings and brooches. These could be of impressive size: the biggest individual pieces contain nearly 500 grams of silver.[130] Objects were both store and symbol of value. An Arab observer, Aḥmad ibn Faḍlān (d. c. 960), described how the wives of successful *Rūs* traders in Russia would wear gold and silver neck-rings, each representing ten thousand dirhams of wealth.[131] The eastern regions where ibn Faḍlān encountered the *Rūs* provided the principal conduit that enriched northern Europe

---

124. Jankowiak 2019; Hårdh 1996, 86–88.

125. Hadley and Richards 2018; Blackburn 2011, 221–64. On the nature of army camps as temporary towns, see Williams 2015; 2020, 84–102.

126. Hårdh 1996, 161–62; 2007, 97–99; Kilger 2008b, 310–12.

127. Jankowiak 2019, 27–28.

128. Hårdh 1996, 176–81; Kershaw 2014, 157. For a helpful summary of the major chronological milestones, see Williams 2011, 342–50.

129. See earlier discussion.

130. Graham-Campbell 1995, 108–10, for several enormous brooches from the tenth-century Skaill hoard (Orkney); very large arm-rings have also been uncovered in the viking East: see Hårdh 2007, 139–40.

131. Lunde and Stone 2012, 46.

with silver; slaves and perhaps other valuable goods such as furs and swords were some of the main commodities that travellers plying this long-distance route apparently took with them in the other direction.[132] The driving force behind this was trade with the Muslim world, via long and fragile routes that passed through several intermediaries in what are now Russia and Ukraine (see map 2.2).[133] Silver derived from dirhams began to spread from east to west in the years around 800, first into the Baltic, then reaching Denmark in the early decades of the ninth century and Norway in the middle of that century.[134] A smaller influx of silver came in from the Carolingian Empire to the west.[135] Thanks to a rapid buildup of silver, the later ninth and tenth centuries were the heyday of the bullion economy as a whole, though it always took regionally distinct forms.[136] Later, difficulties of access to eastern silver from the mid-tenth century prompted a turn toward western (German and English) coins from about 970. Scandinavian rulers in the generation that followed started to issue the first coins in the name of a current king, modelled on English pennies. This has often been read as a, if not the, great leap forward, bringing Denmark, Norway, and Sweden into the monetary mainstream of Europe.[137] More recent assessments have instead laid stress on the slow progress these coins made in circulation: foreign or imitative coins had already started to overtake bullion as the dominant component of hoards in most areas by the later tenth century, before the institution of royal coinages, and it took most of the eleventh century or longer for the latter to become dominant.[138] Royal, western-style coinage constitutes part of a string of institutional developments on the part of Scandinavian kings and was a matter of control and normalization. It should not be construed simply as a natural and rational advance that left behind an outmoded bullion economy.

The onset of wider bullion use hence did not put an end to the "display" element of precious-metal use; nor did the beginnings of local coinage

---

132. For fur, see Howard-Johnston 2020, and other chapters in the same volume for slavery.

133. Noonan 1992, 1994; Jankowiak 2020.

134. Blackburn 2008, esp. 52; Kilger 2008a, esp. 214–28.

135. The most important site relating to this trade is now that of Havsmarken on Ærø in Denmark, where at least seventy-five individual finds of Carolingian denarii have come to light (including one lost part-way through being melted down): Coupland 2022.

136. Gruszczyński 2019.

137. Engel and Serrure 1891–1905, 2:848–49; Fossier 1989, 2:784.

138. Hårdh 1976; Bendixen 1981, 410–11; Gullbekk 2009, 32, 34; Kilger 2011, 269–70; Gruszczyński 2019, 200–11.

quickly eradicate bullion or display elements.[139] Overlap and coexistence of these three models are now recognised within a regionally varied landscape.[140] Furthermore, silver was always just one kind of money or means of exchange alongside others, including commodities as well as gold and copper alloy, which—although widely separated in value—could both be used in ways analogous to silver.[141] It is not helpful to continue to distinguish a separate "bullion economy" or "display economy," or for that matter a "gift economy" or a "commercial economy"; rather, these represent different emphases within a large, interconnected exchange economy, the various components of which could and did work together.[142]

While the categories of display or prestige, as well as commercial, ritual, and others, are useful pigeonholes for the roles money could play in the Viking Age, they all reflect individual moments in the life-cycle of an object, and it is entirely plausible that the same coin or object could enter into all these different roles and uses and move between them rapidly.[143] Coins continued to be pierced and worn as ornaments into the eleventh century, and a significant proportion of those that were pierced or mounted made their way back into circulation, perhaps being cut into fragments along the way for use in a more directly weight-based exchange.[144] One Samanid dirham found on Bornholm had even been broken into fragments but then wired back together to remake a whole coin, possibly one that carried special significance, or where there was a pressing need to symbolically reverse the act that had led to its fragmentation (figure 5.5). The lines between coin, bullion, and display were fluid and could be crossed several times, in different directions, by the same piece of silver. Equally, Ribe and Hedeby were both enclaves of something closer to a coin-based economy between the eighth and tenth centuries.[145] Within their immediate hinterland, coins were probably used

139. Graham-Campbell 2007, 51; Graham-Campbell, Sindbæk, and Williams 2011a, 19, 21.

140. E.g., Kershaw 2014, 157; Williams 2007, 180–85.

141. Kershaw 2019b, 8–12. For viking use of gold, see Fuglesang and Wilson 2006; Kershaw 2019a; Oras, Leimus, and Joosu 2019. It has also been argued that copper alloy played a role as a means of exchange and/or store of wealth: Sindbæk 2003; Williams 2011, 354; Blackburn 2011, 235–36; Pestell 2013, 249–50; Hadley and Richards 2016, 47–48.

142. Williams 2011, esp. 350–56.

143. Williams 2020.

144. Gruszczyński 2019, 16; Audy 2018, esp. 163–65.

145. For the ninth- and tenth-century issues, see Malmer 1966, 2007; Moesgaard 2018; for an important new hoard, see Feveile and Moesgaard 2018. The eighth-century coinage attributed to Ribe has been the object of extensive debate: for a summary with references, see Naismith 2017b, 92–93.

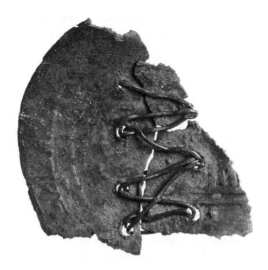

FIGURE 5.5. Samanid dirham found near Kobbegård, Bornholm, broken into fragments but carefully tied back together with silver wire (Find no. BMR 3792x1) (maximum width 22 mm). National Museum of Denmark, Copenhagen.

for a range of purposes; the coins' status beyond that patch is less clear, though the numerous pierced examples in grave finds and the different handling of western-style silver pieces compared to dirhams suggests that they perhaps served a narrower role as a prestige currency.[146] Dublin from the 990s and York a century earlier were also islands of apparently controlled coin-based exchange.[147] These geographically confined monetary economies, associated with key markets and towns, reflect the ability of viking political authorities to mandate what form exchanges should take, or at least to try. That might have applied only to coin-based exchanges, as was perhaps the case at tenth-century Hedeby; bullion and (presumably) commodities went on being used, either following different rules or for different purposes.[148]

In most respects the viking lands were more different from the rest of early medieval Europe in degree than in the basic form of their money. Precious metal was always a commodity as well as a coin; money always

146. Metcalf 1996, 410–22; Moesgaard 2015.

147. For Dublin, see Woods 2013, 1:190–280.

148. Merkel 2016, 118–20, notes that the coins and hackmetal from Hedeby have much the same metallic composition, suggesting a close relationship between the two.

meant many things used in many ways. But there may have been deeper divergences in terms of access and agency. It is only really feasible to focus on silver in this connection. Participation in the weighing of precious metal carried weight in Viking-Age society. In the mountainous Swedish province of Jämtland, some 500 km north of Stockholm, about a third to half of male graves from the mid-ninth to early eleventh centuries included weights and/or scales, often alongside small quantities of silver. These graves probably do not represent members of the elite; nor can they all be construed as professional merchants. Instead, they point to engagement by better-to-do (male) farmers in complex forms of exchange; given the location, this almost certainly meant long-distance exchange, perhaps plied in winter when snowy overland routes connecting Norway and Sweden through the mountains were easily traversable.[149]

Jämtland is important precisely because of its remoteness: this was the end of the line for the silver economy in Scandinavia, marginal in terms of its agricultural sustainability and barely on the radar for inchoate political powers. That makes the use of silver, and the incorporation of weights and scales into mortuary rituals, all the more interesting. Use of silver in this region took effort and carried social significance. It was also not driven from above. The population's involvement in networks of exchange developed without any meaningful input from kings, who did not appear on the scene until much later. Nor was there a prominent local elite: evidence for social stratification in the region is limited.[150] The profile of Jämtland's silver economy breaks sharply from that of many other parts of early medieval Europe, where the driving force in the making and primary use of gold and silver coin is thought to have been the elite.

It might be argued that Jämtland was a peripheral offshoot of the major streams that brought silver to the northern lands, and therefore unrepresentative. Certainly one can point to regions of the North where there is also silver (sometimes plentiful silver) and evidence of more dominant local elites: Vestfold and Hålogaland in Norway, for example, the former home to Kaupang and the Gokstad ship burial, and the latter to the chieftain Ohthere, who told Alfred the Great's court about his life, and also to the massive Borg hall.[151] And of these two, Hålogaland was also

149. Holm 2015, 2017.

150. Holm 2015, 102–4. See Jakobsson 2021 for one of the cemeteries at the upper end of the region's social stratification.

151. Myhre 1998; Skre 2007b; Gullbekk 2014, esp. 342–46; Storli and Roesdahl 2007; Storli 2016. For silver finds in northern Norway in the vicinity of Borg, see Skaare 1976, 172–75 (though there have been new finds since this time).

agriculturally marginal. What distinguishes Scandinavia from most of the rest of western Europe is that richness in silver was not as tightly bound to elite wealth. Gotland is the prime example to set alongside Jämtland. As already noted, this Baltic island is a veritable elephant's graveyard of silver. Its riches are spread across the island, such that in some areas half of all farms have produced a hoard (and some several).[152] The nature of Gotlandic society in the Viking Age has been hotly debated since the 1970s, as a new generation of legal scholars and archaeologists reacted against a romanticized vision of the island as a peasant republic.[153] Yet the consensus that has emerged actually falls closer to the earlier impression: that Gotland was a relatively flat society without a king or aristocracy, nor much evidence of serious internal conflict. That is not to say it was egalitarian. There were slaves and gradations of wealth among the free inhabitants, reflected in the size of farms.[154] If later sources provide a good indication of conditions in the viking period, the leading element in society would have been farmers with larger holdings who dominated local assemblies and the island's *alþing* at Roma.[155] The better literary evidence from Iceland centuries later gives a flavour of the complicated dynamics that could be at work within such a system, though it is less clear how far the inequalities of the twelfth- and thirteenth-century "contemporary sagas" can be projected back.[156] In Gotland, the position of the leading farmers is thought to have been based on informal alliances and obligations rather than tenancy; their property was larger, but still within the same league.[157]

How, then, did so much silver get to Gotland, and what was it used for when it got there? The island's position in the middle of the Baltic made it a natural stepping stone between different regions.[158] That included, most pertinently for the Viking Age, movement of dirhams from east to west, but Gotland has also produced a relatively large number of hoards of Roman denarii from earlier times, which probably came in via what is now Poland.[159] Its connectivity may always have been multidirectional within the Baltic. That traffic was probably in the hands of the Gotlanders

152. Carlsson 2009, 87.

153. The voluminous historiography is laid out in Siltberg 2012.

154. Thunmark-Nylén 1984. For general guidance, see Thunmark-Nylén 1995–2006.

155. Östergren 2004.

156. Wickham 2015b; Orri Vésteinsson 2007; compare with Byock 2001, 75–80, 185–95, 118–41.

157. Andrén 2008, 48–49; 2012, 102–3.

158. E.g., Carlsson 2020, 225.

159. Jonsson and Östergren 1992; Gruszczyński 2019, 227–31.

themselves. Runic inscriptions on the island describe men going off on long-distance military and trading ventures, the difference between which was probably more in outcome than intention.[160] There were also about fifty harbour sites dotted around the edge of the island.[161] Several of these, such as Paviken and Ridanæs, are now known to have been sites of trade and exchange in the viking period,[162] if never on anything like the scale of emporia like Birka, Hedeby, Kauping, Truso and Wolin. Silver did circulate on Gotland, even though it is mostly known in the form of hoards rather than single finds; examples of the latter have now come to light in considerable quantity, including at the possible *alþing* site at Roma, and the mixed contents of the hoards also presuppose a degree of circulation.[163] The hoards also show that silver was used in diverse ways. Jacek Gruszczyński has argued that smaller hoards deposited without a container (which account for 59 per cent of hoards from Gotland with good data) are likely to represent "placed deposits": that is, assemblages of silver buried without intention of recovery.[164] Reasons for their burial can only be surmised, but one plausible possibility is asserting the owner-ship of land. A large proportion of the possible placed deposits occur on thinner, less productive soil.[165] The theory is that these hoards would have been deposited as part of a rite of claiming land by implanting mov-able wealth into it—a sort of inversion of the logic that says whatever is found in the land belongs to the landowner: one comes to own land by depositing movable property into it. Something like this is narrated in the later medieval *Svarfdœla saga* about a ninth-century Icelander who buried three tranches of silver as part of a series of rituals to claim a valley for his own.[166] As an example of how assemblages of silver could factor into peasant society, this hypothesis is persuasive. It moves silver beyond a strictly commercial, "entrepreneurial" context and highlights the close nexus between various means of obtaining silver (commerce, expropria-tion, etc.) and socially embedded, ritual applications. Access to silver could have increased the portion of the population with the ability to participate in key social transactions, such as dowries, compensations, and land pur-chases. It was therefore desirable because it strengthened people's agency

160. Gruszczyński 2019, 205, 209; Kilger 2020a, 50–52.

161. Carlsson 1999.

162. Carlsson 2005, 2016.

163. Gruszczyński 2019, 261, 275–79; 2020, 189, 197–99; Kilger 2020b, 243.

164. Gruszczyński 2019, esp. 268–72.

165. Gruszczyński 2019, 57–60, 65–67. See also Gustafsson 2013, 43–47.

166. *Svarfdœla saga*, c. 11 (Jónas Kristjánsson 1956, 20; trans. Heinemann 1997, 161).

and autonomy in public life as well as their buying power in a commercial setting.

Gotland and to some degree other parts of the northern lands, pose a fundamental challenge to models of monetary circulation in the early Middle Ages that depend on elite interests. There were no real elites on Gotland, and while historically elites in the region had been weak in comparison with counterparts in the Frankish world or even England,[167] this was changing in some regions during the Viking Age. In Scandinavia and the Baltic, aristocrats and kings might patronise towns and raiding or trading ventures. By so doing they leeched off a socially diverse trading system that trafficked in both low- and high-value commodities, including silver, by establishing or—as in the case of the Danish king Godfrid's transplant of the men of Reric in 808[168]—taking over nodes where exchange was already in full flow.[169] Towns and trading centres were more than posts in a command economy: they succeeded because they were open to all-comers, like Ohthere who sailed the length of Norway to reach *Sciringesheal* (Kaupang) without any apparent compulsion and then went on to Hedeby;[170] and because they attracted craftspeople and traders who catered to a wider market of lower-value goods.[171] These characteristics relate to the basis of Scandinavia's exchange economy. Market-oriented exchange reached far beyond the confines of Birka, Hedeby, and Kaupang. It is becoming increasingly apparent that "outfield" resources like tar, fur, and iron, which were produced in the relative isolation of forests, heaths, and mountains, formed part of an integrated whole with towns and markets.[172] Many people in many places were involved with complex, interdependent networks of skills and commodities. The beginning of the viking period witnessed a sort of economic arms race, as goods deriving from long-distance exchange (not least silver) entered society and both broadened and heightened expectations for becoming established in life and setting up a home. A significant share of the population had some access to these goods. But the demand for more, distributed by increasingly well-developed maritime routes of communication, has been claimed as a precipitating factor in the beginning of the viking raids.[173]

167. Wickham 2005, 375–76; 2015b. See also Price 2020, 292–94.

168. *Annales regni Francorum* s.a. 808 (Pertz and Kurze 1895, 126; trans. Scholz and Rogers 1970, 88).

169. McCormick 2007; Skre 2007, 446–47, 452–63.

170. Old English *Orosius*, 1.1.21 (ed. and trans. Godden 2016, 42–43).

171. Skre 2007, 451; Sindbæk 2011, 52.

172. Lund and Sindbæk 2021, 4–6, 35–36; Hennius 2018.

173. Barrett 2008, 676–78; Sindbæk 2011, 52–59; Horne 2022, 113–14, 134–35. For

Peasant society in Scandinavia and the Baltic may have been similar to the coastal societies in eastern England and the Netherlands, as described by Chris Loveluck and Dries Tys, in that they dwelt outside or on the fringe of coercive political units and, through water-based connectivity, had enhanced opportunities to engage in exchange.[174] Structures for trade and warfare at this level were small-scale and embedded in families and local communities. Meeting sites that were used in the Viking Age and for centuries before reflect the deep history of these small to midsize groupings.[175] In war they would coalesce into the following of a single leader, and units of this kind were the building blocks for larger viking armies:[176] *lið*, as such units were known in Old Norse,[177] which can be compared with the "associations" (*sodalitates*) that a viking army divided into to wait out the winter in a Frankish annal for 861,[178] or the "violent gangs" (*hloþe*) into which an army in England broke up in 893.[179] The remains of what may have been members of such a group who met a violent end, buried in two ships at Salme in Estonia in the mid-eighth century, showed through their DNA that they were part of the same kin group.[180] Similar patterns based on groups of men banding together from the same district or family continued into the later Viking Age and are referred to—again, often when the enterprise had ended badly—on runestones from Gotland and elsewhere.[181] Broadly horizontal rather than vertical structures in law, warfare, and trade may well have carried over to the disposal of wealth. According to *Heimskringla*, written by Snorri Sturluson in the early thirteenth century, the farmers of Iceland resolved that each would contribute three pennies to the tenth-century poet Eyvindr skáldaspillir for his composition of a poem in their honour; at the *alþing* these pennies were then refined and made into a brooch supposedly weighing 50 marks. In the event Eyvindr broke up the brooch and used the proceeds to buy himself a farm.[182] Despite this being a late source, the general principles

connectivity, see Sindbæk 2007a; 2007b; and for the individual prestige of travel and long-distance connections, Ashby 2015.

174. Loveluck and Tys 2006; Loveluck 2013, esp. 178–212.

175. Semple et al. 2021.

176. Raffield et al. 2016; Raffield 2016; Jón Viðar Sigurðsson 2017, 103–15.

177. Jesch 2001, 187–89.

178. *Annals of Saint-Bertin* s.a. 861 (Waitz 1883, 56; trans. Nelson 1991, 95–96).

179. *Anglo-Saxon Chronicle* (MSS A, B, C, and D) s.a. 893 (Bately 1986, 56; trans. Whitelock 1979, 202).

180. Peets 2013; Price 2020, 275–78.

181. Kilger 2020a, 50–52.

182. Snorri Sturluson, *Heimskringla: Haralds saga Gráfeldr*, c. 16 (Bjarni Aðalbjarnarson 1941–51, 221–22; trans. Finlay and Faulkes 2011, 135–36).

of the story are believable in a Viking-Age context. It was commonplace to melt coins down to form objects,[183] and collective action represents a plausible context for other hoards. These could represent the accumulated property of a family, warband, or district. In a context such as Gotland, this is arguably a more plausible context for large assemblages than ownership by a single, extremely wealthy individual. The vast Spillings hoard, for example, is probably best explained in this context, though only speculation is possible as to what sort of group put it together, and why.[184]

If communal enterprises were significant to economic structures, a signal advantage of using bullion so freely was that it significantly reduced the economic bottleneck of minting. Melting down dirhams or other items to produce whole objects for redistribution to some extent fulfilled that same role, albeit on a more limited scale. In the Viking World, the large majority of silver effectively went straight into secondary uses, with a rather smaller segment of elite-dominated primary uses. When the men of Iceland supposedly decided to contribute as a group to Eyvindr's reward, they already had the coins they needed and transformed them for presentational purposes. In a sense this too was like the reminting of coinage, with the important difference that the patrons were peasant-farmers, some relatively rich but others not. Freshly made coins in a world where silver could be freely exchanged had to carry some other kind of cachet to make them acceptable, be it a carrot or a stick. The carrot was appeal to preexisting concepts of trust, such as copying a familiar, respected variety of coinage. That is why so many of the first locally minted coinages of Scandinavia were imitative: they tapped into the reputation of other acceptable coins and were probably expected to pass for them, being of good weight and alloy.[185] To issue innovative coinages that adopted even a partially new appearance, such as a king's name, was a significant step: an attempt to insert the issuer as a guarantor for their use. In this respect they offered a response to what Dagfinn Skre has called "threatening trade."[186] Commercial exchange, especially with unknown or less familiar partners, always carried a frisson of uncertainty and danger. Would one be fleeced or score a bargain? It was to help manage this threat that trade gravitated to sites evocative of respect and trust, such as sacred places, and took place under the auspices of an agency powerful enough to

183. Hårdh 1976, 110–27; Merkel 2016, 75–76, 118–20.

184. Carlsson 2009, 104, suggests that it could have been a tribute raised from the island, which for some reason was never paid and ended up being buried on the land of a judge.

185. Malmer 1989, 1997; Kilger 2011.

186. Skre 2007, 450–52.

enforce a degree of security at that location, such as a chieftain or king. The lure of coins issued by that supervisory authority, and the benefit of recognising their fixed value, was that they would be guaranteed where that authority ran, even if they circulated at a possibly lower value elsewhere. There were advantages for the ruler as well. For the rest of the population, this was the stick element of the establishment of local coinage. Encouraging the use of coins easily shaded into demanding their use for payments of tolls or other dues to the ruler, at a rate fixed by them. At first this would apply only in places where exchange and royal oversight could be brought to bear, above all in towns. Rulers also had the option of gifting the coins to favoured followers, who would then have a vested interest in enforcing the same face value in exchanges they could dominate.[187] The circulation of the early native coinages of Scandinavia may therefore have been conceived in personal as well as geographical terms. Crucially, though, that sphere was limited in extent, becoming widespread in Denmark and Norway only later in the eleventh century (and later still in Sweden).[188] The peasant bulk of the population could and did use the new coins, but that meant entering into a more hierarchical structure of exchange, especially at or near the point of production.

The interest of Scandinavia and the Baltic is as a region with weak aristocratic power and still weaker state structures, yet with an impressively rich and deeply embedded exchange economy. Precious metal here was at once money, commodity, and display of wealth. There were specific reasons for this, relating to social structure and emergent networks of exchange, but it nonetheless is an instructive comparison to other parts of Europe where elite interests are the most visible component of the monetary economy.

Case Study 3: Tang and Song China

The concluding case study departs from Europe altogether to consider China during the period roughly analogous to the early Middle Ages: that of the Tang (618–907) and earlier Song (960–1127) dynasties.[189] There

187. Moesgaard 2015, 59–63, 85–89, 90, 101–5. Moesgaard emphasizes a dual role for the (probably royal) Danish coinage issued from c. 950: it functioned as a managed currency within Hedeby, perhaps required for some transactions, and elsewhere was distributed primarily to elites. In an earlier study (2012, 128–31) Moesgaard also allowed for the possibility of minting by a town government or mercantile association.

188. Selected studies include, on Denmark: Bendixen 1981; Steen Jensen 1995; on Norway: Malmer 1961, Skaare 1976, 58–110; Gullbekk 2009, 29–41; on Sweden: Lagerqvist 1968; Malmer 1995.

189. The term "China" is used here for the sake of convenience, although previous

is no claim here to direct contact or influence in either direction.[190] But setting specific aspects of the two regions side by side is stimulating, just as it has been for historians of the ancient and modern periods. Specific developments can be found in both early medieval Europe and contemporary China: a significant overall increase in population, wealth, productivity, and monetisation, albeit at a different pace, from very different starting points and, as will be seen, for distinct reasons.[191] In methodological terms, examining correlations between the two, and how far they can be pushed, helps to decentre western Europe and, having put it out of historiographical stride, reveals new patterns beyond familiar narratives, one of which involves the relationship of coin, bullion, and commodities in exchange contexts. An exclusively coin-based system (or at least one based exclusively on coins and extensions of them such as written instruments of credit) is the telos toward which Western monetary history has traditionally galloped. Yet western Europe's privileging of a high-value, exclusionary coinage should not be seen as normal or universal. In Tang and Song China, with a vastly larger population and significantly more complex economy, coin, bullion, and commodities were all used on a large scale and in distinct ways.[192] They did not stand in a hierarchical relationship: each had its own set of functions. In other words, China was anything but simple or undeveloped, and yet it always had a multipart monetary economy. The interest lies in how those parts worked, in relation to state and other demands, and to each other.

There was, in the first place, a coinage of copper-alloy pieces. The standard coin was the *ch'ien* (*qian*), which was about the same diameter as a

imperial regimes do not map straightforwardly onto the modern polity; the issue is considered in Standen 2019.

190. That is not to say there were no connections, especially between China and the Muslim world (Smith 2015b; Dudbridge 2018; Strathern 2018, 319–24); simply that in the context considered here, there are many parallels but few direct influences. There are two examples known to the author of Northern Song–period coins found in western Europe (from Cheshire and Hampshire in England: PAS HAMP-C2BC79 and LVPL-4F4637), but these are most plausibly explained either as late medieval or modern losses (see Green 2018).

191. Mielants 2002; Moore 2003; Wareham 2012. Studies of the ancient and especially modern comparisons are legion.

192. McDermott and Yoshinobu 2015, 325: the population of China is estimated at ninety-five million in 1080, having perhaps doubled since the mid-eighth century. This figure derives from government fiscal records; information for contemporary Europe is far weaker except in England (Wickham 2016, 123), but a total population in the eleventh century about half that of China is plausible.

FIGURE 5.6. Two examples of Chinese copper coins: *above*, an example of the Kaiyuan Tongbao ("circulating treasure from the inauguration of the new era"), the standard coin across the Tang period (621–907); *below*, a coin of the Song emperor Hui Tsung (1100–1126), made in the period 1107–10, moulded from calligraphy personally executed by the emperor (diameters 24 mm and 41 mm). Private collection and Classical Numismatic Group, LLC, respectively.

European silver penny of the mid-eighth century and after (figure 5.6).[193] Unlike its European counterparts, the *ch'ien* was made by casting and always had a hole through the middle so that it could be threaded onto a string. For large sums, and for state accounting purposes, people dealt in terms of strings of a thousand coins each. To put this in perspective, unskilled or semiskilled urban labourers made one hundred to two hundred coins a day in the eleventh century, while in the late twelfth century (when the cost of living had risen significantly) a weaver, washer, or tailor made one hundred coins a day, a butcher two hundred, and a fishmonger three hundred.[194]

193. Golas 2015, 207.

194. I am extremely grateful to Richard von Glahn for these figures. See also McKnight 1992, 224, 277, 443, who offers rather lower estimates.

The *ch'ien* held a prominent place in political symbolism and discourse. Chinese thought on money going back to the Warring States period (c. 475–221 BC), and codified under the Tang dynasty, emphasised the role of coinage as an expression of imperial authority; another major tenet was that maintaining a reliable, accessible currency represented one of the responsibilities of any good ruler.[195] Some Song coinages were even impressed with characters calligraphically executed by the emperor himself, which were carved in relief and then reproduced through casting.[196]

In general terms, it should be stressed that the Chinese copper coinage was a major operation, especially when compared to contemporary western Europe. Production figures from now lost official records are quoted as supporting detail in historical compilations,[197] and they show that minting was already running at a rate of 327,000 strings per annum in the period 742–56, and 100,000 strings in 834–35. In relative terms, however, the Tang dynasty's minting and coin revenue were small fry next to those of the much more economically complex Song period. Coin gradually became the dominant element of state income, excluding all others by the twelfth century, while minting went into overdrive. A total of 5,949,234 strings (i.e., nearly six billion coins) are said to have been minted in 1080–81 alone.[198] It has been estimated that the Song manufactured up to 260 billion coins altogether.[199]

The emperors faced formidable challenges in keeping this coinage going. The value of the coins qua coins hovered dangerously close to their value as bullion, and at many points the worth of the copper surpassed the face value, meaning that coins disappeared from circulation to be melted down. This led to highly protectionist practices. From the time of the Tang dynasty onward, copper mining was a government monopoly, and all freshly mined copper had to be funnelled into the coinage; mints tended, therefore, to be situated in mining areas (see map 5.1).[200] There were determined efforts to open up new copper mines as old ones were worked out, and under the Song copper production expanded tenfold.[201] Other expedients included restrictions on the domestic use of copper for other purposes, and especially limits on movement with coin, for one of

195. Von Glahn 1996, 21–47; and forthcoming.
196. Yu and Yu 2004, 19–20.
197. Li and Hartman 2011.
198. Ch'en 1965, 619, for production figures.
199. Von Glahn 2016, 235. Golas 2015, 208, offers a somewhat lower estimate: 150–200 billion.
200. Von Glahn 1996, 50.
201. McDermott and Yoshinobu 2015, 378–79.

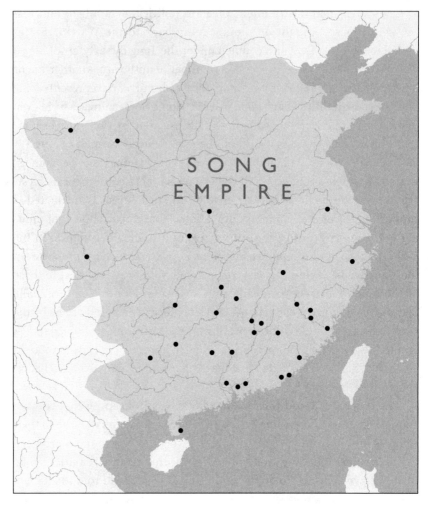

MAP 5.1. The Song Empire, before the major loss of northern territory in 1127; dots represent known copper mines or mining areas (following Ch'en 1965).

the main drains on the supply was export of coin to neighbouring lands, including Japan, the kingdoms to the north, and Southeast Asia.[202] One ploy to combat this scourge was to institute lead, iron, or pewter coin (which were all less attractive for export) in frontier regions or mercantile cities.[203] The first paper money came about as an extension of this scheme, in what is now Sichuan. Iron coinage had been prevalent there since the Tang dynasty, and deposit shops sprang up to save people the

202. Von Glahn 1996, 40–42.
203. Ch'en 1965, 620–21; von Glahn 1996, 49; 2016, 228.

difficulty of actually carrying around huge quantities of iron coins; the notes they issued (*jiaozi*), standing in for so many thousand iron coins on deposit, began to circulate on their own and eventually displaced coins. In 1023 the printing of *jiaozi* was made into a government monopoly. Later issues spread to other parts of the empire, albeit with less success, and in the early twelfth century production ceased when *jiaozi* notes were over-produced to defray government costs and fell prey to inflation.[204] Further initiatives followed in the twelfth century and after.

Who actually used these coins, and for what? The focus has tradition-ally fallen on fiscal payments: coins that were rendered as tax and paid out for state expenditure. There is no doubt that this was substantial, and the proportion of tax paid in coin started to rise from the mid-Tang period, even in rural areas.[205] One of the main points of friction in the specialist literature is how dominant that fiscal cycle was. Did much of the coinage at any one time sit inert in state coffers? Did it also serve a large role in markets?[206] Paying taxes was the sector where other means of exchange came most visibly into play. A shipwreck that came to light in Indonesia, the so-called Intan Wreck, carried ninety-seven large silver ingots from China during the Five Dynasties period (907–60). Several had legible inscriptions, either on the ingot itself or on a silver sheet wrapping, relat-ing to payment of salt taxes.[207] The ingots stated the name of the official responsible for overseeing the payment, and sometimes also the place where this was done and the name of the artisan who had actually made the ingot. In many respects they replicate the range of information that was put onto silver coins in contemporary western Europe.

The Intan ingots, along with a range of others found at sites across China, reflect a sort of subsidiary monetary economy based on silver, one that was focused on efficiently condensing and transferring large sums for fiscal purposes. Silver played a large role in this setting, even more so under the Song, and its significance in the Chinese monetary economy would increase considerably in the twelfth and thirteenth centuries.[208] It did not really serve as a regular means of exchange, just as a store of value. Taxes were therefore probably not actually settled in silver (except when

204. Yang 1952, 53–53; von Glahn 2004, 173–75. No actual examples of Song-era paper money survive, though plates used to print thirteenth-century specimens possibly do (von Glahn 2006).

205. Twitchett 1966; 1968.

206. Von Glahn 2004; 2016, 235.

207. Twitchett and Stargardt 2002, 35–41.

208. Von Glahn 2012.

they derived from silver mines);[209] the presumption is that base-metal coins or commodities were handed over but then commuted for silver by officials. That meant coins could stay local, which matched other Tang and Song policies aimed at limiting the private circulation of coin across the empire.[210] The question that follows is what then happened to the silver after being handed over to the central authorities. Clearly it could and did move over long distances. The Tang capital, Chang'an, had storehouses dedicated to silver, where a few ingots have been found that derive from merchants' taxes.[211] Reserves of this kind could be transferred or liquidated when the need arose, though probably not in a directly monetary way. The ingots from the Intan Wreck may represent silver that had been dispensed with in this way by the Southern Han state and that was being exported as a commodity. The cycle to which they belonged was apparently tight-knit: the ingots include numerous more or less identical specimens, which suggests a tranche that had stayed together from the time of manufacture to deposition and not been broken up by extensive circulation.[212]

Silver formed a separate monetary circuit, primarily shaped by tax revenues, but also extending into high-value commerce. As in contemporary Islamic and viking societies, silver was rated and handled by weight. But textiles, hempen and silken, along with agricultural goods like grain were also used to settle Chinese tax obligations and private payments. Under the early Tang, fabric was the overwhelmingly dominant form of tax payment.[213] Although known and used across the empire, the best picture of its use comes from the western fringe of the Tang domains, in the remarkable finds from Dunhuang, Khotan, and Turfan. Documents from these locations give detailed descriptions of the use of textiles to pay taxes and settle private transactions and even contain examples of fabrics that were used to pay tax. Like silver ingots, bolts of fabric would be paid to the state, marked with inscriptions stating who had paid it, when, and for what, but they would subsequently be paid out and put into circulation again, travelling over vast distances in the process.[214] The Tang government sought to maintain a balance of coin and fabric, alternately stimulating whichever

---

209. Twitchett and Stargardt 2002, 48, 52.

210. See earlier discussion.

211. Twitchett and Stargardt 2002, 51–52.

212. Twitchett and Stargardt 2002, 60–61.

213. Xu 2013; Hansen and Rong 2013, 295. Hansen and Wang 2013, 160, describes how silk was used to pay large transactions, and coin to pay small ones.

214. Hansen and Wang 2013, 157–58.

was not in the ascendant.[215] In 804 it was mandated that cloth and other commodities should be acceptable alongside coins in markets, and from 830 that half of any sum over one hundred strings should be paid in cloth or grain. Yet it is likely that these demands were intended to protect the supply of coin, implying that the inclination was to use copper coinage where possible.[216] Coins had clear benefits over fabric—textiles lost value more easily to damage or wear and tear and also were ill suited to being cut up for smaller payments[217]—and coined money was always used as the standard unit of account to mediate between other kinds of commodity.[218] The coinage provided a fixed and standard unit of account, even though it was one of several acceptable means of exchange.

All this suggests that coin was used extensively for payments *to* the state—but it also featured prominently in payments *from* the state. Military expenditure was undoubtedly massive, arguably eating up 80 per cent of expenditure in the eleventh century, when the Song army peaked at 1,259,000 men.[219] There was a large bureaucracy, paid partly in coin and partly in grain, which helped concentrate monetary circulation in the capital cities (Xi'an under the Tang, Kaifeng under the Northern Song) and made them important contributors to imperial taxes.[220] Some initiatives of the state were calculated to pump money into localities, or keep what there already was within its home region. For a brief period during a time of fiscal shake-up in the 1070s, the imperial government issued cash loans to smallholding peasants in the hard months before harvest (the "green sprouts" initiative) so as to help lift them out of permanent indebtedness to large landholders (who all too often were becoming landlords) and give them the resources to improve their productivity; repayments could be either in cash or in produce.[221] Merchants willingly participated in sophisticated schemes of vouchers, known in the Tang period as "flying money": these facilitated long-distance trade, at first in tea, between the capital and the southern provinces and took the form of bills of exchange that were

215. Xu 2013, 223.

216. Twitchett 1970, 80–81.

217. Xu 2013, 234, noting that Tang officials grasped these difficulties in the early eighth century.

218. Wang 2013, 169–70; Hansen and Wang 2013,

219. Von Glahn 2016, 229; McDermott and Yoshinobu 2015, 378.

220. McDermott and Yoshinobu 2015, 380–81; von Glahn 1996, 56, on a ban on exporting coin south from the Tang capital.

221. Smith 2009, 394–97; von Glahn 2016, 237. For background on the expansion of large estates, many of them held by ambitious and wealthy officials, see Twitchett 1959, 1960; Golas 1980, esp. 300–4.

issued to merchants when they paid in the profits of their sale of tea to a provincial commission in Xi'an. They could be redeemed in the province itself for the same amount of cash. This was beneficial for all involved. The provincial bureaucracy could count the payments in the capital toward their tax liability, and the merchants avoided the difficulty and risk of travelling over a long distance with a large quantity of coin.[222]

On the face of it, the state-driven contexts of coin, silver, and pseudo-monetised commodity circulation appear dominant. This is partly a matter of sources, however, for these privilege the activities of state administration, mostly from a centralised perspective.[223] They therefore downplay the fact that the many different sectors and layers of government could work at odds with one another. Local officials building up estates for themselves were among the main scourges of the peasant farmers, for example, not least because they put together their own private hoards of metal. Personal assemblages were in some cases huge. The Tang government in 817 prohibited hoarding of over five thousand strings (i.e., five million coins), and in the 1030s and 1040s Song officials complained about private individuals hoarding up to thirty thousand or fifty thousand strings of coin.[224] Nothing quite of this magnitude has come to light in the find record, but a few enormous hoards have indeed been uncovered: one from Jingdezhen, Jiangxi province, in 2017 contained about 300,000 Song coins, weighing 5.6 tons,[225] and another of iron coins from Cangzhou, Hebei province, weighed 48 tons.[226]

Importantly, governmental institutions and private individuals, families, or organisations were implicated in hoarding, making this a piece of circumstantial evidence for the use of coin beyond tax and state expenditure. Stockpiling and regional imbalances in distribution are also persuasive explanations for why, even with vast quantities of coin being injected into circulation, shortage of cash was an endemic problem.[227] Other pieces of anecdotal evidence tell the same story: that people wanted and

222. Twitchett 1970, 72–73. At first the state charged a commission on flying money, but this was quickly discontinued.

223. Li and Hartman 2011.

224. Twitchett 1970, 80; von Glahn 2004, 171.

225. "A Staggering 5.6 Tons of Coins Are Unearthed in China and Archaeologists Struggle to Fathom Who Hid Them," *Ancient Origins*, October 27, 2017, https://www.ancient-origins.net/news-history-archaeology/staggering-56-tons-coins-are-unearthed-china-and-archaeologists-struggle-021684..

226. "China Unearths Mountain of Ancient Iron Coins," *People's Daily*, May 20, 2000, http://en.people.cn/english/200005/20/eng20000520_41261.html.

227. Ch'en 1965, 618; von Glahn 1996, 40–42, 49–50; 2004, 176.

expected to use coin for diverse purposes but sometimes had difficulty doing so. Han Gan (c. 706–83), one of the greatest equestrian painters of the Tang period, allegedly started out as a bar worker in the capital and was "discovered" when he was sent to collect the tab from a celebrated poet; it was the men and horses that Han Gan drew in the sand to while away the time as the poet sought out his cash that caught the latter's eye.[228] Under the later Tang and Song, Han Gan would perhaps have remained a barman, for the state authorities made determined efforts to boost the amount of cash in circulation: the poet might have been able to pay for his drinks on the spot, or not spent quite so long tracking down his money when asked to pay. This went well beyond the traditional expectation of a benevolent ruler maintaining a supply of fresh coin and reflects the changing nature of the empire's finances. The later Tang and especially the Song dynasties were exceptional for their dependence on nonagricultural revenue: under the Song, for the first and only time in Chinese history prior to the nineteenth century, more government income derived from commercial taxes and related sources than from agricultural revenue.[229] Monetisation was an important part of this process. Whereas coin accounted for only about 1 or 2 per cent of early Tang tax income (the rest being in the form of textiles), by 1077 that relationship was on the way to being reversed: revenue included forty-eight million strings of cash, estimated to be almost four times the value of in-kind payments.[230] Those coins were all obtained from taxpayers. The state, therefore, was heavily invested in, and increasingly dependent on, a vibrant commercial economy.[231] That relationship had its tensions; as Paul Jakov Smith put it, many Song government initiatives started with good intentions but "metamorphosed into the claws of a predatory bureaucracy whose sole purpose was to gouge new revenues out of the economy."[232] But the central point is that state finances depended on the population of the empire having ready and plentiful access to coin.

Although vastly larger in terms of scale, and much more literate and complex in its governance, China did have important points in common with western Europe when it came to coin and money. Both had unevenly distributed currency. Some regions were richer in specie than others, depending on factors like the presence of mines and mints, or of army

228. Benn 2002, 58.
229. Golas 2015, 148; Liu 2015. For the beginnings of the shift in this direction in the later Tang dynasty, see Twitchett 1968.
230. Liu 2015, 53.
231. Von Glahn 2004, 170.
232. Smith 2009, 394.

units; and even within areas that had coin, access to currency—especially freshly made currency—depended on social closeness to the source. That is to say, wealthier elites were not only richer but better able to liquidate and instrumentalise their wealth, while those with little money to start with faced an uphill struggle in finding and keeping enough of it to meet their needs. Coinage exacerbated preexisting inequalities anywhere it could be found. Another striking parallel is the close yet selective relationship between the monetary role of coin and its identity as bullion (i.e., a commodity). In China, the primary material for money was copper alloy, and this was treated essentially as a fiduciary currency: its role as bullion came into play only if the value of copper crept high enough that it was worth withdrawing coin from circulation.[233]

A larger structural difference that stands out is the much more overt, even overbearing, influence of state structures. On this point Tang and Song China is somewhat closer to the later Roman Empire, where there have been similar disagreements about how tax, military spending, and commerce intermeshed, albeit with the emphasis falling more on precious metal coin than copper alloy. In China, it is also likely that fiscal actions were only one component of the monetary economy, although they had a sort of tent-pole effect, giving shape to other uses that went on around them. Strikingly, and unlike in England or Francia, where governmental controls extended only to silver coinage, the Chinese state perpetuated several discrete monetary spheres or circuits, including those of base-metal coin, precious metal, silk, and agricultural goods, sometimes extending to written instruments pegged to one or more of these monies. Scholars of China read this diversity in a positive light, as part of the remarkable commercial effervescence of the late Tang and Song periods. Money was not one thing, but a mode of thought.

Conclusion

The salient points of this chapter are simple. Coin, bullion, and other commodities were all used as monetary means of exchange, and early medieval societies included elements of each. The three are better conceptualised as a set of preferences along a sliding scale rather than hard-and-fast categories. Different kinds of exchange, varying levels of wealth, or dealing with specific individuals might shift the balance toward one means of payment over another. Even in the most monetised portions of early medieval

233. Von Glahn forthcoming.

Europe, paying in coin would rarely if ever have been the default. The issue should be framed in terms of why coins (or bullion, or commodities) were used, as one of several possibilities.

This is not to deny that the overall balance of exchange would have looked very different region to region. The relationship between separate kinds of "money" would vary too. While precious-metal bullion was used very widely as a store and display of wealth, keyed into units of weight or coinage, its place in Viking-Age Scandinavia, the Baltic, and viking-settled areas elsewhere was unusually developed and deep-rooted, in contrast to the frequently high-status context of gold and silver bullion elsewhere. The background to this viking economic system may relate to socially broad access to long-distance exchange, and competitive behaviours at a local level between farmers of roughly similar status. Silver represented a new, powerful kind of card to play in several different situations.

Finally, there are deep problems with fitting commodity, bullion, and coin together in an evolutionary scheme. Anthropologists have long exploded the myth that exchange systems began with barter, while no "coin-based" economies in this period rejected use of bullion and commodity money entirely, and all three could be found working together. In China they did so on a massive scale, and rich, commercially developed societies in some parts of the empire—such as the oasis of Dunhuang—got by perfectly well with silk, grain, and little or no coinage. To use particular means of exchange was a matter of social and administrative background. Moving from a preference for bullion to a preference for coin in particular is a signal of the controlling efforts of the ruling authorities: it did not mean progression in an abstract sense, for although working with bullion poses challenges, it is extremely versatile and has the potential to move between (and build bridges between) distinct groups and span borders. Trust in any silver—and by extension the bearer of that silver—was thus replaced with trust in a ruler and their silver, be it good or bad.

PART II

CHAPTER SIX

The Roman Legacy

JOHN CHRYSOSTOM (D. 407) won his reputation by doing precisely what his epithet, "the golden-mouthed," suggests: preaching eloquently and often to the Christians of Antioch, his home city. Eventually he was elevated to one of the most prestigious positions in the empire, archbishop of Constantinople, but before that he spent his life immersed in the day-to-day life of Antioch. This great city teemed with markets, and John was a sharp observer of the commercial cut and thrust that he saw as reflective of exploitation, greed, and oppression of the weak by the powerful. Coinage provided a language that he and his urban audience could all readily understand. He described people with gold looking down haughtily on those who stooped to pick up low-value coins that had been dropped. Others gave money to the poor only in return for performing dangerous and humiliating stunts, or spurned formal arrangements for charitable distributions (including through the church) out of concern over peculation by those charged with the task.[1] These experiences made an impression, and John's interpretation of scripture was firmly grounded in the realities of what he saw in the streets beneath the blazing Syrian sun. Christian teaching itself became a sort of currency. He called on people to be like savvy bankers, as the gospels and sayings of Jesus commanded. Their wisdom should be lent out like money, for "if they only store at home the money which they receive, and no longer distribute to others, the whole business of the marketplace will go away." One could, he added, "watch this [cycle of lending and depositing] happen repeatedly all day long."[2] John extended the metaphor to the coin bankers

1. John Chrysostom, *In Corinthianos* 21.5–6 (*PG* 61, col. 177–79). See in general Leyerle 1994.
2. John Chrysostom, *In principium Actorum* 4.2 (*PG* 51, col. 98; trans. Compton 1996, 293).

dealt with, which he mapped onto the teaching of faith. Both needed to have "the complete stamp of the word," and, tellingly, one of the words John used here for coined money, *chrematon* (χρημάτων), derived from the verb for "to use," laying the emphasis firmly on individuals and their decisions in what to do with coin.[3] There was no question of coin being optional; what made it such an effective parallel to faith was the fact that "the use of coins welds together our whole life, and is the basis of all our transactions. Whenever anything is to be bought or sold, we do it all through coins."[4] What mattered for John Chrysostom was *how*, rather than *if*, people used coins.[5]

John's arresting image of the poor scrabbling in the dirt for their copper-alloy coins and the rich who stood apart caressing their gold highlights a monetary chasm in late Roman society. Coin may have been ubiquitous, but not all branches of the monetary system bore equal weight. Base metal in particular was liable to give way, while gold grew stronger all the time. The two competed on a highly uneven playing field, their success or failure dependent on how they gelled with the preferences of the imperial government and the richest citizens of the empire. In an important sense the later Roman Empire did not have a single monetary system: a set number of copper-alloy coins did not always translate to a set number of gold pieces. It was as if modern coins and notes formed separate yet parallel systems, one the domain of mass-market exchange, the other of high-value transactions. The former was tariffed in terms of the latter. What tipped the scales more and more in favour of gold was its stability and its prestige, the two combining to make it the preferred currency of the state and of the elite. These worked hand in glove, and although the state element is much more visible in this period, there was a burgeoning undergrowth of private demand for gold among the wealthy and powerful that laid the groundwork for its vigorous persistence in post-Roman kingdoms with much-reduced governmental machinery.

The emergence of that dynamic is one of the key themes of this chapter. After considering the general outline of Roman money and monetisation, the focus will turn to the relationship of different parts of the currency, and of different elements in society to the currency—in particular the state and the landholding elite. A picture emerges of a monetary system that was increasingly harnessed to accrue wealth and reinforce hierarchical divisions. This was the bedrock on which the early medieval monetary systems

3. Karayiannis and Drakopoulou Dodd 1998, 181–82.

4. John Chrysostom, *In principium Actorum* 4.2 (*PG* 51, col. 99; this translation from Barnish 1985, 37).

5. Singh 2018.

were established. If one wants to know why gold enjoyed such preferential status in the sixth and seventh centuries, one needs to look back to the fourth, to an era when coined money was much more plentiful and much more monolithically imperial—and when the gap between John Chrysostom's users of copper alloy and gold was widening.

Later Roman Coinage: An Age of Gold

The Roman coinage of the fourth and fifth centuries combined baffling complexity in some respects with stunning simplicity in others. In appearance it was exclusively and rigorously imperial. Each coin, of whatever metal, carried the name of the emperor, embedded in a string of abbreviated honorifics. The inscriptions, carved in tiny and exquisite capitals, surrounded an effigy of the emperor. These busts were no longer the highly individual little portraits of the early imperial era. Emperors of the fourth and fifth centuries looked very much alike, contributing to an aura of continuity and stability around the office itself; one that presented a calming antidote to the often rapid and violent turnover of rulers.[6] Imperial authorities jealously guarded the privilege of being represented on coins, extending it only to the emperor himself and select members of his family. Minting was tightly controlled too.[7] Rights to produce coin had narrowed down considerably from early imperial times, when there was a voluminous output of "provincial" issues (as they are now known) on the part of individual cities, mostly in the eastern Mediterranean and mostly in base metal. But this tradition had come to an end by the close of the third century. In its place was a much smaller, more centralised network of mint-places: about twenty places in total for the whole empire, though rarely more than half a dozen at any one time. These mint-places were situated on the basis of administrative geography at the provincial level, not local economic demand. The cluster of mint-places in Thrace and north-western Asia Minor—Constantinople, Cyzikus, Heraclea, Nicomedia, and Thessalonika—reflects the confluence of several provincial jurisdictions, while other mint-towns were also provincial centres, such as Alexandria, Antioch, Aquileia, Arles, London, Lyon, Siscia, and Trier; Constantinople, Milan, and Ravenna, all favoured imperial seats, were special cases, as was Rome (map 6.1). Importantly, there was no hard-and-fast rule that every province or diocese of several provinces should have its own minting

6. Bastien 1992–94; Elsner 1998, 759–60; Prusac 2010, 59–78.
7. Hendy 1985, 371–94; Kent 1994, 23–26.

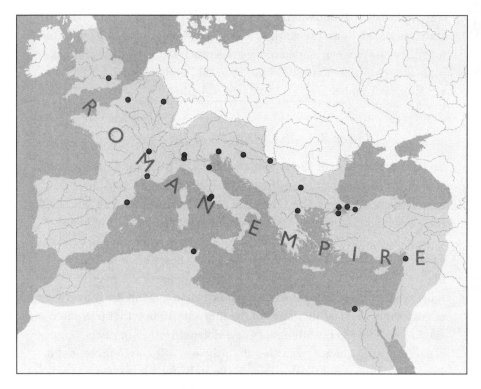

MAP 6.1. The later Roman Empire, with known mint-places active in the period c. 300–450.

centre. Whole areas of the empire such as Africa and Spain were without a regular mint for most or all of this period, and Africa in particular was one of the wealthiest areas of the empire. Yet lack of minting did not translate to a lack of coinage. One of the biggest ever recorded hoards of fourth-century copper-alloy coins came to light at Tomares near Seville (in what was the Roman province of Baetica) in 2016: some 600 kg by weight, contained in nineteen amphorae.[8] Another massive find was in 1981 at Misrata in Libya, consisting of 108,000 fourth-century bronze coins. In North Africa, extensive availability of base-metal coinage was one of the key supports in a dynamic local agricultural economy that included a large element of migratory-season labourers paid with cash wages.[9]

The mint-places of the later Roman Empire took responsibility for different segments of the monetary system. At the apex of their output was the gold solidus and its fractions, the semissis (half) and tremissis

8. Pliego Vázquez forthcoming.
9. Tedesco 2018b, 412–24; Lewit 2009; Dossey 2010, 62–97.

FIGURE 6.1. *Above*: a gold solidus of Constantine I (306–37), minted in 335 at Nicomedia; *below*: a gold tremissis of Honorius (395–423), minted in 403–8 at Constantinople (diameters 21 mm and 16 mm). Both Classical Numismatic Group, LLC.

(third) (figure 6.1). Larger multiples of the solidus existed too, but on a small scale and for ceremonial purposes.[10] The solidus originated in the time of Constantine I (306–37) as a gold piece of about 4.48 grams, or 72 to the Roman pound.[11] Remarkably, the solidus and its fractions were "as fine as it was possible to make them,"[12] and at Constantinople they retained this weight and fineness more or less uninterrupted down to the eleventh century.[13] The solidus quickly became established as the benchmark currency of the empire and a point of reference in systems of account: it rivalled and eventually displaced the silver denarius, reflecting a general shift toward gold and away from silver. Gold being the most valuable and prestigious component of the coinage, its production was the most tightly restricted of all. Only a portion of the mint-places would issue gold, and in the course of the fourth century production of gold started to be restricted to

10. Grierson and Mays 1992, 34–35. See Bursche 2001 on these pieces and imitations of them beyond the frontier.

11. Hendy 1985, 466. Diocletian's gold issues were also referred to as solidi (Hendy 1985, 450), but the weight standard normally associated with the coinage only came in with Constantine. Cf. Banaji 2007, 39–40.

12. Kent 1981, 56.

13. Morrisson 1992, 300.

FIGURE 6.2. Silver siliqua of Magnus Maximus (383–88), minted at Trier (diameter 17 mm). Classical Numismatic Group, LLC.

a so-called comitatensian mint that formed part of the imperial entourage.[14] The comitatensian mint was of a higher status than other "public mints" (*monetae publicae*) and managed by a different administrative department within the "sacred largesses" (*sacrae largitiones*), or managers of public finance.[15]

Denominations below the gold are more difficult to pin down. The main silver coin is known to modern scholars as the siliqua, on the basis that it was meant to correspond to one carob seed (*ceratonia siliqua*) worth of gold (i.e., 1/24th of a solidus), but it is not known if this is what contemporaries actually called the relevant coins (figure 6.2).[16] Another, larger silver coin has been associated with what various texts call a *miliarensis* and came in two slightly different weight brackets.[17] Silver played second fiddle to gold but did have an important niche, especially if one thinks beyond coin to the functions of uncoined bullion as a prestigious demonstration and store of value for the empire's elite.[18] As coined siliquae, silver was common only for a period of about half a century from the 350s, perhaps because of a temporarily elevated valuation relative to gold.[19] But the motives and mechanisms behind silver production are even more obscure than those of gold, as they do not feature in the laws on minting. Nor is it known whether the valuation of silver coin relative to gold remained stable, especially as the weight of the main silver denomination changed several times over the fourth century.[20] Yet the pattern of production suggests a setup not so dissimilar from the gold: minting was concentrated at times and locations where the imperial court was present, as with the comitatensian mint of solidi. That association is never made explicit on the coins, though a small minority of issues incorporate into

14. Kent 1956; Hendy 1985, 386–95. Hendy notes that although the legislation and terminology come from the time of Valentinian I, the coins themselves suggest a similar practice had prevailed since the beginning of the fourth century.

15. Jones 1964, 369. Cf. Delmaire 1989.

16. Carlà-Uhink 2020, 2–5; Grierson and Mays 1992, 27.

17. Carlà-Uhink 2020, 2–5; Guey 1965.

18. Grierson 1992; Hunter and Painter 2013. See also chapter 5.

19. Carlà-Uhink 2020; Guest 2005.

20. Hendy 1985, 468–69; Moorhead 2012, 609.

the abbreviated mint signature the letters sm, usually interpreted as *sacra moneta*, meaning the major establishments of minting in key cities.[21]

Silver might have been especially closely tied to state expenditure, given that there is less evidence for taxes being paid in silver, or of private demand for silver. It therefore might well have been, at times, a favoured way of paying soldiers and other functionaries. A large share of surviving silver coins could reflect military pay and other state disbursements, which would fit with their heavy presence in militarised provinces like Britain, and with references to military pay in silver to soldiers in Gaul and Persia during the 360s.[22] At the same time, siliquae finds from Britain were not restricted to the regions with greatest military presence, so the coins did not stay locked into a fiscal circuit.

By far the largest element of the currency was the copper alloy, which came in a bewildering range of denominations, if the surviving coins are any guide: probably four during the fourth century, with just one very small denomination persisting through most of the fifth (figure 6.3).[23] What contemporaries actually called these coins is a mystery. Only a few terms were used to refer to copper-alloy coins in fourth-century texts: *centenionalis* and (*pecunia*) *maiorina* both come from laws of the mid-fourth century and after, and even if they originally referred to specific coins, they probably took on a looser and more general meaning;[24] while follis, which originally meant "bag," additionally referred to the coins that would be packed into that bag, adding up to a given value.[25] *Bicharacta, dichoneutum*, and similar terms probably denoted coins from early in the fourth century that included a small element of silver alongside base metal, which nefarious metalworkers tried to extract and profit from.[26] Matters were simpler in the fifth century, when the one kind of coin in circulation presumably equated with the low-value nummi that (for instance) Valentinian III fixed at a rate of 7,000 or 7,200 to the solidus in 445.[27] To make matters worse, the famous price-list of Diocletian and many other

21. Kent 1994, 36.

22. Ammianus Marcellinus, *Res gestae* 20.4.18, 24.3.3–4 (ed. and trans. Rolfe 1935–39, 2:26–27, 422–25).

23. Grierson and Mays 1992, 28. Moorhead 2012, 614–24, surveys the relationship of the three metals and their denominations.

24. *Codex Theodosianus* 9.21.6 and 9.23.1 (Mommsen and Meyer 1905 1.2, 473 and 475; trans. Pharr 1952, 243–44).

25. Hendy 1985, 339–41.

26. Hendy 1985, 473.

27. *Novellae Valentiniani III* 16.1 (Mommsen and Meyer 1905, 2:101; trans. Pharr 1952, 530). For earlier rates of exchange, see Moorhead 2012, 621.

FIGURE 6.3. *Above*: a bronze follis of Constantine the Great (306–37),
minted in 310–12 at London; *below*: a bronze nummus of Marcian (450–57),
minted at Constantinople (diameters 21 mm and 11 mm). Both
Classical Numismatic Group, LLC.

sources operate in denarii that were by this stage a purely notional currency, and it is possible that real coins were also at times reckoned as multiples of so many denarii or nummi: numerals designating multiples of
nummi became common on large copper-alloy and silver coins in Italy,
Africa, and the eastern empire during the mid- to late fifth century.[28] The
central point is that, although there are a great many surviving silver and
especially base-metal coins, how exactly they fitted together as a system is
more of a challenge to grasp.

"Money, the Cause and Source of Power and Problems"

It is not possible to put a precise figure on how many coins were in circulation across the later Roman Empire, or even in a single province or
city. But the number is likely to have been huge. The best one can do is
note how many specimens have come to light in modern times. This can

28. Grierson and Mays 1992, 27–28.

be done for only a small number of places. Despite Britain's remoteness, it provides one of the best case studies, as modern England and Wales have a strong set of initiatives in place to analyse and record both single finds and hoards. Even these can still go only so far in revealing the details of original circulation. They include what has been reported by finders in recent decades, or culled from archaeological reports, so are far from complete. Still more problematic is the fact that the find record covers only what was lost or deposited: coins that remained in circulation have vanished without trace, melted down or exported. One has to presume that for every coin that comes to light now, there must have been dozens, hundreds, or even thousands more that passed safely from hand to hand. Those multipliers are the numbers to bear in mind when reflecting on the recorded body of Roman-period single finds from England and Wales, which now extends to over a million coins.[29]

This is an impressive total, but in the abstract it conveys only a very broad sense of scale, like a mountain range seen from afar. To get a better impression of just how thoroughly coin permeated daily life in the later Roman era, one needs to focus in and consider the coins used and lost or concealed on specific sites. One might start where we have already been: John Chrysostom's home city of Antioch. Situated in a rich part of the empire that was just entering a period of economic success,[30] many parts of the city have been excavated, producing over 8,200 coins of the period c. 300–500. Coins have been found in houses, baths, forums, and elsewhere. They point to people using copper-alloy pieces frequently, in domestic and commercial contexts. If there were any doubt about it, the volume and placement of finds from Antioch point to a society in which coin was plentiful.[31] Similar conclusions could be reached with reference to excavations of cities across the empire, from Britain to Iraq, but it is also apparent that coins were not solely an urban phenomenon. Finds from archaeological excavations demonstrate the availability of coinage in the fourth- and fifth-century countryside, and in small towns. Many small bronze nummi had fallen into cracks between the paving stones of the forum of Caesarea in Mauretania (modern Cherchell, Algeria),[32] and peasant sites in central Italy suggest that places of prolonged habitation or commodity production were most likely to see losses of coin in

29. Personal communication with Roger Bland, September 2020.
30. Whittow 2003; Lewit 2020.
31. Personal communication with Alan Stahl.
32. Benseddik and Potter 1993.

this period,[33] while the fort of Richborough in Kent, at the southeastern extremity of Britain, has produced over 27,000 small copper-alloy coins of the fourth and fifth centuries.[34] Smaller sites are represented by the road-side village of Esdraela (now Tel Jezreel in Israel), where about 70 coins from the period have been found,[35] by Kom el-Ahmer in northern Egypt, where over 600 littered a single house and the adjacent stretch of street,[36] and by the single farm of Nador in the former North African province of Mauretania Caesariensis, excavation of which produced 1,131 coins, almost all of them base-metal pieces of the fourth and fifth centuries.[37]

For the inhabitants of these locations, the fourth century was very much a bronze age. Partly that is because there simply was a vast amount of copper-alloy coinage in circulation. There was a genuine explosion in their quantity and spread that began with debasement in the third century but persisted into the fourth. But this would have meant little without there being a receptive market ready to insert those coins into its exchange mechanisms when they became available.[38] It was also not a localised pattern: a similar chronological profile, including the fourth-century blip, has been observed in many parts of the empire.[39]

In contrast, gold and silver are rare among archaeological finds. This is not just a matter of low quantity. High-value coins are poorly reflected by coin finds of many periods.[40] They simply circulated in ways that were less likely to lead to them being deposited in the ground. Gold solidi would have been a rare sight in the handfuls or bags of cash that changed hands every day in the market, or in bathhouses. When gold coins were brought out, it was for big transactions like gifts, taxes, or major purchases, under the spotlight of officialdom or the wide-eyed scrutiny of people well aware of how much value was vested in each coin. Solidi stood less chance of being in the right sort of context to be lost at all, and even if they were, they stood a much higher chance of being looked for and retrieved. It is no surprise that solidi tend to come more from deliberately deposited hoards: stockpiles of wealth squirreled away for safety or for other purposes. One such was hidden in a drain beneath the floor of the House of the Vestal Virgins at the foot of the Palatine Hill

33. Bowes et al. 2021, 544–58.
34. Moorhead and Walton 2014, 103.
35. Moorhead 1997.
36. Asolati, Crisafulli, and Mondin 2019. See also Noeske 2000.
37. Dossey 2010, 85.
38. Dossey 2010, 88. Cf. de Ligt 1990.
39. Reece 1995, 1996; Dossey 2010, 84–88; Moorhead 2020; Collins-Elliott 2019.
40. Cf. Cook 1999; Blackburn 2007, 60–61.

in Rome, around 470. It contained nearly 400 solidi, divided into two distinct groups. One, consisting of about fifty coins, was a mix of issues from various mints and emperors in both east and west, mostly from the forty years or so before the deposition of the hoard. This compares closely to other solidi hoards and resembles the circulating medium in Italy at that stage, which is important in itself: solidi circulated on a large enough scale that they did not remain the stuff of penny packets. That is, in fact, why the second element of the hoard stands out so much: 341 solidi are Rome issues of the ill-fated Emperor Anthemius (467–72), and another ten are Rome issues of his wife Euphemia. Furthermore, 324 of these were struck from a single obverse die and two reverse dies. This degree of homogeneity strongly implies that the coins had stayed together ever since the point of production. It further suggests that whoever put the hoard together was not only a person of considerable means but someone with relatively direct access to fresh coin, so possibly someone involved with Anthemius's regime or the imperial administration. Why it ended up being concealed below the floor in what was by Anthemius's time a defunct temple is anybody's guess. The traditional explanation that it belonged to someone close to the unfortunate emperor, who chose to hide their gold somewhere quiet and accessible from the Palatine when his opponents were battering down the gates of the city in summer 472, is plausible, but nothing more.[41]

The hoard from the House of the Vestals is testimony to why blunt quantitative approaches are an imperfect guide to the impact that various segments of the currency had. Gold combined a circulating component that was used for diverse big-ticket transactions with a strong element of official use. Both were set well apart from equivalent uses of copper alloy. As John Chrysostom put it, a hundred weights of bronze would of course be much heavier than ten equivalent weights of gold. "But the ten measures of gold would be more valuable, since they are more impressive and more honourable according to the laws of nature."[42] Gold in particular was enjoying a boom, its impressive and honourable status reshaping the monetary landscape. Money was indeed "the cause and source of power and problems," to use the words of a fifth-century play.[43]

41. Ungaro 1985; Fischer 2014.

42. John Chrysostom, *In principio apostolorum* 1.1 (*PG* 51, col. 65; trans. Compton 1996, 248–49).

43. "Pecunia, illa rerum ac sollicitudinum causa et caput," *Querolus*, prooemium 2 (Jacquemard-Le Saos 1994, 3; trans. O'Donnell 1980, 215, 295).

Currencies of Inequality

Despite its superficially trimetallic structure, the later Roman Empire had begun to move inexorably toward a monometallic system,[44] in that everything else was worth so much of a solidus, and in turn the solidus was worth its market value in gold. Purity and weight were essential, therefore, but the solidus remained a coin, its gold content and value validated by the minting process. It was not possible to have one without the other. One of the spiritual homilies associated with Macarius of Egypt (d. 391) used this point to elucidate Adam's transgression in the Garden of Eden: "Suppose there were a coin, bearing the image of the king, and it were stamped afresh with a wrong stamp; the gold is lost, and the image is of no value"—in other words, the gold represented his inner nature, the stamp that faculty of choice God bestowed on him.[45] Regardless of the inner quality of the gold, the right stamp was still essential.

Gold solidi came to be seen as a sort of currency within a currency, to be bought and sold in return for other coins. A new law (or "novel") of Emperor Valentinian III in 445 commanded the public "buy" solidi at the same price even if they carried the name of a dead emperor,[46] and St. Augustine (354–430) in his *De musica* could speak of "buying" (*emere*) a gold solidus with just ten nummi as a metaphor for accepting something at dramatically less than its regular value.[47] From the time of Constantine the Great onward, copper alloy did not have the same bullion-based value as solidi: the coins were instead tokens valued in terms of gold,[48] the rate of exchange between them generally allowed to climb up and up, partly due to the decreasing weight of base-metal coins (which culminated in the virtual abandonment of large pieces for several decades) but mostly due to inflation as more gold became available, and more sought after for private and state purposes, in the course of the fourth and fifth centuries.[49] The extent of this inflation was brutal. Under Diocletian (284–305), there were meant to be up to 1,200 denarii to the solidus (in this instance probably equating with the lowest-value coin in circulation).[50] Later, in the fifth

---

44. Banaji 2016, 52; Carlà 2009, 131–57.

45. *Spiritual Homilies* 12.1 (trans. Maloney 1992, 97).

46. *Novellae Valentiniani III* 16.1 (Mommsen and Meyer 1905 II, 101; trans. Pharr 1952, 530).

47. Augustine, *De musica* 1.1 (Jacobsson 2018, 80–81). See also *Sermones* 389 (*De faciendis eleemosynis*) (PL col. 39, 1704) and *Sermones ad populum* 107A (*PLS* 2, col. 774).

48. Banaji 2007, 39–43; Tedesco 2015, 29–31.

49. Tedesco 2019, 561–63.

50. Hendy 1985, 458.

century, the exchange rate in the western empire had gone up to around 7,000–7,200 nummi.[51] The value of the solidus varied geographically, and only a few regions have produced the evidence needed to see how this fluctuation worked in practice. In North Africa at the end of the fifth century, some 14,700 nummi were needed to make up a gold solidus.[52] Egypt apparently had much more extreme inflation than any other known province, as well as uniquely rich documentation to show its progression. Rates of exchange move from 830 denarii to the solidus in 300 to 4,350 in 324, with a series of big leaps in the subsequent century, to about 350,000 in 340, 13,600,000 in 359, and 39,000,000 in c. 423.[53] These colossal sums probably also imply that in Egypt the denarius—now purely a unit of account—had parted ways from the base-metal coinage.

Just as John Chrysostom observed on the streets of Antioch, those who dealt in gold lived in a very different world to those who dealt primarily with base metal. Coined money became highly stratified, gold skewed in favour of elites, base metal in favour of others.[54] The attractions of gold for the wealthy of the empire were numerous. Solidi were stable and predictable in value, as well as highly liquid: everyone was bound to accept them. There was little incentive to store up gold in other forms.[55] The preeminence of gold was, depending on how one looked at it, either a malaise or an opportunity that grew rapidly in the fourth century. The decision to adopt the gold solidus as the benchmark coinage used to rate all others may have been taken as early as the reign of Constantine I.[56] To the anonymous writer of De rebus bellicis (On military matters), a fourth- or fifth-century tract on the ills of the empire and how to solve them, it was as if Constantine had supplanted bronze with gold in public finance.[57] That cannot have been exactly right, but it is indicative of the way contemporaries thought the wind was blowing. Had gold circulated in only a limited way, making it the lynchpin of the whole monetary system could have been an effective check that left the whole in a more balanced state. But it did not circulate in a limited way. Two other key developments saw to that. First, the quantity of gold in circulation expanded, on a modest level in the earlier half of the fourth century, but ballooning thereafter.[58]

51. Grierson 1959b, 77–80.
52. Grierson 1959b, 77.
53. Banaji 2007, 222–23.
54. For the historiography of monetary stratification, see Tedesco 2018a, 123–28.
55. For the contrast with silver, see Hendy 1985, 450–51.
56. Banaji 2007, 39–40.
57. De rebus bellicis 2.1 (ed. and trans. Ireland 1979, 5, 26).
58. Banaji 2016, 112–18.

Where the raw material for this expansion came from is not completely clear: it is likely that a new mine had come online at an unknown location in the empire,[59] but there may have been other factors in play, for the second principal change affecting the gold coinage was that it also began to be used in larger and larger volume. Finds of gold coins, at a low ebb since the early second century, rebounded strongly in the fourth and fifth.[60]

A tidal wave of gold was washing over the empire, and even if it was considerably smaller in real size than the wave of copper alloy, it had a much more destabilising effect. Gold became established as the currency of wealth and power. The richest of the rich disposed of truly staggering amounts of the stuff. Members of the immensely wealthy senatorial families who dominated the western empire, and some up-and-comers in the East, reckoned their wealth in terms of *centenaria*, or hundred-pound units of gold.[61] The historian Olympiodorus marvelled at the sumptuous lifestyle of the Roman super-rich, and claimed that many brought in 4,000 lbs of gold per year, with income in kind mounting to a third that much again in cash value. The next rung down disposed of 1,000–1,500 lbs of gold per annum but could drum up a great deal more for a special occasion, as when Symmachus spent 2,000 lbs on games in celebration of his son's praetorship.[62] Those 2,000 lbs would have consisted of 144,000 solidi alone. It is worth stressing the value of the solidus. Even one of Symmachus's 144,000 gold pieces would have been a small fortune to the poor men and women who watched the games from the topmost seats in the Colosseum. For 1 solidus they could have acquired some 88.5 kg of pork, almost 345 litres of wheat, or about 110 litres of wine (or just over 145 regular modern bottles), based on a set of standard valuations fixed by Emperor Valentinian III in the mid-fifth century.[63] In other words, a single solidus could have bought almost a year's supply of key commodities.

The difference went even deeper than the stark reality of buying power. "A 'poverty line' had come to be drawn in the social imagination . . . between the areas of society where the mighty solidus circulated and a bleak social hinterland where the solidus was absent or difficult to obtain," as Peter

59. Callu and Loriot 1990, 110.
60. Callu and Loriot 1990, 110–15. See also Bland and Loriot 2010, 16–27.
61. Brown 2012, 3–30.
62. Olympiodorus, *Fragment* 41.2 (Blockley 1981–83, 2:205). See discussion of this and other figures in Wickham 2005, 162–63.
63. *Novellae Valentiniani III* 13.4 (Mommsen and Meyer 1905, 2:95–96; trans. Pharr 1952, 527).

Brown eloquently put it.[64] Access to gold was access to a solid world of economic clout, the vast majority of which flowed between members of the empire's elite. Nonetheless, there is considerable evidence that solidi also entered the hands of a wide variety of people. In 373 Flavius Ammon, an Egyptian *speculator* or military scout, sold 2⅛ arouras of land in return for 5 solidi.[65] Augustine told an anecdote in one of his sermons about a "devout man of middling rank" (*quidam religiosus mediocris homo*), who sold his 1 solidus for the sake of his household, subsequently losing all the proceeds to a thief save for 100 folles he had given to the poor.[66] In his vitriolic diatribe against Vigilantius, written in the 390s, Jerome snidely remarked that the son of a tavern-keeper (as Vigilantius was) could not be expected to combine the skills of examining gold coins and discerning good wine with real knowledge of the scriptures.[67] Further north, in the relatively underdeveloped province of Britain, numerous small hoards have been found with a handful of gold solidi alongside more numerous siliquae and copper coins. At Sturmer (Essex) in February 1793 a workman came across a small pot stopped up with tile that contained thirty coins: 1 solidus of Honorius, and 29 siliquae of him and his predecessors.[68] Over a dozen similar assemblages from the late fourth and early fifth centuries have been found in Britain alone, and they plausibly represent little nest eggs put together by relatively humble members of society;[69] people like regular soldiers who could look forward to occasional donatives of 5 solidi and a pound of silver,[70] or the camel driver who worked for the great Apion family in sixth-century Egypt in return for a salary of 1⅓ solidi per annum (plus 16 *artabas* of grain).[71] Handling gold meant something very different when one clung to 1 or 2 solidi rather than hefting hundreds or thousands of them. Dealing in such a dauntingly valuable concentration of wealth forced people of limited means onto the back foot: by investing

64. Brown 2012, 15. Cf. Tedesco 2015, 43–48.

65. Hoogendijk 1995.

66. Augustine, *Sermones ad populum* 107A (*PLS* 2, col. 774). A different version of the same story is in *Sermones ad populum* 389 (Lambot 1948, 48), describing the figure as "not a wealthy man, but even so rich in the fat of charity from his limited resources" (homo non diues, sed tamen etiam de tenui facultate pinguis adipe caritatis).

67. Jerome, *Epistolae* 61 (Hilberg 1910–18, 1:579).

68. Bland and Loriot 2010, no. 184.

69. Bland and Loriot 2010, nos 14, 24, 181, 236, 378, 379, 440, 442, 549, 551, 555, 599, 641.

70. Jones 1964, 624. These took place every time a new emperor took office, and every five years each member of the imperial college had ruled, meaning that in practice they would have happened more often than every five years (assuming, that is, that emperors paid up when they were supposed to).

71. Banaji 2007, 235–37. See also Kelly 2004, 141.

so much in a single transaction, gold constrained as well as liberated. An anonymous soldier in Egypt in the late fourth century wrote a pleading letter to his commanding officer, in which he begged his superior to release 4 solidi that he was due, since the 1 solidus that had been given to him and another soldier had been spent on emergency medical expenses and the pair were now left destitute.[72] Gold was a rich man's currency: the poor did use it, but in relative terms they did so rarely, lightly, and perhaps with a degree of resentment and difficulty as they came, or were forced, into contact with the worlds of wealth and officialdom. The last of these is by far the best evidenced.

"Caesar Seeks His Image on Your Gold": Gold and the State

Gold glinted brightly in the imagination of contemporaries who wrote about taxes. The two seemed to be a natural, inevitable pair. Gold meant taxes, and taxes meant gold. In the hands of an orator as adept as St. Augustine, bishop of Hippo, this rhetorical conjunction came brightly to life. In one of the hundreds of sermons he preached to the people (*sermones ad populum*) of Hippo and Carthage between 391 and his death, Augustine seized on the words of Psalm 4:7, "the light of thy countenance, O Lord, is signed (*signatum*) upon us." *Signatum* was also the word that was used for the striking of coins, and the bishop of Hippo built from this a powerful metaphor grounded in the coins that the congregation would have used every day, imagining that the listeners might become God's coins and be taken up into His treasury. At this point he called on another passage of scripture that all would have known: the parable in the synoptic gospels about rendering unto Caesar the coins that bore his image (and to God the things that were God's).[73] But Augustine playfully recast the roles of man and God around the coin. In his sermon, mankind became the money of Christ (*moneta Christi*), on whom the likeness of God had been stamped, as in the psalm—and Christ himself became a tax collector (*exactor*) as he explained what kind of coin he and Caesar sought.[74] Augustine ended his point with a rhetorical question: "As Caesar seeks his image on your gold, will God not seek his image on your soul?" In doing so he made a small yet telling change to the words of scripture. Whereas the evangelists had

72. Kenyon and Bell 1907, 242–43 (no. 982). Discussed in Underwood 2018, 359.

73. Matthew 22:15–22; Mark 12:13–17; Luke 20:20–6.

74. Hirt 2012.

written of Christ handling a denarius (a silver coin; δηνάριον in Greek) with the image of Caesar on it, for Augustine the defining money of the Roman state was gold.[75]

The evocative image of Christ the taxman coming for coin, and particularly for gold coin, relied on Augustine's congregation sharing an impression that the emperor and his agents expected to receive solidi. Some members of the congregation knew from painful, firsthand experience that this metaphor could be all too real. In one of his letters, Augustine told the sorry tale of one of his congregants, Fascius. Tax collectors had appeared and demanded from him the sum of 17 solidi. Not having the requisite money, Fascius had fled and sought sanctuary in Augustine's church, where the bishop in turn had had to fend off the tax collectors. To avoid Fascius being dragged out and punished after his requisite thirty days of respite were over, Augustine had borrowed the 17 solidi from another man to make the payment—and was now writing a letter to explain the embarrassing situation to his congregation, in the hope that they would have a whip round and pay back the lender. The letter reveals something of the pressure that everyone was under: those who had to pay, those like Augustine who wanted to help, and also those who had to extract what was needed in a timely manner—the urgency came from the fact that the tax collectors (who were probably local *curiales* dragooned into a risky and thankless task) needed to move on in short order so could not afford to wait.[76] What is less clear, however, is what kind of tax Fascius's 17 solidi were going toward. The late Roman imperial government expected several kinds of tax from its citizens; John Lydus in the sixth century listed no fewer than twenty-six varieties of tax.[77] Some were explicitly expected to be paid in gold, such as the *collatio glebalis* (paid by the senatorial class) and the *collatio lustralis* (paid by all engaged in buying and selling).[78] But the most prominent exaction was a tax on land, usually known as the *census* and administered in varied ways between provinces, so that it was sometimes based on land alone, sometimes on land and population.[79]

The starting point was apparently that payments would be reckoned and made in kind, based on registers of tax liability by *caput* (head) and/or

75. "Caesar quaerit imaginem suam in auro tuo, deus non quaeret in animo tuo," Augustine, *Sermones ad populum* 16 (Dolbeau 1996, 128; trans Hill 1997, 71–72).

76. Augustine, *Epistolae*, 20 (ed. and trans. Baxter 1930, 520–27).

77. *De magistratibus* 3.70 (ed. and trans. Bandy 1983, 242–45).

78. Kent 1956, 194–96; Jones 1964, 427–37, 871–72.

79. How taxation was reckoned and carried out are matters of considerable complexity and long-standing debate: for selected views with earlier references, see Tedesco 2015; Banaji 2007; Wickham 2005, 56–80; Jones 1964, 411–69.

iugum (plough) for each *civitas* (city-territory).[80] But a process known as *adaeratio* (literally "metallisation") led to portions of the state's due in kind being commuted into coin of corresponding value. Responsibility for doing so might have lain with the taxpayer, the local tax collector, or indeed the soldier or official who would otherwise have been paid in kind.[81] The process did not in itself create money but rather brought a private world of commerce and currency into contact with the state, for the latter's convenience, and with the probable goal of obtaining gold solidi. Later Byzantine evidence indicates that tax collectors may have rounded up to the nearest gold piece and then paid back the difference in base metal.[82] There was a thirst for cash on the part of the state, although adaeratio could work at several levels and be driven by demand from both sides. Payments in kind would mostly have been destined for supplies to the army or, in Egypt, North Africa, and selected other regions, the population of privileged cities, as part of the *annona* distribution of subsidised food.[83] Adaeratio applied principally to military supplies, and already under Constantine I, soldiers were spurning supplies until they rotted because the procurators and tax collectors took too long to purchase them.[84] Officers were in the habit of rejecting offerings of supplies, or the prices set for them, as not befitting their rank. Problems of managing adaeratio persisted across the fourth century. Emperors did not object to it in principle, but they did seek to avoid provincials having to pay multiple times due to negligence, and also to pin down fair prices and clear time frames for the commutation of supplies.[85]

Of course, all this reflects the logistical problems the military leadership faced. Payments in kind for supplies would have come from the whole populace, meaning that they often lay far from where they needed to be on the frontier. Moving them, as with moving anything overland, was a costly exercise: Diocletian's edict of maximum prices showed that moving a wagon of 1,200 lbs of wheat cost twenty denarii per mile, meaning that

---

80. These units did not translate directly into exact numbers of people or a consistent size of land unit: see inter alia Jones 1957; Goffart 1974.

81. Tedesco 2015, 26–37; 2019, 564.

82. Hendy 1985, 285–89. The twelfth-century text records this practice in relation to a suite of minor taxes, rather than the main land tax, but a similar system is likely in earlier times.

83. Wickham 2005, esp. 708–15; Lo Cascio 1999.

84. *Codex Theodosianus* 7.4.1 (Mommsen and Meyer 1905 1.2, 315; trans. Pharr 1952, 158–59).

85. *Codex Theodosianus* 7.4.18–36, 8.4.6 (Mommsen and Meyer 1905 1.2, 319–24, 368; trans. Pharr 1952, 160–64, 190).

moving it one hundred miles cost more than half the value of the grain.[86] It was massively expensive to pay soldiers in supplies on anything other than a local basis. Sometimes there might have been no alternative to relocating supplies over long distances, when the men were too numerous or the local supplies too scant. Another avoidance tactic was to billet soldiers in rural areas, close to the produce they would eat. But adaeratio came into its own as a way of allowing soldiers to source their own food locally, at fixed prices.[87] Cash also had the advantage of being easier to keep track of and less liable to spoilage. Counterintuitively, payment in kind probably cost the state considerably more than paying in coin.

Taxes were not the only way for the state to obtain gold: there were also mines, and taxes on landholders in metalliferous areas, as well as the revenue from confiscated or defunct property.[88] The state bureaucracy also exercised a prerogative of compulsory purchase from money changers, for whom the senator Symmachus—at that time urban prefect of Rome—had to intercede with Emperor Valentinian II in 384. Solidi at this point were in high demand for "public use" (usus publicus) on the basis of a tariff fixed a few years earlier by the emperor Gratian (d. 383). Now the money changers were being caught out by the rising price of gold on the open market, and the fixed tariff left them out of pocket in their business with the state.[89]

Across the board, the late Roman government was voracious when it came to taking gold. But the limits of that relationship are revealing too. Contexts in which gold was not used tell us more about those in which it was. The picture that emerges is one of a prestige currency that was aligning more and more with the elite's interests. To a significant degree these overlapped with the interests of the state. This is important, for the state's role was critical,[90] but also because it was intertwined with those of its powerful subjects. The imperial administration, as an entity that reached into the lives and pockets of its people, can be seen as a set of detached and depersonalised institutions, though it can equally be thought of as a web of human interactions that was at various times governed by big-picture profit or moralistic checks.

The biggest limitation is what happened, as it were, at the other end. State authorities seem to have been very hesitant about gold expenditure.

---

86. Hendy 1985, 554–61.

87. Treadgold 2014, 307. In North Africa in the early sixth century, a normal year's supply through the annona could be commuted to 5 solidi (Treadgold, 313–14).

88. Jones 1964, 435–36; Burnham and Burnham 2004

89. Symmachus, Relationes 29 (Seeck 1883, 303–4; trans. Hendy 1985, 250–51).

90. Hendy 1989.

Gold would be earmarked for expenses only where, for whatever reason, nothing else would do. Two examples stand out. One is tributes to quell barbarians. Large quantities of gold and silver were handed over year on year to groups beyond the frontier to circumvent the need for military action. These are one explanation for the numerous finds of late Roman gold and silver in what is now central and northern Europe, well beyond the frontiers of the empire.[91] The barbarian recipients of these coins were under no compulsion to accept the emperor's base-metal coins; paying them in precious metal was a necessity. The second expenditure where nothing but gold (and silver) would do was what might be called prestige payments. Late Roman emperors were masters of combining state with ceremonial. The massive Missorium of Theodosius, found near Mérida in Spain, is both a highly accomplished material manifestation of imperial pomp and circumstance and a weighty treasure in itself (figure 6.4): its ring-base carries a discreet inscription specifying the Missorium's weight as 50 lbs.[92] It and similar items of prestige silver plate belong to the world of *largitio*: distribution of gifts by the emperor on important occasions such as anniversaries. Coins, especially gold ones, were also a central part of this ceremony (and, tellingly, the office of the *sacrae largitiones* was responsible for making solidi and siliquae as well as plate).[93] A bowl like the Missorium of Theodosius most likely came to its initial recipient piled high with gold coins: Corippus vividly described "silver vessels full of yellow gold" that the emperor gifted to an array of senators in 566.[94] Lavishness on this scale had to be seen to be marvelled at; gold and silver were part and parcel of what must be described as an experience as much as a simple donation or state expenditure. It was involvement in rituals of this kind that helped define the group consciousness of the highest of the elite.

Status affected how all state expenditures were paid out. Salaries for bureaucrats in Rome, Ravenna, Constantinople, and provincial centres across the empire were reckoned, and probably normally paid in, gold. *Domestici* (personal assistants to every officer of state) expected a solidus a day in the prefecture of the east (Syria and Egypt), while in Africa the *domesticus* and *cancellarius* (who controlled access to the court of the

91. Moorhead 2012, 608; Guest 2008; Fagerlie 1967; Andersson 2011; Klang 2013. For hacksilver handed over across frontiers, see Fraser and Hunter 2013. For wider material context, Bursche 2002.

92. The weight of the Missorium is in fact somewhat less than 50 Roman pounds (15.35 kg, rather than about 16.1 kg), though part of it is missing (Leader-Newby 2004, 11, 14).

93. Leader-Newby 2004, chap. 1.

94. Corippus, *In laudem Iustini* 2.142–47 (ed. and trans. Cameron 1976, 76–77).

FIGURE 6.4. The Missorium of Theodosius (diameter 740 mm; weight 15.35 kg), probably made in 388 and found at Almendralejo, Spain, 1847; it was folded in half when first uncovered. Real Academia de la Historia, Madrid.

official) together shared a stipend of 7 lbs of gold a year (252 solidi each).[95] A higher office, such as the praetorian prefect of Africa in the time of Justinian (527–565), brought 100 lbs of gold a year.[96] Theoretically many bureaucrats were also members of the army,[97] and financing the army is usually seen as *the* key expenditure of the Roman state across its history.[98] The bulk of the soldiery's direct cash income—and the only part of it that was commonly paid in precious metal—arrived in the form of *donativa*: essentially ceremonial bonuses given at the accession of a new emperor, or after five years of a reign. From at least the 360s, donativa typically

95. Jones 1964, 602–3.
96. Jones 1964, 557.
97. Jones 1964, 563–65; Banaji 2007, 54–55.
98. Duncan-Jones 1994, esp. 33–46; Hebblewhite 2017, 103.

consisted of 5 solidi plus (sometimes) a pound of silver.[99] There was also an annual cash payment, the *stipendium*, going back to the days of the Principate when it was supposed to cover living expenses. But inflation meant that this had fallen to a token amount in the fourth century, and it was phased out altogether in the fifth.[100] Theoretically, the main emolument of the military, including officers, was payment in kind via the *annona militaris*, though this was of course often subject to adaeratio.[101] Those who actually served in the emperor's armies probably received much of their cash pay, beyond donativa, in copper alloy. Base-metal coins of the fourth century are plentiful in provinces with a strong military presence, such as Pannonia, Germania, and Britain,[102] and aspects of the more detailed distribution within Britain have been argued to reflect purchases of supplies from the countryside or the billeting of troops in rural areas.[103]

It does not necessarily follow, however, that since soldiers were often paid in base metal that most base-metal coins were made and/or used specifically to pay soldiers. Finds are also numerous in provinces like Egypt, North Africa, and Spain that had few or no regular army units stationed there, and generally no mint. Nor are these provinces outliers in the chronological and geographical profile of their coin finds; if anything, some of them show signs of a very proactive response to ebbs in supply that affected the whole region. At Alexandria, local imitations made by casting regular coins account for a significant proportion of fourth- and fifth-century finds—the majority in the 360s and the early fifth century, when the supply of official coins dropped off across the Mediterranean.[104] The overall impression is that the supply of base-metal coin was fluid and porous, and while there may have been channels that brought batches of fresh coin to these provinces in the same way as to militarised areas— payment of officials and *coemptio* of supplies on the state side, by-products of the *annona* from Egypt and North Africa, and possibly also consignments made and sent at the instigation of individuals or institutions, as happened with base-metal coin earlier in the Roman period[105]—commercial

---

99. Bastien 1988, showing that issues in all metals could probably have been intended as *donativa*—this was far from solely the province of gold.

100. Hebblewhite 2017, 87–90.

101. Jones 1964, 623–66, 643–44.

102. Reece 2003; Callu 1980b, 105–6.

103. Moorhead 2001, 90–96; Moorhead 2012, 615; Walton and Moorhead 2016, 843–44.

104. Marcellesi 2012, 272–74.

105. Katsari 2003; Kokkinia 2000 records an inscription from Rhodiopolis in the second century, which seems to describe a wealthy local's "donation" of copper-alloy coins that he had commissioned from Rome's mint.

redistribution was also an important force in bringing coins from their places of origin and initial expenditure into neighbouring provinces.[106] That point ties into larger commercial dimensions in the late Roman economy as a whole: state and aristocratic actions were important but collectively may still have been outweighed by the production and exchange carried out by the peasant population.[107] Moreover, because copper-alloy coins could stay in circulation for a long time (potentially decades or even centuries), a drip-feed of fresh coin might be enough to sustain a relatively dynamic monetary economy.[108]

This process of monetary osmosis was accepted as part of circulation by the Roman authorities, though their expectation was that it would happen as a natural consequence of interprovincial trade: assembling and transporting copper-alloy coin as a commodity in itself seems to have been frowned on. A law of 356 set out to curtail traffic in copper-alloy coin; no longer would merchants travelling overland be allowed to take more than a thousand folles with them to cover expenses.[109] The passage is confusing because it compresses together concern with several monetary offences (including counterfeiting and use of prohibited coin), but it also recognises that there was a trade in coin, most likely between southern Gaul (where the prefect to whom the law was directed had his base) and neighbouring provinces such as Spain or North Africa.[110] It was this— the carrying of large amounts of coin "in order to sell them" (*vendendi causa*)—that the emperors wanted to halt. Nevertheless, the circulation of copper-alloy coins in general was strongly encouraged, not least because, whatever mechanisms first distributed them, they might very easily come back to the state in the form of tax payments. There is abundant legislative evidence that base-metal coin could be, and was, used to settle accounts with the state.[111]

The manufacture and circulation of gold needs to be looked at critically too. As with base metal, it is not satisfactory to assume that gold was only made and used because of the demands of the fisc. A clue to the limitations of state initiative comes from setting a well-known law of Valentinian I alongside actual finds of gold pieces. Issued in 366, the law

106. Hendy 1985, 379.

107. Carrié 2012; Whittow 2013, 137–43.

108. Dossey 2010, 84–90.

109. *Codex Theodosianus* 9.23.1 (Mommsen and Meyer 1905 1.2, 475–76; trans. Pharr 1952, 244).

110. Hendy 1985, 291–94.

111. See *Codex Theodosianus* 11.1.23, 11.4.1, 11.20.1–3, 11.28.9 (Mommsen and Meyer 1905 1.2, 576, 583, 607, 619; trans. Pharr 1952, 294, 297–98, 311–12, 319).

stated that all the solidi paid by any particular province in tax should be melted down together into one huge ingot for remission to the treasury.[112] If this had happened regularly, and if gold was dominated by the fiscal cycle of tax–treasury/mint–state expenditure, then the result would be a very "young" profile of coins in circulation, with few if any old or worn gold pieces. That is largely true in peripheral areas such as Britain, where the military and administrative cycle may have accounted for a greater proportion of circulation,[113] but less so in the Mediterranean, where hoards of fourth- and fifth-century solidi regularly contain decades-old coins that show evidence of weight loss through wear.[114] The stock of solidi does not, in short, seem to reflect a coinage that was mostly being recycled on a frequent basis. It is possible that Valentinian's law was a dead letter, or a targeted measure intended only to operate for a short time, or in provinces beset with unacceptable levels of fraud and peculation. Alternatively, and perhaps more probably, the amount of gold being handed over in tax— despite looming large in the legislative record—was small in proportion to the overall circulating supply of solidi. This conforms with recent assessments of late Roman taxation being heavy, but far from crippling; large swathes of the empire prospered in the fourth century, and sometimes long afterward as well.[115]

So, while the role of gold had expanded rapidly, neither did gold account for all taxation (let alone all state expenditure), nor did taxes account for all use of gold pieces. To identify what else made gold so popular, it is necessary to examine how its public face interfaced with other kinds of use, above all in the hands of the elite.

State and Private Demands in Dialogue

The Roman state never had a large bureaucracy: at the beginning of the sixth century there was a total of some thirty thousand to thirty-five thousand staff, which is about the same as the number of civil servants in the British Home Office alone as of 2019.[116] The job of those bureaucrats was essentially to handle interactions with central government, most visibly

---

112. *Codex Theodosianus* 12.6.12 (Mommsen and Meyer 1905 1.2, 716; trans. Pharr 1952, 374). A group of fifteen such ingots was found at Crasna in Romania (well beyond the frontier of the empire) in the nineteenth century: see Hobbs 2006, no. 1400.1.

113. Guest 2005, 22, 38.

114. Banaji 2007, 70–75, 77–81.

115. Heather 2005, 78–80.

116. Kelly 2004, 111.

in the form of legal grievances, and to oversee the extraction of resources from the population. But the refined and exclusive caste of imperial civil servants did not sully themselves by engaging directly in the rough-and-tumble business of collecting what was due. The central administration only set the amount each province was to provide: that sum was then portioned out among the city-territories that made up the province, and the task of updating tax assessments and ensuring their payment to provincial-level authorities fell to members of the city-level councils (*curiae*), effectively meaning that tax-gathering was a hot potato dropped into the hands of local elites. Any loss or shortfall came out of the locals' own pockets, at considerable cost: one Egyptian official named Flavius Isidore in 373 lost part of a tax payment from the city of Hermopolis that he had been responsible for delivering to the imperial residence in Syria, and he complained that shelling out the full compensation from his own resources would ruin him.[117]

As might be expected, this was a deeply unwelcome responsibility and contributed significantly to the mass dereliction of duty by members of city councils, known as *decuriones* or *curiales*: they escaped by joining the army or the clergy, or if they could by seeking a high honour in the imperial administration.[118] Those who fled tended to be *curiales* of lesser, more precarious wealth. This proved to be an important ingredient in shaping the nexus between elite wealth and gold, for while departing *curiales* left behind the risk, they also turned away from the power and the potential profit that tax collection entailed. They left that duty to a narrower field of richer counterparts, drawn from the wealthiest town councillors.[119] Processes of adaeratio and coemptio, which depended on ready access to gold among private citizens, provided another way for the locally rich to turn taxation to their advantage.

Power over fiscal liability helped to consolidate the wealth of rich landowners and was manifestly open to abuse; as Salvian bitterly put it with reference to Gaul in the fifth century, "the powerful levy what the poor are to pay; the favour of the rich decrees what the multitude of the wretched are to lose."[120] Even the overall amount of tax to be paid was kept secret,

---

117. Kelly 2004, 150–51; Zuckerman 1998, 86–91; Ward-Perkins 1998, 373–76. In the event Isidore only paid 72 solidi out of a total of 177, and this sum was perhaps not truly debilitating, as he continued to transact land and engage in disputes after 373.

118. Jones 1964, 724–63; Liebeschuetz 2001.

119. Brown 2012, 345–47. On the middling levels of wealth among *curiales*, see Kelly 2004, 145–51.

120. "Decernunt potentes quod solvant pauperes, decernit gratia divitum quod pendat

to protect the interests of those who held the reins. Successful locals operated alongside agents of the mega-rich, who might own property across multiple provinces, and also alongside members of the growing imperial bureaucracy. The latter had interests that tended to extend beyond an individual city-territory, contributing to a tendency to take cash where possible.[121] Bureaucrats' presence was more apparent in some areas than others; broadly speaking, they were a stronger, more prominent force in the East, which had a more regionalised elite.[122] The West, in contrast, seems to have had a starker, steeper distribution of wealth, marked by a class of super-wealthy and highly influential senatorial landowners with property all over the Western Empire, and long-established dominance over major administrative roles.[123] Jaw-dropping though the wealth and landed property of these few families was, it existed alongside multiple layers of lesser elites. Some, like Sidonius Apollinaris (d. 489) in Gaul, descended from senators and prized their status as *clarissimi*, the "entry-level" rank for senators, but their land and resources were concentrated within a single province or diocese; below them were many others, including large numbers of *curiales* like the 283 whose names appeared on an inscribed list at Timgad, or the father of St. Patrick in western Britain.[124]

All these groups worked to bring more gold into their own hands. They could supplement often comparatively small formal salaries in various ways. Those with public office had the potential to make considerably more by exploiting their position. Bureaucrats charged fees for their services, which were perceived, counterintuitively, as a levelling mechanism: anyone who could pay got access to the machinery of the state, rather than having to rely on the more slippery stepping stones of personal networks and reciprocal obligations.[125] That access did not come cheaply, however. Christopher Kelly has calculated that in fourth-century North Africa, it cost 81 *modii* of grain to pursue a fairly straightforward case locally, or 121 if it needed to be prosecuted at the provincial capital (which would translate to between 3 and 6 solidi).[126] John Lydus in the sixth century boasted that he had gained 1,000 solidi in fees one year, at a time when the salary for someone in his position

---

turba miserorum." Salvian, *De gubernatione Dei* 5.7 (ed. and trans. Lagarrigue 1971–1975, 2:334; trans. O'Sullivan 1947, 139).

121. Sarris 2004, 302.

122. Banaji 2007, 101–70.

123. Banaji 2007, 216–17; Kelly 2004, 142.

124. Wickham 2005, 155–65. For the Timgad list, see Kelly 2004, 145–47. For Patrick's father, see *Confessio* 1 (Bieler 1993, 56), with recent discussion in Flechner 2019, 30–39.

125. Kelly 2004, 112, 134–35, 157.

126. Kelly 2004, 107–8.

might have been 9 solidi per annum.[127] Other income streams based on official functions were not so different from fees in practice but were treated more harshly by contemporaries, effectively amounting to peculation. One law of Honorius and Theodosius II chastised the procurators who gathered taxes for upping the rate at which tax was drawn, from the equivalent of 1 solidus per 120 people to 1 per 60 or even 13.[128]

Those with land and resources had additional, more subtle ways of capitalising on late Roman public finance that overlapped with the income that came from being a rich and overbearing landlord. The dark matter of the late antique economy, given the general preponderance of sources dealing with the state, is the activity of private citizens producing, distributing, and marketing. Only in Egypt is that side of the story more consistently visible, and although there are many uncertainties, monetisation on the back of the agrarian economy was considerable.[129] State and private interests fed into one another, even at a very local level. The concentration of local power into fewer hands led wealthier city officials as well as bureaucrats to become vectors of patronage, not least by providing shelter from the full force of obligations to the state. Lesser landowners voluntarily came under the wing of richer ones, the patron claiming ownership of the poorer figure's property for tax purposes. All too often this fiction of ownership graduated into actual ownership, and the payment of more and more onerous dues: a day's work here, a render of money there.[130] Encroachment of this kind was another of the abuses Salvian chastised the rich of Gaul for inflicting on the poor.[131] In more developed form, this process resulted in local lords coming to expect regular rents and labour services from those who lived in the orbit of their property, in return for letting tenants work part of the land while working on others for the lord: a setup very similar to the "bipartite" large estates that emerged in the early Middle Ages. There are hints from Egypt, and more contentiously from Italy and southern Gaul, that large bipartite estates of the sixth century and later had their roots in this reshuffling of control over material resources in the later Roman period.[132] These effects relate to those

127. *De magistratibus* 3.27 (ed. and trans. Bandy 1983, 174–77). For fees, see Kelly 2004, 107–13.

128. *Codex Theodosianus* 7.4.32 (Mommsen and Meyer 1905 1.2:322–23; trans. Pharr 1952, 163).

129. Tedesco 2020 surveys the problems.

130. Sarris 2004, 294–96; Banaji 2007, 112–27.

131. Salvian, *De gubernatione Dei* 5.7–8 (ed. and trans. Lagarrigue 1971–1975, 2:332–44; trans. O'Sullivan 1947, 137–44).

132. Sarris 2004, 310–11; Banaji 2007, 171–89; Halsall 2012 (who emphasises ruptures

who actually lived directly under the thumb of major elite landowners, but the consequences of their actions sent out ripples through society more widely. For example, drawing formerly independent landholding tax payers under the wing of elites meant that the tax burden fell more heavily on others;[133] this was how small-scale figures like Augustine's friend Fascius could end up being pursued by the taxmen of North Africa over a matter of 17 solidi.

The role of gold coin in this shift is less easy to pinpoint. Paying solidi could help to cement the dominance of landowners, particularly in the case of day labourers, who were an important element of the agrarian workforce in Egypt and possibly elsewhere. Paying such workers in gold was an important way for the relatively poor to gain access to solidi. That might have been desirable in some respects: it gave the potential to pay one's own way with the state, and perhaps passed on some of the lustre of exclusivity that gold possessed.[134] Yet stipulating payment in gold, either in advance or in arrears, would also have been an axe held over the heads of labourers, effectively as peonage: payment in advance bound labourers to work until their upfront solidus had been paid off; and payment in arrears forced labourers to work until their efforts added up to a solidus's worth.[135] To turn rents and produce into solidi presented more of a challenge. Many peasant tenants would not have been in a realistic position to pay solidi on their own account, or could only do so with considerable difficulty. Demands of this kind might lie behind a law of the 360s that forbade North African landlords from demanding their *rustici* pay cash instead of produce, implying that this was unwelcome to the producers themselves, but a known problem nonetheless.[136] Produce made directly for the lord's benefit by slaves or through labour obligations would have to be sold off to obtain cash, at rates beneficial for landowners out to get gold.[137] Potential customers included the state itself—the counterpart of adaeratio, in which the government bought supplies in return for offsetting monetary tax obligations, was known as *coemptio*[138]—and soldiers spending their adaeratio-commuted cash for supplies, as well as the population of towns. All these required a lot of legwork on the ground and so

---

in the post-Roman period, meaning that later structures of this kind would be new, albeit similar, formations).

133. Sarris 2004, 296.

134. Banaji 2007, 184–85, 190–212.

135. Banaji 2007, 198–99.

136. *Codex Iustinianus* 11.48.5 (Blume et al., trans. Frier 2016).

137. Tedesco 2015, 47–48.

138. Naismith 2014a, 275–76.

must have been arranged by local agents who set up the assemblage of produce, its sale, and the remission of the proceeds to the landlord. Such was apparently the practice in Spain and Gaul in the seventh century.[139] Nebulous though they now seem, the processes that connected rural production with large-scale monetisation matter considerably as an essential bridge from one economic world to another.

By hook or by crook, the senators, *curiales*, and bureaucrats of the empire were bringing in large quantities of gold. Since they were also the agents of imperial government, these men were in a position to wash one hand with the other. The emphasis so far has fallen on the nexus of elite and state interests with regard to public income, settled using coins which had already been put into circulation for other purposes. There is also a case to be made that the production and initial distribution of coin sometimes arose from the efforts of private individuals. This is not to deny that fiscal forces set their rhythm, or that the minting network remained under close central management: some issues bear inscriptions making it clear they were intended as donativa, for example, and it is possible to tie other issues to donativa, with varying degrees of confidence.[140] But there is a disjuncture between the vast scale of circulation of solidi, not least in fees to bureaucrats and in the income of the mega-rich, compared with the relatively meagre outlays in gold on costs like state salaries. It is possible that part of the cachet of solidi came from the demand for them: the comparison that might be drawn is with fifteenth-century England, where even members of the gentry such as the Paston family of Norfolk were perennially short of precious-metal coin. One night in March 1475, John Paston III wrote to his mother to explain his delay in travelling to her, the reason being that he and his retinue were awaiting their cash payment for service in the king's army, and their paymaster was in turn expecting the money to appear at any time.[141] Another possibility is that some of the business of the late Roman mints responded to direct demand from the elite: those with the resources to send their money or metal over a considerable distance to be minted and then brought back. Two laws in the Theodosian Code appear to address this eventuality. In 369 Valentinian I, Valens, and Gratian wrote to the *comes sacrarum largitionum*, ordering him to put a stop to private individuals bringing their own gold to the "public mints"

139. Naismith 2014a, 298–99; de Ligt 1990, 42.

140. Bastien 1988. For reservations about which coin issues can securely be tied to donativa, see Burnett 1989; King 1990.

141. Davis 1971–76, 1:593–94. For discussion and context, see Mayhew 1974.

(*monetae publicae*) for processing into coin.[142] That of course implies that this had been going on, potentially on a significant scale—indeed, it is possible that the emperors were perfectly happy for the gold to be sent to the central comitatensian mint.[143] What irked them was that the gold at provincial mints came from people trying to circumvent regular fiscal channels. The mints were simply not in the business of providing a service to those who had gold but wanted to turn it into a more convenient, reliable form. Nonetheless, there was a market eager for more direct access to minting facilities. Those demands were heard, because a few years later, in 374, the emperors relented. From now on private gold *could* be coined at imperial mints, and Valentinian and his companions made the best of a bad situation by commanding that two ounces per pound of gold (⅙) be surrendered for the privilege of using imperial mints to turn privately owned metal into coin.[144]

Precedents for this arrangement could be found earlier in the Roman period. A civic-minded magnate from Rhodiapolis in Lycia during the second century paid from his own resources to have bronze coins minted in Rome and then shipped on to his city.[145] Bankers might have done the same thing, albeit not for the same motives. They had responsibilities such as turning soldiers' gold into more readily spendable base-metal coins, for which it would have been helpful to have numerous such coins on hand.[146] By the last quarter of the fourth century, then, imperial mint-places may have been catering to private consignments of gold alongside public requirements. It suggests the depth of demand for gold, and that some unknowable proportion of the gold coins made in the 370s and after (just as they were becoming extremely numerous) might represent the results of private interests piggybacking on the fiscally oriented minting system.

Conclusion

Ambrose (d. 397), the virtuoso bishop of Milan, in the 380s found himself embroiled in a bitter dispute with the imperial authorities, led from behind the throne by Justina, mother of the young emperor Valentinian

142. *Codex Theodosianus* 9.21.7 (Mommsen and Meyer 1905 1.2, 473; trans. Pharr 1952, 243).

143. The interpretation favoured in Hendy 1985, 389–90.

144. *Codex Theodosianus* 9.21.8 (Mommsen and Meyer 1905, 1.2:473; trans. Pharr 1952, 243).

145. Katsari 2003; Kokkinia 2000.

146. Katsari 2003, 142.

II (d. 392). This quarrel had many sides to it, and its progression remains hotly debated. It led to some tense moments, above all when the bishop and his church were surrounded by a steel ring of armed soldiers.

In a powerful sermon he wrote at the height of this dispute, which would have been preached with the clanks of Roman military might audible from just outside the church, Ambrose foregrounded the proper and improper use of gold. He willingly offered up the gold that the emperor required from church estates and also gladly accepted the charge of distributing gold among the poor. This was partly a facet of the current dispute, one charge against Ambrose being that he was priming an uprising, but the accusation had deeper connotations: giving out largesse in gold was supposed to be a prerogative of the emperor, who handed it to senators. By dishing out solidi to the poor of Milan, Ambrose undermined the power play that gold was meant to exemplify.[147] The bishop felt contempt for the lust that gold provoked in base men, and in a text on his deeds as bishop, *De officiis* (On Offices, or On Duty), Ambrose defended his decision to use gold that had been given to the church to redeem captives taken by barbarians; this, he said, was *aurum utile*, "useful gold," or, as the translator of *De officiis* Ivor Davidson more elegantly and insightfully rendered it, "gold that is truly beneficial."[148] The inference was that this kind of gold—gold that adorned the church, redeemed captives, and enriched the poor—stood apart from the regular use of gold that was emblematic of greed and worldly excess.

For Ambrose, Augustine, John Chrysostom, and other Christian literati of the fourth and fifth centuries, gold had become shorthand for wealth so concentrated that its very name conjured up dizzying opulence. Gold as a metonym went far beyond haves and have-nots, evoking something more like have *everything* and have *nothing*. In this capacity, gold featured often as part of a discourse on the deployment of wealth in a Christian society,[149] the participants in which fixed their gaze on the ethereal strands that tied earth to heaven. Thirst for gold as one of the basest sins could be contrasted with rejection of money as an elevated virtue. A rural community of eastern monks imagined by Sulpicius Severus (d. c. 425) had supposedly cast aside "gold and silver, which mankind generally deems the most desirable of things," and its priest refused an

---

147. Ambrose, *Epistolae* 75A (Faller and Zelzer 1968–1990, 2:104–5; trans. Liebeschuetz 2005, 158). For background to the dispute, Liebeschuetz 2005, 124–35; for Ambrose and his views on gold and wealth, Brown 2012, 120–47.

148. Ambrose, *De officiis* 2.138 (ed. and trans. Davidson 2001, 2:344–45).

149. Brown 2012.

offering of 10 solidi as detrimental rather than beneficial to the church.[150] The *Narrationes* of Pseudo-Nilus of Ancyra contains a description of the idyllic life of hermits: "The coin of Caesar has no currency among them . . . they do not know the practices of selling and buying."[151]

Even if they wrote in terms that were deliberately larger than life, these writers captured some of the central points about gold in the late Roman world. Above all, there was a lot of it, and it had been given a preferential status in the monetary system. Gold was more than one component of a multimetallic system. It became the money of account across the board. In practice, the later Roman Empire operated a monometallic monetary system, with everything else being priced in terms of gold. Because of its versatility, the taste for gold particularly favoured the standard gold coin, the solidus and its fractions: since these were guaranteed by the state and continued to be worth their weight in gold, there was a strong incentive to store the metal in this form. The government also allowed more and more of its taxes to be paid in gold, requiring it as a general rule for some, and permitting adaeratio from kind into gold for others. Expenditure in gold was also large, if more targeted.

A whole web of gold-tinted exchange emerged, which was strongly associated with wealth and power. Those with the resources to do so dealt in gold whenever they could. As private citizens, they demanded it from the products of their land, and as subjects of the emperor they finagled their tax assessments and contributions to be in gold. One of the key points to emphasise is that the two worked hand in glove. The unrelentingly imperial face of the coinage conceals a more nuanced background, in which private demand played a large part. This has to be inferred from scattered sources. Much more is known about the public dimension of coinage because legislation on it, in the Theodosian Code and Justinian Code, features so prominently in reconstructing its production and use. These codes of their nature emphasise what *should* happen, from the highest possible vantage point in the empire: that of an emperor intent on keeping order. But this is only one perspective. Taxes in gold should be read as a symptom of a wider world of gold circulation, and a response to private demand as much as an imposition from the state, with the same people doing both the demanding and the imposing. Crucially, this extended to the ability to force gold onto and out of others. Landholding

---

150. "Aurum atque argentum, quae prima mortales putant." Sulpicius Severus, *Dialogues* 1.5 (Fontaine and Dupré 2006, 120–22; trans. Schaff and Wace 1894, 11:26).

151. Pseudo-Nilus of Ancyra, *Narrationes* 3.8 (*PG* 79, 617c; trans. de Ligt 1990, 33).

elites had to obtain their gold from somewhere. Some could have come from selling supplies to the army and other agents of the state. But a lot surely had to come from the products and labours of dependants and workers who toiled on estates, and other private buyers of agricultural produce. In this way, gold could and did penetrate well below the major landowning elite, yet it kept its association with richness, and a high proportion of minor landowners, peasants, and townspeople who handled gold must have done so as part of their dealings with richer neighbours or patrons. They did not necessarily use it willingly or eagerly, and when they did use gold must often have done so briefly: solidi were of such value that they would have been for large transactions (such as tax liability for minor landholders), or quickly broken up with money changers for base metal that could be used in a more granular way.

Gold fell short of being a real mass currency, even if its impact on the monetary system was massive. This is a major part of the story of late Roman currency, especially as it pertains to subsequent developments. Its legacies included an emphasis on gold coin, which in the long run left silver and copper-alloy coinage vulnerable; a firm association between minting and secular authority; and a dynamic relationship between public mechanisms of production and private wealth. These will be pursued in more depth in the next chapter. For now, the final point to reiterate is one noted earlier: that the empire was a big place, and over the two centuries or so considered here it changed a great deal. The emperors strove for a degree of standardisation in denominations and certain policies, but there were still important differences. Individual emperors steered elements of public finance in different directions: Valentinian I undertook important modifications to the minting system and sought to limit the spiralling price of gold;[152] Zeno (476–91) and his top advisers were supposedly masters of office-peddling.[153] Demography and imbalances in the distribution of wealth meant that individual provinces varied widely in the circulation of cash. The prevalence of gold in fiscal contexts tended to reflect the level of liquidity needed in state finance. That is why, counterintuitively, the generally less developed western empire was significantly more demanding of gold in its finances than the East; a process that also suited and played into the hands of the Western Empire's relatively more dominant cohort of large landowners.[154] Italy, home to the senatorial aristocracy of

---

152. Amandry et al. 1982; Hendy 1985, 387–91; Grierson and Mays 1992, 30–31; Tedesco 2015, 42.

153. Kelly 2004, 158–65.

154. Tedesco 2015, 44–45. Cf. Hendy 1989, 16.

"gigantic wealth, possibly . . . greater in relative terms than any other aristocracy ever,"[155] was, in 458, apparently able to make all its tax returns in gold if so desired.[156] Egypt, as discussed earlier, was a special case due to its great agricultural wealth, its unusual geography and, above all, its uniquely rich records. But these also highlight the importance of geography at a much more granular level. Individual city-territories and rural districts could vary in the degree and nature of their contact with the monetary economy. Towns were magnets for the wealthy and for exchange, typically galvanising circulation of coin in surrounding areas, though the fourth and fifth centuries also saw, in many provinces, extension of monetised exchange into more remote rural areas, on the strength of the massive copper-alloy coinage.[157] The presence of large estates, military units, government installations of other kinds, and roads would all also have stimulated use of coinage, mostly in copper alloy but to some extent in silver and even gold. Whether one felt the full force of late Roman monetary pressure depended heavily on where and when one lived in the empire, but there is little doubt that its reach and weight grew during this period.

155. Wickham 2005, 156.

156. *Novellae Majoriani* 7.16 (Mommsen and Meyer 1905, 2:171; trans. Pharr 1952, 559). See Tedesco 2015, 87–92.

157. Dossey 2010, 84–88.

CHAPTER SEVEN

Continuity and Change in the Fifth to Seventh Centuries

PROCOPIUS (D. AFTER 565), a learned and sharp-penned member of the East Roman intelligentsia, had a strongly developed sense of propriety: certain prerogatives were the domain of the Romans, by which he meant the emperors of Constantinople and their subjects. He was, consequently, not impressed on finding out that the Franks had had the temerity to issue gold coins stamped with the image of their own ruler. Even the Persian king, he observed, restricted himself to silver, for "it is not considered right either for him or for any other sovereign in the whole barbarian [i.e., non-Roman] world to imprint his own likeness on a gold stater."[1] Procopius brought up this affront as one of several ways in which these thugs on the western fringe of civilisation (as he saw them) were aping and debasing Roman culture.

The coins Procopius railed against were solidi and tremisses of Theodebert I (533–547/48), king of the eastern portion of the Merovingian Frankish kingdom, known as Austrasia (figure 7.1). In principle Procopius's accusation of stamping the king's image on these coins seems puzzling, for they closely replicate those of recent East Roman emperors. Nothing about the figure on these coins, save the style of its execution, was especially Frankish. The difference lay in the inscription, which broke with the usual Frankish custom of making gold coins in the name of a Roman emperor (either the current one or a former one). Instead, they carry the name of Theobebert himself, sometimes called "king" (REX), "victorious"

---

1. Procopius, *History of the Wars* 7.33.5–6 (Dewing 1914–1928, 4:438–39).

FIGURE 7.1. Gold solidus of Theodebert I (533–547/48), uncertain mint (diameter 19 mm). Fitzwilliam Museum, Cambridge.

(VICTOR), "our lord" (D[*ominus*] N[*oster*]), or even "revered one" (AVG[*ustus*]), implying that the king was staking a claim to Roman authority.[2]

Theodebert's coins exemplify the blend of old and new seen in the former western empire between the later fifth and seventh centuries. Gold coin remained dominant and superficially very much in the same vein as before, at least at first. But behind the scenes important changes were taking place. State-led production in large, centralised mints for distribution as military pay gradually ceased to be the dominant model. This organisation and production of coin instead shifted to more dispersed, localised arrangements. That might at first have meant gold pieces were made at the point of paying taxes rather than when the state spent them, but it also very probably meant that local elites were taking on a larger role. That role embraced their full range of needs and activities, not just as taxpayers and (often) representatives of the state, but as pillars of the agrarian economy and in networks of power and patronage. It is possible, probable even, that this range of uses for gold was far from new. Many of these developments can already be observed in the late Roman Empire. The changing circumstances of the age simply altered the balance. But if there was relative continuity in the use of gold, the rest of the monetary economy entered the early Middle Ages in a much more precarious state. For the mass of the population, access to coined money became a matter of avoidance where possible, stop-gap measures where necessary and engagement with high-value gold coin where unavoidable, as will be seen. This chapter begins with the expedients that arose to negotiate the collapse of the empire's

2. Jenks 2000; Grierson and Blackburn 1986, 115–17. For context, see Collins 1983.

base-metal currency. The spotlight then pivots to the reasons for, and consequences of, concentrating so exclusively on gold. Thereafter, the focus will turn to four more detailed case-studies: Ostrogothic Italy, Merovingian Gaul, Visigothic Iberia, and early Anglo-Saxon England.

Getting By in a Time of Scarcity: Low-Value Coinage

The limitations of the money supply in the post-Roman centuries have long been apparent. In particular, the dominant gold coinage functioned very poorly as a currency for the mass of the population. Its high value suited it only for large obligations, luxuries, and bulk purchases. All these are attested: Gregory of Tours describes merchants in sixth-century Gaul who traded in large quantities of wine with gold pieces, and aristocrats splurging gold and silver in the jewellery boutiques of Merovingian Paris.[3] But the high value of gold inevitably meant use in commercial contexts was limited, and unlikely in itself to have been a driver of production. Gold survived because it fulfilled other purposes. A corollary of its ongoing dominance was the contraction of low-value coinage. The former western empire was fast becoming, as Brian Ward-Perkins put it, "a world without small change":[4] base-metal coinage, the mass-market currency of the Roman Empire. The pace and depth of its retreat varied place to place. In Britain it was especially severe, with only very limited imports and sporadic residual use of old copper-alloy coins after the early fifth century.[5] Some cities in Burgundy and Provence minted bronze into the sixth century, but on a fairly limited scale.[6] Post-Roman issues of small bronze coins have now been identified from certain cities in southern and eastern Iberia and the Balearics; some seem to have been civic issues, and a few bear royal monograms (figure 7.2), but most are anonymous.[7] Italy and North Africa had more substantial base-metal coinages, including a revival of large denominations in the later fifth century (figure 7.3).

---

3. Gregory of Tours, *Historiae* 6.32 (Krusch and Levison 1951, 303; trans. Thorpe 1974, 363); and Gregory of Tours, *In gloria confessorum* c. 110 (Krusch 1969, 369–70).

4. Ward-Perkins 2005, 110–17.

5. Ward-Perkins, 112; Abdy 2006, 91–94; Moorhead 2006, 102–6; Moorhead and Walton 2014, 103.

6. Lafaurie 1973; Brenot 1980; Grelu 1984; Grierson and Blackburn 1986 1, 111–12, 115–16; Stahl 2012, 633–39.

7. This series has been the subject of heated debate, but the emerging consensus is that it does indeed represent a Visigothic-period issue. The coins were first identified in Crusafont i Sabater 1994; the most important recent studies of the topic are Pliego Vázquez 2015–16; 2018a; 2020a; Mora Serrano 2016.

FIGURE 7.2. A small bronze piece probably made in Visigothic-period Seville (diameter 14 mm). Classical Numismatic Group, LLC.

FIGURE 7.3. Revived larger-format bronze coins; *above*: from Rome under the Ostrogothic king Theodahad (534–36); *below*: from Constantinople under Anastasius I (491–518), minted after 498 (diameters 25 mm and 38 mm). Both Classical Numismatic Group, LLC.

These persisted through the sixth century, with supply and use of new coins becoming patchier in later times: Rome still had quite a substantial bronze coinage in the early eighth century,[8] an idiosyncratic local lead coinage was produced at Luni,[9] and Sicily had a vast base-metal coinage in the seventh century and into the eighth.[10]

It is therefore premature to pronounce the low-value coinage of the West dead on arrival in the sixth century, except perhaps for Britain and northern Gaul. In the Mediterranean there were, besides the small issues of new bronze coin outlined earlier, three other strategies that provided continued access to low-value denominations. The first was a resurgence of small silver pieces. Some of these may have been conceived as halves or quarters of old Roman units, but the denominational structure of these coins is largely guesswork, save in Italy and Africa, where the silver coins carried numbers expressing their value in terms of denarii or nummi.[11] A small number of minute silver coins have now been identified from northeast Iberia and assigned tentatively to the mid-sixth century.[12] A much larger but still poorly understood series of small silver pieces, conventionally known as *argentei*, began in Gaul during the last stages of imperial rule in the early to mid-fifth century and continued into the sixth century. Most known finds come from graves, but an increasing number stem from other contexts, and given their tiny size (typically between 0.15 gram and 0.4 gram in weight) they are easily missed or completely lost to corrosion. The appetite for these coins was strong. Finds occur across Gaul, and local issues were supplemented with others brought in from Italy.[13] Silver coins would have been more valuable than equivalent copper-alloy ones, but very small denominations would have been within the regular reach of most members of society, in the same way as farthings and halfpennies of similar size in the later Middle Ages.[14] The will of Abbot Aredius of Limoges, written in 572, describes the wives of unfree

8. Rovelli 2000 and 2001.

9. Ricci 1988.

10. Prigent 2013; Grierson 1982, 129–38, 165–68.

11. Grierson and Blackburn 1986, 19–20, 36–37; Merrills and Miles 2010, 171–73. Values were placed on silver pieces in Italy only after Justinian's conquest in the mid-sixth century and show that the silver coinage played an intermediary role between bronze and gold, fitting into two systems of account based on the different metals: Grierson 1982, 58–59.

12. Crusafont, Benages, and Noguera 2016; Kurt 2020, 117–18. The crucial hoard comes from Les Tres Cales, near Tarragona.

13. Kent 1994, 450–62; McCormick 2013, 343–49; Blanchet 2020; Doyen 2019. See also the important papers in Chameroy and Guihard 2020.

14. Dyer 1997.

tenants (*mancipia*) paying rents of ten *argenti* each per year, or giving five on the church altar.[15] In one of the Tablettes Albertini from what is now inland Tunisia in the 490s, a list of the contents of a dowry includes eight thousand folles in silver: that would have meant at least 336 coins, if paid in the hundred-denarii silver pieces that were the largest denominations of the time.[16] Although separated by hundreds of miles, these two cases exemplify the potential of late and post-Roman silver coinages, which straddled the gap between base-metal and gold issues and enjoyed a degree of popularity in some quarters. Their production also combined features of higher and lower denominations. Some bore names of rulers or cities and stemmed probably from a formal minting operation that discharged state obligations to soldiers or officials (perhaps of lower status than those who received gold).[17] But in Gaul especially there is a large group of silver coins of less fixed fineness and more diverse character, which can plausibly be explained as the output of a more dispersed network of production that catered to a wider range of figures and demands.[18]

The second strategy for negotiating the retreat of larger regular issues in copper alloy was to produce a vast coinage of tiny base-metal pieces referred to by modern scholars as nummi or (for the smallest specimens) *minimi*. Nummi can be found in large numbers across the Mediterranean, including in the East; they are well known from excavations at Antioch, Aquileia, Beirut, Athens, Jerash, Butrint, and Rome, among others. They continued to be made and used even after the authorities of Carthage and Rome, and in 498 those of the eastern Roman Empire, reintroduced large-denomination bronze coins. It is possible that in the East, especially on the Danubian frontier, the large denominations were meant as military pay, the implication being that the morass of nummi instead reflects the still vibrant commercial economy of the Mediterranean.[19] Some of the latter can be assigned to specific rulers or cities. But the bulk of the relevant coins have no intelligible inscription. Their origins are murky; certainly

15. *PL* 71, cols. 1144–46. On the status of *mancipia*, see Wickham 2005, 559–64; Rio 2017, 163–64, 184, 188, the latter stressing that *mancipium* (at least in the Carolingian period) had become quite a vague term for several different kinds of unfree status.

16. *Tablettes Albertini* no. 1 (Courtois 1952, 215). On valuations see Grierson 1959b. The calculation is based on a follis at this time equating to 42 nummi, with silver coins being valued in terms of denarii worth ten nummi each.

17. On the use of late Roman silver coins to supplement military payments in gold, see Banaji 2007, 43, with emphasis on ceremonial uses in Grierson 1992; Moorhead 2013, 609–11; Callu 1980a; Morrisson 1989–91, 240–41.

18. Blanchet 2020, esp. 357–59.

19. Moorhead 2013, 609; Guest 2012; Wickham 2005, esp. 708–20.

there is a large element generally characterised as "irregular" or "unofficial" from outside the network of regular mints.[20] Egypt produced a large series of coins cast from originals in the fifth century,[21] but western (probably mostly North African) coins dominated the small change of the Mediterranean, including the East, in the sixth century,[22] presumably circulating along the same channels that distributed African Red Slip ware.[23] Even the much rarer Spanish examples have turned up in Arles and Sardinia, and as far afield as Greece.[24] Importantly, the same basic production technique was used by makers of nummi, official and unofficial alike, in different regions of the Mediterranean,[25] and from the point of view of users there would have been little apparent difference, if anyone even stopped to check, for it is likely that these minute coins often changed hands en masse in bags or purses (folles) with thousands of them being needed to match the value of a solidus.[26] Another reason for their vibrant circulation was that, as the lowest common denominator in the late Roman monetary system, they could slip easily between the monetary regimes of the period throughout the Mediterranean. In effect, two tiers of base-metal coin came into being.

The final strategy of maintaining access to low-value coin is related to the second. It consisted of protracted—sometimes very protracted—use of existing copper-alloy coins. It is likely that in the fifth century especially a great many coins from the third and fourth centuries or before were still in use.[27] In Italy old bronze coins were extensively used into the sixth century and to a lesser extent the seventh.[28] At most sites it is impossible to gauge the likely date of loss of individual coins: only fine stratigraphy anchored by other materials reveals the extent of ongoing reuse of base-metal coin. At Vieux-la-Romaine (dép. Calvados), where a total of 668 coins were found in the excavation of a large domestic building, the latest layer—dated by ceramics to the fifth century—contained nearly 200

20. Moorhead 2012, 624; Asolati 2016.

21. Moorhead 2012, 624.

22. Guest 2012, 113, 118; Moorhead 2013, 602–3; Birch et al. 2019, 5374–75.

23. Bonifay 2004; Wickham 2005, 709–13, 720–31; Baklouti et al. 2014.

24. Pliego Vázquez 2020a, 147.

25. Canovaro et al. 2013, 1028.

26. Moorhead 2013, 605; for exchange rates of bronze and gold, see chapter 6. The production of imitative nummi in lead, found most often in Italy, perhaps relates to the practice of passing on coins in bags or purses, where a minority of overweight coins would not be noticed: Moorhead 2012, 624.

27. Arslan 2007a.

28. Rovelli 2009, 48–55; 2015–2016; Sagui and Rovelli 2012; Cantilena, Rovelli, and Sagui 2017.

coins. Of these, only 12 had been minted after 364: 13 dated to the second century or before, and the bulk of finds (over 160 coins) came from the later third century, a period of massive monetary productivity.[29] Continuous usage can be seen all over the Roman world, including in urban settings: at Beirut,[30] Nicopolis ad Istrum (now in northern Bulgaria),[31] and Carthage.[32] In some locations older Roman coins were adapted as they entered reuse. At San Martino-Lomaso (Trentino) and a number of other places in both the East and the West, large copper-alloy coins from the early Empire were cut into pieces, usually halves or quarters, and it is not clear whether these should be read as a way of making small change, or as a sign the coins were being treated as scrap metal.[33] Italy and North Africa have also produced extensive finds of early imperial copper-alloy coins with a new denomination (either XLII or LXXXIII) deeply scratched onto the surface, reflecting a more structured re-entry of these coins into circulation (figure 7.4).[34] The scratched coins are mostly of the first-century Flavian dynasty, so they cannot have been extracted from wider circulation and may be the result of a hoard coming to light in late antiquity.

How long this practice continued is an open question. Certainly it was not universal: in the south of Gaul, old Roman bronzes had largely gone out of use by the end of the fifth century.[35] Finds of Roman coins from Anglo-Saxon contexts in England are relatively few and have generally been read as ornaments, apotropaic objects, or weights, though the dominance of grave finds might be a misleading guide.[36] In certain parts of early medieval Europe, however, there was extensive and long-lasting use of Roman base-metal coins. A fourth-century bronze was overstruck as a *fals* at some point during the Muslim rule of al-Andalus, so no earlier than 711, and conceivably later in the eighth century or even the ninth.[37]

29. Blanchet 2016, 88.

30. Butcher et al. 2003, 97–114.

31. Butcher 1995.

32. Buttrey 1976; Reece 1984; 1994.

33. Saccocci forthcoming. For examples in Egypt and Cyprus, see Moorhead 2012, 623.

34. The origin of these coins remains a point of debate, but either Italy or North Africa seems likely. Arslan 2017 has proposed a much earlier date (in the late third century), though there are good reasons to consider the traditional fifth- or sixth-century date more likely (Asolati 2018, 256). Selected discussions include Morrisson 1983; Grierson and Blackburn 1986, 28–31; Gambacorta 2010; Asolati 2012, 113–34; Saccocci 2015.

35. Brenot 2003. For ongoing use of earlier bronze coins in northern Gaul in the fifth century, see Cardon 2015–2016.

36. King 1988, 224–25; Moorhead 2006.

37. The relevant coin is part of the Tonegawa Collection, visible at http://www .andalustonegawa.50g.com/fulus/FrochII_f.jpg (as of 29 August 2022).

FIGURE 7.4. A bronze *as* of Galba (68–69) carved with XLII for circulation in the post-Roman period (diameter 28 mm). Classical Numismatic Group, LLC.

This is no outlier: Roman coins were being used and lost as late as the ninth, tenth, and eleventh centuries. Several ninth- to eleventh-century sites in France have produced significant numbers of Roman coins from (apparently) the same stratigraphic layers as contemporary silver pieces.[38] One of the richest and most closely studied cases in Spain is El Tolmo de Minateda (Albacete). A Roman hilltop settlement, abandoned in favour of the surrounding valley in the second century, was reoccupied in the sixth century and remained important until the later ninth. It is hence very much a site of Visigothic and Muslim date. Yet more than half the coins found there belong to the Roman period, the large majority of them to the third and fourth centuries, when El Tolmo de Minateda was essentially defunct. The stratigraphy again clearly indicates that these are early medieval losses. In other words, Roman coins were brought from elsewhere and used extensively between the sixth and ninth centuries.[39] The scale here is staggering: there simply must have been a large circulating stock of centuries-old coins.[40] These coins could have formed a second layer of monetisation, probably informal in character, like tokens in seventeenth-century England that were made by private individuals to fill a gap in the circulation of small change.[41] They may have fulfilled other roles too,

38. Cardon 2015–2016, 15–20.

39. Doménech Belda and Gutiérrez Lloret 2006; Amorós Ruiz and Doménech Belda 2020.

40. Doménech Belda and Gutiérrez Lloret 2006, 365; Doménech Belda 2016, 742.

41. Valenze 2006, 37–38; Whiting 1971. Several archaeologists working on material from France proposed this interpretation: Cardon 2015–16, 20–23, though Cardon himself ultimately prefers to see the coins as raw material for metalworking (2021, 129–31).

including as a source of bullion for metalworkers.[42] Where Roman bronzes came from is less easily answered. They cannot have been continuously circulating en masse since the Roman period: the mixture of issues from the first century to the fourth seen in early medieval contexts would never have been encountered together in previous times.[43] Rediscovery is the only viable possibility. They may have been stockpiled and curated, most plausibly by local elites on whose property they were found.

The later fifth and sixth centuries are generally perceived as an age of gold, dominated by the solidus and the tremissis. A chasm had opened up between these very valuable coins and the main other coinage produced at that time: the tiny copper-alloy nummus. There is no mistaking the advantage that accrued to those who could deal in gold, which brought much greater price stability. But there were ways of partially bridging the gap. Silver pieces did so most neatly, being between copper and gold in value. Nummi themselves were available in large quantity and offered a degree of versatility on several levels. Individual coins, or handfuls of coins, could be used for small transactions, while bags of them facilitated larger exchanges. Being low-value, they were seemingly viewed in a more relaxed way by contemporary authorities. Nummi circulated very widely, and local and "irregular" production to supplement the offerings of trade and government supply was widespread—a creative, engaged response to demand, a "community currency" that has points of contact with other local efforts to reinforce and particularise a general monetary system.[44] The nummus economy persisted through the sixth century and in some places, such as Iberia, possibly into the seventh. During that time, and beyond, they were used alongside not only larger regular base-metal coins, but a great backwash of older copper-alloy coins, stretching back to the third century or earlier.

On these foundations, people in parts of the western Roman world still had access to a substantial quantity of small change, probably not materially less than their ancestors had done a century earlier.[45] In some regions it can even be taken as an important feature in the economic landscape: commercial farming in North Africa continued to pick up pace from the fourth century into the fifth and beyond, employing a large number of

---

42. King 1988, 227–28; Clément 2015–16, 329.

43. Moorhead 2006, 107–8; Bompaire 2015–16, 6–8; Naismith 2017b, 38.

44. For a reading of German *Notgeld* (local issues of small-denomination paper currency from the First World War and the Weimar Republic) along these lines, see Maynes 2019.

45. Ruggini 1984, 19.

mobile, waged peasant labourers, in part on the back of extensive access to appropriate forms of coined money.[46] It is worth emphasising this point about the larger background. Substantial mass currencies, and efforts to keep them as accessible as possible, arise from complex economic systems. In the elegant breakdown of the Roman economy delineated by David Mattingly, low-value coins were tied most closely to the empire's diverse provincial economies (and large provinces could contain several largely separate economic circuits), or successors of similar scale. These units worked around towns, markets, and their hinterlands and intersected partially with wider networks of state-driven or commercial movement of goods between provinces; low-value coins, along with ceramics, are in fact a good example of how local and long-distance economies of bulk redistribution could dovetail.[47]

How long did all this last? Until at least 600, those parts of the Mediterranean that had possessed a working monetary economy in the Roman period continued to do so. Thereafter the picture breaks up, and generalisation becomes impossible. Small silver issues ended in Gaul at some point in the sixth century, but in Italy both Byzantine and (to a lesser extent) Lombard mints continued to make them across the seventh and into the eighth, in reduced quantity,[48] as was also the case in North Africa and Sicily, though the latter two provinces also had a voluminous local coinage of larger copper-alloy pieces down to the mid-seventh century and ninth century, respectively.[49] The nummus economy started to grind to a halt after about 600. Late issues from after this date can be identified in the eastern Mediterranean and possibly Iberia (where some types may even belong to the later seventh century), but on a smaller and more geographically restricted scale.[50] Old base-metal coins may never have gone away entirely. Building and digging on Roman sites must have always brought more specimens to light. And changes in the nature of the evidence, such as the decline of furnished burial, remove some of the clearer contexts for detecting ongoing use. Nonetheless, there are no grounds to see them continuing in monetary use on a significant level. As the year 700 neared, most denizens of the Mediterranean faced a very different situation in terms of the usable, low-value coins available to them than their grandparents would have known. In many areas there was a lot less coin

46. Dossey 2010, 45–103; Tedesco 2018, 412–24.
47. Mattingly 2011, 138–40.
48. Arslan 2004, 2016; O'Hara 1985; Morrisson and Barrandon 1988.
49. Grierson 1982, 125–29; Morrisson 2016, 181–95.
50. Moorhead 2013, 610; Pliego Vázquez 2020a, 146–49.

around, and even where there was still coin to be had, it tended to be more circumscribed in circulation.[51]

Gold, Taxes, and Barbarian Settlement in the West in the Fifth and Sixth Centuries

There is no getting around the difficulties posed by the emphasis on gold in post-Roman currency. A single gold piece was valuable,[52] and there is no reason to believe that the buying power of the solidus dropped off after the end of Roman political rule; if anything, it may well have gone up. The only concession that minting authorities made to the practical challenges of dealing with such a high-value currency was to move gradually away from the solidus toward its smallest fraction in regular production, the tremissis.[53] The solidus retained its primacy in most written contexts,[54] but in practice newly minted gold solidi from local sources had become a rarity in western Europe by the seventh century.

The late Roman gold coinage was the only segment of the monetary system that survived into the post-Roman centuries on anything like the same level as before. In Gaul the rate of single finds of gold pieces made between about 455 and 575 dipped only a little compared to the period c. 300–455, and it increased significantly in the period c. 575–675.[55] The simple reason why gold persisted was that it stood at the peak of the Roman monetary system. It was the benchmark currency and the preferred medium for payments that had any whiff of prestige about them.[56] Maintenance of gold coin reflected commitment to cultural and institutional *Romanitas*. Yet it persisted at first as a sort of zombie currency. The rulers of the new kingdoms in the west—Burgundians, Merovingians, Ostrogoths, and Visigoths—generally minted gold solidi and tremisses in the fifth and early sixth centuries with no reference to the local ruler or mint-place; on the face of it, these territories still recognised past or present Roman emperors in their coinage and used long-established standards of weight and fineness. It was of course possible to tell these issues apart: a law

---

51. For wider economic system shock in the seventh century, see McCormick 2001, esp. 115–19; Wickham 2005, 819–31, emphasises longer-term change, driven especially by the fate of state-led distribution.

52. See chapter 6.

53. Morrisson 1989–91, 240; Stahl 2012, 646–52; Naismith 2014a, 281–82.

54. Naismith 2014a, 282, lists a few exceptions.

55. Naismith 2014a, 283.

56. See chapter 6 and Naismith 2014a.

from the Burgundian kingdom, probably drafted in the time of Sigismund (516–24), says outright that all solidi are acceptable, save for four groups of poorer quality that contemporaries must have been able to distinguish but that numismatists have struggled to identify.[57] This homogeneity had advantages. As the Burgundian law noted, it meant that gold pieces could circulate over a long distance and across political frontiers.[58] Crucially, adherence to Roman denominations, standards, and even designs and inscriptions is also usually taken as evidence that this part of the machinery of the Roman state had been taken over in functional condition, albeit on a geographically reduced scale, and with two additional caveats: that the reasons for minting coin in the later Roman Empire were probably growing more diverse, and were not just tied to fiscal demands;[59] and that this is largely an argument from silence. Precious little is known about what actually changed behind the scenes of fifth- and sixth-century coinage. All that is certain is that gold pieces were not made "just because": they had not been under the emperors, and even less so under the new kings. To add to the circulating pool of currency meant a specific need for fresh coins. There had to be a patron with the significant resources needed to sustain minting in gold, where even a few dozen coins—let alone hundreds or thousands—represented a considerable sum, well beyond what most peasants, or even ordinary soldiers, might expect to see in a year. Crucially, there also had to be some sort of context that required fresh coins, and not solidi or tremisses drawn from the large pool of circulating coins made under the authority of past or present emperors. Demands that laid emphasis on the physicality and ceremonial of coin distribution were therefore more likely to have prompted fresh minting.

Individual kingdoms each had their own trajectory. The conservatism of gold coinage conceals regional idiosyncrasies, but issues of bronze and silver are more revealing, as they provide more direct reference to contemporary rulers and mints. In Gaul, copper-alloy coins were made on a limited scale at Provençal and Burgundian mint-places into the sixth century,[60] while very small silver pieces were used across the province.[61] The coinage of the Vandals, based in Carthage, was unusual in that it

---

57. *Constitutiones extravagantes* 21.7 (de Salis 1892, 120). On context, see Wood 2016, esp. 5 (where he also raises the possibility of dates for this text in 508 or after 524).

58. Carlà 2010.

59. See chapter 6.

60. Brenot 1980; Grierson and Blackburn 1986, 111–12, 116; Stahl 2012, 633–39.

61. See later discussion.

consisted only of silver and copper, minted on a very large scale.[62] These issues in the name of the king and marked as coming from Carthage represent only one aspect of the monetary economy; the Albertini Tablets reveal a society with its own distinct rates of exchange, suggesting a degree of fragmentation within Vandal-ruled Africa.[63] Italy remained closest to the old Roman order and even elaborated on the narrow range of denominations available by the mid-fifth century. Under Theoderic (493–526), the same mint-places persisted, and gold pieces were minted in the names of the East Roman emperors, while the range of silver and bronze denominations expanded, including a revival of large bronze pieces (also seen in Vandal Carthage). Some of these innovations were retained in Italy even after Roman reconquest, and large bronzes were taken up in the Eastern Empire (figure 7.4).[64]

Significant regional variation is apparent in terms of the numismatic material, but it is difficult to relate this to changes in the organisation of production, and the reasons for which coins were made. In Gaul, for example, there had in the fourth and early fifth centuries been three significant mint-places: Arles, Lyon, and Trier, all of which were important cities in provincial administration.[65] Sporadic use of mint signatures (especially on bronze and silver coins) and written references to mints show that between about 470 and 580, a significant number of new places beyond the three Roman mints produced coins, in two main clusters: the kingdom of the Burgundians, and the eastern portion of the Merovingian realm in the time of Theodebert I (see map 7.1). Not all these attributions are secure, and the mints need not have been large-scale, long-lived operations; nor is it certain that places named on bronze or silver coins must also have minted gold. Moreover, it is likely that other mints were active too, especially in western Gaul; Toulouse, the royal base of the Visigoths in Gaul, may well have been the source of their extensive gold issues from the later fifth century.[66] Seats of kings were one element in this new dispensation, suggesting that structures of minting coalesced in the

62. Betlyon 2008, which shows that the deposition of bronze coin at the commercial harbour of Carthage was as substantial in the Vandal period as in the preceding late Roman period.

63. Merrills and Miles 2010, 173–75; Tedesco 2018b. For wider discussion of Vandal coinage, see Berndt and Steinacher 2008; Hendy 1985, 478–90; Grierson and Blackburn 1986, 19–23. For the Albertini Tablets, see Courtois 1952, esp. 203–5; Grierson 1959b.

64. Hendy 1985, 475–78; Arslan 1993; Metlich 2004.

65. There were also short-lived mints at Amiens and Narbonne, associated with the pressing needs of particular emperors.

66. Guyon 2000; Kurt 2020, 45.

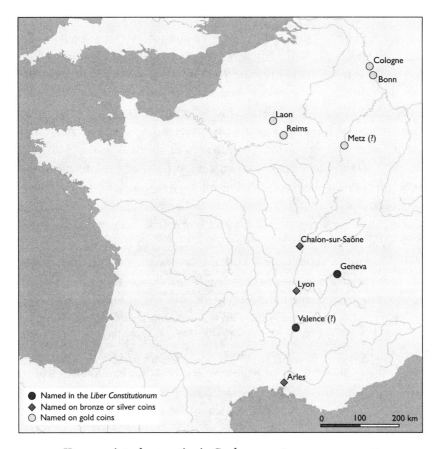

MAP 7.1. Known mint-places active in Gaul c. 470–580.

royal orbit.[67] But that does not account for all the known or likely mints of the period: some were in cities that had no obvious significance save as the centre of their *civitas*-territory, and some not even that. Bonn had been a *castrum* in the late Roman period and remained so into the ninth century.[68] Even though the minting of gold is likely to have been largely a royal prerogative, just as it had formerly been (and, in the East, still was) an imperial one, there may well have been increasing scope for other agencies to avail themselves of the increasingly fragmented minting network.

A more complex monetary landscape was taking shape in Gaul, and probably also Iberia,[69] behind the outward veneer of continuity suggested

67. Bonnet and Reynaud 2000; Dierkens and Périn 2000.

68. James 1982, 66; Ristow 2015; Fehr 2020, 507.

69. There are still fewer hints from Iberian bronze or silver or legal texts, but there must have been at least one and probably several new mint-places in Iberia, certainly after

by the coinage of the later fifth and sixth centuries. The real reasons for this are beyond our grasp except in general terms, though one potential tension stands out. Military pay has been seen as a, or even the, major force behind late Roman minting.[70] In the new order of the fifth century and after, the maintenance of barbarian armies moved toward settlement rather than salary.[71] If soldiers' principal remuneration now came in the form of land, or direct allocation of the taxes from a given territory, then presumably they were no longer receiving a salary, or at least not so much of one.[72] By the late sixth and seventh centuries, only a minority of coinages can plausibly be interpreted as military pay, such as the puzzlingly large output of the southern French *vicus* of Banassac (dép. Lozère), perhaps associated in some way with the bid for power of Charibert II (629–32),[73] or Visigothic issues with inscriptions alluding to military victories.[74] With its main outlet in retreat, both the tax system and the gold coinage risked becoming functionally ornamental, symbols of prestige and a tool of patronage rather than substantive economic and administrative forces.

The question is why coins carried on being made and used at all under such circumstances. Were taxes and central state expenditure still the principal forces stimulating production and primary use of coin? The answer differs for each of the major regions of the post-Roman West, as will be seen below, but the broad trend—with the possible partial exception of Visigothic Iberia—saw manufacture and use of gold coin become detached from taxes by the middle part of the seventh century, if the latter were still being extracted at all. Intermediary stages can sometimes be identified, as in Gaul, where the extreme local atomisation of minting could have begun as a fiscal expedient, but probably ceased in most cases to serve that role as the seventh century wore on. While there is little doubt about the general direction of travel, the survival of gold currency in ossified form yet relatively plentiful quantity reflects a secondary role for fiscal factors

---

507 and probably before: Kurt 2020, 55–59, with Marques, Cabral, and Marinho 1995, 19–21.

70. See chapter 6.

71. Wickham 2005, 60; Lee 2007, 59–60.

72. The mechanisms of barbarian settlement and support have a large, fiercely contentious literature behind them. Debate in recent decades has been driven in large part by the arguments of Walter Goffart (1980; 2006; 2010; 2013), and responses to them (among others, Barnish 1986; Wood 1990, 65–69; Liebeschuetz 1997; Wickham 2005, 84–87; Halsall 2007, 422–47).

73. Metcalf 2006a, 380–83; Strothmann 2008, 371–72; Blet-Lemarquand, Bompaire, and Morrisson 2010, 194; Lafaurie 1973, 128–31.

74. Pliego Vázquez 2009, 1:182–83, 192–93; Kurt 2020, 100–104, 18687, 212–17, 257–72.

and a rise in the relative importance of other kinds of use that fanned out from elite patrons: large payments for land; legal fines; redistribution through gifts and salaries to dependants; expenditure on bulk or luxury commerce; and flows back into elite hands via rents, the commutation for which into gold might have been handled either by individual tenants or by local agents who specialised in collecting and bulk-converting produce into gold.[75] It is significantly easier to lay out some of these possibilities than to assign priority among them. But there is detail enough to see that gold coin and its use persisted in rude health as tax systems tottered and, eventually, decayed; what came next is best seen as the result of elite demand for coins.

Post-Roman Italy

In the early part of this period, the Ostrogothic kingdom of Italy maintained most of the administrative machinery that existed under the fifth-century emperors, including a coinage of gold, silver, and bronze. Gold in particular can be seen to have played an important role in taxes and state expenditure. The raft of taxes administered by the *sacrae largitiones* lost out to an increasingly monetised land tax and revenues from imperial (later royal) lands, all of which were collected by the Praetorian Prefecture. Land and taxation thereby took on a much more markedly military character.[76] A third of land tax revenues, apparently paid in solidi, was earmarked for military support. Land actually occupied by soldiers (*sortes*) was exempt from this payment.[77] There was also large-scale commutation of the rest of the tax, especially for the payment of higher-ranking individuals,[78] while the mass of the army might be paid in gold either for special purposes or as part of occasional donatives. The former is known from the case of a group of Gepid cavalry who were fronted gold by the king as they moved north through Italy toward Gaul. The letter giving this order spells out the reasons for doing so: actual supplies were unwieldy and might spoil on the journey, while giving the men gold encouraged them to deal fairly with the locals rather than just taking food from them.[79] Under normal conditions the Gepids would, it can be inferred,

---

75. Naismith 2014a, 298–99.

76. Tedesco 2015, 118–20.

77. In this I follow Tedesco 2015, 112–14, though there are other readings of both *sortes* and *tertiae*.

78. Cassiodorus, *Variae* 11.35–38 (Mommsen 1894, 349–52; trans. Bjornlie 2019, 455–59).

79. Cassiodorus, *Variae* 5.10 (Mommsen 1894, 149, trans. Bjornlie 2019, 212).

have received only supplies. Some other post-Roman kingdoms had similar practices: a poem in the *Latin Anthology*, probably from Vandal Africa, castigates a military officer for requisitioning "the produce of the people" (*populi pastus*), thereby depriving both the soldiers and the state.[80]

Alongside, or perhaps assembled from, the tax allocations (*tertiae*) were donativa given out ceremonially by the king to his soldiers. This personal dimension provided an especially plausible context for the minting of new coins; donatives were when the ruler's charisma came into play before his men, so coins fresh from that ruler's mint had an inherent attraction.[81] Theoderic's letters refer to donativa several times, for both officials (such as state couriers) and soldiers.[82] As in earlier times, government payouts were hierarchical: high officials and officers or aristocrats could expect more (Theoderic's letters speak of payments of hundreds of solidi per annum), and expect to receive them in gold.[83] Those for regular soldiers still consisted of 5 solidi and may have become more routine than in earlier times. In one case Theoderic summoned Goths from southern and eastern Italy to Ravenna to receive donativa toward the end of his reign;[84] the fact that only one province (or possibly two) at a time was brought in might suggest that the king now gave donatives out frequently, but to only a segment of the serving Gothic population at a time.

It is not possible to know if leaders in other post-Roman kingdoms gave out donativa, or what form any such payments came in. Italy in particular may have retained a stronger association between minting and state expenditure, including on armies. Both Lombard and Roman/Byzantine territory saw a gradual petering out of the land tax system, by the seventh century in the former, probably in the eighth century in the latter, though the evidence for the later stages of this process is meagre and (among the Lombards) suggests a highly varied picture with no regular place for coin.[85] Coins in gold, along with (on a highly variable scale) bronze and silver, continued to be made and used throughout, with no obvious change in form or function, unless in some way the declining fineness of Italian gold

---

80. *Anthologia Latina* 117 (128) (ed. and trans. Kay 2006, 48, 200–205).

81. For the general ceremonial context of donatives, see Lee 2007, 52–60.

82. Cassiodorus, *Variae* 2.31, 4.14, 5.26–27, 36, 11.35–38 (Mommsen 1894, 64, 120–21, 158–59, 163, 349–52; trans. Bjornlie 2019, 105, 175, 225–26, 232–33, 455–59).

83. On the need to accommodate powerful aristocrats and their followers in Ostrogothic Italy, see Heather 1996 236–42.

84. Cassiodorus, *Variae* 5.26–27 (Mommsen 1894, 158–59; trans. Bjornlie 2019, 225–26). Cf. comment in Bjornlie 2019, 105; and in Barnish 1986, 182–84.

85. Tedesco 2015, 133–87; Costambeys 2009; Wickham 2005, 115–20; Pohl 2001; Gasparri 1990, 262–68.

issues relates to the breaking of cycles of taxation.[86] There is a reference to soldiers receiving donativa in the Vandal kingdom, while others received salaries,[87] but there seem to have several tiers in its distribution: officers and officials with close ties to the king and royal apparatus might well receive gold, whereas soldiers of lower rank, and especially those living outside the rich, privileged coastal areas, were more likely to receive donativa in the form of base metal or silver, passed on secondhand via the more favoured layers of the hierarchy.[88] The puzzle in Vandal Africa is that there was no known minting of gold coins. That might be because the kingdom's rich agrarian trade with other regions of the Mediterranean brought in sufficient gold from Italy and the eastern Mediterranean to meet the needs of the kings, and also helped to keep gold as an exclusive resource of the elite.[89] But there were probably other factors: the absence of any tradition of minting in gold in North Africa under imperial rule, and possibly a different kind of relationship between the king and the Vandals that laid more emphasis on landholding and privileged a small, restricted elite.[90]

New Gold 1: Merovingian Gaul

The half-century or so either side of the year 600 witnessed a transformation in the structure of gold coinage in Gaul, Iberia, and England. Imitative coins that had followed in the footsteps of Roman issues came to an end, as did the possibility of substantial circulation of gold pieces across borders. Three distinct new currencies came into being, each reflecting the changing nature of the region that made it. All were based overwhelmingly on the lowest gold denomination in the Roman tradition, the tremissis.

The Merovingian coinage of this period has historically been known, somewhat unhelpfully, as the "national" coinage, though recent assessments have adopted the more neutral term "moneyer coins"

86. The declining fortunes of gold are vividly represented in Blackburn 1995, 540–53. See more generally on the use of coin Bernareggi 1970 and 1976, with (on actual coins and coin finds) Blackburn and Wickham 1986, 55–73; Arslan 2002b (and numerous other works by the same author).

87. Steinacher 2016, 169–72. For donatives, see Fulgentius, *Sermo* 3.2 (Fraipont 1968, 2:906).

88. Steinacher 2016, 169–72; Tedesco 2018b, 409; for supporting numismatic evidence, Morrisson 2016.

89. Tedesco 2011, 125; 2018b, 409–11.

90. For views on the nature of Vandal settlement, see Modéran 2002; 2012; Schwarcz 2004; Merrills and Miles 2010, 63–70; Goffart 2012; Conant 2012; Tedesco 2018b, 404–7.

(*Monetarmünzen*).[91] The latter is an apt description, for the salient feature of the new Merovingian coinage is that each piece carries on it an inscription naming a location and a moneyer. Vast numbers of both are recorded: about twelve hundred different moneyers' names (some of them used by several individuals, of whom there were perhaps two thousand) at between six hundred and eight hundred locations (see map 7.2).[92] The quantity of material is formidable, and much of it still awaits rigorous modern study; place-name attributions in particular need urgent reexamination, along the lines of what has been done for Aquitaine and the Auvergne.[93]

What is missing from the coinage is overt royal involvement: only a small minority of surviving coins bear the name of a king.[94] It is possible, however, that the rarity of explicitly royal coinage is a mirage. The new pattern of coinage had a few precursors from the late 550s onward but seems to have become generalised in the 580s. Its apparently rapid uptake in all parts of the Frankish realm can only reasonably be explained as the result of a directive from the king (or kings); Philip Grierson proposed 587, when there was a peaceful compact between Childebert II (575–96) and Guntramn (561–92) after years of turbulence.[95] Chronology beyond that point is a minefield. Changes in fineness and style provide a broad outline, but it is apparent that there could be considerable variation in both these characteristics.[96] Certainly one can say that coins were produced across the period from the inception of the "moneyer coins" until the switch to silver around 660 or after.[97] Still less clear is *why* the new style of coinage came in. What purpose could such an atomised coinage have served? And why did it take off?

A starting point is that although the distribution of mints was plentiful, it was not haphazard. The places named on the coins run the gamut from cities (of which about ninety are named) to a much larger number

91. Compare Greule et al. 2017 with Grierson and Blackburn 1986, 117–38; the latter remains the best detailed guide in English.

92. These totals are given in Strothmann 2020, 801.

93. Boyer 2018, with Chambon 2001; see also Zadora-Rio 2014. The best overall assessment of mint-places is Kluge 2013, which essentially brings together the contents of the major nineteenth-century catalogues. Moneyers' names have recently received considerable attention from philological scholars: see Felder 2003 along with the papers in Jarnut and Strothmann 2013 and Greule et al. 2017.

94. On the characteristics and circulation of this group, which comes from about seventeen locations, see Naismith 2014a, 295–96; Metcalf 2006a, 378–83; Strothmann 2008, 371–73.

95. Grierson and Blackburn 1986, 92–93.

96. Brown 1981; Stahl and Oddy 1992; Depeyrot 1998, 1:19–27; Pol 2013.

97. See chapter 8.

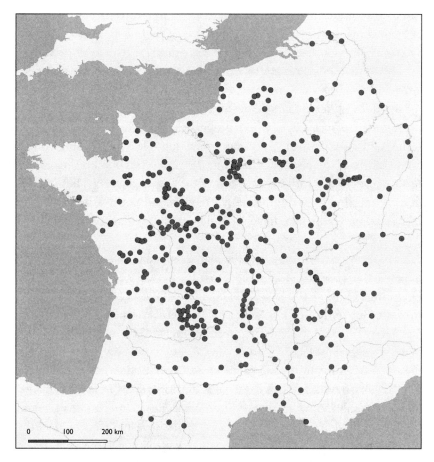

MAP 7.2. Identifiable mint-places in Merovingian Gaul c. 580–670 (based on Kluge 2013).

of smaller places: *vici* most plentifully, but also *castra*, *villae*, and places without any kind of determiner. Cities tended to be active longer and on a larger scale, matching the larger role they played in the economic and institutional landscape.[98] But even though hundreds of minor places are named on the coins, these represent significant nodes in local power structures.[99] Coins of the *vicus* BRIVATE, for instance, have been associated with the modern village of Brive-la-Gaillarde (dép. Corrèze).[100] This place

98. Drauschke 2010, 43.

99. Boyer 2018, 622–26, tabulates correspondences between mint-places and local administrative centres in northern Aquitaine.

100. Stahl 1994, no. 181; Chambon 2001, 357.

was also an important Roman settlement,[101] and the centre of a *viguerie* or *vicaria* in later times.[102] There is every reason to believe that it served as a focal point for the surrounding area in judicial and other respects during the Merovingian era. Minting probably took place in connection with a specific assembly or event at that location—quite possibly in full view of the worthies gathered there, ready for distribution. Other factors included the influence of local elites, whose properties might serve as mints, such as Ardin (dép. Deux-Sèvres), which was both a mint-place and a well-recorded estate centre of the bishops of Le Mans,[103] or a series of places in eastern Austrasia associated with the ancestors of the Carolingians.[104] These conditions of minting were not mutually exclusive: administrative centres in the landscape could take shape around landholdings and their associated dependencies, or vice versa.

It is also worth stressing that the places named on coins normally were mints, in the sense of a place where the coins were made. That is the strong implication of the word FIT[*ur*], found on a significant proportion of coins, which means something like "made at."[105] It is also strongly implied in the one narrative account of minting in Merovingian Gaul to have survived: a much-discussed passage of the *Life of St. Eligius* (588–660), written later in the seventh century by the saint's friend, St. Ouen (Audoin).[106] Essentially a miracle story, the tale revolves around the saint's immunity from the demands of royal taxation. After a property at Solignac, near Limoges, was given to Eligius, either one or two royal officials, *domesticus* and *monetarius*—the wording leaves it ambiguous whether there were two men or one fulfilling both jobs—showed up to exact the public tax (*census publicus*) that was incumbent on the surrounding rural district (*pagus*).[107] It was either paid directly as gold or else commuted to gold, because that was what the official or officials were confronted with: a mass of metal, "so that according to

101. Lintz 1992, 70–76.

102. Boyer 1995, 30–31.

103. Lot 1921; Goffart 1989, 243–46; Magnou-Nortier 1989, 300–306; Sato 2004.

104. Bruand 1997, 48–52; on similar cases elsewhere, see Naismith 2014a, 293–94.

105. Prou 1888, esp. 542–44; Grierson and Blackburn 1986, 99. Other scholars have argued that the coins were normally made at a central location, perhaps from metal gathered at the place named on the coins: Depeyrot 1998, 1:9–10; Durliat 1990, 117–20; Strothmann 2020, 805–6.

106. The surviving text includes some passages that other authors added, though it is now thought that these can be identified, and do not include the passage on minting: Bayer 2007, 466–75; Heinzelmann 2013, esp. 249–56.

107. *Domesticus* referred quite broadly to an inner circle of royal officials responsible for running the palace and the king's estates: Carlot 1903; Strothmann 2008, 363–64. On whether there was one man or two here, see Hendy 1988, 66; Strothmann 2017, 45–46.

custom only the purest and reddened metal may be presented to the king's hall."[108] But try as they might, the gold would not melt; not, at least, until a messenger from Eligius arrived. Again, the text's wording leaves what happened next somewhat open to interpretation. The messenger stopped (*interciperet*) the proceedings and brought them back into Eligius's jurisdiction (*eius dominio revocaret*). At that point the inhabitants rejoiced—a signal that all this, including the intended minting by the moneyer, was supposed to be going on at Solignac itself—and the melting was completed (*opus perfectum est*) and committed to his authority (*eius dicioni commissum*).

Eligius's run-in with the taxman calls attention to the crossover of economic, fiscal, and jurisdictional interests encapsulated by gold coinage, which was still presented as the symbol of taxation par excellence. The will of Bertram, bishop of Le Mans (d. 623), for instance, expected that his numerous estates would produce annual *tributum* or *suffragium* in the form of gold.[109] Taxes in kind still went on, but paying grain and livestock failed to fire the same rhetorical indignation: gold remained a totem of taxation.[110] But those taxes were increasingly negotiable.[111] Paying became a strategy for dealing with the king. Gregory of Tours describes how the bishop of Poitiers invited tax inspectors to come to the city in 589 in order to update the written assessments so as to make tax payments more equitable and relieve the poor.[112] By 614 a capitulary of Chlothar II (584–629), one of the most effective of the Merovingian kings, decreed that he would withdraw any new and unwelcome *census* on request.[113] Consciously engaging with the tax machinery, then, could get results and was also—regardless of the scale of actual payment—a way of building bridges with central authority. It also brought material gain to those charged with assembling and conveying payment, in the form of peculation, or even borrowing against the proceeds of future tax payments: Gregory of Tours tells the sad story of a count and his deputy (*vicarius*) doing precisely that at Tours in the 580s and eventually murdering the man who had lent them the money.[114] Negotiability lent tax payment a

108. "Ut iuxta ritum purissimus ac rutilus aulae regis praesentaretur metallus." Audoin, *Vita Eligii* 1.15 (Krusch 1902, 681).

109. Weidemann 1986, 11.

110. Goffart 1989, 226.

111. Liebeschuetz 2015, 177–79.

112. Gregory of Tours, *Historiae* 9.30 (Krusch and Levison 1951, 448–49; trans. Thorpe 1974, 515–16).

113. Edict of Chlothar II of 614, c. 8 (Boretius 1883, 22).

114. Gregory of Tours, *Historiae* 7.23 (Krusch and Levison 1951, 343–44; trans. Thorpe 1974, 405–6).

new valence as financial *Königsnähe*, at least for those who were in a position to decide to cooperate, to evade, or to resist. Gregory tells the story of the tax payment at Poitiers precisely in order to set up his own decision to resist, on the grounds that his see, Tours, had been granted exemption from "any new tax laws which might be to [the population's] disadvantage" after an earlier count of the city tried to raise tax and take the proceeds to the king, against the wishes of the bishop.[115]

Taxes, like the minting of gold, were also increasingly fragmented and localised. Historically, the principal unit of taxation in the later Roman world had been the city-territory (*civitas*), and indeed Gregory of Tours and others in the sixth century still seem to have thought in terms of taxes being drawn from cities.[116] The circulation pattern of Merovingian coins seems to fit well with this reading. Tremisses tended to circulate very far, even ones from quite minor mint-places, and a plausible mechanism for this was taxes paid to the king, then dispersed through royal largesse, salaries or gifts for favoured dependants, or purchase of luxury goods.[117] But in the generation after Gregory's death (594), the fiscal and administrative role of the *civitas* came unstuck, building on developments that had been brewing in the sixth century.[118] The proliferation of mint-places points to a more granular picture of how actual taxes were being gathered, as does the narrative of the *Life of Eligius*. Another development that ate away at the ubiquity of taxation was immunities. Franks, in return for military service, held their own *mansi indominicati* free from tax payment, and they also held the right, as both a responsibility and a privilege, of collecting and paying tax from dependent peasant lands, some of which they retained to support their military service.[119] Another large constituency of tax-exempt land was that held by the church—not, it seems, as a universal rule, but by increasingly frequent grant. Already before the end of the sixth century, the freedom of Gallic churches from tax had become common wisdom: in 599 Gregory the Great challenged the Merovingian kings on turning a blind eye to simony, when the bishops should be satisfied with

115. "Ullam novam ordinationem . . . quod pertinerit ad spolium." Gregory of Tours, *Historiae* 9.30 (Krusch and Levison 1951, 448–49; trans. Thorpe 1974, 516).

116. Strothmann 2013, 618–22; Loseby 1998, 2454–57; 2020, 589–90. For the late Roman situation, see chapter 6.

117. Metcalf 2006a, esp. 348–49; Naismith 2014a, 295–96.

118. Loseby 2013; 2020, 596–98.

119. Goffart 2008. A slightly different interpretation is offered in Liebeschuetz 2015, 175–77, where it is argued that only land granted by the king to Franks was exempt.

the income that their churches got from tax exemption.[120] That extra income was often channelled into specified functions, such as keeping lights burning on the altar: an expensive operation that was, at this time, usually sustained through cash grants.[121] But the net effect was to make churches relatively cash rich.[122] As Alexander Murray has noted, ecclesiastical immunity from taxation was probably so widespread in the seventh century that it was taken as read in the first surviving written concessions. The latter instead concern judicial immunity, which in effect was another kind of fiscal exemption: freedom from the intrusion of royal officials and the fines or fees they might charge.[123] By the seventh century these two kinds of immunity were probably very widespread. A form letter preserved in the *Formulary of Marculf* stated that only those whose names were not entered in tax registers could be counted as "truly free" (*bene ingenuus*),[124] and at the Council of Clichy in 626/627 those whose names were entered in tax registers were barred from entering into religious life without special permission.[125] Exemption from tax had become a marker of status and a signal of favour.

The fiscal landscape of Merovingian Gaul was increasingly pockmarked in the late sixth and especially the seventh centuries. Taxes were irregular and increasingly targeted at small districts rather than whole *civitas* units. Other kinds of indirect revenue collection such as tolls and fines came to take on more prominence as the basic land tax diminished.[126] It was in this climate that the "moneyer coins" appeared and flourished. Theoretically taxes in gold would have been owed by the whole liable population, but in practice actually raising and paying the requisite gold fell to local elites, whose agents would commute contributions in kind or (less probably) other kinds of coin in the same way as estate managers (*iuniores*) collected together the monetary income of landowners.[127] In effect, the moneyers named on these coins would often, like their counterparts in

120. Gregory the Great, *Registrum epistolarum* 9.216 (Norberg 1982, 2:778; trans. Murray 2010, 920–21).

121. Fouracre 2021, 52–63.

122. Fouracre 2021, 60–61.

123. Murray 2010, 915. Magnou-Nortier 1984 offers a wide-ranging survey of written concessions of immunity, while Brühl 1995 focuses on those of the seventh and eighth centuries. Rennie 2018, 30–48, considers monastic immunity from episcopal control.

124. *Formulary of Marculf* 1.19 (Zeumer 1886, 55–56; trans. Rio 2008, 153). Cf. Goffart 1989, 231.

125. Council of Clichy c. 8 (de Clercq 1963, 293).

126. Fouracre 2021, 60; Stahl 1982, 133–35.

127. *Actus pontificum Cenomannis*, Vallée, Ledru, and Busson 1902, 240–42.

later Anglo-Saxon England, have been "pocket" moneyers, answering indirectly to the demands of powerful patrons.[128] The inception of this new monetary system may well have begun as an attempt to cut through the fiscal system and shift part of the burden (as well as some of the associated benefits) onto individual taxpayers. As time went on, however, the proliferation of mint and moneyer coins came to reflect almost the opposite. It turned into a symbol of the particularism inherent in the system; a signal of the inconsistencies in Merovingian taxation, and how they could be exploited at a local level. For a bishop or secular landholder to choose to pay their taxes, and mint coins to do so, was a statement in itself of buying into royal authority. There may have been a military tax payable in gold, which became increasingly tied to status and the entourage of aristocrats over the course of the seventh century.[129] It is entirely conceivable that some coin issues, although based on a framework that probably went back to tax payments, were not made with the intention of paying tax at all.

New Gold 2: Visigothic Iberia

The Visigothic kingdom in Iberia transformed its gold coinage at very much the same time as Merovingian Gaul. It is even possible that ideas for revamping the coinage passed from one to the other, as there were important similarities between them. Like in Gaul, the Visigothic coinage named a much-enlarged complement of mint-places: a total of at least a hundred locations.[130] Much more so than in Gaul, however, production was weighted toward a small number of these. Córdoba, Mérida, Seville, and Toledo together account for a large proportion of surviving coins; a pattern that is not simply down to the vagaries of hoard finds.[131] And although, when all the mints are mapped (map 7.3), it appears that northwest Iberia (the old province of *Gallaecia*) had the densest concentration of them, most of its complement issued coins on a small scale, and only down to about the 620s. The reasons for this dense and short-lived concentration are debatable. Gold mining had been significant here in earlier

128. On the Merovingian moneyers, see Grierson and Blackburn, 97–102; Boyer 2018, 28–36.

129. Halsall 2003, 53–60.

130. The most up-to-date list is Kurt 2020, 300–303; see also Pliego Vázquez 2020b, 187–90.

131. The entire corpus (as of 2006) is presented in Pliego Vázquez 2009. There have been additions since (e.g., Pliego Vázquez 2012; 2018b), though they do not offset this general pattern.

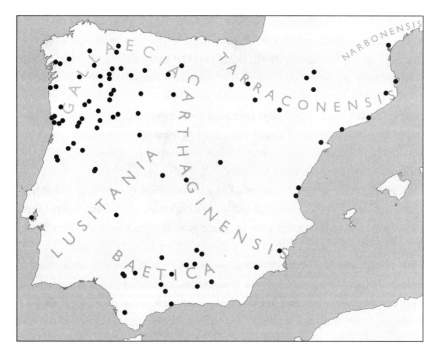

MAP 7.3. Identifiable mint-places in Visigothic Iberia c. 570–711, with former Roman provinces (following Pliego 2009 and Díaz Martínez 2019).

times, though whether this was still going on is unclear.[132] Peculiarities of local geography, with numerous separate cities and bishoprics,[133] might also have been a factor, and major precipitating causes for minting might have been to support the military conquest of the region, as well as to extract tribute and remint coin in a recently conquered area.[134] These features more generally point to a scenario similar to what was sketched above for Merovingian minting: that production was dispersed because the state had shunted the burden of making coins onto local communities.

The most obvious difference between the Visigothic coinage and that of their Frankish contemporaries was the prominence of the king and the degree of standardisation in appearance. While the king was only rarely named on Merovingian coinage, he was all over the Visigothic currency, from the establishment of royal coinage in the course of Leovigild's

132. Hendy 1988, 58–59; for limited evidence of gold mining beyond the fourth century, see Domergue 1990, 215–24.

133. Díaz Martínez 2004.

134. Kurt 2020, 211–20, provides the best recent overview. See also Metcalf 2000. For the character of earlier coin in this area, see Martín Viso 2011, 221–29.

turbulent and bloody reign (568–86) to the end of the kingdom at the dawn of the eighth century.[135] Every single Visigothic tremissis from this period carried the name of the king, and usually also his image. Those who actually made the coins got no look in, and virtually nothing is known about who fulfilled this role or on what terms. Legislation on forgery suggests that both slaves and freemen were involved, the latter perhaps including goldsmiths.[136] From the point of view of the coinage, the king was ostensibly in absolute control, his name and image reaching out to scores of places across the kingdom.

Together, these two features of the coinage—a more localised structure combined with a determinedly royal appearance—have been taken to suggest that the Visigothic coinage was strongly inflected by fiscal demands from the king that were imposed on specific communities.[137] How that translated into direct reasons for minting is less apparent.[138] Some of the many smaller mint-places that operated briefly can be tied to specific military campaigns, implying that these issues were intended for donatives, for compulsory land purchases, or for acquiring supplies—in other words, expenditure by the king and his military commanders.[139] That might explain the preponderance of the South, and its many new, short-lived mint-places, around the time campaigns against the Byzantine province of Iberia were at their most fierce.[140] The surprisingly productive mint of Antequera (*Barbi*) in the South is plausibly interpreted as a creation of the campaign against nearby Málaga under Sisebut (612–21), and Italica near Seville as a product of Leovigild's campaign against the city.[141] There may also have been a symbolic element to some of these coinages: Leovigild's tremisses from Italica compare with those of Seville and La Roda de Andalucia in carrying legends that emphasise their conquest through divine will from his rebellious son.[142] The numerous small mint-places of the late sixth and early seventh centuries in the Northwest

135. For the establishment of the coinage around the time of the revolt of Leovigild's son Hermenegild (d. 585), see Grierson and Blackburn 1986, 49–51; Pliego Vázquez 2009, 2:79–91; Kurt 2020, 112–14.

136. Kurt 2020, 126–28.

137. A case made most forcefully in Barceló Perello 1981; Crusafont i Sabater 1994; Retamero 2011, 200. See more generally Valverde Castro 2007.

138. For good discussion of this point, see Pliego Vázquez 2008; Kurt 2018–2019, esp. 168–74.

139. Kurt 2020, 203–6. On the importance of military prowess and of the armed followings of aristocrats, see Wickham 2005, 98–99.

140. Kurt 2018–2019, 168–72.

141. Kurt 2020, 200; Bartlett and Cores 2005; Pérez and Díaz 1995.

142. Pliego Vázquez 2009, 1:94, 119.

can also plausibly be read as militarily driven operations for supporting armies, extracting tribute, and reminting local coin in a recently conquered area.[143]

Another strand, taxation, has loomed much larger in scholarship, sometimes being touted as the driving force behind the Visigothic monetary system. There is good evidence that Visigothic kings from the sixth century onward raised tax on land, and that this was measured, and potentially paid, in gold coin. Two of the newly discovered Visigothic charters from San Martín de Asán in the foothills of the Pyrenees concern royal taxation reckoned in solidi. One, in the name of Leovigild, remitted 50 solidi that would otherwise have been due on the "annual render" (*annua illatio*) from land in the province of Tarraconensis. Another, in the name of Reccared (586–601), granted to the monastery lands formerly belonging to a bishop for the purposes of either lighting the church or feeding the poor; these properties were rated by their expected tribute to the treasury of 9 solidi.[144] Still more important is a short and unusually lucid letter, preserved as an addendum to a church council and referred to as *De fisco Barcinonensi*, which describes how these payments worked at the *fiscus* (meeting where payment was negotiated and handed over) of Barcelona in the year 592.[145] In this instance payments were reckoned in kind but apparently settled in gold. The letter was addressed by the bishops "who paid their taxes to the *fiscus* of Barcelona" to a set of *numerarii* (accountants or tax gatherers) delegated by the count of the *patrimonium*, meaning here an official in charge of royal properties and interests in the district.[146] The purpose of the letter seems to have been to communicate monetary rates to be paid for grain, the implication being that those rates would change year on year. At this point, the going rate was fourteen siliquae per "canonical modius" of barley (justified as nine for the base rate, one to cover the labour of the *numerarii*, and four to cover unavoidable losses or fluctuation in prices). Assuming this meant gold, fourteen siliquae was 1¾ tremisses, and as in later Byzantine tradition it is possible that the *numerarii* would round up and then repay the

143. Kurt 2020, 211–20, provides the best recent overview. See also Díaz Martínez 2004; Metcalf 2000; Hendy 1988, 58–59, on gold mining. For the character of earlier coin in this area, see Martín Viso 2011, 221–29.

144. Tomás-Faci and Martín-Iglesias 2017, 279–81, 283–84. For discussion, see Fernández 2021 and other chapters in the same volume.

145. For text and translation see Fernández 2006, 218. There is extensive published discussion of this text: see Barbero and Vigil 1978, 111–13; García Moreno 1971, 244–54; Pérez Sánchez 1999, 312–15.

146. García Moreno 1974, 27–28; Díaz Martínez 2012, 97–98.

difference to individual taxpayers, or count it against the next year's payment.[147] Michael Hendy observed that there was a burst of activity at the otherwise minor mint of Barcelona around this time, associating it with a period when the *fiscus* of the region was based there, with references in legislation to similar gatherings or offices in other cities through the seventh century.[148]

It is by no means clear that the circumstances of *De fisco* were matched elsewhere. If anything, having to write a letter such as this, spelling out the current rates, indicates an atypical situation.[149] It paints a picture of taxes being paid by cities (bearing in mind that Iberia, unlike Gaul, was divided up into a vast number of very small city-territories),[150] each represented by a *numerarius*, but within a fluid and changeable framework of larger groupings that probably worked around the remit of individual office-holders (*comites* and *duces*), who operated on behalf of the king.[151] Even the old Roman provincial infrastructure had less and less significance,[152] while the number of city-territories that operated as autonomous entities may have been declining in the seventh century.[153] The old city councils of *curiales* were also gone, or effectively so, as real forces in local organisation by the seventh century, though individuals of equivalent stature may well have been the constituency from whom bishops and clergy, as well as *numerarii* and other lower rungs of officials, were recruited.[154] Locally dominant figures may have provided a new structuring principle.[155] It is also debatable whether the rates in *De fisco Barcinonensi* describe taxes or a rate of adaeratio.[156] The former is more probable, because otherwise (if the "canonical modius" was similar to the modius volume measure used elsewhere) the price quoted is astronomically high: beyond famine levels in contemporary Gaul.[157] But from the point of view of many taxpayers, who are unlikely to have had ready access to gold, adaeratio was probably

147. See chapters 3 and 6.

148. Hendy 1988, 53–56.

149. Fernández 2021, 108–9.

150. Kulikowski 2004, 1–2.

151. King 1972, 53–56, 69–71.

152. Díaz Martínez 2019.

153. Kulikowski 2005, 48–49.

154. Curchin 2018, esp. 231; Fernández 2020. For the situation at the beginning of the sixth century, see Dumézil 2008.

155. Fernández 2017; Retamero 1999; Martín Viso 2008; Kurt 2020, esp. 175–86, 234–36.

156. For a reading of it as adaeratio, see Kurt 2020, 180.

157. King 1972, 70 n. 1, but with a note of uncertainty on the size of the *modius canonicus*.

still a part of the process, for if the *numerarii* required gold from every-one, elites (secular and ecclesiastical) with larger reserves would probably have had to step in to buy grain at or above the assessed rates, essentially providing a private adaeratio service.[158]

Finally, the biggest hole left by *De fisco Barcinonensi* and the other limited sources mentioning Visigothic taxes is what happened to those payments once they had been paid. The kings had no regularly salaried army to support, but there was a growing network of palace and local offi-cials, themselves probably drawn from the elite, and especially from the assertive and well-supported high elite. Donatives or occasional other pay-ments for these groups, as well as gifts to favoured churches or largesse on projects like new cities (e.g., Recópolis), could have been substantial. Garrisons and armies needed supplies, as already noted, which could have been provided from taxes paid in kind, or else bought locally using gold.[159]

The Visigothic laws and church councils show that taxes were still being paid in the last decades before the kingdom was conquered. Some of the complaints made about the difficulty in raising tax belong to a rhetorical tradition stretching back to the Roman Empire and should not be given much credence.[160] Real changes were taking place, how-ever, that tended in different directions. Landholders could hand part of their property over to the state in exchange for tax exemption on the remainder.[161] Taxation still played a symbolic and rhetorical role but may have been becoming marginal in material terms.[162] That provides a possible context for the contraction of the Visigothic coinage in the late seventh and early eighth centuries. Relatively fewer places issued trem-isses, and their gold content was generally lower, regularly below 40 per cent pure by the joint reign of Egica and Wittiza (694–702/3).[163] Lower-ing of the gold content of coins was part of a trend seen across the west-ern Mediterranean in the mid-seventh century. But there was still scope for restoring the standard of the coinage in Iberia at this date: separate types of the late seventh and early eighth centuries display different lev-els of fineness.[164] The coinage, even in its straitened form, was still an important symbolic concern. Changes in fineness seem generally to have

158. Retamero 1999, 288–90; Osland 2011; Martín Viso 2011.
159. King 1972, 72–73.
160. Wickham 2005, 95–96.
161. *Edictum Ervigii* (Zeumer 1902, 479–80).
162. Wickham 2005, 99–100.
163. Pliego Vázquez 2009, 1:211.
164. Marques, Cabral, and Marinho 1995, 145–47; Kurt 2020, 157–72.

applied across the kingdom, which, with ongoing typological unity, indicates a persistent grip on minting.[165]

All this assumes a close nexus between minting and taxation. As in Gaul, however, a coinage that started out as a strongly fiscal tool may not have stayed that way. The coins themselves give little away. Patterns of circulation show a mix of relatively local and long-distance movement, with about a third of finds occurring within 100 km of the place of production.[166] There is of course no way to tell where they had been before deposition, and it is possible that some of these coins could have travelled from their place of production to Toledo and back again, conceivably several times, as part of a well-established cycle. Recent studies have tended to lay emphasis on the fiscal element in movement of coin, though also allowed for the local role of elites, not only in gathering taxes but also in funding military ventures or undertaking charitable or euergetistic enterprises like building projects.[167] Elite demands and pressures, on a local or regional basis, may well have become independent of systems of taxation. Important evidence that points away from the dominance of a tax cycle in minting and circulation comes from the composition of hoards. These suggest a gradual, continuous replacement of the coinage; in other words, that only a small portion of the circulating currency would have been reminted in any short space of time. Coins from the last, most recent ruler are only in the majority in a third of finds, although tremisses from the twenty years before likely deposition accounted for 90 per cent or more of the contents of eleven out of the twelve substantial Visigothic hoards dating to the period c. 570–714 (and 80 per cent in the twelfth).[168] Significantly older coins did survive, but in small numbers, suggesting that their absence was a matter of attrition rather than systematic replacement.[169] This pattern could be read in two ways: either most or all taxes did not have to be paid in fresh coin, which begs the question of what if any nexus there was with minting; or, if coin was reminted to pay tax, only a small portion of the stock passed through the system each year. Both possibilities strongly suggest that the coinage was not completely tax-driven, and that minting was a response to several pressures. Analysis

---

165. Pliego Vázquez 2009, 1:212.

166. Barral i Altet 1976, 168–99; Metcalf 1986; 1988a.

167. Barceló and Retamero 1996; Retamero 1999; 2001; 2011; Kurt 2020, 232–45, 257–72.

168. Pliego Vázquez 2009, 1:231–55, with Pliego Vázquez 2012; 2018b. "Substantial" is here defined as five coins or more.

169. Retamero 2011, 208–10, suggests that reminting of coin was only substantial under Leovigild (568–86) at the beginning of the royal, mint-signed Visigothic coinage.

of bullion reinforces that picture. Most Visigothic tremisses were made from two sources of gold, presumably both mined in Iberia, and often show admixture of gold from those two sources, such as might ensue from reminting of various coins together.[170]

Taxes probably did shape the more dispersed and explicit incarnation of Visigothic coinage after about 570. Like in neighbouring Francia, the burden of minting shifted from state expenditure to income. It may even be that taxes remained relatively more important in the Iberian monetary system. But it is less clear that taxes remained the dominant, let alone the exclusive, force behind minting and circulation across the seventh century.

New Gold 3: Early Anglo-Saxon England

England's earliest coinage (minted from around 600 or shortly after) consisted of gold pieces that were for the most part around the same weight as their counterparts in Francia and Iberia, and Merovingian tremisses in fact circulated in England in larger numbers than the equivalent home-grown pieces.[171] But the similarities stop there. English coins were largely uninscribed, and their iconography more often reached back to Roman coins than to contemporary Frankish ones (see figure 7.5).[172] While mint attributions are inevitably tentative (save for a few groups that name Canterbury and London),[173] more than thirty distinct types can be identified, some now represented by many coins with their own internal subdivisions, others known from only one coin or a handful of coins.[174] This points to a similar range in scale to Francia or Iberia, but probably not to quite the same profusion of mint-places.

The English coinage is especially intriguing because it was, on the one hand, quite large in scale, as metal-detector finds have gradually revealed. More than 370 finds are now known.[175] These completely offset the reading of early Anglo-Saxon coins that Philip Grierson propounded in the mid-twentieth century. At that point, most gold pieces came from burials or hoards and could plausibly be explained as the stuff of highly

170. Riart and Aparicio 1996, 209–11; Guerra, Calligaro, and Perea 2007, 60–67; Guerra and Roux 2002.

171. Williams 2010; Naismith 2017b, 43–45, 57–59. See also Metcalf 1993–94, 1:29–62.

172. Gannon 2013, 88.

173. Blackburn 2006, 127–35.

174. Naismith 2017b, esp. 46–48.

175. Naismith 2014a, 302. The total offered here dates from March 2020; a significant addition from after this time is the "West Norfolk" hoard of over a hundred Merovingian gold coins (Marsden and Pol 2020).

FIGURE 7.5. Anglo-Saxon gold shilling of the "Two Emperors" type, modelled on a Roman solidus of the fourth century (diameter 12 mm). Fitzwilliam Museum, Cambridge.

restricted and specialised uses, such as sums raised to settle a wergild, or even to pay the spiritual oarsmen of the Sutton Hoo ship burial.[176] Those from graves were often pierced or mounted, suggesting a primarily ornamental role.[177] Now coins found in graves or hoards are in the minority. Because of the very different modern legal regimes regarding coin finds in England, France, and Iberia, it is not possible to make a meaningful quantitative comparison between the three, but there is no reason to think that England was particularly poorly off in terms of gold coinage during the seventh century. But there was in England no prior tradition of making and using gold coin on any scale; crucially, there was also no Roman-style fiscal system, at least by the seventh century. Assessments of English government and economy at this time present a very different landscape. Rulers, as well as aristocrats and churches, raised income from large estates that apparently came in kind and may well have been largely consumed at feasts held in the locality.[178] This leaves few obvious openings for coin, although it is conceivable that some rents were being taken in coin, or that income in kind was being sold to obtain gold pieces; certainly there are signs of stability and enclosure being imposed on the previously mobile settlements of eastern England in this period, a process associated with intensification and specialisation.[179] But coins probably circulated

176. Grierson 1959a; 1961; 1970; cf. Stewart 1978, 144–45.

177. Williams 2006, 146–50.

178. Faith 2019, 50–57; see also Faith 1997, esp. 1–14. There is also important forthcoming work on this topic by Sam Leggett and Tom Lambert.

179. Blair 2018, 149–56. For extraction of resources from land more broadly, see Hamerow 2012, 163–68.

alongside other socially charged prestige goods that changed hands as gifts or in other ritualised contexts. This is the world suggested by the gold and silver of Sutton Hoo, Prittlewell, and the Staffordshire hoard.

There was overlap between these circuits—not least in the case of land itself, which was the prestige good par excellence[180]—and both also existed in Francia and Iberia. In England, however, the presumption must be that the second of these two circuits was the primary driver of coin circulation: exchanges among the elite and their direct dependants. Production also needs to be evaluated against this backdrop. It would very probably have been highly personal. It mattered deeply who patronised the making and distribution of coins, even if neither is readily apparent from surviving specimens. In the early to mid-seventh century, the earliest trading centres in England were only just starting to coalesce at Ipswich, London, and elsewhere,[181] and they did not yet present a likely setting for the production of gold coin on a large scale. Minting in the orbit of elite patrons is much more plausible. In practice the work would have been done by someone else, and some of the earliest English laws specifically mention servile smiths who formed part of elite households. Smiths were men of some importance despite their servile status. The laws of Ine spell out that the smith belonged to a special category of slaves who could be taken from place to place with a wealthy family.[182] It is not clear whether these would be exclusively blacksmiths or able to work a variety of metals, though the remains of one smith buried with his tools at Tattershall Thorpe in Lincolnshire show that he worked on gold and silver as well as iron and copper.[183] Moreover, even if a king had a smith on staff who had the requisite skills and raw materials to make gold coins, they did not necessarily do so on a regular basis. Minting that was driven primarily by the social interactions of the patron depended on occasions and contexts of interaction—hence minting and initial acts of distribution would take place in settings like assemblies,[184] such as the celebrated conclave Bede described King Edwin (616–33) holding to discuss the merits of the new religion.[185] This

180. Campbell 2000, 227–46.

181. Scull 2009, 183–212; 2013; Naismith 2018a, 84–87; Blackmore 2002.

182. Ine 63 (Jurasinski and Oliver 2021, 422–23). Cf. Æthelberht 7 (Liebermann 1903–16, 1:3), on the special compensation due for killing an *ambihtsmið* (servile smith).

183. Hinton 2000, esp. 58–67, 74–75. On the status of smiths at this time, see Hinton 1998; von Carnap-Bornheim 2001; Hardt 2012; Wright 2019.

184. Archaeological discussion of possible early assembly sites includes Semple 2004; Baker and Brookes 2015.

185. Bede, *Historia ecclesiastica gentis Anglorum*, 2.14 (ed. and trans. Colgrave and Mynors 1969, 188–89).

may well have taken place at Yeavering (Northumberland), a royal estate where Edwin and his queen met with Bishop Paulinus.[186] Excavations at Yeavering revealed a large complex of high-status buildings, including a possible structure for holding assemblies, a find of a gold coin, and, on a henge monument, signs of precious metalworking.[187] These finds might now be set alongside those from Rendlesham in Suffolk, not far from Sutton Hoo and described by Bede as an estate of the East Anglian royal dynasty.[188] Rendlesham is now known, from a joint campaign of closely monitored metal-detecting and archaeological survey, to have had masses of coins in circulation, and although no decisive evidence of minting as such has come to light, there are (as at Yeavering) traces of precious metalworking.[189]

It is entirely possible that Rendlesham, Yeavering, or places like them were where gold shillings were made and first handed over, to kin, friends, associates, and dependants of the king. Part of the point would have been the occasion: that these particular coins were those given at *that* time and place, as a tangible demonstration of the relationship between giver and recipient. If these gold coins did primarily circulate within a fairly narrow social group, knowledge of that context could have been one underpinning element in their value—that this particular group of gold coins reflected the booty of a specific campaign, the largesse of a celebrated ruler, gifts offered at an important religious festival, or similar.[190] The worth of a coin would rest on more than just its fineness and weight. This might explain a puzzling feature of the early Anglo-Saxon gold coinage: that the fineness of coins from the same hoard, of the same type, and sometimes even struck from the same dies can vary significantly.[191] The implication, especially of the last of these, is that whoever was making the coins had to switch between batches of gold, refined to different levels, all within a relatively short space of time. These circumstances strongly suggest

---

186. On the metalworking site at Yeavering, see Frodsham 2005, 29–31.

187. For the main buildings, including the gold coin and the assembly site, see Hope-Taylor 1977, 119–21, 280–82.

188. Bede, *Historia ecclesiastica gentis Anglorum* 3.22 (ed. and trans. Colgrave and Mynors 1969, 284–85).

189. Scull, Minter and Plouviez 2016, 1600, 1602–1603.

190. For context-dependent handling of money, see chapter 4.

191. Metcalf 1993–94, 1, nos. 18–19, 22–23, 39–40, 43–44, 58–61, etc. The hoard evidence is restricted, and still consists of only one substantial hoard of Anglo-Saxon shillings found at Crondall (Hampshire) in 1828, from which most of the specimens in Metcalf 1993–94 derive. A similar phenomenon can be seen among the coins of certain Merovingian moneyers: Pol 2013.

sporadic production. General shortfalls in supply could be another factor, but finds like Sutton Hoo, the West Norfolk hoard, and the Staffordshire hoard show that the amount of gold available in seventh-century England was probably not quite so small. Indeed, compositional analysis of gold objects of this period from England indicates that many were made from melted-down coins that had flowed into Britain from Gaul, which in turn would often have been made from gold supplied by the Byzantine Empire.[192] Frankish and other foreign gold coins in England were both numerous and not restricted in circulation, which raises the further question of why English coins were minted at all. Production that was driven by the direct social needs of elites stands out as a likely rationale for both these features of the coinage. Local coin issues became significantly more prominent in both absolute and relative terms during the later stages of this period, from about 650, at about the same time that the fineness of gold pieces began to decline sharply. These changes could point to a larger component of commercial use for later, less valuable gold currency, albeit one that still coexisted with a measure of Merovingian coin circulation.[193] The later English gold issues stemmed from control over the incoming supply via ties to the continent, which were increasingly in the hands of mercantile groups.[194]

England's earliest gold coinage is important in showing that it was possible to have a fairly substantial, vibrant gold currency without dependence on fiscal machinery. Minting and circulation probably relied more on a raft of demands among the elite. The roots of this demand can be traced back to the development of Christianised rulership in England—at first more a matter of contact and familiarity with, and respect for, Christian forms of rule rather than conversion itself, though the first actual coin issues in England came as the new religion was making greater strides.[195] Embracing coins also presupposed a niche they could fit into within the increasingly elaborate kingships of the day. This was the age of "princely" burials that imply a grander, more elaborate deployment of material goods to differentiate the most powerful lineages and project their status over the surrounding population in an increasingly

---

192. Blakelock and Fern 2019, 126; Nicolay 2014, 210–32, 238–44, and 250–57. For the circumstances behind the ebbs and flows of this Byzantine gold supply, see Esders 2013.

193. Woods forthcoming.

194. Loveluck and Tys 2006; Fleming 2009, esp. 410–20, 2010, 182–212; Loveluck 2013, 178–212.

195. Williams 2006, 186–88; Naismith 2016b, 285–92; Yorke 2019, 344–48.

assertive fashion.[196] Giving out coins offered something new: a way of distributing numerous, discrete, and yet readily identifiable pieces of largesse that compartmentalised value in a relatively miniature form, highly suitable for the complicated multilevel exchanges that went into building up the first tangible Anglo-Saxon kingdoms from the late sixth century into the early seventh. This was not just a matter of kings—in the sense of the highest overlords—setting themselves up to lord it directly over the rest of society; it was a collaborative, layered process that enriched several strata in a hierarchy of power.[197] Some of these can be glimpsed among the leaders of smaller groups that had been subsumed into larger hegemonies, which still had a flexible, precarious character, being prone to collapse and reconfiguration, as seen in the rise and fall of Kentish, Northumbrian, and Mercian authority.[198] Figures at many steps of this pyramid could probably have called themselves king or something like it, and so in that sense there is a likelihood that many, perhaps most, of the coins of this period were royal, though in comparative terms it is more appropriate to think of most of these figures as aristocrats rather than kings. Bishops and other churchmen were another possible source of the resources, patronage, and connections needed for minting (and in fact one of the earliest inscribed English gold pieces refers to Liudard, the bishop who accompanied the Frankish princess Bertha to her new home and husband in sixth-century Kent).[199]

Conclusion

What stands out in all these case studies is that to fixate on state operations and exactions misses the point of who was actually behind them. We are in this sense misled by the meagre written sources that tend to focus on, or at least be read in, a highly statist framework. The social, symbolic context of coins imbued them with value to those who were aware of their origin. Manufacture on a holy day or at a holy place, or from metal of special origin, could all affect the worth assigned to them.[200] Kings, officials, and aristocrats bought into these valences as much as anyone else, and the legitimacy of virtually all early medieval institutions was encoded in symbolic and religious terms. The more dispersed production of coin

196. Yorke 1990, esp. 9–19, 2003; Scull 1992; Blackmore and Scull 2019, esp. 325–29.
197. Wickham 2005, 340–45.
198. As seen in the Tribal Hidage, see Davies and Vierck 1974; Blair 2014.
199. Most effectively and fully discussed in Werner 1991; see also Naismith 2017b, 50–51; Gannon 2003, 188–91.
200. Theuws 2004, 127–29.

apparent in the sixth century and after also reflects its status as a mediation between local communities and their overlords. Hendy's distinction between public and private is not especially helpful from this perspective.[201] It is more productive to look at how and why agency in the production of coin changed. The overall trajectory of this period saw facilities and networks for making coin become progressively more localised. This happened largely behind the scenes in Iberia and Gaul during the fifth and earlier sixth centuries, though occasional glimpses leave little doubt that it was going on. The process accelerated sharply in the later sixth century. Importantly, both Iberia and Gaul still had some sort of centralising tax mechanism centred on the king and his court, so the regionalisation of minting is best read as a shift in the dynamics of production. Late Roman minting had, mostly if not entirely, been driven by state expenditure, distanced from outside needs and pressures by layers of bureaucracy; the post-Roman coinages were seemingly the result of a much closer nexus between minting and state income, and with the agencies involved in generating that income—a diffusion of "public" needs as well as the enlistment of "private" ones. This might mean Leovigild minting gold pieces to reward his troops or buy supplies, or Charibert II issuing tremisses from Banassac en masse. But it also meant a revolving door of payment and profit for elites through engagement with taxation and other demands of the state. In short, those who paid now had to take on the responsibility of producing appropriate coins, which allowed for and encouraged a plethora of other interests to come into play.

Those other interests collectively were substantial, as seen most clearly in England, where the process outlined earlier worked in reverse: the driving force was socially charged local elite expenditure. This is important when approaching Gaul and Iberia, where the coinage is usually seen in terms of taxation. But tax was, or at least was becoming, a proxy of the relationship between kings and elites, and one of several pressures that could drive the minting of coinage. Iberia probably kept up a stronger element of fiscal minting, with the important caveat that this too played into the interests of elites, whether that meant coins staying in the vicinity or else being transplanted to Toledo for handover to other, more centrally placed figures. Gaul may have been similar, its gold tremisses of profuse mints and moneyers being the product of a system that perhaps started out as a genuine attempt to balance tax demands with complex local realities. In time, these coins became a vehicle for local dominance to play out,

201. Hendy 1988.

providing their gatherers with an opportunity for peculation or to score points with the king as taxes became more negotiable. It is likely too that gold coins were, increasingly, made using this machinery for purposes that were not related to taxes at all.

Production of gold coins is an especially close index of elite and state interests for the simple reason that their value was so high. For them to be made on even a small scale required the mobilisation of substantial resources. Minting was a rich man's game, and a symbolically laden act. In England most clearly, and potentially also at times in Gaul and Iberia, prestige and the desire to have *one's own* coins for *one's own* needs would have been major factors in production. Minting could on these grounds be an act of dominance. The primary uses of gold coin were thus deeply embedded in elite interactions. These extended to dealings with the state, through taxation or (in the opposite direction) as gifts or military bonuses, and to other demands; anything where the actual manufacture of new coins was needed for the purposes of shock and awe, or to placate a more powerful figure. Opportunities for actually injecting new gold coins into circulation were socially and quantitatively narrow, though functionally they were probably growing more diverse over the course of the seventh century. Importantly, these limitations did not apply to the secondary uses of gold to anything like the same degree. Circulation after the manufacture and initial uses of coins was much more varied. Gregory of Tours described merchants spending and gaining gold pieces in commercial transactions,[202] and the *Vitas patrum Emeritensium* mention Bishop Masona (d. c. 600/610) giving away tremisses as alms to paupers, in the expectation that they would be able to spend them.[203] Gold pieces also featured, in a limited way, in seigneurial payments from tenants to landlords. The will of a Frankish abbot, written in the 570s, refers to some servile tenants (*mancipia tributaria*) who owed *trientes* to the monks of St. Martin.[204] But it is unlikely that gold pieces were frequently found in the hands of peasants. One of the miracle stories in Gregory the Great's *Dialogues* concerns a poor man who could not settle a debt of 12 solidi, and even St. Benedict could not help him when the man first came and asked for help (though the coins miraculously appeared in the church a couple of days later).[205] This of course relates to contemporary Italy, which had a minting system much closer to the Roman model of few, centralised places of production, within the increasingly fragmented political framework

---

202. Gregory of Tours, *In gloria confessorum* 110 (Krusch 1969, 369–70).
203. *Vitas sanctorum patrum Emeritensium* 5.7 (Maya Sánchez 1992, 71–73).
204. *PL* 71:1144D, 1146B–C, 1147A.
205. Gregory the Great, *Dialogi* 2.27 (ed. and trans. de Vogüé 1978–1980, 2:214–16).

of the later sixth century—but in its emphasis on high-value gold coins, it was similar to the other regions discussed in more detail here.[206]

There were still bronze coins—mostly old ones, dating back to the days of the emperors—and in some regions small silver ones to cater to more quotidian needs, but one of the basic challenges of this period, for most of the population, would have been negotiating a monetary system that was so heavily geared toward gold. Even secondary circulation would have favoured elites. The precious few examples of gold coins that have come to light from excavated settlement contexts stem from elite sites; at El Tolmo de Minateda, tellingly, old Roman bronzes were found in Visigothic layers from across the city site, while the six gold tremisses all occurred in the vicinity of the palace and basilica.[207] When peasants and others did acquire gold coins, it was probably for specific needs and short periods of time, with the added challenge of variable, often unfavourable rates of exchange between gold and other goods or coins. But the biggest hurdle would probably have been scarcity in relative terms. Gold coinage overall was still comparatively substantial, but the amount of gold coinage actually available in circulation at any one time would have been small. As in the late Roman era (although not on anything like the scale of the senatorial aristocracy), hoarding of gold was normal, and high-value exchanges probably meant handing over a purse or bag of coin. These practices would have had a chilling effect on the currency. Sixth- and seventh-century elites probably did not spend more coin than they had to, and they did so when it suited their needs. Whatever new gold was put into circulation would end up in large part parked in the chests or secret places of the elite, to be drip-fed into the hands of other coin users.

206. On Italy in this period, see Grierson 1982, 138–44; Bernareggi 1976, 1983; Grierson and Blackburn 1986, 58–66; Rovelli 2012; Arslan 2002b (among many others).
207. Martín Viso 2011, 238–41; Doménech Belda 2014, esp. 15–24.

CHAPTER EIGHT

The Rise of the Denarius c. 660–900

ALDHELM OF MALMESBURY (d. 709) wielded the Latin language like a blunt instrument, filling his sentences with the most recherché vocabulary and letting them wander on and on. The result is almost overwhelming in its complexity and rhetorical pyrotechnics. But Aldhelm took great pride in his idiosyncratic Latin, for he was one of the first English students to reach this level of accomplishment in the language of Virgil, Donatus, and (most important for him) the scriptures. One of Aldhelm's showpieces was a letter written, probably in the 670s, to an English friend named Heahfrith who intended to undertake training in Ireland. Aldhelm was having none of this: better masters could now be found in Canterbury in the form of the Syrian Theodore (archbishop of Canterbury 668–90) and the African Hadrian (d. 710). He argued at length that following this advice amounted to Heahfrith making proper use of his God-given faculties. At one point, Aldhelm cited the gospel parable of the talents of silver in his support: "in vain are the profits of the talent barricaded and concealed in subterranean sands, which should have been spent for the plentiful coins of the moneyers."[1] What is striking here is what Aldhelm thought a trip to the moneyer involved. The biblical passages (Matthew 25:27 and Luke 19:23) left open what would happen to the silver once given to the *nummularii*; in the context of the first century, *nummularii* could well have taken it as a longer-term deposit, to accrue interest.[2] None of this is said,

---

1. "Frustra talenti foenora subterraneis clanculantur obstructa sablonibus, quae trapezitarum numerosis monetae oportuissent nummismatibus profligari." Aldhelm, *Epistolae* 5 (Ehwald 1919, 492; adapted from trans. Howlett 1994, 44).

2. On the operations of Roman *nummularii*, see Andreau 1987, 177–220, 445–641.

meaning that the flow of coins that follow are Aldhelm's inference. Taking a talent of silver to the moneyers to change into a large number of coins seemed the natural thing. He could well have been referring to the prospect of profit that would appear in time, or working from what someone (maybe Theodore or Hadrian) had told him about the nature of banking and money-changing in the Greco-Roman world. But his view could also have been shaped by the important changes he and Heahfrith would have seen around them as a new coinage was becoming established in England and its neighbours.

Getting a lot of coins from the moneyer might have been a new experience for Aldhelm and his contemporaries. Far more coins were being produced and used from the late seventh century onward. The numbers of finds in themselves are eloquent testimony to how much things had changed. England, at the end of 2019, had about 6,500 recorded single finds of early pennies minted between about 660 and 750.[3] Many of these are isolated finds from fields dotted across eastern England; others cluster at what numismatists have taken to calling "productive sites," usually of unknown status.[4] A rare example with better historical and archaeological background is Rendlesham in Suffolk.[5] This 150-hectare site, subjected to a long programme of controlled metal detecting and selective excavation, has produced 168 pennies.[6] Another "productive site" at East Tilbury in Essex has produced over 120.[7] But these English examples are dwarfed by some of the productive sites in mainland Europe. About a thousand early pennies and 229 Carolingian pennies come from Domburg in the Netherlands alone,[8] while another major trading port 130 km east at Dorestad (modern Wijk bij Duurstede) has turned up several hundred early pennies and at least 475 Carolingian-era coins.[9]

Not everywhere was touched by this explosion of silver. Italy in particular is a puzzle, for silver denarii became standard in the northern and

3. This total is based on the combined resources of EMC and PAS. EMC had 3,988 coins as of the end of 2019; PAS had 1,680 (with an uncertain degree of overlap between the two databases).

4. The term in itself is not problematic, but the difficulty came when such sites began to be thought of as markets or similar, often without any formal archaeological investigation (Richards 1999; Gardiner 2001; Pestell 2010).

5. For the royal associations of this site, see chapter 7.

6. Scull, Minter, and Plouviez 2016; Woods forthcoming.

7. Blackburn 2003, 26–28.

8. Op den Velde and Klaassen 2004.

9. Coupland 2010; 2018b, 218; personal communication with Simon Coupland and Wybrand Op den Velde.

central parts of the peninsula from the later eighth century yet are hardly more visible archaeologically than the earlier gold coins. But the point to emphasise at this stage is that a significant step up in the scale of the monetary economy is demonstrable in most regions that adopted silver pennies. In England—where large-scale databases allow for confident long-term comparisons—the period c. 660–750 now stands out as the richest in terms of precious-metal coin finds between the fourth century and the thirteenth. The central factor was the prevalent use of silver rather than gold: a material that was less valuable, and much more readily available in western Europe, not least from the mines at Melle in western France. Dealing in silver pennies or denarii opened up the principal coined denomination of early medieval Europe to a much larger constituency. In eastern England and central and northern Francia, it is probably fair to say that all members of society—from slaves upward—would use coined currency at least some of the time.[10] Nonetheless, it should be stressed that the penny did not represent a low-value currency. Far from it: in the time of Charlemagne, one denarius bought a dozen high-quality loaves of wheat bread.[11] What the penny presented was a more middling denomination that now lay within realistic reach of most people, even if many would only see or use them in occasional, specialized contexts.

This downward shift is the central legacy of the switch to silver in the later seventh century. The story of its impact can be divided into two distinct segments. The first, running from the inception of the denarius/penny (itself a debatable subject) to the middle decades of the eighth century, is dominated by silver pieces that superficially still belonged to the world of the earlier gold tremisses and *scillingas*. They were small and thick, and based on similar standards of weight. Visually, the new coins also come out of the same stable as the earlier gold: Frankish specimens include many with the names of mint and moneyer (though not the king), alongside a growing share with no inscription; in England, meanwhile, meaningful inscriptions of any kind remain rare, though in iconographic terms the early eighth century is a high point of diversity, accomplishment, and general ingenuity.[12] The opening decades of the new coinage hence invite the question of how much had changed at all in terms of the background infrastructure. Was this simply a matter of more—sometimes much more—of the same?

10. Naismith 2012b, 281–82.
11. Council of Frankfurt c. 4 (Boretius 1883, 74).
12. Gannon 2003.

That question is no longer appropriate for England and Francia after the mid-eighth century, when a new and longer segment of the early history of the penny began. Although the basic unit was still a piece of silver of about the same weight, outwardly a whole new currency came into being, and the changes of this period were to have an abiding legacy. One aspect of this related to kingship. Over the course of possibly as little as a decade, rulers in Northumbria, East Anglia, Francia, Kent, and Mercia imposed themselves much more forcefully on the coinage.[13] The contrast with earlier times is vivid. Virtually every coin now named the king or emperor, whereas only a tiny minority of earlier silver and gold issues within these regions had done so. This move ushered in an era of much more openly political coinage, in which the design and inscriptions of coins and, where available, written discussions of them strongly emphasised the relationship between minting and the king. In England, the moneyers were cast as direct operatives of the king.[14] Mint-places in the Carolingian world represented locations where a count had under his supervision an established minting organization; the moneyers, often named even in the late Merovingian silver coinage, lost their outward-facing role.[15]

A third change was physical, consisting of the adoption in Francia and southern England of a broader, thinner format of coin (hence why coins of this period and after are sometimes referred to as "broad pennies"). This encouraged bold, clear, and highly literate statements of regnal authority, unlike most early pennies. As a result, the coinage took on, in every sense of the world, an enlarged role in political symbolism. Coined money became a tool in diplomatic as well as economic relations, meaning that adopting silver pennies or denarii, or a given type within them, sent a message about status and power. When the duke of Benevento was ordered to recognize Charlemagne on his coins and in his charters, he also started issuing silver denarii on the same model as the Franks (figure 8.1).[16] His successors continued to issue silver denarii on a small, essentially tokenistic scale for another century; the only ones minted in larger quantity come from another period of northern intervention in the 860s and 870s, and charters from the abbey of Cava dei Tirreni show that after a brief period when silver was used to settle payments in the late ninth century, gold made a comeback in the form of the Sicilian *tarì* and the Byzantine

13. Naismith 2012a.
14. Naismith 2012b, 132–55.
15. See chapter 7.
16. Erchempert, *Historia Langobardorum Beneventanorum* c. 4 (Waitz 1878, 236). Naismith 2012b, 13–14.

FIGURE 8.1. Silver denarius of Grimoald III, duke of Benevento (788–806) (diameter 18 mm). Classical Numismatic Group, LLC.

solidus.[17] In this case military and political pressure were key, as they had been in northern Italy, where an order to replace gold tremisses with silver denarii came in 781, just a few years after the Carolingian conquest, as a statement about cultural and political alignment.[18] It meant that only silver coins would be made going forward, but actual use took time to catch up: charters from parts of Tuscany and the Monte Sabini indicate that gold was still being used into the 790s and 800s.[19] Something similar happened in Saxony and northeastern Spain, where the denarius was imposed in a context of conquest as the new measure of value, even though in both regions actual coins remained scarce.[20] Kent, Mercia, Rome, Venice, and Denmark also started to issue their own versions of silver denarii in response to those of the Franks (see map 8.1). They probably did so for several reasons. At Venice, it may have been primarily a commercial decision, to enable interaction with the monetary economy of the mainland. Elsewhere, it is more likely to have been a political statement, signalling a measure of alignment with the cultural and economic hegemon.

This chapter focuses on the home regions of the new silver coinage: eastern England, Francia, and (after the 770s) central and northern Italy. After considering in more detail how and where the new coinage emerged, it examines issues related to those principal regions. Subsequent sections

17. Rovelli 2012, chap. 16; see also Day 1997, esp. 43–44; with detailed discussion of the relevant coins in Arslan 2002c and 2003. On the early *tarì*, see Grierson and Travaini 1998, 61, 68–69, 74.

18. Capitulary of Mantua, c. 9 (Boretius 1883, 191). Cf. Rovelli 2012, chap. 6, 11–12.

19. Day 1997, 27–29; Wickham 1980, 27–34.

20. Devroey 2015, 204; Rovelli 2012, chap. 6, 12–25; Grierson and Travaini 1998, 70–73.

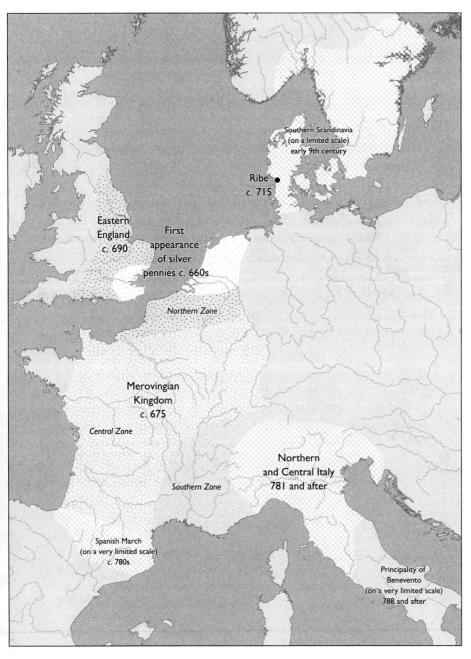

MAP 8.1. The spread of the penny from the later seventh century to c. 800.

will turn to the political and structural background of minting in the Carolingian world, and finally of England in the later eighth and ninth centuries.

From Gold to Silver

Aldhelm wrote at the very cusp of the new era and was familiar with one of the first regions (Kent) to feel its effects. Silver pennies or denarii began to be made in England, Frisia, and Francia around the year 660. This was the final step in a long progression that had already taken the Merovingian and Anglo-Saxon coinages a long way from their late Roman roots. It has been seen as marking a break with Mediterranean tradition and the beginning of a distinct monetary system in northwestern Europe.[21] But it needs to be seen against the background of a Mediterranean in which silver took on a larger monetary role than it had in centuries (figure 8.2). A glance around the Mediterranean in the seventh and eighth centuries shows the variety of roles silver played. Lombard Italy possessed a modest coinage of very small silver pieces in the late sixth and seventh centuries. These formed a flexible lower level of currency that could apparently be issued by bishops and dukes as well as kings.[22] In real terms the impact of these coins is difficult to gauge: although finds come from isolated rural sites as well as cities,[23] they still seem to have been limited in scope, perhaps being primarily intended for ceremonial uses like early Byzantine silver pieces.[24] In the course of the seventh century, silver made a much larger resurgence in the Byzantine Empire. Between the reign of Heraclius (610–41) and c. 680, large silver pieces known as hexagrams were minted, initially as a temporary way of paying salaries using confiscated church treasures, later also finding an important role in tribute payments to neighbouring peoples.[25] Both roles effectively made silver a supplement to gold. After a hiatus, silver *miliaresia* started to be made under Leo III (717–41). These were thinner coins that possibly began with a ceremonial function,[26] and they drew inspiration from a silver denomination that had attained new

21. Pirenne 1939, 244–47 (though he dated this break and the advent of silver coinage to the time of Charlemagne); Hodges 1989, 110–11.

22. Arslan 2002a; 2002c; 2004; Arslan and Uggé 2005.

23. Arslan 2002a, 336–37.

24. Grierson 1982, 56–59, 102–3.

25. Yannopoulos 1978; Hendy 1985, 278, 494–95; Morrisson, Popović, and Ivanišević 2006, 41–73; Brubaker and Haldon 2011, 468, 473.

26. Grierson 1973, 62–64. The quantity of surviving specimens suggests that *miliaresia* took on a significant role in the economy of the eighth to tenth centuries.

FIGURE 8.2. Silver coins of the seventh- and early eighth-
century Mediterranean: a small silver piece of the Lombard
king Perctarit (672–88); a *hexagram* of Heraclius and
Heraclius Constantine (610–41), minted at Constantinope
615–638; a *miliaresion* of Leo III and Constantine V (717–41),
minted at Constantinople 720–41; an Umayyad dirham minted
in AH 79 (AD 698/99) at al-Basra (diameters 13 mm, 25 mm,
25 mm, and 27 mm). All Classical Numismatic Group, LLC.

prominence in the Mediterranean and Middle East: the dirham of the Umayyad Caliphate. Dirhams or drachms had been issued on a massive scale by later Sassanian rulers in the first half of the seventh century, and even in Syria the first Islamic dirhams struck under Caliph Abd al-Malik (685–705) reproduced the design of Sassanian models. But in the early 690s these gave way to a quite different, more strongly Islamic design (i.e., with lengthy Arabic inscriptions and no images) that was before long being minted across Umayyad territory.[27] It should be stressed that both the Byzantine and Umayyad silver worked alongside a continued gold element; equally, it will be apparent that there were different symbolic, ceremonial, and fiscal motives for issuing these new silver coins. They did not form part of a single movement, nor can they be directly linked to the move back to silver in northern Europe.

Indirectly, though, it is likely that ties with the Mediterranean and especially Byzantium did play a part. Subsidies and gifts in the form of gold had flowed from Constantinople to the Franks and Lombards in the sixth and seventh centuries. "Chequebook diplomacy" of this kind is likely to have been a significant source of fresh, high-quality gold in western Europe, with the largest infusions arriving during just a short time in the late sixth century.[28] This cannot have been the only flow, for gold had come in earlier, and some specimens found in the West are unlikely to have arrived through official channels from the empire, such as a single Arab-Byzantine gold dinar from the Buis hoard of the later seventh century.[29] But whatever routes had brought Byzantine gold to the western Mediterranean tightened sharply in the seventh century, especially after the reign of Heraclius.[30] The Arab conquests in themselves probably were not the sole reason; rather, they curtailed Byzantine access to gold from sources on and beyond its eastern frontier and precipitated root and branch realignment in Byzantine finances and infrastructure, which meant that what remained of the empire's resources were turned inward.[31] Monetarily, northwestern Europe was on its own.

27. Heidemann 2011.

28. Fischer 2019. Byzantine payments are known down to 590, while the Lombards also paid a large annual sum in gold to the Franks between 590 and 617/18.

29. Morrisson 2015. The provenance of this coin is not watertight, though Morrisson defends the attribution.

30. Lafaurie and Morrisson 1987, esp. 49–55; Morrisson 2014. In Gaul, finds of Byzantine gold become rare from the late sixth century, though this was probably at first a result of more incoming coins being reminted into the large pseudo-imperial series of Provence.

31. Esders 2013. For the reduced quantity of Byzantine gold in the later seventh century and after, see Morrisson 2002, 936–42; Brubaker and Haldon 2011, 466–70. For

The shift away from gold coin to silver in northwestern Europe was at the same time a response to more local pressures. It represented one more pendulum swing in tastes for precious metals and what to do with them that had been going on for centuries. Elite practices and relationships with other social groups (along with state demands) played a large part in shaping the trajectory of these cycles.[32] In the mid- to late seventh century, gold of some form featured frequently in high-status Frankish burials, though generally in smaller, more routinised forms, with large and ostentatious gold objects now being even rarer and more exclusive;[33] England also shows wider access to smaller amounts of gold and silver, suggestive of attempts at distinction by lower-level elites.[34] Furnished burial in general seems to have been coming to an end in England at about the time of the move from gold coin to silver.[35] In this context, the coins can be read as a strategy in the use of precious metal that emphasized transferability and exchange. Coin offered new possibilities in the construction of social capital, both by smaller, locally important figures and by major magnates dealing with a layered network of subordinates.[36] Other possible channels for elite expenditure would have dovetailed with the onset of silver coinage. The mid- and late seventh century saw a wave of monastic foundation and patronage in England and Gaul, in part as a way of crystallizing the spiritual and material interests of royal and aristocratic families.[37] These churches steered lay society toward alternative ways of expressing status and wealth, including Christian charity, for which coins—especially those of relatively lower value and greater number—were well suited.[38]

Some of these developments may be results instead of causes of changes to the coinage or had a symbiotic relationship with monetary changes, the one stimulating the other. But the central point is that the background to the first emergence of the penny is complex and does not

a contemporary rise in gold output in the emergent Islamic Caliphate, see Shaddel 2021, esp. 290–93.

32. For the late Roman period, especially with reference to silver, see Carlà-Uhink 2020. For the early Middle Ages in the North Sea area, see Nicolay 2014, 101.

33. Périn 2008 (for the Merovingian kingdom).

34. Hines and Bayliss 2013, 541–46.

35. Hines and Bayliss 2013, 526–57.

36. Scull and Naylor 2016, esp. 228–29; Hines and Bayliss 2013, 527.

37. For Francia, see Fox 2014, esp. 302; Wood 2018, 100–101 (though with caution on the impact of "dynastic" foundations); for England, Blair 2005, 84–91, 100–108; Foot 2006, 79–85.

38. Naismith 2017b, 107–8.

stem from any one single cause. Nor is it easily traceable to a single point of origin.

Questions of Origins

There is no doubt that the first pennies appeared in the North Sea world in the second half of the seventh century. What is less clear is exactly when and where. It is not just a matter of assigning a gold (or silver) star for coming up with what would prove to be a watershed in longer monetary history. The question of where silver coinage first appeared has a bearing on what kind of agency and context the new currency sprang from.

The traditional line on the origins of the penny or denarius assigned priority to the Merovingian Franks.[39] One pillar of this argument is that Merovingian coins can be identified that name individuals who can be confidently dated to the 670s. Those of Childeric II (d. 675) from Tours belong to the years 673–75, and several others must belong between then and the early 680s. There may well be other, undatable issues that were made even earlier.[40] But there is also a gold tremissis of Avitus II, bishop of Clermont (676–91), which indicates a degree of regional variation in the transition from gold to silver. A second reason for assigning the earliest pennies to the Franks was simply that the Merovingian kingdom was, in the later seventh century, still the preeminent political, cultural, and economic force in northwestern Europe. Its gold coins had been a powerful influence on the Anglo-Saxons fifty years earlier when the first coinages appeared in England.

A lot of water had passed under the bridge since that point, however. Frankish coins no longer circulated in profusion in England in the early days of the new pennies, while Frisian ones quickly came to be a strong presence. And in any case, Frankish hegemony is not in itself a valid argument for the kingdom having innovative currency or refusing to consider practices from overseas. There are ready examples of precisely the opposite within this period.[41] Furthermore, it is unlikely that all the changes of the later seventh century were commanded at a state level.[42] There are now reasons to challenge both the main reasons for assigning the introduction

39. Rigold 1960–61, 25; Grierson and Blackburn 1986, 186; Hines and Bayliss 2013, 498.

40. A possibility raised in Schiesser 2018, 233–34.

41. E.g., the adoption of large bronze denominations in the East Roman Empire based on practices in Ostrogothic Italy and Vandal Carthage; see chapters 6 and 7.

42. Theuws 2018, 43–48.

of the silver pennies to a central decision undertaken by the rulers of the Frankish kingdom.[43] It is necessary instead to look north, to England and what is now the Netherlands. For the sake of convenience, the latter region is referred to here as "Frisia," though in practice it was a debatable frontier region, the southern part of which had probably lain more or less within the Frankish political sphere for centuries. In practice, "Frisian"' coins were a big part of, and shaded into, the northernmost zone of Merovingian coins, and both showed strong crossover with southeastern England.[44] A frustrating hallmark of this cross-Channel region was rarity of inscriptions, so that the coins can only occasionally be closely dated or attributed to a specific source.

Early studies by Stuart Rigold were shaped by the desire to associate the new English pennies with King Wihtred of Kent (690–725), so he put the shift from gold to silver in the 680s.[45] But two recent projects have together pushed that date back considerably. One assesses evidence for lead production on the basis of pollution traces in Alpine glacial ice, which suggests a series of upticks from about the mid-620s onward; these probably relate to silver that was being used to alloy gold, and later for minting of silver denarii.[46] A second project combines carbon-14 and statistical dating of selected Anglo-Saxon graves (several containing coins). These point strongly to the transition beginning at an earlier date than Rigold postulated, perhaps being largely accomplished as early as 660.[47] There are very few other fixed points in English numismatic chronology in the seventh century, and a shift of this magnitude is entirely plausible within the constraints of current knowledge. It would also put the inception of the first English pennies somewhat before their datable Frankish counterparts.

Three stages can be identified in the relative chronology of the move from gold to silver. The first is reflected in the "preprimary" or "transitional" coinages of southeastern England and Frisia: coherent groups or

43. Others have already queried Frankish precedence: Lebecq 2005, 652–53; Hines and Bayliss 2013, 511.

44. Schiesser 2017, 69–75. Frans Theuws (2018, 57–65) has proposed that the two main "Frisian" groups (Series D and E) were in fact made in England for export. I have doubts about this suggestion, as England was not a primary producer of silver, while late "tertiary"'issues of Series E are a problem in the context of mid- and late eighth-century England, which moved over to broad silver pennies in the names of local kings (though for a different reading of the chronology, see Breternitz 2018; 2020, 111–16).

45. Rigold 1960–61, 25–29.

46. Loveluck et al. 2018. See also Téreygeol 2018, 52.

47. Hines and Bayliss 2013, 493–515.

types with a gold content that fluctuated from 10 or 20 per cent down to virtually nil, in effect making them silver pieces.[48] No such phase is apparent in the mainstream Merovingian coinage: although gradually debased over the seventh century, individual coins rarely dip below about 30 per cent pure, even in the later stages of the coinage.[49] By an apparently organic process, not concerted or centrally impelled, these English and Frisian coinages made the transition from gold to silver. The second stage consists of selective and seemingly more deliberate uptake of silver coinage by individual regions or authorities in Francia. Some of the earliest specimens are associated with the mayor of the palace, Ebroin (d. 680/81).[50] Ian Wood noted that if Ebroin was closely involved in the adoption of the silver denarius, it is odd they were apparently not issued at Quentovic, where he was able to influence cross-Channel traffic.[51] That could be because Ebroin's interests in silver coinage were related to interests in the silver mines of Aquitaine at Melle, for the coins in his name are similar in type to some of the earliest denarii of Melle and could have been struck in the same area.[52]

The onset of much amplified silver extraction at Melle may have been a powerful impetus to the wider adoption of the denarius. This represents the third and final stage of the process, following the more tentative move in this direction that began about 660. No one agency can be said to have imposed the silver denarius at a stroke. It emerged from the interplay of distinct monetary circuits, responding to each other in rapid sequence. The first pennies arose from interregional exchange across the Channel and the North Sea and should be seen as a reaction to the slow attenuation of gold coinage that had been going on already for decades but reached its conclusion in coins that shaded from low gold to no gold (i.e., silver). Responsibility lay with those who made and first used the coins in question: seagoing merchants and coastal landowning elites, who could trust one another to accept these coins.[53] The second stage was piecemeal introduction of a more sharply distinguished silver penny in the "central zone" of coin

48. Naismith 2017b, 48, 56–59, 92; Pol 2008, 2010. In England, the main relevant issues are the "Pada" and "Vanimundus" types; and in Frisia, the "Madelinus" type. A small number of "silver" coins of other early English penny types contain a larger amount of gold, suggesting prolonged overlap between gold, transitional, and silver issues.

49. Pol 2013, esp. 536–38.

50. For his impact on the coinage, see Grierson and Blackburn 1986, 93–94.

51. Wood 1994, 296.

52. Schiesser 2018, 233; Clairand and Téreygeol 2009. For Ebroin's strong involvement in Aquitaine, see Fouracre 1981, 156–57, 212–38.

53. See chapter 3.

circulation in Gaul, under the leadership of various elite patrons;[54] one of these involved the king, but there is no indication of a blanket order to adopt the silver denarius. Again, change took place at the level of regional webs of power and trust. The third part of the process seemingly emerged from the second, in that the making and distribution of denarii in Francia, Frisia, and England picked up steam. Coins from Melle and its region are not especially abundant,[55] which suggests that in practice they were largely melted down again, perhaps alongside late tremisses that would already have mostly consisted of silver.[56] That in itself is important, for coins could circulate freely within and to some extent between a few larger regions—central Francia, southern Francia, and the Netherlands with eastern England—and it is common to encounter a mix of types and mint-places in hoards as well as single finds. This begs the question of why coins were actually minted, or reminted, at all.

The Silver Rush c. 660-750 1: England

The first flush of silver minting in England produced one of the most methodologically challenging coinages in the whole medieval period. Finds are voluminous, with over 6,500 recorded to date and a great many more unreported.[57] Among these, some six hundred major groups of coins have been identified, with much uncertainty over what weight should be put on typological, metrological, and metallurgical features. Their development in broad outline is clear. A small group of large early issues made in southeastern England dominated the early decades of the coinage. These were later joined (probably in the 690s) by large issues traditionally associated with Frisia, as well as by a few new and smaller groups from within England, among them some from well outside the Southeast, including Wessex and Northumbria. Around the 710s these—collectively known as the "primary" phase—gradually faded way, leading to a rather more complicated landscape of numerous coinages, some large and some small, some highly localized in circulation and some not: the so-called secondary phase.[58]

54. For division of Merovingian silver coinage into "northern," "central," and "southern" zones, see Schiesser 2017, 69–75.

55. Clairand and Téreygeol 2009.

56. Geneviève and Sarah 2010, 503–4.

57. Based on 4,900 on EMC and 1,848 on PAS as of 8 January 2022 (with an uncertain degree of overlap between these totals).

58. The best guide to the typology is Abramson 2017. General guides include Metcalf 1993-1994; Gannon 2013, 98–136; Naismith 2017b, 63–110.

This outline gives a numismatist's-eye view; one that reflects the attraction exerted by the tumultuous vista of the early pennies, and the frustration that comes from an endless search for order in apparent chaos.[59] To embrace the chaos is arguably the best way forward. Why are the early pennies the way they are? What kind of infrastructures could have produced them? For those who actually handled early pennies, the first, most obvious, and (for many) only real way to differentiate between them was visual. What coins looked like mattered. As Anna Gannon has noted, the associations encoded in the iconographically elaborate images need to be taken seriously as a constitutive element in the value of a coin.[60] These signals would have been strongest at the point of origin: in the eyes of makers, patrons, and primary users who knew the context the coins came from. It is possible that whoever deposited the highly mixed Woodham Walter (Essex) hoard in the 730s was thinking in terms of groups with this or that image, which to them would conjure up both earthly associations with particular places, individuals, or institutions and spiritual ones: biblical figures, scenes, or ideas, particular saints, or the churches associated with them (figure 8.3).[61] Every subsequent change of hands meant mixing with a wider pool of coinage, and risked eroding the special character of a particular group of coins. Yet in the context of southern England in the age of Bede, where variety was the norm, that bond may have been resilient. Images that necessitated engagement were found on every early penny, above all in the "secondary" phase. There was no break between "real" money and "symbolic" money: all money in the early Middle Ages was real *because* it was symbolic, and especially so in England at this time.[62]

It follows from this that the coinage was deeply saturated with religious knowledge and devotion. Those who produced issues of this kind, and probably many of those who used them, needed the wherewithal to understand them. Church institutions, in England meaning the minsters

59. These coins are often referred to in older literature as *sceattas*, a designation drawn from the laws of Æthelberht that goes back to scholars of the early nineteenth century who mistakenly dated early pennies to the time of Æthelberht and before. Sources from the seventh and eighth centuries suggest the new silver pieces were known from the first as pennies. See Naismith 2017b, 67–68, 361.

60. Gannon 2005, esp. 97.

61. Gannon 2013, 39.

62. Theuws 2018, 77, posits a helpful threefold iconographic division: overtly Christian coins (e.g., with a prominent cross), Christian imagery that requires explanation and could be read in other ways, and imagery that has no apparent Christian referent at all (such as the "porcupine" found on some Frisian coins).

FIGURE 8.3. A selection of early pennies (Series Hc, Qa, and Kc) (diameters 13 mm, 13 mm, and 12 mm). All Classical Numismatic Group, LLC.

that proliferated at exactly the same time as the early pennies, may well have been directly responsible for a significant portion of the coins.[63] But minster sites do not always come across as hubs of production and exchange, and in practice religious institutions would often have been more of a mediator, exercising influence through the minsters' deeply

63. Gannon 2003, 188–91.

embedded relationship with lay society.[64] Indeed, assuming for the sake of argument that many of the early pennies were tied in some way to the political landscape of the day, this too was highly layered. English kingdoms of the late seventh and early eighth centuries remained fluid, especially in the midlands and Southeast where the bulk of the small penny issues are thought to have been made. Mercia rose to be the dominant force under the sons and grandsons of Penda (d. 655), and then under Æthelbald (716–757), and ruled an enlarged sphere that extended to London, Surrey, and the Thames valley; but Kent, Wessex, and East Anglia continued to be important. All these contained many more subkingdoms or other distinct units led by what were now, in effect, subkings or aristocrats. Politics was a matter of personal bonds between the elites of these units, exercised through meetings big and small, and movement through the landscape; royal resources came from a combination of agricultural surpluses and, increasingly, legal revenues and tolls creamed off trade.[65]

Coinage could have fitted into this framework in several ways. Some early penny issues could be associated with the person and resources of a king as largesse for followers or tenants; others might have been made by kingdoms or segments of them coming together in an assembly. It is striking that the area of greatest monetary diversity in the "secondary" period was also one of complicated and fragmented political power, in a broad crescent running from the Wash through London and into Kent.[66] But Frans Theuws has rightly observed that traditional analysis of these coins is vitiated by a determination to set them within a rigid political and institutional framework.[67] Further possibilities for issuers of coin in this and other areas include kin groups, gilds, those who venerated a particular saint or built a church, the dependants of a king or aristocrat, an army, or much else besides. Scale matters here. Major coin issues reflect protracted operations and large mobilisations of wealth, perhaps with an element of coercion and control; smaller ones, in contrast, may not have been made for a long time, or even—if taken type by type—in large quantity. Dies would have been used to make however many coins were needed, which could very probably have been far fewer than they were theoretically capable of making.

64. Theuws 2018, 71–76; Naismith 2014.
65. Dumville 2017, 86–102; Lambert 2017b, 114–36; Yorke 2000; 2003; 2009; Moreland 2000; Wickham 2005, 313–26; Faith 2019, 19–27, 50–76.
66. Naismith 2017b, 70–71.
67. Theuws 2018, 37–51.

What can be inferred from the number and diversity of the early pennies is that, for two or three generations, a large chunk of eastern England had a distinct monetary culture; one in which the making and distribution of coin was a common, well-developed mode of expressing identity. A multiplicity of coin issues coexisted, to the extent that it is difficult to argue for any regnal-level control over circulation. Hoards of early pennies tend to contain a mix of issues, English and Frisian.[68] Single finds from the same region tend to be mixed; this is important because it shows the coins did have a life in secondary circulation and percolated outward from the point of issue. Local types are more dominant in East Anglia but still circulated alongside specimens of the "Frisian" types.[69] Only Northumbria saw the new and overtly regal coinage of Eadberht (737–58) and his brother Archbishop Ecgberht (732–66) (figure 8.4) generally replace the existing stock.[70]

Why, then, were coins made at all? This is an especially puzzling question if, as is likely, most early pennies were made by melting down other early pennies.[71] England probably did not have a substantive source of fresh silver of its own, and the bullion needed for the early pennies most plausibly came from recycling earlier issues, perhaps alloyed with local supplies of lead, tin, and bronze.[72] Yet as already noted, hoards and single finds do not indicate that there was a general requirement for incoming coin to be reminted. Early pennies might therefore be viewed as the result of specific patrons' wish to have fresh and distinctive coin of their own, for purposes that they thought needed or warranted that effort. Spending in a commercial setting is one possibility: familiar coins were a known quantity, and buying and selling invoked trust and prestige. Other contexts should also be considered, however: major purchases by the elite, royal and aristocratic largesse to retinues and dependants, almsgiving to or through the church, funds for construction work, fines or compensation, and more. All these could in principle be settled with preexisting coins and doubtless often were, but any situation that invoked the person, identity, and trustworthiness of the maker is a plausible context for the manufacture of coin.

68. As well as Woodham Walter, see Kent 1972 (an early mixed hoard from Oxfordshire) and Marsden 2013 (two mixed hoards and one of Series E "porcupine" pennies).

69. Woods forthcoming.

70. Naismith 2012a, 301–7.

71. See the comments of Peter Northover in Metcalf 1993–94, 3:649–58. He suggests heavy recycling of silver, often admixed with diverse other metals, some of which could have been sourced locally.

72. Peter Northover in Metcalf 1993–94, 3:649–58.

FIGURE 8.4. Early pennies of Eadberht of Northumbria (737–58), alone and with his brother Archbishop Ecgberht (732–66) (diameters 13 mm and 13 mm). Both Classical Numismatic Group, LLC.

We might be seeing a sort of monetary arms race, in which making coin took on a particular cachet, and the main concern was with "primary" circulation—the immediate expenditure of the patron, driven by social and symbolic pressures. There was probably no real constraint on what coins were used for secondary purposes, save that the appropriate issue had to be used for dealing directly with a specific patron, institution, or group. Tolls that Æthelbald charged in London might have required a particular type of coin, as would any fines paid to the king's agents, while commuting payment of church-scot from kind into coin might plausibly have required using that church's own pennies.[73] For a major figure such as a king, control of this kind could have been a powerful incentive for people to make and obtain the appropriate coin. Multiple networks could have been superimposed on one another: both kings and subkings might have had their own coinages, as would bishops and minsters. Coins from all these

73. Kelly 1992; Blair 2005, 156–60; Tinti 2005.

could mingle in secondary circulation, specific ones being needed only to settle obligations involving the authority in question.

These practices are probably not far removed from the pattern seen with earlier gold *scillingas*.[74] The main difference was one of magnitude: there was just vastly more silver coinage, which multiplied the potential for socially broader use, and for secondary circulation in particular. Use beyond the context of manufacture and its immediate aftermath would have surely been the norm for the mass of the population, as coins of varied origins flowed into a wider market, in some cases as the preferred type of coin for a particular purpose. This implies a rich and commercialised background for the coinage, with minsters as major (and certainly the most visible) stimuli, as well as deep penetration into rural society, which in turn suggests broadened social engagement with coin. Elite patrons should probably still be seen as the leading forces behind production and primary circulation, but smaller issues could plausibly have been patronized by groups of minor landholders or farmers, or of merchants, while the expanded silver economy meant that moneyers working primarily on behalf of a king, aristocrat, or minster could in principle also have produced coin of the same or a related type for smaller patrons who chose to piggyback on the support provided by the larger figure.[75] Finds of early pennies also hint at a changing exchange dynamic around emergent trading towns. Single finds of early pennies in fact diminished in the hinterland of the English emporia as the coins reached their eighth-century peak, suggesting that the kinds of exchange formerly supporting rural coin use in the area were being funnelled into the newly engorged trading centres.[76]

It is likely that at least some coins were made in the emporia,[77] though not perhaps in a very coherent way. The emporia were intersections of multiple interests, with relatively limited evidence of a distinct community identity of their own.[78] Minting and coin use in emporia might have been framed in large part around the needs of more distant lands and agrarian communities in dialogue with the town. How production was structured within the emporia remains unclear and possibly varied case to case.

---

74. See chapter 7.

75. Cf. Wickham 2021, 18, 23–24.

76. Naylor 2012.

77. There is in fact tentative evidence that a building of early eighth-century London was a workshop involved somehow with minting: Malcolm, Bowsher, and Cowie 2003, 148–49.

78. Naismith 2018a, 88–95.

London and the Kentish emporia were probably responsible for several contemporary, overlapping coin issues, whereas Ipswich and Southampton seem to have been dominated by a single major type. Within emporia there is some evidence that stages in precious metalworking took place on different sites and in the hands of different people.[79] Larger productive capacity might, then, have led to minting being broken up into a few larger *chaînes opératoires*, not always sliced vertically into small workshops that did the whole job. Again, this suggests a high level of specialisation and economic complexity.

It should not be assumed, however, that all or even most minting took place at emporia. A coinage based on human networks and geography could accommodate production anywhere that was convenient, so minsters should be considered, as well as places where local or regnal assemblies convened; indeed, the place itself probably mattered rather less than the people involved. A conjunction of patron, demand, and material skills and resources, in a climate that recognised the usefulness of coins, was all that was needed for minting to take place. The putative independent, entrepreneurial moneyer seems less and less likely to be a major figure in the age of the early pennies.[80]

The Silver Rush c. 660–750 2: Frisia and Francia

England's rapid monetisation in the late seventh and early eighth centuries is quite distinct from the experiences of its main neighbours. Frisia shares the large spike in finds of coin but otherwise differs sharply. Where the silver came from is a mystery: metallurgical analysis suggests some degree of similarity with England and also with late Merovingian silver, though this did not all come from Melle.[81] Instead of England's mass of differentiated coin issues, Frisia had only a few major and long-lived groups, albeit with many subvarieties.[82] Its distribution of finds is also much more concentrated than that of England. Fewer coins come from isolated rural locations; instead they cluster thickly in certain hotspots. This can be read

79. Bayley 1996, 89.

80. Naismith 2012a, 300–301.

81. P. Northover in Metcalf 1993–94, 3:649–58; Sarah and Geneviève 2010; Clairand and Téreygeol 2009.

82. Metcalf and Op den Velde 2010 (Series E); Op den Velde and Metcalf 2007 (Series D). Series X is also found in relatively large numbers in Frisia, though its local dominance in finds from Ribe suggests that it should be seen as a Danish issue, or as the work of a network of Frisian traders with interests extending to Ribe (Naismith 2017b, 92–93; Williams 2007, 185–86; Metcalf 2006b; Feveile 2020).

as a hint that silver coins reflected long-distance trade and the activities of a more circumscribed set of communities who handled that traffic.[83] Local exchange with other parts of the region, conversely, was less monetised, and perhaps less integrated in general.[84] The general impression one gets is of disconnection, of a monetary economy that was not as embedded in the full range of local networks, perhaps because production was tied to segments of society somewhat distanced from the social world around them: coastal populations of sailors and traders with loose ties to elites.[85] These groups had counterparts in coastal regions of eastern England, though the latter had less dominance over minting and coin use.

Francia is more difficult to assess because finds are fewer, and the late Merovingian silver coinage in general less well understood. Many denarii perpetuated the pattern seen in gold of naming mint-place and moneyer, indicating continuity in the basic mechanisms of production (not that these are always clear and consistent for gold pieces of the seventh century).[86] Like in England, there were important shifts in detail, for instance in the distribution of finds from specific mint-places, which frequently circulated more locally than in earlier times.[87] Obols began to be struck: these indicate some degree of demand for lower-value denominations, though they are noticeably scarcer than denarii.[88] There was also more coinage issued in the names of churches: this may reflect the changing fiscal and jurisdictional landscape of the kingdom, in which more and more churches enjoyed immunity from taxes and fines that perhaps inclined them to spend generously.[89] Superficially, the most striking break from the English and Frisian picture is the scarcity of finds of denarii from France. The assemblage of single finds published in 2003 by Jean Lafaurie and Jacqueline Pilet-Lemière includes only about 270 denarii, compared to over 900 gold tremisses from the century beforehand.[90] But this total may mislead. It depends on reported finds, especially from antiquarian contexts, which privileged inscribed coins that were more readily identifiable. The small, often less glamorous-looking and uninscribed silver pieces typically received short shrift, if they were recognised

83. Theuws 2018, 58–64.

84. That said, the later eighth century was when weapon burial first appeared in Frisia: Knol 2019, 383.

85. Loveluck and Tys 2006, esp. 143–48; Loveluck 2013, esp. 191–97.

86. Naismith 2014a, 299.

87. Naismith 2014a, 299–300.

88. Dhénin and Schiesser 2007.

89. Naismith 2012a, 318–21; Lafaurie 1998. See also chapter 7.

90. Lafaurie and Pilet-Lemière 2003.

as Merovingian at all. A determined search through private collections and informally reported recent finds has led Philippe Schiesser to identify 219 Merovingian-period denarii, and 20 obols, from the Touraine alone.[91] Similar treatment for other mint-places or regions might redress the surprising gold:silver balance of recorded French finds and pave the way toward a surer picture of the use and manufacture of silver in the later Merovingian kingdom. As things stand, all one can say is that silver pieces are even less likely than gold to have been driven by tax requirements, and that a series of jurisdictional, seigneurial, social, political, and military pressures are the most likely explanations for minting, not so dissimilar from the picture in contemporary England.

Money and Power in the Carolingian Age

Carolingian coins are the symbols par excellence of kingship. They prominently carry the name and title of the king or emperor, or occasionally (yet more impressively) his image. In organisational terms, too, the coins powerfully encapsulate the ambitions of royal government, being standardised in appearance and physical features for much of the period between the accession of Pippin III in 751 and the tenth century, with a high point under Charlemagne (768–814) and his son Louis the Pious (814–40).

This fairly monolithic image is the starting point, but the centralising, standardising achievements of the Carolingian monetary system will form only one element in what follows. The emphasis here is on how and why the coinage worked in the way it did. Two major facets of this will be addressed in turn: circulation and production. In both cases, the coinage raises important questions about the dynamics of economic and social power in the Carolingian world and illustrates how rulers interacted with local elites who patronised and oversaw minting.

AGENCY IN CAROLINGIAN COIN CIRCULATION

When King Louis the German (d. 876) received emissaries from the vikings, he greeted them, so Notker the Stammerer says, with a display of manly, red-blooded bravado, which began with the handover of gold and silver as a signal of loyalty. But Louis was made of sterner stuff. He ordered "that the money . . . be thrown on the ground, to be sneered at by everyone and to be trodden underfoot as if it were dirt." Louis then

---

91. Schiesser 2017.

proceeded to demand the emissaries' swords, which one by one he took and bent double by hand.[92] The point was to show Louis as a strong and supremely disciplined warlord, who valued good iron above mere coin. Notker's pen-portrait of the king is of course a caricature, in a tradition of exaggerated martial prowess stretching from the Spartans to Chuck Norris. It nonetheless attempted to teach a lesson to Charles the Fat (881–88), the patron of the text: in some settings, gestures of contempt for worldly wealth made a powerful impression.[93] A proper king should maintain a degree of distance from coin and not value it too much.

This advice, however, would often have fallen on deaf ears. The Carolingian elites moved in a world that sparkled with silver. An abbot in 841 handed over 1,500s in silver for a land purchase, or 18,000 silver coins.[94] The ability to stockpile on a large scale was one reason why production and the primary uses of coin would largely have remained the purview of the Carolingian elite. That influence can perhaps be seen in the circulation of coin during the apogee of the Carolingian period. In the era from Pippin's accession in 751 (and especially that of Charlemagne in 768) to the death of Louis the Pious in 840, there was a striking degree of long-distance movement of coin. Most single finds occur more than 100 km from their point of origin; indeed, the majority of finds of Charlemagne's monogram type (minted after 793) have turned up at least 400 km from their place of production.[95] In the course of their long peregrinations, the coins became thoroughly mixed. Two small, roughly contemporary hoards from opposite sides of the empire effectively illustrate the blending effect of coin circulation. One from Château Roussillon in the South of France contained denarii from Bourges, Narbonne, Melle, Pavia, Toulouse, and Tours; another from Ibersheim in Germany included ones from Agen, Arles, Lyon, Melle, Milan, Paris, Pavia, and Toulouse.[96] One stream of circulation apparent in both hoards brought money from Italy to the North; so much so that the vast majority of finds of coins minted at Milan, Pavia, and Venice have occurred north of the Alps, while numerous hoards and the vast corpus of single finds from Dorestad contain a

---

92. "Ut pecunia quidem in pavimentum proiceretur et a nullo nisi indignanter aspiceretur, sed potius ab omnibus velut lutum conculcaretur." Notker, *Gesta Karoli* 2.17–18 (Haefele 1959, 88–89).

93. On the nature of the text as a product of Charles's reign, see MacLean 2003, 199–229.

94. Deloche 1859, no. 20. For this and other examples of large expenditures, see Coupland 2014c, 285. For peasant coin use, see chapter 4.

95. Coupland 2018a, 440; 2018b, 218–19.

96. Coupland 2011, nos. 20–21. For discussion, see Coupland 2018b, 218–19.

large Italian element.[97] Other axes brought coins along the Channel littoral, eastward from the Loire valley and north from the Rhône.[98] A striking exception to this general rule is that, with regard to Italy, coins tended to go out rather than flow in; that is to say, denarii from Dorestad and the northern parts of Francia occur rarely among finds from Italy.[99] The prevailing winds of monetary circulation blew northward.

Circulation of coin in the period after 840 shows a rather more circumscribed picture. Hoards within Francia, Aquitaine, and the Middle Kingdom reveal increasingly localised circulation.[100] It is possible that this impression is an illusion created by a new requirement to use coins of the appropriate local king, precipitated by the breakup of the empire into several distinct kingdoms after the death of Louis the Pious. The abbot Lupus of Ferrières (d. 862) around 849 wrote to an acquaintance in Italy asking them to help supply local coin, for he had heard that his west Frankish money was no longer usable in the peninsula. Although Lupus's specific worry may have been ill founded—this is the only reference to a hard barrier in circulation so early and may refer to Rome rather than the kingdom of Italy as a whole—his anxious, indignant tone underscores the visceral reaction that closing off monetary circulation could provoke.[101] If visitors bearing coins intended for local expenditure had to exchange them for legitimate currency, circulation would inevitably appear restricted. Yet the situation of the 840s and after goes further than this: even within the new kingdoms, circulation had become more limited. Exchange of coin between regions undoubtedly still happened but was a matter either of shorter hops from one currency zone to another, or of parcels that were whisked swiftly and directly between widely separated locales, leaving little footprint in between.[102] Large-scale, open fluidity of coin circulation was strongly associated with the period down to 840.[103]

97. Coupland 2010, 24–26; McCormick 2001, 682–86.

98. Bruand 2002, 174–75.

99. Metcalf 1988b, 454–56. Ermanno Arslan's *Reportorio* (updated 30 August 2016), with updates from Simon Coupland (personal communication September 2021), records twenty attributable single finds of coins of Charlemagne from Italy, fifteen of them from Italian mints and five from elsewhere. For Louis the Pious the situation is similar: among attributable coins, sixteen single finds represent coins of Italian mints, and two coins from elsewhere.

100. Metcalf 1990, esp. 78–79, 90; Bruand 2002, 176–77; Coupland 2011, 31–40; 2015, 79–82.

101. Lupus of Ferrières, *Letter* 75 (Levillain 1927–35, 2:18).

102. See chapter 4.

103. Devroey 2015, 201.

The peak in both the scale and the extent of Carolingian coin circulation coincides closely with the peak of political integration in the empire. What the coin finds suggest is that at this point long-distance, interregional exchange played a driving role. That could mean several things. Trade is the obvious and most frequently cited possibility, with the important caveat that interregional trade would normally have focused on luxuries. Long-distance bulk exchange was a rare phenomenon in the ninth century. It did exist: grain, salt, wine, quernstones, and fabrics (among others) sometimes circulated on this basis.[104] The latter reflect widespread diffusion of goods in northern Francia, though none match the empire-wide, trans-Alpine circulation pattern of the coinage.[105] The coinage, in other words, was special. It is possible that the coins and some other luxury goods travelled in such quantities that both passed into the category of "semi-luxuries": goods that approximated luxury items but were available in somewhat larger quantity, such that their consumption became more socially diversified, even routinised.[106] But the crucial point is what kinds of circulation and demand pushed coins across vast distances.

Trade and other forms of exchange did not just happen. Someone, rather than something, should be held responsible. On one level, the answer is quite simply people who moved, be it in a few big steps or many small ones. On another level, the answer is much less straightforward. It is possible that a sequence of locally focused social and commercial networks could take coins from one region to another on their own, though when it happened on a large scale, as it did in the Carolingian Empire, some kind of pull factor was probably at work as well. That pull factor is all but certain when the coins represent a few long-distance movements, especially across arduous and dangerous routes like the Alpine passes. Given the correlation of intense interregional coin circulation with a period of political integration, it is necessary to look closely at those figures and networks most connected with the far-flung geography of the interconnected empire: major churches, and members of the higher aristocracy, above all the so-called *Reichsaristokratie*, who had interests across the empire and benefited from close alliance with the king.[107] These constituencies could all command movement from tenants

104. Verhulst 2002, 97–103. It is not always clear whether these goods circulated over long distances on a large scale, and apart from pottery distribution bulk distribution leaves little archaeological footprint.

105. Wickham 2008, 24–25. On ceramics, see Piton 1993; Thuillier and Louis 2015.

106. An idea developed for a later period in, e.g., Postan 1972, 135, and 204.

107. The formative study is Tellenbach 1939, esp. 42–55; see also Fried 2015, 68–69; Airlie 1995, 433–36.

and the obligations they owed, potentially at properties scattered across the empire, and also represented wealthy and reliable patrons who could support costly long-distance exchange.

The king himself was a powerful force too. He could command large revenues in cash and kind from royal lands as well as from tolls and perquisites of justice. Theoretically at least, this should have meant that large quantities of money and other material destined for the king or the army criss-crossed the empire.[108] What actually happened to those revenues is less clear, especially as they were often raised far away from the main royal stomping grounds in the northern part of Francia, though in the time of Charlemagne and Louis the Pious especially, genuine efforts were made to get the king what he was owed from far and wide, even if it meant an arduous journey.[109] Major abbeys also built up vast patrimonies that stretched over hundreds of kilometres, and their dependants included merchants who traded under ecclesiastical protection, selling goods from their lands or acquiring useful, desirable things from afar, with the potential to act on their own account alongside abbey business.[110] Actual portage of goods from as far afield as Italy was envisaged at this time for the abbeys of Fulda, Saint-Denis, and Tours, which were all granted lands in northern Italy as a source of olive oil to use as lighting in their churches.[111] Aristocrats as well as abbeys had patrimonies that spread across the empire; they may well have had merchants working for them too, though information on most aspects of aristocratic domains is poor. A good example of what one such constellation might look like in practice comes from the will of Eberhard of Friuli (d. 867) and his wife Gisela, which distributes a combination of major, named properties and unspecific collections of estates to the couple's many children. The splitting and sharing of these lands, and of prestige objects, reflected a carefully orchestrated hierarchy among the children, all of which rested on the three kings avoiding any discord, "may it not happen" (the will said) "and we hope it will not."[112] For all that the

108. The key source here—albeit a highly programmatic one—is the *Capitulare de villis*: for discussion, see McKitterick 2008, 149–51; Devroey 2006, 66–67; Campbell 2010; Landau 2018.

109. On the complicated status of royal or public property, see the important collection of papers in Bougard and Loré 2019. For Charlemagne's itinerary, see McKitterick 2008, 171–97; 2011; Davis 2015, esp. 323; Kölzer 2016.

110. Devroey 1993, esp. 378–83; 2003b.

111. Fouracre 2021, 81–83. For another example of long-distance transport of money, see Balzaretti 2019, 513.

112. "Quod absit, et fieri non credo." de Coussemakers 1884, no. 1; trans. West 2018. For discussion, see Bougard 1996; La Rocca and Provero 2000.

division of the empire after 843 did not immediately curtail aristocratic property networks that spanned multiple kingdoms, it did divide interests and enhance vulnerability, leading eventually to more regionalised aristocratic interests.[113] In the context of the mid-ninth century, the key difficulty was that aristocrats could only hold *honores* (offices) in one kingdom, meaning that while families could still span huge distances, individuals had to tie their colours to one mast or another.[114] Reconfiguration of elites to operate in this new, more regional landscape had important consequences for the manufacture of coin as well as its circulation, as will be seen.

REGIONAL DISTINCTIONS IN COIN CIRCULATION

The apex of Carolingian coin circulation between 793 and 840 reflects two or three generations of exceptional political ambition. The empire's rulers played a galvanising role, on the basis of vast, far-flung domains and lucrative patronage. In so doing, they harnessed the monetary economy closely to long-distance exchange. Coins did filter out into wider use, spinning off from these far- and fast-flowing currents, meaning that the benefits of long-distance luxury or semiluxury goods would have been passed on to a relatively larger market. But this was a decidedly secondary current of circulation in the Carolingian Empire, even if economies of scale meant that in relative terms it sometimes still amounted to a substantial injection of cash into the local rural economy.

Variations in the distribution of coin finds can be read against this background of a currency dominated by high rollers. It is a plausible explanation for what one sees in the Netherlands, which has the best single-find data in mainland Europe. There, finds are concentrated along coasts and major rivers and cluster heavily at a few leading trading sites, such as Dorestad.[115] The conclusion that has been drawn is that, as in the era of the early pennies, silver coin was widely available, while still being primarily a facet of long-distance exchange, perhaps with a stronger commercial element in Frisia.[116] A contrast can be drawn with contemporary eastern England, which again has excellent single-find data and in this period was probably similar to the Frankish world in the form of its monetary economy. Coins often travelled far from home, though the fact that

---

113. A process neatly summarised in Fried 2015, 68–69.
114. Airlie 2020, 174–75.
115. Schuurung 2014.
116. See also Theuws 2018, 58–64, for the earlier period.

most were reminted soon after arrival in England conceals the probable links with wider networks that fed silver into the hands of English moneyers.[117] The main difference with English finds is that they are much more ubiquitous in rural contexts, as well as on what must have been arterial routes. It is true that finds are still comparatively rare in settlement excavations. The pattern raises questions about local microeconomies, still difficult to answer, and probably involving secondary distribution of coins through processes like manuring, as well as coins dropped in situ during actual transactions.[118] The central point remains, however, that coins in England were much more visibly embedded in rural communities.

Metal-detected finds from the main part of the Frankish kingdom (represented now by France, Belgium, and parts of Germany and Switzerland) are patchy and recorded under difficult circumstances, meaning that "hot spots" of intense circulation tend to stand out.[119] Finds from French settlement sites are also few, meaning that if their inhabitants did have regular access to coin, they did not use or lose it much at home. But in a few regions with better analysed local finds (Poitou and Upper Normandy), a spread of isolated rural finds is apparent.[120] Concentrations of finds are mostly without archaeological context and could be market, production, or assembly sites, as well as elite residences.[121] Polyptychs, the major written source for rural monetization in the Carolingian era, can be read in different ways, as a source for rich use of coin in a seigneurial context if the emphasis falls on the overall total, or for the paucity of coin in peasant hands if the emphasis falls on coin rent per capita.[122] Taken as a whole, they remain a good spotlight onto one portion of the monetary economy, governed directly by the elite, but involving peasants as well. When set alongside the coin finds from Francia, a pattern closer to that of England can be inferred, with significant local, rural coin circulation as well as long-distance exchange. The more limited evidence

117. Naismith 2012b, 199–251; Metcalf 1998.

118. For the social implications of later medieval manuring, noting that pottery sherds and other finds are denser on land spread with lower-quality peasant manure, see Jones 2009.

119. Coupland 2010.

120. Cardon 2021, 128–35; Moesgaard 1995; Jeanne-Rose 1996.

121. Devroey 2015, 213–14. The importance of rural fairs was highlighted in Despy 1968. But it should be noted that "productive sites" in England without archaeological context are now treated with more caution and not so readily identified with trading sites: see earlier discussion.

122. Coupland 2014c, 289, drawing a contrast between Bruand 2002, 163–64; and Devroey 2003a, 166–67; 2019a, 239–340.

from other parts of the Frankish world points to something more like the Dutch model. Bavaria, for instance, has a relatively small number of finds that cluster around the Danube and its tributaries,[123] known from the Raffelstetten tolls to have been a highway of trade by the later ninth and early tenth centuries.[124]

Bavaria is well represented in comparison with the rest of the eastern Frankish lands beyond the Rhine, where coins are vanishingly rare even though the denarius was now being used as a measure of value;[125] coin finds of the Carolingian era are also extremely few in the Spanish marches and Brittany.[126] But the greatest puzzle is posed by northern and central Italy. As has been noted already, Italian coins from Milan, Pavia, and Venice were a major element in the vast stock of denarii circulating north of the Alps between Charlemagne's coin reform of 793 and the death of Louis the Pious in 840.[127] Among *Christiana religio* coins (minted 822/23–840) from the hoards found at Chaumoux-Marcilly (near Bourges) and Freising in Bavaria, denarii minted in Italy accounted for about a third and 80 per cent, respectively; and among thirty-six single finds of this same type from a productive site in the north of the Isère département, fourteen came from Venice alone.[128] Yet not only did northern coins flow back into Italy rather more rarely, to judge from local coin finds, but hardly any coins at all seem to have been circulating within the peninsula. Urban, rural, ecclesiastical, and secular sites across Italy are virtually bereft of Carolingian coins.[129] Even in the heart of Milan, where excavations in the course of works to build the city's underground railway uncovered a rich and archaeologically important site that was active at this time, no coins of the Carolingian period came to light.[130]

The paucity of Italian finds is exacerbated by several modern factors. Private use of metal detectors is not permitted, and any coins that are uncovered illegally will not be published. Finds are therefore restricted to those from archaeological excavations, antiquarian records, and a few chance discoveries. If the find records of England or the Netherlands were restricted in this way, they too would be dramatically smaller, though

123. Emmerig 2004, 42–43; see also Coupland and Emmerig 2019.
124. Boretius and Krause 1897, 249–52; Ganshof 1966.
125. Devroey 2015, 204. Cf. Kuchenbuch 2019, esp. 54–57.
126. Rovelli 2012, chap. 6, 26–27.
127. Coupland 1990, 32; 2010, 25–26; 2018a, 448. For a more reserved view, see Rovelli 2012 (Addenda and Corrigenda), 4–5.
128. Coupland 2010, 26.
129. Rovelli 2012, chap. 6, 13–23.
130. Arslan 1991.

probably still not so small as those of Italy.[131] There is no need to suspect that coins of this period have been missed in Italian excavations, when small and poorly preserved coins of other periods are now regularly caught by sieving soil.[132] Italy's dearth of Carolingian coin finds does seem to mark a genuine difference, indicative in some way of conditions in the late eighth and ninth centuries. What that difference was is more debatable. In Italy, the new denomination appeared more as a mark of Frankish dominance, and no obols (half-denarii) were minted in the peninsula at this time.[133] The value and utility of the silver coins were incidental. What mattered was that they brought Charlemagne's Italian dominions into line with his others. Yet it is equally clear that there were coins to be had in Italy, lots of them in the right circles, and they typically found their way out of the peninsula and into circulation in the rest of the empire. Documents also show that coins were available in high-value contexts, such as a loan of 12 solidi (i.e., 144 denarii) in Lucca in 813 that was said to consist specifically of Italian coin issues.[134]

A more productive approach is to recognise that, as in the contemporary Netherlands, the mainstream flow of coinage in Italy moved in a distinct and circumscribed path that did not involve a large element of rural and peasant use. This path started with the inflow of distinct sources of silver from the North and possibly, though not certainly, brought in as dirhams from the Caliphate via the Adriatic and Venice;[135] the two streams met in the hinterlands of cities of the North like Milan and Pavia. In these cities, the coins would be reminted and mixed with other sources of silver;[136] here too, and in other towns, were important elites (some transplanted from Francia in the entourage of successive kings),[137] and merchants who travelled between the key cities. Use of coin was probably most common in this region, which may—despite the small number of finds—have

131. Chick 2010, 185–86, shows that about half the corpus of pennies of Offa known in 2010 (365 of 728 coins) had come to light before the advent of popular metal detecting in the 1970s. These probably do not include a large element from hoards.

132. Rovelli 2015–16, 64.

133. Rovelli 2012, chap. 6, 12–13, and chap. 16, 4.

134. Barsocchini 1833, no. 389 (ChLA LXXIV, no. 4). That said, it is possible that many apparent references to money could have allowed the option of payment in kind to that value: Goodson 2021, 140–41.

135. Sarah et al. 2008, 381–91.

136. Sarah 2008 1:413, noting that the Carolingian issues of Italian mints other than Venice tend to be more similar to those from the rest of the empire.

137. The degree of aristocratic migration into Italy from the North remains a matter of debate: the core material is assessed in Hlawitschka 1960, 23–94, 310–21; with varied views in Castagnetti 1995; Gasparri 2002, 72–75; Delogu 1995, 305–8.

been comparable to the southern part of Francia,[138] but there were also side pools of more restricted, localised circulation, with significantly less coin available in general: Tuscany is a perhaps surprising one, for the richness of the Lucchese archives does not change the fact that this area was marginal to long-distance exchange, with virtually no coins from Lucca circulating beyond the Italian peninsula.[139] Lazio and Rome were similar. This regional fragmentation is characteristic of ceramics and other patterns of commodity distribution in early medieval Italy.[140] The northern plains stand out as a conveyor belt that whisked fresh coins rapidly from one elite purse to another, before long leading them to representatives of transalpine interests, in whose hands they would be taken northward. Circulating coins presumably stayed mostly in cities and changed hands rarely and in bulk, which would be one reason why finds are so scarce, even in urban settings: the coins simply were not percolating out into subsidiary networks of circulation on a significant level. Some coins did escape this loop and got into the hands of peasants, to be recorded in Italian polyptychs of the ninth century. The average amount owed is low compared to equivalent documents from Francia (though, as in the North, individual tenants could owe more substantial amounts).[141] It may have been lower still in the generation or two immediately after 781, when the local economy was still calibrated to gold coins. Moreover, tenants (for instance of the bishop of Lucca) were expected to render justice in the city,[142] and they may well have had to pay their rent in the city too, or to an agent who would transplant it there. Centripetal forces thus pulled whatever coins they had quickly back into the major towns of Italy, leaving little visible footprint in the countryside.

That the Carolingian world (for these purposes including England) saw wide variation in the intensity of coin use is well known. But there were several kinds of intense coin use. The core of Francia and eastern England from Kent to Yorkshire represent monetary economies that were deeply

138. Coupland 2022.

139. One monogram coin of Charlemagne (793–813) is known from Wijk bij Duurstede, and one coin of Louis the Pious from the Belvézet hoard in the South of France (personal communication with Simon Coupland, June 2021).

140. Wickham 2005, 33–37, 728–41; Rovelli 2009, 61–68.

141. Devroey 2003a, 167. To this table might be added data from a polyptych in Lucca from the late ninth century (Castagnetti 1979, 205–24), in which the average money rent per head was 9.66d—rather more than other Italian cases, though still lower than most Frankish examples.

142. Wickham 1988, 68–69. For aristocrats and cities see (inter alia) Castagnetti 2009, esp. 616–19; and, for a good recent overview, Goodson 2021, esp. 190–221, with the papers in La Rocca and Majocchi 2015. For polyptychs, see Castagnetti 1979.

plumbed into rural society, with coins being used and lost frequently in the countryside. The Netherlands and Italy, meanwhile, both had lots of coins but stand quite apart in the profile of their finds, indicating that denarii were more the stuff of long-distance exchange rather than intra-regional structures. There was no one model for how coinage, wealth, and exchange mapped onto one another: everything depended on the idiosyncrasies of individual areas.

MINTING AND ROYAL AUTHORITY

The influence of power structures on the Carolingian coinage was also apparent in the organisation of minting. At the most basic level, Carolingian denarii were an emphatically and overtly royal currency.[143] Each coin carried the name and title of the king (the two being effectively synonymous).[144] These were virtually universal and had been since the 750s: already under Pippin III, there was a wide degree of homogeneity in referring on coins to some abbreviation of *Pippinus rex Francorum*.[145]

Beyond this, the vigour of royal input waxed and waned. A low point came in the decades after the civil wars of the early 840s, when the quantity, quality, and homogeneity of the coinage declined across the former empire. In the West, there was a triumphant rebound in 864 when Charles the Bald undertook a bold reform of his coinage.[146] But as with the volume of coins and the distance of circulation, the period from 793 to 840 stands out as exceptional in terms of royal initiative. It witnessed several peaks, all in their own way experimental. Louis the Pious (814–40) went furthest in standardising the currency in 822/23 when he instituted the *Christiana religio* coinage, which dispensed with any reference to the mint-place; instead, the coins carried the name and title of the emperor, plus an invocation of the Christian identity that loomed large in Louis's vision of responsible rulership; it formed a uniquely palpable articulation of "a new wave of imperial confidence."[147] Louis's father Charlemagne (768–814) also instituted a rigorous standardisation of typology, weight, and fineness in 793.[148] The

143. To the extent that, although Pippin had been ensconced as Mayor of the Palace and de facto ruler for a decade, he did not move to change the coinage until after being crowned king: Breternitz 2020, 137–40.

144. Coupland 1985.

145. Garipzanov 2008, 121. For the likely influence of Lombard models on early Carolingian numismatic titulature, see Breternitz 2020, 148–51.

146. Grierson 1990.

147. De Jong 2009, 36–37.

148. Sarah et al. 2008, 381–82.

short-term stimulus probably came from rebellions and famine conditions, and while the new coinage may well have increased royal revenues,[149] it should also be viewed as a robust social and political project, a way for the king to intervene on the side of order and equity in the lives of his subjects. In many ways this reform, which set the tone for the final twenty-one years of the reign, was actually quite a departure from Charlemagne's general practice as ruler, which Jennifer Davis has encapsulated as centralisation that might or might not involve standardisation. As she notes, an expectation of standardisation across the empire was reserved only for "big-ticket" fundamentals like correct forms of prayer and monastic observance.[150] By implication, the coinage fell into this same category. Deviations from its closely regulated norm are special cases that prove the general rule, such as a fascinating little group that replaces the mint name with a longer version of the royal title and adds a Greek monogram, which was probably minted at the royal palace of Aachen.[151] The coinage of Charlemagne thus sat somewhat apart from other aspects of Carolingian governance, and to some extent from other projections of kingship, in that it normally used a distinct and streamlined set of signifiers—name, royal (rather than imperial) title, and monogram—rather than the full current title deployed in diplomas and many capitularies.[152]

For a brief period at the end of Charlemagne's reign this pattern was dramatically shaken up by the emperor's portrait coinage (figure 8.5). Its most notable feature, the portrait, drew on a range of Roman influences to construct something that was actually quite new and distinct,[153] and coupled it with diverse titulature that sometimes comes much closer to that of contemporary diplomas than was otherwise customary with the coinage.[154] Many coins carry a so-called temple that probably represents the Holy Sepulchre in Jerusalem, by implication identifying Charlemagne's rule with one of the key sites in Christendom.[155] These "temple" coins name no mintplace and have been read as the work of a palace mint at Aachen, while only a small and seemingly arbitrary minority of the empire's mint-towns are named among the portrait coins.[156] Close study of the small corpus of

149. Garipzanov 2016, esp. 67–71; Naismith 2012b, 176–77.

150. Davis 2015, esp. 298–303.

151. Rovelli 2012, chap. 17 (pace Thompson 1966, which assigns these coins to Ravenna); see also Coupland 2018b, 227.

152. Wolfram 1973; Garipzanov 2008, esp. 136–39.

153. Davis 2014.

154. Garipzanov 2008, 136–39.

155. Biddle 2014; McCormick 2011, 187–91.

156. Kluge 2002, 374; Coupland 2018a, 428.

FIGURE 8.5. Portrait denarius of Charlemagne (768–814), minted at Quentovic (diameter 19 mm). Fitzwilliam Museum, Cambridge.

coins (fifty-five specimens were known at the time of writing)[157] shows that the dies for it were made at a central source. Those might then have been sent out to individual mints, though Simon Coupland has suggested that *all* the coins, including those with different mint names, were in fact made at a central location in Aachen and then distributed as denarii.[158] Either way, the pattern is a sharp departure from that of the larger coinages immediately before or after, leading to the compelling proposition that Charlemagne's portrait coinage was never meant as a recoinage or general-purpose currency, but rather as a special issue.[159] What made it so special is the emphasis on the person and status of the aged emperor.

A context that would square this dimension of the coinage with the peculiarities of its production can be found in the arrangements of Charlemagne's will, quoted in full by Einhard.[160] This was drawn up in 811, and some of its provisions were enacted over the following years. Two-thirds of Charlemagne's treasure in gold and silver was divided between the twenty-one metropolitan churches of the realm and then further subdivided between suffragan bishops, while the final third would be retained by the emperor until his death, and then subdivided, with a quarter of it also going to the metropolitans and another quarter directly to the poor.

157. Coupland 2014a; Simon Coupland, personal communication.

158. Coupland 2018a, 427–29.

159. Kluge 2002, 373–76; 2014; Coupland 2018a, 429. This interpretation represents a departure from earlier readings, which tended to view the coinage as short-lived but essentially a "regular" issue: Lafaurie 1978; Coupland 2005, 224; Grierson 1965, 524–27; see also Moesgaard 2017.

160. Einhard, *Vita Karoli magni*, c. 33 (Halphen 1938, 93–103; trans. Noble 2009, 47–50). For discussion, see Innes 1997; Scharer 2015; Nelson 2019, 468–71.

Some of Charlemagne's wishes for what should happen to the last third of his wealth were not followed to the letter,[161] but there is no reason to doubt that the first and largest part of his scheme was enacted during his last years. The portrait coinage may have been issued as part of that scheme. Four of the seven named mint-places on the portrait coins are archbishoprics (Arles, Lyon, Rouen, and Trier), and the five letters sometimes found beneath the bust on specimens with no mint name could likewise be associated with archbishoprics.[162] Other archbishoprics could have been supplied with the many coins that have no additional reference to a mint-place. The three named mint-places that were not archbishoprics (Dorestad, Melle, and Quentovic) were all important centres of trade and production and thus plausible venues for the distribution of alms to the poor, or else for taking coins to other locations for the same purpose.[163] There is of course no smoking gun, but a link with the provisions of Charlemagne's will has the virtue of explaining not only when and why such an unusual coinage was produced, but also why it took the form it did in silver and gold.[164] The portrait coins would have been part of a personal, and surely very grand, redistribution of royal wealth, for which parallels can be found elsewhere. Tenth-century English kings commissioned special coinages at their death,[165] and Alfred the Great may well have instituted a special coinage for eleemosynary purposes late in his reign.[166]

MINTING AND LOCAL ELITES

The Carolingian coinage depended on negotiation with those responsible for making coin at mint-places across the empire, which in the Frankish context meant counts. Capitularies from the time of Louis the Pious and Charles the Bald show unambiguously that by the ninth century minting was one of

161. Innes 1997, 848–50.

162. These letters include B (Bordeaux or Bourges), C (Cologne), F (*Forum Iulii/* Cividale), M (Mainz or Milan), and V (*Vesontio*/Besançon or Vienne).

163. Cf. the deliberate choice of Dorestad for the distribution of alms in Rimbert, *Vita Anskarii*, c. 20 (Waitz 1884, 45; trans. Robinson 1921, 71). It may be significant that Dorestad, Melle, and Quentovic lay far from their archdiocese, and in areas where the relevant archdiocese was not clearly named on coins: these centres may have taken on the minting role of the archdiocese in some sense.

164. Just one gold specimen is known: it names Arles but was found in excavations of the palace at Ingelheim and is of rather cruder workmanship than the equivalent silver coins (Martin 1997).

165. S 1515 (Miller 2001, no. 17).

166. Naismith 2017b, 172–73.

the responsibilities of the count.[167] There had been a move in this direction from virtually the beginning of the Carolingian kingdom, but moneyers never went away, and they are referred to occasionally in capitularies, but always in a more subordinate position,[168] and they did not put their names on coins anymore, regardless of how many might have worked in a given mint-place at any point. Recognition of the role of regional aristocrats in patronising and overseeing minting, in collaboration with a resurgent monarchy, can be seen as a natural step from the less visible and less formal yet still very real influence of the Frankish elite behind the earlier Merovingian currency.[169] Hints of it can be detected before 751 in the growing number of ecclesiastical mints, in the activity of mint-places in known power bases of key families and of course a few explicitly signed coinages of elites, most notably in the names of the patricians of Provence.[170]

Pippin and his heirs depended on buy-in from these local potentates, and in terms of coinage they got it in spades. At least a hundred mint-places or authorities issued coins during the period 751–93 (see map 8.2).[171] These reflect the complexities of local power networks. Most early Carolingian mints were cities that possessed walls, a bishop, and a Roman past, though with a significant number of exceptions, especially among smaller mint-places that must have operated briefly and on a limited scale; some of these relate to places of royal power,[172] to strategic (often defended) points on key roads or the coast,[173] to *pagus*-centres,[174] or to powerful individuals.[175] Even the references to place names might in practice have

167. *Capitulare de moneta* c. 1 (Boretius 1883, 299); Edict of Pîtres, c. 8–19 (Boretius and Krause 1897, 314–18).

168. E.g., the earliest reference to minting in a capitulary: *Pippini regis capitulare*, c. 5 (Boretius 1887, 32).

169. See chapter 7.

170. For the patricians and their coins, see Grierson and Blackburn 1986, 146–49. For the Pippinids/Carolingians, see Bruand 1997, 48–52.

171. There are ninety-seven identifiable mint-places in the earlier period, plus at least thirteen that could be either different renderings of the known mints or new ones, and about fourteen in the name of an individual, though with a higher degree of uncertainty. I am grateful to Simon Coupland for up-to-date figures on the number of mints.

172. Andelot, Paderborn (Gai 2001; Mecke 1999), Thionville (Haubrichs 2000), and Valenciennes (Deissen-Nagels 1962).

173. Bingen (Dotzauer 2001, 65), Bonn (James 1982, 66; Keller 2005; Ristow 2007, 152–53), Mouzon, Substantion (Mazel 2009, 361), and Walcheren.

174. Châteaudun, Razès, Roye, and probably Ramerupt.

175. Naismith 2012a, 314–18. A critical assessment that dismisses most of the possible personal names can be found in Breternitz 2020, 122–30. Breternitz is correct that the structures of early Carolingian minting are obscure and may not have been the same as

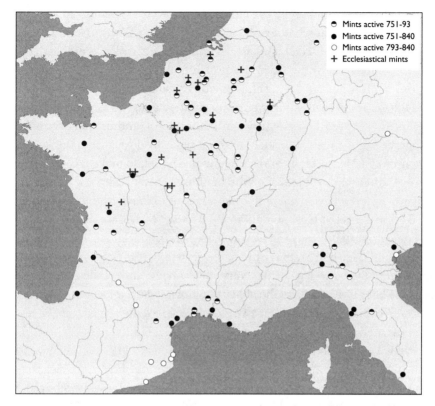

Mints active 751-93
Mints active 751-840
Mints active 793-840
+ Ecclesiastical mints

MAP 8.2. Mint-places active in the Carolingian Empire 751–840.

been shorthand for the individual in control of that location, so the possible references to secular magnates are not necessarily as idiosyncratic as they first appear.

But the most striking special component of the early Carolingian coinage is ecclesiastical. At least eighteen mint-places carry the name of a church (sometimes two in the same city). What these early ecclesiastical "mints" consisted of in practice is obscure. The first grants of minting privileges to churches in the ninth century suggest a moneyer or group of moneyers working under the direct tutelage of an abbot or bishop: they owed profits to them and existed in large part to create coins for the good of the church institution.[176] That may have been the situation in earlier decades, though no formal concessions of such rights have survived, nor

those of the ninth century, but even without most of the personal names, a focus of minting in power bases of regional elites is still likely in the context of the mid-eighth century.

176. See chapter 3.

were they ever claimed by the churches that were named on coins. It is therefore doubtful whether Merovingian or early Carolingian minting grants ever existed. The ecclesiastical mints might be seen as another corollary of the socially embedded nature of minting, in practice not so different from mints primarily serving and sometimes named for secular aristocrats. Monasteries and cathedrals were important poles in the firmament of the elite: they served as repositories of land, wealth, and memory for aristocrats, their leaders as bishop or abbot typically drawn from important families.[177] Moreover, as Frans Theuws has noted, to make gold or silver pieces under the auspices of a saint or church (potentially on the relevant saint's day at a fair or assembly) was a way of to imbue the coins with an additional level of trust and authority.[178] Most early Carolingian ecclesiastical mints name only the patron saint—Mary, Maxentius, Peter, Trond, etc.—and their holy status (with an abbreviation of *sanctus* or *sancta*), as if it were the patronage of the "very special dead" that really counted.[179] In the later ninth century the abbey of Saint-Médard in Soissons actually issued coins in the names of two saints: Médard and Sebastian, whose relics had been installed there in the 820s, and it is difficult to explain this practice without reference to production structured in some way around the feasts, events, and resources of particular saints' shrines.[180] This connection underscores that minting was a "public" business, which in the Carolingian world meant it was open and transparent, something that should perhaps even take place at an assembly or similar, in relation to things like law courts and property transactions.[181] Venues for "public" acts were defined not solely by the nature of the location as by the social networks that coalesced around and between them.[182]

The intersection of minting, comital office, public action, and kingship came under pressure in the central period of Carolingian coinage, from Charlemagne's reform of 793 to the death of Louis the Pious in 840. It was at this point that the scale and unity of the empire's coinage reached their zenith. Yet it was also at this time that the reins were pulled sharply on the minting network, with the number of mint-places falling by half to just over fifty in the early coinages of Louis the Pious.[183] The ecclesiastical

177. Semmler 1974.

178. Theuws 2004, 126–29.

179. P. Brown 1981, 69.

180. Hourlier and Dhénin 1998, 261–64, noting obverse die-links between the Médard and Sebastian coins.

181. Innes 2000, 255–59; de Jong 2018, 486.

182. Innes 2000, 95–105; 2001.

183. Fifty-one mints can be identified (including a "palace" mint), with six that probably

mints mostly disappeared, as did coins in the names of individuals. Almost all the surviving mint-places were cities or major centres of production and trade, such as Dorestad and Melle. This radical contraction probably relates to the reimagined nature of comital responsibility and interaction.with the king. Where Pippin III had relied on winning consensus from regional aristocracies who essentially carried on as they had before, Charlemagne's later reign and that of his son Louis the Pious saw stronger efforts to define the office and duties of counts, and in so doing to frame them as a distinct tier in the Carolingian political hierarchy: their status came to depend on local power harnessed directly to royal command, and no longer as part of a multitiered aristocratic pyramid.[184] What counts did and how they did it now fell under more of a spotlight, and minting became more firmly aligned with comital oversight.[185] A fragmentary capitulary dated to c. 820 stipulated that "the public mint of the city should be under the protection of the count" and that "the public moneyers themselves should not presume to make coins in any location within or outside the city beyond that which is established for them."[186] Minting was fixed in cities, which were already the largest single component of the system. Their prominence was not prompted by the economic importance of cities as such, considerable though this was,[187] or even by the physical presence of the count, because in practice the count often was not present: while counts were frequently associated with cities, or rather with the territories connected to them, they were usually not permanent residents, and in many cases one count would hold multiple counties (and hence multiple cities).[188] Minting took place in cities because of their pivotal, long-established role as points of intersection for surrounding elite networks.[189] By the time of Charles the Bald's Edict of Pîtres in 864, it was

---

or certainly represent unidentified locations. Again, I am grateful to Simon Coupland for details. Coupland (personal communication) also observes that the high degree of stylistic diversity among *Christiana religio* coins from the 820s and 830s could suggest a resurgence in the number of mint-places at that time.

184. Davis 2015, 90–99 (and, at n. 51, arguing for a strong, if not total, shift in this direction from about 790); Innes 2000, 188–89.

185. Cf. Lafaurie 1980.

186. "Ut civitatis illius moneta publice sub custodia comitis fiat. . . . Ut monetarii ipsi publice, nec loco alia nec infra nec extra illam civitatem nisi constituto . . . eis loco, monetam facere praesumant." *Capitulare de moneta* c. 1–2 (Boretius 1887, 299).

187. Verhulst 1999, 47–59; 2002, 91–93.

188. Mazel 2009, esp. 338–39. For the earlier situation, see Claude 1964, 11–32. In the region between Marne and Moselle, ninth-century counts did not have a fixed residence at all: West 2013, 143–44.

189. A good example is the region around Mainz (Innes 2001); such networks would

still assumed that minting would take place in cities under the tutelage of a count. Indeed, minting constituted one of the most explicit links between cities, elites, and, as the c. 820 capitulary stressed, public acts. An important change had taken place here: minting was sequestered and reified as its own sphere of public acts.

The restriction of minting to cities during the most politically ambitious decades of the Carolingian era is easily seen as the norm. In the long run, however, it stands out as an aberration. A penumbra of other, smaller operations that were negligible in their contribution to the currency but important for what they say about the structure of the monetary system returned in the late ninth century and never left. Charles the Bald's later years represent a crucial first step in that direction, with most of the relevant coins being of the *Gratia Dei rex* type instituted in summer 864. These are difficult to treat in isolation because they cannot be readily distinguished from denarii of the same appearance and fabric in the name of Charles the Fat (881–88) or even Charles the Simple (898–923). Across the period 864 to 923 as a whole, three developments stand out (see map 8.3). One is that there were significantly more places making coins—a total of 137 locations named on surviving specimens.[190] These varied vastly in duration and output: some are known from a single surviving coin, others from hundreds. Second is that among these mints, cities remained dominant, and indeed coins were minted at many more cities in this period than before, at a total of nearly sixty places. In Italy, Aquitaine, and Provence in particular, coin production remained overwhelmingly concentrated in the cities. Third, the diverse small mints were concentrated geographically in the North, between the Loire and the Rhine, and in Burgundy—in other words, in the heartland of the Carolingian domain. Here coins were made at royal estates (*fisci*) and palaces; at *castra/castella*, meaning fortified places, often of Roman vintage, rather than castles as such; at *vici*, which like *castra* were important rural agglomerations, often the social and administrative focal point for a *pagus*; at *portus*, meaning in this context riverine trading settlements; and at, or in the name of, a range of ecclesiastical institutions. Some of the latter represent the issues of bishops who had gained control over what had been a comital responsibility, probably or certainly through royal concession (e.g., at Barcelona, Basel, and

---

have been denser in parts of the Carolingian Empire with more cities, such as in the South, though the charter evidence is limited.

190. I am again grateful to Simon Coupland for lists of mints recorded for rulers of this period.

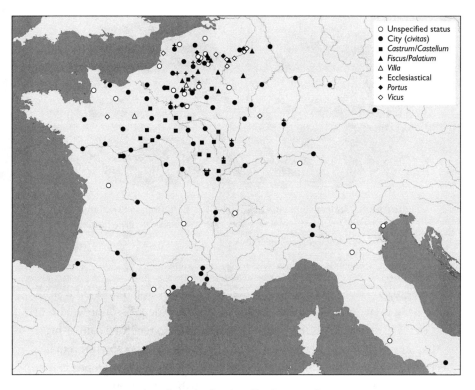

MAP 8.3. Mint-places in the Carolingian Empire 864–c. 923.

Strasbourg);[191] but most carry the name of a saint to whom an important monastery was dedicated, as was actually stipulated in a grant of minting rights to Rethondes in the 880s,[192] or refer to a place where a monastery was the dominant feature.[193] Even in this northern region with a more complicated monetary ecology, cities were generally much more productive and long-lived than the other mints. But there were exceptions. One of the most puzzling is the place referred to as CVRTISASONIEN or similar on coins (figure 8.6). Between the time of Charles the Bald and Raoul

191. For Barcelona, see Crusafont, Balaguer, and Grierson 2012, 72–74. On Basel and Strasbourg, see Schärli 1983.

192. Grat et al. 1978, no. 89, which specifies that coins from Rethondes's mint should be struck in the name of St. Peter (*sub nomine sancti Petri*). GDR coins survive in the name of both Rethondes and St. Peter, though there were several important churches dedicated to the latter, including Corbie.

193. It is not possible to separate with certainty ecclesiastical issues, in the sense of coins issued by and/or under the authority of a church, from those made under other arrangements in an adjoining settlement that was named after the eponymous saint—not that this was necessarily a very meaningful distinction, with the saint's oversight invoked by both.

FIGURE 8.6. Silver denarius of Charles the Bald (843–77) or later, minted after 864 at the mystery location CVRTISASONIEN (diameter 20 mm). Classical Numismatic Group, LLC.

(923–36), it issued denarii in significant numbers, apparently on a similar scale to major cities: in the Chalo-Saint-Mars (dép. Essonne) hoard of c. 879–84, CVRTISASONIEN accounted for 26 of 240 recorded coins—more than any mint except Reims.[194] Yet the identity of CVRTISASONIEN remains contentious: all that can be confirmed with reasonable confidence is that it was an estate centre (*curtis*) that lay somewhere between the Loire and the Seine.[195] It may have been Courcessin (dép. Orne), an estate centre of Saint-Germain (*curtis Saxone* in the polyptych of the early ninth century); if so, its frenetic minting activity could reflect large amounts of silver being channelled there by the monastery and its aristocratic friends.[196] In any case, CVRTISASONIEN shows that the currents of the monetary economy were flowing in new, unexpected directions, not always toward cities.

Superficially, the late ninth and early tenth centuries still saw king and count playing much the same roles in relation to minting as earlier in the century.[197] But behind the scenes, the situation was changing. Within a number of cities, bishops replaced counts as the effective local authority.[198] In this respect they anticipated the local territorialisation of the Frankish aristocracy that was just beginning in the late ninth

194. Coupland 2011, no. 166; Duplessy 1985, no. 79.

195. Dumas 1971, 106–7.

196. *Polyptych of Saint-German*, Breve 12.25 (Elmshäuser, Hedwig, and Hägermann 1993, 1:100). For the identification of CVRTISASONIEN with Courcessin, see Grierson and Blackburn 1986, 248; for Courgeon, see Depeyrot 2017, 313–15; other possible identifications made in the nineteenth century and before are listed in Gariel 1883–84, 2:223.

197. For bishops and minting, see Kaiser 1976.

198. Mazel 2009, 343–55.

century. Firmer control of the landscape by elites was an integral part of this process: castles—in the ninth century more like heavily defended houses—were perhaps the most significant legacy of crystallising "spatial ideology" among the very highest aristocracy,[199] and they can sometimes be set in context as an attempt to use force of arms to take advantage of economic resources, as when the count of Ostrevent set up the castle of Douai early in the tenth century to secure control of the *portus* of Lambres.[200] Local dominance by the aristocracy was of course nothing new (nor was its reflection in the issue of coinage), but in the late ninth and early tenth centuries the rules of the game were being rewritten. Generations of Carolingian rule had reified and solidified elite authority in many parts of the empire, meaning that local communities of aristocrats, abbots, and bishops with interests in the same region could essentially go it alone if they had to, putting established geographical and institutional frameworks under new management.[201] And in the late ninth century, going it alone looked like an increasingly attractive option. The politically fractured, polyfocal world of the late ninth century divided and diluted the attractiveness of court politics, and in any case the prizes that remained were being sucked up by regionally dominant aristocratic families or "super-magnates" who monopolised royal patronage.[202]

Changes in minting need to be seen against this crowded backdrop. New coins and mint-places reflect new patterns of local power. In contrast to the many small mints of early Carolingian times, those of this period can be seen as more unilaterally associated with elite authority over nodal points in the landscape. Bishops, abbots, and counts actively sought to create new mints in places under their jurisdiction. The bishop of Langres in 872 approached Charles the Bald and asked directly for his sanction to set up two new mints, one connected to his church in Langres itself, the other in Dijon.[203] Both are represented by actual coins, though only a few rare specimens from Langres explicitly recognise their episcopal origins.[204] By 887 these *monetae* could be numbered by the bishop among the *res* that pertained to Langres, along with lands, immunities,

199. Creighton 2012, 29, 45.

200. Louis 2012.

201. Innes 2000, 222–34; West 2013, esp. 17–105, 109–38.

202. MacLean 2003, 48–80; West 2013, 109–38; Lösslein 2019; Airlie 2020, 173–79, 287–310.

203. Tessier 1943–1955, no. 365.

204. Morrison and Grunthal 1967, nos. 1019–27, 1471. The episcopal coins (inscribed XPTS VINCIT on the obverse) have only recently come to light in the Neufchâteau hoard of 2008: Coupland 2014b, 331–32.

abbeys, and markets.[205] Other new mints can be tentatively related to the geography of aristocratic power blocs. Blois and Châteaudun, and the counties attached to them, represented strongholds of Robertian power in the late ninth century.[206] Le Talou in Normandy was a *pagus* where the abbey of Fontenelle owned extensive property.[207] The new mint of Château-Landon was where the up-and-coming family who would give rise to the Angevin dynasty in the tenth century acquired their first major *honor* under Charles the Bald,[208] while that of Château-Porcien was probably the central place and namesake of the *pagus Portuensis*, an important frontier county.[209]

From the king's perspective, the rush for new mints on the initiative of the elite must have been a new turn. Charlemagne, Louis the Pious, and even Charles the Bald had all sought to maintain a rather narrower range of mint-places. Charles's early coinage (before 864) had been made at only fourteen places, while the Edict of Pîtres in 864 tried to limit the number of mint-places to ten or eleven locations.[210] But about ten times that number would mint coins over the next five decades. This was not yet a "feudal" coinage (itself a problematic and archaic term), in that precious few issues actually departed from the royal types and inscriptions before about the middle third of the tenth century. The later coins of the Carolingian period remained very much a product of aristocrats working within a regal frame of reference, which allowed and encouraged robust assertions of local power, so long as it was wielded in the name of the king. All the same, the sudden upsurge owes as much to the monetary as to the elite social climate. Charles the Bald's early reign was marked not only by a small number of mint-places, but by variable and often low fineness of coins.[211] Inconsistency might have left both the elite and the wider population lukewarm toward coins. For the former this was perhaps one factor in cooling enthusiasm for production of coin; for the latter, it exacerbated

---

205. Hartmann, Schröder, and Schmitz 2012, 221–23.

206. Werner 2004, 89–97, 158–63, 262–68.

207. Deniaux 2002, 391.

208. *Chronicon de gestis consulum Andegavorum* (Halphen and Poupardin 1913, 28). For discussion, see Bachrach 1989, esp. 16–19; Werner 2004, 51.

209. Longnon 1869–1872, 2:63–86.

210. Edict of Pîtres, c. 12 (Boretius and Krause 1897, 315). The reason for slight uncertainty is that the list says that the mint of Rouen pertained (*pertinet*) to Quentovic by long-established custom, and indeed there are some coins of distinctly Quentovic style with a Rouen mint name: Moesgaard 2010; 2014. For the early coinage, see Coupland 1991.

211. Metcalf and Northover 1989, 114–15, 120; Coupland 1991, 152–53.

a tendency toward caution, leading in 861 to Charles having to despatch *missi* to address endemic rejection of "good" coin.[212]

These problems evaporated after Charles's reform of the coinage in 864. It was his territories in particular that saw the biggest bump in minting; strikingly, numerous mint-places appeared in the former lands of the middle kingdom soon after Charles inherited them in 869. Other parts of the middle kingdom, particularly Italy, followed largely the same pattern as before. This was also true of the East: only the Rhineland and Bavaria had any significant use of coin at all, and they too contained relatively few mint-places. Something was driving rapid uptake of coinage, especially on the part of the western kingdom's elites. Tribute payments to the vikings around this time have sometimes been claimed as a reason for the expansion of minting,[213] but the many middle-kingdom mints actually undermine that proposition: these territories were not part of Charles's domain when the 866 tribute was levied and were explicitly exempt when the next one was called in 877.[214] The attraction of the new coinage was more visceral. A homogenous, high-quality currency could be stockpiled with confidence, like solidi in the fourth century, and many of the coins churned out by the new mints would have been intended first and foremost for the purses of the elite, or for expenditure on direct needs; serving the needs of the general populace was a consideration, and another source of indirect profit for patrons, but a secondary one. The distribution of mints hence followed the geography of local power rather than concentration of population or underlying agricultural production.

Finally, and counterintuitively, increased desire on the part of the empire's elite to mint their own coins for their own purposes could have been tied to shortage of coin in general circulation.[215] That is not necessarily the same thing as less coin being made: there was no fall-off in the scale of silver extraction at Melle in the later ninth century.[216] Rather, more coins were being hived off into a circuit of elite hoarding and restricted circulation, which fed into a vicious cycle: the more aristocrats wanted to

212. *Constitutio Carisiacensis de moneta* (Boretius and Krause 1897, 301–2).

213. Grierson 1990, 60, 63–64.

214. Coupland 1999, 73.

215. It is difficult to assess whether there was a real shortage of coin in late ninth-century Francia, for many coins—especially single finds—cannot be easily assigned to Charles the Bald, Charles the Fat, or Charles the Simple. Superficially it sometimes appears that there was a glut of coin losses under Charles the Bald (e.g., Jeanne-Rose 1996, esp. 250, 255), but if this body of material in fact comes from 864 (or, for some types, 843) to 923 or after, it tells a very different story.

216. Téreygeol 2018, 52.

store up coin, the less there was available for wider circulation, which in turn led more aristocrats to mint their own coin because it was not available on the open market. More people wanted a slice of the pie because it was being eaten straight off the serving plate. Surviving Carolingian grants of minting rights do indeed cite the difficulty of obtaining denarii as a reason for setting up new mints, in the expectation that they would draw out silver and put it into circulation.[217] That may not always have been an effective plan, at least if one hoped for a mint to be a sustained operation of benefit to everyone: if there was no coined money around to begin with, the immediate beneficiaries would have been holders of uncoined silver, probably meaning patrons. New mints appeared, in short, because more agencies with the necessary will and means wanted more coins and could not always get them through existing circuits.

Southern England c. 750–900: A Parallel World?

The emphasis in this chapter has fallen on Francia, in large part because I have written at length about England in this period elsewhere.[218] For present purposes England will be used mainly as a foil to the Carolingian case study, for the English material is richer in certain respects but more limited in others. The main strength is that England has a huge and well-studied body of finds, and there is reason to believe that this reflects a similar pattern to northern Francia of extensive capillary circulation linking rural communities in with long-distance exchange. In contrast, the region with the best recorded finds in mainland Europe, the Netherlands, seems to have had a quite different local dynamic in relation to coin circulation. For this reason, it is significant that England (with the important exception of Northumbria) saw a reduction in the numbers of coins being lost from the mid-ninth century. Francia may have seen the same phenomenon, albeit with a temporary resurgence in Charles the Bald's *Gratia Dei rex* coinage after 864, and considerable uncertainty thereafter, in that many coins cannot be easily divided between Charles the Bald, Charles the Fat, and Charles the Simple. England probably experienced a more modest expansion of minting from about the 870s as well, which lends support to the link between shortage of coin and the opening of fresh mints.[219]

217. See chapter 3.
218. Naismith 2012b.
219. Blackburn 1996; Naismith 2017b, 159–63, 168, 189–93.

Yet here arises one of the key difficulties of English coinage in the time of Offa of Mercia (757–96) and after: places of production are hardly ever named on coins. The emphasis instead fell on king and moneyer, and by extension on the personal origins of coins. It is probable that many Carolingian mints were effectively one-moneyer operations too. But in England there are marked differences of opinion on whether eighth- and ninth-century moneyers would have been concentrated in the few identifiable mint-places, such as Canterbury, London, and York, or were more dispersed.[220] There was probably a continuum between these extremes. Wessex and maybe East Anglia are compatible with dispersed patterns of production already in the late eighth and early ninth centuries. At Canterbury some coinages of the early ninth century struck by numerous moneyers carry the name of the city, suggesting production in one place, while technical features of the mid-ninth-century Northumbrian coinage, above all the extensive sharing of dies among moneyers, are explicable only if they worked in close contact with one another, probably at the same location.[221] A degree of centralisation is likely (and indeed matches developments in contemporary Francia), but the proposition of a tiny number of mint-places comes under strain in the 850s and after, when the number of moneyers notionally working in Canterbury and London expanded dramatically. About fifty moneyers are associated with Canterbury in the years 858–65, and about thirty in 865–71,[222] which is high enough to raise doubts over whether the moneyers all really were specialised, permanent residents of the city. At the same time, the dies used to strike the coins are generally the work of a single source. It is possible that the moneyers of England from the late eighth century and after were not permanent residents of the mint-towns: they could have had their dies sent to them for use in minting on the spot in their home locality, or else they could have journeyed to London, Canterbury, or wherever to mint coins and then returned home to distribute them. Either or both procedures are possible. Elite households routinely undertook journeys to royal assemblies to obtain or ratify land grants at this time.[223] These movements speak volumes about the integration of the English kingdoms.

Those kingdoms went in a markedly different direction from their Frankish counterparts in how they integrated minting with social

220. Compare Blunt, Lyon, and Stewart 1963, esp. 1; Naismith 2010, 78–80; 2017b, 132–33, 139; Williams and Williams 2013, 344.

221. Naismith 2012b, 128–33; 2017b, 114, 132–33, 139–42, 149, 151–53, 163–64.

222. Naismith 2017b, 158–59.

223. Naismith 2021.

FIGURE 8.7. Silver penny minted under Æthelwulf
(839–58), by Dunn, at Rochester, probably between
839 and the early 840s (diameter 21 mm). Classical
Numismatic Group, LLC.

structures. Apart from a small number of issues in the names of bishops
and archbishops, English coins focused heavily on the king and moneyer.
There is a danger here of seeing moneyers solely through this lens, as royal
officials or agents. Almost no evidence exists besides the coins to indicate
who the moneyers of this period were: a possible exception is a moneyer
at Rochester, Dunn, who appears in two documents from the Rochester
archive at the appropriate time (figure 8.7).[224] It is only in his capacity as
a thegn that Dunn ever appears; his role as a moneyer is never mentioned,
and the document in which he features most prominently comes several
years after his likely final act of minting. If Dunn is correctly identified,
he represents a thoroughly local figure, on the edge of the documentary
record, reinforcing the argument for moneyers often being based in the
vicinity of their mint-place. Another way of reading the evidence, however,
is that Dunn was exceptional not just for appearing, but for the qualities
that led to him appearing. He was described as a *minister*, thegn, of the
king at a time when this meant a very direct kind of service, not necessarily associated with high status,[225] and Dunn's will indicates that the estate
it relates to was the only landed property he had to bequeath. Importantly,
Dunn's service to the king did not remove him from his place in the locality; on the contrary, his immersion in local networks was what made him
effective as a thegn and as a moneyer. The moneyers' role in providing

224. S 315 (Campbell 1973, no. 23) is a grant of property in and around Rochester to
Dunn in 855, and S 1514 (Campbell 1973, no. 23) is the vernacular will of Dunn. For further
discussion of this and other possible occurrences of moneyers in texts, see Stewart 1988.

225. Loyn 1955. Blair 2018, 217–19, identifies a small number of thegns who received
strategically important land grants in the eighth century.

access to fresh coin depended less on commercial engagement and more on effective, trusted ties in the community, especially among those with relative wealth. An ealdorman, bishop, or family who needed new coin would have turned to a moneyer for assistance. By this token, the English moneyers would represent office-holders based across the kingdom but supplied from—and regularly in touch with—a small number of minting centres where their dies and perhaps coins were manufactured.

English coinage of the late eighth and ninth centuries thus indicates something important about contemporary government. Anglo-Saxon kings of the later tenth and eleventh centuries benefited from a multilayered form of administration, in which rulers dealt not only with powerful landholders and higher clerics, but also with an array of minor, specialised officials who looked after local and royal interests of diverse kinds. Formal office and status were intertwined with informal networks of power. The full extent of this scheme becomes apparent only in the later period, but it had deep roots, as a relic of the more modest scale of earlier Anglo-Saxon kingship.[226] One of the first places something like this can be seen in practice is with the moneyers. Three stages of development might be discerned. The moneyers of southern England between about the 760s and the 830s emerged out of the era of the early silver pennies and may have been conceived initially in a very direct relationship with the king: they were "his" moneyers, responsible for working as and where he wished, and owing profits to him. That implies a determined and generally successful restructuring of the coinage in the mid-eighth century to get rid of or take over moneyers working for other authorities, with only vestiges being left in the later eighth century (such as the moneyers of the archbishops of Canterbury and York, and the bishop of London).[227] The general contraction of the early pennies in the 740s and 750s would surely have helped by thinning the field of coin issuers.[228] At the same time, it is likely that already by the 760s the king's moneyers were not expected solely to mint the king's own silver and were liaising with elites within their home region. In this respect the earliest phase of broad penny circulation was very geographically focused. When Kent or East Anglia fell under a new regime, the moneyers' coins all changed accordingly, implying that they did not operate outside that kingdom. Conglomerate kingdoms of the kind constructed by Offa, Coenwulf, and Ecgberht saw limited consolidation

226. Naismith 2020b, 660–62.
227. Naismith 2012a, 303–7, 328–29.
228. Naismith 2012a, 295–97.

of the coinage in organisational terms, the main concern being to make sure the right king was named: some rulers were apparently very precise on how they should be represented, while others were content to leave the details to local initiative.[229] The period from around 830 to the mid-870s, and especially the final two decades of this period, was when moneyers proliferated in the Mercian and West-Saxon polities but were still structured around two main bases of operations, provisionally associated with London and Canterbury. East Anglia and Northumbria continued to follow the older pattern of a more regionally focused system. Finally, from around 875 new mint-places become more visible. Some are named on coins, others can be inferred from stylistically distinct groups of coins, and these techniques apply both to issues from the area of English rule (west Mercia and Wessex) and of viking rule (eastern and northern England). Most moneyers still remained aligned toward one or other of a few major centres, but when mint names started to be used regularly in the 920s, it becomes apparent that they were based at a much larger number of locations.[230]

It is important not to lose sight of the fact that while patterns of finds, moneyers, mint-places, and die distribution are all we have to work from, they would have been incidental to more human structures and pressures. These, unfortunately, can only be guessed at. Moneyers moved around to secure coin dies, and potentially (on a more local level) to attend assemblies and liaise with patrons for minting, who would have included ealdormen, bishops, abbots, and indeed the king himself.[231] Also, although there were more places and moneyers making coin, the quantity of pennies in circulation was in sharp decline. Monetisation widened in breadth rather than depth: more people with the resources to patronise minting could get access to coin, but that did not translate to more coins being encountered in markets. As in Francia, this might have been in part a self-sustaining process of shortage generating more, smaller issues of coin. But it can also be associated with rising secular elite interests, carefully managed by kings, at the expense of minster churches.[232] Other manifestations of those interests include the higher proportion of

---

229. Offa seems to have promulgated a specific form of name for his coinage (Naismith 2019c), while Æthelberht of Kent and Wessex (858–865) was normally referred to on coins with the Kentish dialectal form of his name (Naismith 2021, 505–6).

230. Naismith 2017b, 189–93; Metcalf 1992, 82–89.

231. Brooks 2003, 156.

232. Fleming 1985; Blair 2005, 323–29.

grants to high-ranking laymen (especially ealdormen),[233] the development of vernacular documents that would have appealed more strongly to this constituency,[234] and the requirement to raise armies, build fortresses, and pay tributes to the vikings (or debts to others, including the king, who fronted the money for tribute payments).[235]

THE KINGDOM OF NORTHUMBRIA

Unlike southern England, the kingdom of Northumbria stuck with the small, thick model of coin that had emerged in the seventh century. In the ninth century Northumbria's coins were significantly adulterated with copper alloy. It is tempting to write off this kingdom and its small, ugly, and archaic coins as an idiosyncratic throwback. But it had been ahead of the curve in Eadberht's institution of a royally sponsored recoinage in (probably) the 740s, and the later, debased coinage in its way represents an important development: it was the first independently evolved base-metal currency in post-Roman western Europe (i.e., the first that was not a fairly direct continuation of late Roman denominations), and for most of its history it constituted a well-ordered coinage. The main steps in its adulteration took place in the course of relatively long reigns, suggesting they were not knee-jerk responses to political crisis. Importantly, the technical aspects of adulteration point to long-distance bulk trade in metals. Tin and brass (an alloy of copper and zinc) were added to the coins on a large scale in the mid-ninth century. Neither could be found locally: the tin is likely to have come from Cornwall, the brass from the Aachen region.[236] This switch to brass and tin, which were themselves of not inconsiderable value, could have served partially to offset the reduction of silver. Users also did not reject these base-metal coins. Hoards of Northumbrian pennies show that earlier, less adulterated coins did not immediately vanish from circulation, which would again point away from a reading of this coinage as a product of monetary crisis and rampant inflation.[237]

That is not to say, however, that the Northumbrian pennies circulated at parity with silver pennies from southern England. They very likely were worth less, and in principle they could have been a much more functional currency than any other in western Europe at the time. The huge numbers

233. Brooks 2003, 157.
234. Lowe 2008; Gallagher 2018, esp. 233–34.
235. Brooks 1979.
236. Metcalf and Northover 1987, 193–214.
237. Naismith 2017b, 126–27.

of finds broadly support the impression of an extensively used coinage.[238] What is more, die-links within the coinage strongly indicate that the moneyers responsible for it were a close-knit group, probably working at the same location. The existence of coins in the name of the archbishop of York is good evidence that York was the base of operations, though, as in the South of England, it is likely that the moneyers were tied into networks that reached out to other parts of the kingdom. The low value of the coinage may also have opened up the range of patrons who could acquire fresh coin from the moneyers.

Unfortunately, any attempt to develop the significance of this coinage is hampered by the extreme obscurity of ninth-century Northumbria. Even the regnal chronology is murky, and hardly anything is known about the workings of the kingdom and its society. The archaeological record is more helpful in revealing a backdrop of developed exchange systems that persisted through the ninth century. Ceramics include some wheel-thrown groups that were produced in bulk and distributed widely in the region, probably down to at least the late ninth century, which speaks to a degree of complexity in exchange within the kingdom;[239] there was also a rich local tradition of silver and copper-alloy ornamental metalwork, which shows that there was not a dearth of silver for other purposes in the kingdom.[240]

The end of the Northumbrian coinage can best be described as chaotic and is difficult to date, potentially coming at any point between the mid-850s and the 870s.[241] Imitations of various sorts were produced in large numbers, and the low-value Northumbrian pennies apparently continued to be used at many locations. In short, they still had a distinct place in the local economy and were not immediately supplanted by silver. The vikings seem to have used them extensively, presumably for dealing with locals, especially in low-value contexts. They occur in large numbers at Aldwark and Torksey, sites associated with the presence of the viking "great army"

238. As of July 2021, PAS recorded 533 Northumbrian pennies from after c. 810, and EMC 3033; for discussion of find distribution, see Naylor 2004, 37–56. Both figures are likely to be significant underestimates, however: relations between the metal-detecting community and archaeologists have not always been good in Yorkshire, and anecdotal evidence suggests that several sites have produced vastly more Northumbrian pennies than were ever reported: ninety were reported from Aldwark, for example, but one of the detectorists involved reported that hundreds had been found (Hadley and Richards 2021, 214).

239. Hurst 1976, 303–7; Naylor 2004, 56–68.

240. Thomas 2005, 43.

241. Pirie 2006, 225–26.

in the 870s, and potentially even later at York.[242] At Torksey and Aldwark, Northumbrian pennies were used alongside hacksilver and hackgold, as well as precious-metal coins. It has been suggested that some of the many imitative issues originate with the viking incomers who were based at these sites, though this proposition awaits fuller investigation.[243] Even outside Northumbria, Northumbrian pennies enjoyed a role as an unofficial, makeshift fractional coinage. Specimens have occurred as far south as London and Kent; some may have been brought south in connection with viking movements, but not necessarily all.[244] Northumbrian pennies have also been found in diverse locations outside England, in Scandinavia, Poland, Russia, the Netherlands, Germany, Italy, and Spain.[245] Whether they retained an exchange function in these locations is unclear.

Conclusion

The establishment of silver coinage in northwestern Europe brought the possibility of a real material change in how coined money factored into various areas of political, social, and economic life. This was, it should be stressed, a *possibility*: how pennies and denarii were actually used varied significantly depending on local structures of exchange. In Italy things hardly changed at all from the preceding period of gold coinage, except for those involved in long-distance exchange. In eastern England and northern Francia, by contrast, coinage penetrated into rural society in relatively large quantity.

On one level, silver did mean a deepened monetary economy, though this must be kept in perspective. The monetary economy was still small: coins would have factored into a minority of transactions even in the most richly monetised areas of seventh- to ninth-century Europe. The increase in size of that minority, however, brought new opportunities to leverage existing inequalities.[246] Where real change can be seen is in the production of coin. This was not a transformation of basic agency: elites remained the driving force, as they had been in previous times. But in England and Francia the range of participants who entered into the new

242. Pirie et al. 1986, 15–17; Williams 2020, esp. 36–45, 79–80, 130–31.

243. Hadley and Richards 2021, 96–97, 103, 130, 214–15; Williams 2014a, 22; 2020, 42; Blackburn 2011, 225.

244. Metcalf 1998, 177–79.

245. Hadley and Richards 2021, 141–42. The Italian and Spanish finds are both known from personal communication with local finders.

246. See also chapter 4.

currency was surely significantly larger and more diverse. Minting, and the general capacity to get and distribute coin, became a more refined tool for expressing dominance. Kings were the other new factor, as stage managers for this process after the mid-eighth century. Their more direct involvement reflected a combination of fortuitous circumstances, responsive neighbours, and a desire to enhance symbolic and material interests in collaboration with local elites.[247] In England a body of relatively low-status moneyers mediated between kings and the rest of the populace but should not be seen as a realistic alternative to elite involvement; rather, they stand for indirect patronage, and represent a place for the buck to stop in case of fraudulent behaviour. In the Frankish world, it is possible to identify a sandwich approach, albeit with every layer framed around relations between king and aristocracy. This started with a broad and open structure in the late Merovingian and early Carolingian world, resulting in numerous mints that reflected the layered "public" landscape of the day. From about the 790s, Charlemagne and Louis the Pious sought, with some success, to corral a much-expanded monetary system into fewer mints, conceived more narrowly as the responsibility of selected counts. In a sense that equation of counts and minting persisted into the late ninth century, though on quite different terms: far more counts now wanted to operate a mint of their own in support of local interests. It was in that respect that the many late Carolingian mints differed from those of the eighth century.

The eighth and especially ninth centuries set the scene for important developments in years to come, as an increasingly vibrant silver coinage, harnessed to reified and assertive local power, pushed the monetary economy up a gear. In the process, it opened up a range of unintended consequences, including a slew of opportunities on the back of the seigneurial economy.

247. Cf. Naismith 2012a.

CHAPTER NINE

Money and Power in the Tenth and Eleventh Centuries

NO ONE WOULD HAVE BEEN particularly happy when, in the 1060s, Adelaide of Turin (d. 1091) came to deal with the long-standing problem of the mint in Aiguebelle (dép. Savoie). Since the time of her husband, Otto, Margrave of Savoy (d. 1057/60), certain "thieves and counterfeiters" (*latrones et falsarii*) based there had issued a debased version of the coinage of Vienne. This would have been a profitable money spinner: the denarii of the archbishop of Vienne were one of the more popular coinages in eleventh-century France. Debased versions of the archiepiscopal coins could slip into mass circulation and undermine the authentic currency. The latter was important to the interests of the archbishop himself, as both a source of revenue and a tangible manifestation of his authority, so when Archbishop Leudegar (1030–70) learned of the forgers' activities, he arranged for Pope Leo IX (1049–54) to excommunicate the leading moneyer of Aiguebelle, and he made angry representation to Otto. The margrave had supposedly been ignorant of the moneyers' activities, which is difficult to believe since one of his principal castles, Charbonnières, dominates Aiguebelle.[1] Regardless of whether Otto had been blind or turning a blind eye, he put a stop to the mint's mischief. But this was to be only the first of three occasions when the domains of Vienne and Savoy had to reach an understanding about the rogue moneyers of Aiguebelle.[2]

Leudegar, Otto, and Adelaide all evidently took a close interest in the coinage under their jurisdiction. Equally interesting, though less clear, is

---

1. Brocard, Messiez-Poche, and Dompnier 1983, 17–25.
2. *PL* 143, col. 1408. For context, see Creber 2017, 54–55.

the nefarious mint of Aiguebelle. It apparently worked at arm's length from the major authorities of the area but had enough structure for there to be an identifiable chief moneyer, and enough staying power to endure several attempted shut-downs. There was not, however, any name-worthy person the count or the archbishop could turn to, which is in itself suggestive: we are dealing here with a minting operation that had boiled up from below and did not answer reliably to the commands of the margrave or his wife. Aiguebelle's very existence speaks volumes about the scale of local monetary activity. Demand from further down the social scale, from among the local elite or even nonelites, could prompt informal minting operations to spring up on the fringes of more formal ones.

The milieu that produced the situation of Aiguebelle is the focus of this chapter. Production of coin on the basis seen in this picturesque Alpine village would have been difficult to envisage two centuries earlier in the heyday of the Carolingian Empire, let alone in the seventh or eighth century. There had been about a century of important changes in the period before the Aiguebelle mint stirred such anger. From the mid- to late tenth century (and generally more so in the eleventh), there were more coins being made and lost. Coined money featured more often, and with more effect, in the land market, in the seigneurial economy, and in local markets. It also loomed larger in contemporary rhetoric, mostly as a metonym for greed and misplaced love for worldly goods. Across western Europe, the manufacture of these coins was handled in varied ways and with varied effects, by an increasingly varied range of people.

All these themes are well known, and the first part of this chapter considers the historiographical background of "commercial revolution" within which they have traditionally been interpreted. Aspects of that framework are challenged in what follows. First, the actual changes in the number of finds across multiple regions are examined, followed by developments in the production of coin. The second section brings these points together to ask what effects these changes had as a whole, and what might have been driving them forward. The final part examines developments in the making and use of coined money with reference to regional circumstances, looking in turn at Italy, West Francia, East Francia/Germany, and England.

At the Dawn of the Commercial Revolution?

For previous generations of observers, the real home of eleventh-century coinage mostly lay within the walls of towns and the purses of merchants. Money (as coin and later as credit) formed part of the early stirrings of what historians have succinctly described as the "Commercial Revolution": a take-off of commercial trade driven by merchants and towns that began around the turn of the first millennium.[3] Money occupied a special place in this narrative as, in Robert López's words, "the most available and possibly the most sensitive instrument to feel the economic pulse of the Commercial Revolution in its early stages."[4] Expansion of money sat alongside, and bound up with, the resurgence of urbanisation and mercantile trade.

There was a time when the rise of this triad was the main quarry of medieval economic history. The first scholars to pursue the subject at the end of the nineteenth century and in the first part of the twentieth hunted for signs of mercantile life in Flanders, the Rhineland, and northern Italy, listening for the first flutters of European capitalism after the supposedly cataclysmic onslaught of viking, Magyar, and Muslim raids in the ninth and tenth centuries had ended.[5] A line was then drawn from merchant guilds and Jewish moneylenders to modern times, driven by an intangible yet powerful spirit of capitalism. In the formulation of one of the most prominent early researchers of the medieval economy, Henri Pirenne, developments in European towns that began in the eleventh century marked the emergence of "a new notion of wealth" in the hands of "true capitalists."[6] Pirenne's conclusion that the economic changes in and around the towns of this period laid the groundwork for the rise of capitalism seemed all the more impressive for occurring in the teeth of what López summed up as "the unfriendly context of a feudal government and an agrarian society";[7] others fastened on the supposedly debilitating impact of viking, Magyar, and Muslim raids in various parts of ninth- and tenth-century Europe.[8] In the work of Pirenne, López, and others, the commercial changes of the central Middle Ages could be boxed off from the torpor of "feudalism" in which they grew.[9] They took place in spite of,

3. The best overall account of it is López 1976.

4. López 1976, 71. Cf. Bloch 1962, 1:71.

5. The idea that the tenth or eleventh century was a turning point can be traced back to Henri Pirenne (1898; 1913; 1939) in Francophone scholarship, as well as a number of scholars in Germany (von Below 1892; Keutgen 1895; Hegel 1898). See more recently Violante 1993.

6. Pirenne 1925, 159–60; Bautier 1971, 88.

7. López 1976, 89.

8. E.g., Pirenne 1939, 15–38.

9. "Feudalism" here is used to characterise a system of lord-peasant relations that was often conflated with fief-vassal relations and seen as quintessentially rural and antithetical to towns and trade. As Chris Wickham has cogently argued (2021, 3–14), the term can serve as a general label for systems of production based on taking surplus from those who work the land but should be shorn of its other associations.

rather than because of, the social tenor of Europe around the turn of the first millennium.

Julie Mell has cogently identified the deep-rooted problems with these approaches.[10] They inherit the thinking of Werner Sombart and the Historical School of late-nineteenth-century Germany, which chopped up the past into stages of development that unfolded in an evolutionary sequence.[11] In economic history, these stages built toward the emergence of capitalism, which Sombart saw as achieving ascendancy in the sixteenth century, but with an important precursor among the Jews of earlier times, whom he saw as protocapitalistic moneylenders. Other scholars quickly challenged both these arguments. The Jewish side of the story is important and has a complex history, but it will not be pursued here.[12] The emergence of capitalism in the form of a commercial success story, however, has also enjoyed a long legacy. Scholars of the Middle Ages continued to look for the onset of a "spirit of capitalism," or developments that added up to much the same thing, in the milieu of towns and merchants. The period that came before this crucial change—which inevitably comes across as more primitive and alien—was pushed to the edge of "real" economic history and its central narrative.

This evolutionary aspect of Sombart's thinking achieved remarkable staying power by underpinning the "Commercial Revolution." The first use of this term (by Raymond de Roover in 1942)[13] referred specifically to the thirteenth century, and this has generally been seen as the core period of intensification and elaboration of economic processes, first and most impressively in Italy. But a runway was needed before lift-off could be achieved, and in the 1970s the dawn of the first millennium was frequently given as the starting point of that runway.[14] What happened at this time has been construed in different ways: Georges Duby and Lester Little, for example, took a leaf from anthropology in seeing a shift from a "gift economy" to a "profit economy," which was shorthand for money and the economically rational entrepreneurs who wielded it.[15] There are shades here of the "hostile worlds" approach to money as a fundamentally

10. Mell 2007, chap. 5; see also Mell 2017–2018.

11. See especially Sombart 1902.

12. Mell 2017–2018. See also discussion of this work (mostly focusing on its arguments about the Jews) in https://marginalia.lareviewofbooks.org/the-myth-of-the-medieval-jewish-moneylender-a-forum/ (visited 6 September 2021).

13. De Roover 1942.

14. Gies and Gies 1972; López 1976.

15. Duby 1971. Little 1978 developed this influential approach to focus on the religious tension that he saw in the transition from "gift" to "profit."

transformative phenomenon that corrodes and changes everything with which it comes in contact:[16] to identify the start of the transition to capitalism, one had to find the point where a "money economy" began to take shape. This continues to be a line that scholars draw in the historical sand.[17] But, as Michael Postan observed acidly as early as 1944, "'the rise of a money economy' is . . . a *deus ex machina* to be called upon when no other explanation is available," and "historians have frequently taken it for granted that a money economy, like the bourgeoisie, arose at a single point . . . usually at a point best suited to their argument."[18] Postan went on to undercut the identification of particular changes in the availability of cash or credit as a rise of the money economy. To do so implied systemic change and long-term (even permanent) impact. Postan's inference was that any such argument is driven by arbitrary, relative definitions designed to distance what came before and familiarize what came after.

The revival of coinage in late tenth- and eleventh-century western Europe has therefore been tied to a larger raft of developments that together constitute the dawn of the "commercial revolution": merchants, towns, and long-distance trade. It is worth stressing that there undoubtedly were important changes in all these areas that pivoted around the eleventh century. Towns, and the population as a whole, did get bigger. Merchants also became a more significant force, in part by undertaking more long-distance trade, though intensification of local exchange was also important. Ceramics in the tenth century from England, France, and Italy show a gradual increase in complexity of distribution.[19] Herring from the North Sea could be bought cheaply and in bulk fifty miles inland in Cambridgeshire. Storage silos for grain also became more common and important in Francia.[20] All this is suggestive of more elaborate and, at least in part, commercialised networks. But to contextualise these developments properly requires that they be detached from the narrative of emergent capitalism and commercial revolution as an autonomous force. They also need to be seen in relation to other dimensions of the contemporary economy: capillary-level production and distribution, and the place in it of social dynamics, hierarchical and otherwise. Postan saw this point and amplified it in his conclusion: "Increases in the relative volume of money transactions could reflect a whole variety of economic changes . . .

16. See chapter 1.

17. The most sophisticated recent work in this vein is Bolton 2004; 2012.

18. Postan 1944, 123, 124.

19. Cantini 2014; Peytremann 2014; Hurst 1976, 314–42.

20. Peytremann 2013.

which combined with other phenomena to create unique and unrepeatable historical situations."[21] In other words, the monetary economy needs to be seen as a product of its time, embedded in contemporary relations between social groups. That means allowing a larger role for lords, peasants, and rural society as a whole. Points of contact can be identified between them, in terms of higher levels of economic agency lower down the social spectrum. But, as we saw already at Aiguebelle and its mint of ill repute that sat alongside a castle and a newly founded Benedictine abbey, agency still piggybacked on elite wealth and structures; the difference was that the intensity and complexity of those structures extended further downward and created more interstices where others could carve out their own economic space.

A Monetising Economy

Finds of coins from several parts of Europe point strongly toward an uptick in the numbers being deposited in the late tenth and eleventh centuries. In regions with databases of finds from amateur detectorists such as the Netherlands or England and Wales, the pattern is easily discerned: both show a significant increase in finds among coins minted in approximately the 970s and after, relative to the two preceding centuries.[22] The best available database of material from Italy is restricted to archaeological finds (which remain few in this period), chance discoveries, and antiquarian records; it also only runs down to the beginning of the eleventh century. Nevertheless, finds of silver pieces from Rome and the lands to the north are significantly more numerous after about 950, and there is no reason to believe that later coins have been overreported, or early ones underreported.[23] Finds in Italy pick up even more in the mid- to late eleventh century.[24] For Denmark and the southern part of Sweden, a study of single finds has again identified a modest increase among those from the later tenth century and a stronger one in the early eleventh (followed by a sharp drop-off in the later eleventh century).[25] The trend in this

---

21. Peytremann 2013, 134.

22. Naismith 2013a, 201–4; Ilisch 2014a, 67–68. This conclusion is based on (for England and Wales) EMC and PAS, and (for the Netherlands) NUMIS.

23. Arslan 2005 (with updates). A similar picture is sketched for Tuscany in Saccocci 2013 and Benvenuti et al. 2019, 137, with most single finds of silver from the late eighth century to about 1000 being Ottonian denari of the late tenth century.

24. Saccocci 2008 and Arslan 2007b provide good summaries. Rovelli 2010, 168, is even more reserved, stressing that enhanced minting was sporadic until the twelfth century.

25. Von Heijne 2004.

and other parts of Scandinavia can be set alongside the move away from bullion-based silver circulation toward coin, which took a big leap forward in the later tenth century and especially after 1000, coinciding with the sharp contraction in imports of dirhams.[26]

A similar story can be told for some smaller regions where there have been efforts to gather up details of finds in a similar way: in North Rhine–Westphalia, for example, the number of single finds of coins increases somewhat for those dating to the last quarter of the tenth century, but much more markedly for those dating to the eleventh century.[27] Individual sites that were active across all or part of this period again support the general picture. At Mainz, the Hilton Hotel site yielded a rich haul of coins from the last quarter of the tenth century; it was less rich in those from the eleventh century, though this is thought to be a facet of the focus of activity moving within the town.[28] At the hilltop fortress of Tremona near Lake Lugano in northern Italy, numbers of isolated finds picked up with coins of the Ottonians but more significantly in the mid-eleventh century.[29] Further south, at Rome, the *Confessio sancti Petri* contained only a few coins struck between the early ninth century and about 950, but they multiplied gradually in the second half of the tenth century, and much more substantially with coins minted after 1000.[30]

Several sites in France have been rich in later tenth- and eleventh-century coins, including some with quite narrow and well-defined windows of activity. These include locations where building took place on a large scale at the same time, pointing to construction as a possible context of expenditure and loss.[31] Elite sites also stand out. A settlement on the banks of Lac Paladru (dép. Isère) was established in 1003 or soon after and abandoned some forty years later due to rising water levels: the numerous coin finds of that period (twenty-seven coins of late tenth- or early eleventh-century date, plus six Roman pieces) can hence be tied to quite a narrow window.[32] Similarly, the early castle of Andone (dép. Charente) was built around the 970s or 980s as a residence for the counts of Angoulême and abandoned in or before 1028, when the counts transferred their base elsewhere. Again, the total of twenty tenth- and eleventh-century coins (plus

---

26. Gullbekk 2009, 31–35, shows this very effectively for Norway.

27. Ilisch 2012.

28. Wamers, Berghaus, and Stoess 1994.

29. Arslan 2008.

30. Serafini 1951. A new survey of the material from the *Confessio* is in preparation. For the setting in Old St. Peter's, see McKitterick et al. 2013, esp. 163, 214–19.

31. Cardon 2021, 66–74.

32. Colardelle and Verdel 1993, 285–87, 305, plus Colardelle, Moyne, and Verdel 2016.

twenty-four base-metal Roman coins from medieval layers) belongs to a circumscribed period of around fifty years.[33]

Lac Paladru and Andone typify a tendency across western Europe for higher-status archaeological sites of this period to produce concentrations of coins. They can be set alongside English examples at Bishopstone (Sussex), Faccombe Netherton (Hampshire), Goltho (Lincolnshire), and Sulgrave (Northamptonshire), among others.[34] Other French finds come from castles at Blois, Niozelles, and Allemagne-en-Provence (Alpes-de-Haute-Provence),[35] and from rural settlements with high-status characteristics such as la Grande-Paroisse (Seine-et-Marne).[36] In Italy as well as Tremona, there is now the dramatic (*fuori scala* or "off the scale") site of La Vetricella, which has produced no fewer than twenty-one coins minted between about 900 and 1050,[37] and in Germany Bissendorf (Lower Saxony).[38]

From England to Rome, and in a slightly different way in Scandinavia, a broadly similar pattern can be discerned of more coins being lost than before, with hot spots of them in focal points of elite power. In most areas the big increase came with coins minted after about 1000. Some delay needs to be allowed for.[39] Actual losses could have occurred a decade or two after minting, sometimes more. In Italy, the main surge came later in the eleventh century.

Comparison with neighbouring regions emphasises that this is a distinctly western European development. In the Byzantine Empire, a slower, longer-term revival in the number of coin losses began in the ninth century and persisted into the twelfth; at the level of actual excavations, the finds normally consist of base-metal coins.[40] There were significant regional differences, and these become even more marked in the Muslim world. Al-Andalus in the West was relatively similar to the Christian kingdoms

33. Bourgeois 2009, 121–23.

34. M. Archibald in Thomas 2010, 140–41; in Fairbrother 1990, 436–46; and in Beresford 1987, 188; Blackburn 1979.

35. Mouton 2003; 2008; 2014.

36. Mouton 2003. On the material impact of elites at early French castles, see Bourgeois 2013a.

37. Rovelli 2020. Rovelli argues that a cluster of the earlier coins could represent a dispersed hoard, though the archaeological evidence for this is equivocal. This and related sites in Tuscany have been seen as fiscal centres, with evidence of strong activity after about 900: Bianchi and Collavini 2018.

38. Lau et al. 2013.

39. For an attempt to model estimated dates of loss for English single finds, see Naismith 2013a, 205–6.

40. Morrisson 2002, esp. 958–61.

outside Spain (those within Spain being effectively coinless at this time, or only using small numbers of Andalusi coins): finds of coins multiply in the era of the Umayyad caliphate from around the mid-tenth century and remain strong through the eleventh, supplemented in eastern Spain by significant numbers of Fatimid coins.[41] The small corpus of published finds does not permit quantification of coin finds from the Islamic lands extending from Egypt to Iran, but the tenth to twelfth centuries were marked by contraction, debasement, and regionalisation of silver (and, to a lesser degree, gold). Copper coinage was abandoned in most places after the ninth century, and cut fragments of coins served as small change: silver in the tenth century, and gold in the eleventh, alongside local coinages of debased silver.[42] Both whole and fragmentary coins circulated according to standardised weight units that rarely mapped exactly onto the actual number of coins.[43]

There was indeed a rise in the deposition of coins in western Europe from the later tenth century onward, and this survey has underlined that it began at more or less the same time in large parts of western Europe. The most obvious, and most likely, interpretation is that there were simply more coins being put into circulation. Where assessments of the scale of output have been undertaken, especially in England, Dublin, Scandinavia, and eastern Europe, it does indeed seem that the late tenth and eleventh centuries saw an important step-up in production (in some of these cases from a more or less standing start).[44] But an uptick in production could have been exacerbated by modifications in the way coins were used.

There was a chance of coins being lost every time they changed hands.[45] Increased losses of coin, then, could in principle reflect an amplification in the intensity of their use: if coins were circulating more intensively, they stood a higher chance of being lost. More rapid velocity of circulation can be read as a signal of pressure, potentially caused by a rising population, as argued for the early modern period,[46] or by a money

41. Retamero 2006, 307; Doménech Belda 2003.

42. See chapter 5.

43. Goitein 1967–93, 1:230–34.

44. Lyon 2012; Naismith 2013a, 62–68; Woods 2013, 118–53; Suchodolski 1971; Skaare 1976; Hansen 1990; Steen Jensen 1983; Lunden 1999; Gullbekk 2011; Risvaag and Christophersen 2004.

45. This variable is sometimes referred to as the velocity of money, as in the classic Fisher equation of $M(oney) \times V(elocity) = P(rice) \times T(ransactions)$; this is used effectively and sensitively in Mayhew 1995.

46. E.g., Miskimin 1975; Goldstone 1991.

supply that was inadequate to the demands being put on it.[47] It can be interpreted in light of early modern evidence for the tendency of the rich to hoard coins and not let them circulate. Relatively more coins may have been escaping the circuit that led directly from the mint to bulging purses, and that circuit itself may have been giving ground as circulation of coin became more feasible and, perhaps, more desirable. Finally, there is the question of bullion supply. All these coins were made from silver (though some, especially in France, contained very little by the eleventh century), and so supplies of metal needed to be found. Eleventh-century monetisation has sometimes been portrayed as a more or less direct consequence of the fortuitous discovery of new veins of silver in central Germany.[48] Subsequent work on the history of mining in the Harz has undercut this narrative: mining had been going on in the region for centuries, and even if extraction of silver was on a small scale before the mid- to late tenth century, its presence had been known.[49] Here and elsewhere, the opening of multiple new mines was a response to increasing demand, as well as a stimulus to production.

Money, Morality, and the Routinisation of Coin

Money was more on people's minds as well as in their purses. Rejection of real, physical coin turned into a hallmark of the most extreme of ascetics and the most dangerous of heretics.[50] Most famously, it was in the eleventh century that simony, the acquisition of ecclesiastical office in return for payment, came onto the agenda with newfound vigour. Simony was, in the eyes of some, an endemic taint that needed to be expunged. In theory it referred to any material quid pro quo offered for ecclesiastical office, but in practice it was money that attracted the real ire. As one of the most ferocious opponents of simony, Humbert of Moyenmoutier, wrote around 1058, "Where will our freedom flee—the freedom which we accept through you [the clergy] in hope and in which we rejoice in the freedom of the children of God . . . if you yourself are in thrall to the moneyers and a servant of the servants of mammon?"[51] Anxiety over simony, although

---

47. Mayhew 1995.

48. Most prominently Spufford 1988, 74–75.

49. See chapter 2.

50. Naismith 2015, 26–27, 36.

51. "Et quorsum evadet illa nostra libertas, de qua et ipsi per te iam praesumimus in spe et gloriamur in libertate filiorum Dei . . . si ipse nummulariis et servis mammonae servus addictus es?" Humbert of Moyenmoutier, *Adversus simoniacos*, preface (Thaner 1891, 102).

expressed with deafening rhetorical force, needs to be kept in perspective. It can be read as one of several phases of self-critique on ecclesiastical appointments that successive waves of well-placed clergy tried on for size.[52] Accusations of simony enabled select clerical factions to turn on their fellows and conjure heretics everywhere they looked. For this reason, the most shrill reactions to simony were quickly abandoned as impractical. When Pope Leo IX (1049–54) at one point floated at a council the idea of invalidating all simoniacal appointments, it was pointed out that this would leave almost all the churches of Europe without anyone to say mass.[53] Among the "reform" party in Rome, the more moderate approach eventually adopted by Peter Damian won out, which condemned the practice in general but accepted valid simoniac sacraments and appointments.[54]

Committed opposition to simony was never a majority view: it was a minority concern, with limited impact on practice and thought across Latin Christendom as a whole. Crucially, that means the image of rampant commercialism it projected was a rhetorical conceit that needs to be read with extreme caution as an actual mirror of eleventh-century society.[55] What troubled Humbert and Peter Damian was growing awareness of commercialised relations, symbolised by money, where they were not appropriate. Coin became matter out of place, the classic definition of dirt.[56] The movement of monks and priests from relatively less developed regions to more economically complex ones, especially in cities and in Italy, may well have exacerbated the sense of encroaching contamination.[57]

It remains striking that the discourse on simony so readily embraced coin as a metonym for buying and selling.[58] Peter Damian relied heavily on familiarity with coined money: he revived the patristic tradition of using it as a metaphor for the human soul, his language updated to suit the coin of his own day. Thus, bringing a layman to the eremitic life was as difficult as trying to turn a forged penny into a good one just by

52. Leyser 1995, esp. 198–99, 209–10.

53. Peter Damian, *Liber gratissimus* chap. 37 (Reindel 1983–93, 1:498–99).

54. Leyser 1995, 210. See McCready 2011, chap. 3.

55. Pace Murray 1978, 63–67.

56. Fardon 2013 examines the complicated roots of this famous aphorism, popularized by Mary Douglas.

57. West 2015; see also West 2022.

58. Murray 1978, 63–67, which argues for a genuine rise in simony in the period immediately before anxiety took hold.

restamping it.[59] This is one of many cases where, although simony might mean money, money did not always mean simony. It had a proper place and use that needed to be respected. When Peter Damian visited Besançon in 1063 and the archbishop showed him his tomb (built and ready to receive its occupant), he warmly approved of the bishop having already deposited a parcel of coins at each corner of his shroud, as payment for the gravediggers to come.[60] Other anecdotes used coin to exemplify popular charity, equity, and harmony. A poor man with one coin gave it up to a needier pauper, only to be rewarded by a mysterious stranger with twenty shillings in cash.[61] Another tale concerned a man and wife on pilgrimage who lost most of their cash in a lake. They persevered and completed their journey on reduced funds, and on the return trip they stopped by the same lake. There the husband encountered a fisherman from whom he bought a fish, pointedly not haggling when he did so. And when that fish had been cooked, it turned out to contain the couple's lost purse.[62] Coined money had, in religious rhetoric, become a sort of moral litmus test, inviting the good to be virtuous and the wicked to be sinful—which again presumed a society where coin was widely available. As Sylvain Piron has suggested with reference to the emergence at this time of the terms "value" (*valor*) and "cost" (*constamen(tum)*), people were in the grip of a *révolution de l'abstraction monétaire* that led them to see the world around them in terms of its use-value.[63]

Few texts, if any, exemplify this with more vivacity than the bawdy protofabliau *Unibos*, which recounts the adventures of a devious peasant by that name: he of the one ox. The poem concerns the shenanigans that ensue after Unibos takes his one remaining ox to market and then finds a hoard of three pots of silver coins in the woods. Unibos does so while wiping his backside after defecating. This is one of several points in the text where coined money is associated with filth and faeces; there is also a donkey that supposedly excretes silver coins. The juxtaposition of silver and shit contributes to a larger message that the writer of the poem used the wily, Rabelaisian persona of Unibos to convey: money can be a corrupting, destabilising force when it bursts the bounds of status, propriety, and virtue. The poet stresses the vast scale of Unibos's haul, big enough that he has to weigh rather than count its contents, and to undermine

---

59. Peter Damian, *Epistolae* 50 (Reindel 1983–93, 2:127).
60. Peter Damian, *Epistolae* 111 (Reindel 1983–93, 3:248–49).
61. Peter Damian, *Epistolae* 57 (Reindel 1983–93, 2:177–78).
62. Peter Damian, *Epistolae* 169 (Reindel 1983–93, 4:249).
63. Piron 2010, 132–33, 149–50.

the distinction of leading members of his immediate community and tempt them into foolish acts. The mayor, reeve, and priest of the village put themselves into one farcical situation after another: the climax of the story sees them drown themselves in an attempt to reach an underwater pasture rich in pigs. Greed is their great failing, the thirst produced by and slaked with money. That is precisely how the poet introduces Unibos's hoard: when plucking grass to wipe himself, "he finds that which greedy folk love."[64] Still more telling is the final stanza of the poem, which brings the story to a close by encapsulating its moral: "This tale shows for ever and ever that the sly counsels of an enemy must not be believed."[65] The "sly enemy" is of course Unibos, who can be construed as a pseudo-diabolical tempter luring those who are "rich in idiocy" (*fatuitatis diuites*) to destruction with easy, destabilising wealth.[66]

Unibos is a far more subtle work than its toilet humour and magic tricks would superficially indicate. It offers a sustained exploration of how a surfeit of money—and the potential for limitless market purchases—can transform rationality to foolishness, and virtue to vice. Greed itself was nothing new (and nor were admonishments against it in Christian literature), though the prominence of money in those admonishments was.

In addition to the moralistic discussions in written works, coined money took on a stronger role in visual art produced with a similar purpose. Love of coin, exemplified by a purse, became a symbol of avarice on carvings in early Romanesque churches (figure 9.1).[67] A compilation on the struggle of the virtues and vices produced at Moissac around the 1040s succinctly used coin to encapsulate the critical importance of choice and repentance in relation to sin: avarice was represented by someone who clambered roughly on top of a bent over *rusticus* to fill a vase with coins, while "fear of God" (*timor Dei*) properly gifted a coin to a crouching beggar[68] (figure 9.2).

64. "Repperit quod gens auara diligit." *Unibos* v. 18 (Klein 1991, 851; trans. Ziolkowski 1999, 16).

65. "Inimici consilia non sunt credenda subdola: ostendit ista fabula per seculorum secula." *Unibos* v. 216 (Klein 1991, 879; trans. Ziolkowski 1999, 37).

66. This theme has been extensively developed in recent scholarship on the poem: see, among others, Kuchenbuch 2016, 183–90; Ciocca 2012; Mosetti Casaretto 2000; 2002; Bertini 1995.

67. Baumann 1990; Flavian 1995; Bagnaudez 1974; Newhauser 2003, 111–12; see also Little 1971; Murray 1978, 77–80.

68. Paris, Bibliothéque nationale de France, MS Lat. 2077, fols. 165v, 170r. For discussion, see Bradley 2008, 223–31.

FIGURE 9.1. An eleventh-century carving from the church of Ennezat (dép. Puy-de-Dôme) of a usurer, wearing a purse, being apprehended; the inscription on the urn (a container for a hoard of treasure) below is MVNERA DIVES ("treasures [of] the rich man"). Devisme.alain, Wikipedia Commons.

Another book from England around the same time reinforces the routinisation of coin-based exchange, with a subtle hint at the power dynamics it could facilitate. When an illustrator came to decorate the pages of an Old English translation of the first six books of the Old Testament, he or she worked (relatively unusually for the period) directly from the text, making up the images as they went along rather than relying on a preexisting model. This lends the volume rare value as one artist's visualisation of biblical incidents using the resources and understanding of their own time and place.[69] It is therefore significant that when they came to the passage

69. Dodwell and Clemoes 1974, 65–73.

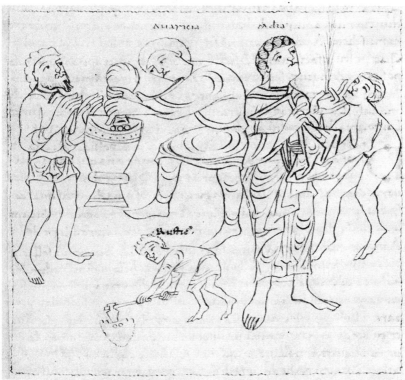

FIGURE 9.2. *Above*: fear of God, represented by a gift of a coin to a beggar; *below*, avarice represented by a person climbing on top of a *rusticus* to deposit coins in an urn, both in Paris, Bibliothéque nationale de France, MS Lat. 2077, fols. 165v and 170r (Moissac, 1040s). Bibliothèque nationale de France.

FIGURE 9.3. Sarai (*above*) and Joseph (*below*) being sold into servitude, with the detail of coin added by an eleventh-century illustrator: London, British Library, Cotton Claudius B.IV, fols. 22r and 55r. British Library.

about Abram and Sarai entering Egypt, and Abram being rewarded in return for Sarai being taken into the Pharaoh's palace (Genesis 12:14–16), they illustrated Abram being paid in coin (figure 9.3), a detail not in the text itself.[70] Again, when Joseph was sold to the eunuch Putiphar (Genesis

70. London, British Library, Cotton Claudius B.4 (Canterbury, s. xi[2/4]), f. 22r. The Vulgate text at this point enumerates the livestock given to Abram, but the Old English paraphrases with *fela sceatta* ("much wealth").

37:36), the transaction took place using coins.[71] Exchanging cash was a helpful way of visualising exchange, but it also speaks to a growing sense that this was a normal and expected way of doing business. And in the context of Genesis, all three illustrated scenes of coins changing hands relate to the unwilling and lamentable trade in human beings.[72] Joseph and Sarai sit mournfully as coins pass back and forth around them.

The panic over simony, and the renewed interest in coined money in other literary and artistic settings, are vivid witnesses to the moralised questions prompted by the monetary economy. Money had the potential to be used well and to do good if used to facilitate fair, equitable exchange, though more interest fell on its proclivity to incite greed and exacerbate differentials in wealth and status.[73] All this must of course be taken with a large pinch of salt as a portrayal of real levels of moral depravity: it is as reliable a guide to eleventh-century economics as *North and South* is to industrial relations in mid-Victorian northern England. Yet at the same time, a strong indirect case can be made for coinage becoming a more familiar part of day-to-day life: it is difficult to conceive of so many different authors and artists calling on the imagery of coined money had it not been commonplace in the society around them, which is just what the coin finds suggest was now the case. Bringing these two classes of material together emphasises the human dimension of coin circulation. To look at the finds in isolation is of necessity to focus on objects, with those who actually held and exchanged them a shadowy background presence. To look at texts is the opposite: we see aspects of the human cost of using coin, the focus falling on who used them and the personal consequences for them as individuals. What is missing is the structural background of why people actually used coins and with what wider social effects. To move in that direction, it is necessary to look first at other indexes of how coins were being used, as well as at who lay behind producing coins and injecting them into circulation.

Money, Markets, and Lands: Mechanisms of Monetisation

The basic uses of coin did not change in the late tenth and eleventh centuries. Coined money probably entered more often into all kinds of interactions. Its spread, however, was not even, either functionally, socially, or geographically,

71. Cotton Claudius B.4, f. 55r.

72. The third scene (Genesis 37:28, on f. 54r) does show a passage with a specific reference to coin in the text: Joseph's initial sale to two Midianite merchants.

73. Cf. Kaiser 1987; Gasper 2015.

and the enhanced distribution of money inclined toward contexts of dominance, as a range of figures sought to gain or strengthen their local superiority. At a basic level that meant accruing land, which was often done with cash in a quickening land market. Land purchases represent a special case in many respects. They are well evidenced because control of land represented one of the most fundamental and important bases of social power in any agrarian society. Possession of land amounted to control of the key means of production and brought power over what happened to it (including, often, those who lived on it and cultivated it).[74] Landed property therefore played a part in defining status, and whether it was handled according to market principles or social imperatives, or a mix of both, is difficult to determine.[75] What can be said is that, in a number of regions, sales of land multiplied from the late tenth century.[76] David Herlihy's pioneering research in the 1950s painted this picture in broad outline for France and Italy. He was able to show that sales swiftly and decisively overtook exchanges, and that a rising proportion of those sales were settled at least partially in money.[77] Subsequent work has emphasised the regional stories behind this broad trend, though tending in the same direction of travel. In Burgundy, in the lands around Cluny, sales began to make up a higher proportion of charters from about the 970s, at about the same time as the average price per unit of vineyards started to go up significantly.[78] Some regions of England also saw an increase in the proportion of sales from the later tenth century, and a wider range of people participated in the land market, including laymen with very local interests.[79] In Italy, the quantity of money paid for lands in and around Bergamo multiplied massively from the mid-tenth century to the mid-eleventh, after which it stabilised to a degree, at the same time as sales also came to account for a much larger share of records.[80] Prices for land also went up in the territory around Milan during the later tenth

74. Feller and Wickham 2005.

75. Feller, Gramain, and Weber 2005 argue for a high proportion of market-led sales; Wickham 1994, 257–74, and Rosenwein 1989 both emphasise social dimensions of sales.

76. For general comment, see Toubert 1997, 84–87.

77. Herlihy 1958, esp. 35; 1957, 14, though the latter is not a point drawn out in the main text, where Herlihy places the emphasis on the high proportion of charters paid partially in kind during the eleventh century—but the underlying data show that the number involving coin rose more consistently.

78. Bois 1992, 44–48; Rosenwein 1989, 69–74, 226–28. For similar conclusions about the Dauphiné, see Falque-Vert 2000.

79. Naismith 2016e, 35–39.

80. Jarnut 1979, 232–34.

century, and sales eclipsed exchanges as the most popular way to acquire property.[81]

Buying and selling across such wide areas had no one explanation. Sometimes it is apparent that purchases were a matter of consolidation: of a single, larger owner trying to bring together a bundle of nearby adjacent properties in a desirable location, with the purpose of more productive exploitation.[82] That in itself was nothing new: in 811, for example, Wulfred, archbishop of Canterbury, exchanged with his own cathedral community a property he had cobbled together from several sources, including the king and a former queen, "so that [the brethren] can more easily work and labour upon them as their own [property], since I have, as it were, united and surrounded them within the fences of a single boundary."[83] But by the late tenth century this might also be done by a layman on a very local level, such as one donor to Cluny in the 990s who had acquired nineteen distinct parcels of land in two adjacent *villae* (Merzé and Valanges), at least nine of which he expressly said had been bought (or "acquired," here probably meaning the same thing) from named "freemen" (*franchis hominibus*).[84] Accumulation of land in this way still, of course, had status connotations: rural property was the next step up for moneyed urban men in the lands around Milan, for example. But they and others, including some large and long-established landholders such as *pieve* (mother churches), also undertook consolidation and physical improvement, such as reducing forest and increasing cereal cultivation.[85]

In terms of exchange, the objective of this process was probably to capitalise on rural and especially urban markets, which developed in symbiosis with rural production. Regular and dependable markets for basic commodities like grain and bread were starting to reappear in cities for the first time since late antiquity.[86] Those markets needed supplies, and they came from the holdings of landowners and cultivators with their finger on the pulse of urban demand. The markets also reflect a rising and more diverse urban population, without gardens or ready-made social networks for obtaining basic sustenance in the city; in other words, they signal migration from rural areas, which might have been spurred by

81. Violante 1953, 99–127; more recently Norrie 2017, 119–20, 123–26.

82. Herlihy 1958, 33–34, with several examples.

83. "Ut facilius elaborare et desudare sua propria in illis potuissent quasi adunate unius termini intra septa conclusi." S 1264 (Brooks and Kelly 2013, no. 43).

84. Bruel 1876–1903, no. 2136. For discussion, see Bois 1992, 47.

85. Norrie 2017, 123–32, 137–38.

86. For Italy, see Norrie 2017, 175–76; Goodson 2021, 136–40.

consolidation and market orientation. Members of local cultivator families perhaps found themselves with fewer opportunities in their old home; they perhaps also had more paths open to them for contacts with towns and cities. Some lords might even have actively encouraged movement between town and country, as in England, where many urban tenements of Domesday Book were attached to specific rural holdings or "urban fields."[87] Peasants who sold all their land might become tenants, though this was not necessarily always so, and in any case they received a significant amount of money that could be used either to buy more land and repeat the cycle on a smaller scale or to engage with those same markets that their lords were filling. The desire to have more and better food or more diverse goods could be a strong one, and a signal of generally upbeat material conditions.[88] This could have been tied up with demographic expansion more broadly, which fed into urban growth as well as rural production. Population growth in a medieval context tended to reflect households starting from a position of relative confidence, potentially because there were increasingly viable prospects for children to relocate to cities or to newly cultivated land.[89]

Development along these lines was driven from above, if not always just by the high elite or by large church institutions. Setting up local dominance in land, and the social relations that went with land, was one strategy adopted by relatively smaller, more intensive landholders. Figures of this general level were a long-standing element of rural society, but while in the past they had effectively stood at the forefront of "peasant" society (in that they were not aristocrats, though they also did not work their own land), they now sought to distance themselves more thoroughly from their neighbours.[90] They did so partly on their own initiative, or as part of the entourage of bigger figures—often bishops in Italy, counts or their equivalents in France, and through royal service in England.[91] The hierarchical background is plain to see if one knows where to look. Conrad Leyser shrewdly noted that the famous observation by Ralph Glaber about France and Italy cladding themselves in a "white mantle of churches" (*candida ecclesiarum*), even though the old ones were fit for purpose, is a

87. Naismith 2018a, 172–73, and references cited there.

88. Dyer 2005, 126–72.

89. Herlihy 1973, 626–32; for a well-developed later parallel, see Langdon and Masschaele 2006 (though the authors argue that the intensity of population growth would have been low in relative terms until c. 1200).

90. Wickham 1988, 40–67.

91. Wickham 2014b; 2015c, 6–11; Campbell 2000, 201–25; Naismith 2020b, 660–62.

veiled signal that material resources were being mobilised and redirected with real force and purpose.[92] These were hardly *fins économiquement improductives*, as Robert López once wrote off church building.[93] Building campaigns created and sustained whole networks of trained craftsmen.[94] Someone had to pay for the building of all those churches, and it was as likely to be a lord or ecclesiastic stamping a collective religious identity onto the surrounding community (and onto their tithes and other renders) as the locals themselves.[95] Castles, and similar monumental buildings for lay lords, were an even more overt assertion of dominance that needed huge investments of labour and resources, almost certain to be amassed form the surrounding rural population under the direction of a militarily active elite implanting itself in the landscape.[96] Richer of Rheims, writing in the 990s, described how two spies sent to Mons arrived to find a construction site on the castle walls and under the guise of itinerant paupers had no trouble joining the work gang in return for a penny a day.[97] Proliferation of fortresses points in the same direction as the multiplication of churches, which is also the same direction as the quickening of land markets and the resurgence of urban and rural markets for other commodities. Commercialisation was closely bound up with lordship, as well as with agrarian production and demographic growth.[98]

Coined money fitted into the feedback loop of seigneurial pressure. Lords acquired and spent coin to get land, and urban dwellers or rural cash croppers who needed to use markets for basic necessities might in turn buy from agents of those lords. On several levels, the game was stacked in favour of those with the greatest measure of control over not only the means of production, but also the mechanisms of redistribution. One brake that limited the ramping up of this pressure was its restricted scale. Even in the later eleventh century there would still have been large areas where lordly intensification and its attendant effects had made little dent. We are still talking about islands of escalating seigneurial economy, denser in favourable

92. Leyser 1995, 199–200. For the quotation, see Ralph Glaber, *Historiae* 3.4 (ed. and trans. France 1989, 114–17). For more on this topic, see Fournier 1982; Gem 1988; Blair 2005, 368–425.

93. López 1952, 438.

94. Vroom 2010; 2015; Cardon 2021, 66–74.

95. The latter did also happen (Zeller et al. 2020, 97–98), though probably not on the same scale in the late tenth and eleventh centuries.

96. Creighton 2012, esp. 45. Cf. Bianchi and Collavini 2017, 199–200.

97. Richer of Rheims, *Historiae* 3.8 (ed. and trans. Lake 2011, 3:10–13).

98. Wickham 2016, 125–26; a point developed in Wickham 2021. See also Feller 2017a, 101–36.

conditions like the environs of towns. On the whole these islands were multiplying in number and growing in extent, but unreconstructed large estates, like the well-known Tidenham in southwestern England, survived alongside them,[99] as did stretches of less heavily burdened land, the inhabitants of which had the option of tapping profitably into the exchange circuits of their neighbours.[100] Escalating monetisation could also play out by other means. Records of renders from the lands of Essen in the early eleventh century show payments only in kind from lands around the nunnery, while another list from later in the century that concerns lands further afield apparently consisted only of money payments.[101] Corvey in the early eleventh century was apparently taking rents in kind, but tithes could be all in money, and potentially quite large: £8 for a series of ten places in the vicinity of Meppen, some 175 km to the northwest.[102]

Another brake was that, even in areas of more dynamic exploitation, the effects were targeted. Information on prices for commodities other than land is thin and often reflects exceptional situations like famine prices;[103] nonetheless, the increase of land prices was probably not proportionately followed for prices of grain and livestock.[104] Nor did money rents always rise: in many parts of southern France and Italy they remained fairly nominal across the eleventh century, and the emphasis fell on exactions in labour and in kind, which tended to be flashpoints of tension between lords and tenants.[105] On the lands of Rheims cathedral, for which both ninth- and eleventh-century surveys survive with details of how much income was expected, the level of monetised income had not changed consistently—some lands owed more money, some less, and most roughly the same.[106] In England, meanwhile, Domesday Book

99. Faith 1994.

100. For an insightful discussion of how this could work in a later period, see Masschaele 1997.

101. Esders 2017; 2021a. Cf. surveys showing an important money element in rents from lands of St. Emmeram both near to and far from the monastery: Kuchenbuch 1991, 206–8; Rädlinger-Prömper 1987.

102. Kuchenbuch 1991, 196–202. For Prüm, see Morimoto 2018 and chapter 3. In both cases it is possible that rents in kind were to be sold off from such distant estates.

103. Slavin 2010, 189–90, suggesting a degree of consistency in the high prices of wheat across several regions in the eleventh century. For further discussion of prices, see chapter 4.

104. Farmer 1988, 716–19; Sáez Sánchez 1946

105. See chapter 4.

106. Devroey 1984. Only a few properties are covered by both surveys. At Courtisols, a total of 92½ free *mansi* and 35 servile ones owed the equivalent of 1,903½d in c. 848, while in the early eleventh century 64 *mansi* (i.e., about half as much) owed the equivalent of

shows that in the two decades after the Norman Conquest, incomes from landed property had gone up overall, in some shires by over 20 or 30 per cent (which under the circumstances is hardly surprising), though it is not possible to isolate exactly how much of this represented increased money rent, and there are also many individual estates that rendered the same amount or even less.[107] Money rents were only one among many paths open to lords for raising cash from their lands: taking income in kind provided potential ammunition for the market; customary dues could be raised; and new tolls could be set up.[108] Elite income worked in layers and depended deeply on integration with (and profit from) others beneath them who travelled their roads and traded in their markets, or lived on their land with otherwise light burdens. Coin featured more heavily in these exactions as the eleventh century wore on. Its fungibility made it versatile; equally, its broad association with agency, promises, and pledges lent coins an air of respectability. It was one thing simply to rough up peasants and take their belongings, but another to demand that they pay a potentially exorbitant fee for a newly conceived toll or custom. Demanding and paying money helped legitimise the tightening of aristocratic screws on the European peasantry.

Coined money was flowing in larger quantities from the late tenth century onward; that much is clear. But it did not flow equally in all directions. Contexts linked to seigneurial exploitation show the strongest effects of the new injection of cash. This included a significant—probably a dominant—proportion of market activity: peasants with no or light burdens had less need for markets to acquire rent, though they might be in a position to piggyback on demand created and primarily driven by seigneurial economic cycles.[109] Other areas of coin use worked in much the same way as in earlier times, sometimes even with similar prices. There was a genuine risk in areas less touched by this seigneurial economy of being left behind by money: that richer neighbours or lords would ride roughshod over those without. Stratification of rural society, and in some areas erosion of peasant autonomy, was hence also tied in with the spread of coin.

1,728d. At Gerson, 10½ leased *mansi* plus one held in demesne included money renders of 126d, while 6 *mansi* at the same location in the early eleventh century owed 78d.

107. Welldon Finn 1971, 35. The best recent discussion of what Domesday values (traditionally a very contentious subject) actually consisted of is Harvey 2014, 161–209; her judicious conclusion is that the *ualet* represented the overall income due to the lord in money, kind, and customary dues, and from demesne exploitation as well as peasant rents.

108. For new tolls set up on roads and bridges in the tenth and eleventh centuries, see Fanchamps 1964, 207–10.

109. See chapter 4.

The Spread of the Penny

It has long been known that coinage on the western European model of silver pennies weighing between about one and two grams and issued explicitly in the name of the local ruler expanded significantly in the later tenth and eleventh centuries. Internal expansion will be considered later, but in this period the penny also extended far beyond its traditional heartland, to places from Dublin in the west to Scandinavia in the North, and Bohemia, Hungary, and Poland in the East (map 9.1). About a dozen distinct regions or states saw the beginning in this period of a substantive coinage, issued under the patronage of a local authority (usually a king), typically taking influential neighbouring coin issues as inspiration. English coinage served as a model in Dublin and the Scandinavian kingdoms, for example, and German and Byzantine coins in Poland; comparisons can also be drawn with the impact of Byzantine coins on the first issues from Kyiv.[110]

This was not the first time the uptake of coinage served as a proxy for increasing cultural and economic contact. England adopted gold coins in the seventh century based on Frankish inspiration, and a limited issue of silver pennies was made in Denmark in the eighth and ninth centuries, modelled on Carolingian precedents.[111] Nor were inscribed, regnal coinages in the tenth and eleventh centuries always the first ones made in these regions: in several cases they were prefigured by silver pennies made in more or less direct imitation of those from elsewhere, copying the most familiar and respected currencies of the day.[112] That implies close contact with foreign coins, mainly from England and Germany, which did indeed circulate widely and sometimes continued to do so alongside the new issues. The key change was the transformation of coinage into a broadly accepted cultural and political phenomenon, marked in most cases by meaningful inscriptions: a textualization of coinage. Minting of this kind represents just one element of a parcel of cultural and institutional changes that Robert Bartlett has described as "Europeanisation." Coinage can be set alongside adoption of Christianity or development of ecclesiastical infrastructure, and in some cases the establishment of towns.[113] Despite coinages of generally

---

110. For a survey of these early traditions, see Kluge 2007, 130–33, 158–63, 165–73.

111. The so-called Hedeby coinage, though probably not just the work of Hedeby: see chapter 5.

112. There is a large literature devoted to these imitative coinages, particularly from Scandinavia, the Irish Sea region, and Poland: for select literature, see Malmer 1989; 1997; Naismith 2017b, 315–22; Paszkiewicz 2006; Lukas 2020.

113. Bartlett 1993, 280–86; Williams 2007, 190–96, for Scandinavia.

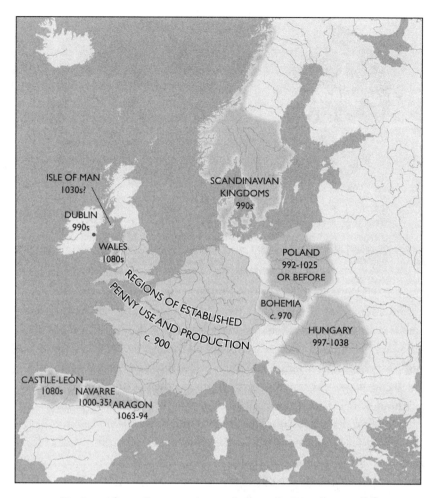

MAP 9.1. Regions where silver pennies on the western European model were adopted c. 950–1100, with the dates of the beginning of production.

similar form appearing widely, they also helped to define and circumscribe individual kingdoms or other units.[114] During their early stages, the new coinages therefore often had more symbolic and institutional than economic significance: those from Denmark and Norway took most of the eleventh century to become established over foreign coin and bullion, while those from Kyiv and the first Piast coinages from Poland proved to be short-lived. There were exceptions. Bohemia and Hungary both rapidly developed significant coinages over the eleventh century. At Dublin, only a minority of coins from early on in the new monetary regime carried literate and

114. Scales 2022, 17–18.

FIGURE 9.4. Silver penny, closely modelled on the English *Long Cross* type, of Sihtric Silkbeard, king of Dublin (989/95–1036), minted at Dublin in the 990s (diameter 20 mm). Classical Numismatic Group, LLC.

meaningful inscriptions: as the city-kingdom's currency became more established—which it quickly did, displacing English material within Dublin—it grew more visually distinct and less literate (figure 9.4).[115] The Dublin coinage's success is presumed to have been backed up by the authority of the local kings, who required that the coins be used for many or all coin-based exchanges in Dublin. This is the sticking point with many of the new coinages: there is little evidence for why they were made and how they circulated. Large issues probably fall closer to the Dublin coinage, mandated for transactions within the issuer's area of authority, or at least within designated places of exchange. Others might be made for distribution to favoured recipients (on either a large or small scale), with the expectation that those coins would then be passed on to secondary recipients on a similar basis, thereby increasing the cachet that attached to the new coins. Theoretically it was possible for a coinage to accomplish both these roles in different locations, reflecting two kinds of regal authority, as with the "cross" coinage from late tenth-century Denmark.[116]

It is worth emphasising that despite this expansion, there were still many important polities in northern and central Europe where no coins were struck. The penny was not universal; nor was its arrival always welcome. Coins started to be produced in Wales only late in the eleventh century in the context of English incursions, while no coins were made at all during this period in the whole of Alba/Scotland or in Ireland beyond Dublin. Minting did not become the default at this time. The popes in

115. Blackburn 2011, 91–117; Woods 2013; Naismith 2017b, 323–36.
116. Moesgaard 2015; cf. chapter 5.

Rome stopped issuing coin around 980, just when the city started to host coronations of Christian Ottonian emperors once again. To make coins on the literate penny model was a statement about ambitious, Christian kingship that often took a cue from England and Germany.

New and Old Mints c. 850–1100

Internal expansion is another matter, traceable in rather more depth and detail within the zone of western Europe where coin had been known since the Carolingian period or before. The coins themselves carry inscriptions naming a great many new mint-places, and in Germany there is also a slew of diplomas that grant minting rights, some for the first time, others restating an existing privilege. Table 9.1 presents the overall number of mint-places recorded in all areas. It shows that there was a small decline in the number of places issuing coin in the first half of the tenth century, relative to the late ninth (though this number is inflated by a burst of new mint-places in Charles the Bald's later years). There was, then, a huge expansion of minting from the late tenth century onward (see map 9.2), such that there were about twice as many places making coins around 1000 as there had been a century earlier. The monetary landscape of Europe had transformed.

The tally of mint-places given here is based on locations known to have issued coin, on any scale, within periods of fifty years. This mitigates the problem of "immobilised" coinages that recycled the same ruler's name like a broken record, for decades, sometimes centuries, after their death, and which can therefore be dated only to a broad period. It does not include places that received the written right to mint coins but are not represented by any surviving specimens. Some mint-places known only from texts could well have minted coinages of which no examples survive, or perhaps their coins are not distinguishable: a grant to Seltz Abbey, unusually, specifies that its coins should adopt the design of either Strasbourg or Speyer, because it sat at the meeting point of these two well-established areas of circulation. But mint-places known from texts include many that for whatever reason never made coins, and so they are not counted. Finally, this total also excludes coinages that cannot be assigned to a specific geographical location. Coin issues that can only be attributed to a region are therefore not factored in. This avoids the danger of counting as just one mint what might in fact be two or more that are simply not distinguishable. In this period, the issue primarily affects areas fairly new to regular coin production in northern and eastern Europe, where imitative coinages were made on a large scale. The upshot of all these reservations

Table 9.1. Total number of recorded mint-places in western Europe in fifty-year intervals, 850–1100

Period	Number of recorded mint-places
850–900	146
900–950	128
950–1000	226
1000–1050	310
1050–1100	336

is that, while the number of mint-places represented here is as confident as possible, it should be taken as a minimum: there would certainly have been more mint-places than are identifiable on these terms.

Other reservations also need to be highlighted, above all in relation to scale. Not all mint-places were equally active. Some operated for only a few years or months or less, either in a burst or on an intermittent basis. For areas with a tradition of fuller studies of individual mints, it is clear there was a world of difference in how much different mint-places might issue. In England, London is known from well over four thousand coins of the period between the early 970s and 1066, while estimates of productivity and its representation among finds suggest it was among the largest, busiest monetary centres in Europe.[117] Conversely, a thorough study of Watchet on the Somerset coast shows that it was a minute operation.[118] These variations reflect the fact that many kinds of places issued coins during the tenth and eleventh centuries. They cannot be measured with the same yardstick, and the temptation to tie them directly to the growing quantity of coin in circulation should be resisted. New mints did not in themselves mean more coin; sometimes in fact quite the opposite.[119] They were a result rather than a cause of increasing monetisation, reflecting more people wanting to make coins on their own terms and their own turf, and sent out a potent statement about the entanglement of economic processes with local structures of power. Additional mints also, in some areas, reflect a new dynamic at work, with more agency and patronage being exercised by new constituencies drawn from lower elites. These divergences are best assessed in relation to local conditions. The social and institutional place of minting will therefore be discussed with reference to specific areas.

117. Naismith 2013b.
118. Blackburn 1974.
119. See chapter 3.

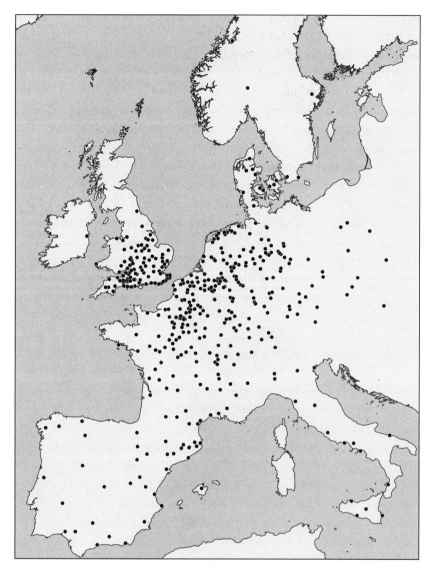

MAP 9.2. All mint-places known to have issued coin between 850 and 1100.

Italy

Italy offers the most extreme case of structural continuity in its mechanisms for producing coin. From Rome to the Alps, more or less the same small number of cities, usually half a dozen or fewer, produced coins from the ninth century until after 1100. These mints were strongly public in character:[120] all were situated in well-established centres of institutional

120. López 1953, 30; Matzke 2011b.

authority, and the coins they made from Carolingian times into the twelfth century generally carried the name of the king or emperor.[121] Relatively few changes upset this basic pattern. Rome, where small numbers of papal coins had been made since about the 770s, represents the main outlier in that it ceased operations in the later tenth century. Verona and Treviso issued coins in the earlier part of this period, and Venice minted coins sporadically too. Lucca, Milan, and Pavia were perennially important and had been so since Lombard times.

The equation of mints with cities in Italy seems so visceral that it might easily pass without comment. In this period, however, the public and urban dimensions of minting complemented one another. Partly that was a matter of inertia: all the mint-towns of this period had been important since at least the Carolingian period. Minting was also one of several administrative-cum-economic ways in which cities tied into the surrounding countryside. Elite interests remained strong in towns, benefiting from a system of extracting and redistributing resources that funnelled a large proportion of rural income through cities. Towns were not yet overwhelmingly dominant, but they were important nodes in the circulation of goods, money, and people engaged in diverse kinds of exchange. Markets in cities had a symbiotic relationship with the redistribution of goods in the orbit of large estates,[122] while fiscal *curtes* typically had their seat in a neighbouring town.[123] State-driven networks only constituted one component of urban relations with the countryside: monasteries located in and near towns supported significant networks of circulation organised along much the same lines, and they were supplemented by a groundswell of aristocratic and smaller secular landowners, mostly from a relatively small area (county- or diocese-scale in size) around each town.[124] That diversity proved important, for it enabled cities to persist as nodes in the regional economy of northern Italy even as the fiscal estates crumbled into smaller units in the eleventh century. If minting had depended on regnal infrastructure, something else kept it going healthily thereafter. The stability of the monetary system therefore belies tectonic shifts in the power structures behind it. Coin production probably came to depend on more localised and durable patterns of commodity distribution and social interaction, and less on large-scale

121. The best recent survey is Day, Matzke, and Saccocci 2016, 30–92.

122. Fiore 2020, 201–2.

123. Fiore 2020, 202–3. On fiscal *curtes* in Italy, see Bianchi, Cantini, and Collavini 2019; Bougard 2019.

124. On the limited scale and economic footprint of Italian aristocratic wealth at this time, see Stoffella 2014; Wickham 2014a, 420–21.

state action or long-distance exchange.[125] In social terms, the networks of demand and distribution that underpinned the production and circulation of coin remained stable in general form if not in configuration.

The point of intersection between all these interests was the moneyers: relatively high-status figures in mint-towns who held responsibility for production and exchange of coin. They did not normally put their names on coins, but their importance in Italy is well known from documentary sources and goes back to the Lombard period.[126] The best insight into how they worked in practice comes from the legal collection *Honorantie civitatis Papie*, dating to the early eleventh century but reflecting institutions in Pavia that went back to before 961.[127] Pavia's minting operation was substantial and, at least as portrayed in this normative text, closely integrated into the other organs of royal government. A *minister monete* was in charge of nine "noble and rich masters" (*magistri nobiles et divites*), who were expected to consult with their counterparts in Milan, where four similar *magistri* could be found.[128] These *magistri* are unlikely to have been the ones actually doing the hard labour of making coins: the *Honorantie* describes them more as overseers of an unspecified number of labouring moneyers. As well as actual minting, the masters of Milan and Pavia handled exchange between the two coinages at a cost of 1d per solidus. This presumably meant the two coinages were not supposed to mingle, and to a large extent they did remain distinct in circulation. In the context of the tenth and early eleventh centuries, when there was rough parity between the products of the main royal mints, restricting what kind of coins could be accepted was a matter of jurisdiction rather than material difference. As the eleventh century progressed, exchange between the coinages of different cities would have become more necessary from an economic point of view as they diverged in metallic quality,[129] while a document of 972 shows that special provision was already being made for Venetian coins, which were treated as worth only half as much as their Milanese equivalents.[130] Milanese coins were supposed to follow

---

125. Wickham 2014b; 2015c.

126. The classic study is López 1953.

127. Brühl and Violante 1983, 20–21. For context, see Majocchi 2010.

128. Four separate moneyers at Pavia can be identified in 899: Bullough 1966, 112 n. 121. *Magistri monete* from Pavia and Milan of Pavia are occasionally recorded in tenth-century documents: Porro-Lambertenghi 1873, nos. 502, 558, 847. One, named Hildebrand, is named in a miracle story in Nalgodus's *vita* of St. Maiolus, abbot of Cluny (d. 994), chap. 4 (*AASS* 11 May, col. 666D–E).

129. Day, Matzke, and Saccocci 2016, 36.

130. Porro-Lambertenghi 1873, no. 738.

the weight and quality as the Pavian coinage, at a rate of five-sixths fine, meaning approximately 83 per cent pure. That is about right for the time of Otto I, though the fineness of Pavian denari declined thereafter and was significantly lower by the time the *Honorantie* was put together.[131] It may be that this command was a dead letter, or more probably the intention was that only payments to the finance office needed to be in Pavian denari, not all coins used in any exchange.

The *Honorantie* treated the moneyers of Pavia and Milan very much as the king's men. They owed an annual rent of £12 to the king's finance office (*camera regis*) and £4 to the count of the palace, who was the leading official in the royal court. There are no points of reference in Italy for how heavy this toll might have been, but it is roughly comparable to the sums expected of moneyers in England according to Domesday Book.[132] It certainly represents a significant sum, but its severity depends on how productive the mint-place was. Finally, in addition to rent, on taking up their position the moneyers owed an entry fee to the finance office of three ounces of gold, which was no small outgoing, and suggests the role they played both in metalworking and in royal administration. Their position had a public dimension to it, which could be passed on from generation to generation, and led to them appearing with relative frequency as witnesses to charters. Behind this lay considerable wealth. Moneyers, alongside merchants and artisans, formed an upper stratum of town-dwellers whose interests tended to be focused within the city walls.[133] Some, either through good fortune or by attaching themselves to the orbit of more powerful patrons, went further by buying land outside the city.[134] A very few hit the big time and established themselves among the urban elite. The Rozo family of moneyers, who included several masters of Milan's mint, were rich enough to patronise the foundation of a church, S. Trinità, near the mint and marketplace in 1030, while other members of the family rubbed shoulders with the sons of the military aristocracy at S. Maria Maggiore.[135]

131. Brambilla 1883; Rovelli 1995; Day, Matzke, and Saccocci 2016, 725–26.

132. Cf. £7 paid annually by the seven moneyers at Chester in 1066 (GDB 262b), or £20 for minting at Gloucester in 1086 (GDB 162a).

133. Norrie 2017, 157; Violante 1953, 70–73; López 1953.

134. López 1953, esp. 25–31; Violante 1953, 41–49; Menant 1993, 655 (though this happened somewhat later in his case study); Balzaretti 2019, 325–30, 520–55. Cf. Wickham 1998, 128–29, on how common it was for rich city-dwellers to buy land in the countryside, albeit with different consequences at different times.

135. Norrie 2017, 75. López 1953, 35–36, identified other moneyers of similarly high standing in Milan and Pavia during the ninth century (cf. Castagnetti 2017, 385–86; Violante 1953, 51–61).

These wider aspects of a moneyer's role were important in creating and sustaining business. That is one of the black holes in the Italian evidence: very little is known about why people actually minted coins at all, and, when they did, how they interfaced with the relatively centralised minting apparatus. We mostly see Italian moneyers surface in the bare-bones context of documents as they witness or participate in land transactions. But there are more than enough indications that they were not simply hardy workmen who kept their nose to the grindstone, under the watchful eye of the mint master, until they had saved enough cash to enter the property market. Even to enter into land transactions, or witness other people's transactions, implied embeddedness in social networks: these often and easily combined with commerce, the one furthering the other.[136] An example comes from a document written in Milan in July 1035. It recounts how Landulf, abbot of S. Ambrogio, had stepped up at what must have been a fairly packed meeting in the house of a merchant named Peter and read out the will of one Peter the moneyer (possibly the same as the merchant who hosted the meeting), who had pledged a series of properties in the countryside around the city to the monks of S. Ambrogio, and while he lived promised an annual rent from those lands of 3s in cash. The whole exercise was a piece of theatre intended to confirm that bequest: Peter the moneyer himself spoke up to agree with its contents, along with a slew of his relatives who were present. Among the latter were his brother Nazarius and a nephew by the same name.[137] It is likely that one of these was the moneyer Nazarius who would, two decades later, be one of the ringleaders of the Pataria:[138] a popular religious movement that united laymen and clerics against perceived abuses in the Church hierarchy.[139] Here is a family of moneyers with bonds that went in several directions: to neighbours within the city, to an abbot and his monastery, and to rural properties (and, doubtless, neighbours, tenants, and potentially landlords who abutted or dwelt on those properties), and later to urban populist factions. The point is that these sorts of connections were precisely how coins would have been made and put into circulation. Minting coins for partners in and around the urban community was one way moneyers could both build and exploit trust and connections, be they with individuals,

136. Wickham 1998, 124–25, 128–29, with examples from a slightly later period in the environs of Lucca.

137. Manaresi 1955–60, no. 339.

138. Andrea di Strumi, *Vita sancti Arialdi*, c. 6 (Baethgen 1934, 1053).

139. The literature on this movement is huge, but on the contribution of laymen like Nazarius, see Violante 1968.

families, ecclesiastical institutions, or others. The benefits of this process cut both ways: mints were few, and it would have been in the interests of patrons to build up ties with a moneyer; while the moneyers gained by attracting a larger share of the coins that were minted or exchanged, as well as cushioning their standing within local society.

Pavia and Milan, along with Lucca, were the most active and best-known mint-towns of Italy. Of the others, Rome was distinctive in that its money-ers, who had issued coins for the popes since the 770s, finally gave up the ghost and ceased producing the so-called *antiquiores* in the later tenth century.[140] No more coins would be made in Rome for about two hundred years. The papal moneyers had since the ninth century been curiously limited in their output, and analysis of the metal in surviving specimens suggests that Rome formed a self-contained and self-sustaining pocket, within which silver was recycled again and again according to long-running local standards.[141] Local silver coin must have occupied a small and specific niche, separate from the large offerings of precious metal that continued to flow into the city.[142] Few specimens of papal coinage have been discovered outside the environs of Rome. One possibility, inevitably equivocal given the paucity of evidence, is that they catered primarily to transactions in and around Rome that involved monetary returns from rural property: the many small rents on ecclesiastical lands lent in emphy-teusis, or the profits from those that remained in more direct control of the popes and their subordinates.[143] Even while the local moneyers still made coins, it may have been that the inhabitants of Lazio supplemented the meagre Roman offerings with currency from elsewhere, sometimes far away (English pennies in the tenth century, French as well as north Italian ones in the eleventh) and with other commodities.[144] This could be why "moneyers" continued to attest charters in Rome after coins ceased to be made: there was still enough demand for exchange to keep them busy.[145]

Of the other mint-places, Verona at times fulfilled a similar role to Lucca, Milan, and Pavia in minting royal and imperial coinage, while

---

140. The last coins, in the name of an Emperor Otto (either I or II) and a Pope Benedict (V, VI, or VII), cannot be dated exactly within this period: Grierson and Blackburn 1986, 265.

141. Naismith, Northover, and Tinti 2015.

142. Naismith, Northover, and Tinti 2015, 200–202.

143. Wickham 2000.

144. Wickham 2015a, 173–76, argues that silver and gold in the form of ingots played a significant role.

145. Ferri 1904, 177; 175 n. 201 collects references to *cambiatores* at Rome in the early eleventh century.

Venice capitalised on its anomalous position, formally outside the jurisdiction of the Carolingian Empire and subsequently the kingdom of Italy but economically tapping into their markets.[146] Two kings of Italy in the early tenth century even confirmed the right of the dukes of Venice to strike coins.[147] It was on this basis that Venice continued to produce coins during much of the tenth and eleventh centuries that fitted in with those of the mainland mint-towns in weight and general appearance, and indeed the *Honorantie civitatis Papie* stipulated that Venetian coins should be the same as those of Pavia in terms of fineness and weight.[148] Despite this injunction, Venice seems to have continued its ninth-century practice of undercutting the coins of other northern Italian mint-towns by issuing silver pieces of significantly lower fineness, and later smaller size.[149] Little is known about the organisation of Venice's mint at this time. A piece of public land where minting had long taken place was sold in 1112, in the parish of S. Bartolomeo along the Canal della Fava. This was, at least in later times, a vibrant commercial district.[150]

Finally, several bishops in northern Italy were given the right to mint coins at this time. Most, including those of Mantua (894 and 997), Ravenna (999), Treviso (905), Ascoli (1033), Padua (1049), and Arezzo (1052), apparently did not exercise that authority.[151] The exception is the patriarch of Aquileia. A diploma granting the right to mint was issued in 1028,[152] resulting in a small issue of coins. These resemble contemporary German coinage and seem mainly to have circulated north of the Alps.[153] Indeed, the principle of issuing episcopal minting rights was to a large extent a German import that failed to catch on.

Italy between Rome and the Alps saw the least change in its minting institutions of any of the regions considered here. Production of coinage remained strongly linked to royal (or, in Rome, papal) authority. Most coins continued to cite the name of the king or emperor, and where there is information about the local organisation of minting, it normally continued to depend on offices and office-holders operating in the name of

146. Ruggini 1992; Berto 2021.

147. Papadopoli 1893–1919, 1:303–7.

148. Brühl and Violante 1983, 18–19.

149. Sarah et al. 2008; Saccocci 1991; 2009. Stahl 2000, 7, notes that Venetian coins in the eleventh century were referred to as *parvi* or *minuti*.

150. Stahl 2000, 8.

151. Schiaparelli 1903, no. 134; MGH DD OIII 255; MGH DD OIII 330; Schiaparelli 1903, no. 52; MGH DD CII 203; MGH DD HIII 234; Day, Matzke, and Saccocci 2016, 20.

152. MGH DD CII 131.

153. Day, Matzke, and Saccocci 2016, 566.

the king. Even in the late eleventh century, as the kingdom collapsed and its institutions withered, this background provided a shared point of reference to adapt or react against.[154] What drove actual minting remains fuzzy.[155] Historically, payments to the royal fisc in denarii could have exerted a significant gravitational pull, though these must have become attenuated in the eleventh century, and quite probably long before. A more persuasive context can be seen in the increasing marketisation and monetisation of urban-rural relations, and the involvement of moneyers in the medium- to high-status networks that drove this process. While the result was a general increase in the scale and use of coin, it would have been patchy both geographically and socially, focused on particular circuits of power and exchange in the orbit of towns (and some towns much more than others). Crucially, this new monetisation derived more from interactions within localised economic systems, and less from long-distance exchange, which seemingly played a larger part in Italy's monetary system in the Carolingian era.

West Francia

In sharp contrast to Italy, West Francia had a profusion of mint-places.[156] They were most numerous in the wealthy and highly contested lands between Flanders and Paris, while in Aquitaine, Brittany, and Normandy they were noticeably thinner on the ground. Some had been active for centuries, but a significant number in Neustria were new establishments, set up during Charles the Bald's very large *Gratia Dei rex* coinage of 864 and after. Their distribution therefore did not originate with, or exactly follow, the boundaries of major power units of the tenth and eleventh centuries, which in West Francia tended to be structured around people and strongpoints rather than hard borders.[157]

The West Frankish network of mints and coin use reflects a pattern that will be seen in several other parts of contemporary Europe of increasing decentralisation and local initiative. Consolidating regional powers harnessed the symbolism, social influence, and economic potential of

---

154. Wickham 2014b, 34–35.

155. Saccocci 2005, 1045, argues that fiscal expenses on military campaigns drove minting in northern Italy by the tenth- and eleventh-century emperors.

156. "West Francia" is here meant as a cultural and geographical approximation. There was only limited political coherence to this area across the whole period 900–1100, and parts of it fell in the Reich, or belonged to the kingdoms of Arles or Burgundy.

157. Mazel 2018.

minting, initially within a royal framework. The main variables in this process were how regional elites actually articulated themselves through coined money—as in, where they made coins, why and through whom—and how they related to other power structures, from the king down to local aristocrats. West Frankish history in this period was formerly seen as a contest between kings and regional aristocrats, the latter's desire to shake off the former being taken as axiomatic, as was the principle that aristocratic gains meant royal losses.[158] More recent scholarship does not foreground centralised authority and its strength or weakness to the same extent, and makes a virtue out of the complex levels and types of relationship that emerged as central authority became more negotiable, especially as these played out on a regional level.[159]

There are good grounds to look at the coinage through this lens too, and to break down the now rather archaic terminological divisions that still define it based on who is named as the issuing authority: royal issues citing the current king; "feudal" issues in the name of a regional magnate; and "immobilised" issues that retain the same design and inscription naming a former king long after they had ceased to be current.[160] Together, these have traditionally been deployed to tell a sorry tale of royal coinage losing out to "feudal" or "immobilised" issues.[161] And in starkly numerical terms of how many places made coins in the name of the current king, it is an effective barometer: coins in the name of Charles the Bald were made at over a hundred locations in the later ninth century, with virtually none acknowledging other authorities, whereas Lothar (954–86) was named at only about fifteen, and his son Louis V (986–87) at two.[162] Historians' and numismatists' interest has traditionally been drawn more to the first coinages of other magnates, including the abbots of Corbie in the late ninth century, and secular magnates in several parts of the kingdom from about 900, though "feudal" coinages remained unusual until late in the tenth century.[163] The immobilised coinages have largely been left to one side.[164]

Dividing the coinage up in this way conceals at least as much as it highlights.[165] Minting became a way of negotiating authority in ways that were

158. The richest, and still most valuable, study to take this approach is Dhondt 1948.
159. Summarised in Hallam and West 2020, esp. 33–35, with references there cited.
160. A total of seven kings, some dead over a century, were being named on coins in various parts of France by 987: Dumas 1992, 173.
161. Lafaurie 1970; Dumas 1973.
162. Grierson and Blackburn 1986, 246–47
163. Grierson and Blackburn 1986, 246.
164. For general guidance, see Bompaire and Dumas 2000, 104–9.
165. The major catalogues of medieval French coinage are based on this approach: Poey

FIGURE 9.5. Silver denarius of Hugh Capet as king (987–96) with Hervé, bishop of Beauvais (987–97) (diameter 23 mm). Classical Numismatic Group, LLC.

fluid, deliberate, and nuanced. Individual issues resist easy classification: Should the coins of Hugh Capet as king, minted in conjunction with Hervé, bishop of Beauvais (987–97), be viewed as royal or "feudal," for example (figure 9.5)? Or those of Louis V, minted in his name at Saintes and Bordeaux but a long way outside his effective jurisdiction? Nor did mints and their masters necessarily remain locked onto one side of a "royal" or a "feudal" cleavage. It was commonplace for mint-places that produced coinages in the name of a count or other magnate to switch back to naming the king at a later point. In Normandy during the 930s and 940s, the coin issues in the name of the counts of Rouen and King Louis IV (936–54) form part of a larger, sometimes violent dialogue: recognition on the coinage was not about embracing or getting rid of the king completely, but rather a way for the counts to show their desire to deal with him from a position of strength.[166]

Crucially, what one did *not* put on coinage could be just as meaningful as what one did, as in the case of the numerous immobilised coinages. Instead of an intractable oddity, they represent a political balancing act. The king's name acted as a sort of guarantee: as one charter of Charles the Simple for the bishop of Tournus put it in 915, the city's moneyers should "stamp the sign of our name and title on all coins, so that there be no debasement of the metal."[167] Even when the current king was not a substan-

---

d'Avant 1858–62; Caron 1875–82; Duplessy 2005. It has fortunately been abandoned in the most recent treatment survey of tenth- and eleventh-century West Frankish coinage: Foucray 2018a.

166. Bruand 2018a, 317–18; 2018b.

167. "Nostri nominis signum singulis imprimant nummis, ne metallorum mixtura adesse valeat." Lauer 1940–1949, no. 82.

tive player in a given region, he might still be invoked on coins when his status suited local needs.[168] Which king's name would be used depended on individual circumstances. Limoges continued to make coins in the name of Odo (888–98), who was by the early eleventh century believed to have been raised to the kingship there, and to have ordered his name placed on the city's coinage instead of his predecessor's.[169] Melle stuck with "King Charles" all the way down to the end of the eleventh century. Recent metallurgical analysis has succeeded in assigning most of these issues to the right Charles (Charlemagne, Charles the Bald, and Charles the Simple). Charles the Bald was probably responsible for "Charles" getting fossilised as the signature of Melle's coinage, as it was during his reign that it became established as the dominant regional coinage of northern Aquitaine.[170] On that basis Melle itself rose in profile, being home to a rich collection of inscribed epitaphs and the centre of its own *pagus* after about 925 (even though by this time the mines' silver output was waning).[171] Such was Melle's dominance of coinage in the county of Poitou that even the mint name was "immobilised": although the coins continued to carry the mint name METALO, later specimens probably come from a number of places in the vicinity, including Poitiers, Niort, and Saint-Jean-d'Angély.[172] At Auxerre, the principle behind immobilised coinage was taken to its logical conclusion in the tenth century with coins that removed any written reference to the ruler behind the coinage, instead leaving a sinister-looking blank space (figure 9.6).[173] Others, including a slew of mint-places in the region of Blois and Chartres, avoided stating their allegiance by switching to an iconographic design of a bust, which could be understood as a generic visual evocation of authority, with a certain amount of latitude over whether it was meant to represent the king, the count, or someone else.[174]

The superficial diversity of West Frankish coinage overlies a sharp concern with authority: those responsible for the coinage paid close attention to the message they were projecting. It is likely that there was rather less variation in the actual running of the coinages than their outward appearance would suggest. Management of minting in West Francia was in some

168. For an example in Catalonia, see Jarrett 2010.

169. Adhemar of Chabannes, *Chronicon* 3.20 (Chavanon 1897, 139).

170. Bruand 2018a, 319–27.

171. Clairand 2009; La Coste-Messelière 1950; Téreygeol 2018; Treffort 2020, 110–28.

172. Grierson and Blackburn 1986, 238.

173. Dumas-Dubourg 1971, 169–73, with Lafaurie 1952, 136, who note that this type was adopted at several other mint-places in the late tenth and early eleventh centuries.

174. Dumas-Dubourg 1971, 196–210.

FIGURE 9.6. Silver denarius minted at Auxerre in the tenth century (diameter 21 mm). Classical Numismatic Group, LLC.

ways not dissimilar to that in contemporary Italy. The majority of mint-places were in well-established towns where coinage had been produced since at least the ninth century. New additions tended to be at sites where the power of the comital elite was concentrated. As discussed in the previous chapter, this process can be traced back to the late ninth century.[175] Brioude (dép. Haute-Loire) was one of the first of these new mints to produce coins in the name the local magnate, from the time of William I (d. 918) or William II (918–26), successive dukes of Aquitaine.[176] Brioude stands out as the only mint-place among several in the extensive lands of both Williams where coins were issued in the name of the dukes, and also as the only new mint of the period (figure 9.7). A *vicus* at the centre of its local *pagus*,[177] Brioude was distinguished by the presence of the important basilica of Saint-Julien, over which William I and II presided as lay abbot, with control (sometimes rising to aggressive exploitation) over its resources.[178] It offered both material advantages and moral prestige that

175. See chapter 8.

176. On the strength of metallurgical and metrological evidence, Geneviève and Sarah 2013 propose that the coinage began under William I (in contrast to earlier scholarship that favoured William II). See also Bruand 2018a, 314–15. The coinage continued to be struck until about 1000, effectively "immobilised" and static in appearance across this time. Interestingly, the title used on the coins was fixed as COMES, while charters of the period apply additional and more expansive styles to successive members of the dynasty (e.g.. *comes, marchio et dux* from 898: Doniol 1863, no. 309; cf. Brunner 1973, 230–35). This could reflect recognition that minting was always a notionally comital power, tied to whoever held the county.

177. Poble 2015, 76, 78.

178. Lauranson-Rosaz 1987; Fontanon 2010; Cubizolles 1980, 100–102; Bouchard 1988, 425–26. For William II's misappropriation of the abbey's resources, see Doniol 1863, no. 66.

FIGURE 9.7. Silver denarius of "Count William" (William of
Aquitaine [d. 918] or one of his heirs in the tenth century)
minted at Brioude (diameter 21 mm). Private collection.

elevated William over his nearby rivals.[179] This office, and with it perhaps the (immobilised) coinage that continued through the tenth century,
afterward came into the hands of the viscounts of Brioude.[180] At Senlis,
reference to an unlocated BERNDO/BERNCO CAS[t]ELLO in or near the
town replaced the name of the king on the obverse of its tenth-century
coins.[181] The Le Puy hoard of the early eleventh century includes coins of
Crépy-en-Valois (as a *castrum*): a castle and attached settlement established by the counts of the Vexin in the tenth century on a strategic road
between Champagne, Flanders, and the Ile-de-France.[182] In 911 a diploma
of Charles the Simple gave the bishop of Cambrai permission to establish a fortress, supported by a market and mint, at Lisdorf in Lorraine.[183]
The same bishop had a similar arrangement at Lambres, where he was
given jurisdiction over all royal perquisites, including a mint.[184] No coins
survive from either Lisdorf or Lambres, and there may never have been
any. An alternative possibility is that some coins with the mint name of
Cambrai actually stem from these locations; that seems to have been the
arrangement when, at the beginning of the eleventh century, the developing *burgus* of Beaulieu was given the right to make coins for Count Fulk
Nerra (987–1040) in the name of the nearby castle at Loches.[185]

179. Lauranson-Rosaz 1987, 67.
180. Lauranson-Rosaz 1987, 125–28.
181. Dumas-Dubourg 1971, 138–39.
182. Lafaurie 1952, 126–27; Mesqui 1994.
183. Lauer 1940–49, no. 67. Cf. Fray 2006, 345–47.
184. Lauer 1940–49, no. 128.
185. Hauréau et al. 1715–1865 14, Instrumenta no. 44. For discussion, see Bachrach
1993, 129–30.

There was no one-size-fits-all model for the mint-places of West Francia. Some new centres were named explicitly, but there is a distinct likelihood that the established centres like Cambrai or Melle lent their name to other, smaller operations that were under the jurisdiction of the same ruler. Just as in the ninth century, the mint name on coins was in a sense a statement of authority in the same way as references to the king: it was shorthand for "whoever holds the mint of," rather than a reference to the place as such.

The charters mentioned earlier are representative of the tenth-century written material on minting in West Francia, which consists predominantly of grants of minting rights to bishops.[186] Frequently that right is framed as part of the *comitatus*, or set of powers and revenues pertaining to the office of count, including market, toll, mint, and other resources,[187] which were all transferred to the bishop: thus at Arles and Le Puy in 920 and 924, respectively, the right of minting was one of "all the things which in that place [the *burgus* alongside the church] are seen to have previously pertained to the lordship and power of the count, including the market, the toll, the mint and all jurisdiction (*districtum*), with the land and habitations of that *burgus*,"[188] while the chronicler Flodoard stated that in 940 Louis IV gave Archbishop Artald (931–40 and 946–61) a charter for "the mint of the city of Rheims . . . and conferred the whole county (*comitatum*) of Rheims on the same church."[189] The transfer of responsibility for minting from count to bishop was not necessarily reflected on the coins, which could continue to name the current king or become immobilised.[190]

Since bishops (and, occasionally, abbots) were thought of as inheriting the functions of counts, the presumption is that minting and coinage otherwise remained within the purview of counts. One starting point for what this meant in practice is the slightly clearer situation in the earlier part of the ninth century, when counts had been entitled to a third of the

186. Prou 1896, liv–lxxxi; Kaiser 1976, 299–307.

187. Kaiser 1976, 290–305 ; West 2013, 20–22, 142–45. By the tenth century *comitatus* was also coming to have a complementary territorial meaning (West 2013, 143–45; Mazel 2018; Panfili 2018).

188. Grat et al. 1978, no. 59; Bautier and Dufour 1978, no. 4.

189. Flodoard, *Annales*, s.a. 940 (Lauer 1905, 75). For context, see Kaiser 1976, 306–7. This grant has been the cause of much debate. Bur (1991, 178) claimed that the comital rights (if not the right to coinage) were interpolations from after the time of Richer of Reims, who makes no mention of them. This interpretation has been challenged (Sassier 1980, xii), but there is reason to believe that the archbishops had wider privileges, including over the coinage, in the decades before 940 (Guyotjeannin 1987, 49; Christophe 2016).

190. E.g., Dumas-Dubourg 1971, 174–75 (Langres), 259–61 (Le Puy)—but see in contrast Arles (275–76).

income that derived from minting and associated activities, the rest being passed on to the king. The counts in return were supposed to watch over the moneyers who produced the coinage, and thereby maintain quality.[191] Another point of departure is to work backward from the concessions that conferred on churches what had, supposedly, been comital prerogatives. Most are plain in formulation, albeit with no obvious sign that profits were still being shared with the king. Some documents imply that when profits were shared, the count was now in the position the king had once been of receiving two-thirds of the revenue. Shares in minting revenue could be given en bloc to churches, or shared among a number of subordinates.[192] The latter possibility is suggested by a grant of minting rights at Châteauneuf to the abbey of St. Martin at Tours in 919, which stipulates that "no minister of the monks from that house may receive a *monetaticum* from the monks' silver."[193] An alternative approach is to turn to the eleventh century, which offers much richer pickings. The emphasis by this point falls on the count or ecclesiastical magnate as master of their coinage, in the same way that the king had been in the ninth. Évrard, abbot of Corbie (1079–85), laid down an agreement with his two moneyers that stipulated the quality of coins they should make and bound the moneyers to weekly checks on their work.[194] At Dinant around 1061, a charter stated bluntly that everything relating to the mint and its coinage belonged to the count: any infringement fell under his jurisdiction, and "when he wants [the coinage] will remain stable; when he wants it will be changed," meaning debased.[195] Counts also freely disposed of and divided the revenues of mints. The count of the Auvergne bestowed the mint of Clermont on the local cathedral in 1044.[196] A string of grants from Cluny record how the dukes of Aquitaine bestowed the mints of Saint-Jean-d'Angély and Niort on the monastery in about 1020 and 1031; a slightly later confirmation (dated c. 1070) implies that this was really a grant of revenues, since the duke also affirmed that the mints would continue to follow the same standards as the coinage of Poitiers, and that any debasement undertaken in response to what happened at Poitiers would be administered without

191. McKitterick 1983, 87–88; Lafaurie 1980.

192. This seems to have been the thinking in tenth-century Catalonia: Jarrett 2010, 224–25. For a 10 per cent share in the income from the mint of Angers, granted to the monastery of Saint-Laud in the period c. 1047–60, see Planchenault 1903, no. 25.

193. Lauer 1940–49, no. 101.

194. Bompaire et al. 1998, 314.

195. "Quamdiu voluerit stabit; quamdiu voluerit mutabitur." Rousseau 1936, 89.

196. Grélois 2002, no. 1.

any profit being taken—a provision highly suggestive of the motives that usually prompted debasement.[197]

So far, the view of coined money and its making has been top-down. Organisation within these mints is much more obscure. As in Italy, there was a strong element of continuity from the ninth century. Moneyers— *monetarii* or, when their exchange role was being emphasised, *trapezitae*— performed the actual work of making and changing coin. They would normally work together in one building. At Abbeville in the eleventh or early twelfth century, three moneyers collaborated closely on alloying and minting coins, and it was precisely this close-knit setup that posed a problem when one adulterated the silver but the culprit could not be identified.[198] At least some larger mint-towns had an official designated as in charge of the mint and its moneyers.[199] Strasbourg at the beginning of the twelfth century had a *magister monetariorum*,[200] and at Barcelona in the 990s a figure referred to as the *custos monetae* probably fulfilled a similar role. The *custos* had responsibility for identifying, and tracing the origin of, forged money and is known only because of a jurisdictional quandary that arose from one of his investigations. A moneyer named Guiscafred turned out to be behind the false coins, but the *custos*, who worked for the count, could not bring Guiscafred to justice because he was the bishop's man.[201] This fascinating case is full of interest. The count was concerned to see justice done in relation to his coinage, and an official existed to do so. There may have been individuals with similar responsibilities elsewhere: an inscription from Rouen cathedral commemorates Radulfus, an official of the town (*publicus urbis*) who had been a foe of thieves and false money (*fures et falsa moneta*) until he was killed by some of said thieves.[202] But the Barcelona *custos* probably was not directly responsible for oversight of mint personnel—if he had been the case is unlikely to have unfolded the way it did—and the status of the count's moneyer as part of the episcopal *familia* implies a looser organisation for the mint personnel than is apparent elsewhere. At Strasbourg *only* members of the bishop's *familia* could become moneyers, while when Geoffrey, count of Angoulême (1032–48), reestablished the mint at Saintes,

197. Bernard and Bruel 1876–1903, nos. 2737 (grant of Saint-Jean-d'Angély), 2855 (grant of Niort), and 3432 (confirmation).

198. *Miracula patrata Abbavillae*, c. 5 (*AASS* 3 Mar, 164).

199. On the location of the mint-building in Pavia, see Bullough 1966, 111; for Milan Norrie 2017, 135; for Strasbourg Naismith 2016c, 57; for Saintes, Grasilier 1871, no. 1. In all three cases it was in a prominent spot, close to a major route or market.

200. Naismith 2016c, 59.

201. Jarrett 2010, 241–42.

202. Undiemi 2014, no. FR21, dated to the late eleventh or early twelfth century.

he did so by bringing in *monetarii* or *trapezitae* from Angoulême and then had them all swear an oath of obedience to the new nunnery, its patron saint, and its abbess, who would be the future masters of the mint.[203] How tightly the moneyers were kept in line evidently varied, but what is equally interesting is that the moneyers themselves generally have precious little identity of their own. When they are mentioned, it is in their capacity as servitors of higher powers, or as very local actors in the same category as craftsmen and peasants.[204] There were a few with greater pretensions, like some moneyers in Normandy who managed to channel their position into rapid advancement; one started out as son of the duke's cook but ended by selling a parcel of land for the large sum of £25, while another, Ranulf, became the progenitor of an important aristocratic lineage.[205] One moneyer at Morlaàs secured from Centule V, viscount of Béarn (1058–90), the office of die engraver for himself and his heirs, though he was able to keep it only after undertaking an ordeal by hot iron and paying a hefty fee to Centule's son, who challenged the grant.[206] But such figures were exceptional. This is a sharp contrast to contemporary Italy and England, where moneyers had a long and still vibrant tradition of being fully engaged members of landholding society and were frequently of higher standing.

Moneyers also sometimes appear on the scene in arrangements made with the aristocratic masters of mints. This could be a contentious process, as the moneyer of Morlaàs discovered, and still more so for those who made counterfeit coins. Fear of forgery features prominently in much writing about coined money, but actual cases are few and far between. At Barcelona in the 1060s and 1070s, two couples were caught and punished for counterfeiting: one pair (who had infringed on the count's gold coins) were probably of fairly high standing, as they gave up to the count a substantial property at the castle of Montfálco Gros, some

203. Grasilier 1871, no. 77.

204. At Vendôme in the 1070s, moneyers witnessed charters alongside monks, *famuli*, bakers, tailors, and peasants (Métais 1893–1904, nos. 239, 246), while another moneyer of Vendôme became embroiled in legal wrangles after selling a mill to Agnes of Burgundy, countess of Anjou, who subsequently divorced the count (no. 177). For donations by a moneyer and his wife of vineyards immediately outside Mâcon in the mid-eleventh century, see Ragut 1864, nos. 448, 450. At Rouen in the mid-eleventh century, a moneyer who was son of the count's cook sold land in the town to an abbot: Deville 1841, no. 60. An enigmatic inscription of the tenth or early eleventh century from Tournus probably records a moneyer named Gerlannus who worked under the abbot of Cluny: Favreau, Michaud, and Mora 1997, no. 84. Another moneyer is commemorated by an eleventh-century inscription at Saint-Hilaire in Poitiers: Favreau, Michaud, and Labande 1974, no. 62.

205. Musset 1959, 291–94.

206. Cadier 1884, no. 19.

70 km northwest of the city; the other couple were said to be *humiliores*, though they owned a considerable urban property in Barcelona itself that they were forced to forfeit for their crime.[207] Other moneyers who kept to the straight and narrow sometimes got a better outcome. Slightly earlier at Barcelona, in the 1050s and 1060s, the count ceded control over the mint for a defined period to consortia of two or three moneyers.[208] In the earliest of these agreements, dating to March 1056, the two lessors agreed to a specified rate of seigniorage (and a reduced one for the count and countess's own silver); strikingly, their annual rent for the mint took the form of five measures of wheat, a good illustration of payment in kind not necessarily resulting from lack of coin. These cases of moneyers assuming a more prominent and concrete stake in the process can be set beside members of the local elite who took it upon themselves to operate mints under the lordship of another, with mixed success. The sorry tale of the mint of Saintes in the early eleventh century illustrates this well. It came to the attention of Geoffrey, count of Angoulême, that the mint at Saintes had been defunct for ten years under the joint tenancy of two men, apparently members of the local elite, distinctly below the count in status.[209] This suggests the local men were responsible for actual running of the mint, not simply for taking profits, though the coins themselves show no obvious sign of change.[210] Geoffrey gave the two tenants three years to get the mint back up and running, or else he would take it away from them. After three years nothing had happened, so the mint was indeed requisitioned, resuscitated, and given to a newly founded nunnery. Reading between the lines, Count Geoffrey or one of his predecessors had farmed the mint out to these two local figures, though whatever conditions this had been under are not specified. Despite the unfortunate outcome at Saintes, Geoffrey was not averse to setting up such arrangements elsewhere: he gave the mint of Vendôme, probably on a similar basis, to Lancelinus of Beaugency around 1040, in return for the church of St. Beatus at Vendôme.[211] Farming out minting to moneyers, townsmen, or *milites* may have been commonplace. One can but wonder about an inscription at Chabanais that commemorates the *miles* Imbertus *de moneta*.[212]

207. Salrach i Marés and Montagu i Estragués 2018, nos. 368, 417.

208. Botet y Sisó 1908–1911, 1:200–202; and Baiges et al. 2010, nos. 468, 520, 678.

209. Francon de Capitolio (the Capitole hill, in Saintes) and Mascelin de Tonnay, on whom see Duguet 1981.

210. They were immobilised in the name of Louis IV until the twelfth century: Dumas-Dubourg 1971, 249.

211. Métais 1893–1904, 1, no. 22.

212. Favreau, Michaud, and Labande 1977, no. 22.

The more reified treatment of minting, and the fact that local elites actively sought to get a foothold in the process, hints that it offered significant reward. Yet very little can be said about why coins were actually made and introduced into circulation in West Francia at this time. Were individual counts or bishops in a position to require that all transactions in their territory use a particular kind of coin? Guibert of Nogent's detailed account of the institution of a new, debased coinage at Laon in 1112 suggests more limited capabilities. The bishop of Laon began by secretly debasing what had been a respected coinage, used in other territories besides his own. Soon its credibility evaporated, and the bishop tried unsuccessfully to make coins of Amiens (also badly debased) current in the city. He then instituted a new coinage marked with an image of a crozier that commanded even less respect than the earlier debased issues. In private transactions these new coins were widely rejected, but within Laon the bishop commanded that they had to be accepted. The many fines that ensued from people who challenged the bishop's substandard coins constituted (in Guibert's view) another way of wheedling money out of the hard-pressed population.[213] The moneyers had been the bishop's allies in all this chicanery. But a monk of Tournai caused more widespread damage by bringing a mass of silver from Flanders and having it turned into the debased coin of Laon; he then went forth and spent his cash, presumably at a higher face value than the recipients would be able to get for the coins once their shoddiness became more widely known. This account suggests that production depended on patrons bringing in silver. Moneyers could have lured them in with enticing rates of exchange or a stable, reputable coinage, or else with good connections in local society. The nosediving mint of Saintes perhaps represents a miscalculation in balancing these demands. Guibert's report is also important for the tension it highlights between two spheres of coin use. On the one hand there was the world of monetary officialdom: this consisted of payments to or made in the sight of the authorities that had to be made using particular coins. The number of these payments was probably high. In Anjou in the decades around the millennium, they ranged from a basic land tax (*census*) to a variety of levies, fines, tolls, and deferments for military service or support.[214] The need to settle obligations of this kind guaranteed a degree of patronage for most mints, as everyone would have had to make such payments, however

---

213. Guibert of Nogent, *Monodies* 2.7 (Labande 1981, 324–26; trans. MacAlhany and Rubenstein 2011, 128–29). For discussion, see Kaiser 1987.

214. Bachrach 1988; 1993, 191–96.

grudgingly. On the other hand, there was a more organic domain of day-to-day coin circulation, in which the many different currencies of France mingled, and sank or swam based on their acceptability. The result was a sort of inversion of Gresham's Law: when many notionally commensurate coinages circulated freely, the good could win out over the bad.[215] That all depends, however, on everyone knowing the reputation and real value of all their coins. Information was at a premium in this situation, for not everyone was in a position to spot bad coins immediately, and the swift and unscrupulous could profit from others' ignorance.

French hoards of the tenth century track the emergence of this mixed, two-tier situation. Two of the largest and most influential on numismatic thinking, those of Fécamp (c. 980–85) and Le Puy (c. 996–1002), included coins drawn from far and wide, although many other finds are more regionally focused.[216] Others, such as the Maffliers hoard of c. 955–65, are almost completely dominated by a single region or authority, in this case coins of the Robertian lands around Paris,[217] while some with a couple of well-defined elements might belong to a person, family, or institution who had to navigate between several neighbouring monetary systems, each of which required use of a particular coin type. The Vignacourt hoard of c. 1065–70 was physically divided along these lines, into two separately wrapped parcels: one from the area of Amiens, the other from that of Orléans.[218] Assemblages of this kind reflect the nature of regional politics in West Francia, which was structured around people and key points rather than lines on a map.[219] A string of zones of circulation can be identified on the basis of these finds, in the same way as for the ninth century, except much smaller.[220] More work is needed on how these zones came into being, evolved over time, and interacted with one another, as well as the extent to which they corresponded with contemporary political divisions. In the tenth century zones of circulation tended to be larger, looser, and more driven by patterns of monetary circulation than political allegiance. Neighbouring lordships adopted similar coin types, which makes most sense if those coinages were already in widespread use.[221] Zones of circulation generally seem to have become less porous over

215. Bridbury 1980; Contamine et al. 1993, 129.

216. Duyrat 2018. Lafaurie 1952, 120–23, is still valuable, with an important update in Pagan 2018. The essential survey of French hoards more broadly is Duplessy 1985.

217. Foucray 2018c.

218. Foucray and Bompaire 2018.

219. Bates 1999, 398; Guyotjeannin 2002, esp. 124–25; Mazel 2018, esp. 86–88.

220. Bompaire 2018, 321–23. For the ninth century, see Bruand 2002, 168–82, and chapter 8.

221. See earlier discussion for the example of Auxerre and its neighbours.

time, so that by the end of the eleventh century hoards more often contained solely local issues. At least some divisions by that point were politically driven. The royal lands of Philip I (1060–1108) are a case in point: during Philip's reign, hoards from his territory gradually came to be dominated by issues from the king's dozen or so mint-places.[222] But not even Philip, and hardly any rulers in West Francia during this period, seem to have operated systematic recoinages that forced users to switch over to new currency, as Charles the Bald had done, and as contemporaries in England still did.[223] Hoards from across France include coins that were several decades old at the time of deposition. The testimony of the hoards can be set alongside that of references to payment in charters, which are plentiful. These rarely stipulate that payments use a particular kind of coin until the latter half of the eleventh century.[224] As far as one can tell, any decent coin was acceptable. Moreover, even when more detailed stipulations about payment appear, they do not always specify the local coinage: one relatively early instance from the Auvergne in the later eleventh century merely stipulates that a potential future payment should consist of 20s "of the coinages which are worth most" (*della moneda que plus valent*).[225]

In this as in so many other respects, it is difficult to imagine that there was ever anything approaching unity across West Francia. There was, nonetheless, common ground in the elaboration of a dense and complex landscape of minting under aristocratic leadership and patronage. Most of these mint-places went back to the ninth century or earlier, and organisation within them was also conservative, based on a cohort of moneyers who laboured under the thumb of whoever the local authority happened to be, with the exception of mints that had been leased out. In these ways the tenth and eleventh centuries were not far removed from earlier times. Strikingly, while the new castles that were springing up in West Francia frequently served as settings for the use of coined money and for control over other economic resources, few ever actually witnessed minting; archaeological signs of nonferrous metalworking at early castles in France (and indeed elsewhere) are very rare.[226]

The overall picture of the West Frankish monetary system is therefore only superficially stable: behind the scenes, a great deal was changing.

---

222. Foucray 2018b, 300.

223. Bompaire 2018, 324, though Moesgaard (2011) argues for more robust type-changes tantamount to *renovationes* in tenth-century Normandy.

224. Bruand 2018a, 315–16.

225. Doniol 1864, no. 650.

226. Bourgeois 2013b, esp. 163–64. See also chapter 3.

Even if many coins still named a king, the initiative now normally lay with counts, dukes, or other regionally dominant figures, and the king's capacity for real, wide-ranging action with the coinage was significantly lower than it had been for Louis the Pious or Charles the Bald. Articulation of authority through money was now a matter of competing for Carolingian spoils, to a large extent through the language of the Carolingian era. But even if the West Frankish monetary landscape had turned into a series of sub-Carolingian systems in miniature, with the stakes in each individual region inevitably being smaller and ambitions narrower, the result can be characterised as intensification as much as disintegration: rights and powers over coinage, and its revenues, generally came into sharper focus. One reason for this is that, even if it was cut up into smaller slices, the pie was larger than it had been in the past. Developments in the running of the coinage need to be seen against the backdrop of a significantly expanding monetary economy.

East Francia/Germany

For East Francia or, as it might be called later in this period, Germany or the Reich, the burst of new minting in the tenth and eleventh centuries effectively brought use of coin to the lands east of the Rhine for the first time. It was only in the West and in Bavaria in the South, that minting and circulation of coined money had been significant in earlier times.[227] These areas boasted a well-established network of mint-places, but also a stronger tendency toward ecclesiastical coinage than their neighbours in West Francia, and more new mint-places that appeared in the tenth and eleventh centuries.

Nonetheless, there is a lot to tie the coinage of this vast and complex area together. At the outset of this period its mints presumably operated in much the same way as those of earlier Carolingian times, issuing coins in the name of the king under the oversight of the local count. The latter could expect a share of the profits of minting but did not put his name or image on the coins.[228] As will be seen, that model may already have been breaking down as minting expanded, and the grip of the king was already rather loose. Little can be said about actual circulation and whether coins from other kingdoms were kept out, for there are no references in capitularies, and precious few finds. From surviving coins, it can be seen that

227. On the fate of this region, see MacLean 2013.
228. See chapter 8.

Louis the Child (899–911) apparently instituted adherence to a common type, though other early kings did not do so, and in the decades following Louis's death the dukes of Bavaria, Lotharingia, and Swabia, along with the bishop of Constance, all started to produce coins in their own name, only sometimes alongside that of the king.[229] This emergent trend toward numerous distinct minting authorities is a signature of the Ottonian and Salian eras. German coinage in this period is a highly devolved phenomenon, but unlike in West Francia, most authorities who had rights over minting were very overt about it on their coins.

The number of mint-places in Germany exploded at this time. Fewer than twenty locations (all but two of them on or west of the Rhine) issued coins in the years 899–936. In the Ottonian era (936–1024) that number went up to seventy, most of them appearing after the death of Otto II (983). Nearly thirty of these lay beyond the Rhine, including Magdeburg and Meissen on the Elbe. Almost twice that many mint-places again, 137, are known to have been operational in the Salian period (1024–1125).[230] The distribution of these is highly uneven. Rich concentrations existed along the central Rhine, in Friesland, central Saxony, northern Franconia, and both upper and lower Lotharingia. The appearance of new mints was not in itself an index of royal weakness. Several of these regions were areas of relative royal strength in terms of land and supporters.[231] Rather, the quantity and distribution of mint-places reflect the nature of the expansion of coinage in Germany. Minting was a political development that rode on the coattails of economic change; a matter of locally powerful figures patronising monetisation and commerce under royal license. The network of coin issuers that took shape over the later tenth and eleventh centuries would not have come into being without the strong and overt interest of local powers.

The norm in Germany was hence for a local or regional magnate to take charge of minting, nominally by concession of the king. Of course, the king or emperor was in his own right one of the more prominent issuers of coin, and he had them produced at mint-places situated in his own lands, such as Deventer, Duisburg, and Tiel in Lotharingia, and Goslar in Saxony, where the Otto-Adelheid coins and Sachsenpfennige (which, unusually for

229. Kluge 1991, 23; Grierson and Blackburn 1986, 228.

230. These numbers are culled from Kluge 1991, 23–78, which is the best overall guide to the coinage of this period. The foundational catalogue is Dannenberg 1876–1905, though it is now superseded on a number of points.

231. E.g., Müller-Mertens 1980; Reuter 1991, 208–20; Bernhardt 1993, 45–70.

FIGURE 9.8. Silver denarius, minted at Liège or Maastricht around 1091, in the names of Bishop Otbert (1091–1119) and Henry IV (1054–1105), with a probable scene of investiture (diameter 16 mm). From the Kose hoard; Estonian History Museum, Tallinn, AM 25159:226.

Germany, do not carry a mint name) were probably also made.[232] It is presumed that, unless stated otherwise, oversight of production at these places lay in the hands of the local count, on the Carolingian model. Kings might also be recognised on coins made in the name of other authorities, especially in the Ottonian period: it was mostly on this basis that kings or emperors were named at a total of at least sixty-three mint-places across Germany.[233] But by the 1070s it was unusual for the king or emperor to be named anywhere outside the few mint-places under his direct control.[234] Naming or showing the king at this point, in the era of the Investiture Controversy, took on new meaning as a statement of support for the royal cause, and at Liège, Maastricht, and elsewhere the king's name and image were actually complemented by pointed scenes of him investing a bishop (see figure 9.8).[235]

Explicit, engaged involvement with coinage on the part of other regional magnates was the norm in Germany. Much more consistently than in other parts of Europe, coins and charters explain the agency behind them. There were few examples of "immobilised" coinage, and dozens of distinct authorities oversaw the production of their own explicitly

232. Hatz et al. 1991; Kluge 2001. Goslar was even claimed as a signal of royal status in the coinage of Hermann of Salm (anti-king 1081–88): Steinbach 2007b.

233. Based on Kluge 1991, 97–99, supplemented with Ilisch 2000 and 2014b for Lower Lotharingia.

234. Kamp 1982, 102–3; Kluge 1991, 68–76, 83–84.

235. Phillips, Freeman, and Woodhead 2013, 293–94; Ilisch 2014b, 332–33.

marked coins or received a diploma granting them the right to do so. At Worms, a tradition of Carolingian royal grants of minting rights was fabricated in the tenth century to provide support for a renewal of minting by the bishop.[236] Inevitably, this situation created an attenuated relationship between king and coinage. Henry IV and V had no real say in the management of most coinages issued in the Reich. Moreover, to grant minting and associated privileges over market and toll was often to give away what the king had never in practice possessed: grants frequently related to new establishments where there would not have been anything to control or derive profit from without the input of the local patrons.[237] In this way, although kings and emperors factored into the production of most coinage only by giving rights over it away, minting was ultimately recognised as deriving from royal dispensation. It was a way of making a grant without actually suffering any material loss. In effect these were licenses to consolidate, and oversee, local economic processes, and even if they never got off the ground—which must have been common, given the number of minting grants that do not correspond to any known coins—the grant still forged a connection between king and recipient.[238]

A large proportion of German minting authorities were ecclesiastical.[239] Some of the most productive mint-places in Germany (to judge from numbers of surviving specimens in Baltic hoards) fell under ecclesiastical authority: in particular, all the main mint-towns of the Rhineland, including Cologne, Mainz, Worms, and Speyer, came under episcopal jurisdiction in the course of this period.[240] Some ecclesiastics operated a whole network of mints: eleven in the case of the bishop of Liège.[241] Church lordship did not in itself bring productivity or prosperity. Other ecclesiastical mint-places are known from only a handful of surviving coins and probably never operated on a large scale. In total at least seventy places in the Reich can be identified as having minted coins for a bishop or archbishop, and another twenty-five for a monastery. Ecclesiastical institutions also dominate the rich German record of charters that pertain to minting. There had been grants of minting rights to bishops and monasteries in East Francia as early as the ninth century, but the Ottonian and

236. Roach 2021, 34–35.

237. Schlesinger 1985; Janssen 1985; Fichtenau 1994.

238. Rosenwein 1999, esp. 137–55.

239. For a general survey of ecclesiastical coinage in Germany in this period, see Steinbach 2007a.

240. Hatz 1974, 41–44.

241. Kluge 1991, 108–11.

Salian kings gave them much more freely:[242] some 139 grants or confirmations of minting rights were given to ecclesiastical recipients between 936 and 1105.[243] It is true that ecclesiastical recipients dominate the corpus of Ottonian and Salian diplomas in general, but as will be seen, there is independent evidence that this was commensurate with their role in minting.

Grants of minting meant that an abbot or bishop took up both the responsibilities and the privileges associated with what had once been royal prerogatives, previously exercised by the local count (or by no one if, as was often the case, the grant related to a *de novo* settlement). A charter of Otto III from 985 that transferred the mint of Huy to the bishop of Liège thus stated that "what remains of royal power, relating to coinage, tolls and, other renders" in the town would now be passed on to the bishop.[244] In a sense they stood in much the same relationship to the king as counts notionally did in West Francia. Having the right to mint coins reflected prestige and responsibility, rather than economic demand as such. Nor was there a systematic policy of vesting coinage rights in the church.[245] The promotion of episcopal and abbatial coinages stemmed from two dovetailing principles: that mints and markets should, if not in the hands of the king, work for the spiritual good of the kingdom and its people by supporting the good works of the church; and that vesting mints and markets in ecclesiastical hands offered the most likely guarantee of equitable management of a public resource. Trade routes were recognised as appropriate places for mints. At Rorschach in 947, the flow of people heading for Italy was cited as a reason for allowing the abbey of St. Gall to establish a market and a mint, while at Seltz on the west bank of the Rhine in 993 the convergence of people crossing the river was given as a motive.[246] In both cases, human traffic was framed as a benefit to the monastic recipients: the point was not to foster local trade, or at least not primarily, but to use that trade to swell the coffers of the monasteries. Protection of the coinage also stands out as a common concern. When Henry II granted market and minting rights at Marbach to the bishop of Speyer in 1009, his charter declared that the coins should follow the standards of one of the

242. Kaiser 1976; Patzold 2008, 84–90; Hardt-Friederichs 1980; the earliest is for Corvey in 833 (MGH DD LdF 328—an original).

243. Kluge 1991, 101–4.

244. "Quod relictum erat regiae ditionis, in moneta scilicet et teloneo reliquisque redditibus." MGH DD OIII 16.

245. Wangerin 2019, 60–63, 75–76, 80–85.

246. DD OI 90 and DD OIII 130. Seltz was a special case, as the intended burial place of Empress Adelheid (d. 999): for context, see Wollasch 1968; Staab and Unger 2005; and Zimmermann 1984–89, no. 324, for a papal privilege secured around the same time.

two major neighbouring coinages, those of Speyer or Worms, "in order to remove false coinages from circulation,"[247] while a charter of Otto III for the abbey of Echternach declared it should have a mint "in which trustworthy coins are struck, as in other places subject to royal authority, for the use of [the abbey's] church and monks."[248] This is not, of course, to say that ecclesiastical lords always lived up to such expectations. In real terms, their management of coinage is unlikely to have been materially different from that of secular rulers. Otbert, bishop of Liège (1091–1119), was accused by his own monks of having changed, diminished, and debased the *legitimae monetae*: an offence that was put alongside simony and infringement of various clerical privileges.[249] The monks may well have had a point, as Otbert's coinages seem to have changed frequently in type, possibly every year,[250] and the bishop undertook several costly building projects that could have provided the impetus for him to increase profits from the currency, as may also have happened at Speyer in the 1080s.[251]

Coin issues of counts, dukes, and other secular powers in their own right are well represented among surviving specimens, which altogether were produced at fifty-nine mint-places at least. The dukes produced coins on a relatively substantial scale in the tenth century but tailed off thereafter.[252] The most powerful dukes of the era, the dukes of Bavaria, minted on the largest scale. Their coins came from a relatively small number of mint-places, though several (Regensburg, Augsburg) were very productive, and their products often carried an abbreviated version of the name of the moneyer. Within their territory, the Bavarian dukes operated an effective monetary monopoly from the beginning of the tenth century until the time of Henry II (1002–24), who had himself been duke before taking the throne as king and later as emperor: other authorities, including the king, did not issue coins, and the dukes' pennies dominated the local currency.[253] Ducal issues from elsewhere were for the most part smaller and less coherent, being particular to individual mint-places. Coinages of the next rung down of the secular elite (*comites*, *Grafen*, more occasionally Palatine Counts, and in one case a monastic advocate) developed from about 1000, beginning with those of

247. "Ad destruendas in circuitu falsas monetas." MGH DD HII 190.

248. "In qua nummi probabiles sicut in aliis locis regiae potestati subditis percutiantur ad usum ecclesiae suae et monachorum." DD OIII 89.

249. *Cantatorium* chap. 96, Hanquet 1906, 249.

250. Phillips, Freeman, and Woodhead 2013, 291–92; Ilisch 2000, 241–48.

251. Steinbach 2015, 22.

252. Kluge 1991, 63–65; 2007, 96–97.

253. Hahn 1976; with Weinfurter 1986 for wider context.

the counts of Stade at the mouth of the Elbe,[254] though written grants of minting to such individuals started earlier: Ansfried the Elder was given the power to hold a market and run a mint at Kessel on the Maas in 950, while his son and namesake in 985 received the rights over tolls and minting that he had already held on behalf of the king at Medemblek.[255] These two are part of a group of just eleven grants of minting rights to laymen in the Ottonian and Salian period, and of those, two are for figures who had the express intention of establishing a monastery,[256] while two are possible forgeries.[257] But given the lower chances of survival for grants to laymen, there is no reason to doubt that many more were once issued.

If the East Frankish kingdom had inherited the normal Carolingian practice of putting production of coins in the name of king under the tutelage of the local count, with two-thirds of the profits being returned to the king, this was by no means so prevalent in the later tenth and eleventh centuries. It may have persisted at mint-places that still answered more directly to royal authority. The grant to Ansfried in 985 describes a situation along these lines: before receiving his grant, the count would still have owed some of the profits of minting, tolls, and trade to the king, probably the two-thirds that would have been expected in the ninth century. But in practice several developments had eroded the baseline comital model. There were very few mint-places to begin with, and most of the established ones in the western part of the kingdom gravitated quickly into episcopal hands, along with associated comital powers.[258] Moreover, Ottonian and Salian counties were more fluid entities than their Carolingian predecessors, overlapping and broken up, with the individual comital offices sometimes going separate ways as they became about a signifier of status as well as oversight of royal governance.[259] Coin production is in fact a good illustration of this process, as many of the grants of permission for minting—including to counts, as well as bishops and others—specify in whose county the location was situated. In other words, they created a small and specific immunity from the surrounding jurisdiction. The claim of local counts to responsibility for minting in their territory was a thing

254. Kluge 1991, no. 301.

255. DD OI 129 and OIII 14. On Kessel, see Ilisch 2014b, 343. For the family, see Baerten 1961; Kersken 2016, 30–43. For the coins of monastic advocates, see Kluge 1991, 68; for a slightly later period, see Lyon 2022, 147–52.

256. DD OII 110; DD OII 325.

257. DD HII 347; DD HIV 60.

258. Heinemeyer 2018.

259. Heinemeyer 2018; Nelson 1999, 121; Reuter 1991, 195, 218; Hoffmann 1990, esp. 456–61.

of the past: coinage had been decoupled from comital office, the emergent practice being for it to fall under the remit of whoever had the where-withal and connections in high places to initiate it.

Germany, in short, developed a highly devolved way of running its coinage. What remains to be considered is how the kings, dukes, counts, bishops, abbots, and others who had their names put on coins actually ran their mint-places and regulated the use of the coins. Strikingly little information is available on either front, despite the numerous charters dealing with minting; these focus heavily on the jurisdictional aspects of coinage and are silent about how recipients would implement their privilege. The assumption is that one or more moneyers took responsibility, albeit mostly under the heavy influence of whoever the patron of the coinage might be. In Bavaria down to the eleventh century, it was customary to put the moneyer's name (or an abbreviation of the name) onto the coins,[260] a practice that was so unusual in Germany, it may well have been prompted by acquaintance with English tradition, where the moneyer's name was standard. It also implies a degree of compartmentalisation in the production process; that is, different aspects and portions of it could be hived off to different figures. A grant of minting rights from the bishop of Verdun to the abbot of Saint-Mihiel in 1099 represented the patronage of a single moneyer, who would be subject to punishment by the bishop for any infractions and would collect his dies from the bishop's mint.[261] Another moneyer, named Otger, temporarily placed his name on coins from Brussels, Maastricht, Tongres, and (probably) Louvain in the mid-eleventh century (figure 9.9). These were issued for several different authorities, but the maintenance of distinct local stylistic traits among surviving specimens in Otger's name suggests that he either joined or, more probably, oversaw local craftsmen at each location.[262] Otger represents a peregrinatory model of minting, in which moneyers might travel to find new opportunities as various potentates undertook bursts of production. He can be compared with Peto, a merchant of Bad Buchau in the early 1020s who also operated as a moneyer, and who the monks of St. Gall feared might fence gold and silver stolen from the abbey.[263] Both might be set alongside other peripatetic artisans who moved around undertaking commissions from diverse patrons.[264]

260. Hahn 1976, 31–43.

261. Lesort 1909–12, 200–201.

262. Boffa 2009; Ilisch 2014b, 129–31.

263. Clavadetscher et al. 1983–, no. 874. For discussion, see Cahn 1911, 56–57.

264. As in the case of the "Gregory Master" (Nordenfalk 1972); see also Hoffmann 1986 more broadly.

FIGURE 9.9. Silver denarius in the name of the counts of Louvain, minted at Brussels in the eleventh century by the moneyer Otger (diameter 20 mm). Jean Elsen & ses fils.

There is a strong likelihood that the seemingly vast monetary world of Ottonian and Salian Germany is to some extent a mirage. In practice, minting would have been brief and intermittent at most locations, driven by temporary needs and pressures, drawing on moneyers who combined this skill with others in order to get by during lulls. The moneyers of major mint-towns were most likely comparatively important members of urban society, like their counterparts in England and Italy. But for the tenth and eleventh centuries this is a matter of inference; it is not until the early twelfth century that one finds, for example, a moneyer recognised as patron of a sculpture in Worms Cathedral,[265] or a moneyer referred to by occupation on a grave slab from Mainz Cathedral.[266] Elsewhere, moneyers are extremely obscure figures who operated within the shadow of their lord.[267] This may be a consequence of the newness of most mint-places in Germany. The picture the diplomas paint of new foundations where mint, market, and toll worked in harmony links the multiplication of mint-places with the governmental and jurisdictional dimensions of expanding urbanisation.

But while figures with minting rights generally had a close grip at the point of production, how far that control extended to what people actually did with their coins is less apparent. Knowledge of circulation of coin in Ottonian and Salian Germany largely depends on study of hoards and single finds from within the Reich itself: although the large majority of

265. Fuchs 1991, no. 18.

266. Arens and Bauer 1958, no. 18 (HEMMO NVMMVLARIVS).

267. Cf. one Bavarian moneyer's son who was bought out of servitude to Agnes of Poitou (d. 1077) by his uncle: Widemann 1943, no. 615; Hahn 1976, 74–75.

surviving coins come from Baltic hoards, these have little bearing on the situation at home. And in fact the two paint quite different pictures. While the Baltic finds are for the most part relatively mixed, with a preponderance of Rhenish and other northern issues,[268] the German finds suggest a multitiered situation.[269] There were some mixed hoards that included issues from diverse mints. An assemblage deposited at Klein Roscharden (Kr. Cloppenburg) in what was the northwestern part of Saxony around 996 or after included specimens from the royal mints of southeastern Saxony alongside appreciable numbers from the Rhenish towns and Verdun.[270] In this and other mixed hoards, the best-represented issues tend to be those of large and productive mint-towns, the ones that also feature prominently in the northern hoards. The mixed finds can be set alongside a cluster of much more localised hoards. At least fifteen or so pools of currency can be identified from them, some large (most of Bavaria), some relatively small (those of Ulm and Speyer), and there undoubtedly were others that do not happen to be represented. On the face of it, these finds point to much more localised circulation. Most were heavily dominated by the issues of a single mint-place (90 per cent or more), sometimes even a single type.[271] But a third part of the material invites caution. Among the many single finds of coins uncovered at the Hilton hotel site in Mainz, coins of the local mint accounted for about two-thirds of the total from this period; Speyer and Worms counted with Mainz accounted for about 80–85 per cent. Single finds from Trier show a similar situation.[272] What these suggest is a currency that was not completely homogeneous. Neighbouring coinages mingled and did not have hard-and-fast frontiers, as implied by the grants of minting rights to Seltz and Marbach.

These single finds cast the hoards in a different light. They do not reflect an entirely self-contained series of currencies that sat side by side, with just a few far-ranging travellers that skimmed across them. It follows that bishops, dukes, counts, and others, confronted with a continuum of coin circulation, were not in the business of restricting all monetised exchanges to just the local issue. People could use coins from neighbouring mint-places even if they fell under different masters, and there was also scope for moving over longer distances without having to change currency systematically as one went. At the same time, the hoards indicate

268. Hatz 1974; Ilisch 1981.
269. Hess 1990; 1993; Blackburn 1993; Ilisch 2016.
270. Hess 1993, no. 21; Hatz 1974, no. 31.
271. Hess 1982; 1988.
272. Blackburn 1993, 45–46; Wamers, Berghaus, and Stoess 1993, 177–89.

that for some purposes there was a much stronger predilection for the local currency. In this regard Germany probably stands close to contemporary West Francia and Italy: the strongest jurisdictional influence rulers could have over the use (and, by extension, minting) of coinage related to what was or was not acceptable payment to the ruler's own agents. Areas of currency could expand and contract; that of Cologne, for example, can be seen to have shrunk as new coinages emerged in the north of what had been its sphere of circulation late in the tenth century and in the eleventh. Individual cities or regions hence need to be looked at separately. But the general picture is strongly suggestive: rulers were closely and energetically involved with minting at all levels but took a less direct hand in guiding the flow of coined money through the kingdom beyond their own expenditure.

England

Like West Francia, Italy, and parts of Germany, England had a long history of making and using coins before 900. England was also like Germany in rapidly gaining an enlarged network of mint-places. It went from having possibly as few as 6 in the mid-ninth century to almost 40 in the time of Æthelstan (924–39) and more than 120 places named in total between the early 970s and 1100 (up to 60 or 70 of them at once).[273] The mint-place was, however, seen as a secondary piece of information. The moneyer remained the principal point of reference. There were approximately 2,500 moneyers active in England between 900 and 1100, heavily weighted toward the period after about 980.

That is one respect in which England stands apart from the other regions discussed here. Although moneyers active elsewhere can be pursued in charters and other texts, England was one of few places where they put their names on the coins systematically. A second distinctive feature of the English coinage was that it remained under firm and, at first glance, undivided royal authority. No aristocrats or bishops issued coins in their own name over this period, even though some did have rights to the profit of one or more moneyers.[274] As far as one can tell from the actual coins,

---

273. Naismith 2017b, 337–56; Allen 2012, 382–96.

274. A law code of Æthelstan (II Æthelstan, c. 14: Liebermann 1903–16, 1:158–59) states that the archbishop of Canterbury, abbot of St. Augustine's, and bishop of Rochester had the profits of some moneyers. The abbot still held this right in the twelfth century (Crafter 2006) so presumably had done so across the intervening period, and the archbishop for even longer. The abbot of Bury had rights to the profit of a moneyer active in the town (S

however, the moneyers were solidly royal. They normally minted the same type and changed over to new issues at the same time. Because of this strongly royal flavour, coinage figures in historical evaluations of tenth- and eleventh-century England in a way it does not for other European regions, because it fits into—indeed, is a major pillar of—the prevailing interest in strong royal government at this time.[275] The coins can also be set alongside royal legislation of the period that makes reference to the coinage in proprietary and moralistic terms: "One coinage shall be current throughout all the king's realm, and no-one shall refuse it" reads one law code of Edgar (959–75),[276] while several of the legal and homiletic writings of Wulfstan of York (d. 1023) encouraged "improvement of the coinage" (*feos bot*) as a form of moral and spiritual defence against divine disfavour.[277]

Wulfstan's rhetoric and other texts of the period imply that recoinage was a safeguard against corruption by forgery, even though there is no evidence for significant counterfeiting in England at this time. Unity in the coinage and protection against the taint of illicit coin had become virtues in themselves by the end of the tenth century. A major reorganisation of the coinage by Edgar in the early 970s amplified the already strong emphasis on royal recognition and instituted kingdom-wide uniformity in design, in contrast to the more variable and often regionalised situation earlier in the tenth century (see figure 9.10).[278] Under Æthelred II (978–1016) an important refinement emerged: frequent and general changes of type. This system took shape only gradually. The first new issue of his reign had significant regional variants and in many ways harks back to the situation in the 960s and before. It is also unlikely that this or later coinages appeared according to a strict and arbitrary timetable, as Michael Dolley argued in the mid-twentieth century.[279] On the contrary, the coinage was highly responsive to concerns of the royal court, and to changing events. When a huge viking army appeared in late summer 1009, the exhausted English could not mount any meaningful military resistance, so the king instead initiated a programme of national prayer and penance, into which the coinage was co-opted: the

1085; Harmer 1952, no. 25). For a layman holding rights to a moneyer at early eleventh-century Stamford, see subsequent discussion. See further Allen 2012, 9–12.

275. Campbell 2000, 7–8, 32–33, 160, 181; Molyneaux 2015, 116–41.

276. "Ga an mynet ofer ealne þæs cynges anweald, [and] þane nan man ne forsace." III/IV Edgar 8 (Liebermann 1903–16, 1:204–5).

277. Keynes and Naismith 2011, 197–98.

278. Molyneaux 2015, 117–23; Naismith 2014d; Jonsson 1987.

279. Expressed most fully in Dolley and Metcalf 1961; Dolley 1964, 24–30; 1976.

FIGURE 9.10. Silver penny of Edgar (959–75), reform type, Derby mint, moneyer Oswulf (diameter 20 mm). Classical Numismatic Group, LLC.

FIGURE 9.11. Silver penny of Æthelred II, *Agnus Dei* type, minted autumn 1009 (?), Stafford mint, moneyer Ælfwold (diameter 20 mm). Gabriel Hildebrand, Collections of the Economy Museum—Royal Coin Cabinet, Stockholm (CC-BY).

result was the remarkable yet very short-lived *Agnus Dei* coinage (figure 9.11). This coinage gave a material expression to the kingdom's brief spiritual offensive. Not all mint-places produced *Agnus Dei* pennies, but those that did were widely scattered in Mercia, Wessex, and the East Midlands. Temporarily abandoning the usual imagery of the coinage in favour of the holy lamb and dove (both symbols of the peace the English hoped God would bring them), and with a high weight standard that had come to be associated with the initiation of a substantive new coin issue, the *Agnus Dei* pennies constitute the high point of moralised monetary policy in England.[280]

280. Keynes and Naismith 2011.

While it was an extreme case, the *Agnus Dei* issue is representative of how the royal relationship with coinage evolved in the decades either side of the millennium. Coinage became one of the primary mechanisms for expressing the moral well-being of English society. This projection of royal anxiety onto the exercise of kingship is quintessentially Æthelredian: the principle of frequent recoinage is a direct result of the climate and turbulence of his court, steeped as it was in Christian thought on royal office and its responsibilities.[281] The process also had the potential to generate a substantial income for the king, though it is doubtful whether this was at first the primary motive. Subsequent rulers did not occupy the same ideological ground as Æthelred and his councillors, and the fact that they maintained the practice of frequent recoinage—and even, from the later 1030s, did so noticeably more often—should be read as a matter of routinisation, very probably on the basis of the financial benefits that accrued to the king. These would have included a share of the income that came directly from fees paid by moneyers (probably two-thirds, with the remaining third normally going to the local ealdorman or earl),[282] but the king's other main source of profit from the coinage might have been the power to exact payments reckoned on the basis of purified silver while others had to pay by tale, which Domesday Book suggests produced a surcharge of 25–30 per cent.[283]

English coinage presents a jarring combination of highly centralised overall conception with deeply localised implementation. The lavish, if highly uneven, provision of mints and moneyers did not correlate straightforwardly with population or agricultural productivity. East Anglia and Yorkshire were quite poorly provided with minting facilities yet had considerable wealth and population (to judge from the record left by Domesday Book); conversely, Somerset and adjacent shires in the Southwest had a surfeit of mint-places that surely went far beyond direct need (map 9.3). Importantly, the mint-places also do not map directly onto the urban geography of England, and it is dangerously circular to use the minting of coins as a definition of urban status (or vice versa).[284] Taking the 112 places with urban features in Domesday as a guide and setting them against the 113 or so named mint-places active in England between the 970s and 1066, about a quarter of towns were not mint-places, and about a quarter of mint-places were not towns. It should be added that many

281. Naismith 2016a, 125–32; Roach 2016.

282. Baxter 2007, 89–97.

283. Naismith 2017b, 252; cf. Harvey 2014, 136–46.

284. As seen in Stenton 1971, 536–37. A more nuanced exploration of the topic is Loyn 1961.

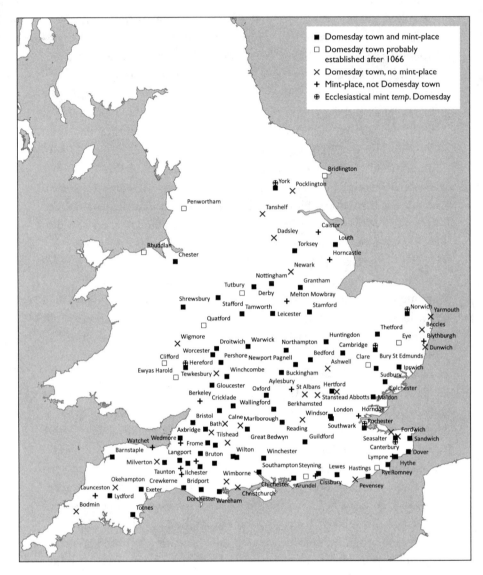

MAP 9.3. Mint-places in England between the early 970s and 1066, correlated with towns in Domesday Book (following Naismith 2017b, 337–56; Darby 1977, 296–97).

mint-places hosted moneyers only briefly or sporadically, meaning that at any one time there were probably a lot of towns with no moneyer.[285]

285. Naismith 2019a, 4–5. Domesday towns include those directly identified as such in (usually) the opening sections of each county entry, as well as settlements with various features suggestive of urban status such as the presence of burgesses (for the full list, see Darby 1977, 297, with more recent discussion in Munby 2011). It is of course by no means

But even if towns were not automatically mints, major towns tended to be the dominant minting centres. Urban settlements in tenth- and eleventh-century England were vital nodes in the jurisdictional and social networks that played a large part in shaping the manufacture of coin. This was especially apparent in the early to mid-tenth century, when the *byrg* (singular *burh*) seem to have been bases for some of the functions later expected to take place at shire and hundred assemblies.[286] At that time virtually all identifiable mint-places were *byrg* (though plenty of *byrg* did not host moneyers). In the midlands, the first appearance of minting at *byrg* plausibly occurred as part of this drive to concentrate administrative functions: most later shire-towns minted coins as early as the time of Edward the Elder or Æthelstan, long before there is any indication of a formalised network of hundreds and shires, and at a time when the large majority of *byrg* were of marginal importance as economic centres.[287]

By the late tenth and eleventh centuries there was only a partial correlation between boroughs and mint-places, especially at the smaller end of the network.[288] This suggests that the manufacture of coin was becoming tied to a wider range of circumstances, shaped by the human and institutional landscape and driven in part by pressure from above to support recoinages, supply armies, and feed demands for taxes and tributes. Some of the mint-places that appeared outside known towns at this time can be plausibly explained for other reasons. Berkeley, Crewkerne, and Melton Mowbray were not described as towns but hosted markets, Launceston was a monastery, and South Petherton and others were the centres of large royal estates. Yet there remains a cluster of mint-places for which there is no obvious explanation, such as Horndon in Essex.[289]

It is likely in cases like this that minting was a product of the workings of justice, administration, and lordship.[290] Horndon (referring to some or all of what is now East and West Horndon, or nearby Horndon-on-the-Hill)

---

certain that the places identified in this way for 1066 and 1086 reflect the urban landscape of the century before 1066.

286. Molyneaux 2015, 106–9, 153–54; Lambert 2017b, 244–47. *Burh* meant "enclosure" or "fortress" but also came to be the standard term for "town" (cf. modern "borough").

287. Astill 1991, 2006; Russo 1998, esp. 193–231.

288. Reynolds 2019 shows very effectively how dispersed power structures were in the countryside.

289. Known from a unique coin in the British Museum (*BMC* 554). The authenticity of the coin has been queried (Freeman 1985, 1:218) and defended (Metcalf and Lean 1993, 223–24); one might also add in support of its authenticity that the form of the mint name (HORNIDVNE) is very close to that in Domesday Book (*Horninduna* and similar).

290. For Domesday lordship and its operation more broadly, see Baxter 2007, 204–69; 2009.

was a large estate where several important landowners held property in 1066 and 1086 according to Domesday Book: one of those, or a predecessor, could have temporarily patronized minting, just as one local aristocrat is known to have done at Stamford in the early eleventh century.[291] A clearer example comes from a rare insight into jurisdictional details of minting from Domesday Book. On the Suffolk coast, the port town of Dunwich had no moneyers before the twelfth century. That is unusual for what appears to have been the largest town in the shire in 1066. Domesday Book reveals two other points of potential relevance. First, Dunwich was not a borough held by the king, unlike Ipswich or the boroughs of adjacent Norfolk. What would normally have been royal rights over the town were in the hands of a wealthy thegn, Eadric of Laxfield. This arrangement was not unique, and other towns that were described simply as estates belonging to lords besides the king could host minting.[292] But there was also an acknowledgement of Dunwich's special relationship with the nearby hundredal centre and royal estate of Blythburgh.[293] The town was meant (like any other settlement) to send representatives to the hundredal meeting, and thieves apprehended in Dunwich would also be taken to Blythburgh for punishment—and while "there was no moneyer there [in Dunwich], there was one in Blythburgh."[294] Dunwich's establishment and growth as a town probably generated the demand that underpinned this moneyer's work, but the nature of the institutional landscape meant that the actual striking of coin took place at Blythburgh.

At all mint-places, large and small alike, the number of moneyers reflects the scale and complexity of demand for coin. Moneyers could appear and disappear in short order, which suggests that their expertise was not solely technical. They were likely implanted in circuits of personal and land-based dependence. Each maker of coin would represent a distinct social network or clientele. Some of these would overlap, some would be restricted to the associates of a single patron, and some would consist of individuals who were effectively the moneyer's own peers (or indeed family). These networks brought ready-made patronage to the moneyers, meaning that relatively few moneyers would rely on

291. Kelly 2009, no. 31 (xi).

292. Maitland 1897, 213–15.

293. Lambert 2017a, 141–42.

294. "T[empore] r[egis] E[dwardi] n[on] fuit ibi ca[m]bitor s[ed] in Blideburh." LDB 312r–v. *Cambitor* or *cangeor* (literally "changer") was used in other documents of this period for moneyers, and the functions of money changer and maker of coin were closely connected in tenth- and eleventh-century England (Naismith 2017b, 242).

commercial or walk-in business, or set themselves up without a known base of clients.[295]

The moneyers seem to have come predominantly from social groups that allowed them to reach both up and down in terms of their connections. The Winton Domesday survey (probably carried out a decade or so before the Norman Conquest) refers to a number of moneyers, some explicitly as *monetarius* or *cangeor*, while others likely appear in their capacity as a goldsmith or priest.[296] A tenth-century collection of miracle stories (also from Winchester) refers to a rich moneyer who would take horses to attend feasts both in and far from the town.[297] It is possible that a small number of moneyers with uncommon names can be traced among the recipients and witnesses of charters, suggesting a degree of local significance, and not just in urban settings.[298]

Some sense of how common it may have been for men of this standing to work as moneyers is provided by comparison of moneyers of the eleventh century with figures recorded in Domesday Book.[299] About 60 per cent of moneyers named on coins between 1042 and 1100 almost certainly do not appear among named Domesday landholders, in that no individual with the same name occurs within twenty miles of the appropriate mint-place. Representation is slightly better among moneyers active earlier, who appear among Domesday landholders of 1066, for there were a great many minor landholders named as possessors "on the day King Edward was alive and dead" (i.e., 4 January 1066), whereas William the Conqueror's reign saw significant consolidation of smaller landholdings into the hands of a few tenants-in-chief.[300] It does not necessarily follow that the other moneyers were simply too insignificant to matter. Domesday is a huge but highly specific document, concerned with landholdings at only a few steps remove from the king, meaning that in most parts of the country sub-subtenants or below are not mentioned, even though they may have been

295. Naismith forthcoming a.

296. Biddle and Keene 1976, 400–407.

297. Lantfred, *Translatio et miracula s. Swithuni*, c. 2 (ed. and trans. Lapidge 2003, 266–67).

298. For examples, see Blackburn 1974, 19–22; Stewart 1988; Naismith forthcoming b.

299. This exercise depends heavily on the breakdown of Domesday individuals represented in PASE Domesday. This database uses a number of criteria (geography, later ownership, etc.) to assign estates to different men or women with the same name. For the first time, it is therefore possible to see various landholders as distinct characters rather than as a vague mass of undifferentiated individuals by the same name.

300. Baxter and Lewis 2017.

an important part of the rural population.[301] The sense that moneyers were often drawn from those who operated only on a local level—men who would have been important in their own village, and perhaps known and respected at the level of the hundred if not the shire—is strengthened when one turns to the 306 moneyers who are probably or plausibly identifiable in Domesday.[302] The large majority of these (73 per cent) had only a small amount of landed wealth, with a total revenue of less than £5 a year. At this marginal level, it is entirely credible that many moneyers would go unnamed in the Domesday survey.[303]

Only a few English moneyers were very wealthy (taken here to mean having lands worth more than £50 per annum), and these identifications are generally less secure, but a more significant cohort (21 per cent) had middling wealth, between £5 and £50. These include some very convincing cases of moneyers with unusual names, who closely match Domesday landholders by name and location. There was Agmundr, who minted coins at Lincoln from about the early 1060s to 1070; this is almost certainly the man of the same name who in 1066 held sixteen properties in Lincoln and its rural vicinity with an annual value of £16 9s 11d, and who in 1086 was described as one of the twelve "lawmen" of the city, in succession to his father Wælhrafn in 1066, who had also served as a moneyer around the beginning of Edward the Confessor's reign and under Edward held two pieces of land that brought in £4 (map 9.4).[304] At Exeter in Devon there was a man who rejoiced in the name Viking and minted coins briefly late in the reign of Edward. One of only two figures named Viking in Domesday Book was Viking "of Awliscombe," who held a series of eleven properties in the environs of Exeter, which brought him income of £7 15s a year.[305] It is highly likely that the moneyer and the Domesday landowner were identical with a thegn (*minister*) who attested a charter associated

301. Baxter and Lewis 2017, 366–67. On the process of composition, see Baxter 2020.

302. "Plausible" identifications represent cases where multiple possible Domesday matches exist for a single moneyer: 184 moneyers find a total of 438 matches among Domesday landholders. Further discussion of this methodology, and full details of the comparison between the coinage and Domesday, can be found in Naismith forthcoming a. Roffe 2018 uses a similar principle.

303. One might compare them with the jurors who swore to the holdings of hundreds in Cambridgeshire in 1086: a mix of English and Norman figures who were considered knowledgeable and trustworthy enough for this important task. Yet only about a third of them appear among named Domesday landholders (Lewis 1993; Baxter and Lewis 2017, 367).

304. PASE Agemund 7 the lawman; Baxter and Lewis 2017, 359–60.

305. PASE Viking 2 "of Awliscombe"; Lewis 2016, 192.

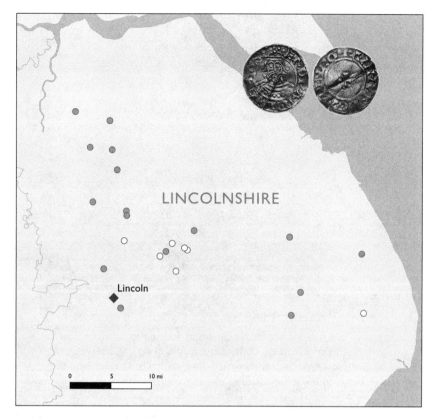

MAP 9.4. Lands of Agmundr in the time of King Edward according to Domesday
Book; grey dots represent properties held by him; white dots, properties of
which he was lord but that were leased to others. Includes a coin of Agmundr,
Lincoln mint, *Facing Bust* type (early/mid-1060s). By kind permission of Halls
Hammered Coins.

with a meeting and property in Devon, and also a manumission that identified him as Viking "the boatswain (map 9.5)."[306]

Men like Agmundr and Viking underscore that there was no single or
simple profile for being a moneyer, save that it seems unlikely that the high
aristocracy served in this capacity, at least by the time they had acquired
their wealth. Moneyers did not necessarily work constantly or long-term.
If Agmundr's father Wælhrafn was indeed still a lawman in 1066, it had
probably been more than twenty years since he minted coins. A contrast
is apparent between moneyers who seem to have devoted more time and
energy to the role and those who acted as moneyers only occasionally.
There was a slight tendency for wealthier moneyers like Agmundr and

306. S 1474 (O'Donovan 1988, no. 17); Pelteret 1990, no. 138.

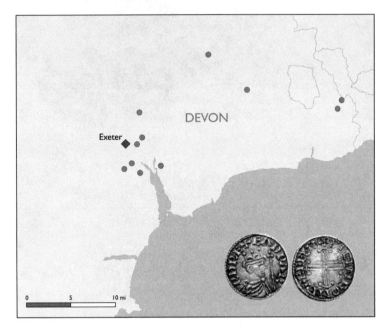

MAP 9.5. Lands of Viking "of Awliscombe" in the time of King Edward according to Domesday Book. Includes a coin of viking, Exeter mint, *Hammer Cross* type (late 1050s–early 1060s). By kind permission of the Fitzwilliam Museum, Cambridge, accession no. CM.ME.590-R.

Viking to issue coins on a briefer, more occasional basis, while a higher proportion of what might be called "established" moneyers who issued coin on a larger scale and for a longer period can be found among the less wealthy moneyers.[307] Exceptions arise on both sides: some established moneyers had greater wealth, and some occasional moneyers held little or no land.

This should probably not be read as a sharp dichotomy between "professional" moneyers who drew their custom from the urban marketplace, and "gentleman" occasional moneyers who minted for landholding elite interests. Most moneyers probably had elements of both these models. The occurrence of potential moneyers among rural landholders in Domesday Book undermines the notion that moneyers were always heavily commercial and urban in their focus, which stems from the presumption that issuing money must also be a commercial and urban operation.[308] If the moneyers represented individuals immersed in networks of lordship, often moving back and forth between town and country as a matter

307. For "established" and "one-type" moneyers, see Freeman 1985, 1:40–46.
308. Save for a few mint-places outside towns: see Naismith 2019a, 4–6.

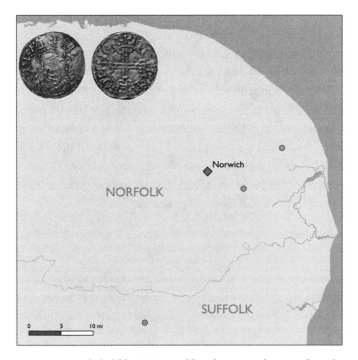

MAP 9.6. Lands held by Hringwulf in the time of King Edward (1042–66) according to Domesday Book. Includes a coin of Hringwulf, Norwich mint, *Pointed Helmet* type (early/mid-1050s). By kind permission of AMR coins.

of course, their work instead comes across as driven by social bonds and contacts, horizontal as well as vertical. Unfortunately, the nature and direction of these links are the hardest part of the story to trace, though the fuller record of "Little" Domesday Book (which covers Essex, Norfolk, and Suffolk) occasionally shows the form they might take. Hringwulf, a moneyer at Norwich under Edward, was probably identical to at least one (and most likely all three) of the recorded individuals in Domesday with this name, who all appear in Norfolk and northern Suffolk. He held one of his estates from Alsige, nephew of Earl Ralph and a kinsman of the king, so he could have provided minting services for Alsige and his men had the need arisen. But on two properties Hringwulf also had a total of ten unnamed freemen and women who held land leased from him; again, this might be one kind of relationship that could lead to minting (map 9.6).[309]

On this basis, tenth- and eleventh-century English coinage stands out as unusually atomised and very tightly woven into the middling strata

309. PASE Hringwulf 9–11, and Alsige 45 nephew of Earl Ralph.

of local society, made up of men with some level of resources and connections who got ahead in part by serving the state in various capacities, which in practice was frequently the same thing as serving members of the local elite. The English kings and their agents were good at taking advantage of this group and using them as a direct ally.[310] This is why, superficially, the English coinage appears to be an exclusive matter of moneyers working under the king. Indirectly, however, it was a very different entity. Most moneyers would have depended for the bulk of their business on established bonds with patrons and clients, sometimes organised around a single powerful figure. In practice, England was not so far removed from contemporary French and German practice.

Conclusion

Adalbero, bishop of Laon (d. 1030/31), found much to put into a poem he wrote about the shortcomings of early eleventh-century society. This text, directed to King Robert II (996–1031), lambasted everyone and everything that deviated from Adalbero's very narrow sense of what was proper. It was right, for example, that the clergy who protected all with their prayers and ministrations, and the fighting secular elite who protected all from earthly foes, should be supported by the hard graft of the third element in his vision of society: those who were of servile condition (*servi*). "Even counting with the figures on an abacus," Adalbero wrote, "who could measure the industry, the work, or the many tasks of the servile? They are treasure, clothing, and sustenance for all, since no freeman can live without the servile."[311] The bishop of Laon's picture of a harried, exploited peasantry is mirrored elsewhere in increasing distaste for *labor*: hard manual labour was now more often a drudge than a virtue, suitable only for those most downtrodden in society.[312]

Treasure (*tesaurus*), quite possibly in the form of coins, was first among the basic perquisites that Adalbero thought the elite could and should expect to reap from peasant labour. Hierarchical pressure of this kind, applied from several converging directions, was an important catalyst in

310. Naismith 2020b, 660–62.

311. "Quis abaci signis numerando retexere possit seruorum stadium, cursus, tantosque labores? Tesaurus, uestes, cunctis sunt pascua servi; nam ualet ingenuus sine seruis uiuere nullus." Adalbero, *Carmen ad Rotbertum regem* (Carozzi 1979, 22–23). There is extensive literature on this text in relation to the tripartite division of medieval society: Carozzi 1978; Oexle 1978; Arnoux 2012, 63–65.

312. Lauwers 2017; for a contrasting view, see Arnoux 2012, 37–97.

the "monetary explosion" that began in the late tenth century and rever-
berated through the eleventh.[313] A lush historiography has grown up
around the evolving social dynamic of the tenth and eleventh centuries
that enabled such casually aggressive extraction of resources. Departing
from Georges Duby's concept of a "feudal revolution," which in turn con-
densed and accentuated the transition between Marc Bloch's first and second feudal ages,[314] the tendency has been to foreground a widening gulf in
rural society: lower elites and even better-off tiers of the peasantry pulled
apart from the rest of the rural population, who were in turn pushed into
a more servile, burdened condition—vividly designated *encellulement* or
"caging" by Alain Guerreau;[315] this process worked alongside the emerging supremacy of a martial elite that was tied up in personal obligations
that fractured old structures of public authority. Lorenzo Tabarrini has
summed it up effectively as the "political" starting to take its cue from the
"economic," stimulated by the formalisation of local power and property
rights.[316] Castles, military followings, and brute force were among the
pieces in this game.[317] Other strategies of dominance took a different
tack. R. I. Moore has argued that renewed accusations of heresy, typically
by elites against nonelites, represent another signal of the potential for
hostility that arose on either side of the growing social and economic gulf.
The Peace of God movement that took off in late tenth- and eleventh-
century France was spurred in part by the appropriation of church land
and misconduct toward ecclesiastics and their tenants: its provisions were
"designed and used to highlight the avarice or brutality of the mighty."[318]

To keep playing their part in this aggressive game, lords needed resources,
and these had to come from below, from the land and those who worked it,
just as Adalbero stressed. Direct, violent expropriation was one way to get
them; other ways included various kinds of squeeze applied through dominance of local landscapes and communities.[319] There are important economic implications to be teased out of seigneurial intensification, from how
all the castles and churches of the era were built to shifts in the mechanics

313. Murray 1978, 50; see also Buc 2019, 286.

314. Duby 1971; 1974; Bloch 1962 (originally published in French in 1939).

315. Guerreau 1980, 201–10; see also Fossier 1989, 288. The translation "caging" comes
from Wickham 2009a, 529.

316. Tabarrini 2020, 26.

317. Other significant contributions (among many) include Poly and Bournazel 1991;
Barthélemy 2009; Reuter, Wickham and Bisson 1997; West 2013; Fiore 2020.

318. Moore 1992, 2000, esp. 14–15 and 22 (source of quotation); 2006, esp. 99–100.

319. Well expressed in Bisson 2008, 41–79; see also West 2013, esp. 107–98, and the
works cited in note 326 of this chapter.

of peasant labour.[320] Lords' assertions of dominance and distinction may not have been undertaken on a capitalistic basis, but the material impact of building local primacy, status, and formal or informal ties with desirable partners must have been considerable.[321] In many areas this meant higher demands on the peasantry and tighter restrictions on their autonomy, in part because there were also more lords: smaller-scale elites with interests concentrated around a single castle or village, who pursued what they took to be their prerogatives with increased vigour. At every level from peasants to high aristocracy and kings there was a firmer, more reified treatment of personal service and rights, and of the material handovers that gave form to them.[322] Coin was a special subcategory of exchanging and storing wealth; one that reflects the character of early medieval monetisation, which was embedded in hierarchical as much as commercial cycles, and that demonstrates how the two overlapped. In this setting, coined money can be read as a function not just of exchange but of production: it presented a means of fluidly redistributing the proceeds of agrarian output. All this must still be qualified with the fact that money factored into only a portion of the exchange economy taken as a whole, and that portion did not overlap exactly with that of seigneurial pressure, which could could ramp up without coin.[323] Even so, the monetised segment of the economy was getting bigger and more important, and it took off in significant part because of, not in spite of, its place in the seigneurial economy of the eleventh century.

The sketch presented here derives largely from French scholarship and (not surprisingly) best represents conditions in France, though other parts of western Europe also experienced similar developments.[324] Evolving forms of lordship and social relations are an important side of the wider economic landscape of the late tenth and eleventh centuries, an underappreciated side, even, especially in relation to coinage. Scholarship on the "feudal revolution" and departing from it in subsequent debates has gradually, and lamentably, moved away from economic history.[325] The latter is still divided, awkwardly and artificially, into an urban and mercantile domain and another of agrarian growth. Coined money represents a bridge between

320. Myrdal and Sapoznik 2016.

321. Arnoux 2017, 139–40.

322. An argument made in West 2013.

323. Rovelli 2010, 168, notes that *incastellamento* in Italy does not correlate with regions experiencing higher monetisation in this period.

324. Wickham 2009a, 541–43; Bates 2000; Coss 2003, 20–43; Menant 1993; Reuter 1991, 226–28, 230–31.

325. Bruand 2018a, 314.

the two. It is arguable that the nexus between seigneurial power and money had a catalytic effect, priming the juggernaut-level changes of the period that would take on a life of their own in due course: commercialisation and especially population growth.[326] Other factors need to be allowed for too. Climate change in particular has long been recognised as facilitating agricultural intensification,[327] though more recent scholarship (of which there is a vast amount) is generally circumspect in turning climatic correlation into causality.[328] This is an important lesson. No single development—demography, production, commercialization, climate, lordly pressure, or others—can be assessed in isolation, or held accountable for all the diverse and widespread changes in European economy and society that began in the tenth century and went on for three centuries thereafter.[329] Human agency played off material and environmental factors.

That is the conclusion to be drawn from the patterns in both circulation and production of coinage. The forms of coin use that show the most visible growth in this period are those tied in with elite action, such as the land market, and building commercial activity in the orbit of towns and castles, the two being linked together. There were probably many others less apparent from surviving sources. Monetisation depended on groups or landholders who plumbed themselves and their dependants or neighbours more firmly into the milieu of markets. Intensity of coin use waxed and waned even within zones of intensifying monetisation. Contexts existed where coin might have been used but without the same impact, such as exchanges that were less directly associated with the elite. This subsidiary tier of secondary circulation among peasants and lords was less tied into aggressive, dynamic practices; a world that had probably always known some coin and thinking in terms of money, but still moved at a slower pace in much the same way as it had probably done for a century or two already. Nonetheless, circulation of this kind remained a by-product of an arena dominated by elite activities.[330]

326. The beginnings and pace of demographic growth remain contentious and impressionistic: Fossier 1989, 88–107; Contamine et al. 1993, 141–46; Wickham 2009a, 543–45; Hinton 2013.

327. Le Roy Ladurie 1971; Duby 1974, 6–11.

328. Select recent discussion with extensive references include McCormick 2019; Preiser-Kapeller 2021; Ljungqvist, Seim, and Huhtamaa 2020.

329. Wickham 2016, 121–40. For selected studies of twelfth-century developments, see Spufford 1988, 109–31; Bolton 2012, 141–223; Wickham 2017, 105–6.

330. On the paradox of peasant access to (and benefit from) exchange systems only increasing at the expense of autonomy, see Wickham 2021, 19–20.

CHAPTER TEN

Conclusion

A SKETCH OF EARLY MEDIEVAL MONEY

THIS BOOK BEGAN BY challenging the claim that early medieval money was negligible in significance and static in its (non)development. These are, I hope, claims that can be safely laid to rest. This book will end by offering something to put in their place. I have broken down the general conclusions into nine principal points.

The first is a basic yet, arguably, important one: people in early medieval western Europe *did* continue to think with money right through this period, in virtually all regions for which we have information. And in a large proportion of that area, coined money continued to be made and used as well. It is flat-out wrong to say that early medieval Europe was not a monetised society. In its own way, it was a rich and layered monetary economy. This should not be read as a knee-jerk defensive reaction, out of bitterness toward those who snub one's own pet period, or as a matter of one-upmanship to try and claim special, primordial economic status for the early Middle Ages (except in the banal sense that each period is special and needs to be read on its own terms). On the contrary, the second point is that this was a time of abject misery and deprivation for many, and of limited horizons for most, with the constrictions of the monetary system being a significant contributory factor. Coins were few, often in high demand, and far from versatile in facilitating either low- or high-value exchange. So much of what modern readers take for granted, in using a range of small change and high-value notes (or, more realistically at the time of writing, cards or electronic payments) would have been impossible or massively cumbersome with the resources available in the early Middle Ages. All the same, people in the ninth or tenth century would never really have known a different situation, and they were geared to view money as a measure of the material world as well as a means of exchange.

These are very general points, and the third major conclusion is that the large areas considered in this book were far from homogeneous. Individual regions all followed different paths, leading to important divergences between the major units considered here: primarily England, the Frankish lands, Italy from Rome to the Alps, Scandinavia, and Spain. But even this allowance for regional distinctions is only a half measure. The form and experience of money varied on a microregional level too. Within each of these bigger segments were areas of more or less coin use, or breaks in how minting was arranged. Rome was quite different from Tuscany, Kent from Northumbria, the Rhineland from Aquitaine. We are looking at a web of smaller economic units that had their own histories. Finally, even on a local level, the penetration and impact of money would vary. Settlement to settlement, even household to household in some cases, circumstances like closeness to towns, access to markets, or involvement in particular social or seigneurial networks might lead to very different experiences of money.

The fourth point follows on closely from the third and relates to the pace and timing of change. Larger developments are easily sketched. Minting and access to coin declined in the post-Roman centuries (fastest in Britain and northern Gaul, more slowly in the Mediterranean), and the onset of the silver penny in the seventh century laid the foundations for a reversal of that trend. Within this narrative, however, were many localised rises and falls that redrew the monetary landscape many times over the early Middle Ages. Production and access to coined money vacillated multiple times, on a level of decades rather than centuries. One generation might well have found, if they talked to their elders, that coin had been much scarcer or more plentiful within recent decades. An inhabitant of Lundenwic in about 700, for instance, would have seen relatively plentiful silver pennies all around them but heard a rather different story from grandparents who could remember growing up in the 650s, when debased gold pieces were the norm. But if the Londoner of 700 survived into old age and told their own offspring about the past in 750 or so, they would have found themselves in a time of renewed scarcity. These pulses did not follow the exact same course everywhere, though there were correlations between some nearby, interconnected regions (such as England, Frisia, and western Francia). They were also not unique to the early Middle Ages: there was a "bullion famine" in the later fourteenth and early fifteenth centuries, for example. As in that case, bullion supply and the fragile structures that carried metal to mints were one factor dictating the scale of coin production and use, though far from the only one. It is also more difficult to explain retreats in minting and circulation than expansions. Fiscal or administrative shocks, as at the end of central Roman rule in the West, are one factor here; other possibilities are wider economic contractions or shortfalls in supply of bullion. The precarious state of early medieval currency meant, on the one hand, that these swings could have a big effect, sometimes to all intents and purposes wiping out the production of coinage; on the other, it meant that people were prepared to cope with the absence of coin. Elites with control over minting and money supply were best placed to weather the storm and take advantage of better fortune in the future.

Early medieval coin was unusual in that its production depended on local *and* long-distance networks coming together, reflected in where and under what circumstances coins were made. The nature of early medieval minting constitutes the fifth concluding point. Elites exercised dominance over production in most of early medieval Europe: dominance over the location of mint-places, dominance over their regulation, and often dominance over their patronage. In some respects, this amounted to a privatised version of minting, though it was generally still seen as public, in that local elites were the agents and representatives of the states of the period, such as they were. This represents one of the sharpest departures from the Roman model inherited by the early medieval kingdoms, in which the production of coin was the preserve of a more centralised state structure, geared primarily toward handling the expenses of the state, as remained the case in Byzantium and the Caliphate. In early medieval western Europe, the onus passed from the state to the patron, from expenditure to income, and before long direct state demands were no longer the exclusive driving force. This new scenario paved the way for elite needs and tastes to dictate production to a very large degree: access to fresh coin became a social bottleneck.

What happened to coins subsequently, however, is more complicated, and the sixth point to emphasise is that "primary" and "secondary" uses need to be kept quite distinct. Primary concerns production and the needs that immediately precipitated and followed it. If a bishop commissioned new coins to engage in a land purchase, that is a primary use. But if those coins were then spent in diverse ways by the recipient, and spent in turn by others, that was secondary use, which could in theory go on for many steps. The two cannot always be distinguished easily in surviving sources. Nor is there any way to tell with confidence how many hands an individual coin had passed through before coming to rest in the ground, either alone or as part of a hoard—though the mixed character of many hoards is highly suggestive of a churning monetary circulation.

Primary and secondary use were nonetheless quite separate phenomena, and the seventh major point relates to the roles of different groups in them. Elites, as noted, were very probably dominant in primary use in most of early medieval Europe. This mainly meant aristocrats and major churches, but lower elites, such as thegns in England and *milites* in post-Carolingian Frankish lands, also played a role, especially in the late tenth and eleventh centuries as the size of the monetary economy increased. Secondary use is more complicated. It may have extended much further not only geographically but also socially, into networks that were really quite distant from their elite origins in manufacture. In such situations, coin became an important component in fuelling peasant-level commercial engagement. Indeed, one of the distinctive features of many early medieval western societies is that the factors that likely drove primary use were not so different from those behind secondary use: essentially, demand for coin to fulfil a range of social, public, and commercial needs. What differed in primary contexts was who had the resources and connections to patronise fresh minting. Moreover, even elites must in practice have depended heavily on secondary circulation too. Even if lords were demanding more rent, or kings more tribute, in the context of the early Middle Ages they could not expect to get it without commercial activity by which peasants obtained the coins they needed to pay. And lords did not demand everything. There was scope for peasants, individually or collectively, to assemble and use coins for their own benefit. Taken as a whole, this secondary level of circulation might be very substantial and economically meaningful—and also, potentially, rather less dominated by the elite than the actual production of coin.

Three broad models can be proposed for how early medieval minting and circulation knitted together:

1. Minting takes place under the auspices of the elite, and the circulation of the resultant coins is largely confined to "primary" uses. In other words, it hardly left the close economic and social orbit of the elite. Noncommercial uses of coin such as taxes, tributes, gifts, and rents probably loomed relatively large; commerce did take place with coin but was mostly restricted to elites and professional merchants. These conditions are most likely in contexts of very high-value coinage (i.e., when gold was

dominant). Gaul and Iberia in the later fifth century and most of the sixth would probably fall into this category, along with Lombard Italy, with only very limited or informal access to lower-value denominations.

2. Minting takes place under the auspices of the elite, but circulation now penetrates beyond the elite and their immediate entourage. That wider penumbra of use remains structured around elite demands: there is not a wider, self-sustaining level of monetisation. Commercial use was more important than in the first model, perhaps accounting for about as much use as other uses put together, and also more extended socially. Secondary circulation is therefore present but limited in scale and only going a few steps beyond production. The surprisingly numerous and widely circulated gold tremisses of seventh-century Gaul might represent this scenario, and it would also have been common for silver coinages, for instance in Carolingian Italy.

3. Minting itself still takes place largely under the auspices of the elite, although coins are more plentiful and, crucially, much more widely used. Most use reflects secondary circulation, which comfortably surpasses primary. A substantial, self-sustaining, and probably market-led sphere of coin circulation can be discerned: one in which elites were still important, surely still the largest individual actors, but collectively no longer the only viable anchor of demand and resources. Importantly, nonelites can now readily be seen transacting with other nonelites using coin. Eastern England and much of Francia west of the Rhine from the late seventh century reflect this stage of development, to be joined by Italy and Francia east of the Rhine in the late tenth century. On a somewhat different basis, silver circulation in some areas of Scandinavia reached this level in the ninth and tenth centuries.

A few caveats are needed. It is possible to imagine a scenario in which coins circulated widely but generally not commercially. If one were reliant on archaeological evidence alone, this would be a realistic possibility: it is now how many specialists interpret, for example, gold and silver coins in Iron-Age Britain.[1] But written sources show a different situation in the early Middle Ages. Commercial use was not always dominant, and never exclusive, but it always went on to some degree, and often a large degree. It should also be stressed that these three models were never set in stone:

1. E.g., Haselgrove 1987.

regions might easily slip from the third to the second, or even the first, if the supply of coin dried up. They could coexist in close proximity, with specific subregions or segments of society being more or less integrated into monetary circulation and all it entailed. Crucially, economic complexity did not hinge on monetisation. It was entirely possible to have a high degree of commerce without coin or precious metal. The opposite is harder to explain: societies with extensive nonelite circulation of coin likely did have elaborate exchange systems, including a large commercial element. Finally, different regions could take different paths to the same destination: not all model-three monetary systems were the same in kind or scale, for example. These models are intended simply to identify structurally comparable regions, and broad similarities in the form of monetisation are meant as a point of departure for considering further parallels and differences. Some of these have been noted in various chapters; others merit further development. It should, for instance, be taken seriously that eastern England in the early eighth century supported monetisation—and by extension commercialisation—on a level comparable to the eleventh century, or (probably) to Carolingian Francia in the ninth century. Yet the prosperity of early eighth-century England proved transitory, which underscores the fact that these regions were not economically identical; just that they both had rich and complex monetary economies that merit further investigation.

The eighth point continues the theme of how coins were used after being put into circulation. They had limitations, certainly, though these were more quantitative than qualitative. Coined money may not have been used for everything, but it *could* be used for most things if one wished or needed to. Some exchange contexts undoubtedly lent themselves especially well to coin. Coinage best suited uses of medium value, large enough to be feasible with the denominations available, but not so large as to be restricted only to elites. In social terms, coinage lent itself to exchanges involving partners with a relationship of what Marshall Sahlins called "balanced reciprocity," meaning openness to exchange, but guarded enough to want to conclude exchanges reliably, swiftly, and discretely, for which coin was a good tool.[2] It was probably not used between close family members (unless one wanted to make a point), and maybe not even with immediate neighbours (for whom informal credit was likely more appropriate); coin was more likely to be used when dealing with others who were known loosely or not at all but who used familiar, trusted mechanisms of exchange. People could put their trust in the coins and their

2. Sahlins 1972, 194–95.

issuers, as well as in the individuals they transacted with. Coined money thus expanded most readily when conditions of relative social and economic complexity prevailed and can (at least in many of the regions considered here) be read as a good proxy for a baseline of commercial activity.

Coins were also used in other kinds of exchange of more formal or social character, including rent, compensation or fine, and gift-giving. These noncommercial uses of coin were not (or at least rarely) dominant in quantitative terms, and they depended to a significant degree on a bedrock of buying and selling, but they are important as a guide to the meaning held by coined money. This is the ninth and final point. Cash supposedly brought a form of equity, and even commercial exploitation was framed more as bullying of the powerless by the powerful. To use coin when it formed a limited and partial component of exchange, and even of money understood more broadly, amounted to a choice and a statement. It was also performative: the act of handing over coins carried weight. Coinage was imbued with ideas of purity, trust, and authority. To use it was to put oneself on the line, for while coins might externalise and reify value, they still had to be transferred between human actors. Handing over money introduced a discrete, balanced quality but did not turn all exchanges into transactions even though there was normally a commercial base to monetary circulation. Calculative expression through coin was deployed within, and subordinated to, other social frameworks of exchange; it did not overwhelm or threaten them. This is almost a reversal of Pierre Bourdieu's observation that "the unstable, artificially maintained structures of the good-faith economy break up and make way for the *clear, economic* (i.e., *economical*) concepts of the undisguised self-interest economy."[3] To deal in coin was not just a neutral and narrowly economic action. It was to participate consciously and meaningfully in a shared web of obligation, horizontal in theory even if frequently vertical and uneven in practice. There is an obvious contradiction here: in principle coin facilitated and levelled up exchange, while in practice being heavily weighted toward those with wealth and social power. That tension lay at the heart of the early medieval monetary economy.

{⟨⟩}

Early medieval money has long been the victim of an inferiority complex. Because it was meagre in quantity and is hence not amenable to most quantitative methodologies, it often fades into insignificance, both in studies of

---

3. Bourdieu 1977, 172 (emphases in the original).

the early medieval economy and in those of the long-term development of monetary history. No early medievalist is ever going to win an argument against the material reality that lies behind this thinking. Even periods and areas of relative monetary plenty, like England, Frisia, and western Francia in the decades around 700 or 800, or a wider area in the late tenth and eleventh centuries, were still very much in the foothills of peaks that had been reached in the Roman period and that would be scaled again in the thirteenth and early fourteenth centuries. But what emerges from this survey of early medieval money is that even a small amount of coined currency could be meaningful. It came and went in cycles rather than on a single linear incline. When there was less of it around, why and when one made or used coin mattered as much as the overall quantity. By reconfiguring to an economy of scarcity, in which even marginal uses and shifts had a deep impact, the character of a very real and historically interesting monetary system comes into focus.

AASS   Societas Bollandiensis, ed., 1643–1925. *Acta Sanctorum*, 68 vols. Antwerp: Ioannes Meursius et al.

ASC   *Anglo-Saxon Chronicle*: for text, see Bately, J., ed., 1986. *The Anglo-Saxon Chronicle: A Collaborative Edition*, vol. 3: *MS A*. Cambridge: Brewer; Irvine, S. E., 2004. *The Anglo-Saxon Chronicle: A Collaborative Edition*, vol. 7: *MS E*. Cambridge: Brewer, with translation in Whitelock, D., 1979. *English Historical Documents*, vol. 1: *c. 500–1042*, 2nd ed. London: Routledge.

BMC   Keary, C. F., and A. H. Grueber, 1887–93. *A Catalogue of English Coins in the British Museum: Anglo-Saxon Series*. 2 vols. London: Trustees of the British Museum.

BSFN   *Bulletin de la Société française de numismatique*

CCCM   Corpus Christianorum: continuatio mediaevalis

CCSL   Corpus Christianorum: series latina

CHECKLIST   Fitzwilliam Museum. *Checklist of Coin Hoards from the British Isles, c. 450–1180*. https://www.fitzmuseum .cam.ac.uk/dept/coins/projects/hoards/index.html.

CHLA   Brucker A., and R. Marichal, eds., 1954–98. *Chartae latinae antiquiores: Facsimile Edition of the Latin Charters*. 49 vols. Olten-Zürich: Urs Graf.

CHLA²   Cavallo, G., G. Nicolaj, et al., eds. *Chartae Latinae Antiquiores. Facsimile-Edition of the Latin Charters. 2nd Series: Ninth Century.* 118 vols. Dietikon-Zürich: Urs Graf.

DOE   Cameron, A., A. Crandell Amos, A. dePaolo Healey, et al., eds., 2018. *Dictionary of Old English: A to I*. Toronto: University of Toronto. https://doe.utoronto.ca.

DOML   Dumbarton Oaks Medieval Library

EETS   Early English Text Society

SS   Supplementary Series

EMC   Fitzwilliam Museum, 1999–. *Corpus of Early Medieval Coin Finds*. Cambridge: Fitzwilliam Museum. https://emc.fitzmuseum.cam.ac.uk/.

EME   *Early Medieval Europe*

GDB   "Great" Domesday Book. Kew, National Archives, E 31/2/1–2.

K   Kemble, J. M., ed., 1839–48. *Codex Diplomaticus Aevi Saxonici*. 6 vols. London: English Historical Society.

LCL   Loeb Classical Library

MGH   Monumenta Germaniae Historica

AUCT. ANT.   Auctores antiquissimi

BRIEFE D. DT. KAISERZEIT   Die Briefe der deutschen Kaiserzeit

CONC.   Concilia

DD ARN   Kehr, P., ed., 1940. *Die Urkunden der deutschen Karolinger 3: die Urkunden Arnolfs*. Berlin: Weidmann.

DD CII   Bresslau, H., ed., 1909. *Die Urkunden der deutschen Könige und Kaiser 4: die Urkunden Konrads II. mit Nachträgen zu den Urkunden Heinrichs II*. Hanover, Ger.: Hahn.

DD HII   Bresslau, H., et al., eds., 1900–1903. *Die Urkunden der deutschen Könige und Kaiser 3: die Urkunden Heinrichs II. Und Arduins*. Hanover, Ger.: Hahn.

DD HIII   Bresslau, H., and P. Kehr, 1931. *Die Urkunden der deutschen Könige und Kaiser 5: die Urkunden Heinrichs III*. Berlin: Weidmann.

DD HIV   von Gladiss, D., and A. Gawlik, eds., 1941–78. *Die Urkunden der deutschen Könige und Kaiser 6: die Urkunden Heinrichs IV*. 3 vols. Berlin, Wien, and Hanover: Weidmann, Böhlau, and Hahn.

DD KAR III	Kehr, P., ed., 1937. *Die Urkunden der deutschen Kerolinger 2: die Urkunden Karls III.* Berlin: Weidmann.
DD LDF	Kölzer, T., ed., 2016. *Die Urkunden der Karolinger 2: die Urkunden Ludwigs des Frommen.* 3 vols. Wiesbaden, Ger.: Harrassowitz.
DD OI	Sickel, T., ed., 1879–84. *Die Urkunden der deutschen Könige und Kaiser 1: die Urkunden Konrad I., Heinrich I. und Otto I.* Hanover, Ger.: Hahn.
DD OIII	Sickel, T., ed., 1893. *Die Urkunden der deutschen Könige und Kaiser 2.2: die Urkunden Otto des III.* Hanover, Ger. Hahn.
EPP.	Epistolae
FONTES IURIS	Fontes iuris Germanici antiqui in usum scholarum separatim editi
LDL	Libelli di lite imperatorum et Pontificum
LL	Leges
LL NAT. GERM.	Leges nationum Germanicarum
SS RER. GERM.	Scriptores rerum Germanicarum in usum scholarum separatim editi
SS RER. GERM. N. S.	Scriptores rerum Germanicarum, Nova series
SS RER. MEROV.	Scriptores rerum Merovingicarum
NUMIS	*NUMIS: Online Database of Dutch Finds.* https://nnc.dnb.nl/dnb-nnc-ontsluiting-frontend/#/numis/.
PAS	*Portable Antiquities Scheme.* https://finds.org.uk/.
PASE	*Prosopography of Anglo-Saxon England.* https://pase.ac.uk/index.html.
PASE DOMESDAY	*Prosopography of Anglo-Saxon England: Domesday,* https://domesday.pase.ac.uk/.
PG	Migne, J. P., ed., 1857–66. *Patrologiae Cursus Completus: series Graeca.* 161 vols. Paris: Ateliers catholiques.

PL Migne, J. P., ed., 1844–64. *Patrologiae Cursus Completus: series Latina*. 221 vols. Paris: Ateliers catholiques.

PLS Hamman, A., ed., 1958–74. *Patrologiae Cursus Completus: series Latina. Supplementum*. 5 vols. Paris: Garnier.

PMH Herculano, A., et al., eds., 1868–73. *Portugaliae Monumenta Historica: Diplomata et Chartae*. Lisbon: Academia das Ciências de Lisboa.

S Sawyer, P. H., 1968. *Anglo-Saxon Charters: an Annotated List and Bibliography*. London: Royal Historical Society.

TTH Translated Texts for Historians

BIBLIOGRAPHY

Primary Sources

Andrade Cernadas, J. M., ed. 1995. *O tombo de Celanova: estudio introductorio, edición e índices. ss. IX–XII).* 2 vols. Santiago de Compostela, Sp.: Consello da Cultura Gallega.

Arnold, T., ed. 1882–1885. *Symeonis monachi opera omnia.* 2 vols. London: Longman.

Bachrach, B. S., and D. S. Bachrach, trans., 2014. *Widukind of Corvey: Deeds of the Saxons.* Washington, DC: Catholic University of America Press.

Baethgen, F., ed. 1934. "Vita sancti Arialdi auctore Andrea abbate Strumensi," in *Monumenta Germaniae Historica: Supplementa tomoroum I–XV,* MGH SS 30.2, 1047–75. Leipzig, Ger.: Hiersemann.

Baiges, I. J., et al., eds., 2010. *Els pergamins de l'Arxiu Comtal de Barcelona, de Ramon Berenguer II a Ramon Berenguer IV.* 4 vols. Barcelona: Fundació Noguera.

Bandy, A. C., ed. and trans., 1983. *Ioannes Lydus on Powers, or, the Magistracies of the Roman State.* Philadelphia: American Philosophical Society.

Barsocchini, D., ed., 1833. *Memorie e documenti per servire all'istoria di Lucca 5.2.* Lucca, It.: Francesco Bertini.

Bartoli Langeli, A., ed., 2005. "I documenti," in *Carte di famiglia. Strategie, rappresentazione e memoria del gruppo familiare di Totone di Campione (721–877),* ed. S. Gasparri and C. La Rocca, 237–64. Rome: Viella.

Bately, J., ed., 1986. *The Anglo-Saxon Chronicle: A Collaborative Edition.* Vol. 3: *MS A.* Cambridge: Brewer.

Bautier, R.-H., ed., 1967. *Recueil des actes d'Eudes, roi de France, 888–98.* Paris: Imprimerie nationale.

Bautier, R.-H., and J. Dufour, eds., 1978. *Recueil des actes de Robert Ier et de Raoul, rois de France 922–936.* Paris: Imprimerie nationale.

Baxter, J. H., ed. and trans., 1930. *Augustine: Select Letters,* LCL 239. Cambridge, MA: Harvard University Press.

Beach, A. I., M.T.L. Shannon, and S. S. Sutherland, trans., 2020. *Monastic Experience in Twelfth-Century Germany: The Chronicle of Petershausen in Translation.* Manchester, UK: Manchester University Press.

Bernard, A., and A. Bruel, eds., 1876–1903. *Recueil des chartes de l'abbaye de Cluny.* 6 vols. Paris: Imprimerie nationale.

Bestall, J. M., and D. V. Fowkes, eds., 1977. *Chesterfield Wills and Inventories, 1521–1603.* Matlock, UK: Derbyshire Record Society.

Bethmann, L., and G. Waitz, eds., 1878. "Pauli historia Langobardorum," in *Scriptores rerum Langobardicarum et Italicarum saec. VI–IX,* MGH, 12–192. Hanover, Ger.: Hahn.

Bieler, L., ed., 1993. *Libri epistolarum Sancti Patricii episcopi.* Dublin: Royal Irish Academy.

Bitterauf, T., ed., 1905–09. *Die Traditionen des Hochstifts Freising.* 2 vols. Munich: G. Himmer.

Bjarni Aðalbjarnarson, ed., 1941–51. *Snorri Sturluson: Heimskringla.* 3 vols. Reykjavík: Hið íslenzka fornritafélag.

Bjornlie, M. S., trans., 2019. *Cassiodorus: The Variae. The Complete Translation.* Oakland: University of California Press.

Blake, E. O., ed., 1962. *Liber Eliensis,* Camden Third Series 92. London: Royal Historical Society.

Bloch, H., ed., 1898 and 1902. "Die älteren Urkunden des Klosters S. Vanne zu Verdun," in *Jahrbuch der Gesellschaft für Lothringische Geschichte* 10:338–449 and 14:48–150.

Blockley, R. C., ed. and trans., 1981–1983. *The Fragmentary Classicising Historians of the Later Roman Empire: Eunapius, Olympiodorus, Priscus and Malchus.* 2 vols. Liverpool, UK: F. Cairns.

Blum, O. J., and I. M. Resnick, trans., 1989–2005. *The Letters of Peter Damian.* 6 vols. Washington, DC: Catholic University of America Press.

Boretius, A., ed., 1868. "Liber legis Langobardorum Papiensis," in *Legum: tomus IIII,* MGH LL 4, 289–585. Hanover, Ger.: Hahn.

———, 1883. *Capitularia regum Francorum: Tomus primus,* MGH Capit. 1. Hanover, Ger.: Hahn.

Boretius, A., and V. Krause, eds., 1897. *Capitularia regum Francorum: Tomus secundus,* MGH Capit. 2. Hanover, Ger.: Hahn.

Bresslau, H., ed., 1915. *Die Werke Wipos,* MGH SS rer. Germ. 61. Hanover, Ger.: Hahn.

Brooks, N. P., and S. Kelly, eds., 2013. *Charters of Christ Church Canterbury,* Anglo-Saxon Charters 17–18. 2 vols. Oxford: Oxford University Press.

Bruel, A., ed., 1876–1903. *Recueil des chartes de l'abbaye de Cluny.* 6 vols. Paris: Imprimerie nationale.

Brühl, C., and C. Violante, eds., 1983. *Die "Honorantie civitatis Papie": Transkription, Edition, Kommentar.* Cologne, Ger.: Böhlau.

Bultot-Verleysen, A.-M., ed. and trans., 2009. *Odon de Cluny: Vita sancti Geraldi Auriliacensis,* Subsidia hagiographica 89. Brussels: Société des Bollandistes.

Butzer, P. L., and D. Lohrmann, eds., 1993. *Science in Western and Eastern Civilization in Carolingian Times.* Basel, Switz.: Birkhäuser Verlag.

Cadier, L., ed., 1884. *Cartulaire de Sainte Foi de Morlaas.* Pau, Fr.: Léon Ribaut.

Cameron, A., ed. and trans., 1976. *Flavius Cresconius Corippus: In laudem Iustini minoris libri IV.* London: Athlone Press.

Campbell, A., ed., 1973. *Charters of Rochester,* Anglo-Saxon Charters 1. London: Oxford University Press.

Carozzi, C., ed. and trans., 1979. *Adalbéron de Laon: Poème au roi Robert.* Paris: Belles lettres.

Castagnetti, A., ed., 1979. *Inventari altomedievali di terre, coloni e redditi.* Rome: Istituto storico Italiano.

Chavanon, J., ed., 1897. *Adémar de Chabannes: Chronique.* Paris: Alphonse Picard.

Chiesa, P., ed., 1998. *Liudprandi Cremonensis opera omnia,* CCCM 156. Turnhout, Bel.: Brepols.

Clavadetscher, O. P., et al., eds., 1983–. *Chartularium Sangallense*. 13 vols. Sigmaringen, Ger.: J. Thorbecke.

Clercq, C. de, ed., 1963. *Concilia Galliae a. 511–695*, CCSL 148A. Turnhout, Bel.: Brepols.

Colgrave, B., and R.A.B. Mynors, eds. and trans., 1969. *Bede's Ecclesiastical History of the English People*. Oxford: Oxford University Press.

Compton, M. B., 1996. "Introducing the Acts of the Apostles: A Study of John Chrysostom's *On the Beginning of Acts*." PhD dissertation, University of Virginia.

Courtois, E.A.C., ed., 1952. *Tablettes Albertini: actes privés de l'époque vandale, fin du V. siècle*. Paris: Arts et métiers graphiques.

Courtois, J., ed., 1908. *Chartes de l'abbaye de Saint-Etienne de Dijon, VIII, IX, X et XI siècles*. Dijon, Fr.: Nourry.

Coussemakers, I. de, ed., 1884. *Cartulaire de l'abbaye de Cysoing*. Lille, Fr.: Société de Saint-Augustin.

Crick, J., ed., 2007. *Charters St. Albans*, Anglo-Saxon Charters 12. Oxford: Oxford University Press.

Davidson, I. J., ed. and trans., 2001. *Ambrose: De officiis*. 2 vols. Oxford: Oxford University Press.

Davis, N., ed., 1971–1976. *Paston Letters and Papers of the Fifteenth Century*. 2 vols. Oxford: Clarendon Press.

Davril, A., A. Dufour, and G. Labory, eds. and trans., 2019. *Les miracles de saint Benoît: Miracula sancti Benedicti*. Paris: CNRS éditions.

Deloche, M., ed., 1859. *Cartulaire de l'abbaye de Beaulieu (en Limousin)*. Paris: Imprimerie impériale.

Deville, J. A., ed., 1841. *Cartulaire de l'abbaye de la Sainte-Trinité du mont de Rouen*. Paris: n.p.

Devroey, J.-P., ed., 1984. *Le polyptyque et les listes de cens de l'abbaye de Saint-Rémi de Reims (IXe–XIe siècles)*. Reims, Fr.: Académie nationale de Reims.

Dewing, H. B., ed. and trans., 1914–28. *Procopius: History of the Wars*, LCL 48, 81, 107, 173, and 217. 5 vols. London: William Heinemann.

Dolbeau, F., ed., 1996. *Augustin d'Hippone: Vingt-six sermons au peuple d'Afrique*. Paris: Institut d'études augustiniennes.

Doniol, H., ed., 1863. *Cartulaire de Brioude*. Clermont-Ferrand, Fr.: F. Thibaud.

———, 1864. *Cartulaire de Sauxillanges*. Clermont-Ferrand, Fr.: F. Thibaud.

Drew, K. F., trans., 1991. *The Laws of the Salian Franks*. Philadelphia: University of Pennsylvania Press.

Dümmler, E., ed., 1895. *Epistolae Karolini aevi: Tomus II*, MGH Epp. 4. Berlin: Weidmann.

———, 1925. "Lupi abbatis Ferrariensis epistolae," in *Epistolae Karolini aevi: Tomus IV*, MGH Epp. 6, 127–206. Berlin: Weidmann.

Dutton, P. E., trans., 1998. *Charlemagne's Courtier: The Complete Einhard*. Peterborough, ON: Broadview.

Eckhardt, K. A., ed., 1962. *Pactus legis Salicae*, MGH LL nat. Germ. 4.1. Hanover, Ger.: Hahn.

Edgington, S. B., ed. and trans., 2007. *Albert of Aachen: Historia Ierosolimitana; History of the Journey to Jerusalem*. Oxford: Oxford University Press.

Ehwald, R., ed., 1919. *Aldhelmi opera*, MGH Auct. ant. 15. Berlin: Weidmann.

Eidelberg, S., ed., 1955. *Teshuvot rabenu Gershom meor hagola.* New York: Yeshiva University.

Elmshäuser, K., A. Hedwig, and D. Hägermann, eds., 1993. *Das Polyptychon von Saint-Germain-des-Prés.* Cologne, Ger.: Böhlau.

Étaix, R., ed., 1999. *Gregorius Magnus: Homiliae in evangelia,* CCSL 141. Turnhout, Bel.: Brepols.

Fairweather, J., trans., 2005. *Liber Eliensis: A History of the Isle of Ely from the Seventh Century to the Twelfth.* Woodbridge, UK: Boydell.

Faller, O., and Zelzer, M., ed., 1968–90. *Sancti Ambrosi opera. Pars 10: Epistulae et acta.* 2 vols. Vienna: Hoelder-Pichler-Tempsky.

Farley, A., ed., 1783. *Domesday Book, seu liber censualis Willelmi primi regis Angliæ, inter archivos regni in domo capitulari Westmonasterii asseruatus.* 2 vols. London.

Feger, O., ed., 1956. *Die Chronik des Klosters Petershausen.* Lindau, Ger.: J. Thorbecke.

Ferri, G., ed., 1904. "Le carte dell'archivio Liberiano dal secolo X al XV," *Archivio della Società Romana di storia patria* 27: 147–202, 441–59.

Finlay, A., and A. Faulkes, trans., 2011–15. *Snorri Sturluson: Heimskringla.* 3 vols. London: Record Commission.

Finnur Jónsson, ed., 1932. *Morkinskinna.* Copenhagen: J. Jørgensen.

Fontaine, J., and N. Dupré, eds. and trans., 2006. *Sulpice Sévère: Gallus; dialogues sur les "vertus" de saint Martin.* 2 vols. Paris: Cerf.

Foulke, D., trans., 1907. *History of the Lombards, by Paul the Deacon.* Philadelphia: University of Pennsylvania, Department of History.

Fraipont, J., ed., 1968. *Sancti Fulgentii episcopi Ruspensis opera,* CCSL 91. 2 vols. Turnhout, Bel.: Brepols.

France, J., ed. and trans., 1989. *Rodulfus Glaber: Opera.* Oxford: Oxford University Press.

Garmonsway, G. N., ed., 1978. *Ælfric's Colloquy.* 2nd ed. Exeter, UK: University of Exeter Press.

Garrigue, G., ed., 1971. *Salvien de Marseille: Oeuvres I–II: Lettres et les livres de Timothée; Du gouvernement de Dieu.* 2 vols. Paris: Cerf.

Gasparri, S., ed. and trans., 1996. *Suger: Œuvres,* Classiques de l'histoire de France au Moyen Age 37 and 41. 2 vols. Paris: Belles lettres.

Gaubert, C., and J.-M. Mouton, eds. and trans., 2014. *Hommes et villages du Fayyoum dans la documentation papyrologique arabe (Xe–XIe siècles),* Haute études orientales: Moyen et Proche-Orient 52. Geneva: Droz.

Gilsdorf, S., trans., 2004. *Queenship and Sanctity: The Lives of Mathilda and the Epitaph of Adelheid.* Washington, DC: Catholic University of America Press.

Glöckner, K., ed., 1929–36. *Codex Laureshamensis.* 3 vols. Darmstadt, Ger.: Hessische historische Kommission.

Glöckner, K., and A. Doll, eds., 1979. *Traditiones Wizenburgenses: die Urkunden des Klosters Weissenburg, 661–864.* Darmstadt, Ger.: Hessische historische Kommission.

Godden, M., ed., 1979. *Ælfric's Catholic Homilies: The Second Series. Text,* EETS SS 5. Oxford: Oxford University Press.

Godden, M., ed. and trans., 2016. *The Old English History of the World: An Anglo-Saxon Rewriting of Orosius,* DOML 44. Cambridge, MA: Harvard University Press.

Goullet, M., ed., 2003. *Adsonis Dervensis opera hagiographica*, CCCM 198. Turnhout, Bel.: Brepols.

Grandmaison, C. de, ed., 1864. *Le livre des serfs de Marmoutier*. Tours, Fr.: Ladevèze.

Grasilier, T., ed., 1871. *Cartulaires inédits de la Saintonge II: Cartulaire de l'abbaye royale de Notre-Dame de Saintes de l'ordre de Saint-Benoît*. Niort, Fr.: L. Clouzot.

Grat, F., et al., eds., 1978. *Recueil des actes de Louis II le Bègue, Louis III et Carloman II, rois de France, 877–884*. Paris: C. Klincksieck.

Grocock, C., and I. N. Wood, eds. and trans., 2013. *Abbots of Wearmouth and Jarrow*. Oxford: Oxford University Press.

Guérard, B.E.C., ed., 1844. *Polyptyque de l'abbé Irminon*. 2 vols. Paris: Imprimerie royale.

———, 1857. *Cartulaire de l'Abbaye de Saint-Victor de Marseille*. 2 vols. Paris: Lahure.

Gwara, S., and D. W. Porter, eds. and trans., 1997. *Anglo-Saxon Conversations: The Colloquies of Ælfric Bata*. Woodbridge, UK: Boydell.

Hadley, J., and D. Singmaster, trans., 1992. "Problems to Sharpen the Young," *Mathematical Gazette* 76:102–26.

Haefele, H. F., ed., 1959. *Notker der Stammler: Taten Kaisers Karls des Grossen*, MGH SS rer. Germ. N. S. 12. Berlin: Weidmann.

Halphen, L., ed. and trans., 1938. *Éginhard: vie de Charlemagne*. 2nd ed. Paris: Belles lettres.

Halphen, L., and R. Poupardin, eds., 1913. *Chroniques des comtes d'Anjou et des seigneurs d'Amboise*. Paris: Auguste Picard.

Hampe, K., ed., 1899. "Frotharii episcopi Tullensis epistolae," in *Epistolae Karolini aevi: Tomus III*, MGH Epp. 5, 240–74. Berlin: Weidmann.

Hanquet, K., ed., 1906. *La Chronique de Saint-Hubert, dite Cantatorium*. Brussels: Kiessling et Cie, P. Imbreghts.

Harmer, F. E., ed., 1952. *Anglo-Saxon Writs*. Manchester, UK: Manchester University Press.

Hartmann, W., ed., 1984. *Die Konzilien der karolingischen Teilreiche 843–859*, MGH Conc. 3. Hanover, Ger.: Hahn.

Hartmann, W., I. Schröder, and G. Schmitz, eds., 2012. *Die Konzilien der karolingischen Teilreiche, 875–911*, MGH Conc. 5. Hanover, Ger.: Hahn.

Hauréau, J.-B., et al., eds., 1715–1865. *Gallia Christiana in provincias ecclesiasticas distributa*. . . . 16 vols. Paris: Coignard.

Haury, J., ed., 1905–13. *Procopii Caesariensis opera omnia*. 3 vols. in 4. Leipzig, Ger.: Teubner.

Heinemann, F. J., trans., 1997. "The Saga of the People of Svarfadardal," in *The Complete Sagas of Icelanders, Including 49 Tales*, ed. Viðar Hreinsson. 5 vols., 4:149–92. Reykjavík: Leifur Eiríksson.

Hellmann, S., ed., 1909. *Pseudo-Cyprianus De XII abusivis saeculi*, Texte und Untersuchung zur Geschichte der altchristlichen Literatur 4.1. Leipzig, Ger.: Hinrichs.

Hilberg, I., ed., 1910–18. *Sancti Eusebii Hieronymi Epistulae*. 2nd ed. Corpus Scriptorum Ecclesiasticorum Latinorum 54–56. 3 vols. Vienna: Tempsky.

Hill, E., trans., 1997. *Augustine of Hippo. Sermons: Newly Discovered Sermons*. Hyde Park, NY: New City.

Holder-Egger, O., ed., 1887a. "Ex Miraculis S. Benedicti auctore Adrevaldo Floriacensi," in *Supplementa tomorum I–XII, pars III: supplementum tomi XIII,* MGH SS 15.1, 474–97. Hanover, Ger.: Hahn.

———, 1887b. "Ex Translatione S. Sebastiani auctore Odilone," in *Supplementa tomorum I–XII, pars III: supplementum tomi XIII,* MGH SS 15.1, 377–91. Hanover, Ger.: Hahn.

———, 1888a. "Ex miraculis SS. Ursmari et Ermini auct. Folquino abate et monachis Laubiensibus," in *Supplementa tomorum I–XII, pars III: supplementum tomi XIII,* MGH SS 15.2, 831–37. Hanover, Ger.: Hahn.

———, 1888b. "Miracula S. Bavonis Gandavensis minora," in *Supplementa tomorum I–XII, pars III: supplementum tomi XIII,* MGH SS 15.2, 589–620. Hanover, Ger.: Hahn.

Holtzmann, R., 1935. *Die Chronik des Bischofs Thietmar von Merseburg und ihre korveier Überarbeitung,* MGH SS rer. Germ. N. S. 9. Berlin: Weidmann.

Huygens, R.B.C., ed., 2008. *Christianus dictus Stabulensis: Expositio super Librum generationis,* CCCM 224. Turnhout, Bel.: Brepols.

Ireland, R., ed. and trans., 1979. *De rebus bellicis: The Text.* Oxford: B. A. R.

Irvine, S. E., ed., *The Anglo-Saxon Chronicle: A Collaborative Edition.* Vol. 7: *MS E.* Cambridge: Brewer, 2004.

Jacob, G., trans., 1927. *Arabische Berichte von Gesandten an germanischen Fürstenhöfe aus dem 9. und 10. Jahrhundert: ins Deutsche übertragen und mit Fußnoten versehen.* Berlin: de Gruyter.

Jacobsen, P. C., ed. and trans., 2016. *Die Geschichte vom Leben des Johannes, Abt des Klosters Gorze.* MGH SS rer. Germ. 81. Wiesbaden, Ger.: Harrassowitz.

Jacobsson, M., ed., 2018. *Augustinus: de musica,* Corpus Scriptorum Ecclesiasticorum Latinorum 102. Berlin: de Gruyter.

Jacquemard-Le Saos, C., ed. and trans., 1994. *Querolus (Aulularia); Le Grincheux, comédie de la petite marmite.* Paris: Belles lettres.

Jesse, W., 1924. *Quellenbuch zur Münz- und Geldgeschichte des Mittelalters.* Halle, Ger.: A. Riechmann.

Johnson, C., ed. and trans., 1950. *Richard, Son of Nigel, Treasurer of England and Bishop of London: The Course of the Exchequer.* London: Thomas Nelson.

Jónas Kristjánsson, ed., 1956. *Svarfdœla saga. Eyfirðinga sǫgur,* Íslendinga sögur 20. Reykjavík: Handritasofnun Islands.

Jurasinski, S., and L. Oliver, eds., 2021. *The Laws of Alfred: The Domboc and the Making of Anglo-Saxon Law.* Cambridge: Cambridge University Press.

Kay, N. M., ed. and trans., 2006. *Epigrams from the Anthologia Latina.* London: Bloomsbury.

Kelly, S. E., ed., 2000–2001. *Charters of Abingdon Abbey,* Anglo-Saxon Charters 7–8. 2 vols. Oxford: Oxford University Press.

———, 2004. *Charters of St Paul's, London,* Anglo-Saxon Charters 10. Oxford: Oxford University Press.

———, 2009. *Charters of Peterborough Abbey,* Anglo-Saxon Charters 14. Oxford: Oxford University Press.

Kennedy, A., and S. Keynes, forthcoming. *Charters of Ely Abbey.* Oxford: Oxford University Press.

Kenyon, F. G., and H. I. Bell, eds., 1907. *Greek Papyri in the British Museum III*. London: Trustees of the British Museum.

Klein, T., ed., 1991. *"Versus de Uniboue*. Neuedition mit kritischem Kommentar," *Studi medievali*, 3rd ser., 32:843–86.

Koder, J., ed. and trans., 1991. *Das Eparchenbuch Leons des Weisen*. Vienna: Österreichischen Akademie der Wissenschaften.

Kramer, J., H. Magennis, and R. Norris, eds. and trans., 2020. *Anonymous Old English Lives of Saints*, DOML 63. Cambridge, MA: Harvard University Press.

Kramers, J. H., and G. Wiet, trans., 1964. *Configuration de la terre. Kitāb Sūrat al-arḍ)*. 2 vols. Paris: Commission internationale pour la traduction des chefs-d'oeuvre.

Krueger, P., et al., eds., 1877–95. *Corpus iuris civilis*. 3 vols. Berlin: Weidmann.

Krusch, B., ed., 1888. *Fredegarii et aliorum chronica, vitae sanctorum*, MGH SS rer. Merov. 2. Hanover, Ger.: Hahn.

——, 1902. *Passiones vitaeque sanctorum aevi Merovingici* [II], MGH SS rer. Merov. 4. Hanover, Ger.: Hahn.

——, 1969. *Gregorii episcopi Turonensis miracula et opera minora*, MGH SS rer. Merov. 1.2. 2nd ed. Hanover, Ger.: Hahn.

Krusch, B., and W. Levison, eds., 1951. *Gregorii episopi Turonensis libri historiarum X*, MGH SS rer. Merov. 1. Hanover, Ger.: Hahn.

Labande, E. R., ed. and trans., 1981. *Guibert de Nogent: Autobiographie*. Paris: Belles lettres.

Lagarrigue, G., ed. and trans., 1971–75. *Salvien de Marseille: oeuvres*. 2 vols. Paris: Cerf.

Lake, J., ed. and trans., 2011. *Richer of Saint-Rémi: Histories*, DOML 10 and 11. 2 vols. Cambridge, MA: Harvard University Press.

Lambot, C., ed., 1948. "Les sermons LX et CCCLXXXIX de Saint Augustin sur l'aumône," *Revue bénédictine* 58:23–52.

Lapidge, M., ed. and trans., 2003. *The Cult of St Swithun*. Oxford: Clarendon.

Lapidge, M., and M. Winterbottom, eds. and trans., 1991. *Wulfstan of Winchester: The Life of St Æthelwold*. Oxford: Oxford University Press.

Lauer, P., ed., 1905. *Les annals de Flodoard*. Paris: Alphonse Picard et fils.

——, 1940–49. *Recueil des actes de Charles III le Simple, roi de France, 893–923*. 2 vols. Paris: Imprimerie nationale.

Lelong, E., ed., 1903. *Cartulaire de l'abbaye de Saint-Aubin d'Angers*. Paris: A. Picard et fils.

Leo, F., ed., 1881. *Venanti Honori Clementiani Fortunati presbyteri Italici opera poetica*, MGH Auct. ant. 4.1. Berlin: Weidmann.

Lesort, A., ed., 1909–12. *Chronique et chartes de l'abbaye de Saint-Mihiel*. Paris: C. Klincksieck.

Levillain, L., ed., 1926. *Recueil des actes de Pépin Ier et de Pépin II, rois d'Aquitaine, 814–848*. Paris: Imprimerie nationale.

Licence, T., ed., 2014. *Herman the Archdeacon and Goscelin of Saint-Bertin: Miracles of St Edmund*. Oxford: Oxford University Press.

Liebermann, F., ed., 1903–16. *Die Gesetze der Angelsachsen*. Halle, Ger.: M. Niemeyer.

Liebeschuetz, J.H.W.G., trans., 2005. *Ambrose of Milan: Political Letters and Speeches*, TTH 43. Liverpool, UK: Liverpool University Press.

Lohmann, H.-E., and P. Hirsch, eds., 1935. *Die Sachsengeschichte des Widukind von Korvei*, SS rer. Germ. 60. 5th ed. Hanover, Ger.: Hahn.

Loscertales de García de Valeavellano, P., ed., 1976. *Tumbos del monasterio de Sobrado de los Monjes*. 2 vols. Madrid: Dirección General del Patrimonio Artístico y Cultural.

Lunde, P., and Stone, C., trans., 2012. *Ibn Fadlan and the Land of Darkness: Arab Travellers in the Far North*. London: Penguin.

MacAlhany, J., and J. Rubenstein, trans., 2011. *Guibert of Nogent and On the Relics of Saints: The Autobiography and a Manifesto of a French Monk from the Time of the Crusades*. London: Penguin.

Macray, W. D., ed., 1886. *Chronicon Abbatiae Rameseiensis*. London: Longman.

Maloney, G. A., trans., 1992. *Pseudo-Macarius: The Fifty Spiritual Homilies and the Great Letter*. New York: Paulist Press.

Manaresi, C., ed., 1955–60. *I placiti del "Regnum Italiae,"* Fonti per la storia d'Italia 92 and 96–97. 3 vols. in 5. Rome: Tipografia del Senato.

Maya Sánchez, A., ed., 1992. *Vitas sanctorum patrum Emeretensium*, CCSL 116. Turnhout, Bel.: Brepols.

Métais, C., ed., 1893–1904. *Cartulaire de l'abbaye cardinale de la Trinité de Vendôme*. 5 vols. Paris: A. Picard et fils.

Miller, S., ed., 2001. *Charters of the New Minster, Winchester*, Anglo-Saxon Charters 9. Oxford: Oxford University Press.

Mommsen, T., ed., 1894. *Cassiodori senatoris Variae*, MGH Auct. Ant. 12. Berlin: Weidmann.

Mommsen, T., and P. M. Meyer, eds., 1905. *Theodosiani libri xvi cum constitutionibus Sirmondianis et leges novellae ad Theodosianum pertinentes*. 2 vols. in 3. Berlin: Weidmann.

Nelson, J. L., trans., 1991. *The Annals of St-Bertin*, Ninth-Century Histories 1. Manchester, UK: Manchester University Press.

De Nie, G., ed. and trans., 2015. *Gregory of Tours: Lives and Miracles*, DOML 39. Cambridge, MA: Harvard University Press.

Noble, T.F.X., trans., 2009. *Charlemagne and Louis the Pious: The Lives by Einhard, Notker, Ermoldus, Thegan and the Astronomer*. University Park, PA: Penn State University Press.

Norberg, D., ed., 1982. *S. Gregorii Magni registrum epistularum*, CCSL 140–140A. 2 vols. Turnhout, Bel.: Brepols.

O'Donnell, R. D., ed. and trans., 1981. "The *Querolus*, Edited with an Introduction and Commentary." PhD dissertation, Royal Holloway, University of London.

O'Donovan, M. A., ed., 1988. *Charters of Sherborne*, Anglo-Saxon Charters 3. Oxford: Oxford University Press.

O'Sullivan, J. F., trans., 1947. *The Writings of Salvian, the Presbyter*. New York: Cima.

Pertz, G. H., and F. Kurze, eds., 1891. *Annales Fuldenses, sive Annales regni Francorum orientalis*, MGH SS rer. Germ. 7. Hanover, Ger.: Hahn.

Pharr, C., trans., 1952. *The Theodosian Code and Novels, and the Sirmondian Constitutions*. Princeton, NJ: Princeton University Press.

Piazzi, P., et al., eds., 1873–2015. *Codex diplomaticus Cavensis*. 12 vols. Naples, It.: Mediolani.

Planchenault, A., ed., 1903. *Cartulaire du chapitre de Saint-Laud d'Angers (actes du XIe et du XIIe siècle)*. Angers, Fr.: Germain & G. Grassin.

Porro-Lambertenghi, G., ed., 1873. *Codex diplomaticus Langobardiae*, Historiae Patriae Monumenta 13. Turin, It.: Regio Typographico.

Poupardin, R., ed., 1905. *Monuments de l'histoire des abbayes de Saint-Philibert*. Paris: Alphonse Picard.

Ragut, M.-C., ed., 1864. *Cartulaire de Saint-Vincent de Mâcon*. Mâcon, Fr.: É. Protat.

Reindel, K., ed., 1983–1993. *Die Briefe des Petrus Damiani*. 4 vols. MGH Briefe d. dt. Kaiserzeit 4.1–4. Munich: Monumenta Germaniae Historica.

Reuter, T., trans., 1992. *The Annals of Fulda*, Ninth-Century Histories 2. Manchester, UK: Manchester University Press.

Rio, A., trans., 2008. *The Formularies of Angers and Marculf: Two Merovingian Legal Handbooks*, TTH 46. Liverpool, UK: Liverpool University Press.

Robertini, L., ed., 1994. *Liber miraculorum sancte Fidis*, Biblioteca di Medioevo latino 10. Spoleto, It.: Centro italiano di studi sull'Alto Medioevo.

Robertson, A. J., ed. and trans., 1956. *Anglo-Saxon Charters*. 2nd ed. Cambridge: Cambridge University Press.

Robinson, C. H., trans., 1921. *Anskar: The Apostle of the North 801–865*. London: Society for the Propagation of the Gospel.

Rolfe, J. C., ed. and trans., 1935–39. *Ammianus Marcellinus: History*, LCL 300, 315, and 331. 3 vols. Cambridge, MA: Harvard University Press.

——, with introduction by K. R. Bradley, 1997–98. *Suetonius*, LCL 31 and 38. Cambridge, MA: Harvard University Press.

Rousseau, F., ed., 1936. *Actes des comtes de Namur de la première race, 946–1196*. Brussels: M. Hayez.

Salis, L. R. de, ed., 1892. *Leges Burgundionum*, MGH LL nat. Germ. 2.1. Hanover, Ger.: Hahn.

Salrach i Marés, J. M., and T. Montagu i Estragués, eds., 2018. *Justicía i resolució de conflictes a la Catalunya medieval: col·lecció diplomàtica, segles IX–XI*. Barcelona: Generalitat de Catalunya; Parlament de Catalunya.

Schaff, P., and H. Wace, trans., 1890–1900. *A Select Library of Nicene and Post-Nicene Fathers of the Christian Church; Second Series*. 14 vols. Oxford: Parker.

Schiaparelli, L., ed., 1903. *I diplomi di Berengario I*. Rome: Forzani.

Scholz, B. W., and B. Rogers, trans., 1970. *Carolingian Chronicles: Royal Frankish Annals and Nithard's Histories*. Ann Arbor: University of Michigan Press.

Schwab, I., ed., 1983. *Das Prümer Urbar*. Düsseldorf, Ger.: Droste.

Schwerin, C. von, ed., 1918. *Leges Saxonum und Lex Thuringorum*, MGH Fontes iuris 4. Hanover, Ger.: Hahn.

Seeck, O., ed., 1883. *Q. Aurelii Symmachi quae supersunt*, MGH Auct. Ant. 6.1. Berlin: Weidmann.

Sheingorn, P., and R.L.A. Clark, trans., 1995. *The Book of Sainte Foy*. Philadelphia: University of Pennsylvania Press.

Sheppard, J. B., and J. C. Robertson, eds., 1875–85. *Memorials for the History of Thomas Becket, Archbishop of Canterbury. Canonized by Pope Alexander III (A.D. 1173)*. 7 vols. London: Longman.

Sitwell, G., trans., 1958. *St. Odo of Cluny, Being the Life of St. Odo of Cluny by John of Salerno, and the Life of St. Gerald of Aurillac by St. Odo*. New York: Sheed and Ward.

Squatriti, P., trans., 2007. *The Complete Works of Liudprand of Cremona*. Washington, DC: Catholic University of America Press.

Tenckhoff, F., ed., 1921. *Vita Meinwerci episcopi Patherbrunnensis*, MGH SS rer. Germ. 59. Hanover, Ger.: Hahn.

Tessier, G., et al., eds., 1943–55. *Recueil des actes de Charles II le Chauve, roi de France*. 3 vols. Paris: Imprimerie nationale.

Thaner, F., ed., 1891. "Humberti Cardinalis libri III adversus simoniacos," in *Libelli de lite imperatorum et pontificum saeculis XI et XII: tomus I*, MGH Ldl 1, 95–253. Hanover, Ger.: Hahn.

Thorpe, L., trans. 1969. *Two Lives of Charlemagne: Einhard and Notker the Stammerer*. London: Penguin.

———. 1974. *Gregory of Tours: The History of the Franks*. Harmondsworth, UK: Penguin.

Tomás-Faci, G., and J. C. Martín-Iglesias, eds. and trans., 2017. "Cuatro documentos inéditos del monasterio visigodo de San Martín de Asán (522–586)," *Mittellateinisches Jahrbuch* 52:261–86.

Trémault, C. A. de, ed. 1893. *Cartulaire de Marmoutier pour le Vendômois*. Paris: Alphonse Picard et fils.

Ubieto Arteta, A., ed. 1976. *Cartulario de San Millán de la Cogolla, 756–1076*. Valencia, Sp.: Anubar.

Vallée, E., A. Ledru, and G. Busson, eds., 1902. *Actus Pontificum Cenomannis in urbe degentium*. Le Mans, Fr.: Société des archives historiques du Maine.

Vogüé, A. de, ed. and trans., 1978–80. *Grégoire le Grand: Dialogues*. 3 vols. Paris: Cerf.

Viðar Hreinsson et al., ed. and trans., 1997. *The Complete Sagas of Icelanders, Including 49 Tales*. 5 vols. Reykjavík: Leifur Eiríksson.

Waitz, G., ed., 1878. *Scriptores rerum Langobardicarum et Italicarum saec. VI–IX*, MGH. Hanover, Ger.: Hahn.

Waitz, G., ed., 1883. *Annales Bertiniani*, MGH SS rer. Germ. 5. Hanover, Ger.: Hahn.

———, 1884. *Vita Anskarii auctore Rimberto, accedit Vita Rimberti*, MGH SS rer. Germ. 55. Hanover, Ger.: Hahn.

———, 1887. "Translatio et Miracula SS. Marcellini et Petri auctore Einhardo," in *Supplementa tomorum I–XII, pars III: supplementum tomi XIII*, MGH SS 14, 238–64. Hanover, Ger.: Hahn.

Warner, D. A., trans., 2001. *Ottonian Germany: The Chronicon of Thietmar of Merseburg*. Manchester, UK: Manchester University Press.

Weidemann, M., 1986. *Das Testament des Bischofs Berthramn von Le Mans vom 27. März 616: Untersuchungen zu Besitz und Geschichte einer fränkischen Familie im 6. und 7. Jahrhundert*. Mainz, Ger.: Römisch-Germanischen Zentralmuseum.

Werminghoff, A., ed., 1908. *Concilia aevi Karolini: tomus I, pars II*, MGH Conc. 2.2. Hanover, Ger.: Hahn.

West, C., trans., 2018. "The Will of Eberhard and Gisela, c. 863." http://turbulentpriests .group.shef.ac.uk/wp-content/uploads/2018/12/The-Will-of-Count-Eberhard-and -Gisela.pdf.

Whitelock, D., ed. and trans., 1930. *Anglo-Saxon Wills*. Cambridge: Cambridge University Press.

———, trans. *English Historical Documents. Vol. 1: c. 500–1042*. 2nd ed. London: Routledge, 1979.

Whitelock, D., M. Brett, and C.N.L. Brooke, eds. and trans., 1964–81. *Councils & Synods, with Other Documents Relating to the English Church. Vol 1*. 2 parts. Oxford: Clarendon.

Widemann, J., ed., 1943. *Die Traditionen des Hochstifts Regensburg und des Klosters St. Emmeram*. Munich: Scientia.

Williams, A., and G. H. Martin, trans., 2002. *Domesday Book: A Complete Translation*. London: Penguin.

Winterbottom, M., ed. and trans., 1978. *Gildas: The Ruin of Britain and Other Works*. Chichester, UK: Phillimore.

Winterbottom, M., and R. M. Thomson, eds. and trans., 2002. *William of Malmesbury: Saints' Lives: Lives of SS. Wulfstan, Dunstan, Patrick, Benignus and Indract*. Oxford: Clarendon.

———, 2007. *William of Malmesbury: Gesta pontificum Anglorum; The History of the English Bishops*. 2 vols. Oxford: Oxford University Press.

Wuensch, R., ed., 1903. *Joannis Lydi: De magistratibus populi Romani libri tres*. Stuttgart, Ger.: Teubner.

Zeumer, K., ed., 1886. *Formulae Merowingici et Karolini aevi*, MGH Formulae 1. Hanover, Ger.: Hahn.

———, 1902. *Leges Visigothurum*, MGH LL nat. Germ. 1. Hanover, Ger.: Hahn.

Zimmermann, H., ed., 1984–89. *Papsturkunden 896–1046*. 3 vols. Vienna: Österreichischen Akademie der Wissenschaften.

Ziolkowski, J. M., trans., 1999. "A Medieval 'Little Claus and Big Claus': A Fabliau from before Fabliaux?," in *The World and Its Rival: Essays on Literary Imagination in Honor of Per Nykrog*, ed. K. Karczewska and T. Conley, 1–37. Amsterdam: Rodopi.

Secondary Literature

Aarts, J., 2005. "Coins, Money and Exchange in the Roman World. A Cultural-Economic Perspective," *Archaeological Dialogues* 12:1–28.

Abdy, R., 2006. "After Patching: Imported and Recycled Coinage in Fifth- and Sixth-Century Britain," in Cook and Williams 2006, 75–98.

Abels, R., 1988. *Lordship and Military Obligation in Anglo-Saxon England*. London: British Museum.

Abramson, T., ed., 2014. *Studies in Early Medieval Coinage. Volume 3: Sifting the Evidence*. London: Spink.

———, 2017. *Sceatta List: An Illustrated and Priced Catalogue of Sceats for Collectors*. London: Spink.

Airlie, S., 1995. "The Aristocracy," in McKitterick 1995, 431–50.

———, 2020. *Making and Unmaking the Carolingians 751–888*. London: Bloomsbury.

Akin, D., and J. Robbins, 1999. "An Introduction to Melanesian Currencies: Agency, Identity, and Social Reproduction," in *Money and Modernity: State and Local Currencies in Melanesia*, ed. D. Akin and J. Robbins, 1–40. Pittsburgh: University of Pittsburgh Press.

Algazi, G., 2003. "Feigned Reciprocities: Lords, Peasants, and the Afterlife of Late Medieval Social Strategies," in Algazi, Groebner, and Jussen 2003, 99–127.

Algazi, G., V. Groebner, and B. Jussen, eds., 2003. *Negotiating the Gift: Pre-Modern Figurations of Exchange.* Göttingen, Ger.: Vandenhoeck & Ruprecht.

Allen, M., 2004. "Medieval English Die-Output," *British Numismatic Journal* 74:39–49.

——, 2007. "The Proportions of the Denominations in English Mint Outputs 1351–1485," *British Numismatic Journal* 77:190–209.

——, 2012. *Mints and Money in Medieval England.* Cambridge: Cambridge University Press.

——, 2016. "The Mints and Moneyers of England and Wales, 1066–1158: Addenda and Corrigenda," *British Numismatic Journal* 86:164–90.

Amandry, M., et al., 1982. "L'affinage des métaux monnayés au Bas-Empire: les réformes valentiniennes de 364–368," *Numismatica e antichità classica* 11:279–96.

Amorós Ruiz, V., and C. Doménech Belda, 2020. "Espacio, tiempo y monedas en el Tolmo de Minateda," in *El sitio de las cosas: la alta edad media en contexto,* ed. C. Doménech Belda and S. Gutiérrez Lloret, 161–73. Alicante, Sp.: Universitat d'Alacant.

Andersson, K., 2011. *Guldålder. Svenska arkeologiska skatter.* Uppsala, Swed: Balderson.

Andreau, J., 1987. *La vie financière dans le monde romain: les métiers de manieurs d'argent (IVe siècle av. J.-C.–IIIe siècle ap. J.-C.).* Rome: Palais Farnèse.

Andrén, A., 2008. "Lies about Gotland," in *Facets of Archaeology: Essays in Honour of Lotte Hedeager on her 60th Birthday,* ed. K. Chilidis, J. Lund, and C. Prescott, 47–56. Oslo: Unipub.

——, 2012. "Servants of Thor? The Gotlanders and Their Gods," in *News from Other Worlds: Studies in Nordic Folklore, Mythology and Culture,* ed. M. Kaplan and T. R. Tangherlini, 101–10. Berkeley, CA: North Pinehurst Press.

Archibald, M., 2011. "Testing," in *The Cuerdale Hoard and Related Viking-Age Silver and Gold from Britain and Ireland in the British Museum,* ed. J. Graham-Campbell, 51–64. London: British Museum.

Arens, F. V., and K. F. Bauer, 1958. *Die Inschriften der Stadt Mainz von frühmittelalterlicher Zeit bis 1650.* Stuttgart, Ger.: A. Druckenmüller.

Arnoux, M., 2012. *Le temps des laboureurs: travail, ordre social et croissance en Europe (XIe–XIVe siècle).* Paris: Albin Michel.

——, 2016. "Manger ou cultiver: *laboratores, oratores et bellatores* entre production et consommation. XIe–XIIe siècle)," in *Les communautés rurales dans l'Ouest du Moyen Âge à l'époque moderne: perceptions, solidarité et conflits,* ed. C. J. Jeanneau and P. Jarnoux, 183–98. Brest, Fr.: Centre de recherche Bretonne et Celtique.

——, 2017. "Rivoluzione industriosa e crescita demografica medievale," in *La crescita economica dell'Occidente medievale: un tema storico non ancora esaurito: venticinquesimo Convegno internazionale di studi, Pistoia, 14–17 maggio 2015,* 137–46. Rome: Centro italiano di studi di storia e d'arte.

Arslan, E. A., 1991. "Le monete," in *Scavi MM3: ricerche di archeologia urbana a Milano durante la construzione della linea 3 della metropolitana, 1982–1990,* ed. D. Caporusso, 71–131. Milan: Edizioni ET.

———, 1993. "La struttura delle emissioni monetarie dei Goti in Italia," in *Teoderico il Grande e i Goti d'Italia. Atti del XIII Congresso internazionale di studi sull'Alto Medioevo, Milano 2–6 novembre 1992*, 517–54. Spoleto, It.: Centro italiano di studi sull'alto Medioevo.

———, 1998. "Mutamenti di funzioni e di struttura degli stock monetari in Europa tra V e VIII secolo," *Settimane di studio del Centro italiano di studi sull'alto medioevo* 45:379–460.

———, 2002a. "La moneta in argento dei re longobardi. Un'emissione inedita di Ariperto I," *Numismatica e antichità classica* 31:327–37.

———, 2002b. "La monetazione dei Longobardi," *Studi Monzesi* 11/12:121–36.

———, 2002c. "Le monnayage d'argent de Bénévent à l'époque carolingienne," *Bulletin de la société nationale des antiquaries de France* 2002:224–39.

———, 2003. "Emissione e circolazione della moneta dei ducati di Spoleto e Benevento," in *I Longobardi dei ducati di Spoleto e Benevento: atti del XVI Congresso Internazionale di Studi sull'Alto Medioevo*. 2 vols., 1031–52. Spoleto, It.: Centro italiano di studi sull'alto Medioevo.

———, 2004. "Una frazione di siliqua con il monogramma di re Grimoaldo nell'anfiteatro romano di Milano," *Quaderni del civico museo archaeologico e del civico gabinetto numismatico di Milano*, 67–81.

———, 2005. *Repertorio dei ritrovamenti di moneta Altomedievale in Italia. 489–1002.* Spoleto, It.: Centro italiano di studi sull'alto Medioevo. Further updates published online subsequently, the most recent on 30 August 2016, though no longer online as of January 2022.

———, 2007a. "Ancora sulla questione della cosidetta 'Moneta in rame dell'Italia longobarda': una replica e problemi di metodo," *Rivista italiana di numismatica e scienze affini* 108:491–507.

———, 2007b. "Ceni sulla moneta e sulla politica monetaria a Milano al tempo di Ariberto," in *Ariberto da Intimiano. Fede, potere e cultura a Milano nel secolo XI*, ed. E. Bianchi and M. Basile Weatherill, 397–415. Cinisello Balsamo, It.: Silvana.

———, 2008. "Le monete di Tremona," in *Tremona-Castello. Dal V millennio a.C. al XIII secolo*, ed. A. Martinelli, 357–86. Borgo San Lorenzo, It.

———, 2016. "Un ottavo di siliqua a nome di Cunincpert nella collezione numismatica dell'Università di Pavia e la moneta longobarda in argento nell'VIII secolo," in *I Longobardi oltre Pavia: Conquista, irradiazione e intrecci culturali. Atti della giornata di studio, Pavia, 13 giugno 2015*, ed. G. Mazzoli and G. Miciele, 73–106. Milan: Cisalpino.

———, 2017. "Ancora sulla riforma di Aureliano. XX e XXI: due nominali distinti?," *Bulletin du Cercle d'études numismatiques* 54:2–17.

Arslan, E., and S. Uggé, 2005. "Ritrovamenti dalla pieve di San Giovanni di Mediliano (AL)," in *L'Italia alto-medievale tra archeologia e storia: studi in ricordo di Ottone d'Assia*, ed. S. Gasparri, 33–54. Padua, It.: Il poligrafo.

Ashby, S. P., 2015. "What Really Caused the Viking Age? The Social Content of Raiding and Exploration," *Archaeological Dialogues* 22:89–106.

Ashby, S. P., and S. Sindbæk, eds., 2020. *Crafts and Social Networks in Viking Towns*. Oxford: Oxbow.

Ashtor, E., 1977. "The Development of Prices in the Medieval Near East," in *Wirtschafts-geschichte des Vorderen Orients in Islamischer Zeit*, ed. B. Lewis, 98–115. Leiden, Neth.: Brill.

Asolati, M., 2012. *Praestantia nummorum: Temi I Note di Numismatica Trado Antica e Alto Medievale*. Padua, It.: Esedra.

———, 2016. "La distribuzione della moneta bronzea ufficiale e imitative in età tardo antica: i casi dei gruzzoli di Gortyna 2011 (IV sec. D. C.) e di Aquileia 2011 (V sec. D. C.)," in Chameroy and Guihard 2016, 199–215.

———, 2018. "Nuove scoperte sulle monete bronzee d'età imperiale con contromarche XLII e LXXXIII," in *Percorsi nel Passato: Miscellanea di Studi per i 35 Anni del Gravo e i 25 anni della Fondazione Colluto*, ed. A. Vigoni, 253–65. Rubano, It.: Quasar.

Asolati, M., C. Crisafulli, and C. Mondin, 2019. *Kom Al-Ahmer—Kom Wasit. II: Coin Finds 2012-2016, Late Roman and Early Islamic Pottery from Kom Al-Ahmer*. Oxford: Archaeopress.

Astill, G., 1991. "Towns and Town Hierarchies in Anglo-Saxon England," *Oxford Journal of Archaeology* 10:95–117.

Astill, G., 2006. "Community, Identity and the Later Anglo-Saxon Town: The Case of Southern England," in Reynolds, Davies, and Halsall 2006, 233–54.

———, 2011. "Exchange, Coinage, and the Economy of Early Medieval England," in Escalona Monge and Reynolds, 253–72.

Audy, F., 2018. *Suspended Value: Using Coins as Pendants in Viking-Age Scandinavia (c. AD 800–1140)*. Stockholm: Stockholm University, Department of Archaeology and Classical Studies.

Bachrach, B. S., 1988. "The Angevin Economy, 960–1060: Ancient or Feudal?," *Studies in Medieval and Renaissance History* 20:1–55.

———, 1989. "Some Observations on the Origins of the Angevin Dynasty," *Medieval Prosopography* 10:1–23.

———, 1993. *Fulk Nerra, the Neo-Roman Consul, 987–1040. A Political Biography of the Angevin Count*. Berkeley: University of California Press.

Baerten, J., 1961. "Les Ansfried au Xe siècle," *Revue belge de philologie et d'histoire* 39:1144–58.

Bagnaudez, M., 1974. "Les représentations romanes de l'avare: étude iconographique," *Revue d'Histoire de la Spiritualité* 50:397–432.

Baiges, J., et al., eds., 2010. *Els pergamins de l'Arxiu Comtal de Barcelona, de Ramon Berenguer II a Ramon Berenguer IV*. 4 vols. Barcelona: Fundació Noguera.

Baker, J., and S. J. Brookes, 2015. "Identifying Outdoor Assembly Sites in Early Medieval England," *Journal of Field Archaeology* 40:3–21.

Baklouti, S., et al., 2014. "Provenance and Reference Groups of African Red Slip Ware Based on Statistical Analysis of Chemical Data and REE," *Journal of Archaeological Science* 50:524–38.

Balaguer, A. M., 1999. *Història de la moneda dels comtats Catalans*. Barcelona: Institut d'Estudis Catalans.

Balog, P., 1970. "Islamic Bronze Weights from Egypt," *Journal of the Economic and Social History of the Orient* 13:233–56.

Balzaretti, R., 2019. *The Lands of Saint Ambrose: Monks and Society in Early Medieval Milan*. Turnhout, Bel.: Brepols.

Balzaretti, R., J. S. Barrow, and P. Skinner, eds., 2018. *Italy and Early Medieval Europe: Papers for Chris Wickham*. Oxford: Oxford Unversity Press.

Banaji, J., 1996. "The Circulation of Gold as an Index of Prosperity in the Central and Eastern Mediterranean in Late Antiquity," in *Coin Finds and Coin Use in the Roman World*, ed. C. E. King, 41–53. Berlin: G. Mann.

———, 2007. *Agrarian Change in Late Antiquity: Gold, Labour, and Aristocratic Dominance*. 2nd ed. Oxford: Oxford University Press.

———, 2016. *Exploring the Economy of Late Antiquity: Selected Essays*. Cambridge: Cambridge University Press.

Baratte, F., 2013. "Silver Plate in Late Antiquity," in Hunter and Painter 2013; 57–73.

Barbero, A., and Vigil, M., 1978. *La formación del feudalism en la Península Ibérica*. Barcelona: Crítica.

Barceló Perello, M., 1981. "A Statistical Approach to Multiple Mint Issues of Royal Coinage: The Case of the Visigoths in Hispania (585–711)," in *Statistics and Numismatics*, ed. C. Carcassonne and T. Hackens, 138–54. Strasbourg, Fr.: Conseil de l'Europe.

———, 1997. *El sol que salió por Occidente: estudios sobre el estado omeya en al-Andalus*. Jaén, Sp.: Universidad de Jaén.

Barceló Perello, M., and F. Retamero, 1996. "From Crops to Coin: Which Way Back?," *Gaceta Numismática* 122:53–60.

Barnish, S.J.B., 1985. "The Wealth of Iulianus Argentarius: Late Antique Banking and the Mediterranean Economy," *Byzantion* 55:5–38.

———, 1986. "Taxation, Land and Barbarian Settlement in the Western Empire," *Papers of the British School at Rome* 54:170–95.

Baron, S., et al., 2006. "Medieval Lead Making on Mont-Lozère Massif (Cévennes-France): Tracing Ore Sources using Pb Isotopes," *Applied Geochemistry* 21:241–52.

Barral i Altet, X., 1976. *La circulation des monnaies suèves et visigotiques. Contribution à l'histoire économique du royaume visigot*. Munich: Artemis.

Barrett, J. H., 2008. "What Caused the Viking Age?," *Antiquity* 82:671–85.

Bartels, C., and L. Klappauf, 2012. "Das Mittelalter: der Aufschwung des Bergbaus unter den karolingischen und ottonischen Herrschern, die mittelalterliche Blüte und der Abschwung bis zur Mitte des 14. Jahrhunderts," in *Geschichte des deutschen Bergbaus. Bd. 1: der alteuropäische Bergbau: von den Anfängen bis zur Mitte des 18. Jahrhunderts*, ed. K. Tenfelde, C. Bartels and R. Slotta, 111–248. Münster in Westfalen, Ger.: Aschendorff.

Barthélemy, D., 2009. *The Serf, the Knight, and the Historian*, trans. G. R. Edwards. Ithaca, NY: Cornell University Press.

Bartlett, P., and G. Cores, 2005. "The Coinage of the Visigothic King Sisebut (612–21) from the Mint of Barbi," *Gaceta Numismática* 158–59:3–21.

Bartlett, R., 1993. *The Making of Europe: Conquest, Colonization and Cultural Change 950–1350*. London: Penguin.

Bastien, P., 1988. *Monnaie et donativa au Bas-Empire*. Wetteren, Bel.: Éditions numismatiques romaine.

———, 1992–94. *Le buste monétaire des empereurs romains*. 3 vols. Wetteren, Bel.: Éditions numismatiques romaine.

Bates, D., 1999. "West Francia: The Northern Principalities," in Reuter 1999, 398–419.

——, 2000. "England and the "Feudal Revolution,'" *Settimane di studio del Centro italiano di studi sull'alto medioevo* 47:611–46.

Bates, D., and R. Liddiard, eds., 2013. *East Anglia and Its North Sea World in the Middle Ages.* Woodbridge, UK: Boydell.

Battilossi, S., Y. Cassis, and K. Yago, eds., 2020. *Handbook of the History of Money and Currency.* Singapore: Springer.

Baumann, P., 1990. "The Deadliest Sin: Warnings against Avarice and Usury on Romanesque Capitals in Auvergne," *Church History* 59:7–18.

Bautier, R.-H., 1971. *The Economic Development of Medieval Europe*, trans. H. Karolyi. London: Thames and Hudson.

Baxter, S., 2007. *The Earls of Mercia: Lordship and Power in Late Anglo-Saxon England.* Oxford: Oxford University Press.

——, 2020. "How and Why Was Domesday Made?," *English Historical Review* 135:1085–1131.

Baxter, S., and C. P. Lewis, 2017. "Domesday Book and the Transformation of English Landed Society, 1066–86," *Anglo-Saxon England* 46:343–403.

Bayer, C.M.M., 2007. "*Vita Eligii,*" in *Reallexikon der germanischen Altertumskunde,* ed. J. Hoops and H. Beck, 35 vols., 35:461–524. Berlin: De Gruyter

Bayley, J., 1996. "Crucibles and Cupels," in *The Gold, Silver and Other Non-Ferrous Alloy Objects from Hamwic, and the Non-Ferrous Metalworking Evidence,* ed. D. Hinton, 86–93. Stroud, UK: Sutton.

——, 2018. "Lead Sources in Early Medieval Britain," in Bompaire and Sarah 2018, 55–67.

Belke, K., 1998. "Von der Pflasterstraße zum Maultierpfad? Zum kleinasiatischen Wegenetz in mittelbyzantinischer Zeit," in *Byzantine Asia Minor (6th–12th Cent.),* ed. S. Lampakis, 267–84. Athens: Ethniko Hidryma Ereunōn.

Bell, S., and J. F. Henry, 2001. "Hospitality versus Exchange: The Limits of Monetary Economics," *Review of Social Economy* 59:203–26.

Below, G. von, 1892. *Der Ursprung der deutschen Stadtverfassung.* Düsseldorf, Ger.: L. Voss.

Bendixen, K., 1981. "The Currency in Denmark from the Beginning of the Viking Age until c. 1100," in Blackburn and Metcalf 1981, 405–18.

Benn, C. D., 2002. *Daily Life in Traditional China: The Tang Dynasty.* Westport, CT: Greenwood.

Benseddik, N., and T. W. Potter, 1993. *Fouilles du Forum de Cherchell 1977–1981.* Algiers: Ministère de la culture et du tourisme.

Benvenuti, M., et al., 2019. "Metals and Coinage in Medieval Tuscany: The Colline Metallifere," in *Origins of a New Economic Union (7th–12th Centuries),* ed. G. Bianchi and R. Hodges, 135–46. Sesto Fiorentino, It.: All'Insegna del Giglio.

Beresford, G., 1987. *Goltho: The Development of an Early Medieval Manor c. 850–1150.* London: English Heritage.

Berkhofer, R. F., 2004. *Day of Reckoning: Power and Accountability in Medieval France.* Philadelphia: University of Pennsylvania Press.

Bernareggi, E., 1970. "Attività economiche e circolazione monetaria in età longobarda nella testimonianza delle "chartae,'" *Rivista italiana di numismatica* 72:117–37.

———, 1976. "Struttura economica e monetazione del regno longobardo," *Quaderni ticinesi* 5:331–76.

———, 1983. *Moneta Langobardorum*. Milan: Istituto Editoriale Cisalpino.

Berndt, G. M., and R. Steinacher, 2008. "Minting in Vandal North Africa: Coins of the Vandal Period in the Coin Cabinet of Vienna's Kunsthistorisches Museum," *EME* 16:252–98.

Bernhardt, J. W., 1993. *Itinerant Kingship and Royal Monasteries in Early Medieval Germany c. 936–1075*. Cambridge: Cambridge University Press.

Bertini, F., 1995. "Il contadino medievale, ovvero il profilo del diavolo: una nueva interpretazione dei *Versus de Unibove*," *Maia* 47:325–42.

Berto, L. A., 2021. *Early Medieval Venice: Cultural Memory and History*. London: Routledge.

Bessard, F., 2020. *Caliphs and Merchants: Cities and Economies of Power in the Near East (700–950)*. Oxford: Oxford University Press.

Betlyon, J. W., 2008. "The Coins from the 1975–1978 Seasons in the Punic Port and Tophet of Carthage, Tunisia," *Revue numismatique* 164:321–53.

Bettenay, L., 2022. "Geological and Mining Constraints on Historical Mine Production: The Case of Early Medieval Lead-Silver Mining at Melle, France," *Metalla* 26.2: 67–86.

Bianchi, G., 2018. "Public Powers, Private Powers, and the Exploitation of Metals for Coinage: The Case of Medieval Tuscany," in Balzaretti, Barrow, and Skinner 2018, 384–401.

———, 2020. "Rural Public Properties for an Economic History of the Kingdom of Italy (10th and 11th Centuries): An Archaeological Survey," in Bianchi and Hodges 2020, 185–96.

Bianchi, G., F. Cantini, and S. Collavini, 2019. "Beni pubblici di ambito toscano," in *Beni pubblici, beni del re. Le basi economiche dei poteri regi nell'alto medioevo*, ed. F. Bougard and V. Loré, 277–322. Turnhout, Bel.: Brepols.

Bianchi, G., and S. Collavini, 2017. "Risorse e competizione per le risorse nella Toscana dell'XI secolo," in *Acquérir, prélever, controller: les ressources en compétition (400–1100)*, ed. G. Bührer-Thierry, R. Le Jan, and V. Loré, 171–88. Turnhout, Bel.: Brepols.

———, 2018. "Public Estates and Economic Strategies in Early Medieval Tuscany: Toward a New Interpretation," in Hodges and Bianchi 2018, 147–62.

Bianchi, G., and R. Hodges, eds., 2020. *The nEU-Med Project: Vetricella, an Early Medieval Royal Property on Tuscany's Mediterranean*. Sesto Fiorentino, It.: All'Insegna del Giglio.

Bianchi, G., and Rovelli, A., 2018. "Production minière et production monétaire en Toscane au Moyen Âge (VIIIe–XIIe siècle): un long chemin . . . ," in Bompaire and Sarah 2018, 111–40.

Biddle, M., 2014. "XPICTIANA RELIGIO and the Tomb of Christ," in Naismith, Allen, and Screen 2014, 115–44.

Biddle, M., and D. J. Keene, 1976. "Winchester in the Eleventh and Twelfth Centuries," in *Winchester in the Early Middle Ages: An Edition and Discussion of the Winton Domesday*, ed. M. Biddle, 241–448. Oxford: Clarendon.

Bijovsky, G., 2010. "A Single Die Solidi Hoard of Heraclius from Jerusalem," in *Mélanges Cécile Morrisson*, 55–92. Paris: Association des amis du Centre d'Histoire et Civilisation de Byzance.

Birch, T., et al., 2019. "From *nummi minimi* to *fulūs*—Small Change and Wider Issues: Characterising Coinage from Gerasa/Jerash (Late Roman to Umayyad Periods)," *Archaeological and Anthropological Sciences* 11:5359–76.

Bisson, T. N., 2000. "Princely Nobility in an Age of Ambition, c. 1050–1150," in *Nobles and Nobility in Medieval Europe: Concepts, Origins, Transformations*, ed. A. J. Duggan, 101–13. Woodbridge, UK: Boydell.

———, 2008. *The Crisis of the Twelfth Century: Power, Lordship, and the Origins of European Government*. Princeton, NJ: Princeton University Press.

Blackburn, M.A.S., 1974. "The Mint of Watchet," *British Numismatic Journal* 44:13–38.

———, 1979. "Wærin: A Northampton Moneyer for Eadgar," *Numismatic Chronicle*, 7th series, 19:217–19.

———, 1993. "Coin Circulation in Germany during the Early Middle Ages: The Evidence of Single Finds," in Kluge 1993, 37–54.

———, 1995. "Money and Coinage," in McKitterick 1995, 538–59.

———, 1996. "Mints, Burhs, and the Grately Code, Cap. 14.2," in *The Defence of Wessex: The Burghal Hidage and Anglo-Saxon Fortifications*, ed. D. Hill and A. R. Rumble, 160–75. Manchester, UK: Manchester University Press.

———, 2003. "'Productive' Sites and the Pattern of Coin Loss in England, 600–1180," in *Markets in Early Medieval Europe: Trading and "Productive" Sites, 650–850*, ed. T. Pestell and K. Ulmschneider, 20–36. Macclesfield, UK: Windgather.

———, 2006. "Two New Types of Anglo-Saxon Gold Shillings," in Cook and Williams 2006, 127–40.

———, 2007. "Gold in England during the 'Age of Silver' (Eighth–Eleventh Centuries)," in *Silver Economy in the Viking Age*, ed. J. Graham-Campbell and G. Williams, 55–98. Walnut Creek, CA: Left Coast.

———, 2008. "The Coin-Finds," in Skre 2008, 29–74.

———, 2011. *Viking Coinage and Currency in the British Isles*. London: British Numismatic Society.

Blackburn, M.A.S., and K. Jonsson, 1981. "The Anglo-Saxon and Anglo-Norman Element of North European Coin Finds," in Blackburn and Metcalf 1981, 147–255.

Blackburn, M.A.S., and D. M. Metcalf, eds., 1981. *Viking-Age Coinage in the Northern Lands: the Sixth Oxford Symposium on Coinage and Monetary History*. Oxford: B. A. R.

Blackmore, L., 2002. "The Origins and Growth of *Lundenwic*, a Mart of Many Nations," in *Central Places in the Migration and Merovingian Periods: Papers from the 52nd Sachsensymposium, Lund, August 2001*, ed. B. Hårdh and L. Larsson, 273–301. Stockholm: Almqvist & Wiksell.

Blackmore, L., and C. Scull, 2019. "Belief, Economy and Society," in Blackmore et al. 2019, 297–340.

Blackmore, L., et al., 2019. *The Prittlewell Princely Burial: Excavations at Priory Crescent, Southend-on-Sea, Essex, 2003*. London: Museum of London Archaeology.

Blair, J., 2005. *The Church in Anglo-Saxon Society*. Oxford: Oxford University Press.

———, 2014. "The Tribal Hidage," in Lapidge et al. 2014, 473–75.

———, 2018. *Building Anglo-Saxon England*. Princeton, NJ: Princeton University Press.

Blakelock, E., and C. Fern, 2019. "Workshop Practice," in Fern, Dickinson, and Webster 2019, 123–85.

Blanchard, I.S.W., 2001–2005. *Mining, Metallurgy and Minting in the Middle Ages.* 3 vols. Stuttgart, Ger.: Franz Steiner.

Blanchet, G., 2016. "Vie et survie du petit numéraire dans le nord de la Gaule: l'exemple des découverttes de la domus au grand peristyle de Vieux-la-Romaine. Calvados," in Chameroy and Guihard 2016, 83–96.

———, 2020. "L'étude des monnayages d'argent des Ve–VIe siècles découverts en Gaule: une démarche interdisciplinaire pour de nouvelles hypothèses," *BSFN* 75:352–60.

Bland, R., and X. Loriot, 2010. *Roman and Early Byzantine Gold Coins Found in Britain and Ireland, with an Appendix of New Finds from Gaul.* London: Royal Numismatic Society.

Blet-Lemarquand, M., M. Bompaire, and C. Morrisson, 2010. "Platine et plomb dans les monnaies d'or mérovingiennes: nouvelles perspectives analytiques," *Revue numismatique* 166:175–98.

Bloch, M., 1933. "Le problème de l'or au Moyen Âge," *Annales d'histoire économique et sociale* 5:1–34.

———, 1962. *Feudal Society,* trans. L. A. Manyon. 2nd ed. 2 vols. London: Routledge.

———, 1967. *Land and Work in Mediaeval Europe: Selected Papers,* trans. J. E. Anderson. London: Routledge.

Blume, F. H., et al., eds. and trans., 2016. *The Codex of Justinian.* 3 vols. Cambridge: Cambridge University Press.

Blunt, C. E., C.S.S. Lyon, and B.H.I.H. Stewart, 1963. "The Coinage of Southern England, 796–840," *British Numismatic Journal* 32:1–74.

Boffa, S., 2009. "Le monnayeur Otger: un spécialiste itinérant dans les Pays-Bas au XIe siècle," *Revue belge de numismatique et de sigillographie* 155:209–18.

Bogucki, M., 2011. "The Use of Money in the Slavic Lands from the Ninth to the Eleventh Century: The Archaeological/Numismatic Evidence," in Graham-Campbell, Sindbæk, and Williams 2011, 133–52.

Bohannan, P., 1959. "The Impact of Money on an African Subsistence Economy," *Journal of Economic History* 19:491–503.

Bois, G., 1992. *The Transformation of the Year One Thousand: The Village of Lournand from Antiquity to Feudalism,* trans. J. Birrell. Manchester, UK: Manchester University Press.

Bolton, J. L., 2004. "What Is Money? What Is a Money Economy? When Did a Money Economy Emerge in Medieval England?," in *Medieval Money Matters,* ed. D. S. Wood, 1–15. Oxford: Oxbow.

———, 2012. *Money in the Medieval English Economy 973–1489.* Manchester, UK: Manchester University Press.

———, 2013. "Reply to Pamela Nightingale's 'A Crisis of Credit,'" *British Numismatic Journal* 83:164–65.

Bompaire, M., 2015–2016. "Trouvailles de monnaies de bronze romaines en contexte médiéval: un bouquet de questions," *Journal of Archaeological Numismatics* 5/6, 1–10.

———, 2018. "Le monnayage en Francie occidentale au Xe siècle. L'apport des nouveaux trésors," in Foucray 2018, 305–27.

Bompaire, M., et al., 1998. "La monnaie de Corbie (XIe–XIIe siècles)," *Revue numismatique,* 6th series, 153:297–325.

Bompaire, M., and Dumas, F., 2000. *Numismatique médiévale: monnaies et documents d'origine française*. Turnhout, Bel.: Brepols.

Bompaire, M., and Sarah, G., eds., 2018. *Mine, métal, monnaie, Melle: les voies de la quantification de l'histoire monétaire du haut Moyen Age*. Geneva: Droz.

Bondioli, L., 2021. "Peasants, Merchants, and Caliphs: Capital and Empire in Fatimid Egypt." PhD dissertation, Princeton University.

Bonifay, M., 2004. *Études sur la céramique romaine tardive d'Afrique*. Oxford: Archaeopress.

Bonnassié, P., 2001. *Les sociétés de l'an mil: un monde entre deux âges*. Brussels: De Boeck Université.

Bonnet, C., and J-F. Reynaud, 2000. "Genève et Lyon, capitals burgondes," in Ripoll López and Gurt Esparraguera 2000, 241–66.

Booth, J., 2000. "Northumbrian Coinage and the Productive Site at South Newbald ('Sancton')," in *Early Deira: Archaeological Studies of the East Riding in the Fourth to Ninth Centuries AD*, ed. H. Geake and J. Kenny, 83–97. Oxford: Oxbow.

Borek, N., 2012. "'Specialized Personnel': The Zygostatēs, the Solidus, and Monetary Technology in the Later Roman Empire." MA thesis, Queen's University at Kingston, ON.

Bornholdt-Collins, K., A. Fox, and J. Graham-Campbell, 2014. "The 2003 Glenfaba Hoard (c. 1030), Isle of Man," in Naismith, Allen, and Screen 2014, 471–514.

Botet y Sisó, J., 1908–11. *Les monedes catalanes*. 3 vols. in 2. Barcelona: Institut d'estudis catalans.

Bothe, L., S. Esders, and H. Nijdam, eds., 2021. *Wergild, Compensation and Penance: The Monetary Logic of Early Medieval Conflict Resolution*. Leiden, Neth.: Brill.

Bouchard, C. B., 1988. "The Bosonids or Rising to Power in the Late Carolingian Age," *French Historical Studies* 15:407–31.

Bougard, F., 1995. *La justice dans le royaume d'Italie de la fin du VIIIe siècle au début du XIe siècle*. Rome: École française de Rome.

———, 1996. "Trésors et mobilia italiens du haut Moyen Age," in *Les trésors de sanctuaires de l'Antiquité à l'époque romane*, ed. J.-P. Caillet and P. Bazin, 161–97. Paris: Université de Paris X.

———, 2002. "Genèse et réception du Mâconnais de Georges Duby," in *Studi sulle società e le culture del Medioevo per Girolamo Arnaldi*, ed. L. Gatto and P. Supino Martini, 33–56. Florence, It.: All'Insegna del Giglio.

———, 2008. "Adalhard de Corbie entre Nonantola et Brescia (813): commutatio, gestion des biens monastiques et marché de la terre," in *Puer Apuliae: mélanges offerts à Jean-Marie Martin*, ed. E. Cuozzo, V. Déroche, A. Peters-Custot, and V. Prigent, 51–68. Paris: Association des amis du centre d'Histoire et Civilisation de Byzance.

———, 2010. "Le crédit dans l'Occident du haut Moyen Âge: documentation et pratique," in Le Jan, Feller, and Devroey 2010, 439–78.

———, 2018. "L'église de Varsi et son chartrier. Pouvoirs, territoires, communauté, VIIIe–Xe siècle," in *La fabrique des sociétés médiévales méditerranéennes: les Moyen Âge de François Menant*, ed. D. Chamboduc de Saint Pulgent and M. Dejoux, 421–32. Paris: Éditions de la Sorbonne.

———, 2019. "Les biens et les revenus publics dans le royaume d'Italie (jusqu'au milieu du Xe siècle)," in *Biens publics, biens du roi. Les bases économiques des pouvoirs royaux dans le haut Moyen Âge*, ed. F. Bougard and V. Loré, 79–120. Turnhout, Bel.: Brepols.

Bougard, F., G. Bührer-Thierry, and R. Le Jan, 2013. "Elites in the Early Middle Ages: Identities, Strategies, Mobility," *Annales. Histoire, sciences sociales* 68:1079–1112.

Bougard, F., and R. Le Jan, 2010. "Quelle mobilité sociale dans l'Occident du haut Moyen Âge?," in *La mobilità sociale nel Medioevo*, ed. S. Carocci, 41–68. Rome: École française de Rome.

Bougard, F., and V. Loré, eds., 2019. *Biens publics, biens du roi. Les bases économiques des pouvoirs royaux dans le haut Moyen Âge*. Turnhout, Bel.: Brepols.

Bourdieu, P., 1977. *Outline of a Theory of Practice*, trans. R. Nice. Cambridge: Cambridge University Press.

——, 1990. *The Logic of Practice*, trans. R. Nice. Cambridge: Polity.

Bourgeois, L., 2009. *Une résidence des comtes d'Angoulême autour de l'an mil: le castrum d'Andone (Villejoubert, Charente): publication des fouilles d'André Debord, 1971–1995*. Caen, Fr.: Publications du CRAHM.

——, 2013a. "Castrum et habitat des élites: France et ses abords (vers 880–vers 1000)," in *Cluny. Les moines et la société au premier âge féodal*, ed. D. Russo and C. Sapin, 471–94. Rennes, Fr.: Presses universitaires de Rennes.

——, 2013b. "Production et distinction: l'artisan au château (Nord-Ouest de l'Europe, Xe–XIIe siècles)," in *Richesse et croissance au Moyen Âge: orient et occident*, ed. D. Barthélemy and J.-M. Martin, 151–82. Paris: ACHCByz.

——, 2014. "Melle: la ville, les pouvoirs et les hommes (VIe–XIe siècles)," in *Du monde franc aux califats omeyyade et abbasside: extraction et produits de mines d'argent de Melle et de Jabali*, ed. F. Téreygeol, 11–28. Bochum, Ger.: Deutsches Bergbau-Museum.

Bourgeois, L., and F. Téreygeol, 2005. "Melle (Deux-Sèvres)," in *Les petites villes du Haut-Poitou de l'Antiquité au Moyen Âge: Formes et Monuments 2*, ed. L. Bourgeois, 77–112. Chauvigny, Fr.: Association des publications Chauvinoises.

Bowes, K., 2021. "When Kuznets Went to Rome: Roman Economic Well-Being and the Reframing of Roman History," *Capitalism* 2:7–40.

Bowes, K., et al., 2021. "Non-Agricultural Production, Markets, and Trade," in *The Roman Peasant Project 2009–2014: Excavating the Roman Rural Poor*, ed. K. Bowes, 543–65. Philadelphia: University of Pennsylvania Museum of Archaeology and Anthropology.

Boyer, J. F., 1995. "Contribution à l'étude des circonscriptions civiles carolingiennes du Limousin," *Bulletin de la Société archéologique et historique du Limousin* 122:23–45.

——, 2018. *Pouvoirs et territoires en Aquitaine du VIIe au Xe siècle: enquête sur l'administration locale*. Stuttgart, Ger.: Franz Steiner.

Brachmann, H., 1992. "Der Harz als Wirtschaftsraum des frühen Mittelalters," *Harz-Zeitschrift* 43/44:7–25.

Braddick, M. J., 2000. *State Formation in Early Modern England c. 1550–1700*. Cambridge: Cambridge University Press.

Bradley, J., 2008. *"You Shall Surely Not Die": The Concepts of Sin and Death as Expressed in the Manuscript Art of Northwestern Europe, c. 800–1200*. 2 vols. Leiden, Neth.: Brill.

Brambilla, C., 1883. *Monete di Pavia*. Pavia, It.: Fratelli Fusi.

Breatnach, L., 2014. "Forms of Payment in the Early Irish Law Tracts," *Cambrian Medieval Celtic Studies* 68:1–20.

Brenner, R. P., 1976. "Agrarian Class Structure and Economic Development in Pre-Industrial Europe," *Past and Present* 70:30–74.

Brenot, C., 1980. "Monnaies en cuivre du VIe siècle frappées à Marseille," in *Mélanges de numismatique, d'archéologie et d'histoire offerts à Jean Lafaurie*, ed. P. Bastien et al., 181–88. Paris: Société française de numismatique.

———, 2003. "Le bronze du Ve siècle à la lumière de quelques sites provençaux," *Revue numismatique* 159:41–56.

Breternitz, P., 2018. "Das Ende der eigenständigen friesischen Münzprägung im 8. Jahrhundert. Beobachtungen zur Chronologie der Porcupinevarianten B, E und F," *Jaarboek voor Munt- en Penningkunde* 105:83–102.

———, 2020. *Königtum und Recht nach dem Dynastiewechsel: das Königskapitular Pippins des Jüngeren*. Ostfildern, Ger.: Jan Thorbecke Verlag.

Bridbury, A. R., 1980. "Review of T. N. Bisson, *Conservation of Coinage: Monetary Exploitation and Its Restraint in France, Catalonia, and Aragon c. 1000–1225 AD* (Oxford, 1979)," *Economic History Review* 33:291–92.

———, 1992. *The English Economy from Bede to the Reformation*. Woodbridge, UK.

Brink, S., 1996. "Forsaringen. Nordens äldsta lagbud," in *Beretning fra femtende tværfaglige vikingesymposium*, ed. E. Roesdahl and P. Meulengracht Sørensen, 27–55. Højbjerg, Den.: Hikuin og Afdeling for Middelalder-arkæologi.

———, 2008. "Law and Society: Polities and Legal Customs in Viking Scandinavia," in Brink and Price, 23–31.

Brink, S., and N. Price, eds., 2008. *The Viking World*. London: Routledge.

Brocard, M., M. Messiez-Poche, and P. Dompnier, 1983. *Histoire des communes savoyardes 3: La Maurienne, Chamoux, La Rochette*. Roanne, Fr.: Éditions Horvath.

Brooks, N. P., 1979. "England in the Ninth Century: The Crucible of Defeat," *Transactions of the Royal Historical Society*, 5th series, 29:1–20.

———. 2003. "Alfredian Government: The West Saxon Inheritance," in *Alfred the Great: Papers from the Eleventh-Centenary Conferences*, ed. T. Reuter, 153–74. Aldershot, UK: Ashgate.

Brown, D., 1981. "The Dating of the Sutton Hoo Coins," *Anglo-Saxon Studies in Archaeology and History* 2:71–86.

Brown, P., 1981. *The Cult of the Saints: Its Rise and Function in Latin Christianity*. Chicago: University of Chicago Press.

———. 2012. *Through the Eye of a Needle: Wealth, the Fall of Rome, and the Making of Christianity in the West, 350–550 AD*. Princeton, NJ: Princeton University Press.

———. 2013. "From *Patriae Amator* to *Amator Pauperum* and Back Again: Social Imagination and Social Change in the West between Late Antiquity and the Early Middle Ages, ca. 300–600," in *Cultures in Motion*, ed. D. T. Rodges, B. Raman, and H. Reimitz, 87–106. Princeton, NJ: Princeton University Press.

———. 2015. *The Ransom of the Soul: Afterlife and Wealth in Early Western Christianity*. Cambridge, MA: Harvard University Press.

Bruand, O., 1997. "Circulation monétaire et pouvoirs politiques locaux sous les Mérovingiens et les Carolingiens (du VIIe au IXe siècle)," in *Actes des congrès de la Société des historiens médiévistes de l'enseignement supérieur public. 28e congrès,* 47–59. Clermont-Ferrand, Fr.: Publications de la Sorbonne.

———, 2002. *Voyageurs et marchandises aux temps carolingiens: les réseaux de communicaton entre Loire et Meuse aux VIIIe et IXe siècles.* Brussels: De Boeck Université.

———, 2018a. "Monnayage et pouvoirs régionaux entre le IXe et le XIe siècle. Réflexions sur le cas de Melle et de quelques ateliers proches," in Bompaire and Sarah 2018, 311–28.

———, 2018b. "Numismatique et hiérarchie politique au Xe siècle: les monnayages immobilisés, antiquaries féodaux, et leur signification," *Bulletin de la Société nationale des antiquaries de France,* 209–24.

Brubaker, L., and J. Haldon, 2011. *Byzantium in the Iconoclast Era c. 680–850: A History.* Cambridge: Cambridge University Press.

Brühl, C., 1995. "Die merowingische Immunität," in *Chiesa e mondo feudale nei secoli X–XII. Atti della dodicesima Settimana internazionale di studio. Mendola 24–28 agosto 1992,* 27–44. Milan: Vita e pensiero.

Brunner, H., 1886. "Die Freilassung durch Schatzwurf," in *Historische Aufsätze, dem Andenken an Georg Waitz gewidmet,* 55–72. Hanover, Ger.: Hahn.

Brunner, K., 1973. "Der fränkische Fürstentitel im neunten und zehten Jahrhundert," in *Intitulatio II. Lateinische Herrscher- und Fürstentitel im neunten und zehnten Jahrhundert,* ed. H. Wolfram, 179–340. Vienna: Böhlau.

Buc, P., 2019. "What Is Order? In the Aftermath of the 'Feudal Transformation' Debates," *Francia* 46, 281–300.

Bücher, C., 1901. *Industrial Evolution,* trans. S. Morley Wickett. New York: Holt.

Bührer-Thierry, G., S. Patzold, and J. Schneider, eds., 2018. *Genèse des espaces politiques IXe–XIIe siècle: autour de la question spatiale dans les royaumes francs et post-carolingiens.* Turnhout, Bel.: Brepols.

Bull, M., 1993. *Knightly Piety and the Lay Response to the First Crusade: The Limousin and Gascony c. 970–c. 1130.* Oxford: Oxford University Press.

Bullough, D. A., 1966. "Urban Change in Early Medieval Italy: The Example of Pavia," *Papers of the British School at Rome* 34:82–130.

Bur, M., 1991. "Le diplôme de Charles le Chauve du 22 novembre 864 relatif à la monnaie de Châlons-sur-Marne. Un faux," in *Villes et campagnes au Moyen Âge. Mélanges Georges Despy,* ed. J.-M. Duvosquel and A. Dierkens, 135–41. Liège, Bel.: Éditions du Perron.

Burnett, A., 1989. Review of Bastien 1988, *Numismatic Chronicle* 149:254–55.

Burnham, B. C., and H. Burnham, 2004. *Dolaucothi-Pumsaint: Survey and Excavations at a Roman Gold-Mining Complex 1987–1999.* Oxford: Oxbow.

Bursche, A., 2001. "Roman Gold Medallions as Power Symbols of the Germanic Élite," in *Roman Gold and the Development of the Early Germanic Kingdoms: Aspects of Technical, Socio-Political, Socio-Economic, Artistic and Intellectual Development, A.D. 1–550. Symposium in Stockholm, 14–16 November 1997,* ed. B. Magnus, 83–102. Stockholm: Kungl. Vitterhets, historie och antikvitets akademien.

———, 2002. "Circulation of Roman Coinage in Northern Europe in Late Antiquity," *Histoire et mesure* 17:121–41.

Butcher, K., 1995. "The Coins," in *Nicopolis ad Istrum: A Roman, Late Roman, and Early Byzantine City*, ed. A. Poulter, 269–314. London: Society for the Promotion of Roman Studies.

Butcher, K., et al., 2003. *Small Change in Ancient Beirut: The Coin Finds from BEY 006 and 045. Persian, Hellenistic, Roman and Byzantine Periods*. Beirut: Faculty of Arts and Sciences, American University of Beirut.

Buttrey, T. V., 1976. "The Coins," in *Excavations at Carthage 1975 Conducted by the University of Michigan. Vol. 1*, ed. J. H. Humphrey, 157–97. Tunis: Cérès Productions.

———. 1994. "Calculating Ancient Coin Production II: Why It Cannot Be Done," *Numismatic Chronicle* 154:341–52.

Byock, J., 2001. *Viking Age Iceland*. London: Penguin.

Cabała, J., et al., 2019. "Pb-Rich Slags, Minerals, and Pollution Resulted from a Medieval Ag-Pb Smelting and Mining Operation in the Silesian-Cracovian Region (Southern Poland)," *Minerals* 2020.

Cahn, J., 1911. *Münz- und Geldgeschichte der im Großherzogtum Baden vereinigten Gebiete. 1. Teil: Konstanz und das Bondensseegebiet im Mittelalter*. Heidelberg, Ger.: C. Winter.

Cahn, K. S., 1969. "The Roman and Frankish Roots of the Just Price of Medieval Canon Law," *Studies in Medieval and Renaissance History* 6:1–52.

Callmer, J., 2015. "The Background and the Early History of the Neck Rings of the Glazov Type (Also Called Permian) and the Beginnings of East-West Connections in Early Medieval Europe in the 8th and 9th Centuries," in *Small Things, Wide Horizons. Studies in Honour of Birgitta Hårdh*, ed. L. Larsson et al., 13–19. Oxford: Archaeopress.

Callu, J.-P., 1980a. "Frappes et trésors d'argent de 324 à 392," in *Imperial Revenue: Expenditure and Monetary Policy in the Fourth Century A.D.*, ed. C. E. King, 175–254. Oxford: B.A.R.

———, 1980b. "Rôle et distribution des espèces en bronze de 348 à 392," in *Imperial Revenue, Expenditure and Monetary Policy in the Fourth Century A.D.*, ed. C. E. King, 41–124. Oxford: B.A.R.

Callu, J-P., and Loriot, X., 1990. *La dispersion des aurei en Gaule romaine sous l'Empire*, Cahiers Ernest-Babelon 3. Juan-les-Pins, Fr.: A.P.D.C.A.

Campbell, D., 2010. "The *Capitulare de villis*, the *Brevium exempla*, and the Carolingian Court at Aachen," *EME* 18:243–64.

Campbell, J., 2000. *The Anglo-Saxon State*. London: Hambledon and London.

———, 2005. "Hundreds and Leets: A Survey with Suggestions," in *Medieval East Anglia*, ed. C. Harper-Bill, 153–67. Woodbridge, UK: Boydell.

Canovaro, C., et al., 2013. "Characterization of Bronze Roman Coins of the Fifth Century Called *nummi* through Different Analytical Techniques," *Applied Physics A* 113:1019–28.

Cantilena, R., A. Rovelli, and L. Saguì, 2017. "Towards a Contextual Approach to Numismatics: A Methodological Reflection," in Pardini, Parise, and Marani 2017, 179–89.

Cantini, F., 2014. "Produzioni ceramiche ed economie in Italia centro-settentrionale," in Valenti and Wickham 2014, 341–64.

Canto, A., and E. Marsal Moyano, 1988. "Hallazgo de moneda emiral de Iznajar (Granada)," *Al Qanṭara* 9:427–80.

Capetillo-Ponce, J., 2004–05. "Contrasting Simmel's and Marx's Ideas on Alienation," *Human Architecture: Journal of the Sociology of Self-Knowledge* 1–2:117–21.

Cardon, T., 2015–16. "Monnaies de bronze en contexte médiéval: la position du problème en France," *Journal of Archaeological Numismatics* 5/6:11–26.

———, 2021. *Pour une approche anthropologique des usages monétaires médiévaux (France du Nord, XIIe–XVIe siècle)*. Caen, Fr.: Presses univeritaires de Caen.

Carlà, F., 2009. *L'oro nella tarda antichità: aspetii economici e sociali*. Turin, It.: S. Zamorani.

———, 2010. "The End of Roman Gold Coinage and the Disintegration of a Monetary Area," *Annali dell'Istituto italiano di numismatica* 56:45–114.

Carlà-Uhink, F., 2020. "Three Metals, but No Trimetallism: The Status of Silver Coinage in Late Antiquity and its Designations," in *Argentum Romanorum sive Barbarorum, Tradition und Entwicklung im Gebrauch des Silbergeldes im römischen Westen. 4.–6. Jh.*, ed. J. Chameroy and P.-M. Guihard, 1–16. Mainz, Ger.: Römisch-Germanischen Zentralmuseum.

Carlot, A., 1903. *Étude sur le domesticus franc*. Liège, Bel.: H. Vaillant-Carmanne.

Carlsson, D., 1999. "Harbours and Farms on Gotland," in *Europeans or Not? Local Level Strategies on the Baltic Rim 1100–1400 AD*, ed. N. Blomkvist, 115–24. Kalmar, Swed.: Centre for Baltic Studies, Gotland University College.

———, 2005. "'Ridanæs': A Viking Age Port of Trade at Fröjel, Gotland," in Brink and Price 2008, 131–34.

———, 2009. "Owner Missing? The Hoard, the Farm and the Community," in Petterson 2009, 65–107.

———, 2016. *Paviken Research Project 2013–2016: Investigation of a Viking Age Trading and Manufacturing Site on Gotland, Sweden*. Visby, Swed.: Arendus.

———, 2020. "Gotland: Silver Island," in Gruszczyński, Jankowiak, and Shephard 2020, 225–41.

Carnap-Bornheim, C. von, 2001. "The Social Position of the Germanic Goldsmith A.D. 0–500," in *Roman Gold and the Development of the Early Germanic Kingdoms: Aspects of Technical, Socio-Political, Socio-Economic, Artistic and Intellectual Development, A.D. 1–550. Symposium in Stockholm, 14–16 December 1997*, ed. B. Magnus, 263–78. Stockholm: Kungl. Vitterhets, historie och antikvitets akademien.

Caron, E., 1875–82. "Catalogue raisonné des monnaies baronales provenant de la découverte de Sierck (Moselle)," in *Mélanges de numismatique*, ed. L. F. C. de Saulcy. 3 vols., 3:240–83. Le Mans, Fr.: E. Monnoyer.

Carozzi, C., 1978. "Les fondements de la tripartition sociale chez Adalbéron de Laon," *Annales* 33:683–702.

Carrié, J.-M., 2012. "Were Late Roman and Byzantine Economies Market Economies? A Comparative Look at Historiography," in *Trade and Markets in Byzantium*, ed. C. Morrisson, 13–26. Washington, DC: Dumbarton Oaks Research Library and Collection.

Carroll, J., A. Reynolds, and B. Yorke, eds., 2019. *Power and Place in Europe in the Early Middle Ages*. Oxford: Oxford University Press.

Casquero, M.-A. M., 2005. "*Pecunia*. Historia de un vocablo," *Pecunia* 1:1–12.

Cassidy, R. J., 2011. "The Exchanges, Silver Purchases and Trade in the Reign of Henry III," *British Numismatic Journal* 81:107–18.

———, 2013. "The Royal Exchanges and Mints in the Period of Baronial Reform," *British Numismatic Journal* 83:134–48.

Castagnetti, A., 1995. "Immigrati nordici, potere politico e rapporti con la società longobarda," in *Kommunikation und Mobilität im Mittelalter. Begegnungen zwischen dem Süden und der Mitte Europas (11.-14. Jahrhundert)*, ed. S. W. de Rachewitz and J. Riedmann, 27–60. Sigmaringen, Ger.: J. Thorbecke.

———, 2009. "Le aristocrazie della Langobardia nelle città e nei territory rurali," *Settimane di studio del Centro italiano di studi sull'alto medioevo* 50:231–98.

———, 2017. *La società milanese in età carolingia*. Verona, It.: GoPrint.

Chaffee, J. W., and D. Twitchett, eds., 2015. *The Cambridge History of China. Volume 5: Sung China, 960-1279 AD. Part 2*. Cambridge: Cambridge University Press.

Challis, C. E., 1978. *The Tudor Coinage*. Manchester, UK: Manchester University Press.

Chambon, J.-P., 2001. "L'identification des noms d'ateliers monétaires mérovingiens (Arvernie et entours): point de vue du linguiste," *Revue numismatique*, 6th series, 157:347–405.

Chameroy, J., and P.-M. Guihard, eds., 2016. *Produktion und Recyceln von Münzen in der Spätantike/Produire et recycler la monnaie au Bas-Empire*. Mainz, Ger.

———, 2020. *Argentum Romanorum sive Barbarorum: Tradition und Entwicklung im Gebrauch des Silbergeldes im Römischen Westen (4.-6. Jh.)*. Mainz, Ger.: Römisch-Germanischen Zentralmuseum.

Charles-Edwards, T. M., 1993. *Early Irish and Welsh Kinship*. Oxford: Clarendon.

Chayanov, A. V., 1966. *The Theory of Peasant Economy*, ed. D. Thorner, B. Kerblay, and R.E.F. Smith. Manchester, UK: Manchester University Press.

Ch'en, J., 1965. "Sung Bronzes: An Economic Analysis," *Bulletin of the School of Oriental and African Studies* 28:613–26.

Chick, D., 2010. *The Coinage of Offa and his Contemporaries*, ed. M.A.S. Blackburn and R. Naismith. London: British Numismatic Society.

Christophe, A., 2016. "Le monnayage de Raoul (923–936) et Séulf (922–925) à Reims," *BSFN* 71:251–52.

Ciocca, R., 2012. "Commercio e denaro nei *Versus de Unibove*," *Studi medievali* 53:667–98.

Clairand, A., 2009. *Une société de pierre: les epitaphs carolingiennes de Melle. Catalogue de l'exposition conçue par la Société archéologique du Mellois et le Centre d'études supérieures de civilisation médiévale*. Melle, Fr.: Direction régionale des affaires culturelles Poitou-Charentes.

Clairand, A., and F. Téreygeol, 2009. "L'atelier monétaire mérovingien de Melle (Deux-Sèvres): premières conclusions," in *Numismatique et archéologie en Poitou-Charentes: actes du colloque de Niort, 7-8 décembre, 2007, Musée Bernard*, ed. A. Clairand, 31–48. Paris: SÉNA.

Clark, P. E., 2017. "Taxation and the Formation of the Late Roman Social Contract." PhD dissertation, University of California Berkeley.

Clarke, H. B., and A. Simms, eds., 1985. *The Comparative History of Urban Origins in Non-Roman Europe: Ireland, Wales, Denmark, Germany, Poland and Russia from the 9th to the 13th Century*. 2 vols. Oxford: B.A.R.

Claude, D., 1964. "Untersuchungen zum frühfränkischen Comitat," *Zeitschrift der Savigny-Stiftung für Rechtsgeschichte: Kanonstische Abteilung* 49:1–75.

Clay, J.-H., 2009. "Gift-Giving and Books in the Letters of St Boniface and Lul," *Journal of Medieval History* 35:313–25.

Clément, N, 2015–16. "Les monnaies du Bas-Empire dans des contextes médiévaux (Ve–XIVe s.) en Vivarais," *Journal of Archaeological Numismatics* 5/6:317–32.

Codine-Trécourt, F., 2014. "Precious Metalwork: Coins and Objects in Merovingian and Carolingian Times," in Abramson 2014, 29–43.

Colardelle, M., J.-P. Moyne, and E. Verdel, 2016. "Éléments archéologiques sur les échanges commerciaux dans le site pré-castral de Colletière à Charavines (Isère, France) durant le premier tiers du XIe siècle," in *Château et commerce: actes du colloque international de Bad Neustadt an der Saale. Allemagne, 23–31 août 2014),* ed. P. Ettel, A.-M. Flambard Héricher, and K. D. O'Conor, 99–112. Caen, Fr.: Presses universitaires de Caen.

Colardelle, M., and E. Verdel, 1993. *Les habitats du lac de Paladru (Isère) dans leur environnement: la formation d'un terroir au XIe siècle.* Paris: Éditions de la Maison des sciences de l'homme.

Collins, R., 1983. "Theodebert I, *rex magnus Francorum,*" in *Ideal and Reality in Frankish and Anglo-Saxon Society: Studies Presented to J. M. Wallace-Hadrill,* ed. P. Wormald, D. Bullough, and R. Collins, 7–33. Oxford: B. Blackwell.

Collins-Elliott, S., 2019. "A Behavioral Analysis of Monetary Exchange and Craft Production in Rural Tuscany via Small Finds from the Roman Peasant Project," *Journal of Mediterranean Archaeology* 31:155–79.

Conant, J., 2012. *Staying Roman: Conquest and Identity in Africa and the Mediterranean, 439–700.* Cambridge: Cambridge University Press.

Constable, G., 1964. *Monastic Tithes from their Origins to the Twelfth Century.* Cambridge: Cambridge University Press.

Contamine, P., et al., 1993. *L'économie médiévale.* Paris: A. Colin.

Cook, B., 1999. "The Bezant in Angevin England," *Numismatic Chronicle* 159:255–75.

Cook, B., and G. Williams, eds., 2006. *Coinage and History in the North Sea World, c. AD 500–1250: Essays in Honour of Marion Archibald.* Leiden, Neth.: Brill.

Coss, P., 2003. *The Origins of the English Gentry.* Cambridge: Cambridge University Press.

Costambeys, M., 2009. "Settlement, Taxation and the Condition of the Peasantry in Post-Roman Central Italy," *Journal of Agrarian Change* 9:92–119.

Coupland, S., 1985. "L'article XI de l'Édit de Pîtres du 25 juin 864," *BSFN* 40:713–14.

———, 1990. "Money and Coinage under Louis the Pious," *Francia* 17:23–54.

———, 1991. "The Early Coinage of Charles the Bald, 840–64," *Numismatic Chronicle* 151:121–58.

———, 1999. "The Frankish Tribute Payments to the Vikings and Their Consequences," *Francia* 26:57–75.

———, 2001. "The Coinage of Lothar I (840–855)," *Numismatic Chronicle* 161:157–98.

———, 2004. "The Carolingian Army and the Struggle against the Vikings," *Viator* 35:49–70.

———, 2005. "Charlemagne's Coinage: Ideology and Economy," in *Charlemagne: Emperor and Society,* ed. J. Story, 211–29. Manchester, UK: Manchester University Press.

——, 2010. "Carolingian Single Finds and the Economy of the Early Ninth Century," *Numismatic Chronicle* 170:287–319.

——, 2011. "A Checklist of Carolingian Coin Hoards 751–987," *Numismatic Chronicle* 171:203–56.

——, 2014a. "The Portrait Coinage of Charlemagne," in Naismith, Allen, and Screen 2014, 145–56.

——, 2014b. "Seven Recent Carolingian Hoards," *Numismatic Chronicle* 174:318–32.

——, 2014c. "The Use of Coin in the Carolingian Empire in the Ninth Century," in Naismith, Allen, and Screen 2014, 257–94.

——, 2014d. "A Supplement to the Checklist of Carolingian Coin Hoards, 751–987," *Numismatic Chronicle* 174:213–22.

Coupland, S., 2015. "Attributing the Melle Coins of Charlemagne (768–814) and Charles the Bald (840–877), Particularly Single Finds from the Netherlands," *Jaarboek voor Munt- en Penningkunde* 102:61–96.

——, 2017. "On Good and Bad Coin in Carolingian Europe," in *Nummi et Humanitas. Studia ofiarowane Profesorowi Stanislawowi Suchodolskiemu w 80 rocznice urodzin*, ed. M. Bogucki, W. Garbaczewski, and G. Sniezko, 91–112. Warsaw: Wydawnictwo Instytutu Archeologii i Etnologii Polskiej Akademii Nauk.

——, 2018a. "Charlemagne and His Coinage," in *Charlemagne: les temps, les espaces, les hommes. Construction et déconstruction d'un règne*, ed. R. Große and M. Sot, 427–51. Turnhout, Bel.: Brepols.

——, 2018b. "The Formation of a European Identity: Revisiting Charlemagne's Coinage," in *Writing the Early Medieval West: Studies in Honour of Rosamond McKitterick*, ed. E. M. Screen and C. West, 213–29. Cambridge: Cambridge University Press.

——, 2018c. "Les monnaies de Melle sous Louis le Pieux," in Bompaire and Sarah 2018, 259–78.

——, 2022. "The Importance of Coinage in the Carolingian World," *EME* 30:384–407.

Coupland, S., and H. Emmerig, 2019. "Neue karolingische Münzfunde aus Bayern und Österreich," *Numismatische Zeitschrift* 125:233–64.

Cowell, M. R., and N. M. Lowick, 1988. "Silver from the Panjhir Mines," in *Metallurgy in Numismatics 2*, ed. W. A. Oddy, 65–74. London: Royal Numismatic Society.

Crafter, T., 2006. "Henry II, the St Augustine's Dispute and the Loss of the Abbey's Mint Franchise," in Cook and Williams 2006, 601–16.

Craig, J., 1953. *The Mint: A History of the London Mint from A.D. 287*. Cambridge: Cambridge University Press.

Creber, A. M., 2017. "Adelaide of Turin (c. 1014/24–1091): Imperial Politics and Regional Power in Eleventh-Century Northern Italy." PhD dissertation, King's College London.

Creighton, O., 2012. *Early European Castles: Aristocracy and Authority, AD 800–1200*. London: Bloomsbury.

Croix, S., M. Neiß, and S. Sindbæk, 2019. "The *Réseau opératoire* of Urbanization: Craft Collaborations and Organization in an Early Medieval Workshop in Ribe, Denmark," *Cambridge Archaeological Journal* 29:1–20.

Crusafont i Sabater, M., 1994. *El sistema monetario visigodo: cobre y oro*. Barcelona: Asociación numismática española.

Crusafont, M. de, A. M. Balaguer, and P. Grierson, 2012. *Medieval European Coinage, with a Catalogue of the Coins in the Fitzwilliam Museum, Cambridge. Vol. 6: The Iberian Peninsula.* Cambridge: Cambridge University Press.

Crusafont, M. de, J. Benages, and J. Noguera, 2016. "Silver Visigothic Coinage," *Numismatic Chronicle* 176:241–60.

Cubitt, C., 2009. "'As the Lawbook Teaches': Reeves, Lawbooks and Urban Life in the Anonymous Old English Legend of the Seven Sleepers," *English Historical Review* 124:1021–49.

———, 2020. "Reassessing the Reign of King Æthelred the Unready," *Anglo-Norman Studies* 42:1–28.

Cubizolles, P., 1980. *Le noble chapitre Saint-Julien de Brioude.* Aurillac, Fr.: Institution Saint-Julien.

Curchin, L. A., 2018. "Curials and Local Government in Visigotic Hispania," *Antiquité tardive* 26:225–40.

Curta, F., 2006. "Merovingian and Carolingian Gift Giving," *Speculum* 81:671–99.

Dannenberg, H., 1876-1905. *Die deutschen Münzen der sächsischen und fränkischen Kaiserzeit.* 4 vols. Berlin: Weidmann.

Darby, H. C., 1977. *Domesday England.* Cambridge: Cambridge University Press.

Davies, W., 2002. "Sale, Price and Valuation in Galicia and Castile-León in the Tenth Century," *EME* 11:149–74.

———, 2012. "Free Peasants and Large Landowners in the West," *Revue belge de philologie et d'histoire* 90:361–80.

Davies, W., and H. Vierck, 1974. "The Contexts of Tribal Hidage: Social Aggregates and Settlement Patterns," *Frühmittelalterliche Studien* 8:223–93.

Davis, J., 2011. *Medieval Market Morality: Life, Law and Ethics in the English Marketplace, 1200–1500.* Cambridge: Cambridge University Press.

Davis, J. R., 2014. "Charlemagne's Portrait Coinage and Ideas of Rulership at the Carolingian Court," *Source: Notes in the History of Art* 33:19–27.

———, 2015. *Charlemagne's Practice of Empire.* Cambridge: Cambridge University Press.

Day, W. R., 1997. "The Monetary Reforms of Charlemagne and the Circulation of Money in Early Medieval Campania," *EME* 6:25–45.

Day, W. R., M. Matzke, and A. Saccocci, 2016. *Medieval European Coinage, with a Catalogue of the Coins in the Fitzwilliam Museum, Cambridge. 12: Italy (1): Northern Italy.* Cambridge: Cambridge University Press.

Deissen-Nagels, F., 1962. "Valenciennes, ville carolingienne," *Le Moyen Âge* 1962:51–90.

Dejardin-Bazaille, C., 2007. "La relation de dépendance entre saint Benoît et ses serfs: contrainte ou protection?," *Le Moyen Âge* 113:383–92.

Delmaire, R., 1989. *Largesses sacrées et res privata. L'aerarium impérial et son administration du IVe au VIe siècle.* Paris: École française de Rome.

Delogu, P., 1988. "Oro e argento in Roma tra il VII ed il IX secolo," in *Cultura e società nell'Italia medieval. Studi per Paolo Brezzi.* 2 vols. Rome, 1:273–93.

———, 1995. "Lombard and Carolingian Italy," ed. McKitterick 1995, 290–319.

———, 1998. "Reading Pirenne Again," in *The Sixth Century: Production, Distribution and Demand,* ed. R. Hodges and W. Bowman, 15–40. Leiden, Neth.: Brill.

Deniaux, E., 2002. *La Normandie avant les normands: de la conquête romaine à l'arrivée des Vikings.* Rennes, Fr.: Ouest France.

Depeyrot, G., 1998. *Le numéraire mérovingien: l'âge d'or*. Wetteren, Bel.: Moneta.

——, 2017. *Le numéraire carolingien: corpus des monnaies*. 4th ed. Wetteren, Bel.: Moneta.

Desan, C., 2014. *Making Money: Coin, Currency, and the Coming of Capitalism*. Oxford: Oxford University Press.

Desnier, J.-L., 1987. "Stips," *Revue de l'histoire des religions* 204:219–30.

Despy, G., 1968. "Villes et campagnes aux IXe et Xe siècles: l'exemple du pays mosan," *Revue du Nord* 50:145–68.

Devroey, J.-P., 1993. "Courants et réseaux d'échange dans l'économie franque entre Loire et Rhin," *Settimane di studio del Centro italiano di studi sull'alto medioevo* 40:327–93.

Devroey, J.-P., 2003a. *Économie rurale et société dans l'Europe franque. VIe–IXe siècles. Tome 1: fondements matériels, échanges et lien social*. Paris: Belin.

——, 2003b. "L'espace des échanges économiques. Commerce, marché, communications et logistique dans le monde franc au IXe siècle," *Settimane di studio del Centro italiano di studi sull'alto medioevo* 50:347–92.

——, 2006. *Puissants et misérables: système social et monde paysan dans l'Europe des Francs (VIe–IXe siècles)*. Brussels: Classe des lettres, Académie royale de Belgique.

——, 2015. "Activité monétaire, marchés et politique à l'âge des empereurs carolingiens," *Revue belge de numismatique et de sigillographie* 161:177–232.

——, 2019a. *La nature et le roi: environnement, pouvoir et société à l'âge de Charlemagne (740–820)*. Paris: Albin Michel.

——, 2019b. "Le paysan consommateur: enjeux d'une problématique," in *Le nécessaire et le superflu: le paysan consommateur. Actes des XXXVIes Journées internationales d'histoire de l'abbaye de Flaran, 17 et 18 octobre 2014*, ed. G. Ferrand and J. Petrowiste, 267–78. Toulouse, Fr.: Presses universitaires du Midi.

——, 2019c. "Le petit monde des seigneuries domaniales. Seigneurs, notables et officiers dans les seigneuries royales et écclesiastiques à l'époque carolingienne," in Kohl, Patzold, and Zeller 2019, 165–201.

Devroey, J.-P., and N. Schroeder, 2020. "Land, Oxen, and Brooches: Local Societies, Inequality, and Large Estates in the Early Medieval Ardennes (c. 850–c. 900)," in Quirós Castillo 2020, 177–202.

Dhénin, M., and P. Schiesser, 2007. "Oboles mérovingiennes," *Revue numismatique* 163:283–313.

Dhondt, J., 1948. *Études sur la naissance des principautés territoriales en France, IXe–Xe siècle*. Bruges, Bel.: De Tempel.

Díaz Martínez, P. C., 2004. "Acuñación monetaria y organización administrativa en la Gallaecia tardoantigua," *Zephyrus* 57:367–75.

——, 2012. "Confiscations in the Visigothic Reign of Toledo: A Political Instrument," in *Expropriations et confiscations dans les royaumes barbares: une approche régionale*, ed. P. Porena and Y. Rivière, 93–112. Rome: École française de Rome.

——, 2019. "El esquema provincial en el contexto administrativo de la monarquía visigoda de Toledo," *Mélanges de la Casa de Velázquez* 49:77–108.

Dierkens, A., and P. Périn, 2000. "Les 'sedes regiae' mérovingiennes entre Seine et Rhin," in Ripoll López and Gurt Esparraguera 2000, 267–304.

Dierkens, A., N. Schroeder, and A. Wilkin, eds., 2017. *Penser la paysannerie médiévale, un défi impossible? Recueil d'études offert à Jean-Pierre Devroey*. Paris: Éditions de la Sorbonne.

Diestelkamp, B., ed., 1982. *Beiträge zum hochmittelalterlichen Städtewesen.* Cologne, Ger.: Böhlau.

Dinkova-Bruun, G., 2015. "Nummus falsus: The Perception of Counterfeit Money in the Eleventh and Early Twelfth Century," in Gasper and Gullbekk 2015, 77–91.

Dodwell, C. R., and P. Clemoes, 1974. *The Old English Illustrated Hexateuch: British Museum, Cotton Claudius B.IV.* Copenhagen: Rosenkilde and Bagger.

Dolley, R.H.M., 1954. "The So-Called Piedforts of Alfred the Great," *Numismatic Chronicle,* 6th series, 14:76–92.

———, ed., 1961. *Anglo-Saxon Coins: Studies Presented to F. M. Stenton on the Occasion of his 80th Birthday 17 May 1960.* London: Methuen.

———, 1964. *Anglo-Saxon Pennies.* London: Trustees of the British Museum.

———, 1976. "A Hiberno-Manx Coinage of the Eleventh Century," *Numismatic Chronicle,* 7th series, 16:75–84.

———, 1978. "An Introduction to the Coinage of Æthelred II," in Hill 1978, 115–33.

Dolley, R. H. M., and D. M. Metcalf, 1961. "The Reform of the English Coinage under Eadgar," in Dolley 1961, 136–68.

Doménech Belda, C., 2003. *Dinares, dirhams y feluses. Circulación monetaria islámica en el País Valenciano.* Alicante, Sp.: Publicaciones de la Universidad de Alicante.

———, 2013. "Tesorillo islámico de la calle Jabonerías de Murcia," *Tudmir* 3:8–24.

———, 2014. "Moneda y espacios de poder en el reino visigodo. Los tremises de El Tolmo de Minateda (Hellín, Albacete)," *Arqueología y Territorio Medieval* 21:9–37.

———, 2016. "Numismática y arqueología medieval: la moneda de excavación y sus aportaciones," in *Actas XIII congreso nacional de numismática. Tomo II: moneda y arqueología. Cádiz, 22–24 de octubre de 2007,* ed. A. Arévalo González. 2 vols., 2:731–60. Madrid: Museo Casa de la Moneda.

Doménech Belda, C., and S. Gutiérrez Lloret, 2006. "Viejas y nuevas monedas en la ciudad emiral de Madīnat Iyyuh. El Tolmo de Minateda (Hellín, Albacete)," *Al-Qantara* 27:337–74.

Domergue, C., 1990. *Les mines de la péninsule ibérique dans l'antiquité romaine.* Rome: École française de Rome.

Dopsch, A., 1923–24. *Wirtschaftliche und soziale Grundlagen der europäischen Kulturentwicklung: aus der Zeit von Caesar bis Karl den Grossen.* 2nd ed. 2 vols. Vienna: Seidel.

———, 1930. *Naturalwirtschaft und Geldwirtschaft in der Weltgeschichte.* Vienna: Seidel.

———, 1937. *The Economic and Social Foundations of European Civilization,* abbreviated by E. Patzelt and trans. M. G. Beard and N. Marshall. London: Kegan Paul.

Dossey, L., 2010. *Peasant and Empire in Christian North Africa.* Berkeley.

Dotzauer, W., 2001. *Geschichte des Nahe-Hunsrück-Raumes von den Anfängen bis zur Französischen Revolution.* Stuttgart, Ger.: Steiner.

Doyen, J.-M., 2019. "La circulation au nord des Alpes du monnayage d'argent des Ostrogoths et de l'exarchat d'Italie (471–584)," in *Mélanges de numismatique et d'archéologie de Byzance offerts à Henri Pottier à l'occasion de son quatre-vingt-cinquième anniversaire,* ed. J.-M. Doyen and C. Morrisson, 43–76. Brussels: Cercle d'études numismatiques.

Drauschke, J., 2010. "The Search for Central Places in the Merovingian Kingdom," in *Trade and Communication Networks of the First Millennium AD in the Northern Part of Central Europe: Central Places, Beach Markets, Landing Places and Trading Centres*, ed. B. Ludowici et al., 26–48. Stuttgart, Ger.: Niedersächsisches Landesmuseum Hannover.

Duby, G., 1971. *La société aux XIe et XIIe siècles dans la région mâconnaise.* Paris: S.E.V.P.E.N.

——, 1973. *Hommes et structures du moyen âge: recueil d'articles.* Paris: Mouton.

——, 1974. *The Early Growth of the European Economy: Warriors and Peasants from the Seventh to the Twelfth Century*, trans. H. B. Clarke. London: Weidenfeld & Nicolson.

Duczko, W., 2002. "Test or Magic? Pecks on Viking-Age Silver," in Kiersnowski et al. 2002, 192–208.

Dudbridge, G., 2018. "Reworking the World System Paradigm," in Holmes and Standen 2018, 297–316.

Duguet, J., 1981. "Un heritage de la famille de Matha: Saintes et Mornac," *Roccafortis*, 2nd series, 4:183–90.

Dumas, F., 1973. "Le début de l'époque féodale en France d'après les monnaies," *Bulletin du Cercle d'études numismatiques* 10:65–77.

——, 1992. "La monnaie comme expression du pouvoir (Xe–XIIe siècles)," in *Pouvoirs et libertés au temps des premiers Capétiens*, ed. E. Magnou-Nortier, 169–94. Maulévrier, Fr.: Hérault.

Dumas-Dubourg, F., 1971. *Le trésor de Fécamp et le monnayage en Francie occidentale pendant la seconde moitié du Xe siècle.* Paris: Bibliothèque nationale.

Dumézil, B., 2008. "Le comte et l'administration de la cité dans le Bréviaire d'Alaric," in *Le Bréviaire d'Alaric: aux origins due Code civil*, ed. M. Rouche, 72–90. Paris: PUPS.

Dumville, D. N., 2017. "Origins of the Kingdom of the English," in *Writing, Kingship and Power in Anglo-Saxon England*, ed. D. A. Woodman and R. Naismith, 71–121. Cambridge: Cambridge University Press.

Duncan-Jones, R. P., 1994. *Money and Government in the Roman Empire.* Cambridge: Cambridge University Press.

——, 2012. "Weights and Measures, Roman," in *The Encyclopedia of Ancient History*, ed. R. S. Bagnall et al. Wiley Blackwell. https//:doi.org/10.1002/9781444338386.

Duplessy, J., 1985. *Les trésors monétaires médiévaux et modernes découverts en France. Vol. 1: 751–1223.* Paris: Bibliothèque nationale.

——, 2005. *Les monnaies françaises féodales.* Paris: Maison Platt.

Durliat, J., 1990. *Les finances publiques de Dioclétien aux Carolingiens 284–889.* Sigmaringen. Ger.: Thorbecke.

Duyrat, F., ed., 2018. *Trésors monétaires XXVII: Monnayages de Francie, des derniers Carolingiens.* Paris: Bibliothèque nationale de France.

Dyer, C., 1997. "Peasants and Coins: The Uses of Money in the Middle Ages," *British Numismatic Journal* 67:30–47.

——, 2005. *An Age of Transition? Economy and Society in England in the Later Middle Ages.* Oxford: Oxford University Press.

Dyhrfjeld-Johnsen, M. D., 2013. "Danish Hacksilber Hoards: A Status Report," in Hunter and Painter 2013, 321–38.

Eaglen, R. J., 2006. *The Abbey and Mint of Bury St Edmunds to 1279*. London: British Numismatic Society.

Edmondson, J. C., 1989. "Mining in the Later Roman Empire and Beyond: Continuity or Disruption?," *Journal of Roman Studies* 79:84–102.

Effros, B., 2017. "The Enduring Attraction of the Pirenne Thesis," *Speculum* 92:184–208.

Effros, B., and I. Moreira, eds., 2020. *The Oxford Handbook of the Merovingian World*. Oxford: Oxford University Press.

Eggert, W., 1975. "*Rebelliones servorum*. Bewaffnete Klassenkämpfe im Früh- und Hochmittelalter und ihre Darstellung in zeitgenössischen erzählenden Quellen," *Zeitschrift für Geschichtswissenschaft* 23:1147–1264.

Ehlers, C., 1997. "Die Anfänge Goslars und das Reich im elften Jahrhundert," *Deutsches Archiv für Erforschung des Mittelalters* 53:45–79.

———, 2007. *Die Integration Sachsens in das fränkische Reich 751–1024*. Göttingen, Ger.: Vandenhoeck & Ruprecht.

Einaudi, L., 2006. *Selected Economic Essays*, ed. L. Einaudi, R. Faucci, and R. Marchionatti. Basingstoke, UK: Palgrave Macmillan.

Eldevik, J. T., 2012. *Episcopal Power and Ecclesiastical Reform in the German Empire: Tithes, Lordship and Community, 950–1150*. Cambridge: Cambridge University Press.

Elsner, J., 1998. *Imperial Rome and Christian Triumph: The Art of the Roman Empire A.D. 100–450*. Oxford: Oxford University Press.

Emmerig, H., 2004. "Der Freisinger Münzschatzfund und das Geldwesen in Bayern zur Karolingerzeit," *Sammelblatt des historischen Vereins Freising* 38:11–75.

Endemann, T., 1964. *Markturkunde und Markt in Frankreich und Burgund vom 9. bis 11. Jahrhundert*. Konstanz, Ger.: J. Thorbecke.

Engel, A., and R. Serrure, 1891–1905. *Traité de numismatique du Moyen Âge*. 3 vols. Paris: Leroux.

Engeler, S., 1991. *Altnordische Geldwörter. Eine philologische Untersuchung altnordischer Geld- und Münzbezeichnungen und deren Verwendung in der Dichtung*. Frankfurt, Ger.: P. Lang.

Ertl, T., and K. Oschema, 2022. "Les études médiévales après le tournant global," *Annales: histoire, sciences sociales* 76:787–801.

Escalona Monge, J., and A. Reynolds, eds., 2011. *Scale and Scale Change in the Early Middle Ages: Exploring Landscape, Local Society, and the World Beyond*. Turnhout, Bel.: Brepols.

Esders, S., 2010. *Die Formierung der Zensualität: zur kirchlichen Transformation des spätrömischen Patronatswesens im frühen Mittelalter*. Ostfildern, Ger.: Jan Thorbecke.

———, 2013. "Konstans II. (641–668), die Sarazenen und die Reiche des Westens. Ein Versuch über politisch-militärische und ökonomisch-finanzielle Verflechtungen im Zeitalter eines mediterranen Weltkrieges," in Jarnut and Strothmann 2013, 189–242.

———, 2014. "Wergeld und soziale Netwerke im Frankenreich," in *Verwandtschaft, Name und soziale Ordnung (300–1000)*, ed. S. Patzold and K. Ubl, 141–59. Berlin: De Gruyter.

———, 2015. "Wergild and Social Practice in the Early Middle Ages: A 9th-Century Reichenau Fragment and Its Context," in *Entre texte et histoire: études d'histoire médiévale offertes au professeur Shoichi Sato*, ed. O. Kano and J.-L. Lemaître, 117–27. Paris: Diffusion de Boccard.

———, 2017. "*Te usero herano misso*: Überlieferungs- und Gebrauchskontext des Essener altsächsischen Heberegisters aus dem 10. Jahrhundert," *Frühmittelalterliche Studien* 51:57–86.

———, 2019. "Amt und Bann. Weltliche Funktionsträger (*centenarii, vicarii*) als Teil ländlicher Gesellschaften im Karolingerreich," in Kohl, Patzol, and Zeller 2019, 255–306.

———, 2021a. "Vernacular Writing in Early Medieval Manorial Administration: Two Tenth-Century Documents from Werden and Essen," in Gallagher, Roberts, and Tinti 2021, 378–411.

———, 2021b. "Wergild and the Monetary Logic of Early Medieval Conflict Resolution," in Bothe, Esders, and Nijdam, 1–37.

Esty, W. W., 2006. "How to Estimate the Original Number of Dies and the Coverage of a Sample," *Numismatic Chronicle* 166:359–64.

———, 2011. "The Geometric Model for Estimating the Number of Dies," in *Quantifying Monetary Supplies in Greco-Roman Times*, ed. F. de Callataÿ, 43–58. Bari, It.: Edipuglia.

Fagerlie, J. M., 1967. *Late Roman and Byzantine Solidi in Sweden and Denmark*. New York: American Numismatic Society.

Fairbairn, H. O., 2013. "The Nature and Limits of the Money Economy in Late Anglo-Saxon and Early Norman England." PhD dissertation, King's College London.

———, 2019. "Was There a Money Economy in Late Anglo-Saxon and Norman England?," *English Historical Review* 134:1081–1135.

Fairbrother, J. R., 1990. *Faccombe Netherton: Excavations of a Saxon and Medieval Manorial Complex*, 2 vols. London: British Museum.

Faith, R., 1994. "Tidenham, Gloucestershire, and the History of the Manor in England," *Landscape History* 16:39–51.

———, 1997. *The English Peasantry and the Growth of Lordship*. London: Leicester University Press.

———, 2019. *The Moral Economy of the Countryside: Anglo-Saxon to Anglo-Norman England*. Cambridge: Cambridge University Press.

Falque-Vert, H., 2000. "La circulation monétaire dans les campagnes du Bas-Dauphiné vers l'an mil," in *Pierres de mémoire, écrits d'histoire: pages d'histoire en Dauphiné offertes à Vital Chomel*, ed. A. Belmont, 45–56. Grénoble, Fr.: Presses universitaires de Grenoble.

Fanchamps, M.-L., 1964. "Étude sur les tonlieux de la Meuse Moyenne du VIIIe au milieu du XIVe siècle," *Le Moyen Âge* 70:205–64.

Fardon, R., 2013. "Citations Out of Place," *Anthropology Today* 29:25–27.

Farmer, D. L., 1988. "Prices and Wages," in *The Agrarian History of England and Wales. Volume 2: 1042–1350*, ed. J. Thirsk, 715–817. Cambridge: Cambridge University Press.

Favreau, R., J. Michaud, J., and E.-R. Labande, 1974. *Corpus des inscriptions de la France médiévale. Vol. 1: Poitou-Charentes; 1: Ville de Poitiers*. Paris: Centre national de la recherche scientifique.

———, 1977. *Corpus des inscriptions de la France médiévale. Vol. 1: Poitou-Charentes; 3: Charents, Charente-Maritime, Deux-Sèvres.* Paris: Centre national de la recherche scientifique.

Favreau, R., J. Michaud, and B. Mora, 1997. *Corpus des inscriptions de la France médiévale 19: Jura, Nièvre, Saône-et-Loire.* Paris: Centre national de la recherche scientifique.

Fehr, H., 2020. "The Transformation into the Early Middle Ages (Fourth to Eighth Centuries)," in *The Oxford Handbook of the Archaeology of Roman Germany,* ed. S. James and S. Krmnicek, 491–519. Oxford: Oxford University Press.

Felder, E., 2003. *Die Personennamen auf den merowingischen Münzen der Bibliothèque nationale de France.* Munich: Bayerischen Akademie der Wissenschaften.

Feller, L., 2005. "Enrichissement, accumulation et circulation des biens: quelques problems liés au marché de la terre," in Feller and Wickham 2005, 3–28.

———, 2007. *Paysans et seigneurs au Moyen Âge, VIIIe–XVe siècles.* Paris: A. Colin.

———, 2011. "Sur la formation des prix dans l'économie du haut Moyen Âge," *Annales: histoire, sciences sociales* 66:627–61.

———, 2014. "Measuring the Value of Things in the Middle Ages," *Economic Sociology* 15:30–40.

———, 2017a. *Paysans et seigneurs au Moyen âge: VIIIe–XVe siècles.* 2nd ed. Paris: A. Colin.

———, 2017b. "Les transactions dans la Vie de Géraud d'Aurillac," in Dierkens, Schroeder, and Wilkin 2017, 69–82.

———, 2018. "Travail, salaire et pauvreté au moyen âge," in Balzaretti, Barrow, and Skinner 2018, 95–109.

Feller, L., A, Gramain, and F. Weber, 2005. *La fortune de Karol: marché de la terre et liens personnels dans les Abruzzes au haut Moyen Âge,* Collection de l'Ecole française de Rome 347. Rome: École française de Rome.

Feller, L., and C. Wickham, eds., 2005. *Le marché de la terre au Moyen Âge.* Rome: École française de Rome.

Fern, C., 2019. "Characterising the Objects," in Fern, Dickinson, and Webster 2019, 29–121.

Fern, C., T. Dickinson, and L. Webber, eds., 2019. *The Staffordshire Hoard: An Anglo-Saxon Treasure.* London: Society of Antiquaries of London.

Fernández, D., 2006. "Quel est l'objet de la lettre *De Fisco Barcinonensi*?," *Antiquité tardive* 14:217–24.

———, 2017. "Statehood, Taxation, and State Infrastructural Power in Visigothic Iberia," in *Ancient States and Infrastructural Power: Europe, Asia, and America,* ed. C. Ando and S. Richardson, 243–71. Philadelphia: University of Pennsylvania Press.

———, 2020. "Transformaciones institutiocionales y liderazgo cívico en la Hispania post-imperial," in *Urban Transformations in the Late Antique West: Materials, Agents, and Models,* ed. A. Carneiro, N. Christie and P. Diarte-Blasco, 259–78. Coimbra, Port.: Coimbra University Press.

———, 2021. "El sistema tributario visigodo y los documentos de San Martín de Asán," in *Nouvelles chartes visigothiques du monastère pyrénéen d'Asán,* ed. C. Martin and J. J. Larrea, 105–24. Bordeaux, Fr.: Ausonius.

Feveile, C., 2020. "Damhus-skatten—en foreløbig præsentation a fen Ribeudmøntning fra tidlig 800-årene," *Arkæologi i Slesvig* 18:51–66.

Feveile, C., and J. C. Moesgaard, 2018. "Damhus-skatten—et fantastisk indspark til den tidlige mønthistorie," *By, marsk og geest* 30:28–30.

Fichtenau, H., 1994. "'Stadtplanung' im früheren Mittelalter," in *Ethnogenese und Über-lieferung. Angewandte Methoden der Frühmittelalterforschung*, ed. K. Brunner and B. Merta, 232–49. Vienna: Oldenbourg.

Fiore, A., 2020. *The Seigneurial Transformation: Power Structures and Political Com-munication in the Countryside of Central and Northern Italy, 1080-1130*. Oxford: Oxford University Press.

Fischer, A., 2019. "Money for Nothing? Franks, Byzantines and Lombards in the Sixth and Seventh Centuries," in *East and West in the Early Middle Ages: The Merovin-gian Kingdoms in Mediterranean Perspective*, ed. S. Esders, Y. Fox, Y. Hen, and L. Sarti, 108–27. Cambridge: Cambridge University Press.

Fischer, S., 2014. "The *Solidus* Hoard of Casa delle Vestali in Context," *Opuscula: Annual of the Swedish Institutes at Athens and Rome* 7:107–27.

Fischer, S., 2019. "From Italy to Scandinavia: The Numismatic Record of the Fall of the West Roman Empire," *Settimane di studio del Centro italiano di studi sull'alto medioevo* 66:805–36.

Fischer, S., and F. López Sánchez, 2016. "Subsidies for the Roman West? The Flow of Constantinopolitan Solidi to the Western Empire and Barbaricum," *Opuscula: Annual of the Swedish Institutes at Athens and Rome* 9:249–69.

Fischer, S., and I. N. Wood, 2020. "Vidracco, Braone, and San Lorenzo: Recruitment or *Dilectio*?," *Opuscula: Annual of the Swedish Institutes at Athens and Rome* 13:165–86.

Fitzpatrick, S. M., and S. McKeon, 2020. "Banking on Stone Money: Ancient Ante-cedents to Bitcoin," *Economic Anthropology* 7:7–21.

Flavian, C., 1995. "Recherches sur le thème de l'avare, de l'usurier et du mauvais riche dans la sculpture du diocèse de Clermont aux XIe et XIIe siècles," *Bulletin de la Société des Amis des Arts et des Sciences de Tournus* 94:107–84.

Flechner, R., 2019. *Saint Patrick Retold: The Legend and History of Ireland's Patron Saint*. Princeton, NJ: Princeton University Press.

Fleming, R., 1985. "Monastic Lands and English Defence in the Viking Age," *English Historical Review* 100:247–65.

——, 1993. "Rural Elites and Urban Communities in Late-Saxon England," *Past and Present* 141:3–37.

——, 2009. "Elites, Boats and Foreigners: Rethinking the Birth of English Towns," *Settimane di studio del Centro italiano di studi sull'alto medioevo* 56:393–426.

——, 2010. *Britain after Rome: The Fall and Rise, 400 to 1070*. London: Penguin.

——, 2021. *The Material Fall of Roman Britain, 300–525 CE*. Philadelphia: University of Pennsylvania Press.

Fluck, P., 1993. "Montanarchäologische Forschungen in den Vogesen. Eine Zwischen-bilanz," in Steuer and Zimmermann 1993, 267–89.

Fontanals, N. R., et al., 2019. "Lead and Copper Mining in Priorat County (Tarragona, Spain) from Cooperative Exchange Networks to Colonial Trade (2600–500 BC)," in Armada, Murillo-Barroso, and Charlton 2019, 147–58.

Fontanon, P., 2010. "Le monnayage carolingien et les deniers de Brioude," in *Brioude aux temps carolingiens: actes du colloque international de Brioude, 13-15 sept.*

2007, ed. A. Dubreucq et al., 407–12. Le Puy, Fr.: Société académique du Puy et de la Haute-Loire.

Foot, S., 2006. *Monastic Life in Anglo-Saxon England, c. 600–900.* Cambridge: Cambridge University Press.

Fossier, R., 1978. *Polyptyques et censiers*, Typologies des sources du Moyen Âge occidental 28. Turnhout, Bel.: Brepols.

———, 1989. *L'enfance de l'Europe (Xe–XIIe siècle): aspects économiques et sociaux*, 2nd ed. 2 vols. Paris: Presses universitaires de France.

Foucray, B., 2018a. "Catalogue des monnaies royales et féodales de Francie des derniers Carolingiens aux premiers Capétiens (936–1108)," in Duyrat 2018, 329–73.

———, 2018b. "Un petit dépôt de monnaies royales du début du XIIe siècle à l'église de Marly-la-Ville (Val-d'Oise)," in Duyrat 2018, 299–303.

———, 2018c. "Le trésor du Xe siècle de Maffliers (Val-d'Oise), Deniers et oboles d'Hugues Capet duc," in Duyrat 2018, 101–27.

Foucray, B., and M. Bompaire, 2018. "Le trésor monétaire double de Vignacourt (Somme). Monnaies et circulation monétaire dans l'Amiénois et l'Orléanais au début du règne de Philippe Ier," in Duyrat 2018, 183–272.

Fouracre, P. J., 1981. "The Career of Ebroin, Master of the Palace c. 657–680." PhD dissertation, King's College London.

———, 2004. "Conflict, Power and Legitimation in Francia in the Late Seventh and Eighth Centuries," in *Building Legitimacy: Political Discourses and Forms of Legitimacy in Medieval Societies*, ed. M. I. Alfonso Antón et al., 3–26. Leiden, Neth.: Brill.

———, 2005. "Marmoutier and its Serfs in the Eleventh Century," *Transactions of the Royal Historical Society*, 6th series, 15, 29–50.

———, 2006. "Marmoutier: *Familia* versus Family. The Relations between Monastery and Serfs in Eleventh-Century North-West France," in Reynolds, Davies, and Halsall 2006, 255–74.

———, 2011. "The 'Book of Serfs' of Marmoutier (Eleventh Century): Reflections on the Development of Servitude," in *Familia and Household in the Medieval Atlantic Province*, ed. B. T. Hudson, 123–39. Tempe, AZ: ACMRS.

———, 2020. "Lights, Power and the Moral Economy of Early Medieval Europe," *EME* 28:367–87.

———, 2021. *Eternal Light and Earthly Concerns: Belief and the Shaping of Medieval Society.* Manchester, UK: Manchester University Press.

Fournier, G., 1982. "La mise en place du cadre paroissial et l'évolution du peuplement," *Settimane di studio del Centro italiano di studi sull'alto medioevo* 28:495–563.

Fox, Y., 2014. *Power and Religion in Merovingian Gaul: Columbanian Monasticism and the Formation of the Frankish Aristocracy.* Cambridge: Cambridge University Press.

Francovich, R., and C. Wickham, 1994. "Uno scavo archeologico ed il problema dello sviluppo della signoria territorial: Rocca San Silvestro e i rapport di produzione minerari," *Archeologia medievale* 21:7–30.

Fray, J.-L., 2006. *Villes et bourgs de Lorraine: réseaux urbains et centralité au Moyen Âge.* Clermont-Ferrand, Fr.: Presses universitaires Blaise Pascal

Freeman, A., 1985. *The Moneyer and the Mint in the Reign of Edward the Confessor, 1042–1066.* 2 vols. Oxford: B.A.R.

Fried, J., 2015. *The Middle Ages*, trans. P. Lewis. Cambridge, MA: Harvard University Press.

Frodsham, P., 2005. "'The Stronghold of Its Own Native Past': Some Thoughts on the Past in the Past at Yeavering," in *Yeavering: People, Power and Place*, ed. P. Frodsham and C. O'Brien, 13–64. Stroud, UK: Sutton.

Fuchs, R., 1991. *Die Inschriften der Stadt Worms*. Wiesbaden, Ger.: Reichert.

Fuglesang, S. H., and D. M. Wilson, eds., 2006. *The Hoen Hoard: A Viking Gold Treasure of the Ninth Century*. Rome: Bardi Editore.

Fumagalli, V., 1964. "Note sulla 'Vita Geraldi' di Odone di Cluny," *Bullettino dell'Istituto storico italiano per il medio evo* 76:217–40.

Gai, S., 2001. "Nouvelles données sur le palais de Charlemagne et de ses successeurs à Paderborn (Allemagne)," *Actes des congrès de la Société d'Archéologie Médiévale* 7:201–12.

Gallagher, R., Roberts, E., and Tinti, F., eds., 2021. *The Languages of Early Medieval Charters: Latin, Germanic Vernaculars, and the Written Word*. Leiden, Neth.: Brill.

Gambacorta, F., 2010. "La 'contromarca' xlii sulle monete imperi di epoca imperial: *status quaestionis*," *Numismatica e antichità classiche* 2010:365–83.

Gannon, A., 2003. *The Iconography of Early Anglo-Saxon Coinage: Sixth to Eighth Centuries*. Oxford: Oxford University Press.

——, 2005. "The Five Senses and Anglo-Saxon Coinage," *Anglo-Saxon Studies in Archaeology and History* 13:97–104.

——, 2013. *Sylloge of Coins of the British Isles 63. British Museum: Anglo-Saxon Coins I: Early Anglo-Saxon Gold and Anglo-Saxon and Continental Silver Coinage of the North Sea Area, c. 600–760*. London: British Museum.

Ganshof, F. L., 1946. "Observations sur le synode de Francfort de 794," in *Miscellanea historica in honorem Alberti de Meyer*. 2 vols. Louvain, 1:306–18.

——, 1959a. "A propos du tonlieu à l'époque carolingienne," *Settimane di studio del Centro italiano di studi sull'alto medioevo* 6:485–508.

——, 1959b. *Het tolwezen in het frankisch rijk onder de Karolingen*. Brussels: Koninklijke Vlaamse Academie voor Wetenschappen, Lettern en Schone Kunsten van België.

——, 1966. "Note sur l'*inquisitio de theloneis Raffelstettensis*," *Le Moyen Âge* 72:197–224.

——, 1968. *Frankish Institutions under Charlemagne*, trans. B. and M. Lyon. Providence, RI: Brown University Press.

García Moreno, L. A., 1971. "Algunos aspectos fiscales de la Península Ibérica durante el siglo VI," *Hispania antiqua* 1:233–56.

——, 1974. "Estudios sobre la organización administrativa del reino visigodo de Toledo," *Anuario de historia del derecho español* 44:5–155.

García Ruiz, G., and L. Ruiz Quintanar, 1996. "Fragmentos de monedas en el hallazgo califal 'Haza del Carmen,'" in *II Congreso de Arqueología Peninsular: arqueología romana y medieval*, 4:723–30. Zamora, Sp.: Fundación Rei Afonso Henriques.

Gardiner, M. F., 2001. "Continental Trade and Non-Urban Ports in Mid-Saxon England: Excavations at Sandtun, West Hythe, Kent," *Archaeological Journal* 158:161–290.

Gariel, E., 1883–84. *Les monnaies royales de France sous la race carolingienne*. 2 vols. Strasbourg, Fr.: G. Fischbach.

Garipzanov, I. H., 2008. *The Symbolic Language of Authority in the Carolingian World (c. 751–877)*. Leiden, Neth.: Brill.

Garipzanov, I. H., 2016. "Regensburg, Wandalgarius and the *Novi Denarii*: Charlemagne's Monetary Reform Revisited," *EME* 24:58–73.

Gasparri, S., 1990. "Il regno longobardo in Italia. Struttura e funzionamento di uno stato altomedievale," in *Longobardia*, ed. S. Gasparri and P. Cammarosano, 237–305. Udine, It.: Casamassima.

———, 2002. "The Aristocracy," in *Italy in the Early Middle Ages 476–1000*, ed. C. La Rocca, 59–84. Oxford: Oxford University Press.

Gasper, G., 2015. "Contemplating Money and Wealth in Monastic Writing c. 1060–c. 1160," in Gasper and Gullbekk 2015, 39–76.

Gasper, G., and G. Gullbekk, eds., 2015. *Money and the Church in Medieval Europe, 1000–1200: Practice, Morality and Thought*. Aldershot, UK: Ashgate.

Gautier-Dalché, J., 1997. "Du royaume asturo-léonais à la monarchie castillano-léonaise. Une histoire monétaire singulière (VIIIe–IXe siècle)," in *Actes des Congrès de la Société des historiens médiévists de l'enseignement supérieur public*, 77–92. Paris: Éditions de la Sorbonne.

Geertz, C., 1979. "Suq: the *Bazaar* Economy in Sefrou," in *Meaning and Order in Moroccan Society*, by C. Geertz, H. Geertz and L. Rosen, 123–313. Cambridge: Cambridge University Press.

Geiger, H.-U., 1986. "Der Münzschatz von Ilanz und die Entstehung des mittelalterlichen Münzsystems," *Schweizerische Zeitschrift für Geschichte* 36:395–412.

Gem, R., 1988. "The English Parish Church in the 11th and Early 12th Centuries: A Great Rebuilding," in *Minsters and Parish Churches: The Local Church in Transition 950–1200*, ed. J. Blair, 21–30. Oxford: Oxford University Press.

Geneviève, V., and G. Sarah, 2010. "Le trésor de deniers mérovingiens de Rodez. Aveyron. Circulation et diffusion des monnayages d'argent dans le Sud de la France au milieu du VIIIe siècle," *Revue numismatique* 166:477–507.

———, 2013. "Le trésor monétaire carolingien," in *Rapport d'opération: fouille archéologique, vol. 3. ZAC de Trémonteix lot 1. Les études*, ed. K. Chuniaud, 297–310. Bron, Fr.: Archives du service régional de l'archéologie de l'Auvergne.

———, 2018. "Un denier de Charles le Chauve à la légende fautive émis à Toulouse appurtenant au trésor d'Auzeville (Haute-Garonne)," *BSFN* 73:402–4.

Georgi, W., 1995. "Bischof Keonwald von Worcester und die Heirat Ottos I. mit Edgitha im Jahre 929," *Historisches Jahrbuch* 115:1–40.

Gerrard, J., 2013. *The Ruin of Roman Britain: An Archaeological Perspective*. Cambridge: Cambridge University Press.

Gianichedda, E., 2008. "Metal Production in Late Antiquity: From Continuity of Knowledge to Changes in Consumption," *Late Antique Archaeology* 4:187–209.

Gibson, M., and J. L. Nelson, eds., 1990. *Charles the Bald: Court and Kingdom*. 2nd ed. Aldershot, UK: Ashgate.

Gies, J., and F. Gies, 1972. *Merchants and Moneymen. The Commercial Revolution, 1000–1500*. London: Barker.

Gillingham, J. B., 1989. "'The Most Precious Jewel in the English Crown': Levels of Danegeld and Heregeld in the Early Eleventh Century," *English Historical Review* 104:373–84.

———, 1990. "Chronicles and Coins as Evidence for Levels of Tribute and Taxation in Late Tenth and Early Eleventh-Century England," *English Historical Review* 105:939–50.

———, 1995. "Thegns and Knights in Eleventh-Century England: Who Was Then the Gentleman?," *Transactions of the Royal Historical Society*, 6th series, 5:129–54.

Glørstad, Z. T., and K. Loftsgarden, eds., 2017. *Viking-Age Transformations: Trade, Craft and Resources in Western Scandinavia.* Abingdon, UK: Routledge.

Goethe, R. L., 2016. "King Dagobert, the Saint, and Royal Salvation: The Shrine of Saint-Denis and Propaganda Production (850–1319 CE)." PhD dissertation, University of Iowa.

Goffart, W., 1974. *Caput and Colonate: Towards a History of Late Roman Taxation.* Toronto, ON: University of Toronto Press.

———, 1980. *Barbarians and Romans, A.D. 418–584: The Techniques of Accommodation.* Princeton, NJ: Princeton University Press.

———, 1989. *Rome's Fall and After.* London: Hambledon.

———, 2006. *Barbarian Tides: The Migration Age and the Later Roman Empire.* Philadelphia: University of Philadelphia Press.

———, 2008. "Frankish Military Duty and the Fate of Roman Taxation," *EME* 16:166–90.

———, 2010. "The Technique of Barbarian Settlement in the Fifth Century: A Personal, Streamlined Account with Ten Additional Comments," *Journal of Late Antiquity* 3:65–98.

———, 2012. "Le début (et la fin) des *sortes Vandalorum*," in Porena and Rivière 2012, 115–28.

———, 2013. "Administrative Methods of Barbarian Settlement in the Fifth Century: The Definitive Account," in *Gallien in Spätantike und Frühmittelalter: Kulturgeschichte einer Region*, ed. S. Diefenbach and G. M. Müller, 45–58. Berlin: De Gruyter.

Goitein, S. D., 1967–1993. *A Mediterranean Society: The Jewish Communities of the Arab World as Portrayed in the Documents of the Cairo Geniza.* 6 vols. Berkeley: University of California Press.

Golas, P. J., 1980. "Rural China in the Song," *Journal of Asian Studies* 39:291–325.

———, 2015. "The Sung Fiscal Administration," in Chaffee and Twitchett 2015, 139–213.

Goldberg, J. L., 2012. *Trade and Institutions in the Medieval Mediterranean: The Geniza Merchants and Their Business World.* Cambridge: Cambridge University Press.

Goldstone, J. A., 1991. *Revolution and Rebellion in the Early Modern World.* Berkeley: University of California Press.

Goodson, C., 2021. *Cultivating the City in Early Medieval Italy.* Cambridge: Cambridge University Press.

Gordus, A. A., and D. M. Metcalf, 1970–72. "The Alloy of the Byzantine Miliaresion and the Question of the Reminting of Islamic Silver," *Hamburger Beiträge zur Numismatik* 24/6:9–36.

Graca, L. da, and A. Zingarelli, eds., 2015. *Studies on Pre-Capitalist Modes of Production.* Leiden, Neth.: Brill.

Graeber, D., 1996. "Beads and Money: Notes toward a Theory of Wealth and Power," *American Ethnologist* 23:4–24.

———, 2011. *Debt: The First 5,000 Years*. New York: Melville House.

Graham-Campbell, J., 1995. *The Viking-Age Gold and Silver of Scotland, AD 850–1100*. Edinburgh: National Museums of Scotland.

———, 2006. "The Rings," in Fuglesang and Wilson, 73–81.

———, 2007. "Comparative Economics: Silver in Viking-Age Britain and Ireland," in *Globalisation, Battlefields, and Economics: Three Inaugural Lectures in Archaeology*, ed. H. Vandkilde, 41–54. Aarhus, Den.: Aarhus University Press.

———, ed., 2011a. *The Cuerdale Hoard and Related Viking-Age Silver and Gold from Britain and Ireland in the British Museum*. London: British Museum.

———, 2011b. "The Discovery and Dispersal of the Cuerdale Hoard," in Graham-Campbell 2011a, 21–38.

Graham-Campbell, J., S. Sindbæk, and G. Williams, 2011a. "Introduction," in Graham-Campbell, Sindbæk and Williams 2011b, 19–24.

———, eds., 2011b. *Silver Economies, Monetisation and Society in Scandinavia, AD 800–1100*. Aarhus, Den.: Aarhus University Press.

Graham-Campbell, J., and G. Williams, eds., 2007. *Silver Economy in the Viking Age*. Walnut Creek, CA: Left Coast.

Green, C., 2018. "An Eleventh-Century Chinese Coin in Britain and the Evidence for East Asian Contacts in the Medieval Period." https://www.caitlingreen.org/2018/03/an-eleventh-century-chinese-coin.html.

Green, T., 2019. *A Fistful of Shells: West Africa from the Rise of the Slave Trade to the Age of Revolution*. London: Allen Lane.

Grélois, E., 2002. "Documents sur la monnaie de Clermont et la circulation monétaire en Auvergne (XIe–XIVe siècles)," *Revue numismatique* 158:279–344.

Grelu, J., 1984. "La découverte monétaire de la rue Dinet à Mâcon," *BSFN* 3:488–90.

Greule, A., et al., eds., 2017. *Die merowingischen Monetarmünzen als interdisziplinär-mediaevistische Herausforderung. Historische, numismatische und philologische Untersuchungen auf Grundlage des Bestandes im Münzkabinett der Staatlichen Museen zu Berlin*. Paderborn, Ger.: Wilhelm Fink.

Grierson, P., 1959a. "Commerce in the Dark Ages: A Critique of the Evidence," *Transactions of the Royal Historical Society*, 5th series, 9:123–40.

———, 1959b. "The *Tablettes Albertini* and the Value of the *Solidus* in the Fifth and Sixth Centuries A.D.," *Journal of Roman Studies* 49:73–80.

———, 1961. "La fonction sociale de la monnaie en Angleterre aux VIIe–VIIIe siècle," *Settimane di studio del Centro italiano di studi sull'alto medioevo* 8:341–85.

———, 1963a. "Mint Output in the Time of Offa," *Numismatic Circular* 71:114–15.

———, 1963b. "Some Aspects of the Coinage of Offa," *Numismatic Circular* 71:223–25.

———, 1965. "Money and Coinage under Charlemagne," in *Karl der Grosse. Lebenswerk und Nachleben*, ed. H. Beumann and W. Braunfels. 5 vols, 1:501–35. Düsseldorf, Ger.: L. Schwann.

———, 1967. "The Volume of Anglo-Saxon Coinage," *Economic History Review*, 2nd series, 20:153–60.

———, 1970. "The Purpose of the Sutton Hoo Coins," *Antiquity* 44:14–18.

———, 1973. *Catalogue of the Byzantine Coins in the Dumbarton Oaks Collection and the Whittemore Collection. 3: Leo III to Niceophorus III 717–1081. Part 1: Leo III to*

Michael III (717-867). Washington, DC: Dumbarton Oaks Centre for Byzantine Studies.

———, 1975. *Numismatics*. Oxford: Oxford University Press.

———, 1977. *The Origins of Money*. London: Athlone.

———, 1979. "Coniazioni per dispetto' nell'Italia medievale," *Quaderni Ticinesi di Numismatica e Antichità Classiche* 8:345–58.

———, 1982. *Byzantine Coinage*. Washington, DC: Dumbarton Oaks Research Library and Collection.

———, 1990. "The *Gratia Dei rex* Coinage of Charles the Bald," in Gibson and Nelson 1990, 52–64.

———, 1992. "The Role of Silver in the Early Byzantine Economy," in *Ecclesiastical Silver Plate in Sixth-Century Byzantium: Papers of the Symposium Held May 16–18, 1986 at the Walters Art Gallery, Baltimore and Dumbarton Oaks, Washington, D.C.*, ed. S. A. Boyd et al., 137–46. Washington, DC: Dumbarton Oaks Research Library and Collection.

Grierson, P., and M.A.S. Blackburn, 1986. *Medieval European Coinage, with a Catalogue of the Coins in the Fitzwilliam Museum, Cambridge. 1: The Early Middle Ages (5th–10th Centuries)*. Cambridge: Cambridge University Press.

Grierson, P., and M. Mays, 1992. *Catalogue of Late Roman Coins in the Dumbarton Oaks Collection and in the Whittemore Collection, from Arcadius and Honorius to the Accession of Anastasius*. Washington, DC: Dumbarton Okas Research Library and Collection.

Grierson, P., and L. Travaini, 1998. *Medieval European Coinage, with a Catalogue of the Coins in the Fitzwilliam Museum, Cambridge. 14: Italy (3); South Italy, Sicily, Sardinia*. Cambridge: Cambridge University Press.

Gruszczyński, J., 2019. *Viking Silver, Hoards and Containers: The Archaeological and Historical Context of Viking-Age Silver Coin Deposits in the Baltic c. 800–1050*. London: Routledge.

———, 2020. "Hoards, Silver, Context and the Gotlandic Alternative," in Gruszczyński, Jankowiak, and Shephard 2020, 187–207.

Gruszczyński, J., M. Jankowiak, and J. Shephard, eds., 2020. *Viking-Age Trade: Silver, Slaves and Gotland*. London: Routledge.

Guerra, M. F., T. Calligaro, and A. Perea, 2007. "The Treasure of Guarrazar: Tracing the Gold Supplies in the Visigothic Iberian Peninsula," *Archaeometry* 49:53–74.

Guerra, M. F., and C. Roux, 2002. "L'or de la Péninsule Ibérique de l'Invasion à la Reconquista," *Revue d'archéométrie* 26:219–32.

Guerreau, A., 1980. *Le féodalisme. Un horizon théorique*. Paris: Sycomore.

Guest, P., 2005. *The Late Roman Gold and Silver Coins from the Hoxne Treasure*. London: British Museum.

Guest, P., 2008. "Roman Gold and Hun Kings: The Use and Hoarding of Solidi in the Late Fourth and Fifth Centuries," in *Roman Coins Outside the Empire: Ways and Phases, Contexts and Functions*, ed. A. Bursche, R. Ciolek, and R. Wolters, 295–307. Wetteren, Bel.: Moneta.

———, 2012. "The Production, Supply and Use of Late Roman and Early Byzantine Copper Coinage in the Eastern Empire," *Numismatic Chronicle* 172:105–31.

Guey, J., 1965. "Ne vaudrait-il pas mieux dire miliarensis que miliarense?," *BSFN* 20:492–93, 504–6.

Gullbekk, S. H., 2009. *Pengevesenets fremvekst og fall i Norge i middelalderen.* Oslo: Museum Tusculanum.

——, 2011. "Norway: Commodity Money, Silver and Coins," in Graham-Campbell, Sindbæk and Williams 2011, 93–112.

——, 2014. "Vestfold: A Monetary Perspective on the Viking Age," in Naismith, Allen, and Screen 2014, 331–48.

——, 2015. "The Church and Money in Norway c. 1050–1250: Salvation and Monetization," in Gasper and Gullbekk 2015, 223–44.

——, 2019. "The Elites and Money," in *Nordic Elites in Transformation, c. 1050–1250,* ed. B. Poulson, H. Vogt, and Jón Viðar Sigurðsson, 161–82. New York: Routledge.

Gurevich, A. J., 1985. *Categories of Medieval Culture,* trans. G. L. Campbell. London: Routledge, Kegan & Paul.

Gustafsson, N. B., 2013. "Casting Identities in Central Seclusion: Aspects of Non-Ferrous Metalworking and Society on Gotland in the Early Medieval Period." PhD dissertation, University of Stockholm.

Gustin, I., 1997. "Islam, Merchants, or King? Who Was Behind the Manufacture of Viking Age Weights?," in *Visions of the Past: Trends and Traditions in Swedish Medieval Archaeology,* ed. H. Andersson, P. Carelli, and L. Ersgård, 163–77. Stockholm: Riksantikvarieämbetet.

Guyon, J., 2000. "Toulouse, la première capitale du royaume wisigoth," in Ripoll López and Gurt Esparraguera 2000, 219–40.

Guyotjeannin, O., 1987. *Episcopus et comes. Affirmation et déclin de la seigneurie épiscopale au nord du royaume de France. Beauvais-Noyon, X.-début XIII (siècle).* Geneva: Droz.

——, 2002. "888–1060: Rois et princes," in *Le Moyen Âge. Le roi, l'Église, les grands, le peuple, 481–1514,* ed. P. Contamine, 120–47. Paris: Éditions du CTHS.

Hadley, D. M., and J. D. Richards, 2016. "The Winter Camp of the Viking Great Army, AD 872–3, Torksey, Lincolnshire," *Antiquaries Journal* 96:23–67.

——. *The Viking Great Army and the Making of England.* London: Thames and Hudson.

Haertle, C. M., 1997. *Karolingische Münzfunde aus dem 9. Jahrhundert.* 2 vols. Cologne, Ger.: Böhlau.

Hageneier, L., 2004. *Jenseits der Topik. Die karolingische Herrscherbiographie.* Husum, Ger.: Matthiesen.

Hahn, W., 1976. *Moneta Radasponensis. Bayerns Münzprägung im 9., 10. und 11. Jahrhundert.* Brunswick, Ger.: Klinkhardt & Biermann.

Haldon, J. F., 1993. *The State and the Tributary Mode of Production.* London: Verso.

——, 1997. *Byzantium in the Seventh Century: The Transformation of a Culture.* 2nd ed. Cambridge, UK: Cambridge University Press.

——, 2009. "The Byzantine Empire," in *The Dynamics of Ancient Empires: State Power from Assyria to Byzantium,* ed. I. Morris and W. Scheidel, 205–54. Oxford: Oxford University Press.

——, 2015. "Mode of Production, Social Action, and Historical Change: Some Questions and Issues," in da Graca and Zingarelli 2015, 204–36.

——, 2016. *The Empire That Would Not Die: The Paradox of Eastern Roman Survival, 640–740*. Cambridge, MA: Harvard University Press.

Hallam, E. M., and C. West, C., 2020. *Capetian France 987–1328*. 3rd ed. Abingdon, UK: Routledge.

Halsall, G., 2003. *Warfare and Society in the Barbarian West, 450–900*. Abingdon, UK: Routledge.

——, 2007. *Barbarian Migrations and the Roman West, 376–568*. Cambridge: Cambridge University Press.

——, 2012. "From Roman *Fundus* to Early Medieval *Grand domaine*: Crucial Ruptures between Antiquity and the Middle Ages," *Revue belge de philologie et d'histoire* 90: 273–98.

Hamerow, H., 2012. *Rural Settlements and Society in Anglo-Saxon England*. Oxford: Oxford University Press.

Hansen, M., 1990. "Udmøntningernes størrelse i Danmark og Skåne i 1000 årene," *Nordisk Numismatisk Unions Medlemblad* 3:50–54.

Hansen, V., and X. Rong, 2013. "How the Residents of Turfan Used Textiles as Money, 273–796 CE," *Journal of the Royal Asiatic Society*, 3rd series, 23:281–305.

Hansen, V., and H. Wang, 2013. "Introduction," *Journal of the Royal Asiatic Society*, 3rd series, 23: 155–63.

Hårdh, B., 1976. *Wikingerzeitliche Depotfunde aus Südschweden. Probleme und Analysen*. Lund, Swed.: Liber-Läromedel.

——, 1996. *Silver in the Viking Age: A Regional-Economic Study*. Stockholm: Almquist & Wiksell International.

——, 2007. "Oriental-Scandinavian Contacts on the Volga, as Manifested by Silver Rings and Weight Systems," in Graham-Campbell and Williams 2007, 135–47.

——, 2008. "Hacksilver and Ingots," in Skre 2008, 95–118.

——, 2016. *The Perm'/Glazov Rings: Contacts and Economy in the Viking Age between Russia and the Baltic Region*. Lund, Swed.: Department of Archaeology and Ancient History, Lund University.

Hardt, M., 2004. *Gold und Herrschaft. Die Schätze europäischer Könige und Fürsten im ersten Jahrtausend*. Berlin: Akademie.

——, 2012. "Edelmetallschmiede in erzählenden Quellen der Völkerwanderungszeit und des frühen Mittelalters," in *Goldsmith Mysteries: Archaeological, Pictorial and Documentary Evidence from the 1st Millennium AD in Northern Europe. Papers Presented at a Workshop Organized by the Centre for Baltic and Scandinavian Archaeology (ZBSA), Schleswig, October 20th and 21st, 2011*, ed. A. Pesch, 271–78. Neumünster, Ger.: Wachholtz.

——, 2018. "Der Ring der Awaren," in *Lebenswelten zwischen Archäologie und Geschichte. Festschrift für Falko Daim zu seinem 65. Geburtstag*, ed. J. Drauschke et al. 2 vols., 1:185–92. Mainz, Ger.: Römisch-Germanisches Zentralmuseum.

Hardt-Friederichs, F., 1980. "Über die frühmittelalterlichen Kaufleute im ostfränkischen Reich bis zum Ende der Ottonen," *Genealogisches Jahrbuch* 20:95–107.

Hart, C. R., 1992. *The Danelaw*. London: Hambledon.

Hart, K., 1986. "Heads or Tails? Two Sides of the Coin," *Man* 21:637–56.

Harvey, S.P.J., 2014. *Domesday: Book of Judgement*. Oxford: Oxford University Press.

Haselgrove, C., 1987. *Iron Age Coinage in South-East England: The Archaeological Context*. Oxford: B.A.R.

Hatz, G., 1974. *Handel und Verkehr zwischen dem deutschen Reich und Schweden in der späten Wikingerzeit: die deutschen Münzen des 10. und 11. Jahrhunderts in Schweden*. Lund, Swed.: Kungl. Vitterhets historie och antikvitetsakademien.

Hatz, G., et al., 1991. *Otto-Adelheid-Pfennige. Untersuchungen zu Münzen des 10./11. Jahrhunderts*. Stockholm: Royal Swedish Academy of Letters, History and Antiquities.

Hatz, G., and U. S. Linder Welin, 1968. "Deutsche Münzen des 11. Jahrhunderts nach byzantinisch-arabischem Vorbild in den schwedischen Funden der Wikingerzeit," in Rasmusson and Malmer 1968, 1–38.

Haubrichs, W., 2000. "Das palatium von Thionville/Diedenhofen und sein Umland im Spiegel frühmittelalterlicher Siedlungsnamen und Siedlungsgeschichte. Eine toponomastische und interferenzlinguistische Studie," in *Septuaginta quinque. Festschrift für Heinz Mettke*, ed. J. Haustein, E. Meinecke, and N. R. Wolf, 171–89. Heidelberg, Ger.: C. Winter.

Hayeur Smith, M., 2019. "*Vaðmál* and Cloth Currency in Viking and Medieval Iceland," in Kershaw and Williams 2019, 251–77.

Heck, G. W., 1999. "Gold Mining in Arabia and the Rise of the Islamic State," *Journal of the Economic and Social History of the Orient* 42:364–95.

Heather, P., 1996. *The Goths*. Oxford: Blackwell.

———, 2005. *The Fall of the Roman Empire: A New History of Rome and the Barbarians*. London: Pan.

Head, T. F., 1992. "The Judgement of God: Andrew of Fleury's Account of the Peace League of Bourges," in Head and Landes 1992, 219–38.

Head, T. F., and R. A. Landes, eds., 1992. *The Peace of God: Social Violence and Religious Response in France around the Year 1000*. Ithaca, NY: Cornell University Press.

Hebblewhite, M., 2017. *The Emperor and the Army in the Later Roman Army, AD 235–395*. London: Routledge.

Hegel, K., 1898. *Die Entstehung des deutschen Städtewesens*. Leipzig, Ger.: Hirzel.

Heidemann, S., 2002. *Die Renaissance der Städte in Nordsyrien und Nordmesopotamien: städtische Entwicklung und wirtschaftliche Bedingungen in ar-Raqqa und Ḥarrān von der Zeit der beduinischen Vorherrschaft bis zu den Seldschuken*. Leiden, Neth.: Brill.

———, 2010. "Numismatics," in *The New Cambridge History of Islam. Vol. 1: The Formation of the Islamic World, Sixth to Eleventh Centuries*, ed. C. F. Robinson, 648–63. Cambridge: Cambridge University Press.

———, 2011. "The Representation of the Early Islamic Empire and Its Religion on Coin Imagery," in *Court Cultures in the Muslim World: Seventh to Nineteenth Centuries*, ed. A. Fuess and J.-P. Hartung, 30–53. London: Routledge.

———, 2015. "How to Measure Economic Growth in the Middle East? A Framework of Inquiry for the Middle Islamic Period," in *Material Evidence and Narrative Sources: Interdisciplinary Studies of the History of the Muslim Middle East*, ed. D. Talmon-Heller and K. Cytryn-Silverman, 30–57. Leiden, Neth.: Brill.

———, 2018. "Coins from the Seaside. An Emiral Silver Coin Hoard from a Harbour Settlement on the Cerro da Vila (Vilamoura, Algarve, Portugal)," *Al-Qanṭara* 39:169–224.

Heijne, C. von, 2004. *Särpräglat. Vikingatida och tidigmedeltida myntfynd från Danmark, Skåne, Blekinge och Halland (ca 800–1130).* Stockholm: Stockholms universitet.

Heinemeyer, C., 2018. "Territorium und Territorialisierung. Ein Konzept der deutschen Forschung und seine Problematik," in Bührer-Thierry, Patzole, and Schneider 2018, 89–117.

Helleiner, E., 2003. *The Making of National Money: Territorial Currencies in Historical Perspective.* Ithaca, NY: Cornell University Press.

Heinzelmann, M., 1981. "Une source de base de la littérature hagiographique latine: le recueil de miracles," in *Hagiographie, cultures et sociétés, IVe–XIIe siècles. Actes du Colloque organisé à Nanterre et à Paris (2–5 mai 1979),* 235–59. Paris: Études augustiniennes.

———, 2013. "Eligius monetarius. Norm oder Sonderfall?," in Jarnut and Strothmann 2013, 243–91.

Hendy, M. F., 1985. *Studies in the Byzantine Monetary Economy, c. 300–1450.* Cambridge: Cambridge University Press.

———, 1988. "From Public to Private: The Western Barbarian Coinages as a Mirror of the Disintegration of Late Roman State Structures," *Viator* 19:29–78.

———, 1989. "Economy and State in Late Rome and Early Byzantium: an Introduction," in his *The Economy, Fiscal Administration and Coinage of Byzantium,* 1:1–23. Aldershot, UK: Ashgate.

———, 2002. "East and West: the Transformation of Late Roman Financial Structures," *Settimane di studio del Centro italiano di studi sull'alto medioevo* 49:1307–70.

Henning, J., ed., 2007. *Post-Roman Towns, Trade and Settlement in Europe and Byzantium.* 2 vols. Berlin: De Gruyter.

Hennius, A., 2018. "Viking Age Tar Production and Outland Exploitation," *Antiquity* 92:1349–61.

Henry, J. F., 2004. "The Social Origins of Money: The Case of Egypt," in *Credit and State Theories of Money: The Contributions of A. Mitchell Innes,* ed. L. Randell Wray, 70–98. Cheltenham, UK: Edward Elgar.

Herlihy, D., 1957. "Hoards in the Italian Economy, 960–1139," *Economic History Review,* new series, 10:1–14.

———, 1958. "The Agrarian Revolution in Southern France and Italy, 801–1150," *Speculum* 33:23–41.

———, 1959. "The History of the Rural Seigneury in Italy, 751–1200," *Agricultural History* 33:58–71.

———, 1973. "Three Patterns of Social Mobility in Medieval History," *Journal of Interdisciplinary History* 3:623–47.

Hess, W., 1982. "Münzstätten, Geldverkehr und Märkte am Rhein in ottonischer und salischer Zeit," in Diestelkamp 1982, 111–33.

———, 1988. "Eine Barschaft des 11. Jahrhunderts von Kirchberg bei Wiebelskirchen im Saarland," *Commentationes numismaticae* 1988:185–93.

———, 1990. "Bemerkungen zum innerdeutschen Geldumlauf im 10., 11. und 12. Jahrhundert," in Jonsson and Malmer 1990, 113–19.

——, 1993. "Pfennigwährungen und Geldumlauf im Reichsgebiet zur Zeit der Ottonen und Salier," in Kluge 1993, 17–35.

Hielscher, S., and Husted, B. W., 2020. "Proto-CSR before the Industrial Revolution: Institutional Experimentation by Medieval Miners' Guilds," *Journal of Business Ethics* 166:253–69.

Hildebrand, B., 1864. "Natural-, Geld- und Kreditwirtschaft," *Jahrbuch Nationalökonomie* 2:1–24.

Hill, D., ed., 1978. *Ethelred the Unready: Papers from the Millenary Conference*. Oxford: B.A.R.

Hill, G. F., 1936. *Treasure Trove in Law and Practice from the Earliest Time to the Present Day*. Oxford: Oxford University Press.

Hilton, R., 1984. "Women Traders in Medieval England," *Women's Studies* 11:139–55.

Hines, J., 2010. "Units of Account in Gold and Silver in Seventh-Century England: *Scillingas, Sceattas* and *Pæningas*," *Antiquaries Journal* 90:153–73.

Hines, J., and A. Bayliss, eds., 2013. *Anglo-Saxon Graves and Grave Goods of the 6th and 7th Centuries AD: A Chronological Framework*. London: Society for Medieval Archaeology.

Hinton, D. A., 1998. "Anglo-Saxon Smiths and Myths," *Bulletin of the John Rylands Library* 80:3–21.

——, 2000. *A Smith in Lindsey: The Anglo-Saxon Grave at Tattershall Thorpe, Lincolnshire*. London: Society for Medieval Archaeology.

——, 2013. "Demography: From Domesday and Beyond," *Journal of Medieval History* 39: 146–78.

Hirt, A. M., 2010. *Imperial Mines and Quarries in the Roman World: Organizational Aspects 27 BC–AD 235*. Oxford: Oxford University Press.

——, 2012. "*Conductores*," in *The Encyclopedia of Ancient History*, ed. R. S. Bagnall et al. Malden, MA: Wiley Blackwell. https://doi.org/10.1002/9781444338386.

Hlawitschka, E., 1960. *Franken, Alemannen, Bayern und Burgunder in Oberitalien (774–962)*. Freiburg, Ger.: E. Albert.

Hobbs, R., 2006. *Late Roman Precious Metal Deposits c. AD 200–700: Changes over Time and Space*. Oxford: Archaeopress.

Hodges, R., 1989. *Dark Age Economics: The Origins of Towns and Trade A.D. 600–1000*. 2nd ed. London: Duckworth.

——, 2006. *Goodbye to the Vikings? Re-Readings of Early Medieval Archaeology*. London: Duckworth.

——, 2012. *Dark Age Economics: A New Audit*. London: Bristol Classics Project.

——, 2020. "The Primitivism of the Early Medieval Peasant in Italy?," in Quirós Castillo 2020, 165–74.

Hodges, R., and G. Bianchi, eds., 2018. *Origins of a New Economic Union: Preliminary Results of the nEU-Med Project: October 2015–March 2017*. Florence, It.: Insegna del Giglio.

Hoffmann, H., 1986. *Buchkunst und Königtum im ottonischen und frühsalischen Reich*. 2 vols. Stuttgart, Ger.: Hiersemann.

——, 1990. "Grafschaften in Bischofshand," *Deutsches Archiv für Erforschung des Mittelalters* 46:375–480.

Holm, O., 2015. "Trading in Viking-Period Scandinavia—a Business Only for a Few? The Jämtland Case," *Viking and Medieval Scandinavia* 11:79–126.

———, 2017. "The Use of Silver as a Medium of Exchange in Jämtland, *c.* 875–1050," in Glørstad and Loftsgarden 2017, 42–58.

Holmes, C. J., and N. Standen, eds., 2018. *The Global Middle Ages.* Oxford: Oxford University Press.

Hoogendijk, F.A.J., 1995. "Zwei byzantinische Landkäufe," *Tyche* 10:13–26.

Hope-Taylor, B., 1977. *Yeavering: An Anglo-British Centre of Early Northumbria.* London: English Heritage.

Horne, T., 2022. *A Viking Market Kingdom in Ireland and Britain: Trade Networks and the Importation of a Southern Scandinavian Silver Bullion Economy.* Abingdon, UK: Routledge.

Horsnæs, H. W., 2006. "Roman Bronze Coins in Barbaricum: Denmark as a Case Study," in *6th Nordic Numismatic Symposium: Single Finds, the Nordic Perspective,* ed. H. W. Horsnæs and J. C. Moesgaard, 53–99. Copenhagen: Nordisk Numismatisk Union.

Houlbrook, C., 2018. *The Roots of a Ritual: The Magic of Coin-Trees from Religion to Recreation.* Basingstoke, UK: Palgrave Macmillan.

Hourlier, M., and M. Dhénin, 1998. "Monnaies médiévales de Soissons," *Revue numismatique* 153:245–95.

Howard-Johnston, J., 2020. "The Fur Trade in the Early Middle Ages," in Gruszczyński, Jankowiak, and Shephard 2020, 57–74.

Howell, M. C., 2010. *Commerce before Capitalism in Europe, 1300–1600.* Cambridge, UK: Cambridge University Press.

Howgego, C., 1990. "Why Did Ancient States Strike Coins?," *Numismatic Chronicle* 150:1–25.

———, 1995. *Ancient History from Coins.* London: Routledge.

Howlett, D., 1994. "Aldhelm and Irish Learning," *Archivium latinitatis medii aevi* 52:37–75.

Hudik, M., and E. S. Fang, 2020. "Money or in-Kind Gift? Evidence from Red Packets in China," *Journal of Institutional Economics* 16:731–46.

Hudson, M., 2020. "Origins of Money and Interest: Palatial Credit, not Barter," in Battilossi, Cassis, and Yago 2020, 45–66.

Hunter, F., and K. Painter, eds., 2013. *Late Roman Silver: The Traprain Treasure in Context.* Edinburgh.

Hurst, J. G., 1976. "The Pottery," in *The Archaeology of Anglo-Saxon England,* ed. D. M. Wilson, 283–348. London: Society of Antiquaries of Scotland.

Ilisch, L., 1990. "Whole and Fragmented Dirhams in Near Eastern Hoards," in Jonsson and Malmer 1990, 121–28.

———, 2004. "Die imitativen *solidi mancusi*: 'Arabische' Goldmünzen der Karolingerzeit," in *Fundamenta Historiae: Geschichte im Spiegel der Numismatik und ihrer Nachbarwissenschaften. Festschrift für Niklot Klüßendrof zum 60. Geburtstag am 10. Februar 2004,* ed. R. Polley, A. Röpcke, and R. Cunz, 91–106. Neustadt, Ger.: Schmidt.

Ilisch, L., et al., 2003. *Dirham und Rappenpfennig. Mittelalterliche Münzprägung in Bergbauregionen.* Bonn, Ger.: Rudolf Habelt.

Ilisch, P., 1981. "German Viking-Age Coinage and the North," in Blackburn and Metcalf 1981, 129–46.

———, 2000. "Die Münzprägung im Herzogtum Niederlothringen. I: die Münzprägung in den Räumen Utrecht und Friesland in 10. und 11. Jahrhundert," *Jaarboek voor Munt- en Penningkunde* 84–85:1–272.

———, 2012. *Münzfunde der Jahr 1999 bis 2010 in Westfalen-Lippe.* Münster, Ger.: LWL-Archäologie für Westfalen.

———, 2014a. "The Development of Coinage in the Northern, Western and Eastern Parts of Lower Lotharingia in the Tenth and Eleventh Centuries Compared," *Revue belge de numismatique et de sigillographie* 160:67–76.

———, 2014b. "Die Münzprägung im Herzogtum Niederlothringen. II: die Münzprägung im südwestlichen Niederlothringen und in Flandern im 10. und 11. Jahrhundert," *Jaarboek voor Munt- en Penningkunde* 100:i–xi, 1–383.

———, 2016. "Les monnaies du Saint-Empire du Xe et XIe siècle: exportation ou circulation interne?," *BSFN* 71:49–56.

Ingham, G., 1996. "Money is a Social Relation," *Review of Social Economy* 54:243–75.

———, 1999. "Class Inequality and the Social Production of Money," *Sociological Review* 47:66–86.

———, 2000. "Babylonian Madness: On the Historical and Sociological Origins of Money," in *What Is Money?*, ed. J. Smithin, 16–41. London.

———, 2004. *The Nature of Money.* Cambridge: Polity.

Innes, A. M., 1914. "The Credit Theory of Money," *Banking Law Journal* 31:151–68.

Innes, M., 1997. "Charlemagne's Will: Piety, Politics and the Imperial Succession," *English Historical Review* 112:833–55.

———, 2000. *State and Society in the Early Middle Ages: The Middle Rhine Valley, 400–1000.* Cambridge: Cambridge University Press.

———, 2001. "People, Places and Power in Carolingian Society," in *Topographies of Power in the Early Middle Ages*, ed. M. de Jong and F. Theuws, 397–437. Leiden, Neth.: Brill.

———, 2009. "Property, Politics and the Problem of the Carolingian State," in Pohl and Wieser 2009, 299–314.

Isla Frez, A., 1991. "Moneda de cuenta y organización monetaria en la Galicia altomedieval," in *Miscellània en Homenatge al P. Agustí Altissent*, 487–510. Tarragona, Sp.: Disputació de Tarragona.

Jakobsson, M., 2021. "Burial Layout, Society and Sacred Geography—a Viking Age Example from Jämtland," *Current Swedish Archaeology* 5:79–98.

James, E., 1982. *The Origins of France: From Clovis to the Capetians 500–1000.* London: Macmillan.

Jankowiak, M., 2019. "Silver Fragmentation: Reinterpreting the Evidence of the Hoards," in Kershaw and Williams 2019, 15–31.

———, 2020. "Dirham Flows into Northern and Eastern Europe and the Rhythms of the Slave Trade with the Islamic World," in Gruszczyński, Jankowiak, and Shephard 2020, 105–31.

Janssen, H. M., 1985. "The Origins of the Non-Roman Town in Germany," in Clarke and Simms 1985, 217–35.

Jarman, C., 2021. *River Kings: A New History of the Vikings from Scandinavia to the Silk Roads.* London: William Collins.

Jarnut, J., 1979. *Bergamo 568–1098. Verfassungs-, Sozial- und Wirtschaftsgeschichte einer lombardischen Stadt im Mittelalter.* Wiesbaden, Ger.: Steiner

Jarnut, J., and J. Strothmann, eds., 2013. *Die merowingischen Monetarmünzen als Quelle zum verständnis des 7. Jahrhundrets in Gallien.* Paderborn, Ger.: Wilhelm Fink.

Jarrett, J., 2010. "Currency Change in Pre-Millennial Catalonia: Coinage, Counts and Economics," *Numismatic Chronicle* 169:217–43.

———, 2011. "Caliph, King, or Grandfather: Strategies of Legitimization on the Spanish March in the Reign of Lothar III," *Mediaeval Journal* 1:1–22.

———, 2014. "Bovo Soldare: A Sacred Cow of Spanish Economic History Re-evaluated," in Naismith, Allen, and Screen 2014, 187–206.

———, 2017. "Middle Byzantine Numismatics in the Light of Franz Füeg's Corpora of Nomismata," *Numismatic Chronicle* 176:513–35.

Jeanne-Rose, O., 1996. "Trouvailles isolées de monnaies carolingiennes en Poitou: inventaire roviso ire," *Revue numismatique* 151:241–83.

———, 2007. "L'histoire économique du Centre-Ouest atlantique d'après la littérature hagiographique (VIIIe–XIIe siècle)," *Revue historique du Centre-Ouest* 6:137–64.

Jenks, M., 2000. "*Romanitas* and *Christianitas* in the Coinage of Theodebert I of Metz," *Zeitschrift für antikes Christentum/Journal of Ancient Christianity* 4:338–68.

Jesch, J., 2001. *Ships and Men in the Late Viking Age: The Vocabulary of Runic Inscriptions and Skaldic Verse.* Woodbridge, UK: Boydell.

Johns, C., 2010. *The Hoxne Late Roman Treasure: Gold Jewellery and Silver Plate.* London: British Museum.

Jones, A.H.M., 1957. "Capitatio et Iugatio," *Journal of Roman Studies* 47:88–94.

———, 1964. *The Later Roman Empire 284-602: A Social, Economic and Administrative Survey.* 3 vols. Oxford: Blackwell.

Jones, R., 2009. "Manure and the Medieval Social Order," in *Land and People: Papers in Memory of John G. Evans*, ed. M. J. Allen, N. Sharples and T. O'Connor, 215–25. Oxford: Oxbow.

Jong, M. de, 2009. *The Penitential State: Authority and Atonement in the Age of Louis the Pious, 814–840.* Cambridge: Cambridge University Press.

———, 2018. "The Two Republics: *Ecclesia* and the Public Domain in the Carolingian World," in Balzaretti, Barrow, and Skinner 2018, 486–500.

Jonsson, K., 1987. *The New Era. The Reformation of the Late Anglo-Saxon Coinage.* Stockholm.

———, ed., 1990. *Studies in Late Anglo-Saxon Coinage in Memory of Bror Emil Hildebrand.* Stockholm: Kungl. Myntkabinettet, Kungl. Vitterhets historie och antikvitetets akademien.

Jonsson, K., and B. Malmer, eds., 1990. *Sigtuna Papers: Proceedings of the Sigtuna Symposium on Viking-Age Coinage 1–4 June 1989.* Stockholm: Kungl. Vitterhets historie och antikvitetets akademien.

Jonsson, K., and G. van der Meer, 1990. "Mints and Moneyers c. 973–1066," in Jonsson 1990, 47–136.

Jonsson, K., and M. Östergren, 1992. "Roman Denarii and Solidi on Gotland: Break or Continuity?," in *Florilegium numismaticum: studia in honorem U. Westermark edita*, 183–87. Stockholm: Svenska numismatiska föreningen.

Jón Viðar Sigurðsson, 2017. *Viking Friendship: The Social Bond in Iceland and Norway, c. 900–1300*. Ithaca, NY: Cornell University Press.

Joranson, E., 1923. *The Danegeld in France*. Rock Island, IL: Augustana Book Concern.

Jussen, B., 2003. "Religious Discourses of the Gift in the Middle Ages: Semantic Evidences (Second to Twelfth Centuries)," in Algazi, Groebner, and Jussen 2003, 173–92.

Kaiser, R., 1976. "Münzprivilegien und bischöfliche Münzprägung in Frankreich, Deutschland und Burgund im 9.–12. Jahrhundert," *Vierteljahrschrift für Sozial- und Wirtschaftsgeschichte* 63:289–339.

———, 1987. "Das Geld in der Autobiographie des Abtes Guibert von Nogent," *Archiv für Kulturgeschichte* 69:289–314.

Kamp, N., 1982. "Probleme des Münzrechts und der Münzprägung in salischer Zeit," in Diestelkamp 1982, 94–110.

Kano, O., 2013. "'Configuration' d'une espèce diplomatique: le *praeceptum denariale* dans le haut moyen âge," *Configuration du texte en histoire*, 41–54. Nagoya, Jap.

Karayiannis, A. D., and S. Drakopoulou Dodd, 1998. "The Greek Christian Fathers," in *Ancient and Medieval Economic Ideas and Concepts of Social Justice*, ed. S. T. Lowry and B. Gordon., 163–208. Leiden, Neth.: Brill.

Kasten, B., 2006. "Agrarische Innovationen durch Prekarien?," in *Tätigkeitsfelder und Erfahrungshorizonte des ländlichen Menschen in der frühmittelalterlichen Grundherrschaft (bis ca. 1000): Festschrift für Dieter Hägermann zum 65. Geburtstag*, ed. B. Kasten, 139–54. Stuttgart, Ger.: Steiner.

Katsari, C., 2003. "Opramoas and the Importation of Bronze Coins in Roman Lycia," *Epigraphica Anatolica* 35:141–45.

Keane, W., 2007. *Christian Moderns: Freedom and Fetish in the Mission Encounter*. Berkeley: University of California Press.

———, 2008. "Market, Materiality and Moral Metalanguage," *Anthropological Theory* 8:27–42.

Keller, C., 2005. "From a Late Roman Cemetery to the *Basilica Sanctorum Cassii et Florentii* in Bonn, Germany," in *The Cross Goes North: Processes of Conversion in Northern Europe, AD 300–1300*, ed. M. Carver, 415–27. Woodbridge, UK: Boydell.

Kelly, C., 2004. *Ruling the Later Roman Empire*. Cambridge, MA: Harvard University Press.

Kelly, F., 1997. *Early Irish Farming: A Study Based Mainly on the Law-Texts of the 7th and 8th Centuries AD*. Dublin: Dublin Institute for Advanced Studies.

Kelly, S., 1992. "Trading Privileges from Eighth-Century England," *EME* 1, 3–28.

Kemmers, F., 2019. *The Functions and Use of Roman Coinage: An Overview of 21st Century Scholarship*. Leiden, Neth.: Brill.

Kennedy, A., 1995. "Law and Litigation in the *Libellus Æthelwoldi Episcopi*," *Anglo-Saxon England* 24:131–83.

Kent, J.P.C., 1956. "Gold Coinage in the Later Roman Empire," in *Essays in Roman Coinage Presented to Harold Mattingly*, ed. R. A. G. Carson and C. H. V. Sutherland, 190–204. Oxford: Oxford University Press.

———, 1972. "The Aston Rowant Treasure Trove," *Oxoniensia* 37:243–44.

———, 1981. *The Roman Imperial Coinage. 8: The Family of Constantine I, A.D. 337–364*. London: Spink.

———, 1994. *The Roman Imperial Coinage. 10: The Divided Empire and the Fall of the Western Parts, AD 395–491*. London: Spink.

Ker, N. R., 1948. "Hemming's Cartulary: A Description of the Two Worcester Cartularies in Cotton Tiberius A.XIII," in *Studies in Medieval History, Presented to Frederick Maurice Powicke*, ed. R. W. Hunt, 49–75. Oxford: Clarendon.

Kershaw, J., 2014. "Viking-Age Silver in North-West England: Hoards and Single Finds," in *In Search of Vikings: Interdisciplinary Approaches to the Scandinavian Heritage of North-West England*, ed. S. E. Harding, D. Griffiths, and E. Royles, 149–64. Boca Raton, FL: CRC Press.

——, 2017. "An Early Medieval Dual-Currency Economy: Bullion and Coin in the Danelaw," *Antiquity* 91:173–90.

——, 2019a. "Gold as a Means of Exchange in Scandinavian England (c. AD 850–1050)," in Kershaw and Williams 2019, 227–50.

——, 2019b. "Introduction: Economy, Currency, and Value in the Viking Age," in Kershaw and Williams 2019, 1–14.

——, 2019c. "Metrology and Beyond: New Approaches to Viking-Age Regulated Weights," in *Weights and Marketplaces from the Bronze Age to the Early Modern Period: Proceedings of Two Workshops Funded by the European Research Council. ERC)*, ed. L. Rahmstorf and E. Stratford, 127–37. Kiel, Ger.: Wachholtz.

——, 2020. "Metals and Exchange in Viking-Age Yorkshire: The Contribution of Single Finds," in Williams 2020, 113–27.

Kershaw, J., et al., 2021. "The Scale of Dirham Imports to the Baltic in the Ninth Century: New Evidence from Archaeometric Analyses of Early Viking-Age Silver," *Fornvännen* 116:185–204.

Kershaw, J., and G. Williams, eds., 2019. *Silver, Butter, Cloth: Monetary and Social Economies in the Viking Age*. Oxford: Oxford University Press.

Kersken, H., 2016. *Zwischen Glaube und Welt: Studien zur Geschichte der religiösen Frauengemeinschaft Thorn von der Gründung bis zur Mitte des 14. Jahrhunderts*. Hilversum, Neth.: Verloren b. v.

Keutgen, F., 1895. *Untersuchungen über den Ursprung der deutschen Stadtverfassung*. Leipzig, Ger.: Duncker & Humblot.

Keynes, S., 1985. "King Athelstan's Books," in *Learning and Literature in Anglo-Saxon England: Studies Presented to Peter Clemoes on the Occasion of His Sixty-Fifth Birthday*, ed. M. Lapidge and H. Gneuss, 143–201. Cambridge: Cambridge University Press.

——, 2003. "Ely Abbey 672–1109," in *A History of Ely Cathedral*, ed. P. Meadows and N. Ramsay, 3–58. Woodbridge, UK: Boydell.

——, 2007. "An Abbot, an Archbishop, and the Viking Raids of 1006–7 and 1009–12," *Anglo-Saxon England* 36:151–220.

Keynes, S., and R. Naismith, 2011. "The *Agnus Dei* Pennies of King Æthelred the Unready," *Anglo-Saxon England* 40:175–223.

Kienlin, T. L., and A. Zimmermann, eds., 2012. *Beyond Elites: Alternatives to Hierarchical Systems in Modelling Social Formations*. Bonn, Ger.: Dr. Rudolf Habelt.

Kiersnowski, R., et al., eds., 2002. *Moneta Mediaevalis. Studia numizmatyczne i historyczne ofiarowane Profesorowi Stanisławowi Suchodolskiemu w 65. rocznicę urodzin*. Warsaw: Wydawn.

Kilger, C., 2006. "Silver Handling Traditions during the Viking Age: Some Observations and Thoughts on the Phenomenon of Pecking and Bending," in Cook and Williams 2006, 449–65.

———, 2008a. "Kaupang from Afar: Aspects of the Interpretation of Dirham Finds in Northern and Eastern Europe between the Late 8th and Early 10th Centuries," in Skre 2008, 199–252.

———, 2008b. "Wholeness and Holiness: Counting, Weighing and Valuing Silver in the Early Viking Period," in Skre 2008, 253–325.

———, 2011. "Hack-Silver, Weights and Coinage: The Anglo-Scandinavian Bullion Coinages and Their Use in Late Viking-Age Society," in Graham-Campbell, Sindbæk, and Williams 2011, 259–80.

———, 2020a. "Long Distance Trade, Runes and Silver: A Gotlandic Perspective," in *Relations and Runes: The Baltic Islands and Their Interactions during the Late Iron Age and Early Middle Ages*, ed. L. Kitzler Åhfeldt et al., 49–63. Visby, Swed.: Riksantikvarieämbetet.

———, 2020b. "Silver Hoards and Society on Viking-Age Gotland: Some Thoughts on the Relationship between Silver, Long-Distance Trade and Local Communities," in Gruszczyński, Jankowiak, and Shephard 2020, 242–54.

King, C. E., 1981. "Late Roman Silver Hoards and the Problem of Clipped Siliquae," *British Numismatic Journal* 51:5–31.

———, 1990. Review of Bastien 1988, in *Journal of Roman Studies* 80:253–54.

King, M. D., 1988. "Roman Coins from Early Anglo-Saxon Contexts," in *Coins and the Archaeologist*, ed. J. Casey and R. Reece, 224–29. 2nd ed. London: Spink.

———, 1972. *Law and Society in the Visigothic Kingdom*. Cambridge: Cambridge University Press.

Kipnis, A., 1996. "The Language of Gifts: Managing Guanxi in a North China Village," *Modern China* 22:285–314.

Kirschbaum, E., 1959. *The Tombs of St. Peter and St. Paul*, trans. J. Murray. London: Secker & Warburg.

Klang, A., 2013. *Guldfynd på Gotland: En jämnförande studie av guldfynden från folkvandringstiden*. Stockholm: Stockholms universitet.

Klappauf, L., F.-A. Linke, and F. Both, 2004. "Grabung Düna, vom Harzrand zu den Lagerstätten," in *Archäologie Land Niedersachsen: Begleitbuch zur Sonderausstellung Archäologie, Land, Niedersachsen. 25 Jahre Denkmalschutzgesetz—400,000 Jahre Geschichte, Oldenburg vom 14.11.2004–27.03.2005, Hannover vom 21.04.2005–31.07.2005, Braunschweig vom September 2005–Januar 2006*, ed. M. Fansa, F. Both, and H. Haßmann, 182–84. Stuttgart, Ger.: Theiss.

Kluge, B., 1991. *Deutsche Münzgeschichte von der späten Karolingerzeit bis zum Ende der Salier (ca. 900–1125)*. Sigmaringen, Ger.: J. Thorbecke.

———, ed., 1993. *Fernhandel und Geldwirtschaft: Beiträge zum deutschen Münzwesen in sächsischer und salischer Zeit. Ergebnisse des Dannenberg-Kolloquiums 1990*. Sigmaringen, Ger.: J. Thorbecke.

———, 2001. "Otto Rex, Otto Imp. Zur Bestandsaufnahme der ottonischen Münzprägung," in *Ottonische Neuanfänge. Symposion zur Ausstellung "Otto der Große, Magdeburg und Europa,"* ed. B. Schneidmüller and S. Weinfurter, 85–112. Mainz, Ger.: Von Zabern.

———, 2002. "Die Bildnispfennige Karls des Großen," in Kiersnowski et al. 2002, 367–77.

———, 2007. *Numismatik des Mittelalters. 1: Handbuch und Thesaurus Nummorum Medii Aevi*. Berlin: Münzkabinett, Staatliche Museen zu Berlin.

———, 2014. *Am Beginn des Mittelalters: die Münzen des karolingischen Reiches 751 bis 814. Pippin, Karlmann, Karl der Große*. Berlin: Münzkabinett, Staatliche Museen zu Berlin.

Knapp, G. F., 1924. *The State Theory of Money*, ed. and trans. H. M. Lucas and J. Bonar. London: Macmillan.

Knol, E., 2019. "Living Near the Sea: The Organisation of Frisia in Early Medieval Times," in Carroll, Reynolds, and York 2019, 369–91.

Kohl, T., 2019. "Ländliche Gesellschaft, lokale Eliten und das Reich: der Wormsgau in der Karolingerzeit," in Kohl, Patzol, and Zeller 2019, 309–35.

Kohl, T., S. Patzold, and B. Zeller, eds., 2019. *Kleine Welten: ländliche Gesellschaften im Karolingerreich*. Ostfildern, Ger.: Jan Thorbecke.

Kokkinia, C., 2000. *Die Opramoas-Inschrift von Rhodiapolis*. Bonn, Ger.: Habelt.

Kölzer, T., 2016. "Ein 'System reisender Schreiber und Notare' in der Kanzlei Kars des Großen," *Archiv für Diplomatik* 62:41–58.

Kool, R., et al., 2011. "A Late Tenth-Century Fatimid Coin Purse from Bct Shc'an," '*Atiqot* 67:31–41.

Kool, R., I. Baidoun, and J. Sharvit, 2018. "The Fatimid Gold Treasure from Caesarea Maritima Harbor (2015): Preliminary Results," in *5th Simone Assemani Symposium on Islamic Coins. Rome, 29–30 September 2017*, ed. B. Callegher and A. D'Ottone, 127–43. Trieste, It.: Edizioni Università di Trieste.

Kovalev, R., 2003. "The Mint of Al-Shāsh: The Vehicle for the Origins and Continuation of Trade Relations between Viking-Age Northern Europe and Samanid Central Asia," *Archivum Eurasiae medii aevi* 12:47–79.

———, 2007. "Circulation of Arab Silver in Medieval Afro-Eurasia: Preliminary Observations," *History Compass* 5:560–80.

———, 2011. "Circulation of Sāmānid Dirhams in Viking-Age Northern and Eastern Europe (Based on the Mints of Samarqand and Al-Shāsh)," https://www.academia .edu/13061016/_Circulation_of_S%C4%81m%C4%81nid_Dirhams_in_Viking _Age_Northern_and_Eastern_Europe_Based_on_the_Mints_of_Samarqand _and_al_Sh%C4%81sh_.

Kruse, S., 1992. "Metallurgical Evidence of Silver Sources in the Irish Sea Province," in *Viking Treasure from the North West: The Cuerdale Hoard in Its Context. Selected Papers from the Vikings of the Irish Sea Confererence, Liverpool, 18–20 May 1990*, ed. J. Graham-Campbell, 73–88. Liverpool, UK: National Museums & Galleries on Merseyside.

Kuchenbuch, L., 1978. *Bäuerliche Gesellschaft und Klosterherrschaft im 9. Jahrhundert. Studien zur Sozialstruktur der Familia der Abtei Prüm*. Wiesbaden, Ger.: Steiner.

———, 1991. *Grundherrschaft im früheren Mittelalter*. Idstein, Ger.: Schulz-Kirchner.

———, 2003. "*Porcus donativus*: Language Use and Gifting in Seigniorial Records between the Eighth and the Twelfth Centuries," in Algazi, Groebner, and Jussen 2003, 193–246.

———, 2016. *Versilberte Verhältnisse. Der Denar in seiner ersten Epoche 700–1000*. Göttingen, Ger.: Wallstein.

———, 2019. "Denar-Druck im Okzident 700–1050. Ein Beitrag zur historischen Anthropologie des Geldes," *Historische Anthropologie* 27:52–74.

Kuijpers, M.H.G., 2012. "Towards a Deeper Understanding of Metalworking Technology," in Kienlin and Zimmermann 2012, 413–21.

Kulikowski, M., 2004. *Late Roman Spain and its Cities*. Baltimore: Johns Hopkins University Press.

———, 2005. "Cities and Government in Late Antique Hispania: Recent Advances and Future Research," in *Hispania in Late Antiquity: Currency Perspectives*, ed. K. D. Bowes and M. Kulikowski, 31–75. Leiden, Neth.: Brill.

Kuroda, A., 2007. "The Maria Theresa Dollar in the Early Twentieth-Century Red Sea Region: A Complementary Interface between Multiple Markets," *Financial History Review* 14:89–110.

———, 2008. "What Is Complementarity among Monies? An Introductory Notes," *Financial History Review* 15:7–15.

Kurt, A., 2018–19. "Visigothic Currency in Its Making and Movement: A Varying State of Circumstances," *Visigothic Symposium* 3:165–97.

———, 2020. *Minting, State, and Economy in the Visigothic Kingdom, from Settlement in Aquitaine through the First Decade of the Muslim Conquest of Spain*. Amsterdam: Amsterdam University Press.

La Coste-Messelière, R. de, 1950. *Recherches sur le pagus, la vigueurie et la châtellenie de Melle (Xe–XVe siècles)*. Paris: École des chartes.

———, 1957–58. "Note pour server à l'histoire de Melle," *Bulletin de la Société des Antiquaires de France*, 269–315.

Lafaurie, J., 1952. "Le trésor monétaire du Puy (Haute-Loire): contribution à l'étude de la monnaie de la fin du Xe siècle," *Revue numismatique*, 5th series, 14:59–169.

———, 1964. "Triens mérovingien avec représentation de monétaire," *BSFN* 19:342–43.

———, 1970. "Numismatique. Des Carolingiens aux Capétiens," *Cahiers de civilisation médiévale* 13:117–37.

———, 1973. "Monnaies mérovingiennes du Gévaudan," *Le club de la médaille* 41:126–33.

———, 1978. "Les monnaies impériales de Charlemagne," *Comptes-rendus de l'académie des inscriptions et belles-lettres* 122:154–76.

———, 1980. "La surveillance des ateliers monétaires au IXe siècle," *Francia* 9:486–96.

———, 1998. "Monnaies épiscopales de Paris à l'époque mérovingienne," *Cahiers de la Rotonde* 20:61–99.

Lafaurie, J., and C. Morrisson, 1987. "La pénétration des monnaies byzantines en Gaule mérovingienne et visigothique du VIe au VIIIe siècle," *Revue numismatique*, 6th series, 29:38–98.

Lafaurie, J., and J. Pilet-Lemière, 2003. *Monnaies du haut moyen âge découvertes en France. Ve–VIIIe siècle*. Paris: CNRS Éditions.

Lagerqvist, L. O., 1968. "The Coinage at Sigtuna in the Names of Anund Jacob, Cnut the Great and Harthacnut," in Rasmusson and Malmer 1968, 383–413.

Laiou, A. E., 2004. "Monopoly and Privileged Free Trade in the Eastern Mediterranean (8th–14th Century)," in *Chemins d'outre-mer. Études d'histoire sur la Méditerranée médiévale offertes à Michael Balard*, ed. D. Coulon et al., 511–26 Paris: Publications de la Sorbonne.

Lallemant, M., 2019. "Max Weber et la monnaie," *Revue européenne des sciences sociales* 57:127–48.

Lambert, T., 2017a. "Jurisdiction as Property in England, 900–1100," in *Legalism: Property and Ownership*, ed. G. Kantor, T. Lambert, and H. Skoda, 115–48. Oxford: Oxford University Press.

———, 2017b. *Law and Order in Anglo-Saxon England*. Oxford: Oxford University Press.

———, 2021. "Compensation, Honour and Idealism in the Laws of Æthelberht," in Bothe, Esders, and Nijdam 2021, 133–60.

Landau, P., 2018. "Das Capitulare de Villis—eine Verordnung Ludwigs des Frommen," in *La productivité d'une crise: le règne de Louis le Pieux (814–840) et la transformation de l'Empire carolingien*, ed. P. Depreux and S. Esders, 259–72. Ostfildern, Ger.: Thorbecke.

Landon, C., 2020. "Economic Incentives for the Frankish Conquest of Saxony," *EME* 28:26–56.

Landreth, D., 2012. *The Face of Mammon: The Matter of Money in English Renaissance Literature*. Oxford: Oxford University Press.

Langdon, J., and Masschaele, J., 2006. "Commercial Activity and Population Growth in Medieval England," *Past and Present* 190:35–81.

Lapidge, M., ed., 1991. *Anglo-Saxon Litanies of the Saints*, Henry Bradshaw Society 106. Woodbridge, UK: Boydell.

Lapidge, M., et al., eds., 2014. *The Wiley-Blackwell Encyclopedia of Anglo-Saxon England*. 2nd ed. Chichester, UK: Wiley Blackwell.

La Rocca, C., and P. Majocchi, eds., 2015. *Urban Identities in Northern Italy, 800–1100 ca.* Turnhout, Bel.: Brepols.

La Rocca, C., and L. Provero, 2000. "The Dead and Their Gifts: The Will of Eberhard, Count of Friuli, and his Wife Gisela, Daughter of Louis the Pious (863–864)," in *Rituals of Power from Late Antiquity to the Early Middle Ages*, ed. F. Theuws and J. L. Nelson, 225–80. Leiden, Neth.: Brill.

Lau, D., et al., 2013. "Vorbericht zu den Ausgrabungen eines mittelalterlichen bis neuzeitlichen Herrenhofes in Bissendorf, Gde. Biddendorf, Ldkr. Osnabrück, 2012," *Nachrichten aus Niedersachsens Urgeschichte* 82:201–22.

Lauranson-Rosaz, C., 1987. *L'Auvergne et ses marges (Velay, Gévaudan) du VIIIe au XIe siècle: la fin du monde antique?* Le-Puy, Fr.: Cahiers de la Haute-Loire.

———, 2001. "Le débat sur la 'mutation féodale': état de la question," in *Europe around the Year 1000*, ed. P. Urbanczyk, 11–40. Warsaw: Wydawnictwo.

———, 2002. "La Vie de Géraud, vecteur d'une certaine conscience aristocratique dans le Midi de la Gaule," in *Guerriers et moines: conversion et sainteté aristocratiques dans l'Occident médiéval (IXe–XIIe siècle)*, ed. M. Lauwers, 157–81. Antibes, Fr.: Éditions APDCA.

Lauwers, M., 2017. "Le 'travail' sans la domination? Notes d'historiographie et de sémantique apropos du labeur des cultivateurs dans l'Occident médiéval," in Dierkens, Schroeder, and Wilkin 2017, 303–32.

Lawson, M. K., 1984. "The Collection of Danegeld and Heregeld in the Reigns of Aethelred II and Cnut," *English Historical Review* 99:721–38.

Leader-Newby, R. E., 2004. *Silver and Society in Late Antiquity: Functions and Meanings of Silver Plate in the Fourth to Seventh Centuries*. Aldershot, UK: Ashgate.

Lebecq, S., 2005. "The Northern Seas (Fifth to Eighth Centuries)," in *The New Cambridge Medieval History. Volume 1: c. 500–c. 700*, ed. P. Fouracre, 639–59. Cambridge: Cambridge University Press.

Lee, A. D., 2007. *War in Late Antiquity: A Social History*. Oxford: Blackwell.

Le Goff, J., 2004. *Un long Moyen Age*. Paris: Tallandier.

——, 2012. *Money and the Middle Ages: An Essay in Historical Anthropology*, trans. J. Birrell. Cambridge: Polity.

Le Jan, R., L. Feller, and J.-P. Devroey, eds., 2010. *Les élites et la richesse au haut Moyen Âge*. Turnhout, Bel.: Brepols.

Lemesle, B., 2008. *Conflits et justice au Moyen Âge: normes, loi et résolution des conflits en Anjou aux XIe et XIIe siècles*. Paris: Presses universitaires de France.

Le Roy Ladurie, E., 1971. *Times of Feast, Times of Famine: A History of Climate since the Year 1000*, trans. B. Bray. London: Allen and Unwin.

Lewis, C. P., 1993. "The Domesday Jurors," *Haskins Society Journal* 5:17–44.

——, 2016. "Danish Landowners in Wessex in 1066," in *Danes in Wessex: The Scandinavian Impact on Southern England, c. 800–c. 1100*, ed. R. Lavelle and S. Roffey, 172–211. Oxford: Oxbow.

Lewit, T., 2009. "Pigs, Presses and Pastoralism: Farming in the Fifth to Sixth Centuries AD," *EME* 17:77–91.

——, 2020. "A Viewpoint on Eastern Mediterranean Villages in Late Antiquity: Applying the Lens of Community Resilience Theory," *Studies in Late Antiquity* 4:44–75.

Leyerle, B., 1994. "John Chrysostom on Almsgiving and the Use of Money," *Harvard Theological Review* 87:29–47.

Leyser, C., 1995. "Cities of the Plain: The Rhetoric of Sodomy in Peter Damian's 'Book of Gomorrah,'" *Romanic Review* 86:191–211.

Li, C., and Hartman, C., 2011. "Primary Sources for Song History in the Collected Works of Wu Ne," *Journal of Song-Yuan Studies* 41:295–341.

Lie, J., 1992. "The Concept of Mode of Exchange," *American Sociological Review* 57:508–23.

Liebeschuetz, W., 1997. "Cities, Taxes and the Accommodation of the Barbarians: The Theories of Durliat and Goffart," in *Kingdoms of the Empire: The Integration of Barbarians in Late Antiquity*, ed. W. Pohl, 135–51. Leiden, Neth.: Brill.

——, 2001. *Decline and Fall of the Roman City*. Oxford: Oxford University Press.

——, 2015. *East and West in Late Antiquity: Invasion, Settlement, Ethnogenesis and Conflicts of Religion*. Leiden, Neth.: Brill.

Lifshitz, F., 1992. "The 'Exodus of Holy Bodies' Reconsidered: The Translation of the Relics of St. Gildard of Rouen to Soissons," *Analecta Bollandiana* 110: 329–40.

Ligt, L. de, 1990. "Demand, Supply, Distribution: The Roman Peasantry between Town and Countryside: Rural Monetization and Peasant Demand," *Münstersche Beiträge zur antiken Handelsgeschichte* 9, 24–56.

Lintz, G., 1992. *La Corrèze*. Paris: Académie des inscriptions et belles-lettres.

Little, L. K., 1971. "Pride Goes before Avarice: Social Change and the Vices in Latin Christendom," *American Historical Review* 76:16–59.

——, 1978. *Religious Poverty and the Profit Economy in Medieval Europe*. London: P. Elek.

Liu, W. G., 2015. "The Making of a Fiscal State in Song China, 960–1729," *Economic History Review* 68:48–78.

Ljungqvist, F. C., Seim, A., and Huhtamaa, H., 2021. "Climates and Society in European History," *Wily Interdisciplinary Reviews: Climate Change* 12:1–28.

Lo Cascio, E., 1999. "Canon frumentarius, suarius, vinarius," in *The Transformations of Urbs Roma in Late Antiquity*, ed. W. V. Harris, 163–82. Portsmouth, RI: Journal of Roman Archaeology.

——, 2006. "The Role of the State in the Roman Economy: Making Use of the New Institutional Economics," in *Ancient Economies, Modern Methodologies: Archaeology, Comparative History, Models and Institutions*, ed. P. F. Bang, M. Ikeguchi and H. G. Ziche, 215–34. Bari, It.: Edipuglia.

Lombard, M., 1974. *Les métaux dans l'ancien monde du Ve au XIe siècle*. Paris: Mouton.

Longnon, A., 1869–72. *Études sur les pagi de la Gaule*. 2 vols. Paris: A. Franck.

López, R. S., 1952. "Économie et architecture médievale. Cela aurait-il tué ceci?," *Annales* 7:433–8.

——, 1953. "An Aristocracy of Money in the Early Middle Ages," *Speculum* 28:1–43.

——, 1976. *The Commercial Revolution of the Middle Ages 950–1350*. Cambridge: Cambridge University Press.

Loseby, S., 1998. "Gregory's Cities: Urban Functions in Sixth-Century Gaul," in *Franks and Alamanni in the Merovingian Period: An Ethnographic Perspective*, ed. I. N. Wood, 239–84. Woodbridge, UK: Boydell.

——, 2013. "Lost Cities: The End of the *civitas*-System in Frankish Gaul," in *Gallien in Spätantike und Frühmittelalter: Kulturgeschichte einer Region*, ed. S. Diefenbach and G. M. Müller, 223–54. Berlin: De Gruyter.

——, 2020. "The Role of the City in Merovingian Francia," in Effros and Moreira 2020, 583–610.

Lösslein, H., 2019. *Royal Power in the Late Carolingian Age: Charles II the Simple and his Predecessors*. Cologne, Ger.: Modern Academic Publishing.

Lot, F., 1921. "Un grand domaine à l'époque franque, Ardin en Poitou: contribution à l'étude de l'impôt," in *Cinquanténaire de l'École pratique des hautes études*, 109–29. Paris: E. Champion.

——, 1924. "Les tributs aux Normands et l'Église de France au IXe siècle," *Bibliothèque de l'Ecole des Chartes* 85:58–78.

Louis, É., 2012. "Les origines urbaines de Douai: un réexamen," in *Château, ville et pouvoir au Moyen Âge*, ed. A.-M. Flambard and J. Le Maho, 215–54. Caen, Fr.: CRAHM.

Loveluck, C., 2013. *Northwest Europe in the Early Middle Ages, c. AD 600–1150: A Comparative Archaeology*. Cambridge: Cambridge University Press.

Loveluck, C., et al., 2018. "Alpine Ice-Core Evidence for the Transformation of the European Monetary System, AD 640–670," *Antiquity* 92:1571–85.

——, 2020. "Alpine Ice and the Annual Political Economy of the Angevin Empire, from the Death of Thomas Becket to Magna Carta, c. AD 1170–1216," *Antiquity* 94:473–90.

Loveluck, C., and D. Tys, 2006. "Coastal Societies, Exchange and Identity along the Channel and Southern North Sea Shores of Europe, AD 600–1000," *Journal of Maritime Archaeology* 1:140–69.

Lowe, K. A., 1998. "Lay Literacy in Anglo-Saxon England and the Development of the Chirograph," in *Anglo-Saxon Manuscripts and Their Heritage*, ed. P. Pulsiano and E. M. Treharne, 161–204. Aldershot, UK: Ashgate.

Loyn, H. R., 1955. "*Gesiths* and *Thegns* in Anglo-Saxon England from the Seventh to the Tenth Century," *English Historical Review* 70:529–49.

Loyn, H. R., 1961. "Boroughs and Mints A.D. 900–1066," in Dolley 1961, 122–35.

———, 1991. *Anglo-Saxon England and the Norman Conquest*. 2nd ed. London: Longman.

Lucassen, J., 2018. "Deep Monetization in Eurasia in the Long Run," in *Money, Currency and Crisis: In Search of Trust, 2000BC to AD 2000*, ed. R. J. van der Spek and B. van Leeuwen, 55–101. Abingdon, UK: Routledge.

Lukas, J., 2020. "The Bohemian Finds of Imitative Coins with the Inscription •VIDV," *Wiadomości Numizmatyczne* 64:231–43.

Lund, J., and S. M. Sindbæk, 2021. "Crossing the Maelstrom: New Departures in Viking Archaeology," *Journal of Archaeological Research*. http://doi.org/10.1007/s10814-021-09163-3.

Lunden, K., 1999. "Money Economy in Medieval Norway," *Scandinavian Journal of History* 24:245–65.

Lyon, B., 1974. *Henri Pirenne: A Biographical and Intellectual Study*. Ghent, Bel.: E. Story-Scientia.

Lyon, C.S.S., 1969. "Historical Problems of Anglo-Saxon Coinage—(3) Denominations and Weights," *British Numismatic Journal* 38:204–22.

———, 2012. "Minting in Winchester: An Introduction and Statistical Analysis," in *The Winchester Mint and Coins and Related Finds from the Excavations of 1961–71*, ed. M. Biddle, 3–55. Oxford: Oxford University Press.

Lyon, J. R., 2022. *Corruption, Protection and Justice in Medieval Europe: A Thousand Year History*. Cambridge: Cambridge University Press.

Maass, U., 2007. *Die Freilassung durch Schatzwurf in den Urkunden der karolingischen, sächsischen und salischen Kaiser und Könige: Studien zur Freilassungspraxis frühmittelalterlicher Herrscher*. Bochum, Ger.: Ruhr Universität Bochum.

MacKay, W., and R. Naismith, 2022. "An Imitative Dinar from Hunmanby, North Yorkshire," in *Interpreting Early Medieval Coinage: Studies in Memory of Stewart Lyon*, ed. M. R. Allen, R. Naismith, and H. E. Pagan, 53–64. London: British Numismatic Society.

MacLean, S., 2003. *Kingship and Politics in the Late Ninth Century: Charles the Fat and the End of the Carolingian Empire*. Cambridge: Cambridge University Press.

MacLean, S., 2013. "Shadow Kingdom: Lotharingia and the Frankish World, c. 850–c. 1050," *History Compass* 11:443–57.

———, 2018. "'*Waltharius*': Treasure, Revenge and Kingship in the Ottonian Wild West," in *Emotion, Violence, Vengeance and Law in the Middle Ages: Essays in Honour of William Ian Miller*, ed. K. Gilbert and S. D. White, 225–51. Leiden, Neth.: Brill.

Maddicott, J. R., 2000. "Two Frontier States: Northumbria and Wessex, c. 650–750," in *The Medieval State: Essays Presented to James Campbell*, ed. J. R. Maddicott and D. M. Palliser, 25–45. London: Hambledon.

Magnou-Nortier, E., 1984. "Étude sur le privilège d'immunité du IVe au IXe siècle," *Revue Mabillon* 60:465–512.

————, 1989. "La gestion publique en Neustrie: les moyens et les hommes (VIIe–IXe siècles)," in *La Neustrie: les pays au nord de la Loire de 650 à 850. Colloque historique international*, ed. H. Atsma. 2 vols., 1:271–320. Sigmaringen, Ger.: J. Thorbecke.

Maitland, F. W., 1897. *Domesday Book and Beyond: Three Essays in the Early History of England*. Cambridge: Cambridge University Press.

Majocchi, P., 2010. "Sviluppo e affermazione di una capitale altomedievale: Pavia in età gota e longobarda," *Reti medievali* 11:169–79.

Malcolm, G., Bowsher, D., and Cowie, R., 2003. *Middle Saxon London: Excavations at the Royal Opera House, 1989–99*. London: Museum of London Archaeological Service.

Malmer, B., 1961. "A Contribution to the Numismatic History of Norway during the Eleventh Century," in *Commentationes de nummis saeculorum IX–XI in Suecia repertis, pars prima: Untersuchungen zu den in Schweden gefundenen Münzen des 9. bis 11. Jahrhunderts*, ed. N. L. Rasmusson and L. O. Lagerqvist, 223–376. Stockholm: Almqvist & Wiksell.

————, 1966. *Nordiska mynt före år 1000*. Stockholm: R. Habelt.

————, 1989. *The Sigtuna Coinage c. 995–1005*. Stockholm: Kungl. Vitterhets historie och antikvitets akademien.

————, 1995. "Från Olof till Anund. Ur Sigtunamyntningens historia," in *Myntningen i Sverige 995–1995*, ed. K. Jonsson, U. Nordlind, and I. Wiséhn, 9–26. Stockholm: Svenska numismatiska föreningen.

————, 1997. *The Anglo-Scandinavian Coinage c. 995–1020*. Stockholm: Royal Swedish Academy of Letters.

————, 2007. "South Scandinavian Coinage in the Ninth Century," in Graham-Campbell and Williams 2007, 13–28.

Manzano Moreno, E., 2018. "Coinage and the Tributary Mode of Production," in Balzaretti, Barrow and Skinner 2018, 402–15.

Manzano Moreno, E., and Canto García, A., 2020. "The Value of Wealth: Coins and Coinage in Iberian Early Medieval Documents," in *Beyond the Reconquista: New Directions in the History of Medieval Iberia (711–1085) in Honour of Simon Barton*, ed. R. Portass, 169–99. Leiden, Neth.: Brill.

Marcellesi, M.-C., 2012. "Les monnaies impériales de la réforme de Dioclétien à celle d'Anastase," in *Les monnaies des fouilles du Centre d'Études Alexandrines: les monnayages de bronze à Alexandrie de la conquête d'Alexandre à l'Égypte moderne*, ed. O. Picard et al., 199–291. Alexandria, Egypt: Centre d'études alexandrines.

Marchand, J., et al., 2019. "L'exploitation de l'or en Égypte au début de l'époque islamique: l'exemple de Samut," in Minvielle Larousse, Bailly-Maître, and Bianchi 2019, 147–59.

Marques, M. G., J.M.P. Cabral, and J. Rodrigues Marinho, 1995. *Ensaios sobre história monetária da monarquia visigoda*. Porto, Port.: Sociedade Portuguesa de Numismatica.

Marsden, A., 2013. "Three Recent Sceatta Hoards from Norfolk," *Norfolk Archaeology* 46: 492–502.

Marsden, A., and A. Pol, 2020. "The West Norfolk Hoard, East Anglia's Trophy Type Thrymsas and Anglo-Saxon Nummular Brooches," *Norfolk Archaeology* 48:394–422.

Martin, P.-H., 1997. "Eine Goldmünze Karls des Großen," *Numismatisches Nachrichtenblatt* 46:351–55.

Martín Escudero, F., J. Mínguez, and A. Canto, 2011. "La circulación monetaria en el reinado de Alfonso III a través de las fuentes documentales," in *Asturiensis Regni Territorium. Documentos y estudios sobre el período tardorromano y medieval en el noroeste hispano*, ed. A. García-Leal, R. Gutiérrez, and C. E. Prieto. 2 vols., 2: 157–205. Oviedo, Sp.: Universidad de Oviedo.

Martin-Kilcher, S., 1977. "Tributum Petri?," *Schweizerisches Archiv für Volkskunde* 73:187–94.

Martindale, J., 1992. "Peace and War in Early Eleventh-Century Aquitaine," in *Medieval Knighthood: Papers from the Fifth Strawberry Hill Conference 1990*, ed. C. Harper-Bill and R. E. Harvey, 147–76. Woodbridge, UK: Boydell.

Martín Viso, I., 2008. "'Tremisses y Potentes' en el nordeste de Lusitania. siglos VI–VII)," *Mélanges de la Casa de Velázquez* 38:175–200.

———, 2011. "Circuits of Power in a Fragmented Space: Gold Coinage in the Meseta del Duero (Sixth–Seventh Centuries)," in Escalona Monge and Reynolds 2011, 215–52.

Marx, K., 1963. *The Eighteenth Brumaire of Louis Bonaparte*. New York: International Publishers.

———, 1964. *Economic and Philosophic Manuscripts of 1844*, trans. M. Milligan. New York: International Publishers.

———, 1971. *Grundrisse*, trans. D. McLellan. London: Macmillan.

Masschaele, J., 1997. *Peasants, Merchants, and Markets: Inland Trade in Medieval England, 1150–1350*. Basingstoke, UK: Macmillan.

———, 2009. "Economic Takeoff and the Rise of Markets," in *A Companion to the Medieval World*, ed. C. L. Lansing and E. D. English, 89–110. Chichester, UK: Wiley-Blackwell.

Mattingly, D. J., 2011. *Imperialism, Power, and Identity: Experiencing the Roman Empire*. Princeton, NJ: Princeton University Press.

Matzke, M., 2011a. "L'attività mineraria e la monetazione," in Travaini 2011, 1:271–92.

———, 2011b. "Il diritto monetario," in Travaini 2011, 1:213–58.

———, 2018. "Medieval Coinages in Mining Areas in South-Western Germany: A Research Project," in Bompaire and Sarah 2018, 141–68.

Maurer, B., 2006. "The Anthropology of Money," *Annual Review of Anthropology* 35:15–36.

———, 2015. *How Would You Like to Pay? How Technology Is Changing the Future of Money*. Durham, NC: Duke University Press.

Maurer, B., T. C. Nelms, and L. Swartz, 2013. "'When Perhaps the Real Problem Is Money Itself!': The Practical Materiality of Bitcoin," *Social Semiotics* 23: 261–77.

Mauss, M., 1990. *The Gift: The Form and Reason for Exchange in Archaic Societies*, trans. W. D. Halls with foreword by M. Douglas. London: Routledge.

Mayhew, N. J., 1974. "The Monetary Background to the Yorkist Recoinage of 1464–1471," *British Numismatic Journal* 44:62–73.

———, 1995. "Modelling Medieval Monetisation," in *A Commercialising Economy: England, 1086–1300*, ed. R. H. Britnell and B.M.S. Campbell, 55–77. Manchester, UK: Manchester University Press.

———, 2013. "Prices in England, 1170–1750," *Past and Present* 219:3–39.

Maynes, E. S., 2019. "Currency and Community: Labor, Identity, and Notgeld in Inflation-Era Thuringia," in *Alternative Realities: Utopian Thought in Times of Political Rupture*, ed. P. F. Lerner, 39–56. Washington, DC: German Historical Institute.

Mazel, F., 2009. "Cités, villes et campagnes dans l'ancienne Gaule de la fin du VIIIe siècle au milieu du XIe siècle," *Settimane di studio del Centro italiano di studi sull'alto medioevo* 56:337–90.

———, 2018. "De quoi la principauté territoriale est-elle le nom? Réflexion sur les enjeux spatiaux des principautés 'françaises' (Xe–début XIIe siècle)," in Bührer-Thierry, Patzold, and Schneider 2018, 65–88.

McComb, M. P., 2018. "Strategies of Correction: Corporal Punishment in the Carolingian Empire 742–900," PhD dissertation, Cornell University.

McCormick, F., 2008. "The Decline of the Cow: Agricultural and Settlement Change in Early Medieval Ireland," *Peritia* 20:209–24.

McCormick, M., 1984. "The Liturgy of War in the Early Middle Ages: Crisis, Litanies and the Carolingian Monarchy," *Viator* 15:1–23.

———, 1990. *Eternal Victory: Triumphal Rulership in Late Antiquity, Byzantium, and the Early Medieval West*. 2nd ed. Cambridge: Cambridge University Press.

———, 2001. *Origins of the European Economy: Communications and Commerce, A.D. 300–900*. Cambridge: Cambridge University Press.

———, 2007. "Where Do Trading Towns Come From? Early Medieval Venice and the Northern *Emporia*," in *Post-Roman Towns, Trade and Settlement in Europe and Byzantium*, ed. J. Henning. 2 vols., 1:41–68. Berlin: De Gruyter.

———, 2011. *Charlemagne's Survey of the Holy Land*. Washington, DC: Dumbarton Oaks Research Library and Collection.

———, 2013. "Coins and the Economic History of Post-Roman Gaul: Testing the Standard Model in the Moselle, ca. 400–750," in Jarnut and Strothmann 2013, 337–76.

———, 2019. "Climates of History, Histories of Climate: From History to Archaeoscience," *Journal of Interdisciplinary History* 50:3–30.

McCready, W. D., 2011. *Odiosa sanctitas: St Peter Damian, Simony, and Reform*. Toronto: Pontifical Institute of Mediaeval Studies.

McDermott, J. P., and S. Yoshinobu, 2015. "Economic Change in China, 960–1279," in Chaffee and Twitchett 2015, 321–436.

McFarlane, D. A., J. Lundberg, and H. Neff, 2014. "A Speleothem Record of Early British and Roman Mining at Charterhouse, Mendip, England," *Archaeometry* 56:431–43.

McHaffie, M., 2018. "Law and Violence in Eleventh-Century France," *Past and Present* 238:3–41.

———, forthcoming. "Mercy and the Violence of Law: Pardoning Fines in Western France c. 1030–c. 1170." *Mediaeval Journal*.

McKitterick, R., 1983. *The Frankish Kingdoms under the Carolingians 751–987*. London: Longman.

———, ed., 1995. *The New Cambridge Medieval History. II: c. 700–c. 900*. Cambridge: Cambridge University Press.

———, 2008. *Charlemagne: The Formation of a European Identity*. Cambridge: Cambridge University Press.

McKitterick, R., et al., 2013. *Old Saint Peter's, Rome*. Cambridge: Cambridge University Press.

McKnight, B. E., 1992. *Law and Order in Sung China*. Cambridge: Cambridge University Press.

Mecke, B., 1999. "Die Pfalzen in Paderborn Entdeckung und Auswertung," in *799— Kunst und Kultur der Karolingerzeit. Karl der Große und Papst Leo III in Paderborn*, ed. C. Stiegemann and M. Wemhoff. 3 vols., 3:176–82. Mainz, Ger.: von Zabern.

Meier-Welcker, H., 1952–53. "Die Simonie im frühen Mittelalter. Begriff und Erscheinung in ihrer Entwicklung von der Spätantike bis zum Investiturstreit," *Zeitschrift für Kirchengeschichte* 64:61–93.

Mell, J. L., 2007. "Religion and Economy in Pre-Modern Europe: The Medieval Commercial Revolution and the Jews." PhD dissertation, University of North Carolina at Chapel Hill.

——, 2017–18. *The Myth of the Medieval Jewish Moneylender*, 2 vols. Basingstoke, UK: Palgrave Macmillan.

Menant, F., 1993. *Campagnes lombardes du Moyen Age: l'économie et la société rurales dans la région de Bergame, de Crémone et de Brescia du Xe au XIIIe siècle*. Rome: École française de Rome.

Merkel, S. W., 2016. *Silver and the Silver Economy at Hedeby*. Bochum, Ger.: Marie Leidorf.

——, 2019. "Provenancing Viking Age Silver: Methodological and Theoretical Considerations and a Case Study," in Kershaw and Williams 2019, 206–26.

——, 2020. "The Richness of Silver Ore in the Middle Ages: A Comparative Study of Historical Descriptions and the Archaeological Evidence," in *Mittelalterliche Bergbautechnik in historischen und archäologischen Quellen. Ein Worskhop für interdisziplinären Arbeit in der montanhistorischen Forschung*, ed. L. Asrih, 39–44. Rahden, Ger.: Marie Leidorf.

——, 2021. "Evidence for the Widespread Use of Dry Silver Ore in the Early Islamic Period and Its Implications for the History of Silver Metallurgy," *Journal of Archaeological Science* 135, https://doi.org/10.1016/j.jas.2021.105478.

Merrills, A., and R. Miles, 2010. *The Vandals*. Chichester, UK: Wiley.

Mesqui, J., 1994. "Le château de Crépy-en-Valois: palais comtal, palais royal, palais féodale," *Bulletin monumental* 152:257–312.

Metcalf, D. M., 1963a. "Offa's Pence Reconsidered," *Cunobelin* 9:37–52.

——, 1963b. "English Monetary History in the Time of Offa: A Reply," *Numismatic Circular* 71:165–67.

——, 1964. "Evidence Relating to Die-Output in the Time of Offa," *Numismatic Circular* 72:23.

——, 1965. "How Large Was the Anglo-Saxon Currency?," *Economic History Review*, 2nd series, 18:475–82.

——, 1986. "Some Geographical Aspects of Early Medieval Monetary Circulation in the Iberian Peninsula," in *Problems of Medieval Coinage in the Iberian Area 1*, ed. M. Gomes Marques and M. Crusafont i Sabater, 307–24. Ávila, Sp.: Sociedad Numismática Avalesina.

——, 1988a. "For What Purposes Were Suevic and Visigothic Tremisses Used?," in *Problems of Medieval Coinage in the Iberian Peninsula 3*, ed. M. Gomes Marques and D. M. Metcalf, 15–34. Santarém, Port.: Sociedade Numismática Scalabitana.

——, 1988b. "North Italian Coinage Carried across the Alps. The Ostrogothic and Carolingian Evidence Compared," *Rivista Italiana di Numismatica e Scienze Affini* 90:449–56.

——, 1990. "A Sketch of the Currency in the Time of Charles the Bald," in Gibson and Nelson 1990, 65–97.

——, 1992. "The Rome (Forum) Hoard of 1883," *British Numismatic Journal* 62:63–96.

——, 1993–1994. *Thrymsas and Sceattas in the Ashmolean Museum, Oxford.* 3 vols. London: Royal Numismatic Society.

——, 1995. "Viking-Age Numismatics 1: Late Roman and Byzantine Gold in the Northern Lands," *Numismatic Chronicle* 155:413–41.

——, 1996. "Viking-Age Numismatics 2: Coinage in the Northern Lands in Merovingian and Carolingian Times," *Numismatic Chronicle* 156:399–428.

——, 1998. "The Monetary Economy of Ninth-Century England South of the Humber: A Topographical Analysis," in *Kings, Currency and Alliances: History and Coinage of Southern England in the Ninth Century*, ed. M. Blackburn and D. N. Dumville, 167–97. Woodbridge, UK: Boydell.

——, 2000. "Many Mint-Places, Few Coins: Visigothic Coinage in Gallaecia and Northern Lusitania," in *Homenagem a Mário Gomes Marques*, ed. M. de Castro Hipólito, 175–94. Sintra, Port.: Instituto de Sintra.

——, 2006a. "Monetary Circulation in Merovingian Gaul, 561–674: à propos Cahiers Ernest Babelon, 8," *Revue numismatique* 162:337–94.

——, 2006b. "Single Finds of Wodan/Monster Sceattas in England and their Interpretation for Monetary History," *Nordisk Numismatisk Årsskrift* 2000-2002:337–93.

Metcalf, D. M., and W. Lean, 1993. "The Battle of Maldon and the Minting of *Crux* Pennies in Essex: *Post hoc ergo propter hoc?*," in *The Battle of Maldon: Fiction and Fact*, ed. J. Cooper, 205–24. London: Hambledon.

Metcalf, D. M., and P. Northover, 1986. "Interpreting the Alloy of the Later Anglo-Saxon Coinage," *British Numismatic Journal* 56:35–63.

——, 1987. "The Northumbrian Royal Coinage in the Time of Æthelred II and Osberht," in *Coinage in Ninth-Century Northumbria: The Tenth Oxford Symposium on Coinage and Monetary History*, ed. D. M. Metcalf, 187–234. Oxford: B.A.R.

——, 1989. "Coinage Alloys from the Time of Offa and Charlemagne to c. 864," *Numismatic Chronicle* 149:101–20.

Metcalf, D. M., and W. Op den Velde, 2010. *The Monetary Economy of the Netherlands, c. 690–c. 760 and the Trade with England: A Study of the "Porcupine" Sceattas of Series E*, Jaarbooek voor Munt-en Penningkunde 96. Amsterdam: Koninklijk Nederlands Genootschap voor Munt- en Penningkunde.

Metcalf, W. E., ed., 2012. *The Oxford Handbook of Greek and Roman Coinage.* Oxford: Oxford University Press.

Metlich, M. A., 2004. *The Coinage of Ostrogothic Italy: A Die Study of Theodahad Folles.* London: Spink.

Meyer, C., 1997. "Bir Umm Fawakhir: Insights into Ancient Egyptian Mining," *Journal of the Minerals, Metals and Materials Society* 49:64–67.

——, 2011. "Ancient Gold Mining, Miners and Ore Reduction," in *Bir Umm Fawakhir. Vol. 2: Report on the 1996–1997 Survey Seasons*, ed. C. Meyer, 161–76. Chicago: Oriental Institute, University of Chicago.

Meyer, C., et al., 2000. *Bir Umm Fawakhir Survey Project 1993: A Byzantine Gold-Mining Town in Egypt*. Chicago: Oriental Institute, University of Chicago.

———, 2003. "Ancient Gold Extraction at Bir Umm Fawakhir," *Journal of the American Research Centre in Egypt* 40:13–53.

Mielants, E., 2002. "Europe and China Compared," *Review* 25:401–49.

Miller, W. I., 2006. *Eye for an Eye*. Cambridge: Cambridge University Press.

Minvielle Larousse, J., M.-C. Bailly-Maître, and G. Bianchi, eds., 2019. *Les métaux précieux en Méditerranée médiévale: Exploitations, transformations, circulations*. Aix-en-Provence, Fr.: Presses universitaires de Provence.

Miskimin, H. A., 1975. *The Economy of Early Renaissance Europe, 1300–1460*. Cambridge: Cambridge University Press.

Mitchell-Innes, A., 1914. "The Credit Theory of Money," *Banking Law Journal* 31:151–68.

Modéran, Y., 2002. "L'établissement territorial des Vandales en Afrique," *Antiquité tardive* 10:87–122.

———, 2012. "Confiscations, expropriations et redistributions foncières dans l'Afrique vandale," in Porena and Rivière 2012, 129–56.

Moesgaard, J. C., 1995. "Stray Finds of Carolingian Coins in Upper Normandy, France," in *Studia Numismatica: Festschrift Arkadi Molvõgin 65*, ed. I. Leimus, 87–102. Tallinn, Est.: Huma.

———, 2010. "Le 'maillon manquant' entre Quentovic et Rouen?," *BSFN* 65:57–61.

———., 2011. "*Renovatio monetae* et la chronologie des monnaies de Richard Ier, duc de Normandie 942/945–996," *BSFN* 66:125–32.

———, 2012. "Hedeby og den danske kongemagt i 900-tallet: Mønternes udsagn," *Kuml* 2012, 111–36.

———, 2014. "The Viking Invasions 885–889 and the Activity of the Mint of Rouen," in Naismith, Allen, and Screen 2014, 427–58.

———, 2015. *King Harold's Cross Coinage: Christian Coins for the Merchants of Haithabu and the King's Soldiers*. Copenhagen: University Press of Southern Denmark.

———, 2017. "Charlemagne's and Louis the Pious' Portrait Coinage: A Special Ceremonial or an Ordinary Currency Issue?," in *Nummi et Humanitas: studia ofiarowane profesorowi Stanisławowi Suchodolskiemu w 80 rocznicę urodzin*, ed. M. Bogucki et al., 115–29. Warsaw: Wydawnictwo Instytutu Archeologii i Etnologii Polskiej Akademii Nauk.

———, 2018. "Den fremadskuende hjort—en hidtil uerkendt fase I Ribes udmøntning i 800-tallet?," *By, marsk og geest* 30:17–30.

Molyneaux, G., 2015. *The Formation of the Kingdom of the English in the Tenth Century*. Oxford: Oxford University Press.

Moore, R. I., 1992. "Postscript: The Peace of God and the Social Revolution," in *The Peace of God: Social Violence and Religious Response in France around the Year 1000*, ed. T. F. Head and R. A. Landes, 308–26. Ithaca, NY: Cornell University Press.

Moore, R. I., 2000. "The Birth of Popular Heresy: A Millennial Phenomenon?," *Journal of Religious History* 24:8–25.

———, 2003. "The Eleventh Century in Eurasian History: A Comparative Approach to the Convergence and Divergence of Medieval Civilizations," *Journal of Medieval and Modern Studies* 33:1–21.

——, 2006. *The Formation of a Persecuting Society: Authority and Deviance in Western Europe, 950–1250*. 2nd ed. Oxford: Blackwell.

Moorhead, S., 1997. "The Late Roman, Byzantine and Umayyad Periods at Tel Jezreel," *Tel Aviv* 24:129–66.

——, 2001. "Roman Coin Finds from Wiltshire," in *Roman Wiltshire and After: Papers in Honour of Ken Annable*, ed. P. Ellis, 85–105. Devizes, UK: Wiltshire Archaeological and Natural History Society.

——, 2006. "Roman Bronze Coinage in Sub-Roman and Early Anglo-Saxon England," in Cook and Williams 2006, 99–109.

——, 2008. "The Coins from the Excavations at Tel Jezreel (Israel)," *Numismatic Chronicle* 168:454–74.

——, 2012. "The Coinage of the Later Roman Empire, 364–498," in Metcalf 2012, 601–32.

——, 2013. "Ever Decreasing Circles. The Nummus Economy at Butrint (Albania) and Beyond," in *Numismatic History and Economy in Epirus during Antiquity*, ed. K. Liampi et al., 601–14. Athens: University of Ioannina.

——, 2020. "The Ancient and Early Medieval Coins from the Triconch Palace, c. 2nd Century BC to c. AD 600," in *Butrint 5: Life and Death at a Mediterranean Port*, ed. W. Bowden, 78–94, 275–319. Oxford: Oxbow.

Moorhead, S., and P. Walton, 2014. "Coinage at the End of Roman Britain," in *AD 410: The History and Archaeology of Late and Post-Roman Britain*, ed. F. K. Haarer and R. Collins, 99–116. London: Society for the Promotion of Roman Studies.

Mora Serrano, B., 2016. "Old and New Coins in Southern Hispania in the 6th Century AD," in Chameroy and Guihard 2016, 139–54.

Moreland, J., 2000. "The Significance of Production in Eighth-Century England," in *The Long Eighth Century*, ed. I. L. Hansen and C. Wickham, 69–104. Leiden, Neth.: Brill.

Morimoto, Y., 2018. "Aspects of the Early Medieval Peasant Economy as Revealed in the Polyptych of Prüm," in *The Medieval World*, ed. P. Linehan, J. L. Nelson, and M. Costambeys, 705–19. 2nd ed. London: Routledge.

Morony, M., 2019. "The Early Islamic Mining Boom," *Journal of the Economic and Social History of the Orient* 62:166–221.

Morrison, K. F., 1963. "Numismatics and Carolingian Trade: A Critique of the Evidence," *Speculum* 38:403–32.

Morrison, K. F., and H. Grunthal, 1967. *Carolingian Coinage*. New York: American Numismatic Society.

Morrisson, C., 1983. "The Re-Use of Obsolete Coins: The Case of Roman Imperial Bronzes Revived in the Late Fifth Century," in *Studies in Numismatic Method Presented to Philip Grierson*, ed. C. N. L. Brooke et al., 95–111 Cambridge, UK: Cambridge University Press.

——, 1989–1991. "Monnaie et prix à Byzance du Ve au VIIe siècle," in *Hommes et richesses dans l'empire byzantin*, ed. C. Abadie-Reynal, V. Kravari, J. Lefort, and C. Morrisson. 2 vols., 1:239–60. Paris: Lethielleux.

——, 1992. "Monnaie et finances dans l'Empire byzantin, Xe–XIVe siècle," in *Hommes et richesses dans l'empire byzantin*, vol. 2, 239–60. Paris.

———, 2002. "Byzantine Money: Its Production and Circulation," in *The Economic History of Byzantium*, ed. A. E. Laiou. 3 vols, 3:909–66. Washington, DC: Dumbarton Oaks Research Library and Collection.

———, 2014. "Byzantine Coins in Early Medieval Britain: A Byzantinist's Assessment," in Naismith, Allen, and Screen 2014, 207–42.

———, 2015. "Odd One Out? The Arab-Byzantine Dinar in the Merovingian Hoard from Bais (Chissey-en-Morvan)," in *Myntstudier: Festskrift till Kenneth Jonsson*, ed. T. Talvio and M. Wijk, 47–50. Stockholm: Svenska Numismatiska Föreningen.

———, 2016. "*Regio dives in omnibus bonis ornata*: The African Economy from the Vandals to the Arab Conquest in the Light of Coin Evidence," in *North Africa under Byzantium and Early Islam*, ed. S. T. Stevens and J. P. Conant, 173–98. Washington DC: Dumbarton Oaks Research Library and Collection.

Morrisson, C., et al., 1985. *L'or monnayé 1: purification et altérations de Rome à Byzance*. Paris: Éditions du Centre national de la recherche scientifique.

Morrisson, C., and J.-N. Barrandon, 1988. "La trouvaille de monnaies d'argent byzantines de Rome (VIIe–VIIIe siècles): analyses et chronologie," *Revue numismatique*, 6th series, 30:149–65.

Morrisson, C., V. Popović, and I. Ivanišević, 2006. *Les trésors monétaires byzantins des Balkans et d'Asie mineur (491–713)*. Paris: Lethielleux.

Mosetti Casaretto, F., 2000. *La beffa di Unibos*. Alessandria, It.: Edizioni dell'Orso.

———, 2002. "Una sfida al lettore: i 'Versus di Unibove,'" in *Latin Culture in the Eleventh Century: Proceedings of the Third International Conference on Medieval Latin Studies; Cambridge, September 9–12, 1998*, ed. M. W. Herren, C. A. MacDonough, and R. G. Arthur. 2 vols., 2:153–86. Turnhout, Bel.: Brepols.

Mouton, D., 2003. "La 'Roca' de Niozelles et les mottes castrales du bassin de la Durance moyenne et ses abords." PhD dissertation, Université de Provence.

———, 2008. *Mottes castrales en Provence: les origins de la fortification privée au Moyen Âge*. Paris: Éditions de la Maison des sciences de l'homme.

———, 2014. *La Moutte d'Allemagne-en-Provence: un castrum précoce du Moyen Âge provençal*. Arles, Fr.: Éditions Errance.

Muldrew, C., 2001. "'Hard Food for Midas': Cash and its Social Value in Early Modern England," *Past and Present* 170:78–120.

Müller-Mertens, E., 1980. *Die Reichsstruktur im Spiegel der Herrschaftspraxis Ottos des Großen*. Berlin: Akademie-Verlag.

Munby, J., 2011. "The Domesday Boroughs Revisited," *Anglo-Norman Studies* 33:127–49.

Munro, J.H.A., 2012. "Coinage Debasements in Burgundian Flanders, 1384–1482: Monetary or Fiscal Policies?," in *Comparative Perspectives on History and Historians: Essays in Memory of Bryce Lyon (1920–2007)*, ed. D. Nicholas, B. S. Bachrach and J. M. Murray, 314–60. Kalamazoo, MI: Medieval Institute.

Münsch, O., 2006. "Ein Streitschriftenfragment zur Simonie," *Deutsches Archiv für Erforschung des Mittelalters* 62:619–30.

Murray, A. C., 1978. *Reason and Society in the Middle Ages*. Oxford: Clarendon.

———, 2010. "Merovingian Immunity Revisited," *History Compass* 8:913–28.

Musset, L., 1959. "A-t-il existé en Normandie au XIe siècle une aristocratie d'argent?," *Annales de Normandie* 9:285–99.

Myhre, B., 1998. "The Archaeology of the Early Viking Age in Norway," in *Ireland and Scandinavia in the Early Viking Age*, ed. H. Clarke, M. Ní Mhaonaigh, and R. Ó Floinn, 3–36. Dublin: Four Courts.

Myrdal, J., and A. Sapoznik, 2016. "Spade Cultivation and Intensification of Land Use 1000–1300: Written Sources, Archaeology and Image," *Agricultural History Review* 65:194–212.

Naismith, R., 2010. "The Coinage of Offa Revisited," *British Numismatic Journal* 80, 76–106.

——, 2011. *The Coinage of Southern England 796–865*. 2 vols. London: Spink.

——, 2012a. "Kings, Crisis and Coinage Reforms in the Mid-Eighth Century," *EME* 20:291–332.

——, 2012b. *Money and Power in Anglo-Saxon England: The Southern English Kingdoms 757–865*, Cambridge Studies in Medieval Life and Thought, 4th series, 80. Cambridge: Cambridge University Press.

——, 2012c. "Payments for Land and Privilege in Anglo-Saxon England," *Anglo-Saxon England* 41:277–342.

——, 2013a. "The English Monetary Economy, c. 973–1100: The Contribution of Single-Finds," *Economic History Review* 66:198–225.

——, 2013b. "London and Its Mint c. 880–1066: A Preliminary Survey," *British Numismatic Journal* 83:44–74.

——, 2013c. "Payments for Land and Privilege in Anglo-Saxon England," *Anglo-Saxon England* 41:277–342.

——, 2014a. "Gold Coinage and Its Use in the Post-Roman West," *Speculum* 89:273–306.

——, 2014b. "Money of the Saints. Church and Coinage in Early Anglo-Saxon England," in Abramson 2014, 68–121.

——, 2014c. "Peter's Pence and Before: Numismatic Links between Anglo-Saxon England and Rome," in *England and Rome in the Early Middle Ages: Pilgrimage, Art, and Politics*, ed. F. Tinti, 217–54. Turnhout, Bel.: Brepols.

——, 2014d. "Prelude to Reform: Tenth-Century English Coinage in Perspective," in Naismith, Allen, and Screen 2014, 39–84.

——, 2014e. "The Social Significance of Monetization in the Early Middle Ages," *Past and Present* 223:3–40.

——, 2015. "*Turpe lucrum*? Wealth, Money and Coinage in the Millennial Church," in Gasper and Gullbekk 2015, 17–37.

——, 2016a. "The Coinage of Æthelred II: A New Evaluation," *English Studies* 97:117–39.

——, 2016b. "Currency, Conversion and the Landscape of Power in the Early Middle Ages," in *The Introduction of Christianity into the Early Medieval Insular World: Converting the Isles I*, ed. R. Flechner and M. Ní Mhaonaigh, 281–304. Turnhout, Bel.: Brepols.

——. 2016c. "The Earliest Strasbourg Laws on Minting in Their Early Medieval Context," *Annali dell'Istituto Italiano di Numismatica* 61:43–64.

——, 2016d. "The Economy of *Beowulf*," in *Old English Philology: Studies in Honour of R. D. Fulk*, ed. L. Neidorf, R. J. Pascual, and T. Shippey, 371–91. Cambridge: Boydell & Brewer.

———, 2016e. "The Forum Hoard and Beyond: Money, Gift, and Religion in the Early Middle Ages," *Viator* 47:35–56.

———, 2016f. "The Land Market and Anglo-Saxon Society," *Historical Research* 89:19–41.

———, 2017a. "The Ely Memoranda and the Economy of the Late Anglo-Saxon Fenland," *Anglo-Saxon England* 47:333–77.

———, 2017b. *Medieval European Coinage, with a Catalogue of the Coins in the Fitzwilliam Museum Cambridge. 8: Britain and Ireland c. 400–1066.* Cambridge: Cambridge University Press.

———, 2018a. *Citadel of the Saxons: The Rise of Early London.* London: Tauris.

———, 2018b. "Pecuniary Profanities? Money, Christianity and Demonstrative Giving in the Early Middle Ages," in *Divina Moneta: Coins in Religion and Ritual*, ed. N. Myrberg and G. Tarnow Ingvardson, 142–59. London: Routledge.

———, 2019a. "The Currency of Power in Late Anglo-Saxon England," *History Compass* 17. https://doi.org/10.1111/hic3.12579.

———, 2019b. "Mints, Moneyers and the Geography of Power," in Carroll, Reynolds, and Yorke 2019, 414–35.

———, 2019c. "Two Important Coins of the Mercian Supremacy," *British Numismatic Journal* 89:203–8.

———, 2020a. "*Denarii mixti*: Debasement and Rhetoric in the Early Middle Ages (Fifth–Twelfth Centuries)," in *Debasement: Manipulation of Coin Standards in Pre-Modern Monetary Systems*, ed. K. Butcher, 195–207. Oxford: Oxbow.

———, 2020b. "Gilds, States and Societies in the Early Middle Ages," *EME* 28:627–62.

———, 2021. "Writing, Communication, and Currency: Dialogues between Coinage and Charters in Anglo-Saxon England," in Gallagher, Roberts, and Tinti 2021, 488–521.

———, forthcoming a. "The Moneyers and Domesday Book." *Anglo-Norman Studies* 45.

———, forthcoming b. "The Aristocracy of Money Reconsidered."

Naismith, R., M. Allen, and E. Screen, eds., 2014. *Early Medieval Monetary History: Studies in Memory of Mark Blackburn.* Farnham, UK: Ashgate.

Naismith, R., P. Northover, and F. Tinti, 2015. "The Fineness of Papal Antiquiores," *Numismatic Chronicle* 175:195–203.

Naismith, R., and F. Tinti, 2016. *The Forum Hoard of Anglo-Saxon Coins. Il ripostiglio dell'Atrium Vestae nel Foro Romano*, Bollettino di numismatica 55–56. Rome: Istituto poligrafico e Zecca dello Stato.

———, 2019. "The Origins of Peter's Pence," *English Historical Review* 134:521–52.

Naylor, J., 2004. *An Archaeology of Trade in Middle Saxon England.* Oxford: British Archaeological Reports.

———, 2012. "Coinage, Trade and the Origins of the English Emporia, ca. AD 650–750," in *From One Sea to Another: Trading Places in the European and Mediterranean Early Middle Ages. Proceedings of the International Conference, Comacchio, 27th–29th March 2009*, ed. S. Gelichi and R. Hodges, 237–66. Turnhout, Bel.: Brepols.

Nelson, J. L., 1992. *Charles the Bald.* London: Longman.

———, 1999. "Rulers and Government," in Reuter 1999, 95–129.

———, 2010. "*Munera*," in Le Jan, Feller, and Devroey 2010, 383–401.

———, 2019. *King and Emperor: A New Life of Charlemagne.* London: Allen Lane.

Newhauser, R. G., 2003. "Avarice and the Apocalypse," in *The Apocalyptic Year 1000: Religious Expectation and Social Change, 950–1050*, ed. R. A. Landes, A. C. Gow, and D. C. van Meter, 109–19. Oxford: Oxford University Press.

Nicolay, J.A.W., 2014. *The Splendour of Power: Early Medieval Kingship and the Use of Gold and Silver in the Southern North Sea Area (5th to 7th Century AD)*. Eelde, Neth.: Barkhuis.

Nightingale, P., 1982. "Some London Moneyers and Reflections on the Organization of English Mints in the Eleventh and Twelfth Centuries," *Numismatic Chronicle* 142:34–50.

———, 2013. "A Crisis of Credit in the Fifteenth Century, or of Historical Interpretation?," *British Numismatic Journal* 83:149–63.

Noeske, H.-C., 2000. *Münzfunde aus Ägypten I. Die Münzfunde des ägyptischen Pilgerzentrums Abu Mina und die Vergleichsfunde aus den Dioecesen Aegyptus und Oriens vom 4.–8. JH. n. Chr.* 3 vols. Berlin: Mann.

Noonan, T. S., 1985. "The First Major Silver Crisis in Russia and the Baltic, c. 875–c. 900," *Hikuin* 11:41–50.

———, 1992. "Fluctuations in Islamic Trade with Eastern Europe during the Viking Age," *Harvard Ukrainian Studies* 16:237–60.

———, 1994. "The Vikings in the East: Coins and Commerce," in *The Twelfth Viking Congress: Developments around the Baltic and the North Sea in the Viking Age*, ed. B. Ambrosiani and H. Clarke, 215–36. Stockholm: Riksantikvarieämbetet and Statens historiska museer.

———, 2000–2001. "Volga Bulgharia's Tenth-Century Trade with Samanid Central Asia," *Archivum Eurasiae medii aevi* 11:140–338.

Nordenfalk, C., 1972. "The Chronology of the Registrum Master," in *Kunsthistorische Forschungen: Otto Pächt zu einem 70. Geburtstag*, ed. A. Rosenauer, 62–76. Salzburg, Aus.: Residenz.

Norrie, J., 2017. "Land and Cult: Society and Radical Religion in the Diocese of Milan, c. 990–1130." DPhil dissertation, University of Oxford.

O'Brien, W., 2015. *Prehistoric Copper Mining in Europe, 5500–500 BC*. Oxford: Oxford University Press.

Oexle, O. G., 1978. "Die funktionale Dreiteilung der "Gesellschaft" bei Adalbero von Laon. Deutungsschemata der sozialen Wirklichkeit im früheren Mittelalter," *Frühmittelalterliche Studien* 12:1–54.

O'Hara, M. D., 1985. "A Find of Byzantine Silver from the Mint of Rome for the Period AD 641–752," *Schweizerische numismatische Rundschau* 64:105–40.

Ohly, E. F., 1999. *Zur Signaturenlehre der frühen Neuzeit. Bemerkungen zur mittelalterlichen Vorgeschichte und zur Eigenart einer epochalen Denkform in Wissenschaft, Literatur und Kunst, aus dem Nachlaß herausgegeben*. Stuttgart, Ger.: Hirzel.

Oliver, L., 2011. *The Body Legal in Barbarian Law*. Toronto: University of Toronto Press.

Olivieri, A., 2011. "Per la storia della circolazione monetaria nell'Italia nord-occidentale tra l'XI e la prima metà del XII secolo. La testimonianza delle fonti documentarie," *Reti Medievali Rivista* 12:53–105.

Op den Velde, W., and C.J.F. Klaassen, 2004. *Sceattas and Merovingian Deniers from Domburg and Westenschouwen*. Middelburg, Ger.: Koninklijk Zeeuwsch Genootschap der Wetenschappen.

Op den Velde, W., and D. M. Metcalf, 2007. *The Monetary Economy of the Netherlands, c. 690-c. 715 and the Trade with England: A Study of the Sceattas of Series D*, Jaarboek voor Munt-en Penningkunde 90. Amsterdam: Koninklijk Nederlands Genootschap voor Munt- en Penningkunde.

Oras, E., I. Leimus, and L. Joosu, 2019. "A Viking Age Gold Hoard from Essu, Estonia: Context, Function, and Meaning," in Kershaw and Williams 2019, 145–68.

Orri Vésteinsson, 2007. "A Divided Society: Peasants and Aristocracy in Medieval Iceland," *Viking and Medieval Scandinavia* 3:117–39.

Ørsted, P., 2000. "Production and Population," in *Africa Proconsularis: Regional Studies in the Segermes Valley of Northern Tunisia 3*, ed. P. Ørsted, J. Carlsen, L. Ladjimi Sebaï, and H. Ben Hassen, 133–70. Copenhagen: National Museum of Denmark.

Osland, D., 2011. "Tribute and Coinage in the Visigothic Kingdom: On the Role of the Bishop," *Anas* 24:71–95.

Östergren, M., 2004. "Det gotländska alltinget och cistercienserklostret i Roma," in *Gotland vikingaön*, 40–45. Visby, Swed.: Länsmuseet på Gotland.

———, 2011. "The Spillings Hoard(s)," in Graham-Campbell, Sindbæk, and Williams 2011b, 321–36.

Pagan, H. E., 2018. "The Le Puy (1943) Hoard Revisited," *Numismatic Chronicle* 178:327–38.

Painter, K., 2013. "Hacksilber: A Means of Exchange?," in Hunter and Painter 2013, 215–42.

Pancer, N., 2001. *Sans peur et sans vergogne: de l'honneur et des femmes aux premiers temps mérovingiens, VIe-VIIe siècles*. Paris: A. Michel.

Panfili, D., 2018. "Comitatus vs pagus. Espaces, territoires, pouvoirs en Septimanie, Toulousain, Quercy et Rouergue (fin VIIIe–fin XIe siècle)," in Bührer-Thierry, Patzold, and Schneider 2018, 201–16.

Paolucci, A., 1977. "Marx, Money, and Shakespeare: The Hegelian Core in Marxist Shakespeare-Criticism," *Mosaic* 10:139–56.

Papadopoli, N., 1893–1919. *Le monete di Venezia*. 3 vols. Venice: Ferdinando Onigania.

Pardini, G., N. Parise, and F. Marani, eds., 2017. *Numismatica e Archeologia. Monete stratigrafie e contesti. Dati a confronto*. Rome: Edizioni Quasar.

Parry, J., and M. Bloch, 1989. "Introduction: Money and the Morality of Exchange," in *Money and the Morality of Exchange*, ed. J. Parry and M. Bloch, 1–32. Cambridge: Cambridge University Press.

Parsons, J., 2014. *Making Money in Sixteenth-Century France: Currency, Culture, and the State*. Ithaca, NY: Cornell University Press.

Parvérie, M., 2007. "La circulation des monnaies arabes en Aquitaine et Septimanie aux VIIIe–IXe siècles," *Aquitania* 23:233–46.

———, 2010. "La circulation des dirhams d'al-Andalus entre la Gascogne et l'Aquitaine carolingiennes," *BSFN* 65:144–49.

———, 2012. "Questions sur l'importation des dirhams d'al-Andalus dans l'empire carolingien," *Bulletin du Centre Européen de numismatique* 49:14–23.

——, 2014. "Corpus des monnaies arabo-musulmanes des VIIIe et IXe siècles découvertes dans le sud de la France," *Revue numismatique OMNI* 1:79–100.

Paszkiewicz, B., 2006. "Anglo-Saxon and Imitative Pennies from the Raciążek Hoard," *Numismatic Chronicle* 166: 251–68.

Patterson, C. C., 1972. "Silver Stocks and Losses in Ancient and Medieval Times," *Economic History Review* 25:205–35.

Patzold, S., 2006. "Rédefinir l'office épiscopal: les évêques francs face à la crise des années 820/30," in *Les élites au haut Moyen Âge. Crises et renouvellements*, ed. F. Bougard, L. Feller and R. Le Jan, 337–59. Turnhout, Bel.: Brepols.

——, 2008. *Episcopus: Wissen über Bischöfe im Frankenreich des späten 8. bis frühen 10. Jahrhunderts*. Ostfildern, Ger.: Thorbecke.

——, 2020. *Presbyter: Moral, Mobilität und die Kirchenorganisation im Karolingerreich*. Stuttgart, Ger.: Anton Hiersemann.

Pedersen, U., 2008. "Weights and Balances," in Skre 2008, 119–95.

——, 2016a. *Into the Melting Pot: Non-Ferrous Metalworkers in Viking-Period Kaupang*. Aarhus, Den.: Aarhus Universitetsforlag.

——, 2016b. "Lead Isotope Analysis of Pewter Mounts from the Viking Ship Burial at Gokstad: On the Origin and Use of Raw Materials," *Archaeometry* 58:148–63.

——, 2017. "Viking-Period Non-Ferrous Metalworking and Urban Commodity Production," in Glørstad and Loftsgarden 2017, 124–38.

Peets, J., 2013. "Estonia: Salme Ship Burials," *Current World Archaeology* 58:18–24.

Pelteret, D.A.E., 1990. *Catalogue of English Post-Conquest Vernacular Documents*. Woodbridge, UK: Boydell.

Pérez Sánchez, D., 1999. "Las transformaciones de la antigüedad tardía en la Península Ibérica: iglesia y fiscalidad en la sociedad visigoda," *Studia historica: historia antigua* 17: 299–320.

Pérez, S. C., and S. S. Díaz, 1995. "La ceca visigoda de Barbi: aspectos historiográficos y arqueológicos," *Numisma* 236: 125–38.

Périn, P., 2008. "Dress and Adornment in Merovingian Times," in *Rome and the Barbarians: The Birth of a New World*, ed. J.-J. Aillagon, 512–15. London: Thames & Hudson.

Pestell, T., 2010. "Markets, Emporia, Wics, and "Productive" Sites: Pre-Viking Trade Centres in Anglo-Saxon England," in *The Oxford Handbook of Anglo-Saxon Archaeology*, ed. H. F. Hamerow, D. A. Hinton, and S. Crawford, 556–79. Oxford: Oxford University Press.

——, 2013. "Imports or Immigrants? Reassessing Scandinavian Metalwork in Late Anglo-Saxon East Anglia," in *East Anglia and its North Sea World in the Middle Ages*, ed. D. R. Bates and R. Liddiard, 230–55. Woodbridge, UK: Boydell.

Pettersson, A.-M., 2009. *The Spillings Hoard: Gotland's Role in Viking Age World Trade*. Visby, Swed.: Gotlands Museum.

Peytremann, É., 2013. "Structures et espaces de stockage dans les villages alto-médiévaux (6e–12e s.) de la moitié septentrionale de la Gaule: un apport à l'étude socio-économique du monde rural," in *Horrea, Barns and Silos: Storage and Incomes in Early Medieval Europe*, ed. A. Vigil-Escalera Guirado, G. Bianchi, and J. A. Quirós Castillo, 49–56. Bilbao, Sp.: Servicio editorial de la UPV/EHU.

———, 2014. "L'apport de l'archéologie de l'habitat rural dans le nord de la France à la connaissance de la première moitié du Xe siècle," in Valenti and Wickham 2014, 397–414.

Phillips, M., E. Freeman, and P. Woodhead, 2011. "The Pimprez Hoard," *Numismatic Chronicle* 171:261–346.

Phillipson, D. W., 2017. "Trans-Saharan Gold Trade and Byzantine Coinage," *Antiquaries Journal* 97:145–69.

Pirenne, H., 1898. "Villes, marchés et marchands au Moyen Âge," *Revue historique* 67:59–70.

Pirenne, H., 1913. "The Stages in the Social History of Capitalism," *American Historical Review* 19:494–515.

———, 1925. *Medieval Cities: Their Origins and the Revival of Trade*, trans. F. D. Halsey. Princeton, NJ: Princeton University Press.

———, 1939. *Mohammed and Charlemagne*, trans. B. Miall. London.

Pirie, E.J.E., 2006. "Contrasts and Continuity within the Coinage of Northumbria, c. 670–867," in Cook and Williams 2006, 211–40.

Pirie, E.J.E., et al., 1986. *Post-Roman Coins from York Excavations, 1971–81*. London: Council for British Archaeology.

Piron, S., 2010. "Albert le Grand et le concept de valeur," in *I Beni di questo mondo. Teorie etico-economiche nel laboratorio dell'Europa medievale*, ed. R. Lambertini and L. Sileo, 131–56. Turnhout, Bel.: Brepols.

Piton, D., 1993. *La céramique du 5ème au 10ème siècle dans l'Europa du Nord-Ouest: travaux du Groupe de Recherches et d'Études sur la Céramique dans le Nord— Pas-de-Calais. Actes du colloque d'Outreau, 10–12 avril 1992.* Saint-Josse-sur-Mer, Fr.: NEA.

Pliego Vázquez, R., 2008. "La acuñación monetaria en el Reino Visigodo de Toledo: el funcionamiento de las cecas," in *Els tallers monetaris: organització i producció: XII Curs d'Història monetària d'Hispania*, 117–41. Barcelona: Museu nacional d'art de Catalunya.

———, 2009. *La moneda visigoda.* 2 vols. Seville, Sp.: Secretariado de Publicaciones, Universidad de Sevilla.

———, 2012. "La moneda visigoda: Anexo I," *SPAL* 21:209–31.

———, 2015–2016. "The Circulation of Copper Coins in the Iberian Peninsula during the Visigothic Period: New Approaches," *Journal of Archaeological Numismatics* 1:25–60.

———, 2018a. "Kings' Names on Visigothic Bronze Coins: A New *Minimus* from Ispali in the Name of Leovigild," *American Journal of Numismatics*, 2nd series, 219–31.

———, 2018b. "A Visigothic Hoard from the Reign of Tulga (639–42)," *Numismatic Chronicle* 178:317–25.

———, 2020a. "Rethinking the *Minimi* of the Iberian Peninsula and Balearic Islands in Late Antiquity," *Journal of Medieval Iberian Studies* 12:125–54.

———, 2020b. "Visigothic Currency: Recent Developments and Data for its Study," in *Framing Power in Visigothic Society: Discourses, Devices, and Artefacts*, ed. E. Dell'Elicine and C. Martin, 181–215. Amsterdam: Amsterdam University Press.

———, forthcoming. "The Tomares Hoard," *Journal of Archaeological Numismatics*.

Poble, P.-É., 2015. "Les structures territoriales qualifiées de pagus dans l'Auvergne du Xe siècle," in *Châteaux, églises et seigneurs en Auvergne au Xe siècle: lieux de pouvoir et forms d'encadrement*, ed. O. Bruand, 69–79. Clermont-Ferrand, Fr.: Presses-universitaires Blaise-Pascal.

Poey d'Avant, F., 1858–62. *Monnaies féodales de France*. 3 vols. Paris: Rollin.

Poggi, G., 1993. *Money and the Modern Mind: Georg Simmel's Philosophy of Money*. Berkeley: University of California Press.

Pohl, W., 2001. "*Per hospites divisi*. Wirtschaftliche Grundlagen der langobardischen Ansiedlung in Italien," *Römische historische Mitteilungen* 43:179–226.

Pohl, W., and V. Wieser, V., eds., 2009. *Der frühmittelalterliche Staat—europäische Perspektiven*. Vienna: Österreichischen Akademie der Wissenschaften.

Pol, A., 2008. "A New Sceat of the Dorestat/Madelinus-Type," in *Studies in Early Medieval Coinage. Volume 1: Two Decades of Discovery*, ed. T. Abramson, 119–22. Woodbridge, UK: Boydell.

———, 2010. "Madelinus and the Disappearing of Gold," in *Dorestad in an International Framework: New Research on Centres of Trade and Coinage in Carolingian Times. Proceedings of the First Dorestad Congress, Held at the National Museum of Antiquities Leiden, the Netherlands, June 24–27, 2009*, ed. A. Willemsen and H. Kik, 91–94. Turnhout, Bel.: Brepols.

———, 2013. "Text mit Bild. Eine Betrachtung über die gegenseitige Abhängigkeit von Sprache und Typ/Stil be idem Studium von Monetarmünzen der Merowingerzeit," in Jarnut and Strothmann 2013, 533–49.

Polanyi, K., 1957. *Trade and Markets in the Early Empires*. New York: Free Press.

Poly, J.-P., and Bournazel, E., 1991. *The Feudal Transformation, 900–1200*, trans. C. Higgitt. New York: Holmes & Meier.

Porena, P., and Rivière, Y., eds., 2012. *Expropriations et confiscations dans les royaumes barbares: une approche régionale*. Rome: École française de Rome.

Portass, R., 2017. *The Village World of Early Medieval Northern Spain: Local Community and the Land Market*. Woodbridge, UK: Boydell.

Postan, M. M., 1944. "The Rise of a Money Economy," *Economic History Review* 14:123–34.

———, 1972. *The Medieval Economy and Society: An Economic History of Britain 1100–1500*. London: Weidenfeld & Nicolson.

———, 1973. *Essays on Medieval Agriculture and General Problems of the Medieval Economy*. Cambridge: Cambridge University Press.

Pracy, S., 2020. "Social Mobility and Manumissions in Early Medieval England," *Haskins Society Journal* 31:1–19.

Pratt, D., 2013. "Demesne Exemption from Royal Taxation in Anglo-Saxon and Anglo-Norman England," *English Historical Review* 128:1–33.

Preiser-Kapeller, J., 2021. *Der lange Sommer und die kleine Eiszeit: Klima, Pandemien und der Wangel der Alten Welt, 500–1500 n. Chr.* Vienna: Mandelbaum.

Prelog, J., 1989. "*Gesta Dagoberti*," in *Lexikon des Mittelalters*. 10 vols, 4:1407. Munich: Artemis.

Price, N., 2020. *The Children of Ash and Elm: A History of the Vikings*. London: Allen Lane.

Prigent, V., 2013. "La circulation monétaire en Sicile (VIe–VIIe siècle)," in *The Insular System of the Early Byzantine Mediterranean*, ed. D. Michaelides, P. Pergola, and E. Zanini, 139–60. Oxford: Archaeopress.

Prou, M., 1888. "Les ateliers monétaires mérovingiens," *Revue numismatique*, 3rd series, 6:542–50.

———, 1896. *Les monnaies carolingiennes*. Paris: C. Rollin et Feuardent.

Prusac, M., 2010. *From Face to Face: Recarving of Roman Portraits and the Late-Antique Portrait Arts*. Leiden, Neth.: Brill.

Py, V., 2009. "Mine, bois et forêt dans les Alpes du Sud au Moyen Âge. Approches archéologique, bioarchéologique et historique." 3 vols. PhD dissertation, Université de Provence Aix-Marseilles.

Py, V., et al., 2014. "Interdisciplinary Characterisation and Environmental Imprints of Mining and Forestry in the Upper Durance Valley (France) during the Holocene," *Quaternary International* 353:74–97.

Quirós Castillo, J. A., 2013. "Archaeology of Power and Hierarchies in Early Medieval Villages in Northern Spain," in *Hierarchies in Rural Settlements*, ed. J. Klápště, 199–212. Turnhout, Bel.: Brepols.

———, 2020a. "An Archaeology of 'Small Worlds': Social Inequality in Early Medieval Iberian Rural Communities," *Journal of Medieval Iberian Studies* 12:3–27.

———, ed., 2020b. *Social Inequality in Early Medieval Europe: Local Societies and Beyond*. Turnhout, Bel.: Brepols.

Rädlinger-Prömper, C., 1987. *Sankt Emmeram in Regensburg. Struktur- und Funktionswandel eines bayerischen Klosters im frühen Mittelalter*. Kallmünz, Ger.: Lassleben.

Raffield, B., 2016. "Bands of Brothers: A Re-Appraisal of the Viking Great Army and Its Implications for the Scandinavian Colonization of England," *EME* 24:308–37.

Raffield, B., et al., 2016. "Ingroup Identification, Identity Fusion, and the Formation of Viking Warbands," *World Archaeology* 48:35–50.

Raftis, J. A., 1996. *Peasant Economic Development within the English Manorial System*. Stroud, UK: Sutton.

Rahtz, P. A., Anderson, F. W., and Hirst, S., 1979. *The Saxon and Medieval Palaces at Cheddar: Excavations 1960–62*. Oxford: B.A.R.

Randsborg, K., 1998. "The Migration Period: Model History and Treasure," in *The Sixth Century: Production, Distribution and Demand*, ed. R. Hodges and W. M. Bowsky, 61–88. Leiden, Neth.: Brill.

Rasmusson, N. L., and B. Malmer, eds., 1968. *Commentationes de nummis saeculorum IX–XI in Suecia repertis, pars secunda: Untersuchungen zu den in Schweden gefundenen Münzen des 9. bis 11. Jahrhunderts*. Stockholm: Almqvist & Wiksell.

Rau, A., 2013. "Where Did the Late Empire End? Hacksilber and Coins in Continental and Northern Barbaricum," in Hunter and Painter 2013, 339–57.

Reden, S. von, 2010. *Money in Classical Antiquity*. Cambridge: Cambridge University Press.

Reece, R., 1984. "Coins," in *Excavations at Carthage: The British Mission 1.1: The Avenue du President Habib Bourguiba, Salammbo: The Site and Finds Other than Pottery*, ed. H. R. Hurst and S. Roskams, 171–81. Sheffield, UK: University of Sheffield Department of Prehistory and Archaeology.

———, 1994. "Coins," in *Excavations at Carthage: The British Mission 2.1: The Circular Harbour, North Side: The Site and Finds Other than Pottery*, ed. R. H. Hurst, 249–56. Oxford: Oxford University Press.

———, 1995. "Site-Finds in Roman Britain," *Britannia* 26:179–206.

———, 1996. "The Interpretation of Site Finds—a Review," in *Coin Finds and Coin Use in the Roman World*, ed. C. E. King and D. G. Wigg, 341–55. Berlin: G. Mann.

———, 2003. "Coins and the Late Roman Economy," in *Theory and Practice in Late Antique Archaeology*, ed. L. Lavan and W. Bowden, 139–70. Leiden, Neth.: Brill.

Rennie, K. R., 2018. *Freedom and Protection: Monastic Exemption in France, c. 590–c.1100*. Manchester, UK: Manchester University Press.

Retamero, F., 1999. "As Coins Go Home: Towns, Merchants, Bishops and Kings in Visigothic Hispania," in *The Visigoths from the Migration Period to the Seventh Century: An Ethnographic Perspective*, ed. P. J. Heather, 271–320. Woodbridge, UK: Boydell.

———, 2001. "*Panes et siliquae*: las condiciones de la producción de moneda en el Regnum Gothorum," in *Visigoti e Longobardi: atti del seminario, Roma, 28–29 aprile 1997*, ed. J. Arce Martínez and P. Delogu, 117–32. Florence, It.: Insegna dell Giglio.

———, 2006. "El estado de la moneda en al-Andalus. A propósito de una obre reciente," *Al-Qanṭara* 27:303–21.

———, 2011. "La moneda del *regnum Gothorum* (ca. 575–714). Una revisión del registro numismático," in *Between Taxation and Rent: Fiscal Problems from Late Antiqutiy to Early Middle Ages*, ed. P. C. Díaz and I. Martín Viso, 189–220. Bari, It.: Edipuglia

Reuter, T., 1991. *Germany in the Early Middle Ages c. 800–1056*. London: Longman.

———, 1995. "Property Transactions and Social Relations between Rulers, Bishops and Nobles in Early Eleventh-Century Saxony. The Evidence of the Vita Meinwerci," in *Property and Power in in the Early Middle Ages*, ed. W. Davies and P. J. Fouracre, 165–99. Cambridge: Cambridge University Press.

———, ed., 1999. *The New Cambridge Medieval History. 3: c. 900–c. 1024*. Cambridge: Cambridge University Press.

———, 2006. *Medieval Polities and Modern Mentalities*, ed. J. L. Nelson. Cambridge: Cambridge University Press.

Reuter, T., C. Wickham, and T. N. Bisson, 1997. "The 'Feudal Revolution': Debate," *Past and Present* 155:177–225.

Reynolds, A., 2009. *Anglo-Saxon Deviant Burial Customs*. Oxford: Oxford University Press.

———, 2019. "Spatial Configurations of Power in Anglo-Saxon England: Sidelights on the Relationships between Boroughs, Royal Vills and Hundreds," in Carroll, Reynolds, and Yorke 2019, 436–55.

Reynolds, A., W. Davies, and G. Halsall, eds., 2006. *People and Space in the Middle Ages*. Turnhout, Bel.: Brepols.

Reynolds, S., 1997. *Kingdoms and Communities in Western Europe, 900–1300*. 2nd ed. Oxford: Oxford University Press.

Riart, O. P., and J. B. Aparicio, 1996. "Apuntes sobre la minería visigótica hispana," in *Actas de la I Jornadas sobre Minería y Tecnología en la Edad Media Peninsular*, 198–216. León, Sp.: Fundación Hullera Vasco-Leonesa.

Ricci, R., 1988. "Le coniazioni altomedievali dei vescovi di Luni," *Giornale storico della Lunigiana e del Territorio Lucense* 39:45–63.

Richards, J. D., 1999. "What's So Special about 'Productive Sites'? Middle Saxon Settlements in Northumbria," *Anglo-Saxon Studies in Archaeology and History* 10:71–80.

Richards, J., Naylor, J., and Holas-Clark, C., 2009. "Anglo-Saxon Landscape and Economy: Using Portable Antiquities to Study Anglo-Saxon and Viking England." *Internet Archaeology* 25. http://intarch.ac.uk/journal/issue25/richards_index.html.

Rigold, S., 1960–1. "The Two Primary Series of Sceattas," *British Numismatic Journal* 30:6–53.

Rio, A., 2012. "Self-Sale and Voluntary Entry into Unfreedom, 300–1100," *Journal of Social History* 23:661–85.

——, 2017. *Slavery after Rome, 500–1100*. Oxford: Oxford University Press.

——, 2021. "Nearly-Not Miracles of the Carolingian Era: A Hypothesis," *Haskins Society Journal* 32:1–22.

Ripoll López, G., and J. M. Gurt Esparraguera, eds., 2000. *Sedes regiae (ann. 400–800)*. Barcelona: Reial Acadèmia de Bonas Lletres.

Rispling, G., 2007. "Ninth-Century Dirham Hoards in Russia and the Baltic Region: A Report on Progress," in *Magister Monetae: Studies in Honour of Jørgen Steen Jensen*, ed. M. Andersen, 101–9. Copenhagen: National Museum, Royal Collection of Coins and Medals.

Ristow, S., 2007. *Frühes Christentum im Rheinland: die Zeugnisse der archäologischen und historischen Quellen an Rhein, Maas und Mosel*. Cologne, Ger.: Aschendorff.

——, 2015. "Die Dietkirche in Bonn—Archäologie und Geschichte ihrer Frühzeit," in *1000 Jahre Kirche im Bonner Norden*, ed. A. Plassmann, 11–26. Neustadt, Ger.: P. Schmidt.

Risvaag, J. A., and Christophersen, A., 2004. "Early Medieval Coinage and Urban Development: A Norwegian Experience," in *Land, Sea and Home: Proceedings of a Conference on Viking-Period Settlement, at Cardiff, July 2001*, ed. J. Hines, A. Lane, and M. Redknap, 75–92. Leeds, UK: Routledge.

Roach, L., 2015. "Feudalism," in *International Encyclopedia of the Social and Behavioral Sciences*, ed. J. D. Wright et al., 111–16. 2nd ed. Amsterdam: Elsevier.

——, 2016. *Æthelred the Unready*. New Haven, CT: Yale University Press.

——, 2021. *Forgery and Memory at the End of the First Millennium*. Princeton, NJ: Princeton University Press.

Roffe, D., 2018. "Unequal Partners in Government? Domesday Moneyers," *Studies in Western History* 269:1–17.

Roover, R. de, 1942. "The Commercial Revolution of the Thirteenth Century," *Bulletin of the Business Historical Society* 16:34–39.

Roseneck, R., ed., 2001. *Der Rammelsberg: Tausend Jahre Mensch—Natur—Technik*, 2 vols. Goslar, Ger.: Franz Steiner.

Rosenwein, B. H., 1989. *To Be the Neighbor of St Peter: The Social Meaning of Cluny's Property, 909–1049*. Ithaca, NY: Cornell University Press.

——, 1999. *Negotiating Space: Power, Restraint, and Privileges of Immunity in Early Medieval Europe*. Manchester, UK: Manchester University Press.

Rovelli, A., 1995. "Il denaro di Pavia nell'Alto Medioevo (VIII–XI secolo)," *Bolletino della Società Pavese di Storia Patria* 95:71–90.

——, 2000. "Monetary Circulation in Byzantine and Carolingian Rome: A Reconsideration in the Light of Recent Archaeological Data," in *Early Medieval Rome and the Christian West: Essays in Honour of Donald A. Bullough*, ed. J. M. H. Smith, 85–99. Leiden, Neth.: Brill.

——, 2001. "Emissione e uso della moneta: le testimonianze scritte e archeologiche," *Settimane di studio del Centro italiano di studi sull'alto medioevo* 48:821–52.

——, 2009. "Coins and Trade in Early Medieval Italy," *EME* 17:45–76.

——, 2010. "Nuove zecche e circolazione monetaria tra X e XIII secolo: l'esempio del Lazio e della Toscana," *Archeologia Medievale* 37:163–70.

——, 2012. *Coinage and Coin Use in Medieval Italy*. Farnham, UK: Ashgate.

——, 2015–16. "The Circulation of Late Roman Bronze Coinage in Early Medieval Italy: An Update," *Journal of Archaeological Numismatics* 5/6:55–72.

——, 2020. "The Coins from the Excavations of Vetricella (Scarlino, Grosseto). Notes on the Pavese Issues of Berengar I," in Bianchi and Hodges 2020, 89–98.

Rüfner, T., 2016. "Money in the Roman Law Texts," in *Money in the Western Legal Tradition: Middle Ages to Bretton Woods*, ed. D. Fox and W. Ernst, 93–109. Oxford: Oxford University Press.

Ruggini, L. C., 1984. "Milano nella circolazione monetaria del Tardo Impero. Esigenze politiche e risposte socioeconomiche," in *La zecca di Milano: Atti del Convegno internazionale di Studio, Milano 9–14 maggio 1983*, ed. G. Gorini, 13–58. Milan: Società numismatica italiana.

——, 1992. "Acque e lagune da periferia del mondo a fulcro di una nuova *civilitas*," in *Storia di Venezia. Dalle origini alla caduta della Serenissima. 1: Origini-Età ducale*, ed. L. C. Ruggini, 11–102. Rome: Istituto della enciclopedia italiana.

Russo, D. G., 1998. *Town Origins and Development in Early England, c. 400–950 A.D.* Westport, CT: Greenwood.

Rustow, M., 2010. "A Petition to a Woman at the Fatimid Court (413–414 A.H./1022–34 C.E.)," *Bulletin of the School of Oriental and African Studies* 73:1–27.

——, 2020. *The Lost Archive: Traces of a Caliphate in a Cairo Synagogue*. Princeton, NJ: Princeton University Press.

Saccocci, A., 1991. "La moneta nel Veneto medioevale (secoli X–XIV)," in *Il Veneto nel medioevo. Dai comuni cittadini al predominio scaligero nella Marca*, ed. A. Castagnetti and G. M. Varanini, 243–62. Verona, It.: Banca popolare di Verona.

——, 2005. "La monetazione del *Regnum Italiae* e l'evoluzione complessiva del sistema monetario Europeo tra VIII e XII secolo," in *XIII Congreso Internacional de Numismática, Madrid 2003: Actas—Proceedings—Actes*, ed. C. Alfaro Asíns, C. Marcos Alonso and P. Otero Moràn. 2 vols., 2:1037–49. Madrid: Ministerio de Cultura.

——, 2008. "I rivtrovamenti monetali e i processi inflativi nel mondo antico e medievale," *Numismatica Patavina* 9:95–111.

——, 2009. "Un denaro veneziano di Ottone III imperatore (996–1002) dagli scavi del monastero di Santa Maria in Valle a Cividale," *Forum Iulii* 33:139–47.

——, 2013. "Rinvenimenti monetali nella Tuscia dell'Altomedioevo: i flussi (secc. VI–X)," in *Monete antiche: usi e flussi monetari in Valdera e nella Toscana nord-occidentale dell'età romana al Medioevo*, ed. A. Alberti and M. Baldassarri, 21–34. Bientina, It.: La grafica pisana.

———, 2015. "Ancora sui bronzi contromarcati XLII e LXXXIII," *Rivista italiana di numismatica* 116: 407.

———, forthcoming. "Monete frazionate: i casi studio delle monete frazionate nel sito di San Martino di Lomaso in Trentino e delle monete *plicatae* nelle fonti Inglesi."

Sáez Sánchez, E., 1946. "Nuevos datos sobre el coste de la vida en Galicia durante la Alta Edad Media," *Anuario de historia del derecho español* 17:865–88.

Sagui, L., and A. Rovelli, 2012. "Residuality, Non-Residuality, and Continuity of Circulation: Some Examples from the Crypta Balbi," in Rovelli 2012, 1:1–22.

Sahlins, M., 1972. *Stone Age Economics*. New York: Aldine de Gruyter.

Salvioli, G., 1901. *Città e campagne prima e dopo il mille*. Palermo, It.: A. Reber.

Sánchez-Albornoz, C., 1965. *Estudios sobre las instituciones medievales españolas.* Mexico City: Universidad Nacional Autónoma de México.

Sanders, P., 1994. *Ritual, Politics, and the City in Fatimid Cairo*. Albany: State University of New York.

Sarah, G., 2008. "Caractérisation de la composition et de la structure des alliages argent-cuivre par ICP-MS avec prélèvement par ablation laser. Application au monnayage carolingien." 2 vols. PhD dissertation, Université d'Orléans.

———, 2020. "The Ilanz Hoard," in *Swiss and Italian Monetary Relations: The Early Middle Ages (VI-XI Centuries): Proceedings of the International Numismatic Workshop, Lugano, September 29th 2018*, ed. L. Gianazza and F. Rossini, 71–86. Lugano, Switz.: Circolo Numismatic Ticinese.

Sarah, G., et al., 2008. "Analyses élémentaires de monnaies de Charlemagne et Louis le Pieux du Cabinet de Médailles: l'Italie carolingienne et Venise," *Revue numismatique* 164:355–406.

Sargent, T. J., and F. F. Velde, 2002. *The Big Problem of Small Change*. Princeton, NJ: Princeton University Press.

Sarris, P., 2004. "The Origins of the Manorial Economy: New Insights from Late Antiquity," *English Historical Review* 119:279–311.

Sassier, Y., 1980. *Recherches sur le pouvoir comtal en Auxerrois, du Xe au début du XIIIe s.* Auxerre, Fr.: Publications de la Société des fouilles archéologiques et des monuments historiques de l'Yonne.

Sato, S., 2004. "À propos de la fiscalité et de l'état mérovingien aux VIe et VIIe siècles," in *Le médiéviste devant ses sources: questions et méthodes*, ed. C. Carozzi and H. Taviani-Carozzi, 171–83. Aix-en-Provence, Fr.: Publications de l'Université de Provence.

Sawyer, P. H., 2013. *The Wealth of Anglo-Saxon England*. Oxford: Oxford University Press.

Scales, L., 2022. "Ever Closer Union? Unification, Difference, and the 'Making of Europe,' c. 950–c. 1350," *English Historical Review* 137:321–61.

Scharer, A., 2015. "Das Testament Karls des Großen," in *Urkunden—Schriften— Lebensordnungen: neue Beiträge zur Mediävistik. Vorträge der Jahrestagung des Instituts für Österreichische Geschichtsforschung aus Anlass des 100. Geburtstags von Heinrich Fichtenau (1912-2000)*, ed. A. Schwarcz and K. Kaska, 151–60. Vienna: Böhlau.

Schärli, B., 1983. "Ein Basler Denar Ludwig IV. des Kindes. 900–911 aus der Ajoie. 1982," *Schweizer Münzblätter* 33:16–20.

Schiesser, P., 2017. *Monnaies et circulation monétaire mérovingiennes (vers 670–vers 750): les monnayages d'argent de Touraine.* Paris: Société d'études numismatiques et archéologiques.

———, 2018. "La réinvention du denier comme monnaie réelle au VIIe siècle," *BSFN* 73:232–40.

Schlesinger, W., 1985. "The Market as an Early Form of the German Town," in Clarke and Simms 1985, 237–47.

Schmidt-Wiegand, R., 2006. "Sprache, Recht, Rechtssprache bei Franken und Alemannen vom 6. bis zum 8. Jh.," in *Leges—Gentes—Regna. Zur Rolle von germanischen Rechtgewohnheiten und lateinischer Schriftkultur bei der Ausbildung der frühmittelalterlichen Rechtskultur,* ed. G. Dilcher, 141–58. Berlin: Erich Schmidt.

Schneider, J., 1973. "Aspects de la société dans l'Aquitaine carolingienne d'après La Vita Geraldi Auriliacensis," *Comptes rendus. Académie des Inscriptions et Belles-Lettres* 1:8–19.

Schroeder, N., 2020. "Peasant Initiative and Monastic Estate Management in 10th Century Lotharingia," *Studia historica. Historia medieval* 38:75–95.

Schulze-Dörrlamm, M., 2010. "Gräber mit Münzbeigabe im Karolingerreich," *Jahrbuch des Römisch-Germanischen Zentralmuseums* 57:339–88.

Schuurung, M. P., 2014. "The Circulation and Use of Coins in the Carolingian Era of the Netherlands: A Distribution Analysis." MA thesis, Leiden, Neth.

Schwarcz, A., 2004. "The Settlement of the Vandals in North Africa," in *Vandals, Romans and Berbers: New Perspectives on Late Antique North Africa,* ed. A. H. Merrills, 49–58. Aldershot, UK: Ashgate.

Scott, J. C., 1985. *Weapons of the Weak: Everyday Forms of Peasant Resistance.* New Haven, CT: Yale University Press.

Scull, C., 1990. "Scales and Weights in Early Anglo-Saxon England," *Archaeological Journal* 147:183–215.

———, 1992. "Before Sutton Hoo: Structures of Power and Society in Early East Anglia," in *The Age of Sutton Hoo: The Seventh Century in North-Western Europe,* ed. M. Carver, 3–23. Woodbridge, UK: Boydell.

———, 2009. *Early Medieval (Late 5th–Early 8th Centuries AD) Cemeteries at Boss Hall and Buttermarket, Ipswich, Suffolk.* Leeds, UK: Society for Medieval Archaeology.

———, 2013. "Ipswich: Contexts of Funerary Evidence from an Urban Precursor of the Seventh Century AD," in Bates and Liddiard 2013, 218–29.

Scull, C., F. Minter, and J. Plouviez, 2016. "Social and Economic Complexity in Early Medieval England: A Central Place Complex of the East Anglian Kingdom at Rendlesham, Suffolk," *Antiquity* 90:1594–1612.

Scull, C., and J. Naylor, 2016. "Sceattas in Anglo-Saxon Graves," *Medieval Archaeology* 60:205–41.

Segers-Glocke, C., and H. Witthöft, 2000. *Aspects of Mining and Smelting in the Upper Harz Mountains (Up to the 13th/14th Century).* St. Katharinen, Ger.: Franz Steiner.

Semmler, J., 1974. "*Episcopi potestas* und karolingische Klosterpolitik," in *Mönchtum, Episkopat und Adel zur Gründungszeit des Klosters Reichenau,* ed. A. Borst, 305–95. Sigmaringen, Ger.: Thorbecke.

Semple, S., 2004. "Locations of Assembly in Early Anglo-Saxon England," in *Assembly Places and Practices in Medieval Europe*, ed. A. Pantos and S. Semple, 145–54. Dublin: Four Courts.

Semple, S., et al., 2021. *Negotiating the North: Meeting Places in the Middle Ages in the North Sea Zone*. Abingdon, UK: Routledge.

Senecal, C., 2001. "Keeping up with the Godwinesons: In Pursuit of Aristocratic Status in Late Anglo-Saxon England," *Anglo-Norman Studies* 23:251–66.

Serafini, C., 1951. "Appendice numismatica," in *Esplorazioni sotto la Confessione di San Pietro in Vaticano eseguite negli anni 1940–1949*, ed. B. M. Apolloni Ghetti et al. 2 vols., 2:225–44. Vatican City: Città di Vaticano.

Shaddel, M., 2021. "Monetary Reform under the Sufyanids: The Papyrological Evidence," *Bulletin of SOAS* 84:263–93.

Shahîd, I., 1995–2010. *Byzantium and the Arabs in the Sixth Century*, 2 vols. in 4. Washington, DC: Dumbarton Oaks Research Library and Collection.

Sheehan, J., 1991. "Coiled Armrings: An Hiberno-Viking Silver Armring Type," *Journal of Irish Archaeology* 6:41–53.

———, 1998. "Early Viking Age Silver Hoards from Ireland and their Scandinavian Elements," in *Ireland and Scandinavia in the Early Viking Age*, ed. H. B. Clarke, M. Ní Mhaonaigh and R. Ó Floinn, 166–202. Dublin: Four Courts.

———, 2019. "Reflections on Kingship, the Church, and Viking Age Silver in Ireland," in Kershaw and Williams 2019, 104–22.

Silber, I. F., 2009. "Bourdieu's Gift to Gift Theory: An Unacknowledged Trajectory," *Sociological Theory* 27:173–90.

Siltberg, T., 2012. "The Conception of an Egalitarian Gotlandic Peasant Society," in *The Image of the Baltic: A Festschrift for Nils Blomkvist*, ed. M. F. Scholz, R. Bohn, and C. Johansson, 203–27. Visby, Swed.: Gotland University Press.

Simiand, F., 1934. "La monnaie, réalité sociale," *Annales sociologiques* 1:1–58.

Simmel, G., 1977. *Philosophie des Geldes*. 7th ed. Berlin: Duncker & Humblot.

———, 2004. *The Philosophy of Money*, ed. D. Frisby, trans. T. Bottomore, D. Frisby, and K. Mengelberg. 3rd ed. London: Routledge.

Sindbæk, S. M., 2003. "An Object of Exchange. Brass-Bars and the Routinization of Viking Age Long-Distance Exchange in the Baltic Area," *Offa* 58:49–60.

———, 2007a. "Networks and Nodal Points: The Emergence of Towns in Early Viking Age Scandinavia," *Antiquity* 81:119–32.

———, 2007b. "The Small World of the Vikings: Networks in Early Medieval Communication and Exchange," *Norwegian Archaeological Review* 40:59–74.

Sindbæk, S. M., 2009. "Routes and Long-Distance Traffic—the Nodal Points of Wulfstan's Voyage," in *Wulfstan's Voyage: The Baltic Sea Region in the Early Viking Age as Seen from Shipboard*, ed. A. Englert and A. Trakadas, 72–78. Roskilde, Den.: Viking Ship Museum.

Sindbak, S., 2011. "Silver Economies and Social Ties: Long-Distance Interaction, Long-Term Investments—and Why the Viking Age Happened," in Graham-Campbell, Sindbæk, and Williams 2011, 41–66.

Singh, D., 2018. *Divine Currency: The Theological Power of Money in the West*. Stanford, CA: Stanford University Press.

Skaare, K., 1976. *Coins and Coinage in Viking-Age Norway: The Establishment of a National Coinage in Norway in the XI Century, with a Survey of the Preceding Currency History.* Oslo: Universitetsforlaget.

Skre, D., 2007. "Towns and Markets, Kings and Central Places in South-Western Scandinavia *c.* AD 800–950," in *Kaupang in Skiringssal*, ed. D. Skre, 445–69. Aarhus, Den.: Aarhus University Press.

Skre, D., ed., 2008. *Means of Exchange: Dealing with Silver in the Viking Age.* Aarhus, Den.: Aarhus University Press.

———, 2011a. "Commodity Money, Silver and Coinage in Viking-Age Scandinavia," in Graham-Campbell, Sindbæk, and Williams 2011b, 67–91.

———, 2011b. "The Inhabitants: Origins and Trading Connections," in *Things from the Town: Artefacts and Inhabitants in Viking-Age Kaupang*, ed. D. Skre, 417–42. Aarhus, Den.: Aarhus University Press.

———, 2017a. "Monetary Practices in Early Medieval Western Scandinavia (5th–10th Centuries AD)," *Medieval Archaeology* 61:277–99.

———, 2017b. "Scandinavian Monetisation in the First Millennium AD—Practices and Institutions," in *Encounters, Excavations and Argosies: Essays for Richard Hodges*, ed. J. Mitchell, J. Moreland, and B. Leal, 291–99. Oxford: Archaeopress.

Slavin, P., 2010. "Crusaders in Crisis: Towards the Re-Assessment of the Origins and Nature of the 'People's Crusade' of 1095–1096," *Imago temporis: Medium Ævum* 4:175–99.

Slootjes, D., 2004. "Late Roman Rule and Provincial Expectations: The Governor and His Subjects." PhD dissertation, University of North Carolina at Chapel Hill.

Smart, V., 1990. "Osulf Thein and Others: Double Moneyers' Names on the Late Anglo-Saxon Coinage," in Jonsson 1990, 435–53.

Smith, P. J., 2009. "Shen-tsung's Reign and the New Policies of Wang An-shih, 1067–1085," in *The Cambridge History of China. Vol. 5: The Sung Dynasty and Its Precursors, 907–1279*, ed. D. Twitchett and P. J. Smith, 347–483. Cambridge: Cambridge University Press.

Smith, R., 2015a. "Calamity and Transition: Re-Imagining Italian Trade in the Eleventh-Century Mediterranean," *Past and Present* 228:15–56.

———, 2015b. "Trade and Commerce across Afro-Eurasia," in *The Cambridge World History. Vol. 5: Expanding Webs of Exchange and Conflict, 500CE–1500CE*, ed. B. J. Kedar and M. E. Wiesner-Hanks, 233–56. Cambridge: Cambridge University Press.

Söderberg, A., 2011. "Eyvind Skáldaspillir's Silver: Refining and Standards in Pre-Monetary Economies in the Light of Finds from Sigtuna and Gotland," *Situne Dei 2011*, 5–34.

Sombart, W., 1902. *Der moderne Kapitalismus*, 3 vols. Leipzig, Ger.: Düncker & Humblot.

Sperber, E., 1996. *Balances, Weights and Weighing in Ancient and Early Medieval Sweden.* Stockholm: Archaeological Research Laboratory, Stockholm University.

Spufford, P., 1988. *Money and Its Use in Medieval Europe.* Cambridge: Cambridge University Press.

Staab, F., and T. Unger, eds., 2005. *Kaiserin Adelheid und ihre Klostergründung in Selz: Referate der wissenschaftlichen Tagung in Landau und Selz vom 15. bis 17.*

Oktober 1999. Speyer, Ger.: Pfälzischen Gesellschaft zur Förderung der Wissen-schaften in Speyer.

Stahl, A., 1994. *Collections numismatiques: Mérovingiens et royaumes barbares (VIe–VIIIe siècles). Fonds Bourgey.* Paris: Éditions Errance.

———, 2000. *Zecca: The Mint of Venice in the Middle Ages.* Baltimore: Johns Hopkins University Press.

———, 2012. "The Transformation of the West," in Metcalf 2012, 633–52.

Stahl, A., and W. M. Oddy, 1992. "The Date of the Sutton Hoo Coins," in *Sutton Hoo: Fifty Years After,* ed. R. Farrell and C. Neuman de Vegvar, 129–47. Oxford, OH: American Early Medieval Studies, Miami University, Department of Art.

Standen, N., 2019. "Colouring outside the Lines: Methods for a Global History of Eastern Eurasia 600–1350," *Transactions of the Royal Historical Society* 29:27–63.

Steen Jensen, J., 1983. "Hvor stor var udmøntningen i Danmark i 1000- og 1100-tallet?," *Fortid og nutid* 30:19–26.

———, 1995. *Tusindtallets Danske Mønter fra Den kongelige Mønt- og Medaillesamling.* Copenhagen: Nationalmuseet.

Steinacher, R., 2016. *Die Vandalen: Aufstieg und Fall eines Barbarenreichs.* Stuttgart, Ger.: Klett-Cotta.

Steinbach, S., 2007a. *Das Geld der Nonnen und Mönche: Münzrecht, Münzprägung und Geldumlauf der ostfränkisch-deutschen Klöster in ottonisch-salischer Zeit, ca. 911–1125.* Berlin: Winter Industries.

———, 2007b. "'Herimannvs Rex': Münzen als Informationsträger am Beispiel der Goslarer Gepräge Hermanns von Salm," in *Text, Bild, Schrift: Vermittlung von Information im Mittelalter,* ed. A. Laubinger, B. Gedderth, and C. Dobrinski, 27–44. Munich: Wilhelm Fink.

———, 2015. "From Heinricus Rex to Rothardus Abbas: Monastic Coinage under the Ottonians and Salians (c. 911–1125)," in Gasper and Gullbekk 2015, 185–96.

Stenton, F. M., 1934. *Norman London: An Essay.* London: G. Bell.

———, 1971. *Anglo-Saxon England.* 3rd ed. Oxford: Oxford University Press.

Steuer, H., 1984. "Feinwaagen und Gewichte als Quellen zur Handelsgeschichte des Ostseeraumes," in *Archäologische und naturwissenschaftliche Untersuchungen an ländlichen und frühstädtischen Siedlungen im deutschen Küstengebiet vom 5. Jahrhundert v. Chr. bis zum 11. Jahrhundert n. Chr.,* ed. H. Jankuhn and G. Kossack. 2 vols., 2:273–91. Weinheim, Ger.: Acta humaniora.

———, 1987. "Gewichtsgeldwirtschaften im frühgeschichtlichen Europa," in *Der Handel der Karolinger- und Wikingerzeit: Bericht über die Kolloquien der Kommission für die Altertumskunde Mittel- und Nordeuropas in den Jahren 1980 bis 1983,* ed. K. Düwel, 405–527. Göttingen, Ger.: Vandenhoeck & Ruprecht.

———, 2003. "The Beginnings of Urban Economies among the Saxons," in *The Continental Saxons from the Migration Period to the Tenth Century: An Ethnographic Perspective,* ed. D. H. Green and F. Siegmund, 159–92. Woodbridge, UK: Boydell.

Steuer, H., and U. Zimmermann, eds., 1993. *Montanarchäologie in Europa. Berichte zum Internationalen Kolloquium "Frühe Erzgewinnung und Verhüttung in Europa" in Freiburg im Breisgau vom 4. bis 7. Oktober 1990.* Sigmaringen, Ger.: Thorbecke.

Stewart, B.H.I.H., 1978. "Anglo-Saxon Gold Coins," in *Scripta Nummaria Romana: Essays Presented to Humphrey Sutherland*, ed. R. A. Carson and C. M. Kraay, 143–72. London: Spink.

——, 1988. *"Ministri* and *monetarii,"* *Revue numismatique*, 6th series, 30:166–75.

Stillman, N. A., 1970. "East-West Relations in the Islamic Mediterranean in the Early Eleventh Century: A Study in the Geniza Correspondence of the House of Ibn 'Awkal." PhD dissertation, University of Pennsylvania.

——, 1973. "The Eleventh Century Merchant House of Ibn 'Awkal," *Journal of the Economic and Social History of the Orient* 16:15–88.

Stoclet, A. J. 1999. *Immunes ab omni teloneo: étude de diplomatique, de philologie et d'histoire sur l'exemption de tonlieux au haut Moyen Age et spécialement sur la praeceptio de navibus*. Brussels: Institut historique belge de Rome.

Stoffella, M., 2014. "Élites locali nell'Italia centro-settentrionale: esempi e confronto," in Valenti and Wickham 2014, 41–76.

Stöllner, T., 2012. "Mining and Elites: A Paradigm beyond the Evidence in European Metal Ages," in Kienlin and Zimmermann 2012, 433–48.

Storli, I., 2016. "Between Chiefdom and Kingdom: A Case Study of the Iron Age Farm Borg in Lofoten, Arctic Norway," in *The Farm as a Social Arena*, ed. L. H. Dommasnes, D. Gusmiedl-Schümann, and A. T. Hommedal, 219–44. Münster, Ger.: Münster Waxmann.

Storli, I., and E. Roesdahl, 2007. "Ohthere and His World—a Contemporary Perspective," in *Ohthere's Voyages: A Late 9th-Century Account of Voyages along the Coasts of Norway and Denmark and Its Cultural Context*, ed. J. M. Bately and A. Englert, 76–99. Roskilde, Den.: Viking Ship Museum.

Straßburger, M., 2006. "Archäologie und Geschichte des Ramsbecker Bergbaus," in *Bergbau im Sauerland: Westfälischer Bergbau in der Römerzeit und im Frühmittelalter*, ed. R. Köhne, W. Reininghaus, and T. Stöllner, 58–82. Münster, Ger.: Westfälischen Heimatbundes.

——, 2013. "Early Medieval Ore Mining in Central Europe and Neighbouring Regions," in *Mining and Cultural Landscape: 8th International Symposium on Archaeological Mining History, Reichelsheim-Odenwald 2013*, ed. J. Silvertant, 6–35. Valkenburg aan de Geul, Neth.: Silvertant Erfgoedprojecten.

Strathern, A., 2018. "Global Early Modernity and the Problem of What Came Before," in Holmes and Standen 2018, 317–44.

Strothmann, J., 2008. "Königsherrschaft oder nachantike Staatlichkeit? Merowingische Monetarmünzen als Quelle für die politische Ordnung des Frankenreiches," *Millennium* 5:353–81.

——, 2013. *"Civitas*-Hauptorte und ihre Behennungen als Quelle für den Wandel der politischen Struktur Galliens bis zum 8. Jahrhundert," in Jarnut and Strothmann 2013, 613–28.

——, 2017. "Merowingische Monetarmünzen und die Gallia im 7. Jahrhundert," in Greule et al. 2017, 11–70.

——, 2020. "The Evidence of Numismatics: 'Merovingian' Coinage and the Place of Frankish Gaul and Its Cities in an 'Invisible' Roman Empire," in Effros and Moreira 2020, 797–818.

Suchodolski, S., 1971. *Pczatki mennictwa w Europie srodkowei, wschodniej i pólnocnej.* Wroclaw, Pol.: Zakład Narodowy im. Ossolińskich.

——, 1983. "On the Rejection of Good Coin in Carolingian Europe," in *Studies in Numismatic Method Presented to Philip Grierson*, ed. C. N. L. Brooke, 147–52. Cambridge: Cambridge University Press.

——, 1990. "Die erste Welle der westeuropäischen Münzen im Ostseeraum," in Jonsson and Malmer 1990, 317–25.

Sundqvist, O., 2016. *An Arena for Higher Powers: Ceremonial Buildings and Religious Strategies for Rulership in Late Iron Age Scandinavia.* Leiden, Neth.: Brill.

Sussman, N., 1992. "Mints and Debasements: Monetary Policy in France during the Second Phase of the Hundred Years War: 1400–1425," *Journal of Economic History* 52:452–4.

——, 1993. "Debasements, Royal Revenues, and Inflation in France during the Hundred Years' War, 1415–1422," *Journal of Economic History* 53:44–70.

Svensson, R., 2013. *Renovatio monetae: Bracteates and Coinage Policies in Medieval Europe.* London: Spink.

Tabarrini, L., 2020. "The 'Feudal Revolution' after All? A Discussion of Four Recent Books," *Storicamente* 15–16:1–29.

Täckholm, U., 1937. *Studien über den Bergbau der römischen Kaiserzeit.* Uppsala, Swed.: Appelberg.

Tange, S., 2012. "La paysannerie indépendante et autonome à côté du grand domaine carolingien," *Revue belge de philosophie et d'histoire* 90:347–60.

Tedesco, P., 2011. "Economia e moneta nell'Africa vandalica," *Annali dell'Istituto italiano di numismatica* 57:115–38.

——, 2015. "Late Roman Italy: Taxation, Settlement, and Economy, A.D. 300–700." PhD dissertation, University of Vienna.

——, 2018a. "Late Antiquity, Early Islam and the Emergence of a 'Precocious Capitalism': A Review Essay," *Journal of European Economic History* 47:115–51.

——, 2018b. "'The Missing Factor': Economy and Labor in Late Roman North Africa (400–600 CE)," *Journal of Late Antiquity* 11:396–431.

——, 2019. "The Political Economy of the Late Roman Empire: An Essay in Speculation," in *Uomini, Istituzioni, Mercati: Studi di Storia per Elio Lo Cascio*, ed. M. Maiuro et al., 559–68. Bari, It.: Edipuglia.

——, 2020. "What Made a Peasantry: Theory and Historiography of Rural Labor in Byzantine Egypt," *Journal of Egyptian History* 13:1–46.

Tellenbach, G., 1939. *Königtum und Stämme in der Werdezeit des deutschen Reiches.* Weimar, Ger.: H. Böhlaus nachfolger.

Téreygeol, F., 2007. "Production and Circulation of Silver and Secondary Products (Lead and Glass) from Frankish Royal Silver Mines at Melle (Eighth to Tenth Century)," in Henning 2007, 1:123–34.

——, 2018. "La quantification de la production argentifère: Melle, un cas d'école?," in Bompaire and Sarah 2018, 39–54.

Teunis, H. B., 2006. *The Appeal to the Original Status: Social Justice in Anjou in the Eleventh Century.* Hilversum, Neth.: Uitgeverij Verloren.

Theuws, F., 2004. "Exchange, Religion, Identity and Central Places in the Early Middle Ages," *Archaeological Dialogues* 10:121–38.

——, 2018. "Reversed Directions: Re-Thinking Sceattas in the Netherlands and England," *Zeitschrift für Archäologie des Mittelalters* 46:27–84.

Thomas, G., 2005. "'Brightness in a Time of Dark': The Production of Secular Ornamental Metalwork in Ninth-Century Northumbria," in *De Re Metallica: The Uses of Metal in the Middle Ages*, ed. R. Bjork, 31–48. Aldershot, UK: Ashgate.

——, ed., 2010. *The Later Anglo-Saxon Settlement at Bishopstone: A Downland Manor in the Making*. York, UK: Council for British Archaeology.

Thome, L., 1972. "Die Salzfabrikation in den lothringischen Salinen bis zur Zeit der französischen Revolution," *Zeitschrift für die Geschichte der Saargegend* 20:45–76.

Thompson, M., 1966. "The Monogram of Charlemagne in Greek," *Museum Notes* 12:125–27.

Thuillier, F., and E. Louis, eds., 2015. *Tourner autour du pot . . . Les ateliers de potiers médiévaux du Ve au XIIe siècle dans l'espace européen*. Caen, Fr.: Presses universitaires de Caen.

Thunmark-Nylén, L., 1984. "Socialgrupper i vikingatiden," *Gotländskt arkiv* 56:105–10.

——, 1995–2006. *Die Wikingerzeit Gotlands*. 4 vols. Stockholm: Kungl. Vitterhets, historie och antikvitets akademien.

Tinti, F., 2005. "The 'Costs' of Pastoral Care: Church Dues in Late Anglo-Saxon England," in *Pastoral Care in Late Anglo-Saxon England*, ed. F. Tinti, 27–51. Woodbridge, UK: Boydell.

Toch, M., 2008. "Economic Activities of German Jews in the Middle Ages," in *Wirtschaftsgeschichte der mittelalterlichen Juden: Fragen und Einschätzungen*, ed. M. Toch and E. Müller-Luckner, 181–210. Munich, Ger.: Oldenbourg.

——, 2012. *The Economic History of European Jews: Late Antiquity and the Early Middle Ages*. Leiden, Neth.: Brill.

Toubert, P., 1973. *Les structures du Latium médiéval: le Latium méridional et la Sabine du IXe siècle à la fin du XIIe siècle*. 2 vols. Rome: École française de Rome.

——, 1997. "Il sistema curtense: la produzione e lo scambio interno in Italia nei secoli VIII, IX e X," in *Curtis e signoria rurale. Interferenze fra due strutture medievali. Antologia di storia medievale*, ed. G. Sergi, 7–94. Turin, It.: Scriptorium.

Toynbee, J.M.C., and J. B. Ward-Perkins, 1956. *The Shrine of St. Peter and the Vatican Excavations*. London: Longmans, Green.

Travaini, L., 2004. "Saints and Sinners: Coins in Medieval Italian Graves," *Numismatic Chronicle* 164:159–81.

——, 2022. *The Thirty Pieces of Silver: Coin Relics in Medieval and Modern Europe*, trans. A.D.R. Colvin. London and New York: Routledge.

Travaini, L., ed., 2011. *Le zecche italiane fino all'unità*. 2 vols. Rome: Istituto poligrafico e Zecca dello stato.

——, 2019. "Coins and Identity from Mint to Paradise," in *Money and Coinage in the Middle Ages*, ed. R. Naismith, 320–50. Leiden, Neth.: Brill.

Treadgold, W. T., 2014. "Paying the Army in the Theodosian Period," in *Production and Prosperity in the Theodosian Period*, ed. I. Jacobs, 303–18. Leuven, Bel.: Peeters.

Treffort, C., 2020. *Épitaphes carolingiennes du Centre-Ouest (milieu VIIIe–fin du Xe siècle)*. Paris: CNRS Éditions.

Treffort, C., and M. Uberti, 2010. "Identité des défunts et statut du groupe dans les inscriptions funéraires des anciens diocèses de Poitiers, Saintes et Angoulême entre le IVe et le Xe siècle," in *Wisigoths et Francs autour de la bataille de Vouillé (507): Recherches récentes sur le haut Moyen Âge dans le Centre-Ouest de la France. Actes des XVIIIe Journées internationales d'archéologie mérovingienne, Vouillé et Poitiers*, ed. L. Bourgeois, 193–214. Saint-Germain-en-Laye, Fr.: Association française d'archéologie mérovingienne.

Truitt, A., 2013. *Dreaming of Money in Ho Chi Minh City*. Seattle: University of Washington Press.

Tsurushima, H., 2012. "The Moneyers of Kent in the Long Eleventh Century," in *The English and Their Legacy 900–1200: Essays in Honour of Ann Williams*, ed. D. Roffe, 33–59. Woodbridge, UK: Boydell.

Twitchett, D., 1959. "Lands under State Cultivation und the T'ang Dynasty," *Journal of the Economic and Social History of the Orient* 2:162–203.

———, 1960. "Documents on Clan Administration, I. The Rules of Administration," *Asia Major*, new series, 8:1–35.

———, 1966. "The T'ang Market System," *Asia Major*, new series, 12:202–48.

———, 1968. "Merchant, Trade and Government in Late T'ang," *Asia Major*, new series, 14:63–95.

———, 1970. *Financial Administration under the T'ang Dynasty*. 2nd ed. Cambridge: Cambridge University Press.

Twitchett, D., and J. Stargardt, J., 2002. "Chinese Silver Bullion in a Tenth-Century Indonesian Wreck," *Asia Major*, 3rd series, 15:23–72.

Udovitch, A. L., 1999. "International Trade and the Medieval Egyptian Countryside." *Proceedings of the British Academy* 96:267–85.

Underwood, N., 2018. "Medicine, Money, and Christian Rhetoric," *Studies in Late Antiquity* 2:342–84.

Undiemi, A., 2014. "Per un corpus delle epigrafi di età normanna (secoli X–XII)." 2 vols. PhD dissertation, Università degli Studi di Padova.

Ungaro, L., 1985. "Il ripostiglio della Casa delle Vestali, Rome 1899," *Bollettino di numismatica* 4:47–160.

Unger, R. W., 2007. "Thresholds for Market Integration in the Low Countries and England in the Fifteenth Century," in *Money, Markets and Trade in Late Medieval Europe: Essays in Honour of John H. A. Munro*, ed. L. D. Armstrong, 349–80. Leiden, Neth.: Brill.

Valci, M., 2021. "Rome after Constantinople: From the First Papal Coins to the Closure of the Mint," *Numismatic Chronicle* 181:189–218.

Valenti, M., and C. Wickham, eds., 2014. *Italy, 888–962: A Turning Point*. Turnhout, Bel.: Brepols.

Valenze, D., 2006. *The Social Life of Money in the English Past*. Cambridge: Cambridge University Press.

Valverde Castro, M del R., 2007. "Monarquía y tributación en la Hispania visigoda: lm arco teórico," *Hispania Antiqua* 31:235–51.

Verboven, K., 2009. "Currency, Bullion and Accounts: Monetary Modes in the Roman World," *Revue belge de numismatique et de sigillographie* 155:91–124.

Verhulst, A. E., 1965. "Karolingische Agrarpolitik: das Capitulare de Villis und die Hungersnöte von 792/3 und 805/6," *Zeitschrift für Agrargeschichte und Agrarsoziologie* 13:175–89.

——, 1999. *The Rise of Cities in North-West Europe*. Cambridge: Cambridge University Press.

——, 2002. *The Carolingian Economy*. Cambridge: Cambridge University Press.

Violante, C., 1953. *La società Milanese nell'età precomunale*. Bari, It.: Laterza.

——, 1968. "I laici nel movimento Patarino," in *I laici nella "Societas Christiana" dei secoli XI e XII: Atti della terza Settimana internazionale di studio, Mendola, 1965*, 597–698. Milan: Vita e pensiero.

——, 1993. "Il secolo XI—una svolta? Introduzione ad un problema storico," in *Il secolo XI. Una svolta? Atti della XXXII settimana di studio, 10–14 settembre 1990*, ed. C. Violante and J. Fried, 7–40. Bologna, It.: Il Mulino.

Von Glahn, R., 1996. *Fountain of Fortune: Money and Monetary Policy in China, 1000–1700*. Berkeley: University of California Press.

——, 2004. "Revisiting the Song Monetary Revolution: A Review Essay," *International Journal of Asian Studies* 1:159–78.

——, 2006. "Re-Examining the Authenticity of Song Paper Money Specimens," *Journal of Song-Yuan Studies* 36:79–106.

——, 2012. "Cycles of Silver in Chinese Monetary History," in *The Economy of Lower Yangzi Delta in Late Imperial China*, ed. B.K.L. So, 17–71. New York: Routledge.

——, 2016. *The Economic History of China from Antiquity to the Nineteenth Century*. Cambridge: Cambridge University Press.

——, forthcoming. "Classical Chinese Monetary Theory."

Vos, J. S., 1997. "Das Agraphon 'Seid kundige Geldwechsler!' bei Origenes," in *Sayings of Jesus: Canonical and Non-Canonical*, ed. W. J. Petersen, 277–302. Leiden, Neth.: Brill.

Voß, H.-U., 2013. "Roman Silver in 'Free Germany': Hacksilber in Context," in Hunter and Painter 2013, 305–19.

Vroom, W.-H., 2010. *Financing Cathedral Building in the Middle Ages: The Generosity of the Faithful*. Amsterdam: Amsterdam University Press.

——, 2015. "Financing Cathedral-Building in the Middle Ages: The Eleventh to Thirteenth Centuries," in Gasper and Gullbekk 2015, 107–20.

Walker, K. E., S. Clough, and J. Clutterbuck, 2020. *A Medieval Punishment Cemetery at Weyhill Road, Andover, Hampshire*. Cirencester, UK: Cotswold Archaeology.

Walton, P., and S. Moorhead, 2016. "Coinage and the Economy," in *The Oxford Handbook of Roman Britain*, ed. M. Millett, L. Revell and A. Moore, 834–49. Oxford: Oxford University Press.

Wamers, E., P. Berghaus, and C. Stoess, 1994. *Die frühmittelalterlichen Lesefunde aus der Löhrstrasse (Baustelle Hilton II) in Mainz*. Mainz, Ger.: Archäologische Denkmalpflege, Amt Mainz.

Wang, H., 2013. "A Study of the Tang Dynasty Tax Textiles (Yongdiao Bu) from Turfan," *Journal of the Royal Asiatic Society*, 3rd series, 23:263–80.

Wangerin, L., 2019. *Kingship and Justice in the Ottonian Empire*. Ann Arbor, MI: University of Michigan Press.

Ward-Perkins, B., 1998. "The Cities," in *The Cambridge Ancient History. Vol. 13: The Late Empire, A.D. 337–425*, ed. A. Cameron and P. Garnsey, 337–425. Cambridge: Cambridge University Press.

Ward-Perkins, B., 2005. *The Fall of Rome and the End of Civilization*. Oxford: Oxford University Press.

Wareham, A., 2012. "Fiscal Policies and the Institution of a Tax State in Anglo-Saxon England within a Comparative Context," *Economic History Review* 65:910–31.

Weber, F., 2012. "Séparation des scènes sociales et pratiques ordinaires du calcul: à la recherche des raisonnements indigèenes," in *Écrire, compter, mesurer 2: vers une histoire des rationalités pratiques*, ed. N. Coquery, F. Menant, and F. Weber, 95–126. Paris: Rue d'Ulm.

Weber, M., 1968. *Economy and Society: An Outline of Interpretive Sociology*, ed. G. Roth and C. Wittich. 3 vols. Berkeley: University of California Press.

Weinfurter, S., 1986. "Die Zentralisierung der Herrschaftsgewalt im Reich durch Kaiser Heinrich II," *Historisches Jahrbuch* 106:241–97.

Weinrich, H., 1958. "Münze und Wort. Untersuchungen an einem Bildfeld," in *Romanica: Festschrift für Gerhard Rohlfs*, ed. H. Lausberg and H. Weinrich, 508–21. Halle, Ger.: M. Niemeyer.

Welldon Finn, R., 1971. *The Norman Conquest and Its Effects on the Economy, 1066–86*. London: Longman.

Werner, J., 1954. *Waage und Geld in der Merowingerzeit*. Munich, Ger.: Bayerischen Akademie der Wissenschaften.

——, 1961. "Fernhandel und Naturalwirtschaft im östlichen Merowingerreich nach archäologischen und numismatischen Zeugnissen," *Settimane di studio del Centro italiano di studi sull'alto medioevo* 8:557–618.

Werner, K. F., 2004. *Enquêtes sur les premiers temps du principat français (IXe–Xe siècles)*. Ostfildern, Ger.: Jan Thorbecke.

Werner, M., 1991. "The Liudhard Medalet," *Anglo-Saxon England* 20:27–41.

West, C., 2013. *Reframing the Feudal Revolution: Political and Social Transformation between Marne and Moselle, c. 800–c. 1100*, Cambridge Studies in Medieval Life and Thought, 4th series, 90. Cambridge: Cambridge University Press.

——, 2015. "Competing for the Holy Spirit: Humbert of Moyenmoutier and the Question of Simony," in *Compétition et sacré au haut Moyen Âge: entre médiation et exclusion*, ed. P. Depreux, F. Bougard and R. Le Jan, 347–60. Turnhout, Bel.: Brepols.

——, 2022. "The Simony Crisis of the Eleventh Century and the 'Letter of Guido,'" *Journal of Ecclesiastical History* 73:229–53.

White, R. H., 2020. "A 5th-Century Hacksilver Hoard from Wem, Shropshire," *Medieval Archaeology* 64:365–9.

Whitelock, D., 1961. "The Numismatic Interest of an Old English Version of the Legend of the Seven Sleepers," in Dolley 1961, 188–94.

Whiting, J.R.S., 1971. *Trade Tokens: An Economic and Social History*. Newton Abbot, UK: David and Charles.

Whittow, M., 2003. "Decline and Fall? Studying Long-Term Change in the East," in *Theory and Practice in Late Antique Archaeology*, ed. L. Lavan and W. Bowden, 404–24. Leiden, Neth.: Brill.

——, 2013. "How Much Trade Was Local, Regional and Inter-Regional? A Comparative Perspective on the Late Antique Economy," in *Local Economies? Production and Exchange of Inland Regions in Late Antiquity*, ed. L. Lavan, 133–65. Leiden, Neth.: Brill.

Wickham, C., 1980. "Economic and Social Institutions in Northern Tuscany in the 8th Century," in *Istituzioni ecclesiastiche della Toscana medioevale*, ed. C. Wickham et al., 7–34. Galatina, It.: Congedo.

——, 1988. *The Mountains and the City: The Tuscan Apennines in the Early Middle Ages*. Oxford: Oxford University Press.

——, 1994. *Land and Power: Studies in Italian and European Social History, 400–1200*. London: British School at Rome.

——, 1995. "Rural Society in Carolingian Europe," in McKitterick 1995, 510–37.

——, 1997. "Lineages of Western European Taxation, 1000–1200," in *Corona, municipis i fiscalitat a la Baixa Edat Mitjana: Colloqui*, ed. M. Sánchez and A. Furió Diego, 25–42. Lleida, Sp.: Institut d'Estudis Ilerdencs.

——, 1998. *Community and Clientele in Twelfth-Century Tuscany: The Origins of the Rural Commune in the Plain of Lucca*. Oxford: Oxford University Press.

——, 2000. "'The Romans According to Their Malign Custom': Rome in Italy in the Late Ninth and Tenth Centuries," in *Early Medieval Rome and the Christian West: Essays in Honour of Donald A. Bullough*, ed. J.M.H. Smith, 151–67. Leiden, Neth.: Brill.

——, 2003. "Space and Society in Early Medieval Peasant Conflicts," *Settimane di studio del Centro italiano di studi sull'alto medioevo* 50:551–86.

——, 2005. *Framing the Early Middle Ages: Europe and the Mediterranean, 400–800*. Oxford: Oxford University Press.

——, 2008. "Rethinking the Structure of the Early Medieval Economy," in *The Long Morning of Medieval Europe: New Directions in Early Medieval Studies*, ed. J. R. Davis and M. McCormick, 19–32. Aldershot, UK: Ashgate.

——, 2009a. *The Inheritance of Rome: A History of Europe from 400 to 1000*. London: Allen Lane.

——, 2009b. "Problems in Doing Comparative History," in *Challenging the Boundaries of Medieval History: The Legacy of Timothy Reuter*, ed. P. Skinner, 5–28. Turnhout, Bel.: Brepols.

——, 2010. "Conclusion," in *The Languages of Gift in the Early Middle Ages*, ed. W. Davies and P. Fouracre, 238–61. Cambridge: Cambridge University Press.

——, 2011. "The Problems of Comparison," *Historical Materialism* 19:221–31.

——, 2014a. "Conclusion," in Valenti and Wickham 2014, 417–26.

——, 2014b. "The 'Feudal Revolution' and the Origins of Italian City Communes," *Transactions of the Royal Historical Society*, 6th series, 24:29–55.

——, 2015a. *Medieval Rome: Stability and Crisis of a City, 900–1150*. Oxford: Oxford University Press.

——, 2015b. "Passages to Feudalism in Medieval Scandinavia," in da Graca and Zingarelli 2015, 141–57.

——, 2015c. *Sleepwalking into a New World: The Emergence of Italian City Communes in the Twelfth Century*. Princeton, NJ: Princeton University Press.

——, 2016. *Medieval Europe*. New Haven, CT: Yale University Press.

——, 2017. "Prima della crescita: quale società?," in *La crescita economica dell'Occidente medievale: un tema storico non ancora esaurito: venticinquesimo Convegno internazionale di studi, Pistoia, 14–17 maggio 2015*, 93–106. Pistoia, It.: Centro italiano di studi di storia e d'arte.

——, 2019. "The Power of Property: Land Tenure in Fāṭimid Egypt," *Journal of the Economic and Social History of the Orient* 62:67–107.

——, 2021. "How Did the Feudal Economy Work? The Economic Logic of Medieval Societies," *Past and Present* 251:3–40.

Widerström, A.-M., ed., 2009. *The Spillings Hoard: Gotland's Role in Viking Age World Trade*. Visby. Swed.: Gotlands Museum.

Williams, A., forthcoming. "Cautionary Tales: The Daughters of Æthelstan Mannesunu and Earl Godwine," *Anglo-Saxon* 2. https://www.academia.edu/462239 /Cautionary_Tales_the_daughters_of_Aethelstan_Mannesune_and_Earl _Godwine_of_Wessex.

Williams, G., 2006. "The Circulation and Function of Coinage in Conversion-Period England, c. AD 580–675," in Cook and Williams 2006, 145–92.

———, 2007. "Kingship, Christianity and Coinage: Monetary and Political Perspectives on Silver Economy in the Viking Age," in Graham-Campbell and Williams 2007, 177–214.

———, 2009. "Hoards from the Northern Danelaw from Cuerdale to the Vale of York," in *The Huxley Viking Hoard: Scandinavian Settlement in the North West*, ed. J. Graham-Campbell and R. Philpott, 73–83. Liverpool, UK: National Museums Liverpool.

———, 2010. "Anglo-Saxon Gold Coinage, Part 1: The Transition from Roman to Anglo-Saxon Coinage," *British Numismatic Journal* 80:51–75.

———, 2011. "Silver Economies, Monetisation and Society: An Overview," in Graham-Campbell, Sindbæk, and Williams 2011b, 337–72.

———, 2013a. "The Circulation, Minting, and Use of Coins in East Anglia, c. AD 580–675," in Bates and Liddiard 2013, 120–36.

———, 2013b. "Hack-Silver and Precious-Metal Economies: A View from the Viking Age," in Hunter and Painter 2013, 381–94.

———, 2014a. "Coins and Currency in Viking England, AD 865–954," in Naismith, Allen, and Screen 2014, 13–38.

———, 2014b. "Why Are There No Coins in the Staffordshire Hoard?," *British Numismatic Journal* 84:39–51.

———, ed., 2020. *A Riverine Site Near York: A Possible Viking Camp?* London: British Museum.

Williams, G., and T.J.T. Williams, 2013. "Minting in Wallingford," in *Transforming Townscapes: From Burh to Borough: The Archaeology of Wallingford, AD 800–1400*, ed. N. Christie and O. Creighton, 343–59. London: Society for Medieval Archaeology.

Willmott, H., et al., 2021. "Rethinking Early Medieval 'Productive Sites': Wealth, Trade, and Tradition at Little Carlton, East Lindsey," *Antiquaries Journal* 101:181–212.

Wilson, D. M., 1964. *Anglo-Saxon Ornamental Metalwork 700–1100 in the British Museum*. London: Trustees of the British Museum.

Winogradoff, P., 1876. "Die Freilassung zu voller Unabhängigkeit in den deutschen Volksrechten," *Forschungen zur deutschen Geschichte* 16:599–608.

Wolfram, H., 1973. "Lateinische Herrschertitel im 9. Und 10. Jahrhundert," in *Intitulatio II. Lateinische Herrscher- und Fürstentitel im 9. Und 10. Jahrhundert*, ed. K. Brunner et al., 19–178. Vienna: Böhlau.

Wollasch, J., 1968. "Das Grabkloster der Kaiserin Adelheid in Selz am Rhein," *Frühmittelalterliche Studien* 2:135–43.

Wood, D., 2002. *Medieval Economic Thought*. Cambridge: Cambridge University Press.

Wood, I. N., 1990. "Ethnicity and the Ethnogenesis of the Burgundians," in *Typen der Ethnogenese unter besonderer Berücksichtigung der Bayern*, ed. H. Wolfram et al. 2 vols., 1:53–69. Vienna: Österreichischen Akademie der Wissenschaften.

———, 1994. *The Merovingian Kingdoms 450–751*. London: Longman.

———, 2013. "Entrusting Western Europe to the Church, 400–750," *Transactions of the Royal Historical Society*, 6th series, 23:37–73.

———, 2016. "The Legislation of *Magistri Militum*: The Laws of Gundobad and Sigismund," *Clio Themis: revue électronique d'histoire du droit* 10:1–16.

———, 2018. *The Transformation of the Roman West*. Amsterdam: ARC Humanities Press.

Wood, S., 2006. *The Proprietary Church in the Medieval West*. Oxford: Oxford University Press.

Woods, A. R., 2013. "Economy and Authority: A Study of the Coinage of Hiberno-Scandinavian Dublin and Ireland." 2 vols. PhD dissertation, University of Cambridge.

———, 2019. "Royalty and Renewal in Viking Age Ireland," in Kershaw and Williams 2019, 73–89.

———, forthcoming. "The Production and Use of Coinage in East Anglia 500–800," *British Numismatic Journal*.

Wright, D. W., 2019. "Crafters of Kingship: Smiths, Elite Power, and Gender in Early Medieval Europe," *Medieval Archaeology* 63:271–97.

Wyatt, D., 2020. "Reading between the Lines: Tracking Slaves and Slavery in the Early Middle Ages," in Gruszczyński, Jankowiak and Shephard 2020, 17–39.

Xu, C., 2013, trans. H. Wang. "Managing a Multicurrency System in Tang China: The View from the Centre," *Journal of the Royal Asiatic Society*, 3rd series, 23:223–44.

Yang, L.-S., 1952. *Money and Credit in China: A Short History*. Cambridge, MA: Harvard University Press.

Yannopoulos, P., 1978. *L'hexagramme: un monnayage byzantin d'argent du VIIe siècle*. Louvain-la-Neuve, Bel.: Institut supérieure d'archéologie et d'histoire et de l'art.

Yorke, B., 1988. "Æthelwold and the Politics of the Tenth Century," in *Bishop Æthelwold: His Career and Influence*, ed. B. Yorke, 65–88. Woodbridge, UK: Boydell.

Yorke, B., 1990. *Kings and Kingdoms of Early Anglo-Saxon England*. London: Seaby.

———, 2003. "Anglo-Saxon *gentes* and *regna*," in *Regna and Gentes: The Relationship between Late Antique and Early Medieval Peoples and Kingdoms in the Transformation of the Roman World*, ed. H.-W. Goetz, J. Jarnut, and W. Pohl, 381–407. Leiden, Neth.: Brill.

———, 2009. "The Anglo-Saxon Kingdoms 600–900 and the Beginnings of the Old English State," in Pohl and Wieser 2009, 73–86.

———, 2019. "Historical Context," in Blackmore et al. 2019, 341–48.

Yu, L., and H. Yu, 2004. *Chinese Coins: Money in History and Society*. San Francisco: Long River.

Zadora-Rio, E., 2014. "Les ateliers monétaires mérovingiens (6e–7e s.)," in *Atlas archéologique de Touraine*, ed. E. Zadora-Rio. http://a2t.univ-tours.fr/notice.php?id=94&menu=Texte.

Zelizer, V., 1985. *Pricing the Priceless Child: The Changing Social Value of Children*. New York: Basic Books.

———, 1994. *The Social Meaning of Money*. New York: Basic Books.

———, 2005. "Circuits within Capitalism," in *The Economic Sociology of Capitalism*, ed. V. Nee and R. Swedberg, 289–321. Princeton, NJ: Princeton University Press.

Zeller, B., et al., 2020. *Neighbours and Strangers: Local Societies in Early Medieval Europe*. Manchester, UK: Manchester University Press.

Zotz, T., 1993. "Schriftquellen zum Bergbau im frühen Mittelalter," in Steuer and Zimmermann 1993, 183–99.

Zuckerman, C., 1998. "Two Reforms of the 370s: Recruiting Soldiers and Senators in the Divided Empire," *Revue des études byzantines* 56:79–139.

.

INDEX

Page numbers in *italics* refer to figures and tables.

A NOTE ON THE TYPE

{⁂}

THIS BOOK has been composed in Miller, a Scotch Roman typeface designed by Matthew Carter and first released by Font Bureau in 1997. It resembles Monticello, the typeface developed for The Papers of Thomas Jefferson in the 1940s by C. H. Griffith and P. J. Conkwright and reinterpreted in digital form by Carter in 2003.

Pleasant Jefferson ("P. J.") Conkwright (1905–1986) was Typographer at Princeton University Press from 1939 to 1970. He was an acclaimed book designer and AIGA Medalist.

The ornament used throughout this book was designed by Pierre Simon Fournier (1712–1768) and was a favorite of Conkwright's, used in his design of the *Princeton University Library Chronicle*.